IRELAND

NATIONS OF THE MODERN WORLD: EUROPE
edited by W. Rand Smith and Robin Remington

This series examines the nations of Europe as they adjust to the changing world order and move into the twenty-first century. Each volume is a detailed analytical country case study of the political, economic, and social dynamics of a European state facing the challenges of the post–Cold War era. These challenges include changing values and rising expectations, the search for new political identities and avenues of participation, and growing opportunities for economic and political cooperation in the new Europe. Emerging policy issues such as the environment, immigration, refugees, and reordered national security priorities are evolving in contexts still strongly influenced by history, geography, and culture.

The former East European nations must cope with the legacies of communism as they attempt to make the transition to multiparty democracy and market economies amid intensifying national, ethnic, religious, and class divisions. West European nations confront the challenge of pursuing economic and political integration within the European Union while contending with problems of economic insecurity, budgetary stress, and voter alienation.

How European nations respond to these challenges individually and collectively will shape domestic and international politics in Europe for generations to come. By considering such common themes as political institutions, public policy, political movements, political economy, and domestic-foreign policy linkages, we believe the books in this series contribute to our understanding of the threads that bind this vital and rapidly evolving region.

BOOKS IN THIS SERIES

Ireland: Historical Echoes, Contemporary Politics, Richard B. Finnegan, Edward T. McCarron

The Netherlands: Negotiating Sovereignty in an Interdependent World, Thomas R. Rochon

Austria: Out of the Shadow of the Past, Anton Pelinka

Albania in Transition: The Rocky Road to Democracy, Elez Biberaj

The Czech and Slovak Republics: Nation Versus State, Carol Skalnik Leff

The Politics of Belgium, John Fitzmaurice

Great Britain: Decline or Renewal? Donley Studlar

Spain: Democracy Regained, Second Edition, E. Ramón Arango

Denmark: A Troubled Welfare State, Kenneth E. Miller

Portugal: From Monarchy to Pluralist Democracy, Walter C. Opello, Jr.

IRELAND

Historical Echoes,
Contemporary Politics

RICHARD B. FINNEGAN
EDWARD T. MCCARRON

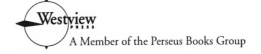
Westview
PRESS
A Member of the Perseus Books Group

In Memory of
Mary Therese Finnegan

Nations of the Modern World: Europe

Copyright © 2000 by Westview Press, A Member of the Perseus Books Group

Published in 2000 in the United States of America by Westview Press, 5500 Central Avenue, Boulder, Colorado 80301-2877, and in the United Kingdom by Westview Press, 12 Hid's Copse Road, Cumnor Hill, Oxford OX2 9JJ

Find us on the World Wide Web at www.westviewpress.com

A CIP record for this book is available from the Library of Congress.
ISBN 0-8133-1400-3 (hc).—0-8133-3247-8 (pb)

The paper used in this publication meets the requirements of the American National Standard for Permanence of Paper for Printed Library Materials Z39.48-1984.

10   9   8   7   6   5   4   3   2   1

Contents

List of Acronyms   ix

Introduction   xi

Three Irelands; Many Interpretations, xi
Ireland: The Place, xv
The Chapters to Come, xvii
Notes, xviii

1   THE QUESTION OF IRISH HISTORY: FROM THE CELTS TO O'CONNELL   1

The Early Peoples, 2
The Norman Conquest, 5
The Shipwreck of the Old Order, 9
The Penal Laws, 12
The Protestant Nation, 14
1798, 17
Union, 21
Daniel O'Connell, 23
Notes, 27

2   FROM THE FAMINE TO THE RISING   31

The Famine, 31
The Famine's Legacy, 38
The Struggle for Home Rule, 42
The Rise of Irish Nationalism, 46
The Easter Rising of 1916, 52
Notes, 57

3   FROM GUERRILLA WAR TO INDEPENDENCE   63

The Rise of Sinn Fein, 63
The Anglo-Irish War and the Anglo-Irish Treaty, 66
The Free State, 72
De Valera's Dream, 75
The Emergency and After, 81
Notes, 85

4   DOORS OPENING AND CLOSING: ECONOMY, EDUCATION, AND THE IRISH LANGUAGE   91

Introduction, 91
The Insulated Economy, 93
The Whitaker Plan and the Planning Period, 1959–1972, 96
Entry into the European Union, 1973–1987, 99
The Emergence of the "Celtic Tiger," 1987–1997, 102
Explaining Ireland's Economic Development, 104
Education: The Traditional System, 107
Education: Reform and Renewal, 109
The Irish Language, 114
Notes, 120

5   MIXED MESSAGES: THE CATHOLIC CHURCH AND THE MEDIA   123

The Catholic Church, 124
The Media, 142
Censorship, 151
Notes, 155

6   VENERATION VERSUS RIGHTS: THE ROLE OF IRISH WOMEN   159

The Suffrage Movement, 159
Venerated But Excluded, 162

The Search for Equality, 165
Controversial Issues in the 1980s, 169
Women's Status in the 1990s, 183
Notes, 194

7   CATHOLIC STATE OR CATHOLIC NATION: POLITICAL CULTURE, CONSTITUTION, AND POLITICAL STRUCTURE   201

Political Culture, 201
Constitutional Foundations, 205
The Structure of Government, 213
Neo-Corporatist Policymaking, 225
The Impact of Europe, 228
Irish Democracy, 230
Notes, 233

8   THE CHOSEN FEW: PARTIES, PRESSURE GROUPS, AND POLICY   239

The Irish Voter, 239
Political Parties, 240
Bases of the Irish Party System, 259
Pressure Groups, 261
Policy Issues: The Environment, 269
Social Problems and Issues, 271
Notes, 278

9   NORTHERN IRELAND: THE GORDIAN KNOT TIED   281

Introduction, 281
The Creation of Northern Ireland, 282
Character of the Conflict, 285
Discrimination and Separation, 288
British Policy in Ulster, 1922–1968, 294
The United States and Northern Ireland, 1922–1968, 295
Years of Violence, 1968–1972, 296

British Policy in Ulster, 1968–1972, 302
The United States and Northern Ireland, 1968–1972, 303
Northern Ireland, 1972–1981, 304
British Policy in Ulster, 1972–1981, 318
The United States and Northern Ireland, 1972–1981, 321
Notes, 326

10   NORTHERN IRELAND: THE GORDIAN KNOT UNTIED?   331

Developments in Northern Ireland, 1981–1992, 331
British Policy, 1981–1992, 336
The United States and Northern Ireland, 1981–1992, 337
External Influences on Northern Ireland, 338
The Peace Process, the Good Friday Agreement of April 1998, and the Prizes of
    Peace, 341
Explaining the Conflict; Explaining the Peace, 367
Notes, 371

11   IRELAND IN THE WORLD: POLICY, PEOPLE, AND THE ARTS   375

Irish Foreign Policy, 375
The European Union, 380
People, 384
Irish America, 388
The Arts, 391
Conclusion, 405
Notes, 406

Select Bibliography   411
Index   419

Acronyms

ADC	Anti Divorce Campaign
ANIA	Americans for a New Irish Agenda
ASTI	Association of Secondary Teachers Ireland
DUP	Democratic Unionist Party
EEC	European Economic Community
EPC	European Political Cooperation
EU	European Union
GAA	Gaelic Athletic Association
ICTU	Irish Congress of Trade Unions
IDA	Industrial Development Authority
IFA	Irish Farmers Association
INTO	Irish National Teachers Organization
IRA	Irish Republican Army
IRB	Irish Republican Brotherhood
IWFL	Irish Women's Franchise League
IWLM	Irish Women's Liberation Movement
IWSF	Irish Women's Suffrage Federation
IWU	Irishwomen United
NICRA	Northern Ireland Civil Rights Association
NORAID	Northern Aid Committee
PLAC	Pro Life Amendment Campaign
RTE	Radio Telefís Eireann
RUC	Royal Ulster Constabulary
SPUC	Society for the Protection of the Unborn Child
TD	Teachta Dala
UDA	Ulster Defense Association
UUUC	United Ulster Unionist Council
WSPU	Women's Social and Political Union

County boundaries
Provincial boundaries
National boundaries

ULSTER

•DERRY
LONDON-
DERRY

ANTRIM

DONEGAL

BELFAST

TYRONE

LEITRIM   FERMANAGH   ARMAGH   DOWN

SLIGO

MONAGHAN

MAYO   CONNAUGHT   CAVAN   LOUTH

ROSCOMMON   LONGFORD

WESTMEATH   MEATH

GALWAY   DUBLIN

GALWAY   OFFALY   DUBLIN
                     KILDARE

LEINSTER   WICKLOW

CLARE   LAOIS

LIMERICK   CARLOW

LIMERICK   TIPPERARY   KILKENNY

MUNSTER

WEXFORD

KERRY   CORK   WATERFORD

CORK•

Introduction

Three Irelands; Many Interpretations

A visitor to Ireland, like Caesar encountering Gaul, will discover at least three Irelands. On this small island can be found some of the most attractive tourist areas in Europe. The jutting cliffs of Moher rival those of the Algarve in Portugal. The Ring of Kerry enchants the eye with its panoramic vistas of mountain and sea. The brooding Carlingford peninsula is redolent with Irish myth and legend. There is a mystique and intimacy to the Irish landscape that provides escape and inspiration to the world-weary traveler. Indeed, within easy reach—often just around the bend or across a field fence—a visual tapestry unfolds: Megalithic tombs, medieval monasteries, Norman tower houses, and Georgian estates. A tour through the west brings one in touch with a slower pace, from the traditional pubs and sessions of County Clare to the remote fishing ports and headlands of Donegal. Much the same spirit of discovery can be found on the urban scene. In Dublin one can sample the treasures of the National Museum, productions at the Abbey Theatre, the Dublin horse show, the Book of Kells at Trinity College, and the narrow streets and trendy shops of Temple Bar—all combined with the warm hospitality of the Irish people.

Another Ireland is that of the Irish people, different from the whirlwind Ireland of the tourist. Although the Ireland of traditional small farms still lingers on in part, a new diversity is apparent on the rural landscape. One can find prosperous Irish farmers driving Land-Rovers and air-conditioned combine harvesters, organic homesteaders from Germany and Holland, and locals trying their hand at chocolate making or ostrich farming, to mention but a few. Dublin, befitting its cosmopolitan persona, likewise plays host to a broad spectrum of people: urban professionals, brightly clad buskers, new immigrants from Romania and Somalia, working class families who seem to spill out of a Roddy Doyle novel, and an army of students drawn to Dublin like pilgrims to Mecca. Ireland is above all a youthful culture. Everywhere there are young people—mobile phone at the ready—who are influenced more by continental Europe, techno-pop, and computers than by the rural agrarian roots of their parents or grandparents.

The quintessential feel of present-day Ireland is change. During the 1990s Ireland enjoyed a booming economy, one that has brought an excitement of possibilities. Jobs abound in high tech and tourism. New housing developments spring up like mushrooms, from Dublin to Dingle. Conspicuous consumption is everywhere in evidence, from luxury cars and holidays in Provence to designer clothes and gourmet food. Yet a closer look reveals another side to Ireland at the new millennium. The "Celtic Tiger" hasn't touched everyone. Indeed, urban slums, unemployment, and poverty coexist with new factories producing pharmaceuticals, chemicals, computers, and electronic components. In Dublin, politicians and bureaucrats struggle with unemployment, economic growth rates, currency fluctuations in the European monetary system, the effect of the Euro, tax policy, agricultural output, foreign debt, crime, drug use, and social welfare programs.

Since the 1960s, the Irish people have confronted new ideas and values in their schools, churches, and homes that have spilled into Ireland from tourists, television, and travel. The settled ways and firm beliefs of the old Ireland were, and are, battered by changing attitudes on sex, religion, work, consumerism, and education. The Irish people are becoming more numerous, better educated, younger, urban and suburban, and more aware of the possibilities for Ireland. They have higher expectations than did previous generations. The politicians run to keep up as the political parties and political leadership attempt to adapt to a new agenda of issues and a new electorate. The clamor of interest groups presses on Dublin: not only labor, farmers, and industry, but also new groups such as women, gays, students, and environmentalists. The Church, a powerful pillar of Irish society, is caught in a wave of change and struggles to reconcile paternal encouragement of piety with internal scandals and secular challenges to traditional practice and doctrine.

A third Ireland is geographically integrated with the first two but is politically separated by an international boundary. Northern Ireland, part of the United Kingdom, is not only divided from the rest of Ireland but divided within itself. The two ethnic communities of Northern Ireland, nationalist Catholics and unionist Protestants, live in a state of persistent tension and conflict that occasionally flares into ruthless bloodshed despite politicians' efforts over the past quarter century to produce peace. Two urban areas, Belfast and Londonderry, contain the bulk of the population. In the 1970s and 1980s each of these cities was marked by rows of burnt-out houses and empty, bricked-up buildings. Streets were closed off at night with giant metal gates. Shoppers were searched at a fence, subsequently removed, that closed off the Belfast city center to potential bombers. The streets were busy not only with traffic but also with the patrols of British armored vehicles. The two communities were not only separated by a barbed-wire-topped "peace line" but were driven apart by wedges of fear and hostility. Hopes for peace have been elevated by different developments, most recently by the 1998 Good Friday Peace Agreement and the elections to a new Assembly, but the two sides are constantly subject to repolarization by events such as the burning of Catholic churches, a bitterly hostile demonstration over marches in Drumcree, the murder of three children in July 1998, and a savage explosion in Omagh in August

1998 that killed twenty-nine women and children shopping for school. Economic decay, high unemployment, an unpopular security apparatus, and skilled terrorists have been the everyday experiences of this Ireland. The economic decisions are made in London. The politicians in Ulster are wed to their respective communities and peace comes only inch by inch.

At the same time, the island, in a cornucopia of creativity emanating from both sides of the political divide, has become the center of a new Irish renaissance, symbolized by the Nobel Prize in Literature given to Seamus Heaney in 1995. Heaney's accomplishments are accompanied by the emergence of poets such as Paula Meehan, novelists like Roddy Doyle, playwrights such as Brian Freil, dancers from *Riverdance*, filmmakers such as Neil Jordan, and musicians ranging from U2 to Enya.

Of the three Irelands, it is the latter two that are the concern of this book. The tourist's Ireland is an attraction that should not be missed, but to see that Ireland alone is to miss the two central dilemmas of contemporary Ireland: the adaptation to the process of rapid economic and social change in the Republic of Ireland and the bitter fruit of political relations between the two communities in Ulster.

The modernization process began in the early 1960s, initiated by a period of relatively rapid economic growth in the Republic. The new crisis in Northern Ireland began in the late 1960s with the inception of a civil rights movement in Ulster. The inhabitants of the island have been caught up in the rapid currents of these two changes, some positive, some negative, but all touching virtually everyone in some way. Sociologist Michel Peillon notes that "to catalogue social change in Ireland under the single label of 'modernization' does not get us very far."[1] Peillon is correct in that the term *modernization* has been used predominantly to refer to nations striving to break the bonds of colonization, politically and socially mobilize their populations, develop an industrial economic base, and foster a sense of nationhood. Ireland had accomplished these goals to some degree in the hundred years from 1848 to the declaration of a republic in 1949.[2] However, the status of the Republic of Ireland in the 1950s, and even up to the present, was hardly that of a modern industrial nation. Not only was Ireland economically a very considerable distance from U.S. or European standards, but social and cultural patterns and values retained a traditional quality as well.

Political modernization involves increasing equality of the people in the political system in areas such as political mobilization and participation, equality before the law, and merit as the criterion for social rewards. Increasing capacity, in part based upon economic growth, involves the development of institutions in the political system to extract resources and provide the services that arise from the increase in participation. Increasing differentiation of social roles such as the division of labor and economic specialization create increasing social complexity. Finally, modernization implies secularization: information based on science, authority based on consent, and decisions based on personal values.[3]

The modernization of Ireland in this context is a process that occurred in the nineteenth century, when the Irish adopted the political ideology of liberalism from Wolfe Tone, were mobilized by O'Connell and Parnell, and developed national identity through Young Ireland and others, in the process of nation building. The values and structures of modern European industrial nations have been thrust onto the Irish political, economic, social, and cultural agenda. The effect has been to generate an unprecedented degree of prosperity coupled with problems of unemployment and international debt; the transformation of the educational system; the decline of rural Ireland; and problems of mass urbanization such as crime, drugs, and inadequate housing. Secular pressures and internal embarrassment are a blunt challenge to the values and role of the Catholic Church; a new political agenda has sprung from the suburban young electorate and from the economic transition. It is difficult to resist labeling this process "modernization" because these social dynamics are certainly closer to those of the most developed nations of North America and Western Europe. Although Ireland has not yet accumulated the capital base and wealth of the industrial nations, the economic, political, and social agenda of issues for this small country is essentially the same as that of the advanced members of the European Union.

When change occurs rapidly in a wide variety of arenas—social, political, economic, and cultural—there arises a wide variety of explanations and interpretations based upon the different opinions and perspectives of those involved. Positive and negative responses come from politicians, journalists, academics, religious leaders, and the population at large as they react to the actual and expected effects of the policies chosen and contemplated. In this book we examine a number of these different interpretations and explanations in the context of historical change, political development, economic development, Church–state relations, social change, and Northern Ireland, as the Irish grappled with the questions of political independence, economic autonomy, the decline of provincialism, the rise of pluralism, and the unsolved conundrum of Irish nationhood: Northern Ireland.

A country rooted as Ireland is in its past has a certain social investment in the preservation of that past and the values that it embodies for the nation. The past in Ireland is a dangerous zone of political and historical contention in which the understanding of events, ideas, and perspectives resonates into the present as part of the meanings people ascribe to their political and cultural identity. Because the history of Ireland is inextricably intertwined with that of the United Kingdom, the political history of Ireland has been seen as a saga of the evolution of a people toward their political, cultural, and economic independence from that omnipresent bulldog to the east. But the history of Ireland can be seen also in different ways that challenge that view of the struggle for independence.

Irish history can be seen also as not so much a uni-linear, uni-dimensional, scripted history as a series of competing stories or interpretations that condition our ideas about the present. The nationalist perspective, for example, treats the history of Ireland as the struggle of an Irish Celtic nation to fight free of the bonds of imperial oppression of England beginning in 1170 and lasting to the present day in Northern Ireland. Judgments made about the people and events in that history are examined in the context of that story, and the heroes and villains are labeled as such based upon whether they advanced the freedom of the Irish nation, compromised it, or retarded it. The practices of the British—whether through the Penal Laws, famine relief, or contemporary judicial practices in Ulster—are evaluated in terms of the meta-story of the quest for freedom of the Irish nation on the island of Ireland. A great deal of Irish history has been framed in this language, which has had a significant impact on the adoption of certain public policies, the role of the Church, the formation of Irish national identity, and, of course, the laying of blame for Ireland's problems.

Irish history reverberates throughout present-day events, determining people's ideas and emotions about historical events. The construction and reading of Irish history is no objective exercise but itself part of the political dialogue (or shouting match) through such events as celebrating the history of the Republic of Ireland, venerating its patriots, and whether one defines Irish Republicans in Northern Ireland as heroes or terrorists. Evaluation of the character of Ireland; the amount, type, and direction of change in Ireland; and Ireland's relationships with the world is focused through the lens of history, so it makes a great deal of difference how thick, to say nothing of what shade of green, red, or orange, those lenses are. The choices made in the second half of the twentieth century in the realms of economic growth, Church–state relations, the role of women, relations with Europe, and Ulster were marked by controversy based upon the competing interpretations of the past and the consequent competing policy positions in the present.

The revisionist school of thought about Irish history was based upon the work of the renowned historians R. D. Edwards and F. X. Moody, who trained a generation of Irish historians to escape the ideological framework of the nationalist model and seek to tell the story of events and people on their own terms, not as part of a larger "drama" or meta-history. Their approach led to a significant breakthrough in Irish historiography and to sophisticated reinterpretations. (See Chapter 1 for an outline of revisionist ideas.) In this book we focus on the competing interpretations of the nationalist and revisionist schools as well as the perspective of a new generation of historians (called the "post-revisionists") who have fashioned a more balanced and often quite different "spin" on the pivotal events of the past.

Ireland: The Place

Ireland itself is small, located on the northwest perimeter of Europe, with Great Britain traditionally both a hovering presence and a barrier to the continent. A visitor can travel from one end of Ireland to the other in a few hours or a day: the distance from north to south is only 302 miles (480 km) and from one side to the other (east to west) only 171 miles (266 km). The total size of the island is 32,595 square miles (84,421 square km). The Republic comprises 27,136 square miles (70,282 square km) and Northern Ireland, 5,459 square miles (14,139 square km). The island's geographical area is approximately the same as that of Austria and slightly less than those of Portugal or Hungary. Compared to the United States, the whole island is the size of the state of Maine, while Northern Ireland is about the same size as Connecticut.

The population of the island in 1996 was 5.2 million people, which is slightly smaller than that of the Commonwealth of Massachusetts. The population density of Ireland is quite low compared to other European states. Belgium has only one-third the area but almost twice the population. In 1991 the number of people per square kilometer of Ireland was fifty-one, the lowest in the European Union, while that of the Netherlands is approximately seven times higher. The population of the Republic of Ireland in 1996 was about 3,621,000. The population distribution of the island, including Northern Ireland, is heavily urban; in the Republic over 60 percent of the population can be considered urban. Dublin, the largest city on the island, has a population, including its suburbs, of over 1 million people, which is slightly less than one-third that of the Republic of Ireland. Cork, Limerick, and other towns and cities are substantial population centers. In Northern Ireland the total population is 1,573,000; the two cities of Belfast (population 280,000) and Londonderry (population over 72,300) account for over 20 percent of the population of that province.

Both regions are characterized by a geographical east–west split that is as distinct as the political north–south split. The province of Ulster is bisected by the River Bann. To the east of the river the Protestants are more heavily concentrated, while the Catholics tend to live in the west and, in fact, are a majority in the city of Londonderry (called Derry by the Catholics).[4] Industry is concentrated in the eastern sector of Ulster, especially in Belfast, which became the first industrial area of Ireland in the nineteenth century. The rural areas of west Ulster have suffered deterioration. Population has declined and little industrial development has taken place. In the Republic the province of Connaught in the west has also suffered decline in population, and despite the efforts of the government to encourage industrial development, it remains less affluent than the more urbanized east. The last remaining Irish-speaking areas are sprinkled in a fringe along the western coast. The decline in the use of that language, even in those areas, accelerated in the last decades of the twentieth century. The decline of the western areas has left a population with more women than men, more old than young, and more poor than affluent, tending relatively inefficient, small farms.

The religious affiliation of the people in the Republic is 92 percent Catholic and 2 percent Church of Ireland, with the remaining 6 percent Methodists, Baptists, and a very small Jewish population. Northern Ireland is composed of 39 percent Catholics, 21 percent Presbyterians, and 18 percent Church of Ireland, with the remaining 23 percent Methodist, Baptist, or other. On the island as a whole the

Catholics make up nearly three-fourths of the population, while Protestants and others constitute the remaining one-fourth.

The major industry in the Republic was for a long time agriculture, which has been supplemented by a vigorous tourist industry and a growing manufacturing base, especially in light industry such as electronics and pharmaceuticals. Services, however, are the fastest growing sector of the economy, with financial services emerging at an unexpectedly rapid rate. The effect has been to replace agriculture as the dominant sector of the economy. The north of Ireland has a good agricultural base, while tourism, understandably, was not a strong sector in the second half of the twentieth century. Nineteenth-century manufacturing strengths such as textiles and ship building were replaced by machine tools, aircraft, and electronics. While both parts of Ireland possess skilled workforces, both have been plagued by high unemployment.

The Chapters to Come

This book, like Ireland and Gaul, has three parts. Chapters 1 through 3 trace how the relationship of Ireland with Great Britain engendered the development of Irish nationalism, which in turn produced Irish independence. That independence, however, revealed the divisions among the Irish people and, in fact, produced the political separation of Ulster. In these chapters we explore the formative power of such events as the Famine and the Rising of 1916.

The ensuing fifty years set the two sections of Ireland on separate paths, the south seeking to realize full independence, the north to consolidate Protestant rule within the United Kingdom. In chapters 4 through 8 the struggles of the Republic for economic development are described and the effects on society of changes in the economic sphere are traced. The impact of economic development on virtually every sphere of society has generated stress and tension as old values conflict with the new forces of urbanization, materialism, and secularism. Critiques of the policies pursued are presented and examined, as are the ideologies of Church–state relations, with an eye to the clash of two very different views of Ireland. The government has had the responsibility of managing this modernization, and these changes have generated new political pressures; a new electorate; a new agenda of issues; and changes in party leadership, structure, and style. The new Irish renaissance and the effect of the creative burst on the global cultural stage compel our attention.

Chapters 9 and 10 cover Northern Ireland and trace the development of that province and the renewal of communal violence that has plagued Ulster for three decades. We look at the players, the role of the United States, the policies of the United Kingdom, and the political developments that have supported peace and those that have undermined it. In these chapters we examine the multiplicity of theories accounting for the conflict. At the end of the twentieth century the violence in

Ulster brought the people of Ireland once again to the question of Irish nationhood and revealed the reciprocal impact on one another of the politics of the two regions. From the dual pressures of modernization and communal violence we return again to the questions raised in the last century when Irish nationalism emerged: What are to be the central social and cultural values of the Irish people? What is the structure of the political order to be?

Notes

1. Michel Peillon, *Contemporary Irish Society* (Dublin: Gill & Macmillan, 1982), p. 1.

2. See Joseph Lee, *The Modernization of Irish Society 1848–1918* (Dublin: Gill & Macmillan, 1973).

3. L. Binder, et al., *Crises and Sequence in Political Development* (Boston: Little, Brown, 1971).

4. Names can convey a lot of information about one's view of Ireland. The Constitution of the Republic of Ireland calls the country Eire, or Ireland in English. That Constitution claims sovereignty over the whole of the island including Ulster. To further confuse matters, prior to 1920 the whole island was called Ireland. Thus the name "Ireland" can refer to the whole geographical unit or to the Republic of Ireland alone. Within the United Kingdom the province of Ulster is called Northern Ireland and the United Kingdom claims sovereignty over it. When Ireland was partitioned in 1922, three counties of the traditional province of Ulster were separated and put into the Free State of Ireland. (Contributing yet more to the confusion over nomenclature, the South of Ireland was called the Free State from 1922 until 1937.) Thus the label "Ulster" can be used to refer to both the current political entity of Northern Ireland and the traditional nine-county province. This distinction leads to the use of the clumsy construction "twenty-six counties of Ireland" and "six counties of Ulster," which at least adds to the precision of language if not its elegance. This terminological morass does not end with the names of places; the anniversary of the potato blight of 1845 to 1850 has prompted a reconsideration of the widely used term "Famine," which implied a lack of food from a natural disaster. There is a suggestion that it should be replaced with the term "Great Hunger," which implies that something could have been done about it but was not, leaving the Irish to starve. Of course, in Northern Ireland one person's "freedom fighter" is another's "terrorist" the former are engaged in an "armed struggle" while the latter are on a "campaign of murder," depending upon one's view of Irish history.

1

THE QUESTION OF IRISH HISTORY: FROM THE CELTS TO O'CONNELL

Henry Ford once said, "History is bunk." This dismissal of history is akin to calling a magnificent tapestry just a collection of threads, which, of course, it is not. A tapestry is a reflection of the lives and ideas portrayed in its composition, and, like art, history is subject to interpretation and reinterpretation as successive generations refocus their collective memories in the light of their current experience. This process is true for the history of any nation, but it is particularly true for the Irish because their experience has been intertwined with the destiny of their largest neighbor to the east.

At least two major historical traditions have competed for attention since Irish independence in 1922. One is the long-standing "nationalist" tradition, with its stress on Celtic, Catholic, and revolutionary dimensions. It emphasizes the centuries-long struggle with the British as the central theme of Irish history and lauds a pantheon of national heroes—Wolfe Tone, the Fenians, Patrick Pearse—who have led Ireland's steady march toward independence. The other tradition is a "revisionist" interpretation, a scholarly approach that seeks to tell a more "objective" history of Ireland, one that is free from partisan and moralistic storytelling. Whereas nationalists view the Great Famine, for example, as the product of parasitic landlords and a near-genocidal British policy, revisionists have softened the rhetoric, opining that the tragedy was the outcome of complex socioeconomic factors that were well under way before 1845. Such debates have captured the hearts and minds of the Irish people and form the backdrop against which they interpret their experiences today and explain changes in modern Ireland. This question of historical viewpoint is particularly acute concerning Northern Ireland, especially when considering the legitimacy of the Irish Republican Army (IRA).

In the 1990s another interpretation began to find a voice. This "post-revisionist" commentary seeks to go beyond the comforting polarities of nationalist and revisionist history to encompass new viewpoints on politics and popular culture. In the following chapters this informing perspective provides an added dimension to our understanding of the Irish story.

This chapter begins our consideration of Irish history with the arrival of early peoples at the dawn of prehistory and progresses through the 1840s. We emphasize the development of Irish institutions and identity and also explore several case studies in light of nationalist and revisionist traditions. The major events examined in this and following chapters are the Penal Laws, the 1798 Rebellion, Daniel O'Connell, the Great Famine, the "Irish Nation," and the Rising of 1916.

The Early Peoples

> Writers of the present have nothing to say of anything
> beyond Ierne [Ireland] which is just north of Britain.
> Natives are wholly savage and lead a wretched
> existence because of the cold. In my opinion it is
> there the limits of the habitable earth should be
> fixed.
>
> Strabo (63 B.C.–21 A.D.)

Strabo's depiction of Ireland on the eve of the new millennium is a chilling one, rooted in classical prejudices regarding "remote countries" and the nature of barbarism. It belies the rich and impressive prehistory that this island, poised on the edge of the North Atlantic, enjoyed. Indeed, Ireland's proximity to Britain and its direct access to Europe contributed to the successive waves of peoples and influences that reached its shores.

By 7000 B.C. hunter-gatherers had arrived from Britain. They entered a country heavily forested and teeming with game. It was their unique adaptation to the environment that forged the first distinctive Irish identity. The first farmers reached Ireland about 4000 B.C., bringing with them cattle, sheep, wheat, and barley, as well as the tools needed to exploit them. Within a few hundred years Ireland had seen the emergence of extensive pasture land and farming, the growth of a substantial population, and the construction of increasingly sophisticated megalithic (great stone) architecture. These megalithic tombs served not only as repositories of human remains but also, arguably, as territorial markers and, in some cases, symbols of power. The major monuments in the Boyne valley—Dowth, Knowth, and Newgrange—rank among the finest achievements of passage tombs in western Europe.[1]

The Celts

With the introduction of metalworking to Ireland around 2500 B.C., Ireland entered a new age of economic advancement. Henceforth the farmer and the craftsman constituted the basis of society. Into this world around 300 B.C. arrived the Celts. Originating in the Bronze Age peoples of central Europe, they brought with them a vibrant assemblage of religion, language, and metalworking. This Celtic culture survived for many centuries in Ireland and parts of Scotland, regions unconquered by the Roman Empire. There is no surviving evidence of a large-scale "invasion" by the incoming Celts. Rather, it is thought that they formed a dominant minority whose language and culture were rapidly assimilated by the indigenous peoples of Ireland.[2]

Socially the Celts lived in loosely knit communities whose elite built defensive hill forts that still dot the Irish rural landscape. Politically, Celtic society was organized along tribal lines, with more than 100 small kingdoms, called tuatha, each with a chief or king. These tribal kingdoms formed shifting alliances among themselves and lived by agriculture and raiding expeditions for land and cattle (which were used as a unit of wealth). The religion of the Celts, Druidism, was filled with pagan mysticism, taboos, and privileges. The different classes of Druids and seers held powerful positions in society and presented a formidable opposition to the new Christian religion initiated by contact with Roman Britain. The encounter between these two worlds is captured satirically in one of the earliest poems surviving in Irish, lampooning St. Patrick (with his bishop's miter) as "an adze head, crazed in the head."[3]

Introduction of Christianity

Patrick was one of many missionaries who brought Ireland more fully into the Roman world, its Latin language, and Christianity. A native of western Britain, he was captured by Irish raiders and enslaved for six years. After escaping his masters he eventually returned to Ireland (he asserts as a bishop) to preach the gospel and evangelize. The process of conversion by Patrick and others spread gradually and fused with many features of pagan Celtic culture. The unique syncretism that emerged in Irish Christianity is particularly notable in the absorption of Celtic customs and festivals into the Church calendar and Christianization of early Celtic sites such as holy wells and royal centers. St. Patrick, especially, understood the symbolic power of place among his Irish converts and thus gained stature through his close association with Ard Macha (Armagh), the capital of the old province of Ulster. Indeed, Patrick's chroniclers would later cite the ancient prominence of this site to support claims that Patrick's church should be the primatial see of all Ireland. Thus, even at an early date, the Irish past was being manipulated to effect contemporary opinion.[4]

This fortuitous blend of Celtic culture, politics, and social structure with the learning and language of Christianity produced the golden age of Ireland in the seventh and eighth centuries. The monasteries were the landmarks of this age: centers of devotion, political power, and scholarship. Indeed, the writing of Irish history began in the monasteries with the adoption of the Latin alphabet to write Gaelic. Thus the ability was developed about the year 600 to record the law of the Gaels, or Brehon Law; the songs, poetry, and scholarship of the bards and monks; and the events of the political and social order. The imprint of this culture upon the Irish gave them a distinctive religious, cultural, and political identity to which they could refer during the long struggle with the British from the twelfth to the nineteenth centuries. British imperialism confronted an integrated, highly developed society and began the slow, uneven process of anglicizing it. The Celtic and Catholic components of Irish nationalism are rooted in that golden age of over two and one-half centuries of Celtic achievement. In the nineteenth century, despite the dominance of the English language in Ireland, it was this cultural heritage, however romanticized, that contributed to the rising nationalist movement.

The Vikings

Irish society and political alignments took on a new pattern as a result of invasions from Scandinavia. The Vikings, chiefly Norwegian in the case of Ireland, began to attack the islands of the north Atlantic in the 790s A.D. Their initial targets in Ireland were Irish monastic settlements, the repositories of valuable and precious metals as well as a potential source of captives, who were pawns in the extensive slave trade carried on by the Norsemen. In the century and a half from 830 to 1014 the Vikings, or Ostmen as they called themselves, controlled the Shannon, founded Dublin, and raided the great monasteries. A ninth-century Irish monk, thankful for a raging storm that made the seas impassable, wrote in the margins of his manuscript:

> *The wind is fierce tonight*
> *It tosses the Sea's white hair*
> *I fear no wild Vikings*
> *Sailing the quiet main.*[5]

New research indicates that this traditional portrait of the Norsemen as raiders and plunderers of the Irish monasteries is incomplete.[6] True, some of the smaller monasteries foundered during the Viking era, but the extent to which the Ostmen were a deciding factor in the decline of the "Golden Age" of Irish saints and scholars is exaggerated. Indeed, prominent monasteries such as

Armagh and Clonmacnoise managed to survive the Viking incursions with their resources intact.

Our view of the Ostmen, particularly by the mid-tenth century, should also include their permanent settlement in Hibernia and their impact on Irish society. Excavations at Dublin's Wood Quay and in Waterford city have indicated their influence on foreign trade, introduction of coinage into Ireland, and role as the first town builders. Indeed, Irish port towns such as Dublin, Wexford, Waterford, and Limerick owe their beginnings and even their names to the Vikings.

By the end of the tenth century, the Ostmen controlled much of coastal Ireland. The Irish challenge to this rule produced one of the most notable figures in the history of the Irish kingship: Brian Boru. Brian Boru began his ascent by defeating the Norse rulers in Munster and becoming king of that province from 976 to 1014. In the north another king, Malachy, rose to defeat the Norse at Tara and then went on to drive the Scandinavians from Dublin. The two Irish kings divided up Ireland; Brian became master of Dublin and Leinster. In 1002 Malachy conceded the high kingship to Brian, who set out to consolidate his power. He spent a week in Armagh, formally acknowledging its ecclesiastical ascendancy over Ireland, and in turn was proclaimed "Emperor of the Irish." One task remained: to defeat an incipient challenge to his rule. At the battle of Clontarf, on Good Friday 1014, Brian defeated a coalition of Leinster Irish and Dublin Ostmen. He was killed in the battle, but his rule had brought significant achievements. He had dominated the high kingship of the Irish people and thus had accomplished what few high kings had achieved: a semblance of unified monarchical authority. His death, however, revived the pattern of political conflict among the provincial kingdoms of Ireland, which now included Hiberno-Norse settlers who had intermarried with the Irish and had integrated into the loose Irish political and social structure.

Brian Boru holds an important place in the nationalist interpretation of Irish history. He is often romantically depicted as a Gaelic champion defending Ireland against Viking domination (even his death on Good Friday symbolically suggests his role as savior). From this perspective the battle of Clontarf is portrayed as the climactic victory of the Irish over a foreign foe, a victory that ended Norse aspirations of conquering Ireland. The reality was more complex. Clontarf was occasioned by long-standing provincial rivalries and pitted the king of Leinster against Brian Boru. It was a battle fought between Irish kings—with Viking allies participating on both sides.[7]

The Norman Conquest

Just as the Irish political climate was unsettled, so too was the identity and direction of the Irish Church. Over the years criticism mounted concerning the vast wealth and temporal power of the monasteries. Complaints of hereditary abbots, married clergy, and the protection of secular and family interests all drew the attention of Rome. By the twelfth century monastic life had reached a low ebb. Major synods reshaped the Irish Church into territorial dioceses and parishes, and native monasteries were increasingly supplanted by foreign orders such as the Cistercians, who brought in new models of monastic rule. While suspect practices such as simony were not eradicated immediately, reforms did succeed in bringing the Irish Church closer to Rome and continental attention.

Ireland also came under closer scrutiny from outsiders in the political sphere. Protest against the evils and abuses in the Irish Church prompted Pope Adrian IV (the only English Pope) to issue the papal letter "Laudabiliter" in 1155, which gave King Henry II of England authority to take possession of Ireland. The immediate impetus, however, for the Norman invasion came from Dermot McMorraugh, a king of Leinster. McMorraugh carries a special burden in the nationalist history of Ireland because it was at his invitation that Richard de Clare, the Earl of Pembroke (known as Strongbow), went to Ireland in 1170 with an invasion force of Welsh-Norman knights and archers. Strongbow's agreement with McMorraugh gained him a wife (McMorraugh's daughter) and designation as heir to the kingdom of Leinster. At this point King Henry II of England began to fear a rival Norman kingdom in Ireland and, under the disputed authority of the papal bull, crossed the Irish sea to claim his title as lord of Ireland.[8] Henry distributed the land in Ireland among his loyal Norman barons and several Irish provincial kings who agreed to pay him tribute. In time, the Normans extended their conquests beyond Leinster, an achievement that was due in part to Norman military skills and superior weaponry. Fortified sites, protective armor, heavy cavalry, and archers (largely unknown in Ireland) gave the Normans a tactical advantage over their Irish foes. Moreover, the invaders were aided by the fragmented resistance and internecine warfare they encountered among Gaelic tribes. As one chronicler remarked: "There has been fighting in all provinces, endless campaigns, cattle raids, burnings, atrocities—Ireland lies like a trembling sod."[9] Norman domination also depended upon more subtle avenues of persuasion such as strategic political and marital alliances. As new historical work suggests these factors may have been equally, if not more, important than military conquest.[10]

While images of the Norman knights emphasize their skill at sword and conquest, we should recall that the Welsh-Norman barons who won land grants from Henry II were primarily interested in promoting commerce and developing market agriculture. They sought out the best land in Ireland (nestled along fertile river valleys to the east and southeast), and some planted rural colonies of Welsh and English farmers to turn a marketable profit. Gerald of Wales, a Norman cleric who visited Ireland about 1185, described the countryside and made an often uncomplimentary comparison between native Irish life and that of their Norman

Tomb Effigy of Cantwell, a fine example of a medieval Norman knight of the fourteenth century in full armor. It stands in the ruined church at Kilfane, County Kilkenny. *Photo by Edward T. McCarron*

betters. He remarked that, "The Irish have no use of castles. Woods are their forts and swamps their ditches." In terms of economy,

> They have not progressed at all from the primitive habits of pastoral living. While man usually progresses from the woods to the fields, and from fields to settlements and communities of citizens, these people despise work on the land. . . . For given only to leisure and devoted only to laziness they think that the greatest pleasure is not to work and the greatest wealth is their liberty.[11]

Gerald also described the Irish as a "barbarous" people who were ignorant of the rudiments of the Christian faith and addicted to vice and outlandish habits. This image of the barbarian, as W. R. Jones points out, was a highly useful cliché "that served equally well as a means of self congratulation and as a rationalization for dispossession."[12] Indeed, the writings of Gerald of Wales were consulted for centuries as an authoritative source on the Irish and provided moral and ideological fuel for English officials intent on the conquest of Ireland.[13]

In time, these deeply felt divisions between the "civilized" Norman lords and the "savage" native Irish began to blur, especially outside the gravitational pull of Dublin, the Anglo-Norman seat of government and administration. Intermittent conflict with the native Irish was accompanied by a slow integration of the Normans into the Irish cultural milieu. Intermarriage, adoption of the Irish language, and general acceptance by the Irish created several layers of Norman influence over the next two centuries. In the Leinster area surrounding Dublin, called "the Pale," the English influence was greatest and was characterized by English law, customs, dress, and administration. The second layer of influence was in the east and south, where the Norman feudal system took hold but where Norman landholders also increasingly adopted the Irish culture. Least influenced were Ulster in the north and areas in the west of Ireland, where the rule remained essentially Gaelic.

Political authority was vested in an Irish Parliament convened in 1297. It was exclusively ecclesiastical and Norman, and no native Irish were invited. The first Parliament condemned the cultural integration of the Normans and labeled as "degenerate English" any people who adopted the Irish language and mores. An often-cited example of the attempt to preserve the Englishness of the Normans is the Statutes of Kilkenny, enacted in 1366. These laws forbade intermarriage, wearing Irish dress, recognizing the Brehon Law, speaking the Irish language, fostering Irish children, and patronage of Gaelic bards and poets. The statutes not only were a reflection of cultural superiority but also signaled the somewhat insecure status of the Anglo-Norman elite in Ireland. By the fourteenth century Norman settlement surrounding the Pale was in a defensive posture, but the traditional political divisions among the Irish prevented the focus of power necessary to drive the Normans out of the country. By the fifteenth century the political arrangement gave the descendants of the original Norman settlers—now known as the "Old English"—substantial home rule (with some areas still under Gaelic rule) and left them resentful of royal authority and inclined to ignore it.

The Shipwreck of the Old Order

The Tudor monarchs observed that the expanding imperial role of Britain was threatened by the vulnerability of Ireland. The lack of English authority beyond the Pale, coupled with the less than total devotion of the Old English aristocracy, was a potential opportunity for England's enemies. This was especially true after the English Reformation in 1534, when Henry VIII severed Britain's allegiance with Rome. The Irish Catholic faith now became an added security risk, a conduit of alliance and complicity with the Catholic powers of France and Spain. England, as one official asserted, must determine not "to have the Pope keeper of the keys of [our] back door."[14] The task of asserting the authority of the English Crown and extending English law to Gaelic Ireland was formidable. Henry VIII tried to garner the adherence of the Gaelic chieftains by having them surrender their lands, whereupon he would return them and grant titles to the chieftains, who would administer the land as tenants-in-chief of the English Crown. Moreover, in 1541, Henry had himself designated king of Ireland by the Irish Parliament.

Of greater consequence in fueling Irish antagonism and deepening the political and cultural gap were attempts by the Tudors to extend the Protestant Reformation into Ireland. Dissolution of the monasteries, attempts to impose Anglican church doctrine, and Edward VI's edict outlawing the Catholic mass all drew the ire of the Gaelic Catholic Irish. Moreover, under the Tudor's, royal power in Ireland was administered in a more partisan fashion, and English-Protestant administrators were increasingly tapped to rule in place of Old English magnates. This developing policy of religious apartheid was resented by the Old English. Catholicism would thus become the hub of Irish identity and later one of the pillars of Irish nationalism.

The Flight of the Earls and Plantation

In the 1590s the Irish came as close as they were going to come to defeating English rule. The earl of Tyrone, Hugh O'Neill, and the earl of Tyrconnell, Hugh O'Donnell, marshaled support from the lesser Gaelic nobles throughout Ireland. For nine years they withstood the English assault but, despite success at the outset, they were finally defeated by superior forces of the Royal Army at the Battle of Kinsale. The struggle ended in 1603 when O'Neill surrendered. (He was subsequently pardoned.) O'Donnell fled to Spain, and a few years later O'Neill and about 100 Irish chieftains from the north, fearing a conspiracy against their lives, left for the Continent.

This "flight of the earls" left the way open for the completion of the English conquest and the decline of a Gaelic Ireland with its own traditions, law, and society. The flight of the earls also led to the plantation of Ulster, a strategy revived by James I to firmly establish English control of the land. Plantation consisted of granting land confiscated by the Crown to "planters," or landlords, who would farm the land. James I seized the O'Neill and O'Donnell lands, which comprised vast tracts of Ulster. Beginning in 1610 English planters and especially Scottish settlers took up land in Ulster, so that by 1641 only one-seventh of the province was in Catholic hands. Thus, despite the fact that many Gaelic Irish remained as tenants, Ulster eventually became a Protestant colony, and the distinct ethnic majority of that region was established.

The pattern of rebellion, defeat, and plantation was to continue. In 1641, during the English Civil War, the native Irish and Old English Catholics mounted another effort to throw off English domination and were quite successful in controlling a substantial portion of Ireland. They formed a government, the Confederation of Kilkenny, which then proceeded to splinter into factions, thus preventing any coherent organization of resistance. The Irish rising of 1641 (like the Cromwellian invasion that followed) is most remembered for its unprecedented sectarian violence. In locales such as County Armagh angry Catholic tenants, many displaced by the Ulster Plantation, took revenge on Protestant settlers—especially at Burntollet Bridge, where more than 100 Protestants were drowned in the river Bann at Portadown. Incidents such as these, which were exaggerated out of proportion by English propagandists, have since echoed down the chambers of history and have helped forge a besieged and defensive consciousness that pervades Ulster today.[15]

Memories of atrocity, in the person of Oliver Cromwell, also seared the Catholic community. Having defeated his royalist enemies in Britain, Cromwell turned to Ireland and ruthlessly crushed the rebellion in 1650. The tone was set by Cromwell's massacre of an Anglo-Irish garrison at Drogheda, a royalist stronghold on the river Boyne. The ensuing sack of the town provided generations of nationalist apologists with historical firepower: images of priests and civilians being murdered, survivors being transported to the West Indies, and violence so intense that laneways such as "Scarlet Street" still attest to the bloodletting.

Land Settlement

The most far-reaching aspect of the Cromwellian conquest, however, was its policy of land settlement. Under the Act of Settlement in 1652, all Catholic estates were confiscated and dispossessed Irish were forced to move to "hell or to Connaught." This transfer of land proceeded rapidly, with expropriated estates being assigned to Cromwellian soldiers and English adventurers.

Catholic "exile" to Connaught, however, was more haphazard. While some Catholic proprietors were transplanted, others remained on the land as tenants, creating a layer of resistance—an "underground gentry"—that would resurface in the century to come. The fact remains, however, that Catholic landholding east of the Shannon was on its way to becoming a memory.[16] It would prove a potent memory, nonetheless, as voiced in the poetry of the dispossessed:

Gerald the Bitter, with your polished smile,
may all be desert up to your door . . .
- for you took my son and you took his father,
you took my dozen cows and the bull.
Your heir, Gerald, may he never inherit![17]

Involvement in English Political Rivalries

In 1688, and not for the last time, English political rivalries played themselves out on the Irish stage. James II, a closet Catholic, had become king in 1685. His pro-Catholic convictions and the fact that his heir was Catholic prompted the British Parliament's decision to depose him and install the Protestant William of Orange on the British throne. James sought his restoration through the back door of Ireland, where he knew he would have Catholic support. James's efforts failed at the siege of Londonderry and on the banks of the river Boyne, where his forces were defeated by the army of William III. While of decisive strategic importance, the Battle of the Boyne was also a symbolic triumph of Protestant forces over Catholic—a victory that is still played out in marches and commemorations in the north. The Catholic forces held out until 1691, when William offered the be-sieged Catholics in Limerick promises that they would be free to practice their religion, their property would remain secure, and they would be free from reprisals. Although William may have concluded the Treaty of Limerick in good faith, his co-religionists in Ireland and England wanted the Irish punished.

The Treaty of Limerick allowed some 11,000 soldiers—predominantly officers and swordsmen—to sail for France. These "Wild Geese," as they are known in Irish tradition, were part of a steady movement of Hibernian immigrants to the Continent, expatriates who sought a place in one of the Catholic armies of Europe or a career in trade.[18] Irish merchant communities emerged at Cadiz, Bordeaux, and Lisbon, and Irish entrepreneurs played an important role in the European wine and brandy trade. The Hennessys of Cork, who built a cognac dynasty in France over several generations, are only the most famous example. Elite Catholic families in Ireland also sent their sons to be educated abroad, including many intended for the priesthood. Indeed, with little opportunity for religious instruction at home, Hibernian clerics founded Irish colleges at Rome, Louvain, and Salamanca. These centers became hotbeds of dissension during the Counter-Reformation and were the staging grounds for Irish apologists and historians abroad. Geoffrey Keating, educated at Bordeaux, wrote *Foras Feasa ar Eirinn*, the first narrative history of Ireland (written in the vernacular) and highly critical of English views on the Irish.[19] Archdeacon John Lynch likewise attacked the prevailing stereotypes of the Irish, particularly those spread by Gerald of Wales. He was especially outraged at charges of Irish inferiority and barbarity, emphasizing the important contributions of early Medieval Irish culture to learning.[20] These works represent some of the first "nationalist" writing in defense of Irish culture and identity and came at a time when Irish rights were quickly eroding.

The Penal Laws

At the close of the seventeenth century the land-owning Protestant elite (a minority in Ireland at roughly 25 percent of the population) approved a series of anti-Catholic measures, fueled in part by prevailing stereotypes and anti-popery. These laws, enacted by the British Parliament and the Irish Parliament between 1695 and 1727, sought to suppress Irish Catholics and prevent their participation in public office, the army, and civil employment. The principal elements included banishment of bishops and religious orders from the country; those priests who remained were to register and disclaim loyalty to the Stuart pretender to the English throne. Catholics were also excluded from Parliament and from the practice of law; they could not found schools or send their children to Europe to be educated. Leasing of property to Catholics was limited to thirty-one years; purchase by Catholics was not allowed. Any property still owned by Catholics could not be left to one son but had to be divided among all sons. If an eldest son, however, converted to Protestantism, the entire family estate became his. These laws were to last in various forms until 1829.

How should we interpret the Penal Laws during the eighteenth century? What role did they play in suppressing religious practice and economic opportunity among Catholics and in galvanizing their resentment and animosity ? These questions have prompted a lively debate in the second half of the twentieth century.

The nationalist interpretation of eighteenth-century Ireland has argued that anti-Catholic legislation, allied with an exploitative landlord class, created a spiritually and economically impoverished peasantry. Popular images abound in early nationalist writing of priest hunters exposing clandestine Catholic activity for bounty and Irish communities clinging precariously to their faith in lonely glens and open fields. Likewise, observers such as Arthur Young, who toured Ireland in the 1770s, described poor wretched souls living in "miserable looking hovels" and everywhere "working as cottiers on lands which were once their own."[21]

Not surprisingly given these images, the nationalist community has underlined the existence of a deeply divided society in eighteenth-century Ireland, one in which the Irish Catholic tenantry, disenfranchised and poverty stricken, were victimized by an Anglo-Irish ascendant class. Daniel Corkery strongly underlines these views in *The Hidden Ireland,* first published in 1924. In his opinion there was little relief for the Gaelic Irish:

> Those Penal Laws that denied him ownership, that forbade him education, that closed the professions to him.—Those laws were as so many nails that held him fast in the bondage where half a century of war had left him—a hewer of wood and a drawer of water—"for his conqueror!"[22]

Here Corkery posits a clear distinction between the Irish peasants who toiled over their patch of rock-strewn ground and the Protestant gentry who lived in the Big House. While the native Irish were "dying of starvation in their cabins," a visit to the landlord's demesne revealed "the wine flushed revelry of the alien gentry, the hunting, the dancing, the drinking, the duelling, with the Big House itself in the background, its half felled woods hanging like dishevelled garments about it."[23]

This view of the Penal Laws and eighteenth-century society has been challenged by revisionist historians since the 1950s. They argue that, whatever the original intent of the Penal Laws, the contention that they created a prostrate Catholic community and an impoverished Irish people is largely overstated.[24] Part of the problem, they suggest, is that nationalists have emphasized a partisan view of past oppression and injustice to suit political purposes. The long-term memory of discrimination under the Penal Laws, for example, was a useful weapon in the armory of the land reform movement of the 1870s. Indeed, as S. J. Connolly reminds us: "The tradition of a parasitic and remorselessly exploited landlord class had an obvious appeal at a time when landlord-tenant relations had become a bitterly contested political issue."[25]

The revisionists have called for a more balanced view of the eighteenth century, one that goes beyond a simple reading of the statute books to explore the local realities of religious experience and economic change.[26] A new "reading" of the Penal Laws suggests that they were, in fact, laxly enforced, particularly after 1730. Many of the cities and towns outside Ulster tolerated "Roman" chapels, which were built unpretentiously along back lanes. Priests likewise enjoyed a practical freedom of movement, cushioned by the fact that Catholics vastly outnumbered Protestants in many districts. Given this disparity it is not surprising, as one contemporary put it, that some priests felt able "to say mass publicly and afterwards put on their swords to dare the country."[27]

A similar reassessment has taken root with respect to economic disabilities. Revisionists have largely rejected the assumption that the Penal Laws created a uniformly impoverished "peasantry." Historians such as Maureen Wall, on the contrary, emphasize the emergence of a Catholic middle class in the eighteenth century, one that was active in manufacturing and overseas trade. She argues that this nascent Catholic elite, prevented from channeling its resources into politics and land holding, refocused its energy into the comparatively fluid and lucrative enterprise of trade.[28] Wall's thesis has recently been modified by David Dickson, who asserts that although a rising Catholic commercial class was in evidence, eighteenth-century urban and maritime trade was firmly in the control of a small cadre of Protestant families and interests.[29]

One finding that has helped to deflate the nationalist position is that penal legislation was not only leveled against Irish Catholics. Eighteenth-century legislation also sought to exclude dissenters and Presbyterians from public office and the military. This religious discrimination, coupled with rising rents, prompted many Presbyterians in Ulster to emigrate to the American colonies. And, in an interesting twist on the Irish nationalist "spin," these Scots-Irish harbored a festering animosity for British and colonial rule in the New World—a consciousness that was expressed most visibly in their enlistment during the American Revolution.[30]

In the late twentieth century a new generation of historians in Ireland has taken issue, in part, with the revisionists. They maintain that in banishing the classic images of penal oppression and injustice, the revisionists may have gone too far on the other side toward whitewashing the evidence of sectarian tension that pervaded eighteenth-century Irish society. Thomas Bartlett, for one, suggests that a central purpose of the Penal Laws was to bring about the conformity of the Catholic elite—a task that would ultimately ensure the safety of the Protestant minority. Most of the legislation that was actually enforced against Catholics—barring them from professions, from political power, and from purchasing land—indicated not a desire to punish an entire people but rather a concern over security and controlling the leadership class of the Irish community. As Bartlett asserts, "In the eighteenth century it was axiomatic that the lower classes of society without elite leadership, could not pose any real threat to the existing social or political order."[31]

While conformity made some inroads into the Catholic elite, recent historical scholarship also reveals that the traditional Gaelic gentry (and the threat from "below") did not simply disappear. Kevin Whelan, in *The Tree of Liberty,* underlines the survival of a uniquely divided and unstable society.[32] "These divisions were due," as one reviewer elaborates, "not just to a history of violent dispossession but to the existence of an 'underground gentry' of middlemen descended from displaced Catholic proprietors. For the Catholic masses this visible survival of the old ruling class provided the basis for continuing disaffection."[33] Perhaps Arthur Browne, the American-born senior fellow at Trinity College, said it best in 1787: "Elsewhere landed title was purchase, in Ireland it was forfeiture. The old proprietor kept alive the memory of his claim. Property in Ireland resembled the thin soil of volcanic countries spread lightly over subterranean fires."[34]

The Protestant Nation

Land redistribution and economic expansion during the eighteenth century led to the establishment of a Protestant "ascendancy," an elite of Anglo-Irish gentlemen who monopolized the legal profession, politics, and land holding. Their attitude of privilege and self-confidence was most notably expressed in their architecture: the fine Georgian houses that dotted the countryside and public buildings such as the Customs House and the Four Courts in Dublin, masterpieces that were designed to rival and even surpass those in London. This self-conscious identity carried over into the world of letters, where intellectuals such as Jonathan Swift sought to transcend their colonial status with England and declare themselves "The Irish Nation."

This Protestant sense of independence shifted to the Irish Parliament in the late 1700s. Increasingly more secure in its position within Ireland, the Protestant minority began to express dissatisfaction with its relationship with Britain. The discontent was directed at two main issues. First was the political restrictions placed upon the Irish Parliament with respect to enacting legislation; the Irish Parliament was a subordinate political entity. Second was the imposition of economic restraints upon Ireland by England. The export of woolen goods to England was restricted, as were other manufactured products. Restraints on the export of livestock, wool, and glass were designed to protect English farmers and manufacturers (linen manufacture was the exception to this policy). Whether these colonial restrictions greatly hampered the growth of trade has been disputed, but the fact remains that these two issues brought the Irish Protestant leadership into opposition with Britain. Although the majority of the Irish Parliament were pro-English (their seats were provided as patronage from the lord justices appointed by the king), a group emerged that was infused by the ideas of John Locke, and it fostered a form of Irish patriotism not unlike the American patriotism of the same period. These "patriots" condemned absentee landlords as parasites who drained Ireland of needed investment and leadership. Just as the American colonists protested the injustice of being ruled by an unrepresentative Parliament, the Irish patriots stressed the need for an independent Irish Parliament, one that would have the exclusive right to legislate for Ireland.

The British were now confronted with a war in North America and Anglo-Irish patriots agitating for Lockean rights at home. Moreover, in 1778 Irish Protestants (along with a few Catholic gentry) organized a national volunteer force, designed to protect against an invasion by the French, who were then allied with the Americans. By 1780 the Irish Volunteers numbered over 40,000, a potent force that began to think of itself not only as a bastion of defense but also as a means to press Irish grievances against Britain. Under these pressures London passed a bill removing the restrictions on Irish trade. The leader of the Anglo-Irish patriots, Henry Grattan, was a liberal who believed in Catholic civil rights, repeal of the Penal Laws, equality of Catholics and Protestants, and an independent Irish Parliament. The liberal Whigs came into power in England in 1782 and, under Irish and international pressure, granted the Irish Parliament legislative independence.

Although Grattan had championed the rights of Catholics, he did not represent the sentiments of the Anglo-Irish. In fact concessions made to Catholics between 1782 and 1800 came at the instigation of the British rather than of the Irish. Fearing the political tumult that was sweeping Europe as a result of the French Revolution, the British urged the Irish Parliament to discourage Catholic disloyalty by limiting the harshest edge of "no popery." Ceding to this pressure in 1792, the Liberals granted Catholics access to civic positions and the legal profession and the right to open schools, vote, and bear arms. Britain also encouraged the opening of a Roman Catholic seminary at Maynooth in 1795. Clearly not motivated by an overwhelming devotion to Catholicism, Protestant British and Irish

Henry Grattan memorialized outside of the gate of Trinity College on Dame Street in Dublin. He was a champion of Catholic emancipation and submitted a bill to end the Penal Laws in 1793 and grant full rights for Catholics. Though that bill failed, Grattan continued his efforts to achieve rights for the Catholic community throughout his career. The Irish Parliament from 1782 to 1800 came to be known as Grattan's Parliament because it was seen by nationalists as a manifestation of self governmment for Ireland. *Photo by Richard B. Finnegan*

leaders feared that the radical ideas of the French Revolution would flow into Ireland through the seminarians trained in Europe. The Irish bishops were in full agreement about creating a seminary at Maynooth because that action was consistent with their long-term interests in controlling education.

Although the bishops and political elites were interested in quarantining the ideas of the French Revolution, there were others who were swept up in the ideas of Tom Paine, Jean Jacques Rousseau, and the American and French Revolutions. In 1791 middle-class dissident intellectuals formed the Society of United Irishmen in Belfast. Adopting the ideas of republicanism, they advocated a democratic Ireland and the elimination of sectarian strife. Because the Ulster Presbyterians had suffered religious oppression under the Anglicans, the idea of a nonsectarian state appealed to the nonconformist Protestants as well as those Catholics who joined the Society. Although the Society united Protestants and Catholics in a common cause, the appearance of unity belied the reality of sectarian conflict in Ireland at that time.

1798

The 1798 Rebellion of the United Irishmen had its prelude in 1796 under the leadership of Wolfe Tone. Tone, the guiding light of the movement, was from Dublin, a Protestant educated at Trinity College. He had a vibrant personality and a keen mind and was totally committed to translating the ideas of republican France to Ireland. He had persuaded the French, then at war with Britain, to send an expedition of 20,000 men to join the Society's force in rebellion. The invasion force, accompanied by Tone, reached Bantry Bay in west Cork but was unable to make a landing due to wild weather. The fleet was scattered and returned to France—one of the great "what ifs" in Irish history.[35]

The Irish Parliament, alarmed by rising tension in the country, created an armed Protestant yeoman corps and instituted a series of coercive measures (house burnings, floggings, mass arrests) to quell unrest. By early 1798 events began to accelerate. In March the government arrested most of the leaders of the United Irishmen in Dublin. Thus, when the Society rose in rebellion several days later, their efforts were hampered by a lack of coordination and focus. Moreover, the scattered conflagrations that erupted were "conducted by local leaders with local reputations, rather than by the better known principals, now dead or in prison."[36]

In May the curtain rose on the first act of the rising in Wexford, where United Irish forces (most drawn from the local countryside) decimated a detachment of militia at Oulart. The victory encouraged many more to join: country folk and "united men" led by strong farmers, priests, and gentry (several of them Protestant). The insurgents fought bravely for over a month before they were defeated decisively at the Battle of Vinegar Hill, overlooking Enniscorthy. The second act unfolded in August 1798 when a small French force under General Jean-Joseph Humbert landed in Mayo and for a month fought alongside local farmers. Despite several electrifying moments—particularly the rout of Irish militia and British regulars known derisively as "the Castlebar races"— Humbert surrendered when he ran out of supplies.[37] In October the final act came to a close when Wolfe Tone was captured off the Donegal coast in a futile attempt to invade Ireland. Rather than be hung as a traitor, he took his own life.

The 1798 Rebellion has been the focus of a substantial body of work and differing interpretations between nationalists and revisionists. Was it a "glorious cause" based on Enlightment ideals of republicanism and inclusiveness, or was it a sectarian fist fight that was distinguished by atrocities and bloody reprisals? The pendulum of interpretation has swung back and forth on these questions over the years, and it may be instructive to explore the various versions because the peal of 1798 still has resonance for our own day.

The personal reflections of Daniel Gahan, a historian of the Wexford rising, open an illuminating window on the impact of nationalist image and the popular history of the period. Gahan recounts growing up in Wexford surrounded by family lore, ballads, and hallowed sites such as Vinegar Hill. The rising, he learned, was a valiant attempt against impossible odds to overthrow the English yoke and to create an independent Ireland. "The schoolroom confirmed it all," Gahan writes. "There the battles of ninety eight took on an even grander significance. There they were part of the great story of the redemption of our nation by men like Tone, O'Connell, Parnell and Pearse."[38] Indeed, one of the important conduits of nationalist tradition in twentieth-century Ireland was the national school system. In 1922 the Free State government instructed history teachers to inspire their students with the aspirations of such men as Thomas Osborne Davis and to emphasize "the continuity of the separatist idea from Tone to Pearse."[39]

This nationalist tradition—passed down in popular accounts, history textbooks, and the national school curriculum—increasingly came under fire in the 1950s and 1960s by the Irish academic establishment. They called for more rigorous scholarship and professional "objectivity" that would carry one beyond the "myths" and "unquestioned assumptions" inherent in the traditional narrative.[40] This revisionist perspective was expressed in several works that became authoritative accounts of 1798. Chief among these was Thomas Pakenham's *Year of Liberty*, a vividly written work that painted a vastly different picture of the Wexford rebels from the heroic accounts of Gahan's youth. Instead of brave amateur soldiers fighting for liberty, the rebels were "a half disciplined mob with little idea beyond plunder."[41] Moreover, they had no serious political aims; they were simply "local peasantry" driven by religious hatred and local grievances.

Pakenham's lead was followed by subsequent works that highlighted the scattered and sectarian nature of the movement. Here, the ideals of the United Irishmen were de-emphasized as simply rhetoric; the reality on the ground in the 1790s was, instead, one of sectarian bitterness. Clashes between the Catholic Defenders and the Protestant Orange Order and sectarian violence by rebels and counter-insurgency troops alike were more representative of the period than the unity of the United Irishmen. Indeed, Roy Foster, in an influential history of Ireland, dismisses the origins of the Rebellion as being due to Catholic land hunger, an increase in taxes, and religious bitterness. "What broke out . . . was a localized jacquerie, taking hold in Wexford and east Leinster, leading to bloodletting and massacre on an appalling scale."[42]

During the bicentennial of 1798, historians debated the merits and the message of the revisionist interpretation. While revisionists have exposed the simplistic and often partisan history of the nationalists, their critics suggest that they were writing in service of an equally politicized reading of history. The escalation of violence in the north after 1970 increasingly led many in the Irish intellectual community to equate nationalism (and its revolutionary icons such as Wolfe Tone) with support for physical force. Indeed, this violence engendered a more sympathetic attitude to British government policy and a consequent disenchantment with the republican movement. In the hands of revisionist historians this alienation with popular revolutionary ideals was translated, unwittingly perhaps, into a negative portrait of the 1798 rebels and a less critical treatment of the role of government during the rising.[43]

The question remains, should the 1790s be viewed as a potpourri of agrarian discontent, old antipathies, and sectarian rivalry? Or was it a defining moment in Irish history, the springboard for new ideas and a developing identity whose trajectory would have a vibrant afterlife in the two centuries to follow? A new wave of historians appears to firmly embrace the latter interpretation. Recent work has focused on the intellectual context of the United Irishmen, the impact of popular politics, and a better understanding of the role of sectarianism in the 1790s.[44] It has also effectively challenged the idea that the Rebellion was a "spontaneous" outburst of peasants without planning or direction. As Kevin Whelan reminds us, the Rising was actually a sophisticated and well-coordinated undertaking, which failed because the key element in the plan, a coup in Dublin, did not succeed, "thereby prompting a disjointed, spasmodic look to the wave of supporting mobilisations in a crescent around the capital."[45]

A central theme in this new scholarship has been the significance of mass politicization. In particular, interest has focused on the rank and file of the movement and the extent to which radical ideology percolated down to the local and parish level. The United Irishmen, while initially a society of radical elites and intellectuals, made it their business to politicize popular culture and penetrate the ranks of ordinary folk.[46] They utilized newspapers, broadsheets, ballads, prophecy men, and hedge schoolmasters to take the message to the people: to "make every man a politician," as Thomas Adis Emmett expressed it.[47] The United Irishmen also moved to incorporate pre-existing clubs into their orbit. Artisan and drinking societies, masonic lodges, and sports teams all served as nurseries for Enlightenment ideas and radical activity. In Wexford, for example, entire United Irish units were based around pre-existing hurling teams. Rather than view participants of the rising as mindless lemmings acting out local grievances, we should appreciate that these groups embraced at least part of the Enlightenment ideas and common cause of their leaders.

In this view 1798 should be remembered not as a sectarian wedge that divided the Irish people but rather as a pivotal moment when strife was laid aside in pursuit of higher ideals. As historians such as Kevin Whelan suggest, we must relinquish our obsession with the atrocities, mayhem, and martyrdom of 1798 and concentrate on "the living principles of democracy and pluralism" that are the lasting legacy of the United Irishmen.[48] Here, then, was a "window of opportunity which opened and was forcibly closed in the 1790s, a window which beckoned to the still unattained prospect of a non-sectarian, democratic and inclusive politics adequately representing the Irish people in all of their inherited complexities."[49] In a time of fragile peace and guarded optimism in Northern Ireland, this is perhaps the most instructive legacy of 1798.

Consequences of the Rebellion

The results of the uprising were both immediate and long term. The immediate impact was the dissolution of the Irish Parliament after 500 years of existence. British Prime Minister William Pitt decided that Ireland would have to be integrated into the United Kingdom. The factionalism of the Irish Parliament, the demands of Catholics for rights, and the vulnerability of Ireland to revolution and foreign influences were too threatening to English leaders. The persuasive skills of Charles Cornwallis and Robert Stewart Castlereagh were turned loose on the Irish parliamentary members. These advocates of union with Britain stressed the need for internal and external security. The Protestants had come to recognize that the maintenance of their power was dependent upon Britain. If the 1798 Rebellion had not been successful, the next one might be. Thus a significant segment of the Protestant elite supported union. The Protestant patriots, however, argued that union would subordinate Ireland's interests to Britain's and relegate Ireland to the status of a mere province. It should also be remembered that the bishops and upper-status Catholics favored union because they were persuaded that the English Parliament would grant Catholic emancipation. This possibility was precisely what the more "anti-popery" Protestants feared, and thus they disliked the idea of union with the British. Their arguments, in the end, proved less persuasive than the mixture of pressures and payoffs to the Irish parliamentarians engineered by the king's lord lieutenant, who handed out peerages to get the vote. Ireland was now to be represented in the British Parliament by 100 members of the House of Commons and 32 peers in the House of Lords. The Irish Parliament ceased to exist in 1800.

The enduring heritage of the 1798 Rebellion was to provide intellectual fuel and emotional ardor to the development of Irish nationalism. Tone's vision of an independent republic free of sectarian privilege provided a modern foundation for the Irish independence movement. No longer was the ideal the restoration of a Gaelic Catholic ascendancy free of English domination, but rather the

Continental and American doctrines of individual freedom, democracy, and representative government.

In the emotional sphere the heroic struggle of the Wexford "croppy boys" meeting British muskets with farmers' pikes provided ample material for the creation of revolutionary myth and lore to be retold, sung, or recited. Finally, the failure of the Rebellion was not seen as irrelevant or fruitless but rather as a heroic sacrifice, the worth being in the act itself and not in its outcome. Thus the pattern of heroic failure was set for numerous Irish revolutionary endeavors, some plausible, others foolish, but all revered with the same ferocity in the collective folk memory. David Thornley notes: "The year 1798 with its curious blend of the political republicanism of the intellectuals and the agricultural suffering of the dispossessed, better perhaps than any other date marks the birth of modern Irish nationalism."[50]

Union

Absorption of Ireland into the United Kingdom may have been seen by Pitt as the answer to British security problems, but he could not foresee that Ireland was to prove to be politically hard to digest. In the course of the next century Irish political energies focused on Catholic emancipation, repeal of the Act of Union, land reform, and Home Rule. The skill of some Irish members of Parliament—such as O'Connell, Parnell, and Redmond—cast Irish interests as the political balance weight in the partisan political conflicts of Britain. Two other threads were to accompany Irish political agitation for Home Rule: new organizations favoring violent revolution and an emerging sense of nationalism. These threads were to weave together in the early years of the twentieth century to bring Britain to the brink of civil war and Ireland into open rebellion.

Background

In the early nineteenth century, Ireland's social and economic character was swiftly changing. Ultimately, much of this can be attributed to growth in population, which exploded from 4 million in 1800 to almost 7 million by 1821. The reasons for this increase are various, but a better diet—based upon the nutritious potato—played an important role. By 1800 Irish society had become highly stratified, with a small but influential gentry at the top of the social pyramid, followed by a tenant farmer class (many of them Catholic), and finally a broad base of cottiers, landless laborers, and rural artisans.

A rising population in rural Ireland meant greater competition for available land. This was reflected in the disproportionate rise of cottiers, who rented small plots from tenant farmers that they paid for in labor services.[51] Other laboring poor moved into previously unsettled upland and marginal areas, particularly in the west of Ireland. The prolific potato and a surfeit of turf for fuel allowed these folks to subsist in extended farm clusters that were often densely populated and subdivided into ever-smaller plots. For many of these people the margin of sub-sistence was quite thin. Two-thirds of the families in Connaught lived on only one to five acres, and opportunistic landlords and head tenants often pushed rents far beyond the real value of the land. This situation was exacerbated by dependence on the potato, which in times of scarcity or blight resulted in localized famines during the early nineteenth century.

Religion in the Union

After the Union was formed the established church was the Church of Ireland. To this alien church the Catholic tenant paid a tithe (although altered in 1838, it was not removed until 1869), which represented one-tenth of the land's produce. This tithe went to support 4 archbishops, 18 bishops, and 1,400 Anglican clergy who ministered to approximately one-tenth of the island's population. If the tenants improved the land through their own efforts, higher rents were charged, and a bill passed in 1816 made capricious eviction easier.

The British politicians in Westminster were either ignorant of, or indifferent to, these conditions because few of them ever visited Ireland. The British leaders per-ceived the conditions as being the fault of the Irish themselves, who were increas-ingly depicted in cartoons and the press as slovenly and ignorant. Moreover, some politicians personally harbored anti-Catholic, anti-Irish prejudices or were sensi-tive to British public opinion, which was characterized by anti-Catholic nativism.

Political Status Under the Union

The Act of Union did not integrate Ireland into the United Kingdom as an equal component. Ireland continued to be treated as a province whose economic inter-ests were to be subordinated to Britain's and whose population was to be subjected to law and order. Sporadic violence continued in rural areas as secret societies such as the Threshers, Caravats, and Shanavests mobilized against tithes; against the in-vasion of common bog or grazing land; and also against other farmers, especially outsiders who took land over the heads of local tenants. This activity prompted the garrisoning of troops in Ireland and in 1822 the establishment of a special con-stabulary. In 1836 this was reorganized into the Royal Irish Constabulary, an armed police force directed at suppressing agrarian discontent.

Within Ireland the liberal Protestant patriots faded away and the Orange Order increasingly became the spokesmen for the Protestant community. Founded in 1795 to counter Catholic secret societies, the Orange Order soon grew beyond its Ulster origins. Characterized by anti-popery of a particularly vivid variety, the Orange Order was now dedicated to the Union because Ulster's economic pros-perity was seen to be tied to it. The Irish unionists allied with the Tory politicians in Britain because they shared religious, property, and class interests with the Irish Protestant ascendancy.

This political environment had a deadening effect on Catholic aspirations and activities for two decades after the Act of Union. One notable and tragic exception was the futile "rebellion" in 1803 by Robert Emmet and his followers. The uprising was less a harbinger of the future than a remnant of 1798, as Emmet had absorbed the ideas of his brother Thomas Addis Emmet, one of the founders of the Society of United Irishmen. After attempting to seize Dublin Castle, Emmet was arrested and convicted for treason. Before he was hung he delivered an emotional speech from the dock, a zealous condemnation of British oppression and a clarion call for Irish revolution. He concluded with the words: "When my country takes her place among the nations of the earth, then, and not till then, let my epitaph be written." Thus, Emmet joined Wolfe Tone in the hagiology of Irish martyrs whose acts were more important than their consequences. Emmet became a heroic figure and thus a contributor to the revolutionary tradition.

Daniel O'Connell

Catholic Emancipation

A far more important figure in the development of political organization among the Catholics and in the achievement of Catholic emancipation was Daniel O'Connell. O'Connell was born in Kerry in 1775 to a well-off Catholic family who could afford to send him to France for his education. Attracted to radicalism in his youth, he was a sometime member of the Society of United Irishmen. He had extraordinary success as a barrister, which established his reputation in Ireland. Earlier he had opposed the 1798 Rebellion because he feared it would provoke bloody reprisals from the British Army. This nonrevolutionary approach to the liberation of Ireland was to characterize his efforts throughout his life (despite his conviction by the House of Lords on a trumped-up sedition charge in 1843). Two great issues shaped O'Connell's career: Catholic emancipation and repeal of the Union with Britain. In pursuit of these objectives O'Connell enjoyed success on the former but fell short on the latter.

The quest for Catholic emancipation was the first item on O'Connell's agenda. The Penal Laws had largely been abandoned by the late eighteenth century, but Catholics were still denied the right to sit in Parliament, advance in the military and civil service, or be appointed to the judiciary. Although civil rights had been virtually promised to Catholics at the time of the Act of Union, Pitt was unable to deliver because King George III refused to agree. Catholics, however, continued to petition the House of Commons for emancipation.

In pursuit of this goal O'Connell welded the Irish Catholic community together in 1823 through the Catholic Association. O'Connell created a mass-based organization using priests as his local grassroots organizers and recruiters. He recognized the strength of the relationship between priest and parishioner, as well as the literary and social eminence of the clergy. The emancipation movement sparked mass enthusiasm and was supported by small contributions (called "catholic rent") collected at mass on Sundays and encouraged from the pulpit by the parish priest. In small ways the Irish peasantry had already been flexing its political muscles. Traditional gatherings such as funerals, sporting occasions, and fairs all gave Catholic tenants a forum for exchanging ideas, affirming their strength, and organizing. These "men of no property," as Wolfe Tone called them, and the threat they posed, ultimately provided O'Connell with the means with which to win emancipation.[52]

The power of the Catholic Association was dramatically demonstrated in 1828 when O'Connell defeated a Tory landlord, William Vesey Fitzgerald, in a parliamentary election in County Clare. The message to the British government was clear. It was faced with a choice between extremely unpleasant alternatives. Either O'Connell's demands for emancipation had to be met, which might provoke anti-Catholic sentiment in England, or they were to be denied, risking, as O'Connell warned, insurrection in Ireland. The Peel government chose Catholic civil rights and passed the Relief Act in 1829. The gain was not without costs to the Irish Catholics: the Catholic Association was outlawed and 180,000 voters (most of them small-holders) lost the franchise.

Seeking Repeal of the Union

The second issue to which O'Connell devoted himself was that of repeal of the Act of Union. Having opposed the Union in 1800, when he urged the Irish not to "sell their country for a price," O'Connell remained steadfast in that position until his death.[53] Echoing Grattan, O'Connell argued that Ireland could never be justly governed from London because British politicians could never respond to Irish needs. Repeal, however, had hardly any adherents in Parliament, and O'Connell was forced into parliamentary alliance with the Whigs to bring about advances in Ireland. In some instances this cooperation worked. Lord Mulgrave, the viceroy, and his undersecretary Thomas Drummond, brought decent, impartial rule to Ireland and outlawed the Orange Order in 1837 (it was revived in 1845). In virtually all other instances, however, O'Connell was frustrated. He hoped for an increase in Irish representation from the reform bill of 1832; none was forthcoming. He expected elimination of the tithe in 1838, but it was simply incorporated into land rents. He expected relief for the poor of Ireland, but Parliament passed a Poor Law that was inappropriate for Irish conditions and added taxes to pay for it.

Mass agitation had worked for emancipation, and O'Connell now believed it was the only road to repeal of the Union. As he had done for emancipation, O'Connell formed a broad-based Catholic organization, the Loyal National Repeal Association, by building upon hostility to the Poor Law. O'Connell had an enormous following, which he excited with promises of freedom, their own parliament and courts, tenant's rights, democracy, and prosperity. The voice of this support can be found in the letters of James Prendergast, a Kerry small-holder who wrote to his children in Boston proclaiming that, "We are all in this country repealers." When O'Connell was later indicted in 1843, Prendergast defended him in no uncertain terms:

> Danl O'Connell the Liberator was on his trial in Dublin this time past for trason against the government for holding Repeal meetings, for enticing the people at those meetings . . . and also for collecting money at home and from foreign lands called America. They say for the dismember-ment of the Empire but they are liers. Danl means no such thing. he means equal laws, equal justice and equal right to Ireland together with some means of support for the poor of all Ireland.[54]

The repeal movement, as suggested in these letters, also flourished among the Irish emigrant communities of the United States. Their organizational zeal and monetary support were the first indications of a potent force that would fuel the manpower, coffers, and arsenals of Irish nationalist societies well into the twentieth century.

In the early 1840s O'Connell organized vast public meetings—called "monster meetings"—to petition for repeal. O'Connell, always the propagandist, staged several of these meetings at historical sites such as Clontarf and the Hill of Tara, shrewdly gauging the symbolic power of place and history in the consciousness of the Irish people. The gathering at Tara, for example, was estimated at over 400,000 souls, a show of strength that implied the force O'Connell could bring to bear against Britain if necessary. As in 1828, O'Connell confronted Prime Minister Peel with the alternative of granting repeal or risking Irish revolution. Peel didn't blink. Emancipation had been costly for the Whigs in 1828 and what they had then conceded was certainly less than Irish self-government. Peel sent troops to Ireland and told O'Connell flatly that he would crush an insurrection rather than grant repeal. O'Connell backed down because he believed the costs of violence to be too high.

Interpretations of O'Connell's Legacy

Since the mid-nineteenth century the perceived image of Daniel O'Connell has changed dramatically, serving as a barometer for measuring Ireland's political atmosphere. While the "Liberator" was idolized by the Irish people during his lifetime, his public stature and legend were diminished in many nationalist circles after his death in 1846. Two of his most vociferous critics were John Mitchel and Charles Gavan Duffy, Young Irelanders who had encountered opposition from O'Connell over the legitimacy of using physical force. Duffy, in particular, sowed doubts about O'Connell's effectiveness as a leader. He argued that O'Connell's political pragmatism—particularly his alliance with the British Whigs, which often slowed the momentum of repeal—was a deviation from the goal of independence to which O'Connell had committed himself and the Irish people.[55] Duffy and Mitchel saved their harshest comments for O'Connell's retreat at Clontarf, the monster meeting in 1843 that the British government had banned. Duffy implied that O'Connell had earlier pledged himself to stand and fight should the government forbid the meeting. His ultimate decision to back down not only showed his own weakness but ultimately derailed the repeal movement.[56]

The barbs unleashed by Mitchel and Duffy had a powerful impact on a generation of nationalists who took center stage in the crucial years between 1900 and 1920. As Donal McCartney points out, Republicans, Socialists, Sinn Feiners, and spokesmen for the Gaelic Revival all found an ax to grind with O'Connell. James Connolly, a union organizer who established the Irish Citizen Army, described O'Connell as an enemy of the Irish working class and their labor unions. Patrick Pearse, a leader of the Easter Rising, criticized O'Connell for his message that physical force had no place in the attainment of political objectives. And, perhaps most telling, supporters of the Gaelic Revival argued that O'Connell "had done more than any other man to kill the language, and the distinctive character of the nation."[57] O'Connell, who was a native Irish speaker, nonetheless saw the survival of Gaelic culture and the Irish language as a badge of inferiority and weakness. He argued that to compete with the British, to best them at their own political game, the Irish people must master English, the language of law, politics, and power.

This opposing image of O'Connell began to change after the 1940s, in large part due to the work of revisionists who wanted to clear away the myth from the man and judge him according to the political climate of his own time. Much of this work has restored the reputation of O'Connell and commends him as a pragmatic leader and political realist.[58] O'Connell's growing stature and "renaissance" also had much to do with events in Northern Ireland. As terrorism and a militant nationalism re-emerged in the 1970s, republicans legitimized their ideal of a united Ireland and the methods to attain that goal by calling on revolutionary role models such as Patrick Pearse, the Fenians, and Wolfe Tone. For political moderates and revisionists alike, O'Connell thus became a prophet whose doctrine of passive resistance and civil rights offered the proper tactics for the struggle in Northern Ireland. The last two decades of the twentieth century saw a spate of O'Connell biographies and studies that laud his political pragmatism, his power sharing in the Whig alliance, and his attention to civil rights, all strategies that take on meaning for Ulster today.[59]

Post-revisionist historians would have us look anew at the O'Connell legacy. While one has to respect his policy of non-violence, several scholars suggest that O'Connell has a lot to answer for. His embrace of Catholicism as a necessary partner of Irish nationalism, they argue, helped drive home the last nails in the coffin of 1798—a spirit and vision that called for a more inclusive, non-sectarian society.[60]

During his lifetime O'Connell's commitment to nonviolent means had come under sharp criticism in the Repeal Association from a group of agitators who called themselves Young Irelanders and who split away and formed the Irish

Confederation in 1847. This movement had sprung up after 1842 and was encouraged and molded by the newspaper *The Nation*. Founded in 1842 by Thomas Osborne Davis, Charles Gavan Duffy, and John Blake Dillon, *The Nation* advocated an anti-industrial cultural nationalism as well as demanding Irish independence. The movement's nationalism flowed from the romantic movement in Europe at the time, which influenced leaders such as Giuseppe Garibaldi in Italy. Its adherents admired Wolfe Tone, Grattan, and liberal political principles but infused them with ideas from the Irish past. Lamenting the retreat of Gaelic before the English language, they urged people to preserve the Irish language and culture.

The Young Irelanders had split with O'Connell over the issues of his cooperation with the Whigs and the question of revolutionary violence and on general differences in philosophy and ideology. The Young Ireland movement itself then split on the question of whether the central issue in Ireland was landlordism and the pursuit of peasant proprietorship, as proposed by James Finton Lalor, or national independence, as proposed by Charles Gavan Duffy. Young Ireland chose the latter course and hoped to extract repeal of the Act of Union from the British Parliament. The Young Irelanders themselves held out little hope for a revolution on the part of the famine-wracked Irish, but the British government was convinced that insurrection was imminent. Parliament passed laws against treason; sent troops to Ireland; and applied martial law to Dublin, Waterford, and Cork. The government began to arrest the leaders of the Young Ireland group and provoked the remainder to "revolution." The constabulary crushed the minuscule attempt at rebellion with little difficulty, and the leaders were transported to penal colonies in Australia. Young Ireland, however, contributed poetry, songs, and a legacy of romantic revolution that would be taken up by subsequent generations of Irish nationalists.

Notes

1. The authoritative account of the first peoples in Ireland is Frank Mitchell and Michael Ryan's *Reading the Irish Landscape* (Dublin: Townhouse Publications, 1997), especially chapters 4 and 5.

2. Barry Raftery, "The Early Iron Age," in *The Illustrated Archaeology of Ireland*, ed. Michael Ryan (Dublin: Country House, 1991), p. 108; and Donnchadh O'Corrain, "Prehistoric and Early Christian Ireland," in *The Oxford Illustrated History of Ireland*, ed. R. F. Foster (New York: Oxford University Press, 1989), pp. 1–3.

3. James Carney, *Medieval Irish Lyrics* (Dublin: Dolmen Press, 1985), p. 3. A sixth-century poem, put in the mouth of a Druidic opponent of St. Patrick.

4. On Ard Macha, see Barry Raftery, *Pagan Christian Ireland: The Enigma of the Irish Iron Age* (New York: Thames & Hudson, 1994), pp. 74–79.

5. Donnchadh O'Corrain, "Prehistoric and Early Christian Ireland," in *Oxford History of Ireland*, ed. Foster, p. 35.

6. See Marie Therese Flanagan, "The Vikings," in *The People of Ireland*, ed. Patrick Loughery (Belfast: Appletree Press, 1988), pp. 55–65; and Ryan, *The Illustrated Archaeology of Ireland*, p. 153.

7. Marie Therese Flanagan, "Irish and Anglo-Norman Warfare in Twelfth-century Ireland," in *A Military History of Ireland,* ed. Thomas Bartlett and Keith Jeffery (New York: Cambridge University Press, 1996), pp. 52–55.

8. Pope Adrian IV was English, and no traces of the bull have been found, thus leading to speculation that it never existed. The Irish Catholic Church, however, was considered to be in need of reform at the time, and Adrian IV was interested in the assertion of strong government in Ireland to bring order to the Irish Church.

9. Mitchell and Ryan, *Reading the Irish Landscape,* p. 173.

10. This point is outlined in Flanagan, "Warfare in Twelfth-century Ireland," in *A Military History of Ireland,* ed. Bartlett and Jeffery, p. 75.

11. Gerald of Wales, *The History and Topography of Ireland* (New York: Penguin Books, 1982), pp. 101–102.

12. W. R. Jones, "England against the Celtic Fringe: A Study of Cultural Stereotypes," *Journal of World History* XIII, no. 1 (1971), pp. 155–171.

13. On this point see W. R. Jones, "Giraldus Redivus: English Historians, Irish Apologists, and the Work of Gerald of Wales," *Eire-Ireland* IX (1974), pp. 3–20.

14. Jane Ohlmeyer, "The Wars of Religion, 1603–1660," in *A Military History of Ireland,* ed. Bartlett and Jeffrey, p. 160.

15. English contemporaries such as Sir John Temple, writing in 1646, inflated the number of Protestant victims in the 1641 rising to as high as 300,000. See Thomas Bartlett, *The Fall and Rise of the Irish Nation: The Catholic Question, 1690–1830* (Dublin: Gill & Macmillan, 1992), pp. 6–9.

16. After the Cromwellian confiscations, Catholic ownership of land in Ireland was reduced to one-fourth of the total. In the century to follow, this total would be reduced to less than 5 percent.

17. Sean O'Tuama and Thomas Kinsella, eds., *An Duanaire* (Philadelphia: University of Pennsylvania Press, 1981), p. 345.

18. See L. M. Cullen, "The Irish Diaspora of the Seventeenth and Eighteenth Centuries" in *Europeans on the Move: Studies on European Migration, 1500–1800,* ed. Nicholas Canny (New York: Oxford University Press, 1994), pp. 113–153; and Harman Murtaugh, "Irish Soldiers Abroad, 1600–1800," in *A Military History of Ireland,* ed. Bartlett and Jeffery, pp. 294–314.

19. On Keating, see Declan Kiberd, *Inventing Ireland: The Literature of the Modern Nation* (Cambridge: Harvard University Press, 1995), pp. 13–15.

20. On the Irish contribution to Counter-Reformation thought and Irish historical writing, see John Silke, "Irish Scholarship and the Renaissance, 1580–1673," *Studies in the Renaissance* XX (1971), pp. 169–206; and W. R. Jones, "Giraldus Redivus: English Historians, Irish Apologists, and the Work of Gerald of Wales," *Eire-Ireland* IX (1974), pp. 3–20.

21. Arthur Young, *A Tour in Ireland, 1776–1779* (Shannon: Irish University Press, 1970, reprint), vol. I, p. 300.

22. Daniel Corkery, *The Hidden Ireland: A Study of Gaelic Munster in the Eighteenth Century* (Dublin: Gill & Macmillan, 1967), p. 39.

23. Ibid., pp. 40–41.

24. ·A good review of literature on the Penal Laws can be found in S. J. Connolly, "Religion and History," *Irish Economic and Social History* X (1983), pp. 66–80.

25. Connolly, "Eighteenth Century Ireland: Colony or Ancien Regime," in *Making of Modern Irish History*, ed. Boyce and O'Day, p. 18.

26. See, for example, Louis Cullen, "The Hidden Ireland: Reassessment of a Concept," *Studia Hibernica* 9 (1969), pp. 7–47.

27. Quoted in Bartlett, *Fall and Rise of the Irish Nation*, p. 48.

28. Maureen Wall, "The Rise of the Catholic Middle Class in Eighteenth Century Ireland," *Irish Historical Studies* XI, no. 42 (1958), pp. 91–115.

29. David Dickson, "Catholics and Trade in Eighteenth-Century Ireland: An Old Debate Revisited," in *Endurance and Emergence: Catholics in Ireland in the Eighteenth Century*, ed. T. P. Power and Kevin Whelan (Dublin: Irish Academic Press, 1990), pp. 85–100.

30. On the Scots-Irish in America, see David Noel Doyle, *Ireland, Irishmen and Revolutionary America, 1760–1820* (Dublin: The Mercier Press, 1981), especially chapters 4 and 5.

31. Bartlett, *Fall and Rise of the Irish Nation*, pp. 22–23.

32. Kevin Whelan, *The Tree of Liberty: Radicalism, Catholicism and the Construction of Irish Identity 1760–1830* (Cork: Cork University Press, 1996), especially pp. 3–56.

33. Connolly, "Review of Kevin Whelan, *The Tree of Liberty*," *History Ireland* 4, no. 3 (Autumn 1996), p. 55.

34. Quoted in Whelan, *The Tree of Liberty*, p. 56.

35. At least one historian of the United Irishmen maintains that had the French landed at Bantry Bay in December 1796, they would in all likelihood have liberated the country. See Thomas Graham, " 'A Union of Power'? The United Irish Organisation: 1795–1798," in *The United Irishmen: Republicanism, Radicalism and Rebellion*, ed. David Dickson, Daire Keogh, and Kevin Whelan (Dublin: Lilliput Press, 1993), p. 246.

36. Thomas Bartlett, "Defence, Counter-insurgency and Rebellion: Ireland, 1793–1803," in *A Military History of Ireland*, ed. Bartlett and Jeffery, p. 278.

37. For an excellent treatment of these events in the form of a novel, see Thomas Flanagan, *The Year of the French* (New York: Holt, Rinehart & Winston, 1979).

38. Daniel Gahan, *The People's Rising: Wexford 1798* (Dublin: Gill & Macmillan, 1995), pp. xiii–xiv.

39. Roy Foster, "History and the Irish Question," in *Interpreting Irish History: The Debate on Historical Revisionism*, ed. Ciaran Brady (Dublin: Irish Academic Press, 1994), p. 139. See also Francis T. Holohan, "History Teaching in the Irish Free State, 1922–35," *History Ireland* 2, no. 1 (Winter 1994), pp. 53–55.

40. A balanced overview of the revisionist position (and its critics) can be found in *Interpreting Irish History*, ed. Brady. See also Boyce and O'Day, eds., *Making of Modern Irish History*.

41. Thomas Pakenham, *The Year of Liberty: The Great Irish Rebellion of 1798* (Englewood Cliffs, N.J.: Prentice-Hall, 1970), p. 131.

42. R. F. Foster, "Ascendancy and the Union," in *Oxford Illustrated History of Ireland*, ed. Foster, p. 182.

43. For a review of this issue, see Connolly, "The Eighteenth Century?", in *Making of Modern Irish History*, ed. Boyce and O'Day, p. 27.

44. See Marianne Eliot, *Wolfe Tone: Prophet of Irish Independence* (New Haven: Yale University Press, 1989); David Dickson and Hugh Gough, eds., *Ireland and the French*

Revolution (Dublin: Irish Academic Press, 1990); Dickson, Keogh, and Whelan, eds., *United Irishmen*; Nancy Curtin, *The United Irishmen: Popular Politics in Ulster and Dublin, 1791–1798* (New York: Oxford University Press, 1994); and Bartlett, *Fall and Rise of the Irish Nation.*

45. Whelan, *Tree of Liberty,* p. 174. For more on this point, see Thomas Graham, "Dublin in 1798: The Key to the Planned Insurrection," in *The Mighty Wave: The 1798 Rebellion in Wexford,* ed. Daire Keogh and Nicholas Furlong (Dublin: Four Courts Press, 1996), pp. 65–78.

46. Whelan, *Tree of Liberty,* particularly chapter 2; Jim Smyth, *The Men of No Property: Irish Radicals and Popular Politics in the Late Eighteenth Century* (Dublin: Gill & Macmillan, 1992); and Curtin, *The United Irishmen.*

47. Kevin Whelan, "The United Irishmen, the Enlightenment, and Popular Culture," in *United Irishmen,* ed. Dickson, Keogh, and Whelan, p. 284.

48. Kevin Whelan, "Reinterpreting the 1798 Rebellion in County Wexford," in *The Mighty Wave,* ed. Keogh and Furlong, pp. 34–35.

49. Whelan, *Tree of Liberty,* p. ix.

50. David Thornley, "Historical Introduction," in *The Government and Politics of Ireland,* ed. Basil Chubb (London: Oxford University Press, 1974), p. 15.

51. Louis Cullen, *Life in Ireland* (London: B. T. Batsford, 1979), pp. 118–119.

52. Bartlett, *Fall and Rise of the Irish Nation,* pp. 311–320.

53. Quoted in Bartlett, *Fall and Rise of the Irish Nation,* p. 256.

54. James Prendergast [Milltown, County Kerry] to Thomas Prendergast [Boston], 3 August 1843 and Prendergast to Prendergast, 3 December 1843, James Prendergast Letters, MS 86–141, Burns Library, Boston College, Chestnut Hill, Massachusetts.

55. Donal McCartney, "The Changing Image of Daniel O'Connell," in *Daniel O'Connell: Portrait of a Radical,* ed. Kevin B. Nowland and Maurice O'Connell (Belfast: Appletree Press, 1984), pp. 19–31.

56. Ibid.

57. McCartney, "Changing Image of O'Connell," in *Daniel O'Connell,* ed. Nowland and O'Connell, p. 27.

58. See, for example, Oliver MacDonagh, *The Emancipist: Daniel O'Connell, 1830–1847* (London: Weidenfeld & Nicolson, 1989).

59. See Fergus O'Ferrall, *Catholic Emancipation: Daniel O'Connell and the Birth of Irish Democracy, 1820–1830* (Dublin: Gill & Macmillan, 1985); MacDonagh, *The Emancipist;* and Charles Chevenix Trench, *The Great Dan: A Biography of Daniel O'Connell* (London: Jonathan Cape, 1984).

60. See, for example, Whelan, *Tree of Liberty,* p. 130.

2

FROM THE FAMINE TO
THE RISING

The Famine

*On the 27th of last month I passed from Cork to Dublin, and this doomed
plant bloomed in all the luxuriance of an abundant harvest. Returning on the
3rd instant, I beheld, with sorrow, one wide waste of putrefying vegetation. In
many places the wretched people were seated on the fences of their decaying
gardens, wringing their hands and wailing bitterly the destruction that had
left them foodless.[1]*

—Theobald Matthew (October 1845)

The middle of the nineteenth century brought an unparalleled human disaster
to the Irish: the Great Famine. Simply put, the single crucial staple food of 8.5
million Irish people, the potato, was struck by a blight that destroyed the crops of
1845, 1846, and 1848. By 1851 approximately 1 million Irish had died of starvation or famine-related disease. Over 1 million emigrated, peopling the mill towns
of England and the burgeoning cities of North America.

It is now established that the potato blight—*Phytophthora infestans*—
originated in the United States and was carried to Europe aboard trading vessels.
By September 1845 the fungus had reached Ireland and spread rapidly throughout
the countryside. As one writer commented in County Kerry:

The Potatoes which were good and healthy a few days since are now rotten in the
Ground. . . . The Newspapers teem with alarming accounts of the same disease

31

throughout the Kingdom. I cannot say whether the loss is equal to the alarm. But dread of the greatest nature pervades all classes.[2]

British Policy During the Famine

The response of Britain ran the gamut from generous humanitarian concern to governmental ideological rigidity and even cruel abuse of the suffering human beings. Sir Robert Peel responded to the Famine by purchasing maize from the United States and distributing it in Ireland. Yet the corn held at state depots was never intended to be a handout to the Irish people. Instead, it would be made available for purchase at cost by local relief committees. Also as part of its relief plan, the government initiated a system of public works designed to give employment and wages to the destitute (a scheme that operated haphazardly at best). Charitable contributions (especially by the Quakers) provided some relief, but by 1846 a second crop was lost, prompting one relief official in County Donegal to exclaim, "Famine is already upon us."[3]

When the Whigs replaced the Tories in 1846, the government's policy lapsed into laissez-faire dogmatism blended with more than a little religious and racial prejudice. The doctrines of laissez-faire economics portrayed the Famine as some inexorable law of nature that was tragic but about which little could be done because it would be counterproductive for the government to interfere with the market forces of supply and demand. What is more, the persistent anti-Catholic, anti-Irish prejudices allowed some British politicians to explain the disaster in terms of Irish laziness, indolence, and popery. These views were inherent in the opinions of Charles Trevelyan, minister of the Treasury, who was entrusted with overseeing relief measures during the Famine. His main concern was "to teach the people to depend upon themselves for developing the resources of the country, instead of having recourse to the assistance of the Government on every occasion."[4]

This policy was driven home in 1847 when Prime Minister Lord Russell determined that his government should leave relief to the local workhouses and make stricken localities pay for their own "able bodied" poor. Their maintenance would come principally from Irish landlords who, according to British opinion, had contributed to the Famine through their parasitic irresponsibility and indifference to the poor. As Trevelyan caustically put it, "Irish property must support Irish poverty."[5] The grim reality of this policy, however, was disaster for the Irish people. Irish proprietors, faced with the burden of supporting defaulting smallholders and paying out relief, often chose to evict their tenants en masse. These "clearances" soared in 1847 and almost 500,000 were permanently evicted during the Famine years. As Peter Gray remarks: "For many, such as the remnants of the 150 families evicted from the Walsh estate in [barony of] Erris [County Mayo], who arrived as living skeletons to beg in Belmullet in late 1847, clearance was a death sentence."[6]

By 1847 the potato blight had brought desolation and distress throughout Ireland. Hardest hit were the marginal and upland areas of the west. In the densely populated farm clusters and cottiers' cabins of Connaught and Munster starvation and disease ran rampant. The Famine knew no boundaries. Even in such relatively prosperous counties as Antrim and Armagh, death was a frequent visitor. This came in the form of Famine fever, which was carried along the roads by streams of refugees from the west looking for food and work. The human and cultural consequences of such a disaster can be heard in the voices of contemporary eyewitnesses. Visiting his west Cork estate in 1846, the absentee landlord Nicholas Cummins found cabins inhabited by "famished and ghastly skeletons . . . such frightful spectres as no words can describe."[7] Similarly, Maurice Prendergast, writing to Boston from Milltown, in Kerry, reported that there was "Nothing to be found in all quarters but death and destitution." He noted that the workhouses, usually the place of the infirm and the destitute, were now thronged "with many a decent person well reared." Even the jails were filled, "people only doing crime to get something to eat or to be transported, preferring it to be a better life."[8]

Emigration

For many, emigration was the sole escape from death or the workhouse. It is estimated that over 1½ million Irish left the island during the decade between 1845 and 1855, many of them bound for Canada and the United States. Although movement out of Ireland was not new, the Famine dramatically accelerated the migrant stream and transformed its character. Whereas earlier migration had come from anglicized areas of Ulster and the southeast, the Famine diaspora flowed out of the west of Ireland: Galway, Mayo, Cork, Kerry, and Donegal (catchment areas that remain strong to this day). The majority of these Famine emigrants were poor and Irish speakers who abandoned their traditional communities only out of desperation and as a last resort. As emigrant letters reveal, many were able to make the trans-Atlantic leap only through communal strategies at home or through the generosity of relations already in "that Yankee country."[9]

The Famine itself left an indelible stamp on Irish America. Many Famine folk experienced a precarious adjustment to life in the New World, and the spectres of poverty, discrimination, and high mortality were their frequent companions. As Peter Gray reminds us, the cultural baggage that Famine immigrants carried to the United States included recollections of the homeland that were frozen in time: images of the Irish landscape, lost friends and family, and a memory of the Famine that was deeply anti-British.[10] This memory, fanned by exiled Young Irelanders and revolutionaries, became the main ingredient in Irish American nationalism—a nationalism that would fund and fuel the growing independence movement in Ireland.

The Famine is a major watershed in Irish history and thus central in disputed interpretations between nationalist and revisionist historians. The event has been to different writers a malicious act of genocide directed at the Irish by the British government or the misguided and tragic choice by policy makers who were prisoners of the ideology of their time. Today, increasingly, it is a reminder of the hunger and poverty that still exist in the modern world.

For the most part, the popular understanding of the Famine in Ireland, and its cultural memory in Irish America, still follows a traditional nationalist model. Much of this viewpoint was nurtured in the years after the Famine by firebrands and polemicists such as John Mitchel, who wrote a savage indictment of the British government's policy. Why, he asks, did potatoes fail throughout Europe yet there was no famine save in Ireland? From his pen emerged images of British ships clearing Irish ports during the Famine years laden with provisions bound for England. "During all the Famine years," Mitchel asserts, "Ireland was actually producing sufficient food, wool, flax, to feed and clothe not nine but eighteen millions of people."[11] Thus, as Mary Daly points out, for Mitchel the Famine was artificial, "caused not by a shortage of food, but by the failure on the part of the British Government to close the ports and by the need to export food to pay rents to profligate, absentee landlords."[12] In the extreme nationalist viewpoint—one that circulated widely in Irish America—this amounted to nothing less than a policy of genocide. As Mitchel concludes, "The Almighty . . . sent the potato blight, but the English created the Famine."[13]

Versions of this interpretation infused public perceptions and nationalist pronouncements in the decades following the Famine. Land League leader Michael Davitt used images of the Famine to fight landlordism in the 1870s and Sinn Fein boss Arthur Griffith contended that the British government deliberately used "the pretext of the failure of the potato crop to reduce the Celtic population by famine and exile."[14] This account of the "Great Hunger"—replete with images of Irish victims and British villains—was also fostered in the National School System during the first half of the twentieth century.

This interpretation came under attack in the 1950s by Irish academics, who called for a more "objective" and sober assessment of the Famine, one based on rigorous historical methods and research in primary sources. Revisionists such as T. W. Moody and R. Dudley Edwards sought to tear down the veils of "mythology" that cloaked the Irish Famine and replace the "interpretive distortions" that punctuated the traditional view. These distortions included exaggerated reports about "coffin ships" carrying emigrants to their doom and the miserliness of Queen Victoria. As one writer commented, "It is the historian's function to debunk these myths, even when they are in the service of a 'good' cause."[15]

One of the key figures among the revisionists has been Irish historian Roy Foster. In his magnum opus, *Modern Ireland: 1600–1972,* he downplays the Famine as a "watershed in Irish history." He suggests that patterns of change such as "demographic decline, large scale emigration, altered farming structures and new economic policies" were actually under way well before the tragedy.[16] Foster also defuses many of the incendiary arguments of Mitchel and the nationalists. He notes that the export of food during the Famine (which nationalists argue could have fed the masses) was an "economic irrelevance." The food that left Ireland between 1846 and 1850 simply would not have been sufficient to stave off hunger and starvation.[17] Likewise, Foster and others have revised our view of Irish landlords—the objects of much blame and criticism (both by British policy makers and in Irish public opinion). While the record yields instances of some landlords who profited from the Famine or met the crisis with brutality and irresponsibility, Foster argues that there were many others who were overrun and went bankrupt because of it. He does admit, however, that "by and large the class that possessed the most did the least."[18]

Perhaps the most striking aspect of revisionist writing on the Famine is its detached and sober tone, one that is far distant from popular best-sellers such as Cecil Woodham-Smith's *The Great Hunger*. Graphic descriptions of starving Irish peasants and ravages of Famine fever are notably absent in the pages of Foster and other revisionists. So too are any hints at English culpability. Instead, one is presented with a dispassionate account, bolstered with statistics, economic patterns, and cool, rational discussion of the inadequacies of British policy. Indeed, Foster and his compeers argue that the British government was a prisoner of its own limited philosophy of laissez-faire economics. Moreover, British policy makers such as Trevelyan were largely ignorant of actual conditions in Ireland during the Famine and lacked the financial capability or administrative command to deal with the crisis.[19]

Until recently there has been comparatively little written concerning the Great Famine. Those who did focus on the period often distanced themselves from the more graphic descriptions and emotional charge inherent in the tragedy.[20] Yet during the 1990s a bounty of new scholarship emerged on the Famine, writing that often takes issue with the cool, dispassionate accounts of Foster and his fellow revisionists.[21] Christine Kinealy, for example, has charged that the revisionists, in their efforts to exorcise the cant of nationalism from historical discourse, have "sanitized and marginalized" the Famine. There has been a tendency to view the Great Hunger and resulting mortality as inevitable, the result of "a long-overdue Malthusian subsistence crisis." More important, the issue of British culpability in the crisis (the linchpin of nationalist accounts of the Famine) is consistently avoided or denied in revisionist accounts.[22] The question remains, why?

Historian Joseph Lee suggests that the revisionist pattern of removing the Great Famine from center stage and exonerating British policy makers from responsibility gained impetus from the renewal of violence in Northern Ireland after 1969. The politically divisive nature of the Ulster conflict led many scholars to shy away from research into the Famine—research that might "provide ammunition for IRA interpretations of Irish history, which drew heavily on the genocidal interpretations of the Famine."[23] Cormac O'Grada, whose research has broken new ground on the Famine, asserts that:

> Nearly 150 years after the event, the Famine is still a sensitive topic, with the result that home-grown academic accounts are rather bloodless, sanitized affairs. But in their quest for "objectivity" some Irish historians—subconsciously perhaps—have tended to trade nationalism for caution and conservatism.[24]

Historical discourse and understanding has changed considerably in today's political climate. The peace initiative of the 1990s and cease fire in Northern Ireland have facilitated a new freedom in the discussion of past events, and historians critical of Britain are no longer seen as providing aid and comfort to the republican cause. Indeed, in the 1990s this political breakthrough cleared a new path toward genuinely "revisionist" scholarship that has illuminated both the mentality of British policymakers and the lives of those "peasants" most affected by the Great Irish Famine.

"Post-revisionist" scholars are revisiting such crucial issues as the role of British policymakers during the Famine. Their approach, however, seeks to move beyond the highly divisive politics of the past to frame the question in a different light. Several historians, Peter Gray in particular, venture to try to understand the mentality and motivations that influenced British officials in charge of famine relief. Gray explains that Lord Russell, Charles Trevelyan, and even Robert Peel were products of an evangelical Protestant ideal that saw the Famine as God's Providence.[25] In extreme cases, this providentialism could interpret the Famine as divine punishment for the religious "error" and popery of the Irish. In official circles, however, it helped to rationalize government endorsement of laissez-faire economic policies and encouraged an extreme reluctance to interfere in market forces in Ireland. In fact, for those like Trevelyan, the destruction of the potato was a "godsend" because it would foster a shift away from the "lazy" habits of the feckless Irish and move Ireland in the direction of modern commercial farming and profits based on grain. In Trevelyan's words, the Famine would produce "permanent good out of transient evil. Even in the most afflicting dispensations of providence, there was ground for consolation and often even occasion for congratulation."[26] As Gray argues, "this concern with the reordering of Irish social structures and habits is central to the history of the Famine." It encouraged officials in London to ignore Irish suffering in the face of unspeakable horror and made them less receptive to heroic relief efforts to ease the catastrophe.[27]

The fact that a favorable outcome was anticipated, however perversely, does not absolve the British administration from any responsibility, according to several scholars. Luke Gibbons, for one, suggests that Britain (in its intractable adherence to political economy) was guilty of "passive injustice" and maintains that some of the horrors of the Famine were preventable.[28] This was made clear in 1847 when Britain launched a remarkable, albeit temporary, program of soup kitchens that produced an estimated 3 million meals a day (significantly, the only time during the Famine that mortality decreased). As Kevin Whelan asserts, it was "an indication of the competence of the state to deal with the starvation issue, had the political will been there to do so."[29] Indeed, government outlays during the period suggest that Britain certainly had the means to deal with the Irish crisis. Joel Mokyr, in an influential analysis, matched Treasury spending on Famine Ireland (£9.5 million) with the cost of the Crimean War (£69.3 million) less than a decade later. In a classic understatement, to quote Cormac O'Grada, government spending came down to a choice between "guns" versus "butter."[30] The important point here is that this assessment is not out of context with the 1840s, when it was widely perceived that famine relief was lean and insufficient. An ailing Daniel O'Connell, for instance, criticized a £20 million compensation to former slave holders in the British West Indies, while a Tory peer sarcastically noted that, if need be, "England could find a hundred millions of money to fight the Grand Turk."[31]

Today, historians of the Famine are seeking to broaden the boundaries of historical research; investigate neglected issues (such as women and the Famine); and forge a history where people, as well as politics, take center stage.[32] New work, for example, has attempted to recover the mindset and the "voice" of ordinary folk—many of them Irish speakers—who lived during the Famine. Personal correspondence, folklore, historical archaeology, and especially vernacular poetry have revealed tantalizing glimpses of the Irish understanding of "An Gorta Mor" and offer perhaps the most authentic record of a disintegrating culture and way of life.[33] In the Famine song "Amhran na bPratai Dubha" ("The Song of the Black Potatoes") one witnesses the depth of emotion and anger that was created by the Famine. It speaks powerfully of a disaster that, in the mind of its county Waterford author, was far from providential:

> 'Twas the black potatoes that scattered our people,
> Facing the poorhouse or overseas emigration,
> And in the mountain cemetery do they in hundreds lie,
> And God in Heaven relieve our situation . . .
> This business was no part of God's plan,
> Scattering the poor in grief and pain,
> The poorhouse gates clanging closed on them,
> And married couples separated for life.[34]

It is this personal memory of the Famine, this chant of anguish and pain, that has been largely forgotten in the historical literature. From a revisionist viewpoint, such "popular history" was based on myth and folklore; historical truth, they argue, lies firmly in the hands of academics who make use of scientific method and hard evidence to fashion an objective narrative of the past.[35] Yet as a new wave of historians have pointed out, it is the "voice" of everyday people and their register of memory concerning such events as the Famine that are often the key to interpreting the past. Indeed, critic Luke Gibbons advises that:

Understanding a community or a culture does not consist solely in establishing "neutral" facts and "objective" details: it means taking seriously their ways of structuring experience, their popular narratives, the distinctive manner in which they frame the social and political realities which affect their lives.[36]

Currently, many scholars are striving to recover (both in historical and personal terms) "the world that was lost" with the Famine and to understand the impact of "famine memory" and trauma on the mores and behavior of later generations.[37] In this way, it is hoped, Ireland and the "survivors" of the Irish diaspora may confront the ghosts of the past and perhaps develop a sensitivity to the injustice and suffering of others today.

This new understanding of the Famine is linked to a more enlightened view of the tragedy. The Famine is not simply about commemorating past victims or pointing accusing fingers. Reclaiming the experience of the Irish Famine is also crucial to understanding the continuing crisis of starvation that touches Third World countries such as Somalia, Rwanda, and North Korea.[38] As Irish President Mary Robinson suggested, perhaps the most powerful legacy of the Great Famine is "to connect us with the terrible realities of our current world. It challenges us to reject the concept of inevitable victims, and having done so, to face up to the consequences of that rejection."[39]

The Famine's Legacy

The effects of the Famine were far-reaching. In the social sphere the Famine prompted a tide of emigration from Ireland that did not stop until more than a century later. From a high of 8.5 million people, Ireland's population declined to approximately 4.5 million before it began to rise again after 1960. The Irish diaspora fueled the Industrial Revolution in the Atlantic world and peopled a variety of destinations, most notably Britain, Australia, Canada, and the United States. Indeed, by the twentieth century a culture of emigration had become fixed and all-pervasive in the Irish experience. This is suggestively expressed by Harold Speakman, a U.S. writer, in his 1931 travel book *Here's Ireland*. Visiting an Irish schoolhouse, he wrote, "Little boys of assorted sizes, resting themselves first on one leg and then on the other, stood against the walls. . . . They seemed to be waiting for something. As I shared my raisin bread with them, there came to my mind the bizarre notion that they were waiting to grow up and go to America."[40]

Decline of the Irish Language and Cultural Tradition

The Famine also dealt a deadly blow to the Irish language and cultural tradition. A vibrant culture that had existed in pre-Famine Ireland—one characterized by a sense of close-knit community; an expressive world of dance, music, and story-telling; and a rich spiritual life connected with landscape, local superstition, and

Harper's Weekly cartoon by W. A. Rogers that caricatured the steady stream of impoverished Irish emigrants who flooded the United States in the wake of the Great Famine.

calendar customs—declined in the wake of the tragedy.[41] Hugh Dorrian, of County Donegal, described this cultural sea change: "In a very short time, there was nothing but stillness, a mournful silence in the villages; in the cottages grim poverty and emaciated faces showing all the signs of hardships. The musicians of all and every description disappeared."[42]

So too the Irish language, the tongue of up to 4 million people before the Famine, disappeared in many locales. This decline can be explained by a variety of factors. First and foremost are demographic realities: A large proportion of those who died or emigrated during the Famine era came from Irish-speaking areas. For those who remained, the trauma of the Famine—and the close association among language, poverty, and suffering—may have helped to silence the native tongue even further. Social aspirations and upward mobility among farmers and shopkeepers also contributed to the abandonment of Irish in the nineteenth century. Ambitious parents saw English as essential to the social and economic advancement of their children. As one country parson commented in County Kilkenny, "The English language rapidly advances, for so anxious are the people to speak it in the country, that the mountain farmers who cannot speak English, and who send their children to hedge schools, will scarcely allow them to speak Irish at home."[43] What was lost in this surrender of Irish, however, was not simply a vocabulary but an entire world view. The Gaelic language was the medium through which the people interpreted history, community, and the landscape. That traditional inheritance was lost with the Famine, and only a shadow of its power survives today in Irish-speaking areas of Connaught and Munster.

Impact on the Economy

The effect of the Famine on the Irish economy was likewise profound. The Famine drove the poorest of the Irish farm workers, laborers, and cottiers off the land and decimated the communal clachans—or farm-clusters—that dotted the landscape in the west of Ireland. In many regions they were displaced by strong farmers and graziers who occupied large holdings, often at the expense of their more impoverished neighbors.[44] The Encumbered Estates Act of 1849, which allowed the courts to sell the land of bankrupt landlords, prompted the eventual sale of one-third of the cultivated land in Ireland by 1880. The purchasers were predominantly Catholics who shifted from producing grains to raising livestock. Meat, butter, and eggs were increasingly exported to industrial Britain, a ready market. The years 1850–1880 saw an economic upsurge for large farmers in Ireland. Prices and agricultural wages rose significantly after the Famine, providing tenant farmers with a much more varied diet and a generally higher standard of living.[45] Because rising expectations more often produce agitation for change than does destitution, the Irish smallholders still clamored for better guarantees of tenant rights with respect to rents and security of tenure and, ultimately, for ownership.

Impact on Political Activity

The political movements that had culminated during the Famine period were all moribund. Popular support of O'Connell's Repeal Association dissolved into sporadic agrarian violence and Famine-induced misery. Likewise, the alternative Young Ireland movement was in dissolution. In 1847 James Fintan Lalor called for a popular uprising of tenant against landlord. As he noted in a series of articles, only by "repealing the conquest" could the Irish people find freedom.[46] The "rebellion" in 1848, however, was a shambles. Poor preparation, the arrest of Young Ireland's leaders, and disintegration of public support resulted in only sporadic clashes between rebels and Crown forces. Yet the Young Irelanders who managed to escape to the United States or France remained committed to the revolutionary path and the overthrow of British rule. Their influence would have a dramatic impact on Irish American nationalism and agitation in the future.

After the Famine an independent Irish group appeared in Parliament, but it was not very effectual. This effort was generated by Charles Gavan Duffy, who formed the Tenants League in 1850. This organization became the focal point of agitation for tenant's rights: fair rents, fixity of tenure, and free sale. Although electorally successful in 1852, it quickly shattered because some members were altogether too willing to serve in the British government. A more telling blow was the lack of support for the Tenants League from Paul Cullen, the archbishop of Dublin, who saw agitation for tenants' rights as the leading edge of Irish revolution. Cullen curtailed the political activity of the clergy who supported tenants' rights at the grass-roots level, so the League lost any chance of building up a mass base in the O'Connell fashion.

Indeed, Cullen pulled the Church in Ireland away from supporting the nationalist movement. He was more interested in extracting concessions from Parliament with respect to disestablishing the Anglican church, thus eliminating the tithe, and establishing Catholic control over education. In these objectives he was successful. In 1869 the Church of Ireland was disestablished; by 1883 elementary education in Ireland was denominational. Cullen also spearheaded an extensive building program and devotional revolution in the Irish Catholic Church. This agenda was highly successful; the more prosperous tenant farmers and the middle class contributed to a visible explosion of churches, rectories, convents, and schools. In the clergy there was a tightening up of authority and, in the laity, a sharp increase in attendance at mass, confession, and the practice of the faith. Under Cullen's reforms such magical beliefs and popular practices as patterns (the celebration of local saints' days), keening, protective charms, and pilgrimages were discouraged. While these older traditions survived in some locales—such as the Lough Derg pilgrimage—their observance became more disciplined and orthodox.[47]

The collapse of the parliamentary road to Irish reform and independence in 1859 left a void that was not to be filled until the rise of Charles Stewart Parnell twenty years later. But people who believed that the liberation of Ireland had to come through force were building a new organization on the crumbled ruins of Young Ireland. Two exiled veterans of the 1848 insurrection, Michael Doheny and John Mahoney, came together in New York. That an organization to instigate a revolution in Ireland should be created in the United States is another reflection of the Famine. The United States absorbed hundreds of thousands of immigrants in its northeastern cities, newcomers who had a powerful hatred for the British and a burgeoning sense of Irish nationalism. Doheny had come directly to the United States in 1849, but Mahoney, along with James Stephens, had drunk deeply of the revolutionary theories and tactics proffered by European revolutionaries at the barricades and in the cafés of Paris.

The Fenian and Irish Republican Brotherhoods

In 1858 Doheny and Mahoney founded the Fenian Brotherhood in the United States, and James Stephens formed a similar secret society in Ireland that later became the Irish Republican Brotherhood (IRB). A newspaper called *The Irish People* accompanied the movement; it featured the writing of two extremely talented men, Charles Kickham and John O'Leary (who became the mentor of poet W. B. Yeats in the 1880s). The Brotherhood and its spokesmen came under immediate attack from the Church, which disliked the existence of clandestine organizations, especially those devoted to violent revolution. Archbishop Cullen led the attack, and he was backed by Rome, which issued a papal condemnation of the Fenians in 1870.

Money from the United States, military expertise provided by Irish veterans of the U.S. Civil War, and popular discontent were the ingredients of a successful Fenian rebellion. In Ireland the government caught wind of IRB activities through informers, and in 1867 it cracked down on the IRB, provoking the leaderless organization to a feeble uprising. The Irish Constabulary put down the Fenians with ease and earned the sobriquet "royal" in front of their name. The people who were arrested were sentenced to long prison terms; some were tortured. The IRB, although battered, did not disappear and remained on the back burner while the battle for Home Rule held the stage. Later, in 1916, the IRB reemerged to play an important role in another insurrection.

Despite clerical condemnation, the Fenians captured the nationalist imagination in Ireland. People flocked to amnesty associations that demanded the release of the Fenians from British prisons. Protest reached a crescendo with the execution of "The Manchester Martyrs," three Irishmen who allegedly killed an English police constable while attempting the rescue of Irish American leader Colonel Thomas Kelly. The failed rising thus provided an array of martyrs for song and story and fresh inspiration to some members of the Irish middle class, who were disenchanted with the pallid politics of the Irish parliamentarians. The Fenians also revealed the degree to which U.S. support was to play a part in the Irish nationalist struggle. Finally, the Fenians, in their conflict with the Church, made it clear that the quest for political independence did not require clerical sanction and that Church interests were not identical to nationalism.

The Struggle for Home Rule

The weight of Irish efforts to change the country's political status within the United Kingdom shifted to the Home Rule party. This movement was played out in two stages, the first of which was under Charles Stewart Parnell and the second under John Redmond.

Isaac Butt, a Protestant lawyer, had developed a reputation in Ireland for his defense of Young Ireland rebels and later the Fenians. He felt that British control of Ireland had hampered Irish economic development, and his nationalism was directed toward a constitutional form of independence for Ireland modeled on U.S. federalism. He appealed to the Protestants to recognize their interest in an independently governed Ireland and stressed the importance of their participation lest they be left behind as Catholic efforts brought about Home Rule. In 1870 he founded the Home Government Association and in 1873 drew a broader base of support into the Home Rule League. Butt was able to attract diverse elements into this league. His Protestant background, defense of the Fenians, and constitutional approach could appeal to landlords, the Catholic middle class, clerics, and rebels. The League formed the Irish Parliamentary Party, which was committed to Home Rule. In the election of 1874 this party elected fifty-nine members to Parliament. Their performance, characterized on the one hand by Butt's cautious leadership and equivocation on agrarian issues and on the other by rock-hard opposition from British politicians, was less than dazzling. Responding to the criticism of militant Catholics, Butt promised to be more aggressive. The task of challenging the British Parliament, however, fell to the more daring leadership of M. P. Charles Stewart Parnell.

Charles Stewart Parnell

Parnell, an astute Protestant landlord from County Wicklow, had a deep commitment to Irish self-government. His strategy was to obstruct the work of Parliament rather than cooperate with the British politicians. The members of Parliament were furious with Parnell; the English press ridiculed him; and finally Butt, still committed to a conciliatory approach, censured him. A split ensued in the movement and it polarized around Butt's and Parnell's approaches to advancing Irish interests, although most members favored Parnell's confrontational approach.

Although the Irish Parliamentary Party concentrated on Home Rule, the nationalist movements also built upon agrarian discontent. In the late 1870s a depression hit Irish agriculture and raised again the issues of rent, security of tenure, and eviction. The response, as it had been so often before, was evictions on the one hand and unorganized, sporadic violence on the other. The crystalization of this populist anger into political action was engineered by Michael Davitt.[48] In 1879 he created the National Land League, which absorbed the various forms of agrarian discontent, agitation, and violence and channeled them into a coherent strategy of militant confrontation and rent strikes. Indeed, tenants used a variety of weapons against the landlords: crippling cattle, leaving evicted farms empty, withholding labor services, and ostracizing unjust proprietors or their agents. This last tactic gained notoriety in County Mayo with the shunning of Captain Charles Boycott, in which the local community refused his family all services, labor, and human contact. It was a "moral" practice that drove Boycott to leave Ireland and added a new word to the English language.

Parnell, impressed by Davitt, more and more supported the position of the League and its tactics. He assumed the presidency of the League when Davitt stepped aside to allow Parnell's luster to add to the agrarian cause. Parnell now led both the Home Rule and agrarian movements. Although Parnell's political goals and social vision were different than those of Irish tenants, he understood how to shape popular opinion and wield images of historical injustice. As Peter Gray reminds us, throughout the ensuing land war Parnell repeatedly tapped the power of living memory and advocated "undoing the work of the Famine" as the supreme goal of the League.[49]

In the years 1880–1882 a virtual land war took place that could not be contained by the constabulary. Funded by U.S. money, it swept the Irish tenant into enthusiastic support of land reform and Home Rule. William Gladstone, the British prime minister, responded with the Land Act of 1881, which granted the demands of Irish tenants. At the same time, however, Gladstone cracked down on the Land League, outlawing it and arresting the leaders, including Parnell. Although a compromise was eventually reached with Parnell, violent acts continued, including the murder of the newly appointed chief secretary, Lord Frederick Cavendish, by a breakaway revolutionary group known as the "Invincibles." Parnell vehemently denounced the atrocity but hinted that the British government had a choice: either deal with him through Parliament or deal with the secret societies.

Parnell then turned his energies to Home Rule. He established a new organization, the Irish National League, to build electoral support for his party. He made a pragmatic accommodation with the hierarchy of the Church under which it would support his constitutional efforts for Home Rule while he would support the effort to create a publicly financed Catholic educational system. Parnell improved the quality of the members of his party and demanded absolute discipline.

The British Parliament unwittingly aided Parnell's cause by passing reforms that extended the franchise to all householders (which tripled the electorate). In 1885 the Irish Parliamentary Party sent eighty-six members to Parliament and held the balance of power between the Liberals and the Conservatives. Gladstone introduced a Home Rule bill in 1886, but his Liberal Party split on the issue and the government fell.

The split in the Liberal Party in Parliament sent the Irish pro-union members (many of them from east Ulster) running to the Conservatives. They stood for an anti-Catholic, anti-Irish, pro-Empire position. This split cast a beam of light on the split within Ireland between the Ulster unionists and the Irish Party. In the 1886 debate on Home Rule Lord Randolph Churchill had highlighted the degree to which Conservatives were in harmony with the industrialized Protestant Ulstermen, symbolized by the influence of the Orange Order. The slogan "Home rule is Rome rule" reflected the nativist sentiment in the north, and "Ulster will fight and Ulster will be right" gave warning of the depth of the Ulster Presbyterians' opposition to Home Rule.

Parnell did not gain the leverage to get another Home Rule bill introduced before a divorce scandal forced him to resign as leader of the party. Originating with the British Protestants and later picked up by the Catholic clerics, condemnation of Parnell grew to such a crescendo that it split the Irish Party. Parnell fought to regain power but failed; his health broke, and he died in 1891.

The Home Rule party was a shambles over the next decade. John Redmond took over the Parnell wing, the anti-Parnell wing split into feuding factions, and the entire movement stagnated. Ironically enough, while the Irish Parliamentary Party languished, the Conservatives (now called Unionists) adopted a policy of Irish reform in the hopes that it would, as Arthur J. Balfour said, "Kill home rule with kindness." In the periods 1886–1892 and 1895–1905 the Unionists encouraged public works projects, technical schools, and democratized local government in Ireland.

In 1869, when the Church of Ireland was disestablished, Church lands were offered for sale to the tenants with loans to aid in the purchase. This act began the process of transferring ownership of land to the tenants, and further acts weakened the landlords' grip on property. The Unionists completed this process with the Wyndham Act in 1903, which offered incentives to landlords to sell their estates. The cumulative effect of these acts was to increase the base of ownership from 3 percent of the Irish people in 1870 to 64 percent by 1916. Conservatives, though traditionally allies of the landlords, had created a peasant proprietorship.

John Redmond

In 1900 the two wings of the Irish Party came together under John Redmond, and the two constituency organizations were merged in the United Irish League. Redmond had over eighty members in Parliament and solid electoral support. Gladstone had introduced a Home Rule bill in 1893, but under Conservative pressure it had been vetoed by the House of Lords. This tactic had been used to check other Liberal legislation, and the conflict came to a head in 1910. It became clear to the Liberals that getting their legislation enacted, including Home Rule, would require restraining the veto of the House of Lords. After the second election of 1910, during which Home Rule had been a central issue, Redmond demanded that the Liberals curb the House of Lords and introduce a Home Rule bill. Herbert Henry Asquith did so, although it took a threat from George V to pack the House of Lords with Liberal peers to persuade the Lords to accept the act. The combination of the Liberals, House of Lords, and Irish Party votes was more than enough, and Home Rule passed in spring 1912. Its passage was the signal for the Conservatives to unleash a torrent of opposition.

The chief opponents to Home Rule were Sir Edward Carson and Sir James Craig. They immediately went to Ulster and fanned the already bright flames of anti-Catholicism into a pledge by 471,000 Ulster Protestants to resist by all means the imposition of Home Rule. If it were enacted, they pledged to not recognize the authority of the Home Rule Parliament. Indeed, pledges were the fashion: 2 million British signed a covenant in support of Ulster. The people of Ulster organized a "provisional government" and an Ulster Volunteer Force to resist Home Rule. Arms began to pour into Ulster for the Volunteers. Notable Conservative figures spoke out against Home Rule and were even willing to accept civil war to preserve the Union.

Irish nationalists were not blind to these developments. They set out to create a force to offset the intimidation by the British government through the Ulster Volunteers. In 1913 the Irish Volunteers were created under the tutelage of the IRB. The government banned the import of arms into Ireland in late 1913, touching off an arms smuggling race between the Irish and Ulster Volunteers in 1914.

The political climate in Ireland was further unsettled by the "Curragh Mutiny," when the British army officers stationed in Ireland indicated that they would rather resign their commissions than fight their compatriots in Ulster. Prime Minister Asquith bowed to the threat of civil war and offered Redmond Home Rule with the exclusion of Ulster. Redmond refused, but he was caught between the Scylla of Irish nationalist wrath at partition and the Charybdis of bringing down the Liberal government and perhaps losing Home Rule altogether. Redmond offered to accept partition if there were plebiscites in the counties of Ulster on Home Rule. The impasse was never resolved because World War I broke out in August; the British government put the Home Rule Act into law but suspended it for the duration of the war.

With this ambiguous evasion the saga of Home Rule ends. For thirty years this effort had commanded the allegiance of some of Ireland's most notable political leaders. The prize was denied them, however, when British politicians, who had urged parliamentary constitutional processes on the Irish and crushed the rebels in 1798, would not support those processes when the Irish won constitutionally and the Unionists were the rebels. To the observant nationalist the message was clear: Tone, Emmet, Young Ireland, and the IRB were correct—Violent revolution was the only road to Irish independence.

The Rise of Irish Nationalism

Militant nationalist sentiments were fueled also by a mixture of organizations and ideas that emerged at the end of the century, interlocked with the political movement, and ultimately swept away Parnell and Redmond's Irish Parliamentary Party. The elements were the revival of Gaelic culture, the Sinn Fein movement, the reawakened IRB, and the creation of citizen armies by the IRB and James Connolly.

The Gaelic Athletic Association

The impetus to search for Irish identity in the legacy of the Celtic past actually began in the 1840s when writers of Young Ireland turned to the Celtic tradition to assert its distinctiveness and superiority over the materialism of the Anglo-Saxon heritage. However, two organizations gave impetus to the movement. The first, the Gaelic Athletic Association (GAA), was founded in 1884 by Michael Cusak. Cusak wanted to revive Irish games and discourage the playing of English sports. The movement had great success, and Gaelic football and hurling had a substantial following. Although encouraging Irish sports would seem to be a marginal contribution to cultural nationalism, in fact it was much more. The GAA grew powerful with strong support from the Church, particularly from Thomas William Croke, archbishop of Cashel. Moreover, it drew its support from, and encouraged, local patriotism in the rural areas of Ireland. In places such as Mooncoin in south Kilkenny, hurling, the maintenance of the Irish language, and cultural nationalism were all potent measures of local identity. Indeed, the GAA had a loose connection with the IRB, which gave a tone of militancy to its attitude toward sports. The expulsion from the GAA of people who played English games such as rugby or soccer indicates the degree of intense commitment this organization had to things Irish. The mixture of Catholicism, sports, and cultural nationalism in the GAA contributed to the growth of the broader movement.

The Gaelic League

In 1893 Eoin MacNeill founded the second organization, the Gaelic League. Restoration of Irish as the language of Ireland was his goal, as well as studying and preserving Gaelic literature. At the turn of the century the League became very popular; people began to learn Irish and visit the Irish-speaking areas in the west of Ireland. Schools were founded to teach Irish, and enthusiasm for the language spilled over into enthusiasm for traditional Irish music, dance, architecture, and literature. One measure of this revival can be seen in the architectural expressions of the period. Catholic churches, such as Dunlewy in Donegal (built in 1877), championed a revival of traditional Irish features such as the round tower and romanesque doorways. Public houses and inns likewise promoted nationalistic themes, incorporating into their design such motifs as the Irish wolfhound, harps, and busts of Irish heroes such as Tone and O'Connell.[50]

Proselytizers such as Douglas Hyde expanded the Gaelic League and by 1908 had achieved some major objectives, including the teaching of Irish in the elementary and secondary schools and, in 1909, in the new National University. The links with Irish nationalism were obvious as the Gaelic League strove to de-anglicize Ireland and retrieve from the Irish past its customs, place names, sports, and, of course, language. The emphasis on an "Irish-Ireland" was a clear step beyond the

Home Rule or independence movements in that it sought the creation of a
Gaelic nation, not merely a politically autonomous Ireland. Patrick Pearse expressed this difference succinctly when he demanded: "Ireland, not merely free,
but Gaelic as well, not Gaelic merely, but free as well."[51] The GAA and the Gaelic
League nurtured virtually every revolutionary who emerged in the period from
1916 to 1921.

The Irish Renaissance

The third leg of the Celtic revival was a literary movement in Dublin that not only
contributed to the growing Irish cultural awareness but also brought forth some
of the greatest writers of modern literature. Unlike Young Ireland writers, who
stressed native cultural issues in their writings but subordinated it to their political aspirations, the Dublin literary movement was composed of artists who placed
their expressive gifts above their politics. The major figures were William Butler
Yeats, John Millington Synge, James Joyce, and Sean O'Casey. The collected work of
these writers and lesser lights drew upon Celtic mythology, folk tales, and peasant
life to create a romantic vision of Irish culture. This vision would have a powerful
emotional impact, as did Yeats's play "Cathleen ni Houlihan," stirring up intense
feelings of nationalism and love of country. Synge and, later, O'Casey went beyond
the romantic image, and their plays caused uproars in the Irish National Theatre because some people in the nationalist movement could not accept a less than glorified vision of the Irish. The literary renaissance, bubbling as it was with controversy, injected the nationalist movement as never before with a vision of Irish
culture that was portrayed by talents as great as those in other nations. Artistic independence, affirmation of Celtic heritage, and political sensitivity were woven
together by the literary renaissance writers to promote the Gaelicization of
Ireland and also produce enduring works of art.

   This Gaelic revival found a new spiritual and geographical focus in the west of
Ireland. In the activities of the Gaelic League and especially through the work of
Yeats, Synge, and Lady Gregory, there came about an idealization of Irish rural life
and a longing for community and simplicity. In the isolation of the Aran Islands
and the fastness of Connemara one found an older communal tradition and experience that introduced a therapeutic alternative to the harsh industrial world of
England. Scholars and writers such as Synge, who spent his summers on the Aran
Islands, flocked to the west to absorb, collect, and "preserve" the traditional lifeways of Gaelic Ireland. Indeed, the poetry of Yeats and the plays of Synge were
meant to be a blueprint for Irish identity: a world of primitive landscape, community, and an "authentic" Irish persona unspoiled by the industrial horrors and
materialism of the modern world.[52] Moreover, this cultural distinctiveness of the
west was transformed into an argument for national independence. Kevin
Whelan suggests that, "By a strategic inversion, the previously despised Celtic
vices—non-materialism, dreaming, instability—were reinvented as virtues, as

Celtic charm, rebuking the stolid, slavish Saxon culture, with its 'filthy modern tide.'"[53] This ideal is reflected in the work of William Butler Yeats, especially "The Galway Plains":

> There is still in truth upon these great level plains a people, a community bound to-gether by imaginative possessions, by stories and poems which have grown out of its own life, and by a past of great passions which can still waken the heart to imagina-tive action. . . . England or any other country which takes its tune from the great cities and gets its taste from schools and not the old custom may have a mob, but it cannot have a people.[54]

Sinn Fein

In the years after Parnell's fall there arose all over Ireland a smattering of small groups, clubs, and societies that were engaged in nationalist political discussions about Irish independence. Partially joined together by a loose national associa-tion, they formally organized in 1905 into the group Sinn Fein ("ourselves"). The Irish Republican Brotherhood, still a secret oath-bound society, had a quiet hand in this group, as it had in the GAA and the Gaelic League.

The mentor of Sinn Fein was Arthur Griffith, who had been offering his own ideas on Irish independence since 1898 in his paper *The United Irishman*. Griffith had mixed an interesting cocktail of ideas in his version of the independence movement. Convinced that Ireland had to be independent but also convinced that a violent revolution would be crushed, Griffith suggested that the tactics for achieving separation from Britain should be withdrawal from Parliament and the setting up of an Irish assembly that would make policy for Ireland. The objective would be to create an Ireland that would be infused with the values of Celtic cul-ture. In the area of economics Griffith wanted protectionism, as advocated by the German economist Friedrich List.

The IRB had languished in the years since 1858; its leaders were old and its sparkle gone. Three men regenerated the organization after the turn of the cen-tury: Denis McCullough, Bulmer Hobson, and Sean McDermott. McCullough was a vigorous organizer and recruiter for the IRB in Belfast. Hobson was a jour-nalist in Dublin. McDermott was an organizer for Sinn Fein after it had absorbed the smaller political clubs. Together with Thomas Clarke, an IRB veteran who had served fifteen years in a British prison, the new leaders quickly moved onto the Supreme Council of the IRB. The IRB was small and financially supported from the United States but was ready to capitalize on political opportunities for revolu-tion as the Home Rule situation deteriorated in 1912 and 1913. Ironically enough it was the Ulster Protestants who gave the IRB impetus when they formed the Ulster Volunteer Force. In 1913 the IRB was behind the scenes in getting the Irish Volunteers organized under the prestigious name of Eoin MacNeill, head of the Gaelic League.

Citizen Armies

The Ulster Volunteers and the Irish Volunteers were not the only citizen armies in Ireland. The Irish Citizen Army, an adjunct to the labor movement, was created in 1913 under tumultuous circumstances. The nationalist movement in Ireland at times converged with the land agitators and at times with the Catholic Church, but never with the urban workers. The task of uniting nationalism and the working class fell to James Connolly, a brilliant and largely self-educated labor leader. Connolly, born in Edinburgh of Irish parents, led a kaleidoscopic life that included a stint in the British Army at age fourteen, emigration to the United States, and a return to Dublin, where he founded the Irish Socialist Republican Party. Connolly was convinced that the nationalist issue and socialism were complementary and that Ireland needed both freedom and collective ownership of property to prevent class exploitation.

Labor

Connolly shared the stage with James Larkin, the most dynamic figure in the labor movement in 1910. Larkin, a charismatic and energetic labor organizer, had been attempting to organize workers in Belfast and Dublin. Urban workers in Dublin, many of them dependent on casual labor and transport jobs, lived in the most squalid conditions in the United Kingdom. While intellectuals like Synge were searching out the Gaelic ideal in the west, Dublin's underclass lived in crowded, run-down Georgian tenements without water or sanitation. Moreover, they were exploited by employers at every turn. The owners were well organized and had their own strikebreakers, as well as the police, to quell labor disorders. Larkin made inroads with his agitation, called strikes, improved wages, and had gained about 10,000 members for his Irish Transport and General Workers Union by 1913.

In that year Larkin took on a formidable foe, William Martin Murphy, owner of the Dublin United Tramways Company. Murphy was determined that he was going to break Larkin and not recognize his union. Murphy was able to gain the support of other employers in a lockout, and by the autumn of 1913, 25,000 men were out of work. Riots and sympathy strikes affecting a wide variety of Dublin industries ensued and both Larkin and Connolly were arrested. The Irish Parliamentary Party did nothing for the workers, and the Catholic Hierarchy opposed the strike because of its radical doctrines of socialism. Thus the strike ultimately failed, and the men drifted back to work in winter 1914. Larkin left for the United States that same year, and Connolly took over the union. After the strike Connolly inherited the Irish Citizen Army, which had been created during the strike to protect the workers but had virtually faded away. Its regeneration was the work of young Sean O'Casey, at that time working as a laborer, not yet as a playwright.

Planning a Rebellion

The socialist side of Connolly gave way to the nationalist side as World War I progressed. He plotted an insurrection with his 200-man army. The outbreak of World War I was a benchmark in the movement toward Irish independence. At the outset of the war Redmond decided that the importance of defeating Germany was greater than the Irish question, and he encouraged members of the Irish Volunteers to serve Britain in the war. His suggestion that the Volunteers enlist in the British Army was simply too much for the IRB. The Volunteers split into two factions, with the majority going with Redmond and about 12,000 of the 180,000 taking the position that Irishmen should not die for British interests. This latter group, still called the Irish Volunteers, was closely connected with the IRB, who had heavily infiltrated the movement.

In 1914 the Irish republican leaders and the Clan na Gael in the United States decided secretly that they would undertake revolution during the war, in line with the dictum that "England's difficulties are Ireland's opportunities." Thus two movements were committed to violent revolution in Ireland: Connolly and his Citizen Army and the IRB with its Irish Volunteers. The prospects for success in each movement depended upon certain conditions. Connolly anticipated that success would come when his men in Dublin ignited a general rising in the whole country. Britain, preoccupied by the war and unwilling to commit troops to Ireland, would withdraw. Connolly also harbored the peculiar belief that capitalist Britain would be unwilling to destroy property in quelling a rebellion.

For the IRB the plan depended upon U.S. money, German arms, and a mobilization of the Irish Volunteers, who would decapitate British authority in Ireland. What would follow the revolution was not clearly defined, but it included the idea that Ireland would participate in a peace conference.

Patrick Pearse, Thomas MacDonough, and Joseph Mary Plunkett were notable not only for the critical roles they played in the 1916 Rising but also for their vision of its purpose and their conception of success. The three were members of the IRB, having shifted, in the years between 1912 and 1914, from Home Rule to revolution as the answer to Ireland's independence. All were steeped in the cultural nationalism of a Gaelic Ireland. Pearse was a poet, a playwright, and an orator of some ability. He was also a highly original educator who sought to inspire his students at St. Enda's school through the medium of the Irish language and the teaching of Irish history and culture.

Pearse shared with his two poet friends a nationalist vision infused with mystical religious overtones. The revolution needed a messiah, and more than that, said Pearse, it needed a blood sacrifice. Only such a sacrifice could redeem the corruption of Irish culture and politics. This redemption would generate a purer nationalism, which would ultimately liberate Ireland. Clearly this vision of nationalism, according to some historians, brought to a breathtaking extreme the romance of failure.[55] In the veneration of Tone, Emmett, and Young Ireland, their failure was ignored and their acts admired. Pearse asked that the failure be admired and serve as an example because only in this redemptive act would success ultimately come. It was his belief, as he exhorted crowds at the funeral of Fenian O'Donavan Rossa in 1915, that "from the graves of patriot men and women spring living nations."[56]

Pearse, MacDonagh, and Plunkett were members of the Central Executive of the Irish Volunteers and, with the old revolutionary Thomas Clarke, were involved in the planning of the 1916 Easter Week rebellion. The two revolutionary movements joined in early 1916, when Connolly was brought in on IRB planning, linking the mystical nationalism of Pearse with the socialist revolution of Connolly.

The Easter Rising of 1916

Not unlike earlier Irish revolutionary efforts at violence, the 1916 Rising was a shambles. The head of the Irish Volunteers, Eoin MacNeill, was hoodwinked by Pearse into giving orders for a general mobilization on Easter Sunday. When MacNeill found out the mobilization was for an insurrection, he canceled his orders, changed his mind, countermanded the cancellation, then changed his mind again. Thus, many Volunteers—especially outside Dublin—simply did not show up for the revolt. A German ship carrying obsolete Russian arms to the Volunteers was scuttled when it was challenged off the coast of Kerry and escorted into Queenstown harbor (Cobh).[57] These events off the Munster coast effectively dashed the original plans for the Rising, which had envisioned simultaneous rebellions in Dublin and the provinces.

Pearse and Connolly were not deterred, and on Easter Monday approximately 1,600 members of the Volunteers and the Citizen Army took up their planned positions at various locations in Dublin, including the Four Courts, St. Stephen's Green, and the General Post Office (GPO), which served as general headquarters. The Proclamation of an Irish Republic was read by Pearse the first day to a small, uncomprehending crowd gathered in front of the GPO. The document drew on the historical tradition of rebellion, affirmed the republican commitment, and—in the tradition of Wolfe Tone and the United Irishmen—rejected sectarianism. The new republic would resolve "to pursue the happiness and prosperity of the whole nation and of all its parts, cherishing all the children of the nation equally, and oblivious of the differences carefully fostered by an alien government, which have divided a minority from the majority in the past."[58]

The British, initially taken by surprise, moved troops and artillery into Dublin and steadily maneuvered to take the rebel positions. The administration, contrary to Connolly's belief, did not hesitate to use artillery against property and reduced much of central Dublin to fire and ruins. Caught in the crossfire was the civilian population who lived in poor neighborhoods and tenements surrounding the GPO. Numbers of them were killed while looting and others perished when their homes came into the line of fire. Stories would abound for years in working class Dublin of atrocities at the hands of British troops.[59] Although the rebels held their position for close to a week and displayed a fierce resolve, they were hopelessly outnumbered. On Saturday, April 29, Pearse surrendered, an action that was repeated at other rebel strongholds.

The insurrection was seen by the relatively content Irish people, some with sons fighting in France with the British Army, variously as a nuisance, a foolish suicidal act, or treason. Indeed (according to some eyewitness accounts), when the captured rebels were marched through the streets they were abused and jeered by the people of Dublin. New research, however, suggests that this backlash against the rebels was not universal. Joseph Lee suggests that some Dubliners, especially the poor, identified with the rebels, and other, more prominent observers confided that it was a pity that they did not succeed.[60] Many, no matter what their sympathies, gradually sympathized with the rising in the wake of British response and reprisal.

Most of the rebels were shipped to prisons in England. The leaders, however, were kept in Dublin, and military trials were begun. Of the 160 sentenced, 97 were to be executed. The British commander, General Sir John Maxwell, began the executions while the trials were going on and had 15 men shot in twos and threes over a period of ten days. Among them were seven men who had signed the Proclamation: Thomas Clarke, Sean McDermott, Thomas MacDonough, Joseph Plunkett, Eamon Ceannt, Patrick Pearse, and James Connolly. Connolly, having been wounded in the revolt, was propped up in a chair to be shot. Although the Rising prompted mixed reactions among the public, the executions were considered a particularly brutal response and outraged prominent Irish and British figures such as George Bernard Shaw and the bishop of Limerick. As some of the events of Easter Week became clear, such as the brutal murder of activist (and non-combatant) Francis Sheehy-Skeffington by a British officer, opinion grew even more negative, and the executions were stopped.

The Easter Rising and its legacy in Ireland and Northern Ireland have been the focus of heated debate for several decades. Should figures like Pearse and Connolly be considered heroes in the pantheon of Irish nationalism, or are they dangerous role models who incite terrorist response in Northern Ireland today? Is the message of the rising—which champions independence and an insular Gaelic Ireland—relevant in a world where Ireland has become increasingly integrated into Europe and the European Economic Community (EEC)? These questions have riveted a generation of historians and journalists and have prompted a variety of responses.

Well into the 1960s the Easter Rising was a symbol of Irish independence and a touchstone of nationalist identity in Ireland. In a political era dominated by Eamon de Valera (who commanded Volunteer forces at Boland's Mills during the rebellion), Dublin and 1916 were given pride of place in the story of the Irish nation. As D. George Boyce reminds us, praise was especially lavished on Patrick Pearse, who was described by one early biographer as "a virtuous man" who "possessed all the qualities which go to the making of a saint."[61] This adoration was echoed as late as 1967 by David Thornley who, while suggesting that much about Pearse was wrapped up in "national mythology," nonetheless admitted that it was "not merely difficult but almost blasphemous to discern a human being of flesh and blood."[62] In men like Pearse and Connolly one found worthy descendants of Tone, Young Ireland, and the Fenians, links in an unbroken chain of resistance to British rule.

Landmarks and public monuments mirrored the nationalist reverence for the men of 1916. During the 1960s, for example, they were remembered in the re-dedication of a trio of railway terminals that serve Dublin: Pearse, Connolly, and Heuston stations.[63] Moreover, commemorative artwork and sculpture eloquently communicate the power and near-religious reverence that the rebel leaders commanded. This is most potently expressed in a mosaic in the new Catholic cathedral in Galway, which displays the praying figures of Patrick Pearse and John F. Kennedy flanking the image of the risen Christ.[64] The image is clear: Pearse was a martyr, a savior whose Easter sacrifice led to the redemption of the Irish people.

Beginning in the 1970s this nationalist interpretation was challenged by revisionist historians in Ireland. Drawing insight from new documentary evidence and touting "a non-judgmental approach," they suggested that popular understanding of the Easter Rising and the heroic image of rebel leaders might be oversimplified, distorted, or factually wrong. Indeed, several writers questioned the motives and "blood agenda" of those like Patrick Pearse. Conor Cruise O'Brien asserted that the rising was a minority-led "putsch" that did not represent public sentiment in Ireland.[65] Likewise, Father Francis Shaw, in an article published in 1972, declared that the arrogance of the rebel leaders and their glorification of violence closed the door to any peaceful settlement over partition and ultimately led Ireland into civil war.[66] Perhaps most damning were revisionist allegations that renewed Irish Republican Army (IRA) terrorism in Northern Ireland during the 1970s was in part attributable to the nationalist glorification of the rebels.[67]

Several factors underlay this shift in perspective concerning the Easter Rising. First, as historian Michael Laffan notes, it was promoted by changes of mood and values in the Republic during the 1960s and 1970s. Ireland and its people were becoming less insular; with new economic expansion and industrialization they began to acquire a measure of prosperity and self-confidence that was unknown in the Ireland of the past.[68] Moreover, Ireland's membership in the United Nations and the EEC prompted the feeling that the Republic had begun to jettison the British inheritance and had finally "taken her place among the nations of the Earth."[69] Independence, concludes Laffan, was now a fact that many Irish could take for granted and older, self-conscious symbols of that identity—such as the Easter Rising—were seen as redundant and no longer necessary.

Changing interpretations of the Easter Rising were accompanied by, as Declan Kiberd reminds us, changing attitudes toward nationalist and colonial conflicts around the globe. Until the mid-1960s Western writers tended to support the anti-imperial struggles of such nations as Algeria, Palestine, and Iran. This patronage disintegrated in the following decade with the emergence of Khomeini in Iran, Pol Pot in Cambodia, and Idi Amin in Africa. "The image of the freedom fighter was gradually replaced by that of the terrorist."[70] Similarly, in Ireland renewed IRA violence and mayhem in the 1970s led to a revulsion against republican activism and a distancing from traditional role models such as Wolfe Tone and Patrick Pearse. Indeed, some writers suggested a direct connection between the message and glorification of Easter heroes such as Pearse and the recruitment of a new generation of IRA volunteers.[71]

Patrick Pearse

Over the years a spirited debate has centered on the life and legacy of Patrick Pearse. In the hands of nationalist writers, Pearse was virtually a patron saint of Irish independence, a faultless exemplar of right ideas and righteous action. Revisionist historians have painted a much more ambiguous picture. Ruth Dudley Edwards, in an influential biography written in 1978, brings Pearse back down to earth. Edwards argues that, while Pearse was a man of ability and character, he was also a deeply flawed individual. He had an overriding obsession for martyrdom, a blood sacrifice that would redeem the corruption of the Irish people and its culture. According to Edwards, this "triumph of failure" was a fitting and self-fulfilling epitaph to Pearse, whose personal life and achievements "never measured up to his inflated aspirations."

As Edwards concluded:

> Through his adult life he had been consistently disappointed in the response of his countrymen to the visions he laid before them, yet this never led him to question his own judgment. He wrote, acted and died for a people that did not exist; he distorted into his own image the ordinary people of Ireland, who lacked his own remarkable qualities, but who had complexities of their own that he could never understand.[72]

Recent historical writing has challenged the revisionist dogma on Pearse. Joseph Lee, in particular, defends Pearse on several counts. In answer to charges that Pearse had a blood obsession, Lee argues that one has to understand him within the context of Europe during World War I. It was an environment, particularly at the outbreak of the war, in which European correspondents, writers, and poets gloried in the excitement and "sanctifying properties of bloodshed."[73] Pearse was no different. Lee also challenges the accepted idea that martyrdom and blood sacrifice were an integral part of Pearse's long-range plans for the insurrection. He contends that the Rising was planned to occur when the rebels felt they had the maximum chance of success, and they set about to acquire the weapons necessary for such a victory. It was only with the failure of the German arms mission, argues Lee, that the hopelessness of their efforts became apparent and justified in Pearse and others the rhetoric of blood sacrifice and saving Ireland's honor.[74]

Mosaic in the Catholic cathedral in Galway City. The praying figure of Patrick Pearse on one side of the risen Christ underlines Pearse's role as martyr and his Easter redemption of the Irish people. Joining Pearse on the other side is a mosaic of John F. Kennedy revealing the pride in the connection to the United States through immigration.
Photo by Richard B. Finnegan

A new wave of Irish scholars is forging a fresh perspective on the Easter Rising. Recent scholarship has focused attention on the art and imagery associated with the Rising; like historical writing, it has tended to reflect the politics and mindset of the time in which it was created.[75] Irish historians have also set out to reclaim the history of women in the nationalist movement, an important theme but largely ignored in an earlier age dominated by male academics and polemicists. This movement included such luminaries as Lady Gregory, who contributed to the literary nationalism of the Gaelic revival, and Countess Markievicz, an officer in the Irish Citizens Army who, along with thirty-seven other women, took part in the Easter Rising. Alongside them were thousands of women whose roles at the turn of the century have been unrecognized: messengers, nurses, and combatants in the rising; trade unionists and suffragettes; and members of Inghinidhe na hEireann (Daughters of Ireland), an anti-establishment front dedicated to "complete independence" and the eradication of "low" English literature, theater, and entertainment.[76]

Irish scholars and post-revisionists are also developing a more balanced portrait of the leaders during the Rising. While the revisionists helped tear down the cardboard heroes erected in the nationalist tradition, their critics maintain that they often replaced them with an equally one-dimensional picture of violence, deceit, and military obsession. In reality, the lives and legacy of Pearse, Connolly, Plunkett, and McDermott embrace a complexity that has been lost in the debate. Connolly, for example, was a social thinker of the first order. Pearse was a champion of Gaelic culture and effectively brought attention to the Irish language. He was also a "gifted teacher and educationalist" who did much to develop that quality of inquiry and independence that we equate with Irish students today. At St. Endas, as Lee notes, "The object of education was to develop to the full the character and intellect of every individual pupil. The school must foster the talents of the pupil, rather than trying to mould him or her according to some regulation-type identikit personality."[77] These are important legacies of the generation of 1916 that go beyond the martial image that is indelibly stamped in the history books.

Indeed, a new generation of writers in Ireland refuses to be fixed and stereotyped within a single version of past events such as the Easter Rising. This is perhaps most important today in Northern Ireland, where history has been wielded by loyalist and republican alike to shape their understanding of the present and their vision of the future. There are changes in the air. It is perhaps fitting that at this time of the peace accord that Easter has taken on, for some, a new meaning. Rather than being a remembrance of the 1916 Rising (a rallying call blazoned on republican murals in Belfast and trumpeted over the Internet), it is now the new Peace Accord, agreed to over Easter weekend, 1998, that may take precedence. This accord holds the fragile promise of peace for the future, a rare and evolutionary vision in Northern Ireland. As Seamus Heaney suggests:

> If revolution is the kicking down of a rotten door, evolution is more like pushing aside the stone from the mouth of the tomb. There is an Easter energy about it, a sense of arrival rather than wreckage, and what is nonpareil about the new conditions is the promise they offer of a new covenant between people living in this country. For once, and at long last; the language of the Bible can be appropriated by those with a vision of the future rather than those who sing the battle hymns of the past.[78]

Notes

1. Rev. Theobald Mathew to Charles Trevelyan, 7 August 1846, in Noel Kissane, *The Irish Famine: A Documentary History* (Dublin: National Library of Ireland, 1995), p. 47.

2. "Bloodlines: Letters by James and Elizabeth Prendergast," *Boston College Magazine* 51, no. 1 (Winter 1996), p. 27.

3. Peter Gray, *The Irish Famine* (New York: Harry N. Abrams, 1995), p. 45.

4. Kissane, *Irish Famine*, p. 50. Politicians and British public opinion alike believed that Ireland abounded with resources that required only hard work and entrepreneurship to unleash.

5. Gray, *Irish Famine*, p. 49.

6. Gray, *Irish Famine*, p. 69.

7. Kerby A. Miller, *Emigrants and Exiles: Ireland and the Irish Exodus to North America* (New York: Oxford University Press, 1985), p. 284.

8. Maurice Prendergast to Cornelius Riordan [Boston], 26 December 1847, in James Prendergast Letters, MS 86-141, Burns Library, Boston College, Newton, Massachusetts.

9. On Famine migration, see E. Margaret Crawford, ed., *The Hungry Stream: Essays on Emigration and Famine* (Belfast: Institute of Irish Studies, 1997); Robert James Scally, *The End of Hidden Ireland: Rebellion, Famine, and Emigration* (New York: Oxford University Press, 1995); and Miller, *Emigrants and Exiles*, especially chapter 7.

10. Gray, *Irish Famine*, p. 113.

11. Quoted in Mary Daly, "Revisionism and Irish History: The Great Famine," in *Making of Modern Irish History*, ed. D. George Boyce and Alan O'Day, p. 72

12. Ibid.

13. Quoted in Kissane, *Irish Famine*, p. 174.

14. See Michael Davitt, *The Fall of Feudalism in Ireland* (London, 1904), pp. 52–53; and, concerning Arthur Griffith, Gray, *Irish Famine*, p. 179. For a review of the nationalist literature, see Daly, "Revisionism and Irish History," pp. 71–89.

15. Cormac O'Grada, *Ireland: A New Economic History, 1780–1939* (Oxford: Clarendon Press, 1994), p. 174.

16. R. F. Foster, *Modern Ireland, 1600–1972* (New York: Allen Lane, 1988), chapter 14, pp. 318–325.

17. Ibid., p. 325.

18. Ibid., p. 330.

19. Ibid., pp. 326–327.

20. See, for example, R. Dudley Edwards and T. Desmond Williams, eds., *The Great Famine: Studies in Irish History, 1845–1852* (Dublin: Browne and Nolan, 1956); Mary E. Daly, *The Famine in Ireland* (Dundalk: Dundalgan Press, 1986); and Foster, *Modern Ireland*.

21. An incisive review of this question can be found in Kelly Candaele and Kerry Candaele, "Revisionists and the Writing of Irish History," *Irish-America Magazine* (July/August 1994), pp. 22–27.

22. Christine Kinealy, "Beyond Revisionism: Reassessing the Great Irish Famine," *History Ireland* 3, no. 4 (Winter 1995), pp. 30–34.

23. Joseph Lee, "The Famine as History," in *Famine 150: Commemorative Lecture Series*, ed. Cormac O'Grada (Dublin: Teagasc/UCD, 1997), p. 166. Lee's essay provides a stimulating comment on the historiography of the Famine, arguing that each successive generation of historians has "rewritten" the Famine to suit its own particular needs and agenda.

24. O'Grada, *Ireland: A New Economic History*, p. 176.

25. See Peter Gray, "Punch and the Great Famine," *History Ireland* 1, no. 2 (Summer 1993), pp. 26–33; "Ideology and the Famine," in *The Great Irish Famine*, ed. Cathal Poirteir (Cork: Mercier Press, 1995), (Dublin: 1993), pp. 86–103; and "Potatoes and Providence:

British Government Responses to the Great Famine," *Bullan: An Irish Studies Journal* 1, no. 1 (Spring 1994), pp. 75–90.

26. Charles Trevelyan, *The Irish Crisis* (London: Longman, 1848), p. 1.

27. Gray, *Irish Famine*, p. 39.

28. Luke Gibbons, "Doing Justice to the Past: The Great Famine and Cultural Memory," in *Irish Hunger: Personal Reflections on the Legacy of the Famine*, ed. Tom Hayden (Boulder Colo.: Roberts Rinehart, 1997), pp. 258–270.

29. Kevin Whelan, "Interpreting the Irish Famine," (unpublished paper in the author's possession), p. 49. On this point see also Kinealy, "Beyond Revisionism," p. 32.

30. O'Grada, *Ireland: A New Economic History*, p. 176. For Mokyr's telling analysis of government spending, see Joel Mokyr, *Why Ireland Starved: A Quantitative and Analytical History of the Irish Economy, 1800-1850* (London: George Allen & Unwin, 1983), p. 292.

31. O'Grada, *Ireland: A New Economic History*, p. 191.

32. For a review of some of the new avenues in Famine research, see O'Grada, "New Perspectives on the Irish Famine," *Bullan: An Irish Studies Journal*, 3, no. 2 (Winter 1997/Spring 1998), pp. 103–115.

33. See Cormac O'Grada, *Black '47 and Beyond: The Great Irish Famine* (Princeton: Princeton University Press, 1999); Cathal Porteir, *Famine Echoes* (Dublin: Gill & Macmillan, 1995); Charles E. Orser, Jr., "Of Dishes and Drains: An Archaeological Perspective on Irish Rural Life in the Famine Era," *New Hibernia Review* 1, no. 1 (Spring 1997), pp. 120–135; Margaret Crawford, "The Great Irish Famine 1845–9: Image Versus Reality," in *Ireland: Art into History*, ed. Brian P. Kennedy and Raymond Gillespie (Niwot, Colo.: Roberts Rinehart Publishers, 1994).

34. This Famine song, by Maire Ni Dhroma of Ring, County Waterford, is reproduced in Gray, *Irish Famine*, p. 163.

35. For a seminal statement on this viewpoint, see T. W. Moody, "Irish History and Irish Mythology," in *Interpreting Irish History*, ed. Ciaran Brady (Dublin: Irish Academic Press, 1994), pp. 71–86.

36. Luke Gibbons, *Transformations in Irish Culture* (Cork: Cork University Press, 1996), p. 17.

37. On famine memory and its impact on Irish society, emigrant culture, and nationalism, see David Lloyd, "The Memory of Hunger," in *Irish Hunger*, ed. Hayden, pp. 32–47; and Joseph Lee, "The Famine as History," in *Famine 150*, ed. O'Grada, pp. 167–173.

38. For a comparative analysis of the Great Famine and more recent tragedies in Africa and Asia, see Cormac O'Grada, "The Great Famine and Other Famines," in O'Grada, *Famine 150*, pp. 129–157.

39. Quoted in Gray, *Irish Famine*, p. 183.

40. Speakman's quote can be found in Kevin Whelan, "Bitter Harvest," *Boston College Magazine* 55, no. 1 (Winter 1996), p. 25.

41. The loss of this world is powerfully lamented in Nuala Ni Dhomhnaill, "A Ghostly Alhambra," in *Irish Hunger*, ed. Hayden, pp. 68–90. See also Robert Scally, *End of Hidden Ireland*.

42. Quoted in Whelan, "Interpreting the Irish Famine," p. 78. Dorrian's account is based on folk memory and the recollections of eyewitnesses to the Famine. See Hugh Dorian, "Donegal, Sixty Years Ago: A True Historical Narrative" [1896], National Library of Ireland, Ms 2047, photostat copy.

43. Miller, *Emigrants and Exiles*, p. 77.

44. For a brilliant visual depiction of land changes in Ireland during the Famine era, see F. H. A. Aalen, Kevin Whelan, and Matthew Stout, eds., *Atlas of the Irish Rural Landscape* (Toronto: University of Toronto Press, 1997), pp. 79–93.

45. O'Grada, *Ireland: A New Economic History,* pp. 236–250.

46. Gray, *Irish Famine*, p. 76.

47. James S. Donnelly Jr., "Lough Derg: The Making of the Modern Pilgrimage," in *Donegal History and Society,* ed. William Nolan, Liam Ronayne, and Mairead Denlevy (Dublin: Geography Publications, 1995).

48. Land agitation was one arm of a strategy called "the new departure," advocated by John Devoy, an Irish American spokesman for Clan na Gael, the successor organization to the Fenian Brotherhood in the United States. The other arm of the strategy was parliamentary agitation for Home Rule. Together these strategies would lead to an independent Ireland by 1882, either conceded by the British or established by the Irish and backed with guns and money from the United States. Parnell accepted the strategies of the plan—agrarian agitation and parliamentary pressure for Home Rule—but rejected the leadership of the Americans and the idea of ultimate revolt.

49. Gray, *Irish Famine*, p. 125. See also S. J. Connolly, "The Great Famine and Irish Politics," in *The Great Irish Famine*, ed. Porteir, p. 49.

50. On architecture and the Celtic Revival, see Jeanne Sheehy, *The Rediscovery of Ireland's Past: The Celtic Revival, 1830–1930* (London: Thames and Hudson, 1980).

51. F. S. L. Lyons, *Ireland Since the Famine* (London: Collins, Fontana, 1973), p. 635.

52. For a stimulating discussion of Synge and the west of Ireland, see Luke Gibbons, "Synge, Country and Western: The Myth of the West in Irish and American Culture," in *Transformations in Irish Culture,* especially pp. 28–35.

53. Whelan, "Interpreting the Famine," p. 108.

54. W. B. Yeats, *Essays and Introductions* (New York: Macmillan, 1961), p. 213.

55. See especially Ruth Dudley Edwards, *Patrick Pearse: The Triumph of Failure* (New York: Taplinger Publishing, 1978).

56. Patrick Pearse, *Political Writings and Speeches* (Dublin: Talbot Press, 1966), pp. 136–137.

57. Sir Roger Casement, an Anglo-Irish Protestant committed to the Irish rebellion, was to arrange for arms to be smuggled to the Irish Volunteers in 1914 and to attempt to enlist German aid in the Rising of 1916. The latter assignment was a comedy of errors in which Casement first tried to recruit Irish POWs to fight for Ireland and succeeded only in designing uniforms for a bunch of brigands who never left Germany. Casement was also to enlist German artillery and expertise in the Rising; instead he received 20,000 obsolete weapons. Casement returned to Ireland to try to call off the rebellion because it did not have adequate German support. He was arrested three days before the Rising and was hanged for treason in August.

58. Foster, *Ireland: 1600–1972,* Appendix.

59. For an overview of events in Dublin during the rising, see F. S. L. Lyons, "The Rising and After," in *A New History of Ireland, Vol VI,* ed. W. E. Vaughn (Oxford: Clarendon Press, 1996), pp. 207–223.

60. Joseph Lee, *Ireland 1912–1985: Politics and Society* (Cambridge: Cambridge University Press, 1989), pp. 28–33.

61. D. George Boyce, "1916: Interpreting the Rising." in *Making of Modern Irish History,* ed. Boyce and O'Day, p. 166.

62. Quoted in ibid., p. 166. Boyce's point is to illustrate that even in the 1960s—a decade of increasing historical sophistication and critical analysis—one still witnessed the lingering influence of traditional interpretation and idolization. See also David Thornley, "Patrick Pearse—The Evolution of a Republican," in *Leaders and Men of the Easter Rising: Dublin 1916,* ed. F. X. Martin (Ithaca, N.Y.: Cornell University Press), p. 151.

63. Interestingly, many who grew up in Ireland before the 1960s still refer to the older names of the terminals: Westland Row, Amiens Street, and Kingsbridge.

64. Michael Laffan, "Insular Attitudes: The Revisionists and Their Critics," in *Revising the Rising,* ed. Mairin ni Dhonnchadha and Theo Dorgan (Derry: Field Day Press, 1991) pp. 107–108.

65. Quoted in Kelly Candaele and Kerry Candaele, "Revisionists and the Writing of Irish History," *Irish America Magazine* (July/August 1994), p. 25.

66. Father Francis Shaw, SJ, "The Canon of Irish History: A Challenge," *Studies* 61 (1972), pp. 113–153. See also D. George Boyce, "1916: Interpreting the Rising," pp. 178–179.

67. See Candaele and Candaele, "Revisionists and the Writing of Irish History," p. 25.

68. Laffan, "Insular Attitudes," in *Revising the Rising,* ed. ni Dhonnchadha and Dorgan, p. 109.

69. Ibid., pp. 109–110.

70. These points are made in Declan Kiberd, "The Elephant of Revolutionary Forgetfulness," in *Revising the Rising,* ed. ni Dhonnchadha and Dorgan, pp. 7–8.

71. Conor Cruise O'Brien, *States of Ireland,* p. 150.

72. Edwards, *Patrick Pearse,* p. 343.

73. Joseph Lee, "In Search of Patrick Pearse," in *Revising the Rising,* ed. ni Dhonnachadha and Dorgan, pp. 132–133.

74. Lee, *Ireland 1912–1985,* pp. 24–26; and Lee, "In Search of Patrick Pearse," p. 127. As Lee concludes, the actual course of the Rising, and the subsequent execution of its leaders, suited the type of interpretation and mystique that would carry the most historical punch.

75. Sighle Bhreathnach-Lynch, "The Easter Rising 1916: Constructing a Canon in Art and Artifacts," *History Ireland* (Spring 1997), pp. 37–42.

76. Foster, *Modern Ireland, 1600–1972,* pp. 449–450. On the women's movement see Margaret Ward, *Unmanageable Revolutionaries: Women and Irish Nationalism* (Dingle: Brandon Press, 1995); and Margaret MacCurtain and Donncha O'Corrain, eds., *Women in Irish Society: The Historical Dimension* (Westport, Conn.: Greenwood Press, 1979), pp. 46–57.

77. Lee, "In Search of Patrick Pearse," p. 135.

78. Seamus Heaney, "Sweet Unheard Melodies," *The Boston Sunday Globe,* 12 April 1998, pp. 1, 26.

3

FROM GUERRILLA WAR
TO INDEPENDENCE

The Rise of Sinn Fein

The 1916 Rising was like a crack in a dam. At first slowly, then increasing into a great cascade, Irish opinion began to support the rebels. The initial negative reaction to the executions was followed by a growing appreciation of the heroism of the outnumbered rebels and their commitment to their cause.

The British were under pressure from the United States because of the Irish issue both before and after U.S. entry into World War I. David Lloyd George, prime minister of Great Britain, made two offers of Home Rule to John Redmond. The first offer, in 1916, provided for a "temporary" exclusion of six Ulster counties, but at the same time Lloyd George was secretly assuring the Ulster unionists that the exclusion would be permanent. The offer collapsed. In 1917 Lloyd George tried again, offering Home Rule with the permanent exclusion of the six Ulster counties. Redmond initially refused the offer but agreed to try to work out the differences at a conference. Redmond apparently was willing to accept further constraints on Home Rule, but he died during the conference.

Another British move to placate Irish and U.S. opinion was to release "rebels" who had been interned after the Rising. From Britain's point of view this decision was a mistake that was to come back to haunt the government; the released prisoners were welcomed home as heroes. The prisoners provided the backbone of a rebuilt Irish Volunteers and became committed activists for Sinn Fein. Political activity blossomed despite the imposition of martial law in Ireland. The IRB was rebuilt under the direction of released internee Michael Collins, who played a major role in the war with England and the treaty that ended it. In 1917 leaders of the Irish Volunteers rapidly took over Arthur Griffith's Sinn Fein and used it as the political arm of the republican movement.[1] Griffith remained president.

The event that revealed the strength of Sinn Fein and the weakness of the Irish Party was an election in early 1917 in which Count Plunkett, father of the poet who had been executed in 1916, ran against an Irish Party candidate and won handily with Sinn Fein support. Plunkett declared that he would not take his seat in Parliament. This pattern was followed by three other Sinn Fein victors, including one Sinn Fein candidate who was still in jail. The culmination of this policy occurred in June 1917 when Sinn Fein put up Eamon de Valera as a candidate. De Valera's leadership emerged in this election, a leadership more influential on Irish politics than any other in the following forty years.

De Valera was born in the United States, the son of an Irish mother and a Spanish father. He was brought up by his grandmother in rural County Limerick, however, and became a mathematics teacher. As a young man he became involved in the Gaelic League, and he joined the Irish Volunteers in 1913. His enthusiasm and talent earned him the rank of commandant, and his garrison at Boland's Mills was the last rebel unit to surrender in the Easter Rising. During the military trials that ensued he was sentenced to death, but his U.S. birth (and technical U.S. citizenship) probably saved him from execution.[2] De Valera emerged as an informal leader of the men who were imprisoned in England after the rising. Although personally aloof and spartan in temperament, de Valera inspired great loyalty as a leader. One of the last prisoners released because of his rank, de Valera went back to Ireland in June and won an election in East Clare in July by a more than two-to-one margin. Because de Valera was now seen as a hero of 1916, his victory was a victory for the Easter Rising and its proclamation of an Irish republic. In October, at a party conference in Dublin, de Valera was elected president of Sinn Fein. Two days later he was elected president of the Irish Volunteers. He now held the reins of leadership of the republican movement.

Mistakes of British Policy

The British in 1918 undertook two actions that, first, infuriated all of Ireland (save Ulster) and, second, created great sympathy and support for Sinn Fein. It is an overstatement to say that the British never remember Irish history and the Irish never forget it, but clearly few lessons had been learned in Westminster. In April 1918, as the Great War raged on, Parliament passed a bill authorizing the draft in Ireland. The reaction was immediate and explosive. The Irish Party walked out of Parliament, and Sinn Fein, the Labour Party, and all other parties condemned conscription. The Irish Congress of Trade Unions called a general strike and the Catholic Hierarchy proclaimed that the Irish people should resist the draft "by every means that are consonant with the laws of God."[3] Indeed, a pledge was taken by thousands of people outside their parish churches on

Sunday, April 21. Sinn Fein used this broad spectrum of anti-conscription activity to build political support and legitimize its existence in the political arena.

The British authorities also aided Sinn Fein through wholesale arrests of Sinn Fein leaders, including de Valera and Arthur Griffith. The British claimed that the arrests were a result of Sinn Fein's plotting with Germany. The "evidence" was scanty at best, but it provided a justification for the arrest of hundreds, and Sinn Fein was outlawed. For Irish nationalists it must have seemed that to ensure election to Parliament one must be in a British prison; in May Griffith won a resounding victory from his jail cell. In short, the British plan to destroy opposition in Ireland backfired: Sinn Fein gained popular support and, while outlawed, expanded under the leadership of Michael Collins.[4]

Declaring an Independent Republic; the Dail Eireann

The scene was set for the December 1918 general election, which was to select 105 members of Parliament. The outlawed Sinn Fein movement ran candidates who were in jail or on the run from the police. The program put forth to the people consisted of four points: withdrawal from the British Parliament, resistance to British authority, the creation of an Irish assembly, and recognition at the post-war peace conference in Paris of Ireland's independence. Sinn Fein swept the election.

A significant feature of the election, and a boon to Sinn Fein, was a change in the electoral laws that expanded the franchise to encompass all men over twenty-one and women over thirty. These new voters increased the Irish electorate from approximately 700,000 to just under 2 million—a youthful shift that was felt on election day. The Irish Parliamentary Party entered the election with sixty-eight seats; Sinn Fein, with seven. The former came out of the election with six seats; Sinn Fein, with seventy-three.[5] Although the Ulster unionists increased their strength to twenty-six seats, their influence was only felt in the north of Ireland. Outside Ulster, Sinn Fein dominated the election, gaining 65 percent of the vote and sweeping large sections of Munster, the Midlands, and Connaught.[6]

The winners of seven by-elections in 1917 and 1918 had vowed not to take their seats in Parliament. In January 1919 those who had been elected in the general election went further and invited all elected, including unionists, to a meeting in Dublin to establish a new Irish assembly. All except Sinn Fein members refused to come, and Sinn Fein could only produce twenty-seven members—the rest were in jail or in hiding. Those who showed up designated themselves Dail Eireann (Assembly of Ireland) and issued a declaration of independence that stated that the Dail was an affirmation of the Republic declared in 1916. A government was set up and a "Message to the Free Nations of the World" was enunciated, which looked to Irish recognition at the post-war peace conference at Versailles (where self-determination and the rights of small nations were high on the agenda of U.S. President Woodrow Wilson).[7]

The Dail created arbitration courts, a land bank, and an Industrial Disputes Board, essentially setting up a parallel government to the British administration. Its efforts to get recognition at the Paris peace talks failed, however, because the delegates there were unable to persuade the United States to support the Republic. The second session of the Dail elected de Valera as president. He had recently escaped from Lincoln jail in England, a daring flight engineered by Michael Collins. De Valera immediately took ship to the United States to seek money and political support. In his absence the power of Sinn Fein centered around Michael Collins.

Collins was born in west Cork in 1890 and emigrated to London at age sixteen. There he became involved with the Gaelic League and the GAA and went on to join the IRB. He fought in the 1916 Rising and was imprisoned at Frongoch, one of several English internment camps for the Easter rebels. Like de Valera, Collins emerged as a leader in prison. When he returned to Ireland he set out to rebuild the IRB and the Irish Volunteers. He was a bright, powerful, and charismatic leader whose influence permeated the politics of the Sinn Fein movement. In September 1919 the British government outlawed the Dail. De Valera was in the United States, and the success of the provisional government very often depended upon the ability of Collins as minister of finance (he secured the Dail Loan, which financed the Irish alternative government). Moreover, in his IRB role, Collins's responsibilities increased as the Republic slowly slid into guerrilla war with the British authorities in Ireland. His development of counter-intelligence networks and his ruthless command of terrorist squads were significant in the success of the movement.

The Anglo-Irish War and the Anglo-Irish Treaty

The War with Britain

At the outset of the war (or civil disturbance as the British chose to see it), guerrilla actions by the Irish Volunteers (now known as the Irish Republican Army or IRA)[8] were directed at the Royal Irish Constabulary. Armed intimidation and assassinations of police, such as the celebrated ambush of two constables at Soloheadbeg in Tipperary, were designed to instill fear in the constabulary and prompt widespread resignations. Yet, as David Fitzpatrick suggests, there was little overall policy or direction from Sinn Fein "headquarters." Instead, much of the republican action in the countryside was based on local initiative and was initially confined to "arson, arms raiding, and intimidation."[9] In County Clare, for example, locals attempted to isolate and browbeat policemen, no longer supplying food or turf to the barracks, cropping the hair of girlfriends and potential recruits, and in time subjecting police to physical attack.[10] Local Sinn Fein courts were established to hear criminal cases and civil claims and to monitor the "moral" persuasion in the community. They meted out republican justice and often looked the other way in cases of withholding rent, cattle driving (in which herds belonging to wealthy graziers were illegally scattered or taken away), and forced emigration of Protestant families.[11]

Throughout 1919 and into 1920 assaults on and murders of police increased throughout the country. Large numbers of the Royal Irish Constabulary resigned, and new recruits did not clamor for a dangerous job that had no future. In an effort to curb the action of the IRA the government introduced a specially created armed force, the Black and Tans, and recruited ex-army officers to serve as auxiliaries to the police force. These aggressive units and their often brutal repression against the civilian community only served to escalate the war and precipitated a vicious cycle of terrorism and counter-terrorism. Bombings, shootings, executions, and torture were common under this paramilitary expansion, and Black and Tan atrocities—such as the burning and sack of Balbriggan in north County Dublin—only served to further alienate the Irish people.[12]

Escalation of the war under the Black and Tans forced many armed Volunteers (who were significantly outnumbered) to band together for protection.[13] Local IRA units took to the countryside, forming "flying columns" that waged a hit-and-run campaign against paramilitary forces. Their stock-in-trade of ambush, sabotage, kidnappings, and assassinations kept many areas of Ireland—such as southwest Munster—ungovernable in 1920 and 1921.[14] In this guerrilla campaign the flying columns were aided and abetted by local communities, an important factor in their success. Local sympathizers in Inistioge, County Kilkenny, for example, provided safehouses for the IRA, stockpiled arms, and provided willing auxiliaries—such as the village blacksmith who fashioned nails in his forge to be strewn in front of pursuing Crossley tenders.[15] Such communities, of course, were frequently the targets of the Black and Tans, who sought to root out IRA support. Raids on local farms and the round up and interrogation of young men from the parish were continuing catalysts for local sympathies for the Irish cause.

In 1920 an election took place that displayed Sinn Fein at its greatest strength but also created an insurmountable barrier to its objective. Lloyd George had enacted a bill in 1920 titled, no doubt by someone with a sense of humor, the Better Government of Ireland Act. It was Home Rule and partition again. Six counties in Ulster were to have their own parliament, as would the remaining twenty-six counties. The bill also created a Council of Ireland to deal with matters of concern to both north and south. The act went into effect, and elections were held. In the south the results were a massive landslide for Sinn Fein, which captured 124 out of 128 seats in what was supposed to be the new parliament. Sinn Fein, however, used the election to select the Second Dail Eireann, held to its position of abstention from British-created assemblies, and continued the war. Partition was now a fact as the unionists took 40 out of 52 seats in the Ulster election. The Parliament of Northern Ireland began to function, but it was dominated by Presbyterian unionists with strong overtones of the Orange Order.

The latter part of 1920 saw some of the most brutal acts and reprisals of the war. In Dublin on the morning of November 11, Michael Collins unleashed a special squad of assassins who murdered thirteen officers of the Dublin Metropolitan Police suspected of being intelligence agents. That same day—known as "Bloody Sunday"—the Black and Tans responded by shooting into the crowd at a Gaelic football game at Croke Park, killing fourteen people and wounding sixty.[16] In Cork a similar pattern of "assassination and reprisal" took shape. In late November IRA flying columns ambushed several government forces, inflicting heavy losses. Black and Tans retaliated by setting fire to the Cork city center, an episode characterized by the drunken looting of shops and the torching of city hall.

The Treaty

For another six months the savagery continued. Although the IRA were responsible for their fair share of violence, the draconian excesses of the paramilitary forces inevitably led the Irish people to identify with the Irish Republic. The actions of the auxiliaries and the Black and Tans, as one author reveals, also "served to diminish further the moral authority of the government in the face of world opinion."[17] Public sentiment in Britain and the United States was negative toward the "war" against the Irish and critical of the repressive policies of London. The death of Terence MacSwiney, the mayor of Cork, after a seventy-four-day hunger strike in a British prison, stirred public opinion for the Irish cause and released a great wave of protest throughout the world. Bowing to this chorus of complaint, Lloyd George called a truce in July 1921 and prepared to negotiate with Sinn Fein.

Partition was to be the rock upon which the Sinn Fein movement foundered. In 1921 de Valera and Lloyd George met, and the British prime minister set out his conditions for Ireland. They provided for dominion status but included partition and a number of other conditions primarily directed at British military security, such as the custody of air and naval bases in Ireland and the recruitment of soldiers in Ireland. De Valera flatly rejected these conditions but reported them to the Dail. Lloyd George wanted to continue negotiations, so de Valera appointed five men, among them Arthur Griffith and Michael Collins, to return to London to negotiate the Anglo-Irish Treaty. The Treaty would require final approval from the Dail. De Valera's decision not to attend is perplexing in that, to a certain degree, he was sending lambs to slaughter.[18] Lloyd George skillfully persuaded the Irish delegation to accept partition by offering the promise that the boundaries would be open to later negotiation, implying that they would shrink and ultimately disappear. Lloyd George also persuaded the Irish delegation to accept dominion status, with its oath of loyalty to the Crown, by threatening resumption of war. For Michael Collins, who knew that IRA resources and manpower were nearly exhausted, the threat of renewed hostilities must have been a telling factor. The delegates signed the Treaty establishing the Irish Free State and returned to Dublin.

Debate on the Treaty in the Dail, ironically enough, focused more on the dominion status of Ireland and less on partition, military facilities, and compensatory payments to Britain. The hardline republicans, de Valera included, argued that a partitioned, semi-sovereign Ireland and the requirement of making an oath to the Crown were not what the Irish had died for since 1916. The pragmatists, notably Collins, argued that the Free State was a beginning, that the IRA could not continue to fight against the full might of Britain, and that the Treaty was the best that could be obtained. The Dail, on a narrow vote of sixty-four to fifty-seven, accepted the Treaty. De Valera resigned, symbolically setting the stage for the next confrontation: Irishman against Irishman over acceptance of the Treaty. The feeling of those who rejected the Treaty was expressed by Ernie O'Malley, an IRA commander, who considered the Treaty a sell-out:

> All that evening I walked from street to street. I was sick at heart. The splendid dream we had built up was toppling like a house of cards. . . . What would the Fenians have done in their day if the heritage of their trust had been violated? What [of] the poor dead generations, who had toiled, landless, starved, homeless, beaten to their knees, cowed, disheartened, with the vision in their hearts. They did not barter. We were to become part of the British Empire and lose our souls.[19]

The British began to dismantle their administrative machinery in Ireland, and Collins and Griffith began to set up the government of the Free State. The anti-Treaty members of Sinn Fein, however, were ready to continue the fight and established headquarters around the country, including one in the Four Courts in Dublin. In this tense atmosphere an election was held, which resulted in thirty-five seats in the new Free State Assembly for the pro-Treaty wing. An additional thirty-one seats could also be considered pro-Treaty because they went to parties that were going to accept the Free State. The majority of Irish people, it appeared, were ready to put an end to bloodshed and accept a new state.

Civil War

The tension could not last, and the new government eventually attacked the IRA "irregulars" in the Four Courts in Dublin. British artillery was used in the bombardment, which went on for two days before the garrison surrendered. Among the symbolic casualties of the flames were the documents of British colonialism in Ireland: Irish census records, wills, and probate inventories (some of which were stacked up as barricades by IRA defenders). Their destruction, while a great loss for history, was one of the ironic twists in this age of British departure and post-colonialism. The flames of civil war continued to burn for over a year in Ireland, with the same ugly brutality displayed earlier against the Black and Tans. Moderates such as de Valera, who attempted to maintain a republican political organization, were brushed aside by more hardline military leaders such as Liam Lynch, chief of staff of the irregulars. It was only after Lynch was killed in action that de Valera was able to reassert some control. Republican opposition was strongest in Dublin and in Munster, where many of the flying columns joined the anti-Treaty forces and employed the familiar tactics of ambush and assassination. Yet the very independence that distinguished the flying columns worked to their disadvantage—Free State forces exploited a lack of coordination between rebel units to defeat them one by one.[20]

During the Civil War Michael Collins hastily organized a new national army, and with his continued control over the IRB managed to keep the irregulars on the run.[21] General Richard Mulcahey of the Free State Army advised the Cabinet to introduce emergency measures against the rebels, including military courts and capital punishment for a variety of offenses. Indeed, the Free State was tough on its old compatriots. The government executed seventy-eight IRA irregulars, including Rory O'Connor, who commanded the rebel garrison at the Four Courts, and Erskine Childers, a republican leader who was apprehended carrying a pistol (ironically a gift from Michael Collins) in violation of Mulcahey's "murder bill."[22] The Civil War also took its toll of Free State leadership. On August 12, 1922, President Arthur Griffith died of a cerebral hemorrhage, and Collins was killed a week later in an ambush near his birthplace in west Cork. In all, Irish dead at the end of the Civil War numbered over 1,000. These losses left behind many scars in local communities and a divisiveness that has not yet been completely erased.[23]

The anti-Treaty republicans could not spark public support, were condemned by the Catholic Church, and eventually called off the armed struggle in May 1923. In August 1923 there was a general election, and the anti-Treaty forces, despite open hostility from the Church and press, managed to win forty-four seats. The Free State government supporters, now called Cumann na nGaedheal, took sixty-three seats. The remaining forty-six seats were split among the Labor, Farmers, and other smaller parties. Even as it was holding to the position that the government was illegitimate, Sinn Fein could still muster the second-largest block of seats in that government.

The Civil War had profound repercussions in Irish society. The depth of the divisions that split the nation had a lasting effect on local communities and helped shape the Irish political scene for generations.[24] Indeed, events and personalities surrounding the Civil War still polarize argument and debate today, and none more readily than the legacy of Michael Collins. Should Collins be remembered as the man who bartered away a united Ireland, as hardline republicans argue, or was he a hero, "the man who made Ireland," as a popular biography declares?

Michael Collins

In the decades following the Civil War Michael Collins was gradually airbrushed out of the political picture, largely the result of the long tenure of power of Fianna

Fail, the party of de Valera and anti-Treaty supporters. Collins was seen as a turn-coat whose treaty negotiations with Britain sold out nationalist momentum and the goal of a thirty-two county Ireland. In recent years, however, Collins's legacy has been rehabilitated, both in the historical literature and in popular opinion. Research now suggests that Collins was a pragmatic realist who viewed the Treaty as only a stepping stone toward the eventual unification of Ireland.[25] Moreover, he was a charismatic leader who commanded loyalty and respect from many who came within his orbit.

The recovery and public acclaim of Collins is nowhere more vividly expressed than in the blockbuster film *Michael Collins* (1996). The film has been widely ac-claimed by audience opinion and several historians have called it "courageous," "epic," and "well balanced."[26] Controversy, however, has followed the film, partic-ularly in its attention to historical detail but also in the fear (largely expressed in British opinion) that it will be used for propaganda purposes to push the message of violence. One cannot deny that violence was an integral part of Collins's world, but the film, argues director Neil Jordan, transcends that image. Collins was, after all, a leader who made a heroic transformation from guerrilla fighter to arbiter of peace; his legacy speaks for the possibility of political tolerance, compromise, and change.[27] This message has particular resonance today in Northern Ireland and mirrors the current agenda of peace, negotiation, and compromise that those like Gerry Adams have brought to the peace accord.

Having said this, there is a cult of admiration that has grown around Collins, one that embraces the military mystique and warrior image of Collins. Posters of "the General" in his military uniform sell briskly in Dublin's city center, and Irish American students appreciate Collins chiefly as the "minister of general mayhem" who choreographed the guerrilla war in Dublin and directed the IRA counter-intelligence campaign. Yet Collins, historians remind us, was much more. As John Regan argues, Collins brought to the revolutionary stage an administrative genius as minister of finance and a genuine commitment at the peace table, and his po-litical leadership during the birth of the Free State was forthright and effective.[28] Indeed, we need to look beyond the man in the uniform to understand his full legacy for Irish history.

Over the years several scholars have speculated on what Collins would have achieved had he survived the Civil War. Joseph Lee, in particular, suggests that of all the leaders lost during the revolutionary era only Collins had the potential to influence the future course of history.[29] Such speculation emphasizes Collins's view of the Treaty as a stepping stone to a thirty-two-county state, a goal he worked toward both politically and covertly before his death.[30] Moreover, Lee suggests that Collins's social agenda for Ireland, as hinted in his speeches, was far-reaching. He would have an Ireland distinguished by educational opportunity, political tolerance, and economic prosperity for the many, rather than for the elite few. Collins wanted, in the words of Lee, to embark on massive housing schemes to abolish the hideous urban slums, to harness the Shannon for electricity, to industrialize rapidly, to implement worker participation in management, and to generally foster a flourishing economy in the hope that "a prosperous Ireland will mean a united Ireland."[31]

While we need to avoid both idealizing Michael Collins and portraying him as the man who "single-handedly defeated the British forces," his untimely death is another of the great "what ifs" of Irish history.

The Free State

Despite a healthy showing in the 1923 general election, Sinn Fein members would not take their seats in the Free State Assembly and adopted the position that the Second Dail Eireann, elected in 1920, was the true government of Ireland. Although satisfying their commitment to political principles, this position left Sinn Fein politically powerless because the Free State, under William Cosgrave, slowly built up the machinery of government. De Valera had been jailed by the government in 1923 but had been released about a year later, and he watched as the Free State negotiated the border issue in 1924. Cosgrave's efforts on this matter seem to deserve less than a standing ovation. The Ulster unionists were absolutely intransigent, and when a Boundary Commission finally began its work the chairman, a South African judge, interpreted the effort as being a "correction of irregularities." The Free State delegate, Eoin MacNeill, resigned when it appeared that there would be no significant adjustments, especially in heavily nationalist and Catholic areas of Fermanagh and Tyrone, but that Northern Ireland would, in fact, gain some territory. Cosgrave hastily agreed to revoke the commission and in 1925 signed an agreement to leave the border as it was in exchange for relief of debt to London. Certainly not a victory, it was not even a very good fight. De Valera and the republicans pounced on this agreement with intense criticism, and de Valera announced that he would enter the Free State Dail if the oath of allegiance were removed.

In 1926 de Valera formed a new party out of his Sinn Fein followers, called Fianna Fail (Warriors of Ireland). This move was a result of his growing impatience with Sinn Fein republican abstention and his attraction to the reality of power in the Free State government. The IRA, Sinn Fein, and the Second Dail all repudiated de Valera as an apostate for his willingness to participate in the Free State. There remained only the question of de Valera's opposition to the oath to the British Crown.

In the first general election of 1927 Fianna Fail won forty-four seats and the government forty-seven. Labor held twenty-two seats and smaller parties the remainder. Cosgrave, the prime minister, forced de Valera's hand when he sponsored legislation that would require the oath to be taken to run for office as well as for membership in the Dail. De Valera and his party signed the clerk's book containing the oath, waltzed around taking the oath, and entered the Dail. When asked later how he could justify taking the oath given his stand during the Civil War, de Valera remarked "I didn't really take an Oath. My fingers didn't touch the Bible."[32] De Valera's explanation raised equivocation to an art form, but at least now he was a participant in the real power of the state.

During the next five years Fianna Fail was the opposition to the government, threading its way through the maze of participating in the Free State government while trying to preserve the posture of viewing the Free State government as not quite legitimate. Sean Lemass aptly summed up this position when he described Fianna Fail as a "slightly constitutional" party. At the grassroots level Fianna Fail still had strong ties to the IRA, and thus its entry into the Dail was accompanied by an increase in IRA violence. The IRA had not withered away after 1923; on the contrary, it had become convinced that acceptance of partition had revealed the true colors of the Cosgrave government. The IRA bitterly contested the Free State, sometimes with violence, throughout the 1920s.[33] Moreover, the IRA became convinced that partition would never end in a peaceful manner and that only physical force could liberate the province of Ulster, a position that was, in part, a foundation of the difficulties in Northern Ireland in the last third of the twentieth century.

Upon assuming power, the Cosgrave government had a full plate of problems. Required to fight a civil war, the government also had to build a structure that would be credible to the Irish people. The achievements of the Cosgrave years cannot be lightly dismissed. In the economic and social spheres the government was timid, hesitant, and conservative. Unemployment was not lowered; agriculture, not improved; and industry, hardly developed. Emigrants still filled the docks as the population of Ireland declined in the Free State to under 3 million in 1926. However, taxes were not raised, and debt was kept to a minimum. To be fair, the last years of the Cosgrave government were a time of worldwide depression that also affected Ireland. Overall the record was one of stability rather than progress. In the social sphere Cosgrave did little because both his lack of a social policy or ideology and the basic conservatism of his supporters did little to encourage social welfare policies.

There were, however, some innovative ideas expressed in culture and education (with varying degrees of success). Several members of Cosgrave's Cabinet, notably Eoin MacNeill, the minister for Education, had been members of the Gaelic League and grafted their ideals onto government policy. An emphasis was placed on preserving the Irish language, and in this effort a series of Gaeltachts—Irish-speaking hearth areas—were established in Ulster, Munster, and Connaught. This Gaelic ideal also carried over into education. The Free State envisioned a society in which the Irish language was a centerpiece of national identity and enacted a policy of language immersion in the schools, particularly in the primary grades, to achieve that goal. While this ideal was commendable, the reality was less than encouraging. As Joseph Lee maintains, the government did not practice what it preached: It failed to provide the opportunity or obligation to carry the Irish language beyond the schools into the everyday spheres of commerce, politics, and social interaction.[34]

In the international sphere the Free State government achieved successes that were inadequately appreciated by people who were preoccupied with the Treaty/anti-Treaty split in Irish politics. In many ways Cosgrave set out to dismantle the Treaty a full decade before de Valera's more dramatic new constitution. The Free State took an active role in the League of Nations, appointed ambassadors, and took a foreign policy position that was different from that of the United Kingdom. Within the Empire Ireland worked with Canada to pass resolutions that gave the member states equal status. In 1931 these efforts were acknowledged by the United Kingdom in the Statutes of Westminster, which granted the dominions the right to reject the legislation of London. The "empire" became the "commonwealth," and the dominions became sovereign and equal states.

Perhaps the most difficult task the Free State government faced was that of maintaining civil order. The government took a hard line toward the rebels in the Civil War. Shortly after the war the IRA followers of Michael Collins in the Free State Army demanded that the government cease postwar demobilization and move more rapidly toward becoming a unified republic. Dissident officers led by Liam Tobin formed a secret clique, the "Old IRA," to further their aims and issued an ultimatum to the government. This mutiny was rapidly crushed by Minister of Justice Kevin O'Higgins.[35] O'Higgins held extensive powers under a 1923 Public Safety Act and did not hesitate to use them to control the lawlessness and violence that were rampant at the time. O'Higgins renewed the 1923 Act in 1926, but an even more draconian law came about as a result of his own death. O'Higgins, who often flaunted his own safety, was gunned down in the street by IRA assassins in 1927. The government reacted by outlawing associations designed to overthrow the state by force and by authorizing special courts and extensive powers of search and detention. This legislation lapsed in 1928, but when violence surged in 1930 and 1931, Cosgrave responded with the harshest law of the decade. Under this act military tribunals could impose the death penalty on members of illegal organizations. The IRA and other republican groups were soon declared illegal, and the law drove many republicans underground and out of Ireland. The law was also quite unpopular, and along with high unemployment, widespread poverty, and the accumulation of past blunders, it exhausted the Cosgrave government's political support among the Irish electorate.

In 1932 Fianna Fail won seventy-two seats and Cummann na nGaedheal only fifty-seven. With Labour Party support Fianna Fail then undertook a limited program of social reform, an area Cosgrave had left untouched, and allocated money for housing, old age pensions, and welfare benefits. In the economic sphere de Valera imposed tariffs on foreign goods and enlarged the subsidies to farmers and to industry. In many ways de Valera's program of social reform and economic self-sufficiency was integrally linked to his larger vision and aspirations for Irish society and Irish identity.

Road sign at the border of County Clare and County Galway. The village of Boston County Clare suggests the continuing migration between the west of Ireland and the United States and the strong cultural connection to the "next parish west of Galway." *Photo by Edward T. McCarron*

De Valera's Dream

De Valera's Ireland, as outlined in his speeches and radio broadcasts, would be predominantly rural, Catholic, and Irish speaking. He placed value on the self-sufficiency of the Irish farming family and the opportunity for as many Irish families as possible to be rooted in the soil. Catholicism would also distinguish Ireland, especially from its neighbor across the Irish Sea. A sense of spirituality, nurtured in the copse of close-knit country parishes, would offset the greed and materialism seeping into Ireland from industrial countries. Above all, Ireland would be Gaelic in its identity and language. De Valera was dedicated to restoring Irish as a living language and envisioned the spoken vernacular as a symbol of the Irish nation. Indeed, it would differentiate the Irish from other countries and personify the character and culture of Ireland.[36] Moreover, the Irish language was an important link with the past, especially the pre-Conquest world of "saints and scholars" that took the lead, as de Valera expressed it, in "Christianizing and civilizing the barbarian hoards that had overrun Britain and the west of Europe."[37] De Valera's message was clear, as historian Michele Dowling suggests: Just as Irish missionaries had once rescued Europe from the clutches of barbarism, so could a modern pastoral Ireland provide a civilizing influence on a world polluted by materialism, warfare, and greed.[38]

De Valera's vision for Ireland was pursued through a vigorous government policy. He continued the gaelicization of education begun under Cosgrave and championed the protection of regions where Irish was still a primary medium of communication. Irish-speaking "hearth" areas—the Gaeltacht—were encouraged in parts of Waterford, Cork, Kerry, Galway, Mayo, and Donegal. These islands of Gaelic culture would serve as archetypes, proof positive of the rural spirit, communal values, and creative unity to which de Valera aspired.[39] To encourage their survival, the Gaeltacht were allocated government monies to establish employment schemes and incentives. Irish colleges were also established at such locations as An Rinn, County Waterford, and Ceann Clogher, County Louth. Here students from around the country would come during the summer to learn Irish and experience Gaelic games and culture.[40] Although the number of native Irish speakers steadily declined during the Free State era (200,000 in 1922 to 100,000 in 1939), this was as much a commentary on continuing emigration from the west of Ireland as it was on the conscious abandonment of the language.

De Valera's espousal of the rural ideal and his advocacy of small-scale tillage farming were promoted by the Irish Land Commission. This agency continued the process of transfer of ownership from landlord to tenant, dividing the land into small family farms (20–30 acres) that echoed the "frugal comfort" championed by de Valera. Indeed, as Kevin Whelan asserts: "Large holdings were deemed to be immoral, because they deprived people of the opportunity of owning their own holding." In the long run, however, this landscape of small family units was inefficient to take advantage of expanding opportunities in dairying and grazing.[41] Nevertheless, there were some notable advances by the Land Commission during de Valera's tenure. The most ambitious was the policy of "transplanting" families from congested farm clusters in Connaught to small farms carved out of confiscated land in Leinster. This was embodied by the vibrant colony of Rath Cairn in County Meath, an Irish-speaking seedbed that, it was hoped, would help germinate the spread of Irish along the anglicized east coast.[42]

In many areas of Ireland, de Valera's arcadian vision was alive (if not completely well) during the 1930s and 1940s. The country was still predominantly rural and Catholic. In the west, for example, small farms dotted the landscape and in quiet rural townlands one could still experience lifeways largely undisturbed by modernism and progress. One such pocket of tradition was on Great Blasket, the largest of a group of islands off the west Kerry coast. These remote islands of fishing families had long been emblems of the social cohesion, Celtic identity, and purity of spirit espoused by cultural nationalists.[43] In the 1930s this island world, with its 150 Gaelic-speaking inhabitants, was described by its own writers, notably Tomas O'Criomthain, Peig Sayers, and Muiris O'suilleabhain. In *Twenty Years a-Growing* (1933), O'suilleabhain delineated an evocative landscape of ocean, cliff face, and hard-scrabble field. His was a village of whitewashed houses connected by well-worn paths and intimate landmarks such as "the big red patches on the Sandhills made by the feet of boys and girls dancing."[44]

Economic Hardship and Emigration

This world was not to survive. While de Valera's dream for Ireland championed places like Great Blasket, the lack of economic opportunities in the 1930s could not staunch the flow of migrants leaving such traditional strongholds. Many from the Blaskets, faced with poverty and the decline of the fishing market, left for the shores of the United States. Most journeyed to Springfield and Holyoke, Massachusetts, following a chain migration of islanders who had earlier put down roots in these New England mill towns.[45] Indeed, for many the writing was on the wall or, more accurately, on the blackboard. Among the subjects taught at the Blasket Island school were English and U.S. geography, a fitting choice for many young students destined for the New World. As one schoolmistress remarked:

> I would not have wanted to let the students finish school without a fairly good knowledge of English. I knew quite well what was in store for them, and it was not fenian tales or the like at school which would stand to them, even if they were never go to America.[46]

This cycle of leave-taking was completed in 1953 when the Irish government, admitting the inevitable, resettled the remainder of Blasket's people on the mainland. As Tomas O'Criomthain said at the end of his diary, "the like of us will never be again."[47]

As exemplified in the Blaskets, not all was well in the rural Eden imagined by de Valera. Many people in country areas suffered from poverty, poor housing, and limited opportunities. The thatched cottages that were so admired by outsiders often had no running water and only one in twenty had an interior lavatory. Disease was also a common companion. Ireland had one of the highest rates of tuberculosis in Europe, a scourge that only began to ebb in the 1950s.[48] Given these conditions, emigration out of Ireland was endemic. This movement could involve seasonal migration to the potato harvests of Scotland, relocation to the industrial cities of Britain, or a search for opportunity in the United States.[49] Many of these journeys were accompanied by a silent rejection of rural life and the subsequent attraction of the metropolis. As early as 1907 the parish priest of Knock, County Mayo, noted an increasing willingness of Irish folk to leave the home farm: "A great change is coming over the peasantry. . . . They are becoming more practical and less sentimental, owing, no doubt, to their intercourse with social life in America, and to the number of emigrants who return each year [for a visit] from that country."[50] Emigration was especially pronounced among young single women, who sought "independence" from an Irish experience characterized by a decline in marriage partners, rigid Catholic morality, and de Valera's belief that women's place was in the home. Indeed, women represented just over 50 percent of the emigrant stream leaving Ireland during the early twentieth century, a pattern unique among European nations.[51]

Conflict with Britain

While de Valera's vision of Ireland was characterized at home by insularity, economic stagnation, and emigration, his goal of self-sufficiency and independence nonetheless had a powerful impact on the political stage. Indeed, two of de Valera's major efforts touched off conflict with Britain. The first was the refusal in 1933 to pay the land annuities that were due Britain as a result of land purchases by tenant farmers after the Wyndham Act of 1903. The British response was to put a tariff on Irish imports, principally cattle and dairy produce. De Valera responded with tariffs on British coal, machinery, and iron, and the result was "the economic war." As a war it was no contest. Ireland's fragile economy was so dependent on Britain that the burden fell far more heavily on Ireland as imports dropped by one-half and exports by three-fifths. For five years this state of affairs continued until Neville Chamberlain, the British prime minister, concluded a treaty with de Valera in 1938 that not only ended the economic war but also transferred to Ireland the naval bases Britain still had as a result of the 1921 Treaty. Additional trade agreements were predominantly to the advantage of Ireland.

The second provocation to Britain was a series of steps de Valera took to dismantle the 1921 Treaty. Beginning in 1932 de Valera informed Britain that he was dropping the oath to the Crown on the grounds that it was a domestic matter for the Irish people to decide. The same year de Valera, through a series of petty embarrassments and political pressure, forced the dismissal of the governor general and replaced him with an insignificant political figure. In 1933 the Irish government removed the right of appeal from Irish courts to the Judicial Committee of the British Privy Council and in 1936 eliminated the king from the Irish constitution (except in a very limited way in foreign affairs) and abolished the position of governor general. All of these actions were a prelude to the development of a new constitution for Ireland (discussed fully in Chapter 7), which was a mixture of various political and social doctrines with a large dose of de Valera. The most controversial parts of the document drafted in 1937 were the stated role of women ("within the home") and the special relationship accorded to Catholicism in the Irish nation.

In the new Constitution the political doctrine of liberal democracy and Catholic social thought coexisted uneasily. The structure of the state was democratic and parliamentary, and liberal principles of tolerance, civil rights, and liberties were guaranteed. However, Catholic thought was manifest in the special position of the family, the prohibition on divorce, and the primacy of the Catholic Church "as the guardian of the faith professed by the great majority of its citizens." When the Constitution was presented to the people for ratification the vote was 685,105 for the document and 526,945 against it. The new constitution took effect in 1937.

Civil Disorder

De Valera was not exempt from the inexorable fact that the people who govern are responsible for civil order, and he found himself, as had Cosgrave, in the position of trying to crush the IRA revolutionaries he had associated with only a few short years before. Upon taking office de Valera had removed the restraints on the IRA enacted by the Cosgrave government. The result was a rapid escalation of IRA drills and meetings, which on occasion took the form of intimidation of the supporters of Cumann na nGaedheal.

As de Valera was contemplating how to deal with this resurgent Left, his attention was also riveted by the emergence of the political Right in Ireland. In 1933, an innocuous organization of veterans of the Free State Army, concerned primarily with veterans' benefits, was quickly transformed from the Army Comrades Association into a semi-fascist political organization. The Blueshirts (as they were popularly called) brought together an array of anti-IRA supporters in defense of free speech and assembly, which they perceived were threatened by the IRA. Right-wing intellectuals espoused doctrines on the corporate state and issued warnings about the dangers of communism from Leftist IRA groups. In early 1933 the Army Comrades Association turned its leadership over to General Eoin O'Duffy, recently dismissed by de Valera from the position of commissioner of police. Under O'Duffy the members took to wearing berets and blue shirts (black and brown having already been adopted in Italy and Germany) and giving fascist salutes; they also adopted the name "National Guard."[52]

The social base of the Blueshirts, which at its height numbered 120,000, was farmers hurt by de Valera's economic policy. Indeed, the "economic war" was a disaster for Irish farmers because they had no English market for their livestock. The government continued to collect the annuities from the farmers, however, leaving them still paying the taxes but bereft of an outlet for their goods. The farmers responded by non-payment of the taxes, whereupon the government impounded cattle and sold them off, often to their own supporters. The Blueshirts intervened in this situation, answering government "tyranny" with their own measure of justice: blockading roads, preventing the sale of cattle, and intimidation. As O'Duffy declared, "We must make life intolerable for those who don't meet our demands."[53]

Two events transformed the Blueshirts. First, de Valera's government outlawed the organization after it had engaged in violent clashes with the IRA and threatened a Mussolini-style march on Leinster House (the seat of Irish government). Second, in September 1933 the banned National Guard, Cumann na nGaedheal, and the Centre Party merged to form Fine Gael (Tribe of Gaels) and reconstituted the Blueshirts as the Young Ireland Association. Eoin O'Duffy was named president of Fine Gael while William Cosgrave remained leader of the parliamentary party. It soon became apparent, however, that O'Duffy was a poor choice. His erratic leadership and his increasingly strident and violent rhetoric caused turbulent waves within the sea of interests that made up Fine Gael. Yet they tolerated O'Duffy and his Blueshirt organization as necessary because of continuing IRA intimidation, violence, and murder.

Whether the Blueshirts were molded in the style of European fascism remains open to question. One recent study argues that while the organization was fascist in rhetoric its growth was largely a reaction to Irish circumstances: namely, the revived Irish Republican Army's association with the governing political party in Ireland.[54] The Blueshirts were a counterweight to the IRA; a mirror, if you will, of militant pro-state activity to match the anti-state IRA. Indeed, the movement was quite unlike continental fascism in content if not in symbolism. Supported mainly by farmers hurt by the economic war, it lacked a broader base of support. Its doctrines were in part derived from Catholic social thought, and its greatest fear, a communist Ireland, was so implausible as to be amusing. And, while the Blueshirts adopted the trappings of fascist groups on the continent, there was also a unique "Irish" flavor to the movement. They adopted the flag of St. Patrick; they often assembled at historic sites or cemeteries accompanied by fife and drums; and they attracted the support of the most "Irish" poet of his generation, W. B. Yeats, who contributed marching songs to the cause.[55]

The Blueshirt threat continued through 1933, but when O'Duffy failed to lead the Fine Gael party to victory in the local government election in June, the days were numbered for the coalition between the Blueshirts and the opposition party. Internal dissension brought about the resignation of the "Irish Duce" in September 1934.[56] The Blueshirts continued in existence for a couple of years, albeit under various new names, before they faded away. They last entered the public arena in 1936 when, under O'Duffy's leadership, they made up most of the 700-strong Irish Brigade that left to fight for Franco in the Spanish Civil War. This crusade, supported by the Catholic bishops, ended in disarray and disillusion. They were poorly trained and did not see much action. Indeed, the rector of the Irish college in Salamanca called them "a regular frost and a complete washout."[57]

The IRA in the 1930s, however, was quite another matter. Continuing violence in Ireland and several brutal murders caused the de Valera government to declare the organization illegal in 1936, and its chief of staff was arrested. The IRA turned its attention to Britain and began a bombing campaign. As Thomas Hachey suggests, their prime objective was to rekindle the Anglo-Irish conflict and rivet world attention on the partition of the north.[58] The most serious incident took place at Coventry, where a bomb planted in a busy thoroughfare killed five people and badly injured twelve. In 1939 de Valera responded with the Treason Act and the Offenses Against the State Act. The former prescribed the death penalty for treason; the latter reconstituted military tribunals and internment without trial. Both acts were directed at the IRA.

The Emergency and After

Neutrality

The most crucial test of the de Valera government, however, came at the outset of World War II when he held that while partition existed Ireland would be neutral in the war. Terming this an "emergency," the government adopted powers to censor, control prices, and regulate resources. The overwhelming majority of the Irish people supported neutrality, if only for the practical reason that it would spare them the horrors of war. As one official commented: "Small nations like Ireland do not and cannot assume the role of defenders of just causes except their own."[59] Yet for de Valera's government neutrality was much more. It became a national symbol of autonomy from Great Britain and marked an important watershed in Ireland's political relationships with the Western world.

While Ireland steered a neutral course, Northern Ireland played an active role in the war. Although army recruitment from Ulster was somewhat disappointing, Belfast's plants and shipyards produced a significant number of cargo vessels, supplies, and armaments for the war effort. In addition, Northern Ireland played host to a string of allied airfields, and the port of Derry served as a major base for North Atlantic convoy escorts.[60] Ulster's contribution to the war effort, however, did not come without a price. In April and May 1941 Belfast was hit by two German air raids (called the "Belfast blitz") that leveled much of the city and caused over 1,000 fatalities. For many unionists this wartime sacrifice underlined Northern Ireland's commitment to the United Kingdom. Indeed, as Winston Churchill opined, "The bonds of affection between Great Britain and the people of Northern Ireland have been tempered by fire," and are now "unbreakable."[61]

One of the fears of the Allies early in the war was collaboration between the IRA and Nazi Germany and the concomitant threat of German invasion of Ireland. In point of fact, there were liaisons between the Axis and the IRA (which embraced the German cause as a means of ending partition). Indeed, early in the war several IRA leaders traveled to Berlin and fifteen Nazi spies briefly infiltrated Ireland. However, their attempt to lay the groundwork for a German invasion came to nothing.[62] Still, a Nazi beachhead in Ireland was a distinct threat early in the war, especially in the eyes of Britain, which planned an invasion of its own to forestall the Germans. Throughout these dangerous months de Valera steered a masterful course and kept a formal commitment to neutrality. After U.S. entry into the war in December 1941 and the subsequent billeting of over 240,000 U.S. soldiers in bases throughout Northern Ireland, the threat of German invasion decreased. Yet there remained among the Allies a lasting distrust of Irish neutrality, particularly among U.S. officials.

On the home front during the war, Ireland's experience could best be described as sobering. While some middle class people lived comfortably in their isolation, many Irish remember the war years as a time of scarcity. Bread, tea, butter, and

sugar were rationed and fresh fruit and vegetables were largely unavailable, leading to outbreaks of rickets and scurvy due to poor diet. Even Guiness stout was
rationed during part of the war, with pub patrons limited to two bottles per night.
Coal and other fuels were also in short supply, leading to the wartime expedient
of tapping the midland turf bogs (a venture that evolved into a successful postwar
enterprise under Bord na Mona). The economy as a whole declined during the
war years, with industrial production dropping 30 percent due to shortages in raw
materials. Unemployment remained high, leading upwards of 100,000 Irish to
seek temporary jobs in Britain to make ends meet. Many of these sojourners
never returned to live in Ireland after the war.

De Valera replied a few days later, pointing out that Churchill had elevated
Despite these hardships, most Irish men and women agreed with Irish neutrality, even though it was a neutrality that was clearly benevolent to Britain. Over
50,000 Irishmen volunteered to fight in the British army (significantly more than
recruits in Northern Ireland), Irish secret intelligence cooperated with British security forces concerning enemy aliens in Ireland, and Allied aircraft stationed in
Fermanagh were allowed to "overfly" Irish airspace on their missions over the
Atlantic.[63] Perhaps the most striking example of "friendly neutrality" was the
practice of returning Allied pilots downed in Ireland to Northern Ireland while
downed German pilots were interned for the duration of the war.

Despite Ireland's "friendly neutrality," de Valera's adherence to diplomatic for-
mality did not endear him to the Allies. His refusal to expel Axis diplomats from
Ireland, for example, raised the ire of both U.S. and British officials.[64] At the end
of the war Winston Churchill could not resist taunting de Valera about Irish neutrality and British patience:

> However, with a restraint and poise to which, I venture to say history will find few
> parallels, His Majesty's government never laid a violent hand on them, though at
> times it would have been quite easy and quite natural, and we left the de Valera gov-
> ernment to frolic with the German, and later Japanese representatives to their hearts
> content.[65]

De Valera replied a few days later, pointing out that Churchill had elevated
Britain's necessity to a moral plane superior to Ireland's rights. But de Valera went
on to remind Churchill just how deeply the Irish felt about those rights:

> Could he not find it in his heart to acknowledge that there is a small nation that has
> stood alone not for one year or two, but for several hundred years, against aggression,
> that endured spoliations, famines, massacres in endless succession, that was clubbed
> many times into insensibility but each time, on returning to consciousness took up
> the fight anew; a small nation that could never be got to accept defeat and has never
> surrendered her soul.[66]

Neutrality was for Ireland the ultimate display of its independence and its
sovereignty.

Post-War Political Developments

After the war the program for economic recovery bogged down and Ireland slipped into a moribund political and economic state. Fianna Fail had been in power continually since 1932 and was suffering from hardening of the arteries, ineffective economic policies, and a weariness on the part of the electorate. Fine Gael was a rather anemic competitor, having lost considerable support over the previous sixteen years. The electorate, and the political arena, were brought to life by the creation of a new party, which in some ways resembled the Fianna Fail of twenty years earlier. Led by Sean McBride, a veteran of the anti-Treaty forces, Clann na Publachta (Republican Family) was formed in 1946. The party's program combined a fresh emphasis on the republican tradition with social and economic reform. The party drew its support from the republican veterans of the 1930s and 1940s but broadened its appeal to disillusioned Fianna Fail and even Fine Gael supporters. Clann na Publachta seemed to be a new wind in politics and promised to have a fresh impact on policy. Contesting many seats in the 1948 election, Clann won ten, a good showing but disappointing in view of the high expectations of its partisans. Although Fianna Fail still had the largest number of seats in the Dail, it had lost eight in the election, and the opposing parties formed a coalition government. It was a strange mixture, but one that managed to last over three years in power.

Since the days of Wolfe Tone the idea of an independent republic of Ireland had burned brightly. In 1948 Ireland was clearly an independent sovereign nation, but it did not bear the title "republic" in de Valera's constitution. The realization of Tone's dream came about in a manner that no doubt would have amused him: John Costello, the prime minister of Ireland, announced the fact at a press conference in Ottawa, Canada. Some people have suggested that Costello did this because he was insulted by the governor general of Canada, but the matter had been discussed in the cabinet of the coalition government. However, a matter as important as the final severing of ties to the Commonwealth would seem to have warranted some discussion and debate among the Irish people before being announced to Canadian journalists. The reticence de Valera had shown in 1937 displayed more wisdom than Costello's act. The British government also issued the Ireland Act of 1949, which was an explicit guarantee that Northern Ireland was part of the United Kingdom and would not cease to be so without the consent of the Parliament of Northern Ireland. What little bridge had existed in the Commonwealth between Ireland and Northern Ireland was broken.

Although far greater attention had been directed to social welfare policy since the Cosgrave years, there were still enormous gaps in the support people received from the government. The coalition government appointed Dr. Noel Browne of Clann na Publachta as minister of Health, and his initial success included an imaginative use of finances to create a collection of sanitariums that virtually eradicated tuberculosis from Ireland. Browne, however, was to flounder on the rocks of Catholic social doctrine in his notable endeavor to provide maternal education and medical care for mothers and children up to the age of sixteen. Drawing upon a plan developed by Fianna Fail that had already attracted clerical hostility, Browne began to implement the scheme and ran into a blizzard of opposition. The medical profession considered the plan unwarranted interference in its area of concern and reacted negatively to the idea that the program would have no means test, or test of poverty, and thus be free to all comers. The most powerful opposition, however, came from the Church. Noting that the constitution stated that the family was the basic unit of society, the Church maintained that the bill was an invasion of family rights and that provision of health care to children was a family responsibility. Browne made efforts to bridge the gap between himself, the Irish Medical Association, and the bishops. All efforts failed, and Browne lost support within the government, eventually resigning from the Cabinet.[67] This episode demonstrated the political power of the Catholic Church in independent Ireland. Under the next government Fianna Fail enacted most of the provisions of Browne's plan, excluding only those families in the highest income bracket.

The election of 1951 brought Fianna Fail back into power for several years, but the government was confounded by economic problems of stagnation, unemployment, and emigration. An election in 1954 resulted in a coalition government of the Fine Gael, Labor, and Farmers parties; Clann na Publachta had disintegrated after the Mother and Child Plan controversy and won only two seats. The coalition had no more success with the depressed economy than had the previous government and was burdened also by an increase in IRA activity, which it had difficulty controlling.

In 1957 Fianna Fail came back to power with a much stronger majority of seventy-eight seats. De Valera was seventy-five-years old, and it appeared that the wheel had come full circle as the man who had once been a young revolutionary now presided over a Cabinet of old men in a government that lacked luster and over a country that was socially, economically, and politically stagnant. Appearances were deceptive, however, because the old leadership was being augmented or replaced by a rising generation of politicians who were far less influenced by the Treaty debate and the events of the 1920s and 1930s. Molded in a rapidly changing post-war world, they were more concerned with economic and social issues than with the traditional concerns of nationalism and partition. In Fianna Fail these new figures included Jack Lynch and Charles Haughey, both later to become prime minister. In Fine Gael were Liam Cosgrave and Garrett FitzGerald, also both later to become the nation's leader.

In 1959 Sean Lemass became prime minister. De Valera retired to the presidency of Ireland, serving two seven-year terms. De Valera's death in 1975 ended one of the most extraordinary careers in modern political history. Once only a day or so away from a British firing squad, de Valera eventually made a greater mark on Irish politics than had O'Connell or Parnell. His dedication to his values, to Catholicism, to the Irish language, and to simple Irish life was combined with a pragmatic toughness that carried him through the rough and tumble years of 1916 to 1932. His astute leadership carried him from 1932 to 1959. Excoriated as anti-democratic and anti-modern, de Valera was just as often praised for his patriotism and leadership. He once remarked that when he wanted to know what the people of Ireland thought, he had only to look in his own heart. Such hubris from anyone else would be intolerable. In the case of de Valera, it was, for most of his life, not far from the truth.

The stage was set for the post-de Valera era of Irish politics, which would witness the rise of Lemass, the initiation of the Whitaker Plan in 1958, a new generation of leaders in Ireland, and a new generation of voters more interested in looking forward to living in a modern society than backward to events that formed less and less a part of their personal experience.

Notes

1. Not long after Sinn Fein was created it became the name the British press, the British military, and even the Irish party used to lump together those people who were more militantly nationalist. The Rising of 1916 was erroneously labeled a Sinn Fein action. The secret IRB, of course, was most important in stimulating revolutionary republicanism and in undertaking the 1916 revolt. Only after 1917 did the popular label and the political reality coincide as Sinn Fein became the broad political front for all nationalists and republicans.

2. David Fitzpatrick, "Ireland Since 1870," in *Oxford History of Ireland,* ed. Foster, p. 241. The importance of de Valera's birth and technical U.S. citizenship has been debated. Several historians suggest that his stay of execution was simply the result of good timing as the British realized that the executions were counterproductive.

3. F. S. L. Lyons, "The New Nationalism, 1916–18," in *New History of Ireland, Vol VI,* ed. W. E. Vaughn, p. 235.

4. In 1918 alone, membership in Sinn Fein clubs throughout Ireland expanded from 66,270 to 112,020, largely through the efforts of Collins's associate Harry Boland, a Dublin tailor.

5. The Irish Parliamentary Party, ironically enough, did not lose much voting strength compared to the 1910 general election, but the majority of the new voters clearly supported Sinn Fein.

6. For a bird's-eye view of the distribution of the Sinn Fein vote in 1918, see Sean Duffy, ed., *Atlas of Irish History* (New York: Simon & Schuster/Macmillan, 1997), p. 115.

7. This tack, as Joseph Lee reminds us, was a problematic one because Wilson, of Ulster Presbyterian stock, had "little instinctive sympathy for the Irish." Moreover, he was an avowed Anglophile, a persuasion that influenced his decisions even during the United States' "neutral" stance at the outset of the war. See Lee, *Ireland 1912–1985,* p. 41.

8. The Irish Volunteers were in somewhat of an ambiguous position with respect to the Dail, which produced a great deal of tension between the minister of defense, Cathal Brugha, and Michael Collins, who was adjutant general, director of intelligence of the Volunteers, and, to complicate matters, president of the IRB. Brugha tried to assert authority over the Volunteers and eventually persuaded the Volunteers as individuals to take an

oath to the Dail. Thus the Volunteers became the Army of the Irish Republic or the Irish Republican Army.

9. Fitzpatrick, "Ireland Since 1870," in *Oxford History of Ireland*, ed. Foster, pp. 248–249.

10. David Fitzpatrick, *Politics and Irish Life, 1913–1921: Provincial Experience of War and Revolution* (Dublin: Gill & Macmillan, 1977), pp. 6–17.

11. Ibid., pp. 174–197.

12. In September 1920 a brawl broke out in a Balbriggan pub in which two Black and Tans were shot. One hundred fifty paramilitaries encamped nearby responded in vicious fashion, burning down a hosiery factory, torching over fifty homes and four public houses, and killing two townspeople during a drunken night of looting and mayhem. Such Black and Tan reprisals echoed throughout 1920 in the Munster towns of Fermoy, Mallow, and Lismore, and in Ennistymon and Lahinch in County Clare.

13. Fitzpatrick, "Ireland Since 1870," in *Oxford History of Ireland*, ed. Foster, p. 249.

14. F. S. L. Lyons, "The War of Independence, 1919–21," in *New History of Ireland, Vol. VI*, ed. Vaughn, pp. 240–259. For a case study of guerrilla activities in County Clare, see Fitzpatrick, *Politics and Irish Life 1913–1921*, pp. 198–231.

15. Information on Inistioge was drawn largely from interviews with Michael Foley in 1988. Foley, born in Ballyshane, County Kilkenny, in 1900, was interrogated and briefly interned by the Black and Tans at Woodstock House during the war. On Inistioge, see also Ernie O'Malley, *On Another Man's Wound* (Dublin: Anvil Books, 1979), pp. 221–235.

16. A narrative description of "Bloody Sunday" can be found in Tim Pat Coogan, *The Man Who Made Ireland: The Life and Death of Michael Collins* (Niwot, Colo.: Roberts Rinehart, 1992), pp. 157–162.

17. Duffy, *Atlas of Irish History*, p. 114.

18. As Lawrence McCaffrey suggests, there are several possible explanations for de Valera's non-attendance. He may have believed that since he and Lloyd George "were at loggerheads," other negotiators might be more effective. He also may have believed he was more constructive in Dublin, where he could restrain non-conformists in the republican ranks and also review the progress of the London negotiations from a less contentious vantage point. See Thomas E. Hachey, Joseph M. Hernon Jr., and Lawrence J. McCaffrey, *The Irish Experience: A Concise History*, rev. ed. (Armonk, N.Y.: M.E. Sharpe, 1996), pp. 163–164.

19. Ernie O'Malley, *The Singing Flame* (Dublin: Anvil Books, 1978), p. 45.

20. S. J. Connolly, ed., *The Oxford Companion to Irish History* (New York: Oxford University Press, 1998), p. 265.

21. The superiority of the Free State forces, however, was not a given early in the war. Sources point out that the most able men in the IRA allied with the anti-Treaty forces, and that the Free State Army was at first largely untrained and officerless. Given this initial superiority of anti-Treaty forces, their occupation of the Four Courts (and other strongholds) was a tactical blunder that needlessly sacrificed many of their best fighting men. See Tom Garvin, *1922: The Birth of Irish Democracy* (New York: St. Martin's Press, 1996), p. 31.

22. Childers, born in Britain, was an active supporter of Irish independence. He was involved in the Howth gun-running, served as minister of Publicity in the Dail 1919–1921, and acted as the first secretary of the Irish treaty delegation to London, a treaty he avidly denounced. Despite pleas on his behalf by Church leaders such as the Archbishop of Dublin, he was one of the first republicans to be summarily executed by the Free State.

23. The legacy of the Irish Civil War, both political and personal, is still a sensitive issue, so much so that historical research on the subject lags behind other comparable events of the era, such as the Anglo-Irish war. Even the highly acclaimed work of Bartlett and Jeffery, *A Military History of Ireland*, contains at best only a few pages on the Civil War.

24. The longstanding divisions and enmity that poisoned local communities are captured in Cathal Black's film *Korea* (1990). This is the story of a fisherman in rural Cavan, an "irreconcilable" during the Civil War, who cannot live with his son's intention to marry the daughter of a Free State family in the early 1950s.

25. See especially Coogan, *The Man Who Made Ireland.*

26. In "The Collins Movie: The Verdict," *The Irish Times,* 9 November 1996, historians and relations of Collins and de Valera offer their opinions (mostly positive) of the film. Criticism tends to focus on the negative characterization of de Valera and the inattention of the film to other leaders such as Richard Mulcahy. See especially the opinion of David Fitzpatrick.

27. "Neil Jordan Tries to Untangle Irish History," *Boston Globe,* 20 October 1996.

28. John Regan, "Looking at Mick Again: Demilitarising Michael Collins," *History Ireland* 3, no.2 (Autumn 1995), pp. 17–22.

29. Lee, *Ireland 1912–1985*, pp. 63–66.

30. Evidence suggests that Collins worked behind the scenes to destabilize Northern Ireland and had a secret arrangement with anti-Treaty IRA members to supply arms to the north. See Coogan, *The Man Who Made Ireland*, pp. 349–351, 362–363; and Fitzpatrick, "Ireland Since 1870," in *Oxford History of Ireland*, ed. Foster, p. 252.

31. Lee, *Ireland 1912–1985*, p. 64.

32. Coogan, *The Man Who Made Ireland*, p. 427.

33. For details on IRA activities during the 1920s, see Tim Pat Coogan, *The IRA: A History* (Niwot, Colo.: Roberts Rinehart, 1993), pp. 29–47; and James Bowyer Bell, *The Secret Army: History of the Irish Republican Army 1916–79* (Dublin: Academy Press, 1979), pp. 40–96.

34. Lee, *Ireland, 1912–1985*, p. 135.

35. On the Army Mutiny, see Eunan O'Halpin, "The Army in Independent Ireland," in *Military History of Ireland*, ed. Bartlett and Jeffery, pp. 410–411; and Maryann Gialanella Valiulis, *Almost a Rebellion: The Irish Army Mutiny of 1924* (Cork: Tower Books, 1985).

36. Michele Dowling, " 'The Ireland That I Would Have': DeValera and the Creation of an Irish National Image," *History Ireland* 5, no.2 (Summer 1997), p. 40.

37. Quoted in ibid., p. 40.

38. Ibid., p. 41. One detects here a post-colonial spin on de Valera's Gaelic pastoral Ireland: It trumpets a moral superiority that is typical of countries that have emerged from colonialism. As Dowling adds, "They cannot compete with the former metropolitan powers at the level of production or living standards, so they redefine the standards of 'greatness.'"

39. On the idea of the Gaeltacht as cultural oasis, see Terence Brown, *Ireland: A Social and Cultural History, 1922–76* (Glasgow: Fontana, 1981), pp. 92–96.

40. The Irish colleges were established in the late 1920s by Cumann na nGaedheal and continued under the patronage of Fianna Fail. The summer school at Ceann Clogher (St. Ita's) was the only Irish college outside the Gaeltacht and attracted the sons and daughters of Dublin professionals and the Irish middle class.

41. Kevin Whelan, "The Modern Irish Landscape," in *Atlas of the Irish Rural Landscape*, ed. Aalen, Whelan, and Stout, p. 96.

42. On the background of colony migration and Irish Land Commission activities, see William Nolan, "New Farms and Fields: Migration Policies of State Land Agencies, 1891–1980," in *Common Ground: Essays on the Historical Geography of Ireland*, ed. William J. Smyth and Kevin Whelan (Cork: Cork University Press, 1988), pp. 296–321.

43. The Blaskets were explored by John Millington Synge in 1905, a visit that inspired both poems and prose. The best and most accessible portrait of the Blaskets by an outsider remains the work of Robin Flower, especially *The Western Island* (Oxford: Oxford University Press, 1944).

44. This quote is located in the introduction to Tomas O'Crohan, *Island Cross-Talk: Pages from a Blasket Island Diary* (New York: Oxford University Press, 1986), p. 6.

45. Peig Sayers is emblematic of this movement. Her autobiography is punctuated by stories of islanders leaving for the United States. Of her six surviving children born on Great Blasket, five went to the United States and only one died in Ireland, unmarried. Thus, a direct link to one of Ireland's most gifted storytellers survives in the industrial world of New England. See Muiris MacConghail, *The Blaskets: A Kerry Island Library* (Dublin: Country House, 1987), pp. 156–159, 164.

46. Ibid., p. 40.

47. O'Crohan, *Island Cross-Talk*, p. 9.

48. In the early part of the twentieth century tuberculosis was responsible for upwards of 16 percent of all deaths in Ireland. See S. J. Connolly, *The Oxford Companion to Irish History* (New York: Oxford University Press, 1998), p. 553.

49. Some of those who chose to remain in rural Ireland, ironically, were not the stalwart farming families envisaged by de Valera but those who remained unmarried. Indeed, in some counties of Ireland such as Wexford, upwards of 30 percent of middle-aged people at the turn of the century never married. In country areas, especially, one found a marked incidence of bachelor farmers, a pattern that has slowly disappeared. On this phenomenon, see Timothy W. Guinnane, "The Vanishing Irish: Ireland's Population from the Great Famine to the Great War," *History Ireland* 5, no. 2 (Summer 1997), pp. 34–35; and O'Grada, *Ireland: A New Economic History*, pp. 214–218.

50. David Fitzpatrick, "Emigration, 1871–1921," in *New History of Ireland, Vol VI*, ed. Vaughn, p. 624.

51. There is a growing literature on Irish women's migration. See especially Janet Nolan, *Ourselves Alone: Women's Emigration from Ireland, 1885–1920* (Lexington: University of Kentucky Press, 1989); see also Pauric Travers, " 'There Is Nothing for Me There': Irish Female Emigration, 1922–71," in *Irish Women and Irish Migration*, ed. Patrick O'Sullivan (London: Leicester University Press, 1995), pp. 146–167. On women's roles under the de Valera constitution, see Lee, *Ireland 1912–1985*, pp. 206–207.

52. On the history of the organization, see Maurice Manning, *The Blueshirts* (Dublin: Gill & MacMillan, 1970).

53. Richard B. Finnegan, "The Blueshirts of Ireland During the 1930s: Fascism Inverted," *Eire-Ireland* XXIV, no. 2 (Summer 1989), p. 92.

54. Ibid., pp. 79–99. See also Lee, *Ireland, 1912–1985*, pp. 181–182.

55. See Finnegan, "The Blueshirts of Ireland During the 1930s," p. 97; and Foster, *Oxford Illustrated History of Ireland*, p. 258, especially the depiction of a Blueshirt rally at a Dublin

cemetery. On Yeats's association with the Blueshirts, see Brown, *Ireland: A Social and Cultural History, 1922–79*, p. 163.

56. The decline of the Blueshirts and the marginalization of O'Duffy was made possible, ironically, by activities of Eamonn de Valera to suppress the IRA. Escalating violence by republican extremists initiated a government policy of arrests, military tribunals, and the eventual suppression of the movement. This Fianna Fail crackdown on the IRA led conservative leaders of Fine Gael to conclude that their growing opposition to the Blueshirts was at last justified and that the Blueshirts were less necessary than they had been in 1932 and 1933.

57. Dermot Keogh, *Twentieth Century Ireland: Nation and State* (Dublin: Gill & Macmillan, 1994), p. 95.

58. Hachey, Hernon, and McCaffrey, *The Irish Experience*, p. 206.

59. Quoted in Keogh, *Twentieth Century Ireland*, p. 108.

60. For a concise view of Northern Ireland's contribution to the war effort, see Keith Jeffery, "The British Army and Ireland," in *Military History of Ireland*, ed. Bartlett and Jeffery, pp. 437–445. See also Brian Barton, *Northern Ireland in the Second World War* (Belfast: Ulster Historical Foundation, 1995).

61. Bartlett and Jeffery, *Military History of Ireland*, p. 442.

62. Keogh, *Twentieth Century Ireland*, pp. 111–113. The significance of German spies in Ireland during World War II is largely the stuff of folklore and action novels such as Jack Higgins, *The Eagle Has Landed*. With one exception, Herman Goertz, who remained at large until late 1941, all of the fifteen spies who landed in Ireland were captured.

63. Keith Jeffery, "The British Army and Ireland," in *Military History of Ireland*, ed. Bartlett and Jeffery, pp. 445–446.

64. Duffy, *Atlas of Irish History*, p. 118.

65. Quoted in Tony Gray, *The Irish Answer* (London: Heinemann, 1966), p. 114.

66. Ibid.

67. On the Mother and Child Plan controversy, see Browne's own account in Noel Brown, *Against the Tide* (Dublin: Gill & Macmillan, 1986), pp. 141–172.

4

DOORS OPENING AND CLOSING: ECONOMY, EDUCATION, AND THE IRISH LANGUAGE

Introduction

In a famous and widely quoted speech in 1943, Eamonn de Valera presented his vision of family, society, and economy in Ireland:

> The Ireland which we have dreamed would be the home of a people who valued material wealth only as a basis for right living, of a people who were satisfied with frugal comfort and devoted their leisure to things of the spirit; a land whose countryside would be bright with cozy homesteads, would be joyous with the sounds of industry and with the romping of sturdy children, the contests of athletic youth, the laughter of comely maidens; whose firesides would be forums for the wisdom of serene old age. It would in a word be the home of a people living the life that God desires men should live.[1]

Inviting criticism, if not derision, de Valera's omniscient projection (as he apparently was privy to God's intentions) tells us more about de Valera's and Fianna Fail's bucolic ideology than about the people of Ireland. That ideology held that, given the chance to create a Gaelic society, the Irish would forego the same level of consumption as, say, the British. However, the "plain people" of Ireland, as Flann O'Brien noted cynically, tended to elevate the virtues of the frugal life only when they had no money. When they had the opportunity to seek a better life, materialistic though it might be, they sought it with alacrity. De Valera's Ireland of the 1950s was scarred by massive emigration, social stagnation, parochial insularity, and economic decay. The people, especially in the west of Ireland and among intellectuals, sensed that Ireland had no future because of emigration and the economic stagnation. Disease and poverty were widespread. At the time of de Valera's speech Ireland had one of the highest rates of tuberculosis in Europe and one of the lowest per capita incomes. The Church was willing to cast its weight against government activity in the social sphere. Ineffective governments of the 1950s, made timid by fidelity to fiscal orthodoxy, were less than bold in addressing social and economic policy. The deadening hand of the Censorship Board gave aspiring writers little room to express their creativity; they joined the emigrants departing Ireland. The values for which Sinn Fein had fought—an independent autonomous, Gaelic, Catholic Ireland—seemed betrayed as young people packed their Gladstones to flee a life of poverty and a culture drained of its imaginative energy. The Fianna Fail governments in the 1930s and 1940s had sought economic autonomy and a pastoral Gaelic society. The result had fallen so far short of the ideal that the idyllic dream of independence was betrayed.

The tides of economic and social change in the relatively rural, poor, organic community of Ireland moved toward the features of advanced industrial democracies after 1960. The rapid change in Ireland after 1960 produced the metamorphosis of a hierarchical, clerical, communal political culture into a more pluralistic, secular, individualist political culture, a "modern" political culture.

Modernization can of course be both descriptive and normative; as a form of social change it was seen by some in Irish society as a deleterious transformation to be avoided at all costs. Such change eroded the fundamental conception of community and values that the Irish chose in law and practice for themselves. The resulting transformation was questioned both by the Church and by adherents to de Valera's bucolic view of the spiritual, traditional, rural Ireland. These critics saw the changes not as ascent to the standards of affluence, information, behavior, and choices of western Europeans but as a descent into the secular, urban, shallow values of a homogenized, "Americanized" or "Europeanized," philistine global culture.

Conversely, modernization can be seen as normatively good in that it is a liberation from a world in which the values of the community are held to be superior to the choices of the individual. The range of possible choices that the individual may exercise is expanded by the advancement of economic growth; exposure to a wider world through educational opportunities; the potential of social mobility through ambition, education, and work; and the ability to formulate one's own values and convictions through an exposure to different ideas, information, values, and ideologies. The process of modernization, as C. E. Black has shown, always destroys some of the old as it generates the new.[2] The new is more susceptible to being shaped by the choices of those exposed to modernization because expanded choice is part of modernization, and thus the forms of the market, the media, the society, and personal behavior are more in flux. Hierarchy is undermined in matters big and small as elite control over social structures diminishes.

Slowly in the late 1950s Ireland opted for a different form of economic order, which whisked it into a process of economic and social modernization. The transformation in the society and economy of Ireland occurred over a relatively brief period and was nothing short of startling. We begin with the rejection of the bucolic dream.

The Insulated Economy

The Irish economy in the 1950s was predominantly agricultural and essentially unchanged since the 1930s. The economic growth rate for the years 1922 to 1938 has been estimated at 1.2 percent per year, at 0 percent during the war years, and at only 1.8 percent after the war. That rate of growth was considerably slower than other European nations and was supported not by investment in industry but by government spending on social services, agriculture, and housing. The loss of jobs in agriculture during the period was also accompanied by a loss of jobs in industry, contrary to the usual pattern of industrial growth. Compensating increases in tourism after the war reached a peak in 1948 and declined thereafter, thus proving inadequate to make up for the slow growth in critical sectors. The reliance on agriculture as the driving wheel of economic growth missed the point that increases in agricultural productivity were not accompanied by increases in agricultural employment. The goals set during the period were wildly optimistic, and there was an expectation that surpluses in agricultural products would be exported to the United Kingdom. However, the stagnant British economy did not import as much as expected, and stiff foreign competition diminished demand for Irish produce. Total agricultural output grew only 8 percent in the fifteen years from 1945 to 1960.

Industry

In the industrial realm the Irish effort was composed of unfounded aspirations such as those expressed in the 1948 *European Recovery Plan*, the Irish document prepared to obtain Marshall Plan funds from the United States, which asserted that "many new factories" would be built in "provincial towns" and that those factories would prosper protected from foreign competition in "light of the well known justification for protection of infant industries."[3] How this industrial growth was to find capital, access skilled workers, acquire technology, and develop markets and distribution systems was left to the imagination. The Industrial Development Authority (IDA) was created in 1949 to review tariffs; in 1952 it was given the authority to seek out foreign investment for Ireland. At the same time Coras Trachtala, the Irish Export Board, was created to foster Irish exports to the United States and Canada. The notion that the IDA might actually project and plan industrial development flew in the face of the economic orthodoxy of the time. The Department of Finance, which dominated economic policy, considered a governmental role in capital development or in providing tax incentives as heresy. The IDA also constituted, at the very least, a potential threat to the bureaucratic turf of the Department of Finance. Thus the IDA was only the embryonic acorn of the mighty bureaucratic oak that it was to become in later years. Consistent with its mission the IDA sought a U.S. consulting firm, IBEC Technical Services Corporation, to assess industrial growth in Ireland. *Industrial Potentials of Ireland: An Appraisal* was issued in 1952 by IBEC.

Evaluations of the Economic Situation

The IBEC report found that Ireland's relative performance (at best pallid) was weakening because what capital was available was invested in non-productive ends. Ireland needed production for export to overcome balance of payments difficulties. In addition, the development of agriculture could not provide more employment, and adopting a policy of protectionism had stunted growth and created deadening price controls. The causes for these policies were not in the economic policy realm but in the philosophical domain. The *Report* noted: "In fact declarations of expansive purpose are frequently qualified by expression of an anti-materialist philosophy, of an asceticism that opposes material aspirations to spiritual goals and hence writes down the former as unworthy."[4] Price controls were criticized for being used, not for economic purposes such as controlling inflation, but based upon "a highly moralistic approach that has tended to turn into a profits control system—attacking high profits as an inherent evil." [5] The unkindest cut of all, in light of Irish aspirations, was the assertion that economic growth was curtailed by dependence on Britain: "The effectiveness of political sovereignty will continue to be vitiated while the Irish economy remains so decisively dependent upon the United Kingdom."[6] Nothing could be more painful for nationalists to hear.

As if this diagnosis was not sufficiently discouraging, another report, designed to assess the potential for export to the United States and titled *Dollar Exports,* was published in 1953, also by U.S. consultants. The U.S. economists discovered that Irish business leaders harbored a series of "illusions" about their products and the U.S. market, including: "The illusion of superior quality; The illusion of appealing to sentiment; The illusion of insufficient capacity; and The illusion of . . . sales without effort."[7] The Irish business owners apparently felt that demand for their high-quality goods from Irish Americans who wanted to "buy Irish" would occur automatically once those goods were placed before the U.S. consumer and that the increased demand would actually put a strain on the capacity

of Irish plants to produce those goods. Rather than straining the production capacity of Irish manufacturing plants, this approach strained the credulity of the
consultants.[8]

This glimpse into the Irish economy of the 1950s reveals that the governments
of the day were not particularly adroit at stimulating a policy of growth. The in-
terparty government that led the country from 1948 to 1951 was willing to engage
in active government expenditure to stimulate growth, but the time period was
too short and the resources too slender to trigger anything more than a rise in
consumer imports. As these were not matched by a corresponding rise in exports,
the next government was presented with a balance of payments problem. The de
Valera government elected in 1951 returned to the economic orthodoxy of the
Department of Finance and deflated the economy in the budget of 1952 with increased taxes, cutting of expenditures, and removal of government subsidies for
products. That the medicine was harsh is noted by economists Kieran Kennedy
and Brendan Dowling, who also felt, in fact, that it was unnecessary because the
economy was potentially on the brink of renewed growth.[9] Unemployment and
emigration were exacerbated by these policies, which were pursued in every budget until 1959. The gross national product (GNP) in 1958, as a result, was 2.5 percent smaller than it was in 1955. What little growth had occurred from 1945 to
1952 was lost in the recession years of 1952 to 1959. Employment in agriculture
and industry from 1951 to 1958 dropped by 12 percent, leading to extensive unemployment. The economic slump was matched by a surge in emigration and a
sense that Ireland was stagnant and inert and that the culture was dying.

Migration

The tide of emigration from Ireland continued at a rate not seen since the
Famine hemorrhage began in the late 1840s. From 1846 to 1946 approximately
5,827,000 left Ireland, a figure larger than the total number of people who had
lived on the island since the early 1850s. The number leaving had diminished
somewhat in the fifteen years prior to 1951 (about 200,000 had left). The economic policies of the 1950s, however, pushed the number taking to the boat up
to 408,766 in the decade from 1951 to 1961, a number larger than any ten-year
period since 1891–1900. Obviously the dismal economic conditions were driving
the Irish to the factories of Britain, Canada, and the United States. Most of the
people emigrating were young and also from the west of Ireland. Thus the economic atrophy of the entire country was accompanied by an acute decline and
demoralization of the people of the west.

The external migration was accompanied by an internal migration to the city
of Dublin, which was in effect colonized by people from the west who were looking for work. Thus, despite the overall population decline, the cities of Ireland
grew during this period. Had emigration not occurred, the problems of unemployment, education, and social services would have challenged the capacity of

the government of the Republic to respond without a serious breakdown in legitimacy.[10] The aspiration to create an ideal Gaelic state for the people of Ireland was
defeated by having a majority of those people leave the country. Because a high
percentage of those emigrants came from Irish-speaking counties—for example,
44 to 55 percent of the emigrants from 1856 to 1910 came from counties that had
from 10 to 59 percent Irish speakers[11]—the Irish language suffered the erosion
that prevented de Valera's Gaelic state from being Irish speaking.

The Whitaker Plan and the Planning Period, 1959–1972

A series of policies that were to bear fruit later in the 1960s were being shaped at
another level of government. In 1954 the Commission on Emigration and Other
Population Problems issued a report concluding that agriculture, while needing
development, would not provide employment for the population, which meant
the development of industry was necessary.[12] In 1956 the Industrial Grants Act
allowed the IDA to subsidize up to 66 percent of the cost of land and buildings
for industrial development in rural areas. More important was the 1956 Finance
Act, which allowed a 50 percent tax relief on increases in profits from exports
from the prior year. The stimulus to export-focused industry was clear. That
largesse was increased in the Finance Acts of 1957 and 1958, to the point that
new or increased profits from exports were tax free for ten years. In 1958 the protectionist measures embodied in the 1938 Control of Manufactures Act, which
excluded foreign investment, were relaxed, and foreign investment for development was encouraged. In addition, the Capital Investment Advisory Committee's
third report in 1958 made an explicit call for the government to generate economic growth in Ireland through the tools of planning, coordination, capital investment, tax policy, and education.[13]

Whether the government would undertake this responsibility in light of past
policy was another question. The trigger was a report prepared by the secretary of
the Department of Finance, T. K. Whitaker.[14] His 1958 report, *Economic
Development*, was, according to historian F. S. L. Lyons, a "watershed in the modern history of the country." If this was an overstatement, it was not by much.[15]
The report cited the failures of the protectionist policies enacted by the government since the 1930s. Agriculture was oversupported by public money and was
backward compared to other countries; industry was feeble, lacking capital and
bold entrepreneurs and hampered by a small domestic market. Emigration
drained Ireland of those who could find no employment, and government expenditure on socially valuable construction projects such as housing, hospitals, and
roads was unproductive in terms of economic growth. *The Programme for
Economic Expansion,* a white paper that accompanied *Economic Development,*
called for the government to take an active role in demand management. The key
was to generate the production of goods for export; the development would come
from incentives that would bring foreign capital to Irish industry. Protectionism

was to be discarded as a policy of development, and domestic industry and agriculture were going to have to compete without special tariff protection. Import quotas and protective tariffs, some as high as 60 percent, were to be gradually eliminated. Much of this planning was done with an eye to entering the European Economic Community (now the European Union, EU) because Ireland had applied for membership in 1961.

Foreign capital was to be attracted by generous incentives which, when coupled with advantages already present in the country, would produce profitable industries and increase employment. Ireland's resources included a plentiful supply of labor at a relatively low labor cost; a relatively convenient location with respect to Britain and Europe; and convenient access to water, power, and ports. For U.S. and British investors the fact that Ireland was an English-speaking country was an advantage, and Ireland's political stability and administrative sophistication compared favorably to the risks of investment in less-developed nations. The drawbacks were obvious as well: Ireland's infrastructure needed work. Transportation and communication were backward; the telephone system in the early 1960s, for example, was an antiquated relic that was incapable of basic person to person communication, let alone what modern industry would need. Roads were narrow, no highway (or "dual carriageway") system existed, and the facilities for shipping were at best very basic.

The principal incentive for investment, however, was the promise of generous grants and loans to companies willing to locate in Ireland and generous tax breaks on their earnings for years after their initial investment. For the first ten years a company's earnings would be tax free, and taxes were to be kept at a reduced level for the following five years. The government would also underwrite up to two-thirds of the cost of building factories and purchasing land and equipment. In addition, the government would assist in the training of workers needed for specific industries. The plans also set aside grants for Irish firms to increase their efficiency and improve their capacity for export sales. Agriculture was not to be ignored: Grassland farming was to be improved to increase exports. The government would assist also in improving marketing, disease control, and agricultural education to improve agricultural management. The Industrial Development Act (Encouragement of External Investment) of 1958 instituted a five-year plan, to last from 1959 to 1964, and set the relatively modest goal of an increase in the GNP of 2 percent per year. The results of the plan were much more impressive, with a growth rate of 4.5 percent per year, new factories built, and approximately 27,000 new jobs created. The GNP had increased by 15.5 percent by 1962, reflecting the jump in production, employment, and exports. The incentives to foreign investors had manifestly paid off. Of the 200 factories established during that period, the British accounted for one-half, the Germans for one-fourth, and the rest were spread among U.S. (later to increase dramatically), Dutch, French, Italian, Belgian, Swiss, Canadian, and Japanese firms. The products ranged from chewing gum to airplane parts.

Still there was grumbling about some aspects of the economic growth. The Bank of Ireland worried that the size of government expenditure and the "unproductive" nature of the public spending would lead to budgetary and balance of payments problems. As the rate of foreign investment grew, the IDA paid out more Irish tax money to assist in putting plants in Ireland. The Left wing argued that the Irish economy was being sold to multinational corporations that would repatriate their profits and then close down when their ballooning profits diminished. By 1985, 47 percent of the top manufacturing companies were foreign owned, and the U.S. firms were making a profit of over 30 percent from their firms located in Ireland, their highest rate of return in the world. Those profits were not reinvested in Ireland and were repatriated at a very high rate (for example, $750 million in 1983). Not only was the Irish taxpayer subsidizing the plant, equipment, and training of the workers, but Ireland was getting no tax revenue on the profits from exports up to 1981.[16] Critiques from the Left in Ireland did not compel much attention from the general public, which, of course, was benefiting substantially from the growth in per capita income.

The government did not neglect the domestic sector. Among the efforts to revive the west of Ireland and to keep Irish business competitive was the Shannon Free Airport Development Company, set up in 1959. Designed to prevent the slow death of Shannon Airport as long-distance jets began to bypass that stop, the Airport Development Company undertook to create an industrial area within the customs boundary. No duties were paid on raw materials entering the area and there were no export duties on products flown out. This generated a spate of light industry in the area. The Company also took to promoting tourism and generated significant business in the area that later took advantage of the burst of interest in visiting Ireland in the 1990s.

The first plan was so successful that Sean Lemass, the prime minister of Ireland, proposed a second plan, much more ambitious than the first, that was to run from 1963 to 1970. The amount and variety of exports to Britain from Ireland was such that the imposition by the British of a tariff on Irish imports in 1964 was deadening to Irish growth. A treaty signed in 1965 removed the restrictions in 1966, and Irish restrictions on British imported goods were slowly reduced and eliminated by 1975. The treaty was a watershed event: The Irish abandoned the use of tariffs and quotas with their largest trading partner. The Second Programme, while stimulating employment, did not staunch the flow of emigration as hoped. The numbers remained high in the 1960s, with 134,500 leaving during that decade. In the 1970s job creation and the improved economic potential of Ireland brought a cessation of the emigration and a return to Ireland of 109,000 people.

The incentive planning depended upon government capital expenditure in the areas of infrastructure, roads, ports, telephones, and subsidizing foreign investment. Moreover, the increasing demands for more services and programs from government increased government expenditure in the non-capital realm. This triggered a round of borrowing from Irish, international, and U.S. banks. Taxes were also increased, and there was a cut in the amount targeted for capital investment. The budget to run the country every day, the operating budget, was in the red, as was the budget of expenditures on economic development, the capital budget. As the amount of debt rose, borrowing began on the current operating budget as well as the capital budget. The high cost of debt service began plaguing the budget process. The borrowing, begun in the mid 1960s, got out of control in the late 1970s and early 1980s and reached nearly 16 percent of the GNP in 1982. The borrowing remained high relative to Ireland's economic growth until 1987, then dropped steadily over the next fifteen years to only 2 percent of the GNP in 1995.

In 1968 the Second Programme was abridged after a relatively disappointing performance in which the overall growth rate of 3.3 percent for the years 1964 to 1967 fell one point below the projected rate of 4.4 percent. Agricultural growth was disappointing, and industry posted a rate of growth of only 5.8 percent instead of the projected 7 percent. Job creation goals were not met and were revised downward. In March 1969 the Second Programme was dropped and the Third Programme, *Economic and Social Development 1969–1972,* was adopted. Again the targets of the Third Programme were not reached, in part because expectations had been set too high, in part because of the increases in inflation and population growth that occurred after the initial growth spurt. The rate of inflation in the early years of the planning period was 4.2 percent, to be followed in the period from 1968 to 1972 by a rate of 8.5 percent. Again, although the rate of economic growth on average for these years was 3.7 percent, the rate of growth in the population was 1 percent per year. Chronic unemployment was not alleviated and the rate of non-agricultural unemployed rose from 6.7 percent to 8.1 percent in the same period. A dramatic increase in the balance of payments problem was caused by a decline in tourism (which, not surprisingly, coincided with the explosion of violence in Northern Ireland) and an increase in the purchase of imported goods.

Entry into the European Union, 1973–1987

On January 1, 1973, Ireland entered the European Economic Community (now the EU). An economic milestone, this step not only fastened the Irish economy to those of the states of the EU but also symbolically diminished the primacy of the link to Britain. The Irish negotiated a five-year transition period and received some dispensations from the EU to continue to foster industrial development. The expected benefits from membership were obvious: agricultural subsidies and price supports from the Common Agricultural Policy (CAP), direct grants from the Social Fund and the Regional Fund, and access to the large European market. The disadvantages were the loss of some autonomy in the sphere of economic policy and the vulnerability of Irish industry to a wave of manufactured products from Europe that would sweep aside domestic products. Although the Irish government tried to prepare domestic industry for what was coming, domestic producers were decimated by competition in the following decade.

The balance of trade was shifted from an almost exclusive focus on the United Kingdom to a more balanced distribution. In 1960, of Irish goods exported, 75 percent went to Britain; of goods imported, 50 percent came from Britain. By 1980, 43 percent of Irish exports and 51 percent of imports passed each other on the Irish Sea. By 1995, 25 percent of exports and 35 percent of imports were passing between the two countries. The volume of Irish exports to the EU increased from 7 percent to 47 percent in the same period, while by 1995 imports to Ireland from the United States had increased by two and one-half times and from the EU by one-third.

In March 1979 Ireland opted to join the European Monetary Fund, which tied together the currencies of the EU members. Britain, reflecting Thatcher's arm's-length policy with respect to Europe, chose not to enter. The punt was severed from the pound for the first time since 1826 and ran the risk of substantially altering the balance of payments because so much of Ireland's trade was with the United Kingdom. The effects, of the event, were relatively minor because the British devalued the pound as the Irish did the punt, and Ireland gained grants of £250 million ($375 million) and loans of £1,250 million ($1,875 million) to cushion the shock of exposure to the currencies of the EU.

Farmers were major beneficiaries from 1973 to 1979 as the price support system of the European Common Agricultural Policy triggered a cascade of income from Brussels to Dublin, reaching £365 million ($547 million) in 1978. These supports were reduced by Brussels in 1978; by 1980 farmers' incomes had plummeted by one-third. By 1988 per capita farm income was no higher than it had been in 1978 even though the number employed in farming had decreased by one-third.

Evaluation of Ireland's entry into the EU is complicated by the fact that it was accompanied by massive jumps in oil prices and the worldwide economic recession. The country was dependent on foreign oil for 70 percent of energy needs. When the price of oil quadrupled in 1974–1975, the negative balance of payments surged and the rate of inflation ascended to a staggering 25 percent. The portion of disposable income for consumer goods was absorbed by the high cost of oil, so consumer demand contracted. In 1979 another oil crisis, prompted by the revolution in Iran, displayed again the vulnerability of Ireland's economy to energy-induced inflation. Payments for oil were made in U.S. dollars; the appreciation of the dollar meant that it took more and more punts to purchase the dollars to purchase the oil. Energy conservation measures were adopted and the use of peat was increased, but the effects on government borrowing and inflation were clear: the rate of inflation in 1980 was 18.2 percent, and government borrowing reached 15.6 percent of GNP in 1982.

Oil prices were an obvious element in the inflationary spurt, but the adoption of national pay agreements among the government, the employers, and the unions began at about the same time (in 1970). The first agreement was designed to last only eighteen months, but it had greater implications in that it signaled the adoption of an explicit corporatist model of economic management. Corporatism has many meanings (see Chapter 7) but in this instance it meant the movement away from laissez-faire arrangements in the setting of wages and even prices. Governments in Europe moved in this direction in the 1970s with national wage agreements, signaling the explicit partnership of labor, government, and industry. The postwar years had seen varieties of corporatism in Europe as governments sought stability, labor sought security, and industry sought profits. The implicit or explicit bargain was that each would cooperate to the degree necessary to achieve its ends: social welfare programs for the workers, subsidies and tax benefits for industry, and political parties that would maintain the bargain whether in power or out. The control of inflation was to be managed not only by the government's control of the money supply but also through the control of wages and prices through agreements. Control of wage-pushed inflation would diminish as workers agreed to a non-inflationary increase in their pay that would in turn allow manufacturers to predict wage costs and thus limit price increases. As historian Joe Lee has labeled them, the agreements were a "flight from reality." The first agreement of 1970 allowed a wage increase of 12 percent per year, which was 4 percent above the rate of inflation. This gap appears modest, however, in light of the 1972 agreement, which granted a 14 percent increase in wages. The rate for 1975 was 29.4 percent, in 1976 16.6 percent, and in 1980, for government employees, 30 percent. Despite the argument that these wages were chasing a runaway inflation rate, which reached, for example, 21 percent in 1975, they were in fact exceeding both the rate of inflation and the rate of growth in productivity and thus were contributing to the cycle of inflation, spending, and borrowing that marked the period.

The election of 1977 brought a new Fianna Fail government to power that was elected on the program of lowering taxes and increasing government benefits and services. This formula of government borrowing and deficit spending, "voodoo economics" in U.S. political parlance, could only be avoided by a massive increase in economic growth and a corresponding increase in tax revenues. The government put forth a white paper, *National Development 1977–1980*, which called for an increase in jobs by a figure of 80,000, a drop in inflation, a growth in GNP of 7 percent per year, and a drop in government borrowing to 8 percent as a percentage of GNP. "Voodoo economics" this turned out to be: the figures in 1980 came in at 18.2 percent inflation, 2.2 percent growth in GNP, and a government borrowing rate that was 13.5 percent of GNP.

The government from 1982 to 1987, a Fine Gael/Labour coalition, did not improve on the record of overspending in both the capital budget and the operating budget. The targeted goals for the period were not met, and two other national economic policy documents, *The Way Forward: National Economic Plan 1983–1987* and *Building on Reality 1985–1987*, identified the problems of inflation, unemployment, borrowing, and spending. In practice the policies of the governments of the day tended to move the economy backward rather than forward on economic growth, with negative rates in 1985 and 1986, and appeared to be "building on unreality" with respect to jobs as the unemployment rate in 1985 and 1986 hovered at 15.5 percent. The government of the day began to recognize reality, moving toward austerity, but could not obtain agreement among the parties in the coalition on the level of pain. The wave of emigration began again: the number leaving Ireland rose from 14,000 in 1983 to 29,000 annually in 1986 and 1987.

The National Economic and Social Council commissioned a study, which was completed in 1981 by the American firm Telesis and titled *A Review of Industrial Policy*. Because the report was critical of the IDA, the premier government agency, it was not published until 1982 and provoked significant bureaucratic infighting and damage limitation by the IDA. The IDA had depended so heavily on the strategy of foreign investment for job creation, the report noted, that it had neglected indigenous industries, especially those with export potential. The foreign firms, as critics had noted earlier, repatriated profits and had few links to the rest of the economy. The firms did little research and development and were only engaged in assembly and packaging. More explosive, however, were the Telesis conclusions that the IDA was not having success with its chosen development strategy of foreign capital investment. Noting that Puerto Rico did better than Ireland, Telesis indicated that the capital grants to companies were too generous, had no sanctions for non-performance, did not produce the number of jobs promised, and paid too much for each job created, an average of £14,600 ($23,000 in 1983.)[17] The number of jobs that had been created by 1981 was only 30 percent of what had been promised since 1970. In 1984 *Industrial Policy*, a planning document, incorporated the Telesis recommendations for industrial development: fund research and development and fund export-oriented indigenous industry.[18]

While some of these numbers tell a distressing story, there were unquestionably positive developments during the period from the 1960s to the 1980s. More than 300 foreign firms invested $3.6 billion in Ireland, they created over 100,000 jobs and the real income of the Irish people almost doubled. The basis of economic growth had shifted from agriculture to export-based industry fueled by foreign investment and then to the development of indigenous industry, financial services, and a service economy.

The Emergence of the "Celtic Tiger," 1987–1997

In 1985 the National Economic and Social Council "had become extremely concerned at the scale of the economic and social problems facing the country and was worried about the consequences of continuing present policies."[19] An election brought the Fianna Fail party under Charles Haughey to power in February 1987. In 1980, in a television address, then Prime Minister Haughey had stated: "As a community we are living beyond our means, we are living at a rate that is not justified by the amount of goods and services we are producing. To make up the difference we are borrowing enormous amounts of money, borrowing at a rate which just cannot continue. . . . We have got to cut down on government spending."[20] But his administration, and the one that followed, continued to borrow; seven years later, back in power, he faced a £25 billion ($38 billion) debt and the nearly £2 million ($3 million) per year attendant debt service. Haughey began a series of austerity measures that were notable for their contrast with the past two decades. The easier path of expanding benefits, expanding borrowing, and expanding debt had been the preference of politicians in the past. The government produced *The Programme for National Recovery 1987–1990* (which followed very closely the alarm bell sounded in the NESC report *A Strategy for National Development 1986–1990*). Recognizing the seriousness of the situation, the government negotiated pay raises limited to 2.5 percent per year, which was under the rate of inflation. The government agreed to this rate for a three-year period and the unions in turn gave a no strike guarantee. These initial negotiated agreements were part of a social partnership that emerged in Ireland as an approach to managing Ireland's economic well-being in the international economy.

The strategy, according to political scientist Brigid Laffan, was part of a learning process for Irish decision makers in managing internationalization. The key sectors—employers, unions, and farming interests—negotiated agreements with government for a three-year period. Moderate wage growth was seen as the key to controlling public debt and remaining competitive. In 1990 the agreements were continued with a rate of 4 percent per year. That rate was a shaky compromise because it exceeded the rate of inflation and the government agreed only under the pressure of a threatened strike. The government slashed spending in the public sphere, including closing hospitals, cutting services, and eliminating government jobs. The decrease in government spending was painful and politically unpopular, but the response of the public was not as hostile as might be expected. As the social partnership developed, other social policies were included, such as health spending and tax reform. *The Programme for National Recovery 1987–1990* also established a Central Review Committee, which was to monitor implementation of the Programme and continue the dialogue among the partners, further establishing a neo-corporatist model of policy making. The 1987 effort was followed by three other agreements. *The Programme for Economic and Social Progress 1990–1993* called for fiscal and monetary stabilization, tax reform, and sectoral development. *The Programme for Competitiveness and Work 1994–1996* and *Partnership 2000: 1997–2000* each were three-year plans and contained agreements on public and private wage increases, sweetening the deal for labor with the promise of social equality and tax breaks favorable to workers. The agreements moved toward limited privatization of state enterprises. The most significant change was the fact that *Partnership 2000* included in the negotiations representatives of the unemployed and of women and broadened the discussion to issues beyond wage agreements such as education, poverty, and social exclusion.[21]

The results of these plans were more than anyone expected and surpassed the growth rates that had occurred when the first *Programme for Economic Expansion* was adopted in 1959. The average growth rate from 1988 to 1995 in real terms was

5.1 percent, approximately twice that of the rest of the EU members. Between 1993 and 1997 the Irish economy grew 40 percent, about three times the rate of the industrialized world. The rate of inflation (over 20 percent in 1980) hovered at just over 2 percent in 1996. The borrowing requirements of the government dropped from almost 10 percent of GNP to about 2 percent of GNP. The per capita GNP of people in the Republic went from £4,200 ($6,300) in 1987 to £13,170 ($19,750) in 1997. Employment grew at a rate of 4 percent per year. Dublin became the most sought-after tourist location in west Europe, with over 2.5 million visitors in 1996, while overall tourist revenues were almost 6 percent of the gross domestic product. Industries were drawn to Ireland's generous incentives. Electronics and software companies—Intel, Analog Devices, Phillips, Dell, Gateway, and Motorola, among many others—put plants in Ireland that employ 30,000 people and provide 25 percent of Irish exports.

The employment in overseas companies is dominated by electronics and engineering, which employ 45,510 people. Of the more than 1,000 foreign firms in Ireland, 400 are from the United States, more than twice the number of the next largest investor, Germany. The cold statistics reveal the rapid growth, but the visitor to Ireland could tell the difference without ever looking at a column of numbers. The construction in Dublin and around the country is extensive, the cars are newer and more luxurious, the clothes are newer and more stylish, and the stores glisten with consumer goods. Restaurants abound and are more cosmopolitan. New hotels have sprouted up in Dublin and around the country. Visitors to Ireland after the changes of the 1960s have said "You would not recognize the place"; in the late 1990s there is one person, no doubt, who would not recognize the place at all: Eamonn de Valera.

Explaining Ireland's Economic Development

Looking back over seventy-five years, the path of Irish economic development has been unsteady, to say the least. Scholars seeking to assess the performance of Ireland have found that from 1926 to 1985 the average annual growth rate for Ireland was 2 percent. That rate compares favorably with the United Kingdom at 2.1 percent; however, the performance of the United Kingdom was the worst in Europe over the same period. Moreover, merely to keep pace with the United Kingdom was not to catch up and narrow the gap; per capita GNP was approximately half that of Britain in 1913 and only 60 percent of it in 1987. In the same period, Norway went from about one-half the GNP per capita of Britain to 127 percent of it.[22] Overall Ireland's economic development, except in the last decade of the twentieth century, has been mediocre. Finally, we have to acknowledge that, while the course of human events is never smooth, Ireland's struggle for independence, the Civil War, the Great Depression, and World War II (in Ireland, The

"Emergency") served to disrupt the effects, and thus the assessment, of particular economic policies.

Several explanations have been offered for the Irish pattern of development, with a number taking into account the fact that Ireland was a post-colonial society. Economic historian R. Crotty, in a quirky but insightful book, *Ireland in Crisis*, argues that Ireland was the only European country to be "capitalist colonized" and is better understood in the framework of the undeveloped world.[23] The colonizer imposes a social and economic structure that prevents indigenous development. After independence the local elites, who benefit from the maintenance of the prevailing institutions, keep those structures to preserve their power. Thus for Crotty the post-colonial state is not the tool of liberation and development but rather a barrier that must be dismantled. While we do not agree with Crotty chapter and verse (few would), Ireland's political and economic dependence on Britain cannot be denied. Ireland's economy was tied to Britain in a host of direct and indirect ways. The pattern of land ownership after the Famine and the ties to the U.K. banking system are examples. The absence of capital in the nineteenth century was not overcome because the Irish economy had a feeble manufacturing sector and relied on agriculture for both jobs and exports. Dependence on the United Kingdom and the weaknesses of the process of economic growth were masked by the waves of emigration, which relieved the pressure on elites (English up to 1922 and Irish thereafter) to provide not only work but a decent life for the people of Ireland. The legacy of British imperialism was attitudinal, structural, and debilitating.

Economist E. O'Malley, in *Industry and Economic Development: The Challenge of the Latecomer,* argues that Ireland is but one of several cases of the problem of industrial development in the face of the industrial base of more advanced countries.[24] Indigenous firms in less-developed countries face the entrenched strength of established firms in the advanced countries with their economies of scale, advanced technology, extensive marketing and distribution, product differentiation, and management expertise. The late developer must utilize the government to assist in generating capital and legislation to overcome the disadvantages facing small or new firms. Even with government assistance, deficiencies in investment capital, management skills, and entrepreneurial energy were noted in a 1992 report on industrial failures in Ireland.[25] O'Malley argues that Ireland fits into this pattern. Government assistance in generating foreign investment created firms involved in assembly and processing, not high value-added economic activities. Moreover, those factories essentially stood alone. While providing jobs, they did not spill over into other sectors and generate growth. The firms repatriated profits, exporting potential investment capital. The Telesis report noted above identified some of these deficiencies in 1982, indicating that it was necessary for the Irish government to create strong companies, not strong agencies to assist weak companies.[26]

One can only agree with economist Kieran Kennedy that historian Joe Lee's magisterial *Ireland 1912–1985: Politics and Society* is "always fascinating," as are his theories about Ireland's development.[27] Lee examines Ireland in the twentieth century in terms of its potential and performance. His conclusion, using the development of other European countries as a basis of comparison, is that Ireland fell far short of its potential. Why this poor performance? Lee's answer is cultural, rooted not merely in macro-economic factors but in Ireland's institutions, intellect, character, and identity. [28] Most prominent is the failure of the institutions of the state. Lee argues that the development of the party system after the founding of the Free State conspired to trade off growth for stability. The leaders of both parties chose the short-term solution of establishing legitimacy, consolidating blocs of support, and winning elections, which Lee views as creative in politics but sterile in government. Turning to the senior civil service, Lee agrees with a number of reports indicating that the government bureaucracy of Ireland was, and is, bloated, rigid, over-centralized, conservative, and ineffectual. Evidence of the poor quality of decisions, the lack of creativity, the influence of party pressure groups, and bureaucracy in policy choices is detailed in Lee's history of policy decisions in the twentieth century.

In the realm of intellect, the lack of receptivity to alternative ideas and policies, Lee argues, was exemplified by the Department of Finance, which could not be moved from neo-classical orthodoxy no matter what information or arguments it encountered. Lee examines the roles of the universities, historians, and economists and concludes that there was insufficient intellectual imagination or institutional support of intellectual creativity to address the social and economic problems of economic development in the Free State and Republic.

In the dimension of character, Lee examines the moral base of the social order and concludes that personal envy (the begrudger mentality), social self-deception, and the paternalism of the Church create Irish character. That character lacks self-confidence and manifests a possessor mentality rather than an entrepreneurial, performance mentality. The possession–performance dichotomy, he notes, is rooted in the insecurity of the nineteenth century, based upon the lack of land ownership and threat of emigration. The fear of loss and the disparagement of achievement have been passed down through the generations, resulting in a preoccupation with the holding of small amounts of worth and avoiding the opprobrium directed at success. When the Irish actually acquired land and small businesses they adopted risk-aversive behavior rather than engaged in wealth creation. In the IBEC report of 1952 the consultants, affirming Lee, found: "The talk is of economic expansion but the actions of government, business and labor alike are too often along the lines of consolidating present positions rather than accepting the hazards inherent in the changed practices upon which expansion depends."[29] Across forty years an echo is heard in a 1992 report on the causes of failure in industrial firms: "The objective of many owners and managers of Irish companies appears to be to preserve the status quo and their current life style rather than to seek opportunities and to take risks."[30]

Crotty, O'Malley, and Lee lay bare three central facets of Ireland's slow economic development: the crippling colonial heritage; late industrial development from a competitively weak position; and (until recently) a passive, uncreative, risk-aversive culture.

Those impediments were finally overcome when Sean Lemass pragmatically rejected the cultural isolation of Gaelic Ireland and embraced the idea of Ireland-in-Europe as the means to genuine political and economic independence. The sense that a new Ireland was in the making became prevalent and swept away the inert economic, cultural, and social attitudes that prevailed in the 1950s.[31] The country began to measure itself by the standards of Europe; self-awareness increased, as did receptivity to change. The Church itself was changing and access to information was increasing as more Irish eyes were glued to the television, which came to Ireland in the 1960s. Modernization was nowhere more evident than in the areas of education and the Irish language.

Education: The Traditional System

The Irish educational system had remained essentially unchanged since the end of the nineteenth century, with the exception of the Irish-language question (discussed below). The British had created a system in 1831 that was to be non-denominational. Within twenty years, however, the system, under pressure from the Church Hierarchy, was essentially denominational. Schools at the local level were run by the teaching orders that had come to provide schools for Catholics in the early nineteenth century, such as the Presentation Sisters, the Mercy Sisters, and the Christian Brothers. Any efforts to impose central direction on these schools by the British administration were resisted by the Hierarchy, which maintained control of the schools at the local level.

After 1922 little changed. The Church was not unsatisfied with this arrangement because the system was to be run by Catholics who would essentially leave it alone. The creation of the Department of Education in 1924 did not signal a move toward centralization; on the contrary, it appears that the more centralization and control were talked about the less they occurred. Thus two of the three levels of Irish education, primary and secondary, were run by the Church and paid for by the state, a situation that remained unchanged until the 1960s.

The curriculum was rigidly prescribed in a classical mode that was designed, in the words of a 1962 report by the Council of Education, to promote the "religious moral and cultural development of the child." The order of these goals was clearly transitive and intellectual development is notably absent. Intellectual development was defined in this context as the mastery of a classical curriculum marked by a deeply conservative and anti-intellectual Catholicism. Learning was defined by rote memorization particularly directed at exams. The schools used set texts and students took a common external exam, the results of which were published, driving the teaching and learning into a very fixed and rigid mode. Modern languages and science were not emphasized; only one secondary school in six in 1960 taught chemistry up to the leaving certificate level.[32]

The teachers were sternly authoritarian in both their control of behavior and their transmission of information and dogma. The Christian Brothers came to be identified with secondary education of boys in Ireland, and their less-than-enlightened educational philosophy appears in many an Irish novel and story. The sexes were rigidly segregated; substantial physical punishment was seen as a pedagogical tool; and Irish, Latin, and Tridentine Catholicism undergirded the curriculum.

Management of the schools was left to the local boards of the Orders that ran them, giving substantial power to the priests in charge. In 1915 the local priest in charge of the school in Fanore removed Michael O'Shea from his position as a teacher because he preferred to marry the woman to whom he was engaged instead of the woman that the priest suggested he marry. The Bishop of Galway, after an appeal from O'Shea, expressed regret at his dismissal but endorsed it. He had a letter read from the pulpit in the parish ordering the parents who had supported O'Shea to stop doing so or their children would be denied confirmation and the sacraments.[33] Fifty years later John McGahern, a primary school teacher and budding novelist, published a novel, *The Dark*, which was banned by the Censorship Board. Upon returning to his Dublin primary school he was told by the school manager, the local parish priest, that he no longer worked there. When queried by the Irish National Teachers Organization about the dismissal, the priest would not explain his action but did indicate to the press that McGahern's novel was not a factor in his decision. Not everyone was persuaded (although an unintended consequence of that priest's actions, and many others, was to enrich the world of literature).[34]

Those students who went beyond the secondary level went to the National University of Ireland, with its three branches at Galway, Cork, and Dublin. Some went to the University of Dublin, Trinity College, the traditionally Protestant establishment institution. Founded in 1592, Trinity had a deeply Protestant character and educated some of the most distinguished political, literary, and philosophical figures in Ireland, including Swift, Burke, Wilde, and Beckett.[35] Until 1970 relatively few Catholic students went to Trinity. Catholics were expressly forbidden to attend Trinity up to the year 1793 (not that there was a really large number of landless Catholic peasants clamoring to go to Trinity in the seventeenth and eighteenth centuries). After 1875 the Catholic Church forbade attendance under the pain of mortal sin. Permission from the Bishop of Dublin could allow a Catholic to attend once he was assured that there would be "guarantees against the danger of perversion." After the creation of the Free State in 1922, Trinity remained out of the mainstream of Irish educational life, suffering both political and denominational isolation, and was more in the orbit of provincial British universities educating students from the United Kingdom (about 40 percent of its students), Northern Ireland, Europe, the Empire dominions, and the Anglo-Irish ascendancy of Ireland.

The National University of Ireland absorbed that small number of Catholic students who had the grades and the money to pursue third-level education. Britain founded the non-denominational Queen's University of Ireland in 1848, with branches at Belfast, Galway, and Cork. The ever-vigilant Catholic Hierarchy, fearing the corruption of the faith at Trinity, did not trust these institutions either. In 1908 the National University of Ireland was created by Parliament, with clerical participation on the governing boards and accepted by the Hierarchy. Queen's University in Belfast was made independent. The constituent colleges at Cork and Galway now included Dublin.

University College Dublin was the successor to the Catholic University of Ireland founded in 1854 by Cardinal Paul Cullen with Cardinal John Henry Newman as rector. Cullen sought to create a Catholic university to provide an Irish Catholic education, while Newman sought to provide a liberal arts education to Irish Catholics. The conflict was not resolved and Newman went back to Oxford. The University was not empowered to grant degrees until 1879 (under the authority of The Royal University). The Jesuits ran the Catholic University until it was incorporated into the National University.

Saint Patrick's at Maynooth, now part of the National University, was founded by the British in 1795 as a seminary for Catholic priests. Such a peculiar development might seem paradoxical in light of the Penal Laws, but by the late 1700s some of the restrictions on Catholics were being removed. The Crown's fear of the radicalism of the French Revolution proved to be more of an incentive for allowing Irish sons to take holy orders in Ireland than fear of popery. Teaching priests at home quarantined them from the poisonous threat of French liberal ideology. Maynooth was long both the symbol and the center of the Church power.

Higher education after 1922 produced a small elite to fill the civil service and other positions in the leadership cadre of Irish society. There was little or no emphasis on the utilitarian skills that might be productive in the economic sphere. After 1922, apart from the language issue, there was little that could be labeled national policy at the level of higher education.

Education: Reform and Renewal

In 1962 Professor Patrick Lynch was appointed head of a small commission sponsored by the Irish government and the Organization for European Cooperation and Development to examine Irish education. After working quietly for three years, the commission published a report in 1965 titled *Investment in Education*.[36] Along with *Economic Development*, *Investment in Education* is seminal in its impact. "One of the most important documents in the history of modern Ireland," journalist Fergal Tobin observed.[37]

The report delineated a litany of deficiencies in the schools that belied the prevalent assumption of quality. By implication, it was an indictment of Church management and state support, which had presided over, and paid for, the system. There were more than 1,000 one- and two-teacher schools. Of these, 70 percent had no piped-in drinking water, and more had no flush toilets. The buildings, erected in the nineteenth century and poorly maintained, were in ramshackle condition. The teachers were powerless and treated with disdain. When teachers asked in 1952 that the local authorities clean, light, and heat the school buildings, the Bishop of Clogher attacked the teachers, referring to them as "these lords who are coming for a few hours" who should remember that they are "ordinary people like the rest of us."[38] Water, toilets, and bricks and mortar were, however, the least of the problems. The report noted that in 1962–1963, although 28 percent of the students had passed the primary certificate, another 18 percent had failed and more than half of the students could not be located at all. Of approximately 17,500 students in primary school, some 8,000 never reached the sixth grade.

The situation was not any better in secondary schools, where 45 percent of the classes had an average of more than forty-five students. Half of the curriculum was devoted to languages, but only 5 percent of boys and 12 percent of girls went on to modern languages. As noted above, science was not taught and one teacher out of five was teaching a subject that he or she had never studied. Twenty-five percent of students left school before sitting for their intermediate certificate. Of those who were in secondary education, a majority came from more affluent backgrounds and urban settings. Children of large farmers and professionals were 80 percent more likely to go to secondary school, and 85 percent of those in higher education came from this class. Third-level education was restricted because only a few could pay the fees and send their children to school for an additional three years. Only one of five students who sat for the leaving certificate ended up in universities.[39]

Although some reform of the education system actually began before the publication of *Investment in Education*, the changes gained significant support from the public after the report. Patrick Hillary, George Colley, and, most important, Donagh O'Malley, ministers for Education from 1959 through 1968, created comprehensive schools with additional vocational subjects for those who had no access to post-primary education. They also created regional technical colleges, consolidated one- and two-teacher schools into larger units, and began government subsidies for the building of new schools. The number of scholarships increased almost fourfold by 1966. The most ground-breaking policies were those of O'Malley (1966–1968.) He announced the removal of fees for secondary education without consulting the Cabinet, the Department of Finance, or the Church (thus circumventing the political friction that would have either watered down the proposal or eliminated it, but also revealing the degree to which power over public policy was, and is, highly centralized in the Irish government). He raised the age of leaving school from fourteen to fifteen and provided buses for children to get to school, removing the travel barriers to education for children in rural areas. The managers of schools were mandated to provide adequate sanitation and heating, with the government subsidizing two-thirds of the cost. The primary certificate was abolished, facilitating movement into secondary school at age twelve without the barrier of the exam. O'Malley died suddenly at the age of forty-seven in 1968. It can be said that the education revolution that followed these reforms was a testimony to his efforts.

The effects of these reforms were dramatic and laid the foundation for the transformation of the Irish economy and society for years to come. The number of children in secondary education escalated from 96,056 in 1957–1958 to 118,807 in 1967–1968 to 239,000 in 1974–1975 and to 362,230 in 1993–1994.[40] The increase in numbers in schools did not eliminate the advantage of those from more privileged backgrounds. Students were still three times more likely to be in third-level education if they came from professional, urban, or well-off families. The changes in numbers also did not change the fundamental structure of the system. The Department of Education sets the curriculum and pays the salaries and 85 percent of the operating costs of the schools. The parish pays the remainder and, at the primary level, supplies the manager of the school, usually the parish priest. The secondary schools are under the same arrangement with, for example, 80 secondary schools under the aegis of the Christian Brothers and 150 under the Mercy or Presentation Nuns.

The major developments of the last third of the twentieth century have been a decline in vocations, changes in management, and increased influence of the lay teachers. The decline in vocations, coupled with an increase in enrollments, shifted the number of lay teachers in secondary schools from less than half in 1960 to nearly 90 percent by 1997. All of the principals of secondary schools were from the sponsoring Order in 1960; by 1999 that figure was two-thirds. Although in 1934 the position of the Church was that, "no lay committee of any kind was to be associated with the manager in school management," in 1985 the minister of Education created a National Parents' Council to formalize the voice of parents in education policy.[41] The school management boards on the local level have been expanded to include parents and teachers, and in many schools the absolute writ of the local priest is no more. The boards are now asked to take on more responsibility for the school's budget, annual reports, and planning. In 1987 a National Council for Curriculum and Assessment was created. Curriculum has been revised to provide for more continuous assessment; child-centered learning; and emphasis on subjects such as science and technology, ecology, and modern languages.[42]

The increasing size of the lay teacher's organizations has also increased their influence. The Irish National Teachers Organization (INTO) was founded for teachers in the national school system in 1868. Most of the primary teachers in INTO have taken an active, if somewhat underwhelming, part in shaping educational policy. The teachers went on an eight-month strike over salaries in 1946 which, despite popular support, was a failure. The long-term effect of this action, how-ever, was to more effectively mobilize the political presence of the teachers. They have exercised influence on promotion and tenure and the control of schools.

While the number of national schools decreased between 1929 and 1981 by 40 percent, the number of convent and monastery schools doubled as a result of the state creating larger schools in urban areas and turning them over to religious or-ders. The effect was to freeze lay teachers out of leadership positions. Eventually INTO gained some ground on this issue when the Ryan Commission in 1968 or-dered that administrative positions in the school be allocated in proportion to the ratio of lay and clerical faculty; thus new lay administrative positions were cre-ated. In 1968 INTO hastened the repair of schools in dismal physical condition by withdrawing the teachers from five schools until they were fixed. The political ef-fect on the school managers who had let these schools atrophy was significant.

The secondary teachers are represented by the Association of Secondary Teachers Ireland (ASTI), founded in 1909. The Association was politically active from the start. With a very small lay minority—in 1934 it had fewer than 300 members—ASTI struggled with issues of pay, tenure, and curriculum in a system that viewed the teachers' presence as extraneous and their views as unimportant compared to the views of the religious superiors and the bishops. By 1942 ASTI represented 42 percent of the teaching staffs and had, after long and painful strug-gles, achieved a contractual relationship with the schools. On pay issues ASTI had not supported INTO because secondary teachers earned on average 15 percent more than primary teachers. When the Ryan Commission in 1968 proposed a common pay scale and remuneration for services and credentials, ASTI resisted to the point of a strike in 1969, but eventually accepted the common scale in 1973. The organization's growth in numbers, and its affiliation with the Irish Congress of Trade Unions, have produced success on issues such as teacher representation on management boards, salaries, and the elimination of discrimination against women in pension plans.[43]

The reforms suggested in the *White Paper on Educational Development* in 1980 and the 1984 *Programme for Action in Education 1984–1987* foundered on the cutbacks in spending on education. Funding had escalated so sharply in the prior decades (From 1963 to 1973, educational expenditures rose from 3.4 per-cent of GNP to 6.3 percent.) that it was vulnerable during the period of national debt in the 1980s. *The Green Paper on Education* of 1992, however, promised to address the issues of a decreasing school population, educationally disadvan-taged students, greater emphasis on technical education, school management boards, school community relations, and the degree of Church authority over the schools.

In the realm of higher education the changes were as dramatic if somewhat quieter. A *Report of a Commission on Higher Education* was issued in 1967 as a re-sult of work done by a Commission appointed in 1960. The Commission recom-mended making each of the universities independent, the creation of a greater base of technological education, an increase in financial aid for students, and the appointment of a permanent Higher Education Authority. O'Malley, minister for Education at the time of the report, proposed the merger of Trinity College and University College Dublin to eliminate duplication. This plan was resisted by every major group involved and was dropped, revealing the age-old political truth that the configuration and depth of political interests, not the reasonableness of a proposal, determine the outcome.

Five regional colleges of technology were founded between 1968 and 1970, followed by six more in the 1970s. These schools offered diplomas in art and design, commerce, science, catering, and technical education. The National Institutes for Higher Education were founded at Limerick in 1972 and at Dublin in 1980 (their names were later changed to University of Limerick and Dublin City University), offering degrees in engineering, computer science, business, chemistry, industrial design, and management. Limerick is more like U.S. universities in subject matter, business internships, and semester exams. The former president and founder of NIHE Limerick, Edward Walsh, explicitly sought to move the university, as he said, "closer to the marketplace."[44]

The increase in scholarships, in students attending secondary school, and in parents' awareness of the importance of education led to expansion at the university level. That expansion was linked to the type of education that was offered at Limerick and triggered debates between those favoring functional and employment-oriented education (the Department of Education) and those favoring the classical education in the liberal arts (the university faculties). The numbers enrolled in university education exploded: in 1965, 15,000; in 1975–1976, 22,000; in 1985–1986, 34,000; and in 1991–1992, 44,000. While less than 5 percent of students received grants in 1968, over 55 percent of students benefited from some form of grant in 1996. The expansion of courses created a surge in faculty hiring and the creation of new programs and degrees.

Maynooth, with its seminary tradition, was not exempt from these changes and added faculties and departments in 1960. In 1966 Maynooth began enrolling lay male and female students; at the end of the century only one-tenth of the 3,500 Maynooth students are seminarians. At Trinity, after 1970, when the clerical ban on Catholics attending was removed, the student body eventually became 90 percent Catholic and expanded to nearly 10,000 students. Trinity slowly shed some of the veneer of its Anglo-Irish "cricket and cucumber sandwiches" image. In 1995 a Catholic, Thomas Mitchell, was chosen to be provost, and he has been aggressive in integrating Trinity with Irish third-level education. This is symbolized by the partnership with University College Dublin and Notre Dame University forged in 1997. The constituent colleges of Cork, Dublin, and Galway also have felt the pressure of increased numbers, going from 19,200 to 24,800 in the five years from 1987 to 1992, which put extraordinary pressure on their resources. Those institutions have responded with internal transformations that have modified curriculum and management.

After 1964 there was a revolution in Irish education in the domains of secularization, accessibility, levels of completion, curriculum, management, and expansion. The revolution has had an important effect on society as a whole. The transformation corresponded to, and augmented, the rise of economic growth and industrialism. The increase in the level of education has had an effect on the authority of the Church, the role of women, the creation of a middle class, and corresponding shifts in policy demands made on the government.

The educational transformation has provoked different responses from people holding different sets of assumptions about the role of education and the future of Ireland. The language issue (discussed below) was the litmus test for traditional cultural nationalists. Their view is that the education system failed and has contributed to the erosion of the Gaelic nation that was the dream of nineteenth-century nationalists. Left-wing cultural nationalists also lament the emphasis placed on technical education because in their view it transforms young people into a technological labor force for multinational corporations, whose interests lie in their competitiveness in the global economy, not in Ireland or the Irish people. The Church resisted the shift of control of the schools from clerical management and the changes in curriculum, which challenged the central place of religion. University educators preferred a classical liberal education and felt pushed toward commercial and technical education by the government. The governments of the last four decades of the century favored the increase in functional, vocational, and technical education because it served the interests of the broad public (increased employment). The middle class preferred professional education in computers and high technology, engineering, and management because it served the career advancement of their children. Despite these conflicting interests, the education system fundamentally has been bent to the latter two goals.

The Irish Language

The Irish language had been in a state of decline throughout the eighteenth and nineteenth centuries. The rate of loss accelerated in the twentieth century. Language is a powerful mark of identity and is widely used as a central marker of an ethnic community. Irish aspirations for independence were based on the distinctiveness of Irish identity; thus the language was closely tied to Irish nationalism and freedom.

Reasons for the Decline in the Use of Irish

Why in fact the language had declined in Ireland when other relatively small linguistic groups in Europe had not changed their language is a good question. The conventional wisdom was that the expansion of economic activities into the periphery of Ireland from the metropolises of England prompted the shift to English. Classic Irish gave way to a profusion of peasant dialects in the 1700s, and the lack of standardization and the absence of literature, courses, texts, and facilities to print in Irish contributed to the decline. Even so distinguished a figure as Daniel O'Connell noted: "The superior utility of the English tongue, as the medium of modern communication, is so great that I can witness without a sigh the gradual disuse of the Irish." [45] Practical pressure on parents to have their children learn English for employment in England or emigration to the United States accounts for the spread of English. However, as J. J. Lee points out, it does not account for the loss of Irish. [46] Far more likely is that Irish was seen as a symbol of second-rate status by some parents, who sought to ensure that their children would have the tool of social acceptance, the English language.

Moreover, all transactions of importance with the state, services, and patronage were in English. The state was thus an instrument of anglicization in the period of language decline. By 1851 only 25 percent of the Irish spoke Irish as a first language; by 1911 only 12 percent did. English imperialism created ambivalence in the identity of the Irish because the English language was not an epiphenomenal veneer over the Irish language but actually sought to displace it. If to be Irish was to speak Irish, then to be Irish meant more than merely the discontinuation of the use of English: It meant the much more difficult task of the restoration of Irish. The fact that English became the global language of power, commerce, and science made the task all the more difficult.

Reviving Irish

From the time of the founding of the Gaelic League in 1893 the policy of Irish-language revival was to haunt Ireland. The Gaelic League had become associated with Sinn Fein in the early part of the twentieth century because they identified the quest for an independent Ireland with the creation, or restoration, of Gaelic Ireland. The crux of the Gaelic Revival was the revivification of Gaelic, or Irish. Douglas Hyde, co-founder and the first president of the League, had argued in his now famous 1892 manifesto, "The Necessity for De-Anglicizing Ireland," that the authentic Ireland was Gaelic Ireland and that the central facet of that authenticity was the Gaelic language. Through the increasing anglicization of Ireland the nation had lost its true cultural identity. Ireland without her own language, as Hyde and others saw it, was spiritually deficient and the prevalence of English had corrupted Ireland's cultural uniqueness. Restoration of Irish would, for the gaeilgeoiri (the language revivalists), allow the individual to flourish within his or her native culture and allow that culture to flourish among other cultures. While rather sanguine about the blossoming of Gaelic Ireland, Hyde recognized that identity is undoubtedly a less compelling conundrum for a people when all speak the same language, a language that is different from that of their imperial master.

The clear, visible symbol of being non-English was the Irish language, and it was appropriated as part of the Irish identity by Irish nationalism. In the years from 1916 to 1921, when Sinn Fein became politically predominant, the political thrust for independence from Britain was inculcated by the cultural quest to be Catholic and Gaelic. Patrick Pearse felt that the Irish language was an essential element of Irish nationality and that if it disappeared the Irish nation would also. De Valera saw the restoration of Irish as just as important as the elimination of partition.

When the Cosgrave administration took power in the Free State it undertook to revive the Irish language in the hopes, at least for the most dedicated partisans of Gaelic, of replacing English with Irish as the vernacular language. In the schools, the government mandated that the Irish language be the medium of instruction for at least one hour a day and that history and geography be taught in Irish. In 1926 a policy was introduced indicating that Irish should be the medium for instruction in as many subjects as possible and that the time spent on other subjects should be reduced to allow more time for Irish. In effect, a movement of nationalist rebirth was to be realized through the education of the children in the Irish language. The difficulty of, in effect, making the schools the single pillar supporting the groaning weight of such a grand goal was lost in the often dogmatic and authoritarian efforts of the language revivalists. The policy ignored the lack of prepared teachers, the degree to which English had become widespread, and the lack of reinforcement of the Irish language at home or in the everyday world. The country had become part of the orbit of Britain, however much resisted or denied.

Along with the schools, the preservation of the language depended upon the preservation of the regions in which Irish still prevailed as the native tongue. The number of Irish speakers was in steady decline even before the Famine, first from the pressure of pragmatic accommodation to an English-speaking country and second as a result of emigration. From 1881 to 1926, the period of the Gaelic League's greatest influence, the number of Irish-speaking persons dropped 41 percent. The problem then, as now, was a choice between ineffective alternatives. To preserve the language in the Gaeltacht the best policy may have been to leave the region alone. This choice, however, simply meant continuing the disproportionate emigration from the depressed rural areas of the declining west. Development schemes, however, invariably meant introducing commercial ventures, improved management of fishing, and training for new forms of employment, which directly or indirectly would stimulate the use of English. This end was to be avoided. The development projects could be productive in economic restoration but counterproductive for linguistic preservation.

Eventually people began to object to the amount of teaching in Irish and felt that all other educational values were being sacrificed at the altar of a laudable but nearly unachievable goal. The decline in population in the west and the increasing use of English in Ireland persuaded a majority of the teachers to oppose the policy of using Irish as the sole medium of instruction to children of English-speaking families. In fact, the decline of the west was a crisis for the language revivalists, who saw the authentic Ireland in the Gaelic-speaking Catholic people on the land. Emigration was a cultural crisis because the national and cultural ideal was turning out to be no more than a manpower pool of laborers for the factories of Leeds, Birmingham, and London. Absent was crucial reinforcement from the state and its leaders. While the schools labored to carry the burden of a language revival, the leaders of the state often gave no more than lip service to Irish and conducted all the business of the state in English, a policy that did no more to revive the language than it did to dispel the impression among the "plain people of Ireland" that their leaders were more than a little hypocritical about the matter.

The 1940s and 1950s brought about little change in the language situation; the overall number of Irish speakers continued to decline. The one bright light was the development in the 1950s of new words and standardization of Irish in dictionaries and language texts. For the first forty years after independence there was little change in language policy despite the fact that it was not working and that restoration was the professed goal of the state. Garret FitzGerald pointed out in the late 1950s that Radio Eireann's Irish-language news was listened to by only 1 percent of the total audience and plays and other cultural programs in Irish by less than 1 percent.[47] By 1969 there were less than 50,000 native speakers of Irish as rural disintegration took its toll on the Gaeltacht. A government commission's report in 1964 and a government white paper in 1965 both detailed the dismal situation and indicated that Irish could die out as a spoken language in a few decades. There was nothing inevitable about this, of course: Hebrew was not a spoken language 100 years ago but was revitalized and adopted by the Jewish people as the language of Israel.

Both in the schools and in the handling of the Gaeltacht the governments since the 1960s have waffled on the language question. In the face of the persistent decline of Irish speakers and looking to a future in Europe, the goal of restoring the Irish language and creating a dual-language state has shifted to preservation of the Irish language. In 1969 Comhairle na Gaelige was created. This council was to advise the government on the preservation and extension of the Irish language. At the same time, however, the government closed down the all-Irish teacher training colleges in the late 1960s.

The mid-1970s brought about further setbacks to the language revivalists. In 1973 it was no longer necessary to pass an exam in Irish to achieve the secondary school leaving certificate (diploma). The same year brought the elimination of the requirement that civil servants pass Irish in their leaving certificate. Only the requirement that students who wish to enter the National University must take and pass in Irish preserves the language, however indirectly, in an influential strata of society, university graduates. The rapid changes in Ireland after the early 1960s dealt the language movement a blow; if people were concerned about the issue at all, they thought they should be learning French and German, not Irish. Journalist Fergal Tobin notes: "As ever, there was an ocean of good will toward the language, exceeded only by a determination not to speak it or listen to anyone speaking it if that could be avoided."[48] The ambivalence of the populace was revealed in a survey done by the Committee on Irish Language Attitudes. Approximately two-thirds of those responding believed that the Irish language was important to Irish cultural identity, that the Gaeltacht should be supported, and that children should still be taught the language. At the same time, almost the same number of respondents indicated that they were not convinced the language could be passed on to the next generation, they did not know or use much Irish, and they thought the language inappropriate for modern commercial life. This position has been argued by the commercial class throughout the life of the state, despite the fact that people in other countries manage to carry out business activities in languages other than English. By 1975 the number of native Irish speakers had declined to approximately 32,000, and the 1956 definition of the Gaeltacht was obsolete as the area diminished. About 1 percent of the Irish use Irish as a daily first language; the comparable figure for the population of Wales using Welsh is 12 percent.

By the late 1970s partisans of the Irish language, however vigorous or imaginative their efforts, were seeing Irish in the schools, the government, and the Gaeltacht diminish. Recently Irish speakers have taken to demanding that their civil rights be respected because they believe they are being discriminated against in the educational realm, the use of Irish in the media, and the development of the Gaeltacht. This is a substantial distance from Douglas Hyde's call for a de-anglicized, Gaelic-speaking Ireland.

Irish-language pressure groups, even operating in a very sympathetic public and governmental environment, were unable to overcome the inexorable pressures extinguishing Irish in the first four decades after independence. In the last two decades of the century Ireland has undergone substantial economic modernization, a communications explosion, and entry into the European economic and political arena. The probability of a Gaelic revival has scarcely been improved by these changes. Nollaig O'Godhra wrote of the first direct elections to the European Parliament: "The most significant thing about all this, from a language point of view, was the almost total lack of debate about Irish language matters in any of the contests." [49] A supporter of Irish language, O'Godhra reveals more than he intends in juxtaposing the new door to Europe with the utter lack of concern for the Irish language.

Sometimes the effort to preserve the language inadvertently reveals the degree to which it is at the margins of Irish life. The Joint Committee on the Irish Language, in a 1984 report on the extension of the use of Irish in the Dail and Seanad, urged that the members submit one of their questions for Parliamentary Question Time in Irish. Such a pathetic recommendation hardly seems destined to make Ireland monolingually Gaelic. Other than in formalities, the cupla focal, scarcely a word of Irish is heard in the Dail; if it were used most members would be at a loss to comprehend what was said. This is the legislature empowered under a constitution that declares Irish to be the national language. In 1983 the Bord na Gaeilige issued a report, *Action Plan for Irish 1983–1986*, calling for one-third of the people of Ireland to be competent Irish speakers, one-third to have basic ability in speaking Irish, and the remaining third to have a basic knowledge of Irish by the year 2000. In 1991 the goals remained unfulfilled and the number of Irish speakers, defined as speaking Irish only or Irish and English, was about 31 percent of the population. (This number is about 4 percent higher than in 1961, and the growth is greater in cities.) Impressionistic evidence would support the idea that Irish is being used more and more. It is certainly apparent in Galway, where the proximity to the Gaeltacht and the vibrant cultural life of the city present Irish as more than a quaint nationalist artifact. Yet the fact remains that those who speak Irish most are in school and between the ages of ten and nineteen. Of the adults, two-thirds indicate that they never speak the language or use it less than once a week.

Successes in Reviving Irish

The most notable advances in Irish are the creation of the all-Irish schools outside of the Gaeltacht which, while funded by the government, have come about due to the pressure of parents. Since 1972 the number of all-Irish primary schools has increased from eleven to eighty and the number of all-Irish secondary schools increased by twelve from 1980 to 1994. The parents support these schools because they consider them better than the regular schools and because they are committed to the preservation of Irish. The question is, will there be enough media, enough speakers of Irish, and enough common use to reach a critical mass, or will the use of Irish by these graduates decline to the point where it is used only in somewhat contrived circumstances or just dusted off for use in an occasional play?

The students do have one advantage from having gone to Irish schools: They can watch Telefis na Gaelige. Credited to the diligent efforts of Minister of Arts, Culture, and the Gaeltacht, Michael D. Higgins, the station began broadcasting in October 1996. The project at the outset faced the paradox of incandescent support from Irish-language partisans but general political and public indifference. The cost was seen as too high and questions were raised about what programming would be available to fill the broadcasting hours. Higgins was successful in getting the government to fund the station at 10 million punts ($15 million) a year. Initial problems were poor reception and a lack of programming, but the station turned out to be far more attractive to viewers than originally thought. Scheduled to put on two hours of Irish-language broadcasting per day, the station has put on four and one-half per day. The remaining four hours of broadcasts are in English, including live coverage of the Dail. The daily audience in 1999 was 310,000 people, more than for MTV and SKY News. The programming has been imaginative, to the delight of the producers, and is attracting those who do not speak the language as viewers. Three programs have won international awards.

The increase in the numbers of speakers of the Irish language appears to be a function of the renaissance in Irish culture, which occurred in literature, music, dance, and drama over the last decade of the century. The number of prominent writers in Irish has increased and their works have been recognized. The number of books published in Irish has increased, with 2,400 titles available in Irish in 1990. But the language has more vitality in traditional Irish music and poetry than it does in the day-to-day life of Ireland. In a 1994 survey reported by James Blake, the Irish people reflected that persistent combination of admiration for the language and recognition of it as a cultural symbol with an utter lack of interest in using the language. Only 10 percent can conduct a conversation in Irish, only 43 percent are Irish speakers, and 70 to 80 percent do not use Irish at all.[50] Modernization both creates and destroys, but no society ever abandons its old culture completely. The Irish language will live on, probably more sung and recited than spoken, and will be preserved as an important symbol more by conservators of culture than by government policies. The inexorable pressures of Europeanization and globalization will counterbalance the language resurgence, and the Irish language will still be an issue of ambivalence as the Irish find a new identity outside the orbit of English cultural imperialism. Ultimately the global culture will create more pressure than the English culture; Douglas Hyde could not have foreseen that the Irish language would be far more "Los Angelesized" than anglicized.

Notes

1. Quoted in Thomas J. O'Hanlon, *The Irish: Portrait of a People* (London: Andre Deutsch, 1976), p. 167, and numerous other places. Michele Dowling, in "The Ireland That I Would Have . . . ," pp. 37–41, argues that de Valera was putting forth an aspiration that was a product of Irish history and culture and thus his statement should not be derided as merely a personal, highly romantic, and distorted image of Ireland at the time.

2. C. E. Black, *The Dynamics of Modernization* (New York: Harper & Row, 1966). The concept of modernization is itself contentious as a tool of analysis to assess political and economic change and went through a period of scholarly ascendancy and then decline. In this work the term is used to identify the changes between two conditions of the Irish society at different times but is not to be seen as fidelity to a monocausal political and social theory.

3. *The European Recovery Programme: Ireland's Long Term Programme (1949–1953)* (Dublin: Department of Foreign Affairs, 1948), p. 21.

4. *Industrial Potentials of Ireland An Appraisal* (Philadelphia: IBEC Technical Services Corporation, 1952), p. 80.

5. Ibid., p. 80.

6. Ibid., p. 92.

7. *Dollar Exports: Report of U.S. Consultants* (Dublin: Stationery Office, 1953), pp. 5–6.

8. Richard B. Finnegan and James L. Wiles, "The Invisible Hand or Hands Across the Water: American Consultant's and Irish Economic Policy," *Eire-Ireland* 30, no. 2 (Summer 1995), p. 48.

9. Kieran Kennedy and Brendan Dowling, *Economic Growth in Ireland, The Experience Since 1947* (Dublin: Gill & Macmillan, 1975), p. 216.

10. Brown, *Ireland: A Social and Cultural History*, p. 212. Brown points out that in 1957 there were 54,000 emigrants, yet 78,000 people were unemployed that year.

11. Kerby A. Miller, *Emigrants and Exiles: Ireland and the Irish Exodus to North America* (Oxford: Oxford University Press, 1985), p. 578.

12. *Commission on Emigration and Other Population Problems, 1948–1954 Reports* (Dublin: Stationery Office, 1954).

13. *Capital Investment Advisory Committee Third Report* (Dublin: Stationery Office, 1958).

14. What the actual turning point was is a question that is examined in James L. Wiles and Richard B. Finnegan, *Aspirations and Realities, A Documentary History of Economic Development Policy in Ireland Since 1922* (Westport Conn.: Greenwood Press, 1993), pp. 69–94.

15. F. S. L. Lyons, *Ireland Since the Famine* (London: Fontana, 1973), p. 628.

16. See Ronnie Munck, *The Irish Economy: Results and Prospects* (London: Pluto Press, 1993), pp. 41–46; and D. O'Hearn, "The Irish Case of Dependency: An Exception to the Exceptions," *American Sociological Review* 54 (1989), pp. 578–596.

17. Richard B. Finnegan, "Irish Drive for Growth Is Working," *Patriot Ledger*, 16 June 1986, p. 23.

18. This represents an important shift in Irish government policy. Wiles and Finnegan, *Aspirations and Realities*, pp. 157–165.

19. National Economic and Social Council, *A Strategy for Development 1986–1990* (Dublin: National Economic and Social Council, 1986).

20. Quoted in Lee, *Ireland 1912–1985*, p. 501.

21. Brigid Laffan and Rory O'Donnell, "Ireland and the Growth of International Governanace," in *Ireland and the Politics of Change*, ed. W. Crotty and D. E. Schmitt (New York: Longman, 1998), pp. 164–165.

22. Kieran A. Kennedy, "The Context of Economic Development," in *The Development of Industrial Society in Ireland*, ed. J. Goldthorpe and C. T. Whelan (Oxford: Oxford University Press, 1992), p. 7. Much of this section is drawn from Kennedy's excellent essay.

23. Raymond Crotty, *Ireland in Crisis: A Study in Colonial Capitalist Underdevelopment* (Dingle: Brandon, 1986).

24. E. O'Malley, *Industry and Economic Development: The Challenge of the Latecomer* (Dublin: Gill & Macmillan, 1989).

25. *The Causes of Industrial Failure in Ireland and Suggestions for Action* (Dublin: Industrial Policy Review Group, Ministery for Industry and Commerce, 1992), pp. 2, 3.

26. Finnegan and Wiles, "The Invisible Hand," p. 53.

27. Kennedy, "Context," p. 17.

28. Lee, in *Ireland 1912–1985*, in the section on identity, roams far from economic variables, examining the place of the Irish language as a marker of Irish identity and citing the New Ireland Forum as an example of the difficulty of addressing identity not only in the homogeneous Republic but with respect to the whole island.

29. *Industrial Potentials of Ireland*, p. 80.

30. *The Causes for Failure in Industrial Projects in Ireland and Suggestions for Action* (Dublin: Industrial Policy and Review Group, Ministry for Industry and Commerce, 1992), p. 3.

31. The sense of excitement and energy is captured in Fergal Tobin's *The Best of Decades: Ireland in the 1960s* (Dublin: Gill & Macmillan, 1984).

32. Ibid., p. 167. Tobin notes that Professor T. S. Wheeler of UCD, addressing Irish science teachers in 1962, indicated that a student trained in the 1880s would have a good chance of passing the science matriculation exam.

33. Brendan OhEithir, *The Begrudger's Guide to Irish Politics* (Dublin: Poolbeg, 1986), pp. 28–38.

34. Tobin, *Best of Decades*, pp. 11–119.

35. Although in 1903, when proposals for the creation of a Catholic university were being discussed, Trinity made the offer to include more Catholics and to put safeguards on their faith and morals in place, the offer was rejected by the Hierarchy. Seamus O'Buachalla, *Educational Policy in Twentieth Century Ireland* (Dublin: Wolfhound Press, 1988), p. 55.

36. *Investment in Education, Report of a Survey Team Appointed by the Minister for Education in Conjunction with the OECD,* 2 vols. (Dublin: Stationery Office, 1965, 1966).

37. Tobin, *Best of Decades*, p. 169.

38. Quoted in the *Times Educational Supplement,* 13 June 1952; reproduced in A. C. Hepburn, ed., *The Conflict of Nationality in Ireland* (New York: St. Martin's Press, 1980), p. 140.

39. Tobin, *Best of Decades*, pp. 169–170: Keogh, *Twentieth Century Ireland*, pp. 272–273: Lee, *Ireland 1912–1985,* p. 397; and O'Buachalla, *Educational Policy,* pp. 72–73.

40. Keogh, *Twentieth Century Ireland*, p. 276.

41. O'Buachalla, *Educational Policy*, p. 320.

42. R. North and J. Coolahan, "Education," in *Political Issues in Ireland Today,* ed. Neil Collins (Manchester: Manchester University Press, 1994), pp. 178–179.

43. O'Buachalla, *Educational Policy*, pp. 122–132.

44. Quoted in John Ardagh, *Ireland and the Irish* (London: Hamish Hamilton, 1994), p. 220.

45. Brown, *Ireland: A Social and Cultural History,* p. 273.

46. Lee, *Ireland 1912–1985,* p. 662.

47. Garret FitzGerald, "Radio Listenership and the TV Problem," *University Review* 2, no. 5 (1968), p. 44; quoted in Gibbon, *Transformations*, p. 76.

48. Tobin, *Best of Decades.*

49. Nollaig O'Ghadra, "Language Report: The Fortunes of Irish 1979," *Eire-Ireland* 15 (1980), p. 129.

50. James Blake, "Irish in Education and the Media, 1994," *Eire-Ireland* 29, no. 4 (Winter 1994, pp. 161–163.

5

MIXED MESSAGES: THE CATHOLIC CHURCH AND THE MEDIA

Two institutions, not at all similar, have conveyed the messages about the same things to the Irish people since the 1960s. For the better part of the twentieth century the Catholic Church held what sociologist Tom Inglis called the "moral monopoly" in Ireland. The Church possessed the capacity not only to set moral standards but, in a more comprehensive way, to establish the language of morality; the social as well as theological measure of appropriate behavior; and the clerical, social, and even governmental sanctions that would maintain beliefs and behaviors.[1] The Church dealt with both the simplest matters of ordinary life and the most profound questions of human existence. The depth of the Church writ, moral authority, and legitimacy was more profound than any other social institution. In the 1980s and 1990s that authority and legitimacy eroded with startling rapidity.

The media, on the other hand, are an institution defined in many ways by their lack of profundity because it is focused on the present, provides entertainment and distraction, and presents the events of the day in an endless succession of images that flatten out meaning. Under the hand of the censor for the better part of the century, the media in Ireland emerged after the 1960s to provide a Niagara of messages to the Irish people. The media channeled ideas, values, and information from outside Ireland; pierced the veil of synthetic uniformity in behavior and belief; and exposed the gaps between the words of politicians and their actions, the moral precepts of the Church and the behavior of priests, and the social norms of people and social behavior. In doing so they increasingly shifted the legitimacy of messages from reliance on a single source to a multiplicity of voices.

The Catholic Church

The Roman Catholic faith in Ireland emerged from the eras of the Penal Laws and the independence movement tenaciously bonded to the Irish people. The conjunction of political oppression and religious oppression under the Penal Laws and of the Church's fight for religious liberty with the Irish quest for political liberty associated devotion to the Church with devotion to the country. Moreover, the Gaelic Ireland movement connected Catholicism with Irish cultural identity. The convergence of these forces created a religious institution that was more revered and powerful than in virtually any other European state.

The evolution of the Church in the late nineteenth century created a structure that was by the turn of the century profoundly hierarchical, paternal, and authoritarian. Religious doctrines were theologically rigid and absolutist in character. Rather Manichaean and puritanical, the Irish Catholic Church had historically stressed the inviolability of established dogma and practice, the purity of the soul, the degradation of the flesh, the authority of the hierarchy, and the importance of devotional expressions. It had not always been so. The structure of the modern Irish Church is the work of Cardinal Paul Cullen and the devotional revolution that took place between 1850 and 1875.

Were this merely a matter of the interaction of the Church with its parishioners, our interest would be limited to the Catholic culture of Ireland. In fact, the Catholic Church and its Hierarchy was deeply intertwined with the structure and policy of the Free State of Ireland, the 1937 Constitution, and critical policy debates on Church–state relations up to the 1990s. The Church was directly active on numerous pieces of legislation. More important, the Church created the climate of values and morality that would exclude other types of legislation from being considered. The result was the convergence of liberal democratic and Catholic values in Church–state relations in Ireland.

The Catholic Church is at once an institution, a theology, and a collection of individuals, leaders, and followers. Every aspect of the Church has had an impact on the Irish State, north and south, and the interface between the Church and the state is considered in many areas of this book, from education to women's rights.

Church and State

In the framework of the Free State, the Church had undergone a difficult period during the struggle for independence as it opposed the actions of the anti-Treaty forces and found itself traversing those bitter divides during the Civil War. After the Civil War the Church not only actively sought to have its policies adopted but was pressing its case on a most receptive Cosgrave administration. Cosgrave advanced legislation in accord with Irish Catholic principles and dogmas on divorce, censorship, school management, and curriculum. The assertion of Catholic identity and Catholic legislation can be seen as an opportunity on the part of Irish nationalists to differentiate themselves from their colonial master and shape the society in accord with their dominant values. Clearly not at odds with the interests of the Church, the convergence produced legislation that was satisfying to all but liberals, who perceived a threat to ideas and beliefs in this comfortable elision of a Catholic nation into a Catholic state.

The 1937 Constitution (discussed below) would only have made the state more subservient to the Church were it not for de Valera's need to have a document that he saw as eventually accommodating the Protestants of Northern Ireland. The de Valera years produced little friction in the realms of censorship, social policy, and family law. In practice the influence of the Church took the form of enforcing a sexual puritanism, supporting the legislation of Church doctrine in family matters, and opposing state intervention in social policy.

The Church saw the temptations of a secular, atheistic, and modern world everywhere, and these temptations invariably assumed a sexual form. Every conceivable human situation was fraught with the danger of sexual license, and the Church sought to extirpate such lures of the flesh. In the rigid sexual segregation of the county's school systems, as well as in other social settings, Irish Catholic paranoia was enforced. The dance hall was deemed particularly dangerous; the Church persistently insisted that dance halls be regulated because they "lent themselves not so much to rhythm as to low sensuality."[2] "Imported dances" seemed particularly dangerous to moral probity; native Irish dances seemed free of these temptations unless coupled with drink, which could then lead to concupiscent consequences. Thus the Church did not discourage the legislation of 1924 and 1927 limiting the hours and the number of "pubs" or public houses.

The support for the censorship laws of 1923 and 1929 reflected clerical concern with the temptations of "evil literature" from Britain, which was seen as destroying parental authority and eroding the morals of the young. The censorship laws reflect a concern with doctrine as well because literature that contained any treatment of contraception, especially a favorable view, was also denied to the people of Ireland. The pressure of the Church regarding sexual purity was reinforced in a thousand direct and indirect ways, from the stern glance of the priest at a young couple holding hands to novenas and retreats filled with preaching against the sins of the flesh. The only voice of opposition to censorship came from a small clique of intellectuals, such as Yeats and O'Faolain, who made no dent in the public's attitude and who were roundly condemned by authoritarian Catholics.

The second area of Church concern was the realm of doctrine. The Church's doctrine on marriage holds that marriage is an inviolate and permanent union (holding aside the granting of annulments, in which the Church holds that the marriage never existed in the first place). Thus the Church opposed divorce and supported the Cosgrave government's 1922 Act precluding legal divorce. In the

1937 Constitution this law was elevated to a constitutional directive in Article 41, which states: "No law shall be enacted providing for the grant of a dissolution of marriage." Thus to legalize divorce in Ireland required a constitutional amendment rather than simply legislative change. In Catholic doctrine the primary purpose of marriage is procreation of children and only secondarily the companionship of the marriage bond. Thus contraception was considered a violation of the natural law. Consequently, in 1935 legislation was passed that included a ban on the importation and sale of contraceptives.

The Church's position on education was reflected in the extensive clerical control of the educational system and the intensity with which the Hierarchy preserved that domain. Ninety-eight percent of the schools were run by the Catholic Church or orders thereof. The education of children in the faith was firmly in the hands of the teaching orders, especially the Christian Brothers. Any threat to the transmission and reinforcement of the faith was to be eliminated. The Church's ban on attending Trinity College is illustrative. Trinity, as a Protestant ascendancy school, was viewed with a jaundiced eye by the Hierarchy. In 1927 the National Council of Bishops stated: "Since there are within the Free State three University Colleges sufficiently safe in regard to faith and morals, we, therefore strictly inhibit, and under pain of grave sin, we forbid all clerics by advise or otherwise, to recommend parents or others having charge of youth to send young persons in their charge to Trinity College."[3] This ban was made more explicit by the Archbishop of Dublin John C. McQuaid, in 1944, when he forbade attendance at Trinity College without his permission to those in his diocese under pain of mortal sin. In 1956 this position was endorsed by all the bishops in Ireland when they forbade students from any diocese from attendance without the archbishop of Dublin's permission. The permission would be granted if there were sufficient "guarantees against the danger of perversion."[4] This ban included not only Trinity College but all non-Catholic schools because only the Church was competent to determine what training augmented or corrupted Catholic education.

The third area of Church influence was social policy. The general thrust of the Church was anti-statist. Not only was this reflected in the 1937 Constitution, where the right to private property is enshrined, but also in the vocational emphasis adopted by the Church during this period. In 1944 a report was issued by a commission chaired by the bishop of Galway, calling for diminishing the centralization of bureaucratic control in Irish government because it was inefficient and insensitive.[5] The state, the report declared, should instead operate through the already existing vocational organizations. That same year the bishop of Clonfert called for reorganization of the medical services and other social services into a social insurance scheme supported, not by the state, but by the contributing members. The report was ignored by the Fianna Fail government, but it did reflect Church thought on the role of the state bureaucracy in the vocational or social sphere during the period. Essentially the Church wanted to deny the state the

In ironic juxtaposition the abandoned Church of Ireland Chapel at Inchigeelah, County Cork, is surrounded by a host of Catholic graves as indicated by the footstones and the Celtic cross in the foreground.
Photo © 1999 Clare O'Neill

role of supplanting the family or the vocational sectors of society in the provision of social services.

In the realms of education, social life, and family law, the Church's moral vision and doctrine held sway. This is not to suggest that such positions were imposed upon a recalcitrant people. On the contrary, the Cosgrave and de Valera administrations, including the Labour Party, embraced these norms wholeheartedly. The devout public offered no resistance. Observers repeatedly noted both the intensity of the devotion of the Irish people and its comprehensiveness. Paul Blanchard, a sharp critic of Irish Catholicism, noted in the 1950s the domination of the Catholic Church and then commented that "the majority of the Irish people do not resent this domination. They accept it as organic and established parts of Irish life." [6] (Raising the question as to the meaning of his word "domination.") Church attendance exceeded that of other Catholic countries (90 percent of the population); confession, novenas, stations of the cross, and other devotional practices were ever-present. The telling of beads, the doff of the hat at a church, pilgrimages, books, and pious phrases in conversation all added to a pervasive presence of Catholicism, which infused the political culture with a disposition toward Church authority and, more broadly, authoritarianism in other realms of life such as school and politics. Sociologist Tom Inglis notes the disposition of the Irish toward two types of religiosity: the magical-devotional and the legalistic-orthodox. The Irish display the first type of practice not only in the Church's liturgy with the transubstantiation of bread and wine into body and blood but also in the "myriad little rituals" used to appease God; please God; or open a special channel to the transcendental, such as holy wells, special appeals to the unique powers of saints, and healing rituals.[7] Special shrines or places attract large numbers of people; penitential acts of mortification and fasting were common at Croagh Patrick and other sites.

The legalistic approach to religious behavior was focused on the rules and regulations of the institutional Church. Salvation came not only in the form of faith but also in the necessity to adhere to the formal rules of the Church. The Church has returned to a new catechism, but the Irish had adhered to a catechismic form of religion for more than 100 years. Lists of do's and don'ts; lists of sins; estimates of the severity of sins; and specific obligations such as attending Mass, receiving communion, going to confession, and fasting all were spelled out by the Church in great detail. Adherence to these rules was widespread and highly formalistic because people believed that to not follow the rules as exactly specified would vitiate the benefits of the behavior. Belief was subsumed into a programmatic legalism enforced by the watchful eye of the pastor, mother, or teacher. Resentment or rebellion was suppressed and people adopted a docile posture with respect to the Church and its authority. The result of this particular combination of Church organization, doctrine, and devotion made Ireland among the most Catholic of Catholic countries, with a powerful institutional Church at the top level of society and a strong grassroots connection to the people at the level of the parish.

Confrontation in the social sphere between the Church and the state arose on the matter of providing health care in the early 1950s. The Mother and Child Health Plan brought the Church's doctrinal opposition into the public arena. The plan was advanced by Doctor Noel Browne, the minister for Health, who had been monumentally important in the effort to control tuberculosis in Ireland. Headstrong, and at the same time naive about political infighting by heavy-weights, Browne supported a plan put forth by his predecessor to provide pre- and post-natal care to mothers and medical care to children up to the age of sixteen, without a test of low income. The Cabinet had developed an accommodation with Archbishop McQuaid of Dublin, a personal friend of Prime Minister Costello, which gave him "the unsolicited but effective power of veto over government action in certain spheres."[8] The Church opposed the expansion of the state into the social sphere in general. This opposition to the state's right to legislate on matters the Church considered doctrinally important was reflected in the statements of the Bishop of Tuam to the prime minister during the controversy: "The right to provide for the physical education of the child belongs to the family and not the State. Experience has shown that physical or health education is closely interwoven with important moral questions on which the Catholic Church has definite teachings. Education in regard to motherhood includes instruction in regard to sex relations, chastity and marriage. The State has no competence to give instructions in such matters."[9]

In this case the Church was concerned with two crucial issues. The first was the extension of state services into what the Church regarded as the inviolate sphere of the family. The potential danger was so great that James Staunton, the secretary to the Hierarchy, had written to the prime minister that the plan was "an instrument for future totalitarian aggression." [10] The incipient threat of totalitarianism aside, the plan also created the potential for that service to introduce ideas that might be at variance with Church doctrine on that apparently most compelling of matters, sexual behavior. Staunton writes that the idea that local medical authorities could have the right to tell women how to behave concerning "sex relations, chastity and marriage" would be viewed by the Church with "the greatest apprehension."[11] That the Mother and Child Health Plan was to be administered by doctors who were overwhelmingly Catholic did not moderate the Church's opposition.

Browne had met with the archbishop and was under the impression that he had satisfied the Hierarchy; however, he went ahead with his plan without being sure he had the full backing of the Cabinet. The bishops rejected the plan, repeating their objections to Browne, and the Cabinet would not support Browne on the issue because most members were not ready to cross the Hierarchy in 1951. Prime Minister Costello stated in the Dail: "I am an Irishman second: I am a Catholic first" and declared that he would "accept without qualification in all respects the teaching of the hierarchy and the Church to which I belong."[12] The telling aspect of this declaration, and that of Cosgrave on the matter of divorce thirty years earlier, was the utter lack of consideration of the possibility that the state was an autonomous actor that could independently determine that natal care might be in the public interest and thus a public responsibility.

Browne was forced to resign from the Cabinet, his departure brought on by the Mother and Child Plan but abetted no doubt by the members of the government growing tired of his brusque personality. Sean McBride, the head of Browne's party Clann na Publachta, did not support Browne and in correspondence to him said, "It was impossible to ignore the view of the hierarchy." Browne reminded McBride of his earlier anti-clericalism and described his position as "a model of the two faced hypocrisy and humbug so characteristic of you."[13] When the next election was held Clann na Publachta was decimated, falling from ten seats to two, with McBride barely holding his seat, but Browne was re-elected as an independent, providing him some sort of symbolic revenge.

Lost in the issues of Church opposition to the issues of sexuality and gynecological information was the fact that the plan called for these services to be paid for by the state for everyone. The plan was opposed by doctors, who saw the fact that the state would set the fees as a threat to their income and declared that it would bring about socialized medicine. The mustering of opposition to the plan by the medical profession was as much as important to the defeat of the plan as was the opposition of the bishops. Another bill was passed by the subsequent Fianna Fail government of de Valera that was also opposed by the Irish Medical Association and the Hierarchy. De Valera's symbolic concessions to the Hierarchy in the form of amendments were, of course, far more politically deft than Browne's intransigence.

The Church and a Changing Irish Society

As Ireland stood on the brink of rapid economic and social changes, the Church was fixed in a mode not substantially different from that of a century earlier: pervasive, powerful, and puritanical. Just as Cardinal Paul Cullen shaped the Irish Catholic Church in the latter part of the nineteenth century, so Archbishop John Charles McQuaid of Dublin put his imprint on the Church for thirty-two years. Serving from 1940 until 1972, McQuaid encouraged a wide range of Church building and Catholic charitable organizations but coupled his ministrations with a rigid sexual and theological code. Determined to preserve Ireland from the rapidly moving currents of modernization, McQuaid imposed his chaste taste on newspaper advertisements, editorials, films and film advertising, plays produced in Dublin, and sports and social activity among young people. McQuaid is noted for his oft-quoted remark upon returning to Ireland from the Second Vatican Council: "Allow me to reassure you no change will worry the tranquillity of your Christian lives."[14] McQuaid was wrong, of course; neither he nor anyone else could hold back the hands of the clock. Not only was Ireland changing, but the Church itself, under the impetus of the Vatican Councils, was destined to undergo substantial transformation.

The signs of change in the Church actually began in a slow trickle. In the early 1950s new Catholic periodicals such as *The Furrow* (1950) and *Doctrine and Life* (1951) began to identify the principal features of Irish Catholicism— anti-intellectualism, dogmatism, and authoritarianism—and questioned whether these would serve a new Ireland in extensive contact with a wider, and obviously more secular, European world. John Kelly, a Jesuit priest, put the matter rather bluntly: "To many people in Ireland today we are trying to make do with a peasant religion when they are no longer peasants anymore. We are a growing and developing middle-class nation, acquiring a middle-class culture and we must have a religion to fit our needs."[15]

External and internal impulses for change produced a series of intended and unintended consequences. The same generational change that had occurred when de Valera passed the torch to Sean Lemass in politics was also occurring in the Church, albeit more slowly. Those bishops who had worked their will on Irish moral life and social policy in the 1930s and 1940s were giving way to another generation of clerical leaders who were somewhat more flexible than, say, Archbishop McQuaid. The self-analysis of the Church begun by clerics in the 1950s took the form of sociological analyses in which writings on the Church and Irish society slowly shifted from accumulating litanies of purportedly immoral acts to examining the empirical foundations of Irish society and Irish religious life.

Concomitant with shifting sociological perspectives was the changing posture of the Church on the role of state intervention. As a more realistic portrait of Irish society emerged—the declining west with its desperate poverty, poor health conditions, and ramshackle housing—Irish churchmen began to reverse their anti-statist doctrines and to call for more state intervention. This "volte face" not only called for increased state activism but also criticized the government for lapses in its support of decent economic standards of living. In 1966 Cardinal Conway, archbishop of Armagh, noted in a speech that the expansion of the state into the social sphere depended on the political and economic conditions and that the fears expressed twenty years earlier about state activism were exaggerated.[16] That exaggeration had been a hallmark of the Church's fear that totalitarianism in Ireland would come from the Left and be a threat to human liberty. The reality was that the threat to liberty was far more likely to come in the form of authoritarian Catholicism and nationalism.

Notable in terms of the Church's changing position was the 1977 pastoral letter "The Work of Justice," which called for alleviation of the problems of poverty and unemployment. Such a reversal of views reflected the impact of Pope John XXIII, who initiated great changes in the Catholic Church through his personal actions, the Second Vatican Council (1962–1965), and his encyclical "Mater and Magistera" (1961). The Vatican Council examined all those doctrines that were characteristic of the tridentine, rigid, and dogmatic Church and attempted to find a place for the Church in the modern world. The encyclical jettisoned vocationalism and accepted the valid role of state responsibility in the social welfare sphere. These changes were absorbed by the Church in all countries but more slowly in Ireland.

The Irish bishops did not meet with President Ronald Reagan on his visit to Ireland in 1984. It was not an oversight. They refrained from meeting with the president in solidarity with Bishop Eamonn Casey and his opposition to the abuse of human rights by the United States in Central America. The irony of the bishops' absence was that Reagan was the quintessential Cold War president, whose opposition to atheistic communism the bishops would have admired. The bishops' position came from the increasing concern for social justice as part of the Church's mission and the particular affinity the Irish Church had with the developing nations because of the number of missionaries who had worked in Latin America. The younger priests, shaped to a greater degree by Vatican II and by the ideas of liberation theology, came to focus on the ills of Irish society as well as the abuses of human rights and economic injustices in the less-developed world. The anti-statist position of the Church, which corresponded to the position of business and governmental elites in Ireland in the 1950s, began to change, and in the next twenty years the idea that government had responsibility for addressing social injustice emerged.

Within the Church the position on censorship began to change, at least among the younger clergy. Reviews of literature and films banned in Ireland were published in the early 1960s in *The Furrow*. The approach of some authors, such as Peter Connally and John Kelly, was to ignore the polemics over censorship and evaluate the aesthetic or artistic merit of the works. This open confrontation with what Father Connally called a juvenile standard of censorship indicated that moral principles need not be compromised in appreciating and learning from modern literature and film. Brian Lenihan, minister for Justice, liberalized the process of censorship for film in 1964 and for books in 1967. The ban on literature discussing birth control was simply overwhelmed by the avalanche of debate on that topic that was spurred by Vatican II and by the publication in 1968 of Pope Paul VI's encyclical on birth control, "Humanae Vitae." Virtually every magazine and newspaper in Ireland, to say nothing of television, would have fallen under the ban were it applied. Archbishop McQuaid and Bishop Lucey spoke out against the liberalization of censorship, of course, but they represented a view with which many younger clergy were out of sympathy at the time.

The government undertook extensive reform in education during the 1960s. These efforts transgressed on a heretofore sacrosanct area of Church control. Surprisingly, the transformation of curriculum, management, state support, and the creation of new schools was remarkably free of the acrimony that would no doubt have accompanied such events had they occurred in the 1920s or 1930s. The ban on Catholic students attending Trinity College was lifted in 1970. Increasingly lay control was increased as parents, now themselves university educated and more cosmopolitan, were willing to challenge, however gently, the power of the clerics over the schools.

One of the most concrete symbols of the Catholicity of the Irish Republic was Article 44 of the Constitution, which enshrined the Catholic Church in a special position in the state. A 1967 report of an all-party committee of the Dail, charged with a review of the Constitution, recommended the elimination of this section.[17] The recommendation was based on the recognition that the article was especially offensive to Ulster Protestants and thus exacerbated differences between the north and south of Ireland. Contrary to expectations, fulminations were not forthcoming from the Hierarchy. The bishops concurred with the recommendation and in December 1972 the Constitution was amended. By 1972 the intensity of the conflict in Northern Ireland was such that the constitutional change did little to soften the utterly intransigent attitude of Ulster unionists. Revealing, however, was the lack of opposition on the part of the Church on a matter that on the face of it would seem to have been central to its traditional position.

The same 1967 report on constitutional reform also raised an issue that confronted Church doctrine directly: divorce. The committee argued that the blanket prohibition on divorce was unjust to the Protestant minority in the Republic, for whom divorce was not theologically unacceptable. Again, the differences between Northern Ireland and the Republic were raised because the ban on divorce was read by Northern Protestants as evidence of discrimination by a Catholic state against religious minorities. The committee recommended that the Constitution be amended to allow divorce for those who were married in a religion that held divorce acceptable.

The Church responded quickly and sharply to this suggestion. Divorce, Archbishop McQuaid flatly stated, is contrary to the law of God. Cardinal Conway chose to speak for the Protestant community when he noted, "few of them believe in divorce still fewer of them want it," a bold presumption on his part to be sure.[18] The brunt of the Church's argument, however, was that allowing divorce for Protestants would rapidly expand to allowing divorce for all people in the Republic and would result in grave evils and suffering for society. In the late 1960s the established view prevailed, but in the ensuing decades the pressure for a divorce law accelerated in three ways. First was a marked shift in public opinion about the acceptability of such a law. Second was the rise of women's groups, who saw the need for a divorce law to provide rights and legal status for separated women, who existed in a legal limbo. Third was the recognition by the political parties, such as Fine Gael, that the problems created by marital breakdown had to be confronted. As noted in Chapter 6, the Church's opposition to a change in the Constitution was sufficient to defeat the 1986 amendment on allowing divorce but was insufficient to change the 1996 referendum.

The response of the Church was crystal clear on the question of contraception. The 1935 Act prohibiting the importation and sale of contraceptives was the backdrop for the developments of the 1970s. Although forbidden, the use of contraceptives was in fact increasing in Ireland, and in 1969 a family planning clinic opened in Dublin that distributed contraceptives. The first formal challenge to the law came in 1971 when then Senator, and later President, Mary Robinson and two other senators, John Horgan and Trevor West, introduced a bill to facilitate the availability of contraceptives. They argued that, as with divorce, a blanket prohibition penalized those who had no religious strictures against contraceptives. The Lynch government had little interest in grasping this nettle and it was voted down in the Senate, as was a similar bill in the Dail in 1972.

The redoubtable Archbishop McQuaid had a letter read from the pulpit against this bill, noting that it was contrary to Church doctrine. McQuaid also indicated the deleterious effects contraception would have on that perennial concern, sexual morality: "Given the proneness of our human nature to evil, given the enticements of bodily satisfaction, given the widespread modern incitement to unchastity, it must be evident that an access, hitherto unlawful, to contraceptive devices will prove a most certain occasion of sin."[19] The question of the relationship of Church and state was still one in which the Church defined the objective moral law; a law making contraceptives available would be a matter of public morality and thus a "curse upon our country." McQuaid indicated that a right to contraception was a "right that cannot even exist."[20]

The introduction of a contraceptive bill again in 1973 prompted a strong statement from the Hierarchy, which painted a bleak portrait of the ills that would result in the Republic of Ireland from the availability of contraceptives. Infidelity, illegitimate children, abortion, disease, and the destruction of marriage would prevail, according to the bishops. The concern, stated the bishops, was not the moral question of using contraceptives, because the Church had spoken already on that matter, but the effect such a law would have on the quality of life in Ireland. The state was not bound to limit the sale of contraceptives just because the Church said so. The Church thus defined its role differently in this instance, self-consciously adopting the posture of a pressure group advocating for a policy that was for the common good rather than that of a transcendental institution claiming the right to instruct the state about what to do on matters involving morality. The Church had made clear its enduring position opposing birth control, but the message was being directed at the people as a matter of their faith and conscience rather than at the state.

This is not to suggest that the Church was so naive as not to realize the obvious connection that what people were told from the pulpit could obviously be enacted at the ballot box, but it did represent an important shift in the assumptions and expectations of both the Hierarchy and the legislators. The days of the Mother and Child Plan, when the Hierarchy could assume control of the behavior of the government and Dail members as subservient Catholics, were departing.

The tentative legislative debate on contraception was abruptly accelerated in 1973 when the Supreme Court of Ireland declared the pertinent sections of the 1935 Act unconstitutional and legalized the importation of contraceptives. The government had to come to terms with the problem of legalization of contraceptives and their availability and sale. The debate ranged from condemnation of the

Court's decision and pressure for a complete ban from such conservative groups as the Irish Family League to pressure for unrestricted availability of contraceptives from such groups as the Contraceptive Action Programme. The thorniest point for most legislators was that of liberalizing availability but restricting that availability to married couples. In 1974 the coalition government under Liam Cosgrave introduced a bill that legalized import and sale of contraceptives but restricted their availability with numerous conditions on licensing, advertising, and sale to unmarried people. The Cosgrave government waffled on the issue and after having introduced the legislation allowed a free vote to the coalition deputies. Cosgrave did not tell his party his position and contributed to an embarrassing defeat when he himself voted against the bill that his government had brought forward.

The debate continued over the next five years, with the bishops reiterating their position in 1978 on the social damage that would follow from legalization. In that statement, however, the bishops also outlined some of the legal difficulties that had to be resolved and thus indicated that they were not in support of the absolute negative position on a contraception law. In 1979 the Fianna Fail government introduced a bill drawn up by then Minister of Health, later Prime Minister, Charles Haughey. The bill was quite restrictive and required a doctor's prescription, limited advertising, and placed a ban on abortifacients. The bill was opposed by some Labour and Fine Gael deputies because it was too restrictive, but the bill passed into law in 1979.

Thus another tenet of Catholic doctrine was changed by the state. The Church had found the courts, legislators, pressure groups, media, and segments of the public considerably less willing to accept the murky blend of a liberal state enforcing Catholic doctrine that was so important in the 1930s. The Church had shifted its position on this question and, while attacking the immorality of contraception and the consequences of the law, tolerated the right of the state to pass laws not in accord with Catholic doctrine.

Emerging from the troubles in Northern Ireland, the multiparty Forum for a New Ireland met in 1983 to discuss the future of Ireland as a whole and to discuss the possible arrangements for a connection between the north and the south. The question of the Church's position on the legislative support for Catholic doctrinal precepts arose because they were present in the south but not in the north. The Church made submissions on a number of topics, but with respect to pluralism it was clear that the Catholic values imbedded in the law were preferable to accommodation of the minority in Northern Ireland. The statement said: "A Catholic country or its government, where there is a substantial Catholic ethos and consensus, should not feel it necessary to apologize that its legal system, constitutional or statutory, reflects Catholic values. Such a legal system may be represented as offensive to minorities, but the rights of the minority are not more sacred than the rights of the majority."[21] While reiterating the 1973 position that Catholic moral teaching need not be enacted into law, the statement was clear that the rights of the minority were in fact no rights at all because "Catholic values" in statutory law historically had meant excluding Protestants from contraception, divorce, abortion, good books, and non-denominational schools. The statement was cold comfort to Protestants of the north as to the character of the law in a united Ireland. The appearance before the Forum of four bishops in February 1984 had the effect of clarifying the position of the Church. The bishops offered repeated assurances that the Church would respect the civil and religious liberties of northern Protestants and did not seek a "Catholic State for a Catholic people." Ultimately the bishops' statements revealed that the Church still did not make a clear distinction between the Church's moral teachings and the laws supporting them. Nor did they make clear why such laws were necessary in the Republic but not necessary if Ireland were united. Their first position was in fact more consistent with their long-term view that the laws of the state must contain Catholic doctrine even though it is not consistent with a liberal state. The issue of whether an individual Catholic was apparently subjected to less temptation in a state with more Protestants was never addressed at all.

Thus on a wide spectrum of issues—education, state services, the special position of the Church, censorship, divorce, contraception, and a united Ireland—the Church has been confronted with demands for change. The Church had to cede a great deal of ground on many of these matters and had to change its views on a number of them. The major decline was yet to come, however, as the differences over specific policies culminated in a larger question of the decreasing legitimacy of the Church in the society as a whole.

From its position of moral arbiter of the Irish society the Church found itself under the pressure of an avalanche of information, ideas, and messages about material consumption, alternative values, and expanding possibilities presented by the media. The balance of power shifted in Irish society and the Church found its dominant position no longer taken for granted although the deference given to the faith by 96 percent of the people was still formidable. At this point the Church began to adapt to the changing circumstances and realized that the posture of aloof authoritarianism did not have as much traction in a better-educated, more sophisticated society. The new Ireland was the product of the education and communication revolutions; rather than accept edicts it sought explanations for the Church's position on women, or gays, or contraception, or school management.

Often the language of the Church and the language of modern pluralism were simply unintelligible to one another. In an article on the controversy between archbishop of Dublin Desmond O'Connell and Professor Anthony Clare on homosexuality, journalist Fintan O'Toole points out that their understanding of the words used was as much a product of their completely different philosophical underpinnings as a difference in objective conclusions.[22] O'Toole notes that the archbishop's statement that homosexuality is a "disorder" means that it is a deviation from a teleological order in human nature and in God's law. In the Church's moral order the ideal is the monogamous family, and anything that detracts or deviates from that end is not in accord with the natural law (God's design for nature as discovered by human reason) however present it may actually be in human society. The evidence suggests that homosexuality is present in all societies at a rate of about 3 to 5 percent of the population. Professor Clare was using the language of medicine and psychology, which rejects the designation that homosexuality is a disease and sees it as a condition that is present in society, no more, no less. The society as a whole has no more right to condemn homosexuality as immoral than to condemn height or red hair as immoral. Society, in fact, has an obligation to prevent discrimination against homosexuals and lesbians because their condition does not warrant invidious exclusion.

Each moral position is drawn from a different perspective. The modern pluralist perspective accepts a multiplicity of values and ideals and seeks to establish a baseline consensus that allows people to live together in harmony while maximizing individual freedom. This language is increasingly prevalent in Ireland and makes the Church's Thomistic moral discourse with the contemporary language of moral relativism a dialogue of the deaf.

The Church Under Fire

The question of moral judgment arose in a series of cases of reprehensible moral behavior on the part of priests and of the Church. In 1992 Bishop of Galway Eamonn Casey was found to have fathered an illegitimate child who was then eighteen years old. He had had an affair with an American, Annie Murphy, when he was bishop of Kerry in 1973 and 1974. When she became pregnant Casey urged her to give the child up for adoption, but she refused and went back to the United States. Casey would have nothing to do with the boy, Peter, although he sent the mother his own money as well as £70,000 ($105,000) of diocesan money (subsequently repaid by benefactors after Casey resigned). When the facts came to light Casey made a statement that he had wronged Peter and his mother, went to a monastery in the United States for several months, and then went to Ecuador as a missionary until 1998, when he returned to Ireland.

The case was shocking because Bishop Casey, like so many other clerics, had spoken out repeatedly against sexual immorality, leaving himself open to the charge of hypocrisy. Casey was particularly visible because he had a larger-than-life personality and an unalloyed commitment to the poor and disadvantaged. He was a widely recognized voice of the Church on television and in other media and was widely admired by the Irish people. His elevation of his career as a cleric over his responsibility to the child was morally distasteful and his use of the diocesan funds reprehensible. The Irish people sorted out the different aspects of the case and came to different conclusions. Some saw it as the failing of one man only, which should be dealt with and forgotten. Others saw the demand that a priest be unmarried as outdated and unrealistic, raising the issue of priestly celibacy. Still others, remembering the stern lectures of their parish priest and their humiliation at the hands of the Christian Brothers, saw Casey as a symbol of the classic hypocrisy of the double standard "Do as I say not as I do" when it came to drink, fast cars, and, most of all, women. The Church, exacting in its demands on the moral behavior of others and in seeking confession to transgressions, silenced Casey and sent him out of the country. By 1998 the Irish public thought it was fine that Casey return to Ireland, probably because additional revelations made between 1992 and 1998 made Casey's transgressions look minor by comparison.

The Irish public identified two incidents that had most undermined their trust and respect for the Church.[23] The first was the case of Bishop Casey, the second that of Father Brendan Smyth. The exposure of Casey's affair opened the flood-gates for revelations about the shabby behavior of priests, with Smyth being per-haps the most egregious example. Smyth, a Norbertine priest, was sentenced to jail for twelve years at the age of seventy after pleading guilty to seventy-four charges, relating to acts committed from 1962 to 1997, of indecent behavior and sexual assault on children. A number of these sexual assaults on children took place in the United States when he spent five years in parishes in Rhode Island and North Dakota. While he was in Ireland he was moved from parish to parish in both north and south, and in those parishes he assaulted children repeatedly.

Smyth's case became widely known when he was charged with sexual abuse in Northern Ireland and the Irish government was asked to extradite him for trial. Attorney General Harry Whehelan delayed the extradition for seven months. A governmental crisis caused the exposure of the delay in Smyth's extradition. As the case became more widely known it became clear that the Church had protected Smyth, moving him from one parish to another, knowing that the same thing was going to happen and covering it up when it did. The complete inability of the Church to behave morally, covering up pedophile rape while at the same time preaching to society on premarital sex and birth control, was not lost on the Irish public. The Church was quick to point the finger at political parties, the media, secularization, or the United States for the ills of society while adopting the posi-tion that it was blameless. Yet the Church proved incapable of addressing, in a manner satisfactory to the public, its responsibility for the behavior of its priests.[24]

Priests were not the only clerics to come under scrutiny. The treatment of chil-dren in orphanages and convents that cared for "fallen women" was portrayed as cruel and abusive. In 1996 Madonna House, run by the Sisters of Charity, was questioned about its treatment of children, and a Dublin orphanage run by the Sisters of Mercy was shown to have displayed relatively little mercy in the care of children in the 1950s. The head of the Sisters of Mercy apologized on television and placed advertisements in newspapers doing the same. In the 1950s the Church and the state operated a system whereby the illegitimate babies of unwed mothers in Ireland were exported to the United States for adoption. Despite the events having taken place decades before, the public was only made aware of them in 1977, amidst the welter of stories about sexual abuse of children, and the news contributed to criticism directed at the Church. The transfer of the babies had been approved by the archbishop and was managed by the nuns who cared for the young women. The Department of External Affairs had effected the transfers.[25]

Like Icarus the Church began its fall, which came in two stages. The Church had held a moral monopoly over the Republic of Ireland from the founding of the state into the 1960s. The next two decades were a period of significant adjustment in the Church as it tried to adapt to changes in Irish society and in its own structure and doctrine after Vatican II. Dr. Gabriel Daly, OSA, summed up the transition aptly when he noted that the Roman Catholicism that had triumphed after the creation of the state was not the Church of Vatican II but rather was triumphalist, philistine, and unecumenical. "We continue to pay a price for our former authoritarianism and uncritical faith," he stated, "an increasing number of our people are passing from a totally uncritical faith to a totally uncritical unbelief."[26]

As difficult as that period was, the 1990s saw a collapse of deference to the Church and the Church's authority that is nothing short of breathtaking. One of the principal reasons has been the prevalence of sexual scandals about priests and brothers, which by 1996 had become a steady stream of accusations and admissions. So great was the outrage that in 1998 the Christian Brothers, in an unprecedented move, took out advertisements in newspapers to apologize to some of the half million students who had attended their schools. They indicated that the order had received serious complaints of "ill-treatment and abuse" and that they sought to respond to people who had been hurt while in the care of the Christian Brothers. But scandals have not been the only cause of the change in the relationship of the Irish to their Church and in the diminution of the Church's writ.

The Church's Position Today

Inglis identified several changes in the way Catholics in Ireland connect to their Church: a view of their religion as spiritual, not institutional; God as a transcendental force rather than a personal one; seeking the Church's voice on social issues but rejecting its absolute authority on personal morality, especially sexual matters; and a rejection of a fear-, guilt-, and damnation-mongering religion.[27]

These changes have occurred in a variety of domains. There are clear indications of a decline in belief and practice. Those believing that the Catholic Church is the one true Church dropped from 83 percent to 73 percent in the decade from 1974 to 1984, with a corresponding drop from 90 to 61 percent in those who believe in Papal infallibility. A 1998 poll for the "Prime Time" television show indicated that more than half the respondents disagreed with the Church's positions on divorce, contraception, clerical celibacy, and women in the priesthood. Attendance at mass dropped from 91 percent in 1974, to 85 percent in 1990, to 77 percent in 1995, to 60 percent in 1998. Monthly confession dropped from 47 percent in 1974 to 14 percent in 1995.[28] Moral worth is increasingly based on the behavior of people and the values they hold rather than on the marker of overt religious practice. As Inglis aptly puts it: "At one time being a good person was easily equated with being a good Catholic."[29] This is no longer true as people have come to rely more on their conscience in guiding their behavior rather than the teaching of the Church.

The presence of the Church in Irish society in the form of clerics is rapidly diminishing. As deference toward clerics is declining the number of clerics is declining as well. The most notable dropoff is in the number of religious brothers, nearly 60 percent from 1970 to 1995. The largest absolute drop in number was in sisters: there were over 6,500 fewer nuns in 1995 than in 1970. Counting religious orders and diocesan priests, the overall drop in the number of religious in Ireland was 35.3 percent over twenty-five years.

The situation for the future looks worse because the number of vocations has been diminishing. From 1966 to 1996 the decrease in vocations was over 92 percent. Those selected for religious life are leaving before ordination at a high rate, and clerics are dying at such a rate that, for example, in 1995 there was a loss of over 700 clerics while vocations numbered just over 100.[30] The numbers reveal two facets of the Church's position in Ireland. The first is the lack of interest on the part of young people in spending a life as a cleric because it no longer commands the respect and deference it once did. With the opening up of the economy of Ireland, the Church is no longer one of a few avenues of educational and social advancement. The status associated with having a priest, nun, or brother in the family and the pious atmosphere that encouraged vocations have diminished since 1960. The lack of human resources means more than just convents up for sale, it also means that the presence of clerics in Irish life, and the moral gravitas they carried, is no longer prevalent. The Church's former uniformity of moral perspective has been eroded by secularization, and its former pervasive presence has been eroded by the decline in the number of priests and nuns. Schools, parishes, hospitals, orphanages, and nursing homes cannot help but experience a change in ethos as lay personnel replace clerical workers. Institutional clout will erode as institutions become more secular.

In education the Church has been challenged on school management, curriculum, sex education, and the building of new schools, but the declining number of priests, nuns, and brothers will be the ultimate determinant of the shape of schools. This is not to suggest that teachers are not good Catholics or do not respect the beliefs of the children, but rather that lay people—married, having children, growing up in the communications revolution, and university-educated in the late twentieth century—will not share the same view as the nuns and brothers who preceded them. Hospitals will change and nurses will replace nuns. Social workers educated by the state will replace clerics in social service agencies.

The diminished role of the Church in political life is manifest in the shifting roles of Church and state and in the adoption of statutes contrary to Church doctrine on contraception, divorce, and homosexual behavior. The increasing social distance between politicians and the Hierarchy has diminished the bishops' influence. The drop in deference has eliminated, for example, the kissing of bishops' rings in public by politicians. The prime minister, separated from his wife, appears with his woman partner at functions of state.

Despite the development of a more Left-wing social agenda from the 1960s to the 1980s, the Church still does not have a coherent social vision.[31] The Church was comfortable with rural, self-sufficient, Gaelic, Catholic Ireland (even though it never seemed to be sufficiently bleached of sexuality). After the social changes in Ireland began in 1960 the Church seemed to have no more to offer than the criticism that liberal values would create a permissive society, with the clear implication that society was better before these secular values intruded. The Church's social vision is thus defined as a negation of the present and the glorification of a society that was viewed by many Irish as poor, inert, authoritarian, repressive, and static. The Irish people, it appears, were more than happy to kiss the Ireland of the 1950s good-bye. The more left-wing, liberation theology, social activist Church of the 1960s and 1970s came under criticism from the Pope and the emphasis on doctrinal fidelity has de-emphasized that social agenda. For all the criticism of vocationalism, or corporatism (the Church's social doctrines of the 1920s and 1930s), it held out a social ideal that was in contrast to individualist capitalism and collectivist communism. There is no such touchstone in the Church today. The Church's position on women, its own non-democratic, hierarchical organization, and its relative inhospitableness to debate and discussion leave it outside of the values, structures, and processes of modern political discourse.

This is not to suggest that there is rampant secularization of Ireland. Attendance at mass is high by international standards and 80 percent of those asked in 1998[32] indicated that religion was still important in their lives. Nor does the analysis of the diminution of the power of the Church imply a decline in the spirituality of the Irish people. Institutionally the Church is not pallid and powerless. What is conclusive is that the institutional Church and the beliefs, deference, and structures that supported its pervasive power in Ireland have eroded to a significant degree. Simply put, the moral monopoly of the Church is gone. The principal reasons are the surge of economic growth that allowed the possibility of a different kind of life and a different kind of society; the education revolution that occurred after 1965; the change in the status of women, who were the bearers of the traditional religious values; the rise of the media as alternative sources of information, values, and different points of view; and the cascade of sex scandals and other deleterious information about the Church that surfaced in the 1990s.[33]

The Church finds itself in a difficult position as its institutional power diminishes because its strength was derived from the penetration of the institutions of society. Widespread devotion and belief of the people; deference from the press, the parties, the politicians, and business elites; legal support for its doctrinal positions; and direct control of social institutions such as schools and hospitals by priests and nuns all undergirded the Church's power. As the influence of the Church leached out of each of those domains, what remained was the isolated institutional Church structure and support from some lay groups. Oddly, the most

Catholic of European countries had no Catholic party, no Catholic newspaper, and no Catholic trade unions. Fianna Fail was the closest approximation to a Catholic party, but the structure of Irish parties is such that the policy agenda of Fianna Fail would secularize to acquire the votes necessary to hold power. Thus the Church moved, or is moving, from a dominant power position in Ireland to a marginal position. The lack of intermediate structures has prevented the Church from holding an intermediate position.

The Catholic Church in Ireland will not lose importance as a social entity even though it has as a political entity. The importance and strength of the Church may ultimately be more in its deep connection to the spirituality of the people and less in its claims to order them around. A medieval epistemology and organization may find the road rough in the twenty-first century; on the other hand, it may turn out that holding to certitudes in a kaleidoscopic world of hyper-relativity may be the strongest appeal of all.

The Media

There are a host of influences on the Irish people's information, attitudes, and values. Especially important in Ireland has been the impact of television, coming as it did at the same time as other changes in Ireland. Two facets of television were problematic for Ireland: the degree of government control of the content and perspective of shows and news and the impact of television on the character of Irish culture, Irish language, and religion.[34]

Radio and Television

Radio broadcasting, under government authority, had existed in Ireland since 1925. The hallmark of the radio was its conservatism and timidity; it was under the minister of Post and Telegraphs and thus under the control of bureaucrats and subject to parliamentary scrutiny (although a weak five-member advisory council did exist after 1952). Radio was seen as an instrument of the state and its content was to be supportive of government policy. The effect was not so much bipartisan as nonpolitical. In 1960 when the government decided to engage in television broadcasting, radio and television were placed under a single nine-person Authority responsible to the sponsoring minister of the government, Radio Telefis Eireann (RTE), a state-sponsored body modeled after the British Broadcasting Corporation (BBC). RTE was a national broadcasting authority and was responsible to the state. The first chair of the Authority was Eamonn Andrews and the first director general of broadcasting was from the United States, Edward M. Roth of Boston. The creation of the Authority was intended to liberate radio as well as television from the direct oversight of a cabinet minister. The degree of autonomy of the Authority would produce controversy later because the Broadcasting Act called for RTE to be "responsive to the concerns of the whole community, be mindful of the need for understanding and peace within the whole island of Ireland . . . and have special regard for the elements that distinguish that culture and in particular for the Irish language." In addition, the Authority was to present the news in a fair and impartial way and refrain from presenting anything that could "undermine the authority of the state." Should the RTE present anything that did the latter, the minister was authorized to order the Authority to "refrain from broadcasting the matter."[35]

No sooner had the glow appeared on the screen than the impact of television on Irish culture was questioned. The decision to broadcast television at all was opposed by some because they feared it would be a channel of alien culture into Ireland. Some wished it delayed, while others had misgivings about its effects on the west of Ireland. The president of the Gaelic Athletic Association, for example, wanted assurances that it promoted Irish games and was not an instrument of anglicization.[36] Broadcasting began on New Year's Eve in 1961. Eamon de Valera's speech of dedication reflected the government's reservations. The new medium could be a positive force, de Valera noted, which could "build up the character of the whole people," but he also feared that it could lead "through demoralization, to decadence and dissolution" of Irish culture. Cardinal Dalton added in the same broadcast a warning to parents not to let their children become television addicts.[37]

From the start in 1962 the content of programming was the subject of controversy. As soon as RTE began broadcasting complaints surfaced that there were not enough Irish-language broadcasts. The Broadcasting Act of 1960 called for the Authority to advance Irish language and culture and mandated that RTE produce Irish broadcasts. Although £2 million was allocated to begin the network, half of RTE's revenues were to be raised by advertising. This created a tension immediately between the revenue stream and the preservation of culture. The commercial dimension of RTE had to generate enough advertising to fund competition with the BBC, which was received by televisions on the east coast of Ireland. Fergal Tobin notes about the 1960s: "As ever, there was an ocean of good will toward the language, exceeded only by a determination not to speak it or listen to anyone speaking it if that could be avoided."[38] Moreover, the producers who ended up at RTE—bright, well educated, urban, and iconoclastic—were not disposed to put Irish-language programming as their top priority. The novelty of television made the viewers seek out shows that were foreign and new to them, that entertained them, or that shocked them, but few wanted RTE to be filled with documentaries on Gaelic kings and poets in Irish, nor would advertisers support such shows.

Ernest Byrne, a senior producer, resigned during the first year because there was not enough emphasis on Irish; Edward Roth resigned in 1963 because there was too much. Eamonn Andrews resigned in 1966, also citing the conflict between the two goals of popular programming, which drew advertisers, and Irish-language shows, which did not. Individual shows in Irish were popular, such as the "Buntus Cainte" show in the late 1960s, which taught basic Irish, and the bilingual "Trom agus Eadrom." The conservators of Irish culture were inevitably going to be disappointed, however, if they saw the medium as a tool for the restoration of Irish. Television was more likely to hasten the already clear decline in the language that had begun before the Famine. In 1976, fourteen years after the initiation of RTE, only 5 percent of the programming was in Irish, almost half of it news. The advent of the Irish-language channel on RTE in 1997 (discussed in Chapter 4) redressed the balance to some degree.

RTE initially was dependent on U.S. television shows because there were insufficient Irish shows to fill the viewing hours, drawing the immediate criticism that RTE was presenting too many of these shows. Approximately half of the hours broadcast in the first few years were imported. This criticism is, in fact, still valid today because, although Irish-produced shows have increased fourfold, the total number of hours of broadcasting has also increased fourfold since 1962. More than half the programs are still purchased from abroad, and U.S. shows such as "Beverly Hills 90210," "NYPD Blue," "Baywatch," and "ER" are seen regularly on RTE. The appeal of the imported shows, especially movies, is widespread. Ireland is part of the Americanized global culture in which people at the far corners of the Earth care who shot J. R., watch "The Fugitive" apprehend his wife's murderer, say good-bye to "M*A*S*H," and lament the departure of "Seinfeld." The most-watched shows, however, are not U.S. produced. In 1995, for example, the particular shows watched by over 1 million people at one time included the "Eurovision Song Contest" (the once-a-year European broadcast), "The Late Late Show," "Glenroe" (a rural soap opera), the "Rose of Tralee Contest," "Coronation Street" (the long-running British comedy soap opera), and "Fair City" (a suburban soap opera), as well as three football (soccer) matches: Ireland, of course, versus England, Portugal, and Holland (although not all at once).

The most-watched show on Irish television, "The Late Late Show," began in 1962 and embodies the impact of television on the culture of Ireland. Designed to be a topical show, it evolved into a combination of late night light entertainment and serious discussion. The host, Gay Byrne, became a national institution, hosting the show from its inception. The particular importance of this show, and Gay Byrne, was its social and political impact. Byrne was willing to bring on a wide variety of guests and ask them questions about topics that had hitherto been off-limits in the Irish media. Drawing mass audiences, Byrne's skilled interrogations brought out controversial points of view on crime, corruption, divorce, broken marriages, contraception, homosexuality, the Church, and a host of other topics. Byrne had the skill to evoke these discussions and control them, while himself not coming across as a ranting liberal, and this skill "made adult debate accessible to a mass audience."[39]

The Church, like Irish-language advocates, also felt inadequately represented and ill used in the 1960s and 1970s, when the subjects of sex, marriage, divorce, and birth control were discussed on the screen. The most famous episode is revealing in that what was seen as shocking in 1966 is so thoroughly pedestrian today. Bishop Thomas Ryan of Clonfert, in "fairness to Christian morality," objected strenuously to a guest on the "Late Late Show" saying that she had not worn a nightie on her wedding night. That the bishop lacked any sense of proportion, let alone a sense of humor, is not as surprising as the revelation of what had previously been excluded from acceptable comment and the bishop's easy assumption that he could speak as the conscience of the country.[40]

The Church, which had taken for granted its position as the arbiter of morality and behavior, was confronted with guests on television who not only did not display the traditional deference but were openly questioning, defiant, and, on occasion, insulting. Playwright Brian Trevaskis, on the "Late Late Show," referred to the Bishop of Galway as a "moron" (assessing the bishop's preference for the architecture of Galway Cathedral) and criticized the priest who fired the novelist John McGahern from his teaching post. A sharp reaction from clerics and the populace condemned RTE for that episode. Oliver J. Flanagan, a most pious member of the Dail, summed up the traditionalist and religious perception of the role of the "Late Late Show," and television itself, in the oft-quoted phrase, "There was no sex in Ireland before television." Flanagan's reaction indicates the degree to which the "Late Late Show" was closing the gap between the actual beliefs, opinions, and behavior of the people and the synthetic moral uniformity assumed by the Church. [41] The RTE Board, even though it issued an apology for the "Bishop and the nightie" incident, came under pressure to curb the "Late Late Show" but generally supported Byrne and left the show alone.

As television raised questions on matters of social and moral concern, the authority of the Church and the state to define the existence and nature of problems and the way people were to think about them was subtlety eroded. The Church was forced to respond or let its position go unheard. The government and politicians did not develop sophisticated media skills until the late 1970s, but the Church, in response to the advent of television and the changes stimulated by Vatican II, set up the Catholic Communications Institute of Ireland in 1969 and a Press and Information Office in 1973. The Church recognized that it had to adapt to the new technology; it trained priests to effectively communicate on television by dropping the traditional stern judgmental tone for a warmer personal connection. The Catholic Communications Institute of Ireland created a documentary program on RTE called "Radharc" (Look), which dealt with devotional topics from the 1960s to the 1990s. "Radharc," under Father Joseph Dunn, took on social issues that were significant in the context of the 1960s, shooting shows in Irish prisons and in the streets and dealing with crime and poverty. In presenting such social problems "Radharc" was also part of the process of closing the gap between the illusionary Ireland, which rarely acknowledged such conditions, and the reality of youth crime and homelessness in the actual Ireland.

The relationship between the Church and the media did not improve significantly in the following decades; each has viewed the other as responsible for all the ills of Irish society. The media see the Church as retrogressive, authoritarian, and preoccupied with sex, and the Church views the media as liberal, hedonistic, and preoccupied with sex. The Church's initial view that the media were a vehicle for its messages of undebatable truth has been altered, but not very much. As censorship eroded, the function of the media in Ireland, as in any country, was to offer lots of information and lots of different opinions and to turn its gaze on the institutions of society, all of which ran counter to the mode of communication of the Church. Eventually different points of view on moral questions were aired and inevitably the media turned to an examination of the behavior of the Church itself. The protection of authority, silence, and deference was gone.

Starting in 1971 Gay Byrne also had a radio call-in talk show that had its moments in closing the gap between the pain in the lives of ordinary Irish people, mostly women, and the surface uniformity of Irish morality and behavior. After the death of Anne Lovett in 1984, Byrne devoted a broadcast to the experiences of women with pregnancy and childbirth. Lovett, fifteen, died in childbirth and it turned out that her parents, teachers, and friends all were aware of the pregnancy. The shame of an illegitimate birth precluded their helping her. Byrne prompted an outpouring of heartbreaking stories from all over Ireland about self-abortions, marital violence, incest, and secret childbirths that revealed both the moral immobilism and the dark recesses of Irish life.[42] Such events go beyond the merely voyeuristic to shape a deeper change in the awareness and attitudes of the Irish people that came to light on such issues as divorce, domestic violence, and abusive clergy.

The expansion of television was rapid. The number of sets in Ireland went from 201,000 in 1963 to 867,500 in 1994, and the broadcast hours quadrupled as cable and satellite added more. Television contributed to the acceleration of changes in attitudes about consumerism, social values, and the west of Ireland. Advertising, both on the British channels available in the east of Ireland and on the Irish channels, opened the world of material goods to the Irish people as the first wave of prosperity hit Ireland. Television urged people to purchase more and more. New styles of dress, new places to go, new trends in music, new household goods, and a new way of life were presented to the Irish people. De Valera's vision of frugal asceticism was not highly regarded by the people of Ireland once they had heard the siren call of the consumer culture portrayed in pixels on the persuasive little screen. Calls from the pulpit to reject materialism and the hedonistic ways of Britain and the United States were not as compelling as they had been in the past when the Irish had little choice in the matter.

More than consumer values were encouraged by television. British television had been accessible in the east of Ireland before 1962 and was, obviously, free from the Irish censor's hand. Thus a way of life, characterized by critics as the "permissive society" and by others less critical as modern liberal society, was presented in Irish homes. Values that had been taken for granted in domestic life, work, and religion were now open to examination as television exposed far more fluid attitudes to family, sex, religion, drugs, and pornography. While the Irish censor laboriously worked condemning books and snipping films until the 1980s, the BBC was showing those same films, and others, uncut, night after night. Sky TV added its numerous channels, some all-sports but others offering the dubious benefits of the U.S. Fox Network style programming (excepting of course "The Simpsons"). Programming, television, and movies from the United States, with its California lifestyle, expensive cars, lavish restaurants, flashy homes, and trendy clothes, or the reverse images of bleak violence and urban decay, contributed to this expanded perspective as well. Such shows often have as little to do with the lives of the vast majority of U.S. residents as they do with the people of Ireland, but they are invidious in extending into the global culture the U.S. images of Arnold Schwartzenegger and his muscular mayhem or "Friends" with their apparently relentless sexual preoccupations.

The impact of television on the west of Ireland, already suffering depletion from emigration, was most acute. Television not only opened up to the young people the world beyond Mayo but in fact treated rural life with derision. There is little place in the values of the sophisticated urban world for rural life. While sometimes romanticized, more often rural life is portrayed as a world of tedium inhabited by bumpkins and fools. Television brought both the allure of the new and disdain for the old to the west of Ireland.

Although television is repeatedly condemned as superficial, violent, and vacuous in Ireland, as well as in Britain and the United States, it has replaced the newspaper as the principal source of news. Newspaper reading in Ireland has declined in the last decade and television has become the center of entertainment for the family. The effects of television on the Irish will continue to reinforce the other changes in the country and contribute their own shallow luster to contemporary Irish values. Virtually no subject is taboo any longer, and programs about drugs, AIDS, domestic violence, and clerical sexual abuses regularly splatter the screen. Although such content draws conservative criticism, the government has left this area alone. The number of channels continues to increase but the quality of television is not improved thereby any more than the quality of water is improved by increasing the number of spigots.

The history of radio and, to a lesser degree, television in Ireland is one of firm government control. Thin-skinned politicians chaffed under criticism and also exerted control over programming. This created a politically sanitized, purportedly impartial, approach to public issues, but in reality political issues were basically ignored on the radio in a pallid concession to political and ecclesiastical pressure. Television has fared better in that political events were reported and investigated in a somewhat more aggressive British or U.S. style, but it falls far short of the degree of independence of British and U.S. television.

A series of controversies over the content of television brought the government in conflict with RTE. The hierarchical culture of the Republic produced the tradition of a few people getting things done through a word in the right place to the right person. The world of Church and business decisionmaking in the 1950s was secretive and the world of party politics only somewhat less so. The media were not seen as disseminators of information to enlighten the public but rather as meddlers who did not know how to play by the rules and were out to embarrass politicians. Conversely, the journalists of the period were moved by the icono-clastic and radical spirit of the 1960s and saw their task as not only revealing the dynamics of Irish politics but also transforming the country. As one administra-tor put it, they thought that Ireland was "rotten" to the core and expected RTE to pay them while they "rushed to build the new Jerusalem." The resulting clash was as unedifying as it was predictable.

In 1966 then Minister for Agriculture Charles Haughey criticized RTE because when his statement about some aspect of agricultural policy was put on the news it also had the temerity to include a statement from the National Farmer's Association that disagreed with him. The Farmer's statement was withdrawn from later broadcasts, which led to the resignation of the news director and then in turn a condemnation of the RTE Authority by the National Union of Journalists. In 1968 the minister for Local Government attacked a priest, Austin Flannery O. P., who hosted a late-night, five-minute religious show called "Outlook," because he put on a panel of radical activists who condemned the government's housing policy. A show called "Home Truths," which challenged the veracity of advertising claims, was withdrawn, allegedly under the pressure of RTE sponsors.

In 1968 the Fianna Fail government put a referendum on the ballot to change the Irish electoral system from proportional representation to the plurality system used in the United States and Britain. The public defeated the amendment. The result was in no small part due to a "Seven Days" show broadcast before the refer-endum, which demonstrated that if the new system was adopted Fianna Fail would win nearly 100 seats in the 150-member Dail. This did not endear RTE to Fianna Fail which, as the governing old-boy party of patronage and insider deals, did not trust the media anyway. In early 1969 three producers resigned from RTE, charging that material had been excluded from the content of shows in deference to the advertisers or the management (that is, the government was watching over their shoulder). In late 1969 Minister for Justice Micheal O'Morain criticized a "Seven Days" show on money lending, accusing the producers of paying for inter-views and getting the answers they wanted by plying those interviewed with drink. An investigation was launched into the show, intimidating the creative people at RTE and increasing the control of the content of shows by an Authority that was responsive to government sensitivities.

As early as 1966 Sean Lemass had reasserted the provisions of the Broadcasting Act to remind the producers of news and public affairs programs that "the gov-ernment rejected the view that Radio Telfis Eireann should be, in general or in re-gard to its current affairs programmes, completely independent of government supervision."[43] In 1968 "Seven Days" was moved to the news division, where it was watched more closely. The crisis in Northern Ireland brought, along with its violence, a controversy over Section 31 of the Broadcasting Act. That section forbids the broadcasting of any matter that promotes the aims of any organization that "engages in, encourages, or advocates the attaining of any political objective by violent means."[44] In 1972 Kevin O'Kelly broadcast an account of an interview with Sean MacStiofain, a leader of the Provisional IRA. Prime Minister Jack Lynch dismissed the entire nine-person RTE Authority under Section 31 of the 1960 Act. O'Kelly was put on trial and convicted but was later freed after his appeal.

Conor Cruise O'Brien, a figure noted for his keen intellect, highly visible public persona, and literary achievements, was in 1976 the minister for Posts and Telegraphs. He sponsored an amendment to the Broadcasting Act that would require the approval of the Dail if the government—that is, the party in power—were to remove the RTE Authority, thus restricting political abuse of the RTE Authority. O'Brien, who had a long record of opposition to censorship and had criticized the Church for advocating censorship of information on contraception, held a position where it would be his job to censor others. O'Brien surprisingly upheld the application of Article 31, such was the ferocity of his opposition to the IRA. O'Brien added more precision to the definition of "broadcasting of any matter that promotes the aims of any organization that engages in, encourages, or advocates the attaining of any political objective by violent means"and added a time limit (one year) to the ban, which could be reviewed by the government within three weeks of its issuance. Despite limiting the ban, O'Brien had implied in an interview that the government would crack down on newspapers that were sympathetic to the IRA. He caused an explosion of criticism about censorship and free speech that almost brought down the 1973–1977 coalition government.

The ban on broadcasting statements made by the IRA and IRA supporters and parties was maintained by successive governments of different parties on the basis that the state broadcasting network was not a forum for those who would use violence. Sinn Fein and the IRA actually drew comfort from the ban because it allowed them to convince themselves that the government so feared the compelling power of their message that it had to prevent the Irish people from hearing it. Sometimes the ban seemed silly, as when actors were used to read the words of Sinn Fein political figures; sometimes it was serious, as when Martin Galvin, a U.S. leader of Northern Ireland Aid (NORAID), visited Belfast to be a pallbearer at the funeral of an IRA man. The journalists at RTE held a one-day work stoppage because the network refused to broadcast an interview with Galvin. Eventually the peace process brought about the demise of the ban in 1994, but the fact remains that for over twenty-five years, in a matter of great historical importance about which the Irish were knowledgeable and concerned, the presumption of the government was that it could and should judge what political views the public should hear.

The transformation of the world of broadcasting, technical innovation, and expanding commercial control came to Ireland as it did elsewhere, and the government eventually responded with the 1988 Radio and Television Act. A commission was created, similar to the Authority of RTE, to integrate the commercial sector into broadcasting. The commission negotiates contracts for issuing radio bands and channels to private companies to operate at the national and local level. The minister of Communication then issues a license to broadcast. The commercial station must include public affairs programming and is subject to the same types of rules as was RTE with respect to fairness, editorializing, and party broadcasts. In 1990, to divert advertising revenue to the new commercial stations, the Dail put a cap on the amount of advertising that could be broadcast on RTE and on the annual advertising revenue. This was politically abrasive to the Left because it was seen as favoring private industry at the expense of RTE. Moreover, it did not work because the expected shift in advertising revenues did not materialize even though RTE was deprived of needed revenues to operate. In 1993 the provisions were rescinded and the 1976 provisions were restored. Commercialization did not alter the basic features of Irish broadcasting, which was a small, state-controlled broadcasting authority faced with the avalanche of new technologies, the explosion of information, the Europeanization and globalization of media, and the dominant position of the United States.

The preservation of identity and culture in the face of such a world was the subject of a 1996 green paper, *Active or Passive: Broadcasting in the Future Tense.*[45] The report identified the problem for Ireland as "how to reconcile the pressure to make information merely a commodity with the need to retain its value as a public good." Citing the example of U.S. media policy in the 1980s, the report notes that there was a demonstrable decline in public affairs programming and the "interest of advertisers being prioritized over the interests of viewers." Concerned that the same could happen to Ireland through the advent of new technologies, the report asks what mix of private and public programming best serves the common good: "What policies promote citizenship rather than passive consumerism?"[46] For RTE the answer has not yet been found.

Newspapers

The most widely read newspapers in Ireland are the morning *Irish Independent,* with an average circulation of over 160,000; the evening *Evening Herald,* with over 121,000 circulation; and on Sunday the *Sunday Independent,* with nearly 340,000 circulation. These do a good job of presenting political news and public information as well as all the other contents of a modern newspaper. The tabloids are the *Irish Press,* with a circulation of about 60,000 and the *Star,* with 70,000. The highest quality newspaper is the *Irish Times,* with a circulation of about 99,000. The *Daily Mirror* and the *Sun,* English papers, have a daily circulation of about 60,000 each. The largest regional paper outside of Dublin is the *Cork Examiner,* with a circulation of about 54,000.

Each paper has an ideological flavor. The *Irish Times,* founded in 1859, was the unionist paper of the nineteenth-century Anglo-Irish elite. It adjusted to the changes in Ireland to become the voice of urban liberal cosmopolitanism. It has the largest circulation among the middle and upper classes and the most well educated. Marked by excellent reporting, more international news, and quality commentary, the *Irish Times* is to Ireland what *The New York Times* is to the United States. While a great paper, it is not one you would seek to get a feel for the grassroots sensibility of the Irish.

The *Irish Independent* (which also includes the *Evening Herald* and the *Sunday Independent*) was founded by Charles Stewart Parnell in 1891 after the split in the Irish Parliamentary Party. Parnell, however, died before the first issue appeared. John Redmond controlled the paper in the 1890s. After running low on money and readers, it came under the control of William Martin Murphy, whose views were diametrically opposed to those of Parnell. In the post-Treaty 1920s the paper supported Cumann na Gaedheal and in the 1930s that party's successor, Fine Gael. It was the voice of strong farmers, sturdy burghers, and businessmen, Ireland's conservative Catholic middle class. The paper now is owned by Tony O'Reilly, the CEO of the Heinz Corporation, who has used the Independent group as a base to build a media empire. The readership crosses a wide spectrum of classes and interests while still retaining the tone of its political origins.

The *Irish Press* (also publishing the *Evening Press* and the *Sunday Press*) was founded by Eamon de Valera in 1931 to be a voice for Fianna Fail nationalism. De Valera controlled the editorial content and was followed as editor by his son Vivion de Valera. The paper displays a more nationalist perspective than the others and in the years of the Northern crisis was most sympathetic to Sinn Fein. The readership of the *Press* is from the skilled working class and the lower middle class. The sale of newspapers in Ireland has dropped overall and that has placed the *Irish Press* in jeopardy. More Irish people, as elsewhere, now get their news from television rather than papers. The place of newspapers in the Information Age is an open question. Declining readership and alternative sources of information threaten the end or transformation of some of the Irish papers.

Censorship

Written Materials

Television is not the only realm of communication subject to government control. Censorship of periodicals and books persisted in Ireland after independence, to the dismay of civil libertarians and the disgust of artists and writers. Censorship, like family law, is an area in which the ideal of the liberal state and the ideal of a Catholic state collided and the Catholic state prevailed. The law was originally generated from a committee appointed by Kevin O'Higgins in 1926 to examine "Evil Literature," mainly British newspapers with their lurid treatment of sexual matters. The pressure to create the Committee came from the Irish Vigilance Association, the Catholic Truth Society, and the Priests' Social Guild. The Censorship of Publications Act of 1929 included books as well as newspapers and magazines preoccupied with crime. Books "suggestive of, or inciting to, sexual immorality or unnatural vice" or containing any treatment of, let alone advocacy of, abortion or birth control were to be banned forever. The legislation had strong clerical support and the conservative, puritanical thought at the time prevailed.

Popular intolerance supporting such legislation was clear before censorship laws were passed. When Brinsley MacNamara published *The Valley of the Squinting Widows* in 1918, his hometown in Westmeath burned the book publicly and humiliated the author. Not satisfied, the townsfolk drove the author's father, a schoolteacher, out of town.[47] Ireland set out to isolate itself—in the name of one of the nation's social pillars, Catholicism—from the contaminating influence of secular cultures. The mixture of independence, the conservative male perspective of the Irish elites, and the Irish Catholic Church of the 1920s produced a monomaniacal obsession with personal sexual matters. A Church unwilling to let young people dance found no difficulty in censoring their reading. A Catholic conservative strata of politicians, whom Sean O'Faolain saw "as having as much cultivation as the heel of your boot," were more than ready to enforce this prudish morality through the law.[48] A pious public was ready to accept the authority of its own institutions, embodying its sentiments as opposed to the debased values of the English.

A five-member Censorship Board began in 1930 to assess not only periodicals and paperback novels but also the works of some of the world's greatest literary figures, including Maxim Gorki, Simone de Beauvoir, John Steinbeck, Arthur Koestler, Theodore Dreiser, Guy de Maupassant, Sigmund Freud, Laurence Durrell, John Dos Passos, Truman Capote, Ernest Hemingway, W. Somerset Maugham, Alberto Moravia, Andre Gide, Jean Paul Sartre, F. Scott Fitzgerald, Andre Malraux, Doris Lessing, and George Orwell. Also embarrassing was the banning of Irish writers such as Austin Clark, Sean O'Faolain, George Bernard Shaw, Frank O'Connor, J. P. Donleavey, Sean O'Casey, Brendan Behan and Edna O'Brien, and John McGahern, denying these artists the audience of their own countrymen. The Censorship Boards were excluding blatant sexual material but they were also excluding point of view, differences of values, and philosophy that they did not approve. They excluded Irish writers for breaking the silence on the synthetic, epiphenomenal, moral uniformity of Ireland and telling about the contradictions, hypocrisies, and pain that were part of the lives of real people.

The operation of the censorship process put literary and moral judgment in the hands of the disgruntled. Those who were offended need merely underline the passage and send the book to the Board. The Board members were volunteers and could hardly have read the cascade of books sent to them each year. Thus the underlined passages determined the fate of such works as Sartre's *Age of Reason* or Hemingway's *For Whom the Bell Tolls*. Irish intellectuals, especially Sean O'Faolain in his magazine *The Bell*, fought a lonely battle against this law, charging not only that it was illiberal but also that it made Ireland look foolish in the eyes of other

Western nations. By 1943 1,700 had been banned. A 1946 act allowed customs officials to seize books that they felt should be reviewed by the Censorship Board. This
hardly seemed to be a step forward because it expanded the censorship authority
to the Department of Customs and Excise, which, as journalist Thomas J.
O'Hanlon cynically noted, "assign[s] import duties on inner tubes one day and become literary critics the day after."[49] In 1956, at the prodding of the Irish
Association of Civil Liberties, the Board was liberalized by the Minister for Justice
James Everett and his successor, Oscar Trainor. Book banning dropped off somewhat. In 1958 the Church Hierarchy, convinced that there was some slippage in the
monitoring of "evil publications" and "foul books," called for an expansion of the
Censorship Board and for a more vigorous application of the law by the police.
This request was rejected by de Valera who, in consultation with the opposition,
concluded that the law was adequate and that there had been no perilous decline in
sexual morality in the 1950s probably because those most interested in sex, young
people, were leaving Ireland in droves.

Censorship during World War II was a special case because all countries, including liberal democracies, censored media during wartime. During the
"Emergency" in Ireland, however, Frank Aiken, with his Mikado-like title,
Minister for Coordinating Defensive Measures, interpreted the flow of virtually
any information as a threat to Irish neutrality. Films, news, mail, and telegraphs
were all censored; the Irish people did not see any information on German atrocities, concentration camps, or any discussion of Irish neutrality policy. Charlie
Chaplin's film *The Great Dictator* was banned, as were stories in the magazine
Irish Golf. The latitude was generous and Aiken took it, banning postcards, board
games, posters, and, of course, books. Wartime censorship was a manifestation of
the same attitude that allowed literary censorship, further justified by the threat of
national danger. If people were allowed to read little but murder mysteries and
westerns during peacetime, they were unlikely to read anything of worth during
the "Emergency."

Liberalization of the practice of censorship came in the 1960s and 1970s. In the
early 1950s the Board banned about sixty books a month and in the early 1960s
about thirty books a month. Legislation in 1967 amended the Censorship Act to
remove all books banned for more than twelve years and limited new banning to a
similar time period. The change released 5,000 books to the Irish people, although books could be banned again by the Board. In 1970 about thirteen books
a month were banned, but in 1991 only one book was banned and in 1992 there
were only eleven. In 1993 the Board banned Madonna's book *Sex.* (Even a stopped
clock is right twice a day.) About 800 books remain banned. After 1992 the criterion of the presence of information about abortion justifying a ban was no longer
applied due to a constitutional amendment. (This had represented only about 5
percent of all books banned.)

Film

Film fared no better in Ireland. The government appointed a film censor after passage of the Censorship of Film Act of 1923. The Act was the result of pressure from the Irish Vigilance Association, supported by the Church, which sought to censor all films shown in Ireland. They asserted that "everything contrary to Christian purity and modesty should be banned mercilessly." Devoid of any film expertise or background, the Boards were dominated by conservative lay organizations such as the Knights of Columbus, the Catholic Truth Society of Ireland, and the Catholic Vigilance Association. The practice of the film censor had been to edit out all objectionable scenes until the result was bland enough to pass muster in a country dominated by rural, Catholic values. While not exactly "socialist realism" in the service of the state, the result was something considerably less than art for art's sake. Eventually the showing of movies on the BBC channels in the east of Ireland circumvented the censors and the Irish were able to view the excised scenes of many movies. A Film Appeal Board was appointed in 1964 to overthrow some of the most egregious decisions. The general opening of media discussed above caused the erosion of film censorship, but it is not completely gone. In the late 1990s the films *Whore* and *The Bad Lieutenant* were banned.

Censorship and National Development

Censorship has been excused by some, who suggest that it is an honor for an author to be banned, that the Irish market is so minimal the author would not lose much money, that banning actually helped the artist's reputation, that the Irish want censorship because they are puritan in outlook, or, finally, that no intelligent person would want to read most of what was banned anyway.[50] Censorship, however, can also be seen as a manifestation of a particular stage of national development. Nationalism in Ireland after 1922 took the form of the values that had defined the Irish as different from the English.

Catholicism was so integral to Irish identity that the formal expression of its values was inevitable. Developing new policy for the state in the presence of the prepackaged moral and value system of the Church prompted the realization of the first (developing new policy) with the content of the second (the Church's value system). Irish autonomy allowed the Irish to concretize those values in the form of law and policy. The Church also was a powerful player in policymaking through its connection to the people via the pulpit and the ear of the devoutly Catholic political leaders. The Irish people, who were asserting their definition of Irishness, welcomed decisions on the boundaries of their freedom of speech by the political leadership. The leadership in turn conceded to the Church the authority to set those boundaries. The Church in turn defined the boundaries as exposure to temptations of the flesh and the maintenance of Church doctrine. The job of maintaining these boundaries was then turned over to pious Censorship

Board members (or customs officials) to judge the greatest works of Western literature on the basis of a phrase, a passage, or the book cover. Thus an important defining component of Irish national identity was distorted into sexual prurience enforced by zealots responding to the disgruntled. The assertion of Catholic triumphalism from the 1920s to the 1950s becomes more understandable, if no less narrow and intolerant, but certainly this period was not a high water mark for freedom of speech in Ireland.[51]

That stage of national development, marked by the economic policy of protectionism and efforts to restore the Irish language, eventually was superseded by the stage in which the Irish people gained a wider contact with the outside world and experienced an educational revolution. The manifestations of the earlier stage of development were re-assessed and the concession of censorship to the Church and the government was reclaimed, so to speak, by the people. The exaggerated, absolute censorship defined by the Church was no longer necessary. Censorship became a primitive badge of difference for a newly independent people that had lasted too long and thus retarded the very goal it set out to achieve. National identity in Ireland has manifested itself in economic growth, cultural revival, and self-confident assertiveness. Expansiveness and international connection within Europe and the world, not the withered shibboleths of cultural isolation, have vitalized Irish national identity.

The demise of censorship marked the demise of provincial paternalism and the rise of open access in the areas of books, television, theater, and film. From the 1970s to the 1990s the media provided access to virtually every topic in the world, which in turn had the effect of showing the Irish their own society, sexual behavior, poverty, drug abuse, and other social damage in a light that had at best been dim in prior decades. Finally, the Church and its clerics themselves came under a scrutiny that had been precluded in the past by the stern paternal eye of the local priest. In part this affected the Church not only in its capacity to control but also in adapting to a new Ireland.

NOTES

1. Tom Inglis, *Moral Monopoly: The Rise and Fall of the Catholic Church in Ireland* (Dublin: University College Dublin Press, 1998), pp. 1–15.

2. Archbishop Gilmartin of Tuam in 1927, quoted in J. Whyte, *Church and State in Modern Ireland 1923–1979*, 2nd ed. (Dublin: Gill & Macmillan, 1980), p. 25.

3. Whyte, *Church and State*, p. 305.

4. Ibid., p. 307.

5. *Report of the Commission on Vocational Organization* (Dublin: Stationery Office, 1944).

6. Quoted in ibid., p. 5.

7. Inglis, *Moral Monopoly*, pp. 24–30.

8. Dermot Keogh, *Twentieth Century Ireland*, p. 209.

9. Whyte, *Church and State*, p. 424.

10. Keogh, *Twentieth Century Ireland*, p. 210.

11. Ibid., p. 211.

12. Ibid., p. 209.

13. Quoted in John Cooney, *The Crozier and the Dail: Church and State 1922–1986* (Cork: Mercier Press, 1986), p. 22.

14. Whyte, *Church and State*, p. 690.

15. Quoted in Brown, *Ireland: A Social and Cultural History*, p. 295.

16. Whyte, *Church and State*, p. 335.

17. *Report of the Committee on the Constitution* (Dublin: Stationery Office, 1967).

18. Ibid., p. 343.

19. Quoted in ibid., p. 406.

20. Cooney, *Crozier and the Dail*, p. 33. Although it may not have been true that no orgasms existed west of the Shannon, as Andrew Greeley once suggested, it was true that the Irish repressed the sexual aspect of their lives to a startling degree. In tandem with the rapid economic transformation of Ireland came an equally startling new set of attitudes and behavior regarding sexual and family matters. From all the evidence, the amount of premarital sex has increased considerably. The dubious joys of paid-for sex seem to be more in demand. Prostitution had not been absent from Ireland in the past, but it definitely has increased of late. The indoor version of the street corner, the massage parlor, has appeared in Dublin and other Irish cities.

21. Cooney, *Crozier and the Dail*, p. 74.

22. Fintan O' Toole, *Black Hole, Green Card* (Dublin: New Island Books, 1994), pp. 145–149.

23. Inglis, *Moral Monopoly*, pp. 218–219.

24. Ibid., p. 219. Such actions are not confined to Ireland. In Boston, after a series of revelations of child sexual abuse by a priest in Fall River, Massachusetts, who had also been moved about repeatedly after it was clear what he was doing, Cardinal Bernard Law blamed the *Boston Globe* for looking for Church scandals.

25. M. Milotte, *Banished Babies: The Secret History of Ireland's Baby Export Business* (Dublin: New Island Books, 1977); and Inglis, *Moral Monopoly*, pp. 228–230.

26. Quoted in Cooney, *Crozier and the Dail*, p. 86.

27. Inglis, *Moral Monopoly*, p. 203. This section draws heavily on this source, which is an absolutely first-rate analysis of the Church in Ireland.

28. Ibid., pp. 208–209.

29. Ibid., p. 211.

30. Ibid., pp. 211–212.

31. Ibid., p. 222.

32. Ibid., pp. 203–204.

33. This is a summation of some the factors Inglis sees as most important—women, the media, and scandal—and those that I see as most important: the media, economic growth, education, and scandal.

34. The tortured path of Irish television in terms of its private or public character and its structure and policy is covered in Robert Savage's excellent *Irish Television: The Political and Social Origins* (Cork: Cork University Press, 1996).

35. Basil Chubb, *The Government and Politics of Ireland*, 3rd ed. (New York: Longman, 1992), p. 65.

36. Tobin, *Best of Decades,* p. 19. The fear of anglicization was more correctly directed at the BBC, which could broadcast into Ireland and was putting transmitters into Ulster. The *First Supplemental Report of the Television Committee* in 1956 pointed out that the BBC, not surprisingly, put a "constant emphasis on the British way of life, the British view of world affairs and the British (including the Six County) achievements." Quoted in Savage, *Irish Television,* p. 46.

37. Tobin, *Best of Decades,* p. 61.

38. Ibid., p. 65.

39. Ibid., p. 142.

40. Inglis makes the point that the Catholic Church had a moral monopoly in the sense that there was no alternative to the Church's power to define moral norms for the society.

41. The *First Supplemental Report* on RTE stated that the BBC attitude toward sex was quite alien to Ireland, warning RTE that it should avoid sexual content. Savage, *Irish Television,* p. 46.

42. Ardagh, *Ireland and the Irish,* pp. 181–182.

43. Keogh, *Twentieth Century Ireland,* p. 254.

44. Chubb, *Government and Politics,* p. 70.

45. Department of Arts Culture and the Gaeltacht, *Active or Passive: Broadcasting in the Future Tense* (Dublin: Stationery Office, 1995).

46. Ibid., pp. 143–144.

47. Keogh, *Twentieth Century Ireland,* p. 31.

48. Ibid., p. 75.

49. Thomas J. O'Hanlon, *The Irish: Portrait of a People* (London: Andre Deutsch, 1976), pp. 48–49.

50. Michael Adams argues for the validity of some form of censorship and, while acknowledging the stature of authors banned, he notes that censorship was successful in keeping pornography out of Ireland because "most of the 1,900 titles banned in the first seventeen years read as if they came out of a sex-shop catalogue." "Censorship of Publications," in *Morality and the Law,* ed. D. M. Clarke (Dublin: Mercier Press, 1982), p. 75.

51. Ronan Fanning, in *Independent Ireland* (Dublin: Helicon, 1983), p. 58, notes the racism of an Irish Radio News music critic in his discussion of jazz as "nigger music" in 1928, and Keogh notes the anti-semitism of some Irish during the 1930s, quoting Oliver J. Flanagan, TD, as wanting special orders directed against the Jews who "crucified our saviour 1900 years ago."(*Twentieth Century Ireland,* p. 130).

6

VENERATION VERSUS RIGHTS: THE ROLE OF IRISH WOMEN

The *Report to the Minister of Finance* in 1972 ushered in a new era of social policy in Ireland. It not only articulated the agenda of women's rights but also symbolized the political activism of women. Not since the women's suffragist movement early in the century had a demand for women's rights emerged in such a self-conscious manner. Over the next twenty-five years a variety of women's groups emerged, influenced by British and U.S. feminism. These groups generated pressure that resulted in changes in policy and law. Confronting the traditional political culture and Church-influenced legislation of Ireland was not an easy task. The question of women's rights with respect to birth control, divorce, and abortion policy in the Church–state context flared into bitter political contests. The demand for women's rights was not confined to one specific policy domain. Women's issues eventually engaged virtually every aspect of Irish public policy, from the media to schools and the workplace, from the bedroom to the boardroom. The issues on the agenda for women's equality mirrored the agenda of individual rights in modern pluralist societies. Women's rights were, and are, a pervasive critical pressure in a modernizing Ireland.

The Suffrage Movement

A feminist agenda accompanied the struggle for Irish women's suffrage from 1908 to 1916. To the detriment of Irish women's suffrage, nationalist aspirations for

Home Rule were culminating at the same time and the two struggles became intertwined. (Success in any case would not be easy; in 1898 women had gained the
vote in local elections in Ireland only after The Irish Women's Suffrage and Local
Government Association, formed in 1876, had lobbied for twenty-two years.)[1]
The Church opposed feminism and women's suffrage as a challenge to the central
role of women in domestic life. Irish politicians opposed suffrage because it challenged the primacy of men in the home, the marketplace, and the corridors of
power. Men were ready to condemn the idealism and the militant strategy of feminists in the struggle for women's rights even though they approved of the same
idealism and strategies when they were in the service of the nationalist struggle.

In Ireland the women's suffrage movement could not simply follow the lead of
the British Women's Social and Political Union (WSPU), founded by the
Pankhursts in 1903. The Irish Parliamentary Party at the time was in a position to
extract Home Rule from the Liberals in the British Parliament because they held
the votes to keep the Liberals in power. However, the leader of the Liberals, Prime
Minister Asquith, opposed women's suffrage, as did the leader of the Irish
Parliamentary Party, John Redmond. The women's position was seen as a threat
to the achievement of Home Rule. To place suffrage on the agenda above Home
Rule would mean bringing down the Liberal government to achieve the vote.

The Irish Woman's Franchise League (IWFL) was founded in 1908 by Hannah
Sheehy-Skeffington and Margaret Cousins. The IWFL adopted the slogan
"Suffrage First—Above All Else."[2] Willing to support any legislation that gave
women the vote, the IWFL also sought to have the vote for women included in
any Home Rule bill to reconcile the two goals.

The women of the IWFL were willing to adopt "unladylike" behavior, to speak
from the back of trucks, be arrested, demonstrate, and confront politicians. A less
militant organization, the Irish Women's Suffrage Federation (IWSF), was
formed in 1911 by Louie Bennett. It consolidated a large number of suffrage
groups with a non-militant posture.[3] The IWSF did not adopt tactics that would
ultimately risk the loss of Home Rule and therefore loss of the support of the Irish
people. In 1911 a women's suffrage bill passed the British Parliament but was defeated in 1912 when Redmond and the Irish Parliamentary Party voted against it.
Redmond in fact saw his opponents, Sinn Fein and the Ulster unionists, as the
beneficiaries of the women's franchise, which would be electorally damaging to
his leverage with the Liberal Party in London.

In 1912 the militancy of the IWFL increased when they realized that women
would be frozen out of the Home Rule bill. Members were arrested for breaking
windows of government buildings in Dublin; their trials became occasions to mobilize others into the suffrage movement through mass meetings and later
through hunger strikes. In July 1912 militant activity increased when Irish women
were excluded by Redmond from an open meeting with Asquith when he visited
Dublin. A mass meeting of women was organized in protest that included a wide
spectrum of women's organizations. Unfortunately a hatchet was thrown at

Asquith by militants of the English Women's Social and Political Union and two women attempted to set fire to the theater in which he had spoken. These actions triggered a backlash; violence against suffrage demonstrations increased and women were attacked by both police and mobs of citizens.[4] The suffragists' actions had little political impact; in November 1912, when the Home Rule Bill was enacted, Redmond prevented the inclusion of female suffrage.

The issue of Home Rule divided Ireland on unionist versus nationalist lines, of course, and that fissure ran through the women's movement as well. Ulster women sought the franchise but only in the context of the United Kingdom because they were hardly sensitive to the nationalist quest for Home Rule. When World War I broke out in 1914 Ulster women by and large put patriotism and national unity before their demands and the WSPU suspended operations to support the British government. In Ireland, however, the members of the militant IWFL opposed the war as both pacifists and feminists. Other women from all classes and from all regions of Ireland were drawn to Cumann na mBan, the women's group organized to support the militant efforts of Sinn Fein to gain independence for Ireland. The Rising of 1916 and the British response drew the women's groups somewhat closer together, although the middle class suffragists had always seen the women of Cumann na mBan as having subordinated themselves to men. Cumann na mBan could hardly be considered a feminist organization, but it was popular and certainly was capable of mobilizing more women than the suffragists.[5]

In 1918 London granted the franchise to women over age thirty (who owned property) and allowed women to stand for election to Parliament. This catalyzed Irish women's efforts to elect Countess Constance Markievicz to the British Parliament from Ireland, the first woman so elected. Because she was in prison she never took her seat.[6] In that 1918 election women's votes by and large went to Sinn Fein as a reaction against Redmond's opposition to suffrage.

The rise of the nationalist tide from 1918 to 1921 had the effect of subsuming the suffrage movement into the national movement. The movement for women's suffrage was broader than merely seeking the vote. It included demands that women be participants in the legal system, sought reform of the laws concerning child abuse and domestic violence, and advocated women's rights in the workplace. The rush of events—World War, the partition of Ireland, the Civil War—and the primordial claims of religion, nationalism, and paternalistic sexism created political pressures that overwhelmed feminist strategy and solidarity.

The Proclamation of 1916 called for equal citizenship of Irish men and women. The government of Ireland in 1922 included the franchise for women in the Constitution. That victory was real but rang hollow because of the actual place of women in Ireland in the following decades. Margaret Ward notes: "The pity was in losing the suffrage movement, Irish women lost their only independent voices as nothing emerged in its place. With no organization to give priority to women's needs, post partition Ireland was able to implement, with little resistance, highly reactionary policies in relation to women, whose domestic roles within the family became endowed with almost sacramental qualities."[7]

Venerated But Excluded

Legislation in Ireland after 1922, when the Irish gained autonomy from the United Kingdom, included restrictions on the freedom of women in a variety of dimensions of public policy, including reproductive rights, marriage, family law, education, employment, and social welfare. Such policies were supported by the more subtle permeation of the institutions of society with sexist attitudes, reinforced by paternal religious authority. The state created in 1922 has come to be seen by feminists as a replication of the state of the colonial power, with the local paternal elites substituted for those based in London. The economic structures, the political structures, and the cultural climate placed women in a subordinate position with respect to power, opportunity, and money. The pattern of colonial domination was replicated within the new state; those who were advantaged by the political and economic institutions excluded from power disadvantaged groups and classes in a manner no less complete than had the structures of the former colonial master.[8]

Such values have consequences, and they created a tension in the Constitution of Ireland between the ideal of a liberal state—centrality of individual freedom and guarantees of individual rights and liberties—and the ideal of a Catholic state: elevation of a particular community vision and Church doctrines woven into the fabric of the Constitution. The ideal of individual, inalienable rights initially excluded women and was basically confined to males with power and property. The fight for women's suffrage was the first effort to redefine the idea that the shift of power from London to the Irish people meant *all* the people, not just men. Thus, in terms of the liberal ideal, the women of Ireland were in effect twice removed: first because the practice of liberal democracy through the mid-twentieth century excluded women and the recognition of their rights and second because the values of the Catholic Church were embodied in the 1937 Constitution.

Women in Ireland were politically oppressed but at the same time culturally elevated. The deprivation of rights of women was accompanied by a culture that venerated woman as wife and mother, the touchstone of the family, and the temporal exemplification of Mary the Mother of God. If women were stereotyped in one way as gentle homemakers who had to be sheltered from the hard worlds of politics and commerce, they were also idealized as the dominant figures in the home and the repositories of the enduring religious and social values that bound Irish society together. The reasons for this dichotomy are imbedded in the authoritarian and traditional political culture. The paradoxical combination, veneration and deprivation, is evident when the position of the Catholic Church in Ireland is brought into the social equation. The Marian emphasis of the Church in Ireland brought a particular sensitivity to the status of women at the same time that both Church and state were insensitive to the rights of women. This is no better illustrated than by the words of David Barry, STL, writing in 1909 on women's suffrage from the Church's point of view. The Church, by honoring the Mother of God, was responsible for the "present honorable, and even privileged position that is accorded women in all civilized societies." Barry asserts that the Catholic Church "was the pioneer, and still is, and will ever be the mainstay of the rights of women," yet when it comes to the right to vote he notes: "Again it seems plain enough that allowing to women the right of sufferage is incompatible with high Catholic ideal of domestic life."[9]

In respect to women's position in Irish society, the greatest advancements in the period of modernization in Ireland from 1960 to 1998 have been in the areas of attitudes and the legal rights of women. The position of women in the workplace, although better than in the past, has seen less change than has occurred in the area of their rights. Affluence, education, and social mobility after 1960 destroyed older patterns; new values and patterns took their place. The threat to the gemeinschaft of organic Irish culture was posed by the gesellschaft of contractuarian liberal individualism. Liberalism was the vehicle by which women overcame exclusion from the rights that would allow them to participate in the life of the society on equal terms, to be able to make their own choices about their lives and bodies free from a pre-ordained role in Irish society set down by the Constitution. Finally, it is on the basis of individual rights claims that women challenged sexism in the broader society, which had kept women in that paradoxical state of "venerated exclusion."

After 1922 the traditional political and social values that made up the political culture and religion of Ireland were nourished and women were seen in terms of their maternal capacity. The practice of legislating divorce through private bills was ended by the Cumann na Gaedheal government in 1925 after extensive consultation with the Hierarchy, which advised "that it would be altogether unworthy of an Irish legislative body to sanction concession of such divorce." The government excluded the possibility of any legislative avenue for divorce.[10] The censorship of literature in 1929 also precluded access to any information on birth control. In 1935 the Criminal Law Amendment Act prohibited the importation and sale of contraceptives and also prevented importation for personal use. Women's occupations were excluded from unemployment compensation by the 1920 Unemployment Insurance Act and the 1952 Social Welfare Act.[11] A law excluded women from jury duty. Women could not have their own bank accounts or borrow money without the permission of their husbands (until 1957, when the Married Women's Status Act gave independent contractual freedom to a married woman and allowed her to sue and be sued and hold property as if she were unmarried).

Eamonn de Valera and the Fianna Fail, reflecting the political, religious, and social values of the Catholic Church and Irish society, shared the perspective of the prior government when they came to power. The Constitution of 1937 enshrined, for example, the illegality of divorce. Articles 40.3.3 and 40.2.1 and 40.2.2 identified the role of women in terms of the social good and the common good that would follow from their place in the home as mothers. The right, and in fact the duty, of the family to provide for the intellectual, moral, physical, social, and religious education of the children defined the family as having priority over the rights of the individual; the mother was the centerpiece of the family. These normative directives laid down a set a values that the legislature was to take as guiding principles in creating the law, the courts were to consider in their deliberations on the law, and the society was to hold precious beyond quotidian pressures.

Political participation and organization among women in the years after the Free State was founded were minimal. The number of women in the Dail, in the elections from 1923 to the election of 1977, went from a low of three (1.9 percent) to a high of six (4.1 percent).[12] Often these women were the relatives of male members of the Dail who had died or were heroes of the 1916–1922 period. None of the political parties made any effort to develop and recruit women into their leadership cadres. The female members of the Senate were limited as well, with few appointed by the prime ministers from the advent of the 1937 Constitution to the first election of a woman, Mary Robinson, to the Senate in 1969.[13] The associations embodying women's organizational energy were the Irish Housewives Association and the Irish Countrywomen's Association. Founded by Protestant women in 1941 and 1910, respectively, these associations were designed to address social issues such as the treatment of the poor and the improvement of the life of rural Irish women. While accomplishing meritorious ends, it is clear that they did not represent the entire spectrum of women, to say nothing of addressing the spectrum of women's issues. These organizations clearly did not have a feminist agenda.

The period before the Whitaker reforms has long been identified as one of stagnation in the political, economic, and religious spheres. What was the place of women during that period? With respect to work it was assumed that women's place was in the home and that the pay of women should be less than that of men. Women's income in Ireland was less than half that of men in the period before 1960 because their limited access to education relegated them to work of drudgery and low wages. The law forbidding married women from working was targeted at teachers in 1933, but it was adopted by the civil service, local authorities, and businesses thereafter. In the civil service the attitude was that a woman in the job was "blocking the way of a man who could give the State good value for the service in question."[14] Protective restrictions were also present in the industrial sector that created exclusions in the employment of women. With respect to pay, the regulations in the civil service graded pay differently based on both gender and marital status: single men and women were paid less than married men in the lower grades and women were paid less than men (married or single) in the higher grades. These practices were emulated in the private sector as well.

The Commission on the Status of Women's *Report to the Minister of Finance* in 1972 notes a number of attitudes that undergirded the restrictive laws on work and pay for women. Management surveys indicated that managers, virtually all male, described jobs with intellectual content as difficult, harder, and requiring decision making and therefore better suited to males. Women were seen as staying only a short time between school and marriage and thus did not warrant a high investment of time, training, and pay. Management also saw women as indifferent to promotion even though surveys of women at the same period indicated that they were interested in promotions and advancement.[15] With respect to pay it was also clear, all agreed, that men should be paid more because they had a family to support. Majorities of men favored higher pay for married men than single men, higher pay for married men than married women, and higher pay for men than women overall. But when women were surveyed in the same period, most of them favored equal pay for single men and women and equal pay for a married man or woman, but more for a married man with dependents than for a single woman. All of these attitudes reflect sexism, but it should be pointed out that they also embody a different notion of social justice, which viewed remuneration as tied to social role as well as market value. The report notes, "there is a feeling that persons with dependents should have a higher total income than those without dependents."[16] In 1960 the pay of women was no more than 53 percent of that of men.

The data are clear on the degree of women's participation in the workforce: from 1926 to 1960, 26 percent to 29.7 percent. In 1970 the figure dropped to 28.2 percent. This was the lowest figure in Europe except for Spain. In 1960 the rate of married women at work in Ireland was 5.2 percent; it had increased to 7.5 percent by 1970. Women's limited mobility in the workforce and access to promotion and higher positions is reflected in the percentages of women in the three highest grades of the civil service. In 1960 and 1965 the number of women in the higher grades did not exceed 3.6 percent of the total, while in the bottom grade women represented over half of the total. Professionally, women were in the majority in two jobs, nurses and teachers. In 1966 the percentage of women engineers was 0.0017, architects 0 .034, and accountants 0.033.

The Search for Equality

How did demands for a change in the status of women emerge? Catherine Shannon identifies five factors that converged in the late 1960s: exposure to international feminism; the 1972 *Report of the Commission on the Status of Women*; pressure from the European Economic Community (now the European Union); an expanding economy; and the effects of increased access of women to education.[17] Exposure to women's groups' actions and feminist ideas outside of Ireland began in the 1960s. In 1967 the United Nations called for governments to set up National Commissions on the Status of Women. The Irish Housewive's Association and the Association of Business and Professional Women formed an ad hoc committee on women's rights in January 1968. This group of more than twenty women's organizations represented a liberal feminist middle class position concerned with the equal treatment of women (one of the three strands to emerge in articulating the women's perspective). In response to the research done by this group and the pressure they exerted, the 1970 Fianna Fail government appointed the Commission on the Status of Women, with senior civil servant Thekla Beere in the chair. The Commission issued its report in December 1972. The report called for action on forty-nine recommendations to eliminate discrimination against women in the realms of employment taxes, education, social welfare, the law, and public life.[18] The ad hoc Committee on Women's Rights became the Council for the Status of Women in 1973, a voluntary lobbying association of about twenty women's groups to assess the implementation of the 1972 report. The Commission later came to be the established, and establishment, voice of Irish women; it was structured into the governmental process of dealing with women's issues.

A somewhat more left-wing and republican approach emerged in the same period as a result of the exposure of women to the explosive ferment of the international feminist movement, which called attention to the marginal status of women in Ireland. Cosmopolitan women in Dublin, such as Mary Maher of the *Irish Times* and Mary Kenney of the *Irish Press,* were instrumental in increasing women's awareness and in organizing the Irish Women's Liberation Movement (IWLM) in 1971. The manifesto of the organization, *Chains or Change? The Civil Wrongs of Irish Women,* published in 1971, reflected both the middle class emphasis on equality and the more radical demands of militant feminists, calling for one family, one house; equal rights in law; equal pay and removal of the marriage bar; justice for widows, deserted wives, and unmarried mothers; equal educational opportunities; and access to contraception as a human right.[19] This group's appearance on Gay Byrne's "Late Late Show" in March 1971 triggered shouting matches and provoked a vigorous public response. A mass meeting in the Mansion House a month later mobilized a large number of women into the women's movement. The IWLM's "Condom Train" in May caused further explosive public response as women went to Belfast and purchased condoms, then flaunted them in front of the police, who were too embarrassed to arrest anyone. All three events certainly put women's issues on the public agenda. Single-issue groups emerged at this time, collecting women around a particular issue. Examples are AIM (Action, Information, Motivation), which focused on family law reform; Women's Aid; The Rape Crisis Center; Cherish, which lobbies for unmarried mothers; and the Women's Political Association, designed to elect women to office.

The Council for the Status of Women represented the liberal feminist, reformist, "remove the legal impediments on women" point of view; the IWLM represented a more militant feminist agenda reflected in *Chains or Change;* and the most radical point of view was advocated by the Irishwomen United (IWU), created in 1975. Although short lived and ultimately transformed into other organizations, the IWU sought to create an autonomous, politicized, and radicalized women's movement. Supported by the Movement for a Socialist Republic, The Communist Party of Ireland, the Irish Republican Socialist Party, and the International Lesbian

Caucus, members of IWU initiated the Contraception Action Programme in 1976 and the Women's Right to Choose Campaign in 1980, the latter advocating a woman's right to choose an abortion. The radical politics of the IWU hardly endeared them to the mainstream of Irish politics, let alone Irish women. The positions they held—self-determined sexuality and the opportunity to choose abortion, for example—were unlikely to draw enthusiastic encomiums in the chatter after Sunday Mass. The IWU did, however, influence the women's movement through its organizational work, its strategy of confrontation and demonstrations, and its ideological critique of the traditional norms of Irish society.[20]

Laws were rapidly changing as a result of the pressure of the women's movement, both in response to the *Report of the Commission on the Status of Women* and to conform to the directives of the European Economic Community. Ireland entered the European Economic Community in 1973. The 1957 Treaty of Rome, in Article 119, called for "equal pay for equal work" for women. In 1972 Ireland passed an amendment to the Constitution that gave primacy to European law in employment and social welfare. Thus Ireland was compelled—by pressure from both the women's movement within and the European Union without—to change its laws. The most notable piece of legislation in this period was the 1974 Anti-Discrimination (Pay) Act, which entitled women to the same remuneration as men for work that is interchangeable, "the same work under the same or similar conditions," work of a "similar nature," or work that is of "similar value" in terms of the demands it makes. In the National Wage Agreements of 1972, pay differentials between men and women based on gender or marriage were narrowed by 17.5 percent and in 1975 by an additional 50 percent.[21] Other traditional strictures were falling as well. In 1972 in a case involving trade unions picketing to prevent the hiring of women, *Murtaugh Properties Ltd. v. Cleary,* the Court held that the right to earn a livelihood without discrimination on the basis of sex is a personal right protected by the Constitution. In 1973 the Civil Service (Employment of Married Women) Act removed the ban on married women working in the civil service. This was followed by the removal of the marriage ban in semi-state bodies, schools, local government, and other agencies and, after passage of the 1975 Anti-Discrimination (Employment) Bill, in the private sector.

In 1975 the Supreme Court struck down the provision whereby jury duty was confined to taxpayers and eliminated the specific exemption of women from jury duty. In response to the 1976 EEC Directive 76/207 calling for equal access to work and promotion, the Dail passed the 1977 Employment Equality Act, guaranteeing access to jobs equally for men and women and rejecting discrimination on the basis of gender or marital status.[22] This Act created the Employment Equality Agency to monitor the 1977 Act. Also in 1977 the Dail passed the Unfair Dismissals Act, which prevented the unfair dismissal of women for maternity leaves. In 1979 the Defense (Amendment)(2) Act provided for the enlistment of women in the armed forces. In 1981 the Maternity (Protection of Employees) Act granted every female employee who is insurable up to fourteen weeks of maternity leave if she qualifies.[23]

In the domain of social welfare, the 1979 European Economic Community Third Equality Directive (Council Directive 79/7/EEC) ordered the member states to implement by December 1984: "no discrimination whatsoever on ground of sex directly or indirectly by reference to marital or family status." This applied to matters of social security; social insurance; and social assistance schemes concerning sickness, invalidity, old age, accidents, occupational diseases, and unemployment for the working population. However, shortly thereafter the Irish government passed the controversial 1981 Social Welfare (Amendment) Act, which provided that a married woman was precluded from claiming unemployment assistance unless her husband was dependent upon her, in effect deeming all married women dependent on their husbands as long as they were living with them. Exclusion from unemployment benefits also meant exclusion from any job training program based on receiving those benefits. Despite the obvious inequality of that Act, the government did not implement the European Economic Community directive until the 1985 Social Welfare (#2) Act, which standardized the levels of unemployment, disability, and injury compensation for men and women. Women began receiving unemployment assistance in November 1986.

In *Carberry v. The Minister for Social Welfare,* the High Court in 1989 overturned an earlier decision as discriminatory, thus affirming the same benefits for married women as were given to married men. In 1986 the European Economic Community issued the Fourth Equality Directive (86/378/EEC), which called for equal treatment for men and women in occupational social security schemes, compelling Ireland to bring its policies in line with Europe's.

Changes in other dimensions of Irish life were beginning to have their impact on women. The education revolution provided increased access for women to all levels of education, and better-educated women were far more conscious of the role and status of women. The second generation of changes in the place of women in Ireland came after 1985, when women's organizations shifted their focus from the achievement of rights to addressing issues of gender inequality in the practices and norms of the society as well as in its laws. The changes in the Irish economy that had occurred since 1960 were expanding urban clusters, increasing industrial employment, and increasing population in the suburbs. These changes provided women with more opportunities to break down traditional gender role expectations.

The years up to the mid-1980s were marked by high visibility on women's issues. Women held national meetings in 1977 and 1978, ran campaigns to create a Women's Centre and a Rape Crisis Center and to make contraceptives available to women, held a demonstration against violence against women in 1978, formed magazines, and held meetings on issues from lesbianism to equal pay. The political parties could not help but take notice of this growing movement, and the number of women candidates for the Dail in the 1977 election was twenty-five, fourteen more than in 1960. Of these twenty-five, six were elected. Prime Minister Jack Lynch appointed three women as senators and in 1977 Maire Geoghegan-Quinn became the first woman Cabinet member when she became minister for the Gaeltacht. In 1982 the Fine Gael government under Garret FitzGerald appointed a minister for Women's Affairs and Law Reform, Nualla Fennell, TD, in the Department of the Taoiseach. In 1983 a Joint Parliamentary Committee on Women's Rights was created; it later issued influential reports on education, social welfare, media, and sexual violence.

Controversial Issues in the 1980s

A continuing legislative controversy and two referenda in this period reveal the jagged intersection between the place of women in Ireland, the doctrines of the Church, and the policy of the state. The first issue was the legal status of birth control, the second was the 1983 referendum constitutionally prohibiting abortion, and the third was the 1986 and 1995 referenda to rescind the constitutional prohibition on divorce. These issues were central to the politics of the women's movement and were also important in the context of Church–state relations.

Birth Control

The first important development shaping Church and state relations in regard to women's rights occurred in 1973 when the Supreme Court in *McGee v. Attorney General* struck down by a three to two margin the part of the 1935 Criminal Law Amendment Act (17.3) that made it unlawful to "sell, or expose, offer, advertise or keep for sale . . . or import . . . contraceptives." Mrs. McGee had four children and was advised by her doctor that another pregnancy would endanger her life. She attempted to import contraceptives for her personal use but was forbidden to do so by Customs officials. The Court found a right to marital privacy in Articles 40 and 41 of the Constitution and based its judgment on that principle. The issue of contraception had been part of the women's movement agenda and they had exerted pressure for liberalized access. The McGee decision opened up the issue for the state to legislate a new policy on contraception. The first legislation was the relatively restrictive Health and Family Planning Act of 1979, which allowed distribution of contraceptives only by a doctor's prescription to married couples over eighteen years of age and restricted outlets. A second, more liberal law in 1985 eliminated the prescriptions for those over eighteen years old and expanded the number and type of outlets. In 1992 an Act allowed access to condoms by seventeen year olds at an expanded but still limited number of locations. Access to oral and spermicidal forms of medical contraceptives remains restricted.

The contraception issue brought to the surface the conflicts that emerge when the doctrines of the Church and the laws of the state collide with the interests of women. The Church's doctrinal position was that each act of sexual intercourse be in principle open to the possibility of conception. The use of contraceptives, however, had increased dramatically in Ireland and the Church was losing the battle over people's behavior long before the political issue came to the Dail. The pressure for liberalization of the laws on contraception came only in part from the women's movement. The spreading secular liberalism in Ireland also defined the contraception issue as one of individual rights. The Church had to shift its justification for opposition to the law from asserting its doctrinal position to secular terms, arguing that contraception would cause a deterioration of the moral character of society. Finally, the potential spread of AIDS brought a new realism to the issue in the 1990s. The debate on contraception had begun in the 1970s based on the Church's doctrinal issue, had shifted to the issue of the social effects of potential promiscuous behavior, and ended on the issue of the deadly potential of unprotected sex.

Abortion

The movement to place an anti-abortion law in the Constitution can be attributed to, among other things, the rise of the radical wing of the women's movement, which generated a reaction among conservative religious groups.[24] At the founding conference of the Pro Life Amendment Campaign (PLAC) in 1981, for example, John O'Reilly, of the Society for the Protection of the Unborn Child (SPUC) cited the Dublin Well Women's Centre and the Women's Right to Choose group as part of a pro-abortion movement; both were associated with Irishwomen United.[25] In the view of the PLAC, the Responsible Society, Opus Dei, and other conservative groups, a rising tide of secularism and moral decadence threatened to overwhelm Ireland. Even though abortion was already forbidden by the 1861 Offences Against the Person Act, their efforts were designed to preempt the possibility of the right to an abortion emerging in the future. In fact most people in Ireland, and most women's groups, were not pro-abortion, a position without much traction in natalist Catholic Ireland. The anti-abortion campaign provided a focal point, however, for those who resented the extent and speed of social change in Ireland.[26]

The opposition to the amendment was led by the Anti-Amendment Campaign (AAC). Sixteen organizations, later to grow to sixty, including the Well Women's Centre, the Democratic Socialist Party, the Irish Council for Civil Liberties, and the Trade Union Women's Forum, were loosely associated, with Senator Mary Robinson as spokesperson.[27] They opposed the amendment on a variety of grounds. Some groups sought a woman's right to choose an abortion. Others were opposed to the state preventing a woman from having control over her own body and to the wording of the amendment, which could potentially be interpreted as valuing a woman's life as secondary to that of a fetus. Anti-abortion advocates noted the failure of adequate policies with respect to sex education and contraception. The Protestant churches opposed the amendment as unnecessary, divisive, and sectarian.

Fine Gael, under the leadership of Garret FitzGerald, was in power at the time and was caught in a maelstrom that went far beyond what was at first imagined to be a straightforward matter. The issue centered around the wording of the amendment formulated by the earlier Haughey government: "The state acknowledges the right to life of the unborn and, with due regard to the equal right to life of the mother, guarantees in its laws to respect, and, as far as is practicable, by its laws to defend and vindicate that right." In the opinion of Attorney General Peter Sutherland, recorded in a detailed 100-page report in 1982, that wording was capable of being interpreted by the Supreme Court as preventing any operation on the mother no matter what the nature of the pregnancy, such as cancer of the womb or an ectopic pregnancy. Another less likely but possible interpretation was that the Court would read the amendment as allowing abortion under certain circumstances because the word "unborn" was undefined. The Catholic Church preferred the original wording because it would exclude any abortion and considered the moment of conception to be the beginning of life. When Prime Minister Garret FitzGerald sought an alternative wording that addressed Sutherland's concerns, the result was seen as not explicit enough by the PLAC or the Church and was resisted by Fianna Fail. The Dail legislation calling for the referendum went forward containing the original wording.

The Church took the position that although Irish voters should vote their consciences it was the obligation of the Church to inform the conscience of good Catholics on matters of faith and morals. The political parties took the position that this was a nonpartisan issue, but the head of Fianna Fail, Charles Haughey, supported the amendment and its wording while the head of Fine Gael, Garret FitzGerald, and Dick Spring, the head of the Labour Party, opposed the wording and the amendment altogether. Throughout 1983 the campaign was so divisive that Tom Hesketh called his book on the subject *The Second Partitioning of Ireland* and likened it to the Irish Civil War.[28] Turnout at the polls in September 1983 was 55 percent. The people voted two to one (66.9 to 33.1 percent) in favor of the amendment. The vote in Dublin was very close and the only five constituencies returning "no" votes were in Dublin. Rural Ireland was overwhelmingly clear in its endorsement of the amendment.

The Irish courts initially took the amendment to mean that no information could be presented to the Irish people about abortion or about travel for pregnancy termination. In both the 1988 case, *Attorney General v. Open Door Counseling et al.*, and a 1989 case, *SPUC v. Grogan et al.*, the SPUC brought suit against clinics that offered non-directive abortion information and counseling. The Irish Supreme Court decided that it was illegal under article 40.3.3 of the Constitution to provide information that would assist a pregnant woman to travel abroad for an abortion. The defendants, represented by Mary Robinson, appealed to the European Court of Justices, which decided in 1991 that the pregnancy services available in one European Union country could be advertised in another (*SPUC v. Grogan*). In 1992, on the basis of Article 10 of the European

Convention on Human Rights, which guarantees free expression, the European Court of Human Rights decided in favor of the clinics (awarding them $38,000) on the basis that the provision of information does not necessarily assist abortion and that the protection of the rights of the unborn could not preempt the rights of freedom of expression (*Open Door Counseling, Well Women Centre et al. v. Ireland*).[29]

The information and travel issues provoked one of the more explosive reactions of Irish public opinion. In 1992 a young woman of fourteen (Miss X) was raped by a family acquaintance. After charges were filed the family sought an abortion in London and notified the Garda of their departure in case medical evidence was needed. The Garda in turn notified the attorney general. He issued an injunction that prevented the girl from leaving Ireland on the basis of the anti-abortion amendment to Article 40.3.3. In fact, the young woman was already in England, but the parents complied with the order and returned to Ireland. The young woman was threatening to take her own life if she had to complete the pregnancy. The attorney general's decision was upheld by the High Court, which based its decision on the grounds that while it was uncertain that the distraught young woman actually would carry out a threatened suicide, it was certain that the unborn child's life would be terminated.

An outburst of elite, media, and public opinion caught government officials and the pro-life movement by surprise in its intensity and the sense of outrage expressed that the full authority and institutions of the state were being put to use to prevent a distraught, suicidal fourteen year old from choosing not to go through the ordeal of a pregnancy and childbirth that was the result of a rape. The parents sought a clarification from the Supreme Court. In the *X et al. v. Attorney General* decision, the Supreme Court, by a four to one vote, chose to overturn the High Court based on the "real and substantial risk" to the mother's life from suicide. While this decision solved the *X* case, it left ambiguities about the understanding of Article 40.3.3 on travel and information, which were resolved to some extent by two amendments to the Constitution passed in 1992.

One of these amendments established that Article 40.3.3 could not prevent the provision of information about abortion services available in another state of the European Union and the other established that Article 40.3.3 could not limit travel from state to state (a possibility that the *X* case had not precluded). A third amendment to Article 40.3.3, supported by the Catholic Church and the AAC, was designed to counter the *X* decision by limiting the grounds for termination of a pregnancy to the basis of a "real and substantial risk" to the life of the mother (not merely to her health), stating that the risk of suicide by the mother was not sufficient. The public adopted the first two amendments but did not accept the third. Between 1981 and 1990 there had been a shift in public opinion with respect to abortion. The number of women approving of an abortion if the mother's life was in danger increased from 43 percent to 63 percent and the number of men supporting that position increased from 49 percent to 67 percent.[30] The AAC and the SPUC, which had sought to make the provisions against abortion more absolute, were dismayed because the result of the rejection of the third amendment was that the prevailing decision remains the *X* case which, while restrictive, explicitly rejected the argument that "it is only where there is an immediate risk of the mother's death that termination of a pregnancy is constitutionally permitted."[31]

The abortion controversy affected the latitude that a woman had to seek information on abortion or to travel; affected constitutional interpretation of the degree of danger that a mother must bear; polarized Church–state relations;[32] and divided the country on the questions of pregnancy and cancer, ectopic pregnancy, and rape and suicide. Abortion was also drawn into the 1992 vote on the question of Ireland's degree of integration into the European Union through accession to the Maasticht Treaty.[33] The Maastricht Treaty called for a common currency, eliminated a wide range of trade restrictions, strengthened the European Parliament, and further coordinated the member states' foreign policy. The Haughey government had quietly negotiated a separate protocol to the Anglo-Irish Treaty that exempted Ireland from any liberalization of access to abortion in the European Union based on Article 40.3.3. When the Treaty was up for a vote in a referendum in June 1992 the protocol became an issue because of the *X* case. The SPUC and the AAC urged a rejection of the Treaty on the basis that the Supreme Court's judgment allowing abortion under certain limited circumstances would be bound into a Treaty obligation. The protocol "protected" the amendment, which was now interpreted more liberally than the original intent of the AAC. Anti-amendment supporters opposed the protocol for the opposite reason, fearing that it would circumscribe both travel and information about abortion. The Fianna Fail government of Albert Reynolds strove to cleave the abortion issue from the debate over the issues of Ireland's role in an increasingly integrated Europe. The abortion protocol, however, was woven into the debate, with both supporters and opponents of the anti-abortion amendment urging a "no" vote. The Maastricht provisions passed in June 1992 by a margin of 70 percent to 30 percent due to the overall pro-Europe sentiment in Ireland.

In the final analysis the Irish people remain opposed to abortion as an unfettered choice and their preference is unquestionably to retain provisions that make it illegal in Ireland except under very circumscribed circumstances. Thus the difficulties faced by women confronted with an unwanted pregnancy are essentially dealt with in the same way that unemployment was dealt with in the De Valera years: by going abroad. Irish women went to England to terminate pregnancy on an average of 3,800 times per year from 1980 to 1990; estimates run to 5,000 per year for the 1990s. They pay about $750 for an abortion, a price that allows more well-off women than poor women to make this choice. No doubt this is, as the aphorism has it, an Irish solution to an Irish problem.

Divorce

Bills had been brought forward in the Dail in the 1980s to eliminate the constitutional prohibition against divorce. Although not successful, they prompted the Fine Gael government under FitzGerald to propose a bill to offer a referendum to the people on the question of allowing divorce legislation. The issue of divorce had been lurking on the social agenda for some time as a series of demographic and social changes occurred in Ireland. Marriage in Ireland in previous generations had been a union of older people who had not had much opportunity to know each other very well; it was based on property and stability and was often lacking in emotional connection between the partners. The options for women other than marriage were few, and there was an expectation that fulfillment would come from children, not necessarily from love and companionship. The male-dominated ethos sometimes made violence a part of the relationship, and alcohol and the male companionship of the pub were preferred to the cultivation of the marriage. The lack of divorce meant that succor for pain in a relationship for women came from female companionship. The Church saw the necessity for sacrifice and suffering as more important than self-fulfillment and prayer as more effective than dissolution of the union. More than a few writers paint a picture of this bleak emotional landscape, including John McGahern in *Amongst Women* and William Trevor in his short story "The Ballroom of Romance."

The growth in the women's movement had corresponded to growth in educational and employment opportunities and the weakening grasp of the Church on a no longer traditional rural society. Young people changed their patterns of socializing with the other gender, their expectations of happiness from relationships, and the alternative choices available in career and family.[34] As with birth control, where the behavior of the Irish people had far outpaced the doctrinal strictures of the Church and the legal strictures of the state, the changes in relationships, marriage, and the family were becoming apparent by the 1970s. In 1979 the census included a category for separated people and revealed that by the early 1990s, 40,000 to 60,000 people were affected by the breakdown of their marriages.[35] These numbers exposed the difficulties of people's lives. The law in Ireland concerning divorce and remarriage, the purchase of property, inheritance, child custody, and the like were all based on the idea that divorce was not an option; that all marriages, however difficult, were retrievable; and that women's place was in the home.

The discontinuities became obvious as time passed; for example, civil divorces received by Irish Catholics while living abroad were recognized by the Irish state but not by the Church. Conversely, when the Church granted an annulment the individuals were no longer recognized as married by the Church but were by the state, which had no provision for divorce. If that person remarried in the eyes of the Church it was a first marriage, while in the eyes of the state it was a second marriage made while the first was still in force. When new relationships were formed the issues of property, inheritance, and child custody became unclear and many were left in a legal limbo.

The effects on women of an "Irish divorce," that is, separation or desertion, were severe. The trials of lone parenthood included a higher likelihood of being poor: 88 percent of households headed by lone parents were in the lowest socio-economic group, compared to only 14 percent of two-parent households. Ninety percent of lone-parent households depend on social welfare for 80 percent of their income. The circumstances of poverty and unemployment generate a panoply of problems associated with those conditions—crime, homelessness, and low achievement—which fall disproportionately on the shoulders of women.[36]

The attitude of Irish society to divorce, especially in cities, was increasingly to live and let live; the traditional social sanctions of shame and disapproval were diminishing. The traditional response of the Church was condemnation, the denial of sacraments, and the marshaling of social disapproval. Such actions have less and less effect and the clergy is confronted with increasingly open non-married couples living together, to say nothing of the increase in open gay and lesbian relationships.

In the face of these circumstances the government sought to rationalize the legal status of the breakdown of marriage and divorce. FitzGerald consulted the churches in Ireland and found support for a limited divorce law among all but the Catholic Church which, not surprisingly, had reservations about the change.[37] At that point the opposition party, Fianna Fail, did not oppose the bill and the other parties favored it, so it passed the Dail in May 1986 with no difficulty. The bill called for the dissolution of a marriage by a court if the marriage had failed for at least five years, there was no reasonable possibility of reconciliation between the parties, and the court was satisfied with the provisions for the dependent spouse and children.

Public opinion polls had increasingly supported a change in the ban on divorce since 1980, and in May 1986 as many as 61 percent of the population favored the change.[38] The Divorce Action Group had been pressing the issue since 1980 and had brought the liberal wing of Fine Gael, including FitzGerald who personally supported a change, and the Labour Party around to its view. The liberal media and Dublin elites all shared this view, as did the Right to Remarry Campaign, the Irish Council for Civil Liberties, the National Women's Council, and Women's Aid, while the opponents of change in the law were quiescent until the referendum. This apparent support and lack of opposition masked the amount of resistance to the change that actually existed. In addition, FitzGerald and Fine Gael blundered in their handling of the issue.

The opposition that had been mobilized by the earlier anti-abortion campaign was again evoked. In May the Anti Divorce Campaign (ADC) was launched, run by Senator Des Hanafin, a leader of the PLAC in 1983, and others from the Anti-Abortion Campaign. They were advised by Professor Mary MacAleese of Trinity College (who was to replace Mary Robinson as president of Ireland in 1997).

Organizations that rallied in opposition to the amendment included the Responsible Society, the Family League, and the Public Policy Institute of Ireland. The latter conducted research on public policy issues on the basis of natural law and Christian principles. All these organizations shared a commitment to traditional values as delineated in the Constitution and in Church doctrine. They argued that the availability of divorce destabilized marriage and led to marital breakdown.[39] The ADC based its opposition on secular grounds, not Church doctrine. They argued that the preeminent place of the family in the Constitution would be threatened and that the primary protection of the law would pass to the second family of a divorced person while the first family would loose its rights of succession. The ADC pointed out that there were no criteria for establishing the failure of a marriage and that divorce could be granted even when the spouse and children were on social welfare.[40]

To appeal to women the ADC adopted a language that spoke to traditional values, even though the subtext depicted women as either helpless victims or predators seeking financial security. Women in happy marriages, it was surmised, would succumb to the temptation of monetary gain by dumping their husbands and marrying older men. Men were seen as ready to selfishly jettison their spouses to secure a younger trophy wife; they would waste no time in abandoning their families. The slogan "Hello Divorce, Goodbye Daddy," used by anti-amendment groups, succinctly conveyed this idea. The image of marriage presented was at the same time sacred and central to society, to be revered and preserved, and brittle and ready to be torpedoed by people in a nanosecond in a quest for status, sex, or money. People so very susceptible to temptation had, in the ADC's view, to be forced to be good.

The ADC gained support and mobilized the public against the amendment on the basis of traditional values while the government was making its case on the basis of the practical necessity to provide remedies for people in marriages that were irretrievably broken down. The government, unwilling to argue against the prevailing Church doctrine and popular sentiment, reiterated its fidelity to family values and treated the campaign not as a matter of principle—that is, by asserting the right of an individual to make a decision to divorce and remarry—but as a form of technical fix for special cases. The necessary legislation to support the referendum was absent and left people feeling that they would be voting for something that was both unknown and threatening.

In addition to handing the initiative to the opposition, FitzGerald let the members of his party, Fine Gael, become leaders of the opposition. Patrick Cooney, the minister for Education, worked actively against the referendum. FitzGerald's party at best did not mobilize adequately and at worst were in open opposition to their own government's position. The opposition Fianna Fail officially had no position on the amendment but, because a majority of their members opposed divorce legislation, the party and the party apparatus were mobilized in opposition. Finally, the Catholic bishops issued a statement in June that voters should vote their consciences but that the Church's view was that the amendment would weaken the family. In fact, letters were read from pulpits decrying the amendment, especially in rural Ireland.

Public support for the amendment drained away in a startling reversal of sentiment that represented a twenty-seven point shift from positive to negative in a period of little more than two months. The results of the referendum, held on June 27, 1986, were 63.5 percent opposed and 36.5 percent for, with a turnout of 62.7 percent of the electorate. The only constituencies that voted for the amendment were in Dublin, and the rural vote was overwhelmingly negative. The results mirrored the abortion referendum results to a remarkable degree, with the difference that a pro-abortion position never had any significant support prior to the vote, while the divorce issue had been supported by a majority of the public up until the referendum. The public had in fact made a distinction between the removal of the divorce prohibition from the Constitution and the rules and laws that would apply in the specific circumstances of divorce. The latter were supported by considerably fewer people (51 percent) than was the former (71 percent).[41] The government mistook support for divorce for support of the specific laws on divorce, a misstep that would be corrected in 1995.

Understanding Ireland's Attitudes Toward Birth Control, Abortion, and Divorce

Many interpretations have been offered to make sense of the unfolding issues of birth control, abortion, and divorce in Ireland in the 1980s. All involve interpreting the three issues as symbols of change in Irish society. The British press, for example, archly observed after the 1986 divorce referendum that the Irish were too backward, too provincial, and too pious to step into the modern world. Ulster unionists asserted that the Roman Catholic Church was omnipotent in the Republic and that the Irish voters were rejecting unionist values. Fianna Fail's Charles Haughey read the results as requiring that Garret FitzGerald resign. All these explanations placed the agenda of the observer on the shoulders of the Irish voters and assumed that they went to the polls to send a message on that issue. This perspective prevails among cosmopolitan liberal elites, both within and outside of Ireland, who set as a benchmark for themselves and others the standards of highly individualistic and pluralistic advanced democracies. Often their reference point is the values and lifestyles of the most advantaged of those societies, such as the "chattering classes" of the Donnybrook set.[42] In this view values in Ireland with respect to politics, women, religion, lifestyle, and individual choice are by definition backward and change is at best marginal and inadequate or simply absent. Clerics get the clever whack in the press from the pundit's word processor, country people are admired for their simplicity in the abstract while their values and behavior are seen as backward, religious conviction is seen as religiosity, religion is viewed at most as an individual preference but certainly not a source of social values. The clumsy political evolution of contraception policy is stressed (with religious politicians such as "Father" Oliver Flanagan at stage front), as are the similarity of the percentages by which abortion and divorce were rejected in 1983 and 1986 (except of course in the more worldly environs of Dublin). Intellectually biting as this perspective may be, it does not go very far toward explaining the response of the Irish people to these issues. The gradations of differences in response to the three different issues, the changes in responses over time, and the differences in depth of intensity are lost in the casting of the Irish into "us" versus "them" (the backward).

An interpretation involving more nuances can be expressed as the friction between traditional society and the liberalizing trends that have occurred since 1960. In this conception the assertion of individual rights collides with the traditional values of the Church and the broader social values, and, in the tension between these positions, the particular policies on specific issues are established only as part of an ongoing change in Ireland from traditional to modern. Thus the abortion and divorce referenda create a parallelogram of pressures between Church dogma, a pluralist Ireland, a united Ireland, and a "cheapened" secular Ireland. The Irish voters were not, as portrayed, trying to dent Prime Minister FitzGerald's reputation, reject the dream of a united Ireland, or oppress Protestants, but rather were trying to prevent the loss of something they cherish: the connection between their religion, their identity, and their community.[43] Brian Girvin, Tom Hesketh, Joe Lee, and Carol Coulter, among others, share this position to varying degrees. In this conception the nature of the issue, and the depth of its place in the traditional culture, makes a difference in the response of the Irish people. The nature of the issue and the arguments and interests are joined in a debate in which the liberal democratic dimension of the Irish Constitution is asserted against the notion of a Catholic state. The linear evolution, in this view, will produce a liberal state of individual rights imbedded in a Catholic nation. The liberalization efforts were eventually successful in the realm of contraception; limited divorce emerged after two referenda (1986 and one in 1995, discussed below); and the attempt to preclude any abortion, as well as the X case, oddly enough produced a narrow band of circumstances in which it was allowed. In this construction the modernization of Ireland produces a demand for individual autonomy that pushes aside demonstrably outdated traditional social and cultural values and laws. The process of change is located in the modernizing values and attitudes of the Irish people, especially the young and the more well educated and well traveled.

Tom Garvin and J. P. O'Carroll highlight two facets of the referenda campaigns that placed them in wider historical and psychological contexts, with a much greater emphasis on tradition as active and assertive rather than passive. Garvin sees the campaigns as manifestations of a much longer political and moral war against the external secularism that was polluting the purity of traditional Catholic nationalism, while O'Carroll holds that Irish traditional thought had

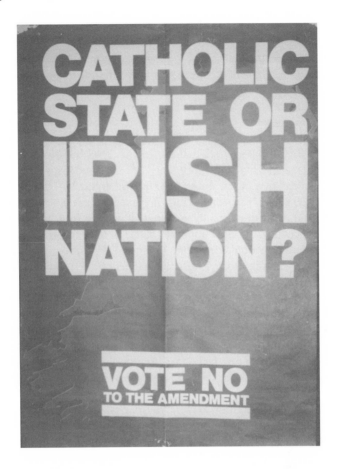

Poster urging voters to reject the 1983 Amendment to the Constitution, which would elevate the prohibition on abortion from the statutory to the constitutional level. The poster addresses the degree to which Church doctrine should be embodied in the constitution and produce a Catholic state rather than specific issues of the morality and legality of abortion. *Photo by Richard B. Finnegan*

certain defining characteristics and was aggressive in defining and attacking perceived threats.[44] Garvin argues that a nineteenth-century puritan image of Ireland was fostered by fundamentalist Catholicism and reinforced by institutions and laws that fostered parochialism. This matched up well with the nationalist image of Ireland as a bucolic agricultural utopia portrayed by de Valera. Law and policy after 1922 reinforced this alliance of values until Irish nationalists recognized the deadening effects of emigration and Irish life in the 1950s. They reversed their policies and sought engagement with Europe, economic growth, and educational reform and thus came into conflict with the puritan Catholic image of Ireland. Garvin argues that the anti-divorce and anti-abortion movements adhered to that puritanical parochial panorama and were marked by a pattern of denial that prevented the acknowledgment of the change that had occurred in Ireland over the past thirty years and thus promoted a "politics of cultural defense" that could ignore change and sanctify a static past.[45]

O'Carroll also develops the features of the traditional culture that mobilized pro-life forces. The political culture of independent Ireland (the cluster of political values, beliefs, and behaviors that undergirds Irish politics) was monolithic and cohesive, marked by conformity, puritanical attitudes toward sex, and authoritarian control by Church and state. O'Carroll argues that the traditional position is marked by the incapacity to imagine an acceptable alternative position to its own; traditionalists thus tend to be absolutist in their assertions and intolerant of any other point of view because it must, *prime facie,* be incorrect. For traditionalists the Constitution would "enshrine" the pro-life position, which would preclude any other "morally wrong" option. Change, to the traditionalists, is highly anxiety producing. They see the present as defiled, and defend a non-existent past in which everything was the way it should be, conjured up as an alternative to the present. Denial of changing values and behavior ensures that there will always be a period that can be cited by traditionalists when "such things" (whatever they may be: unwanted pregnancies, broken marriages, pre-marital sex) didn't happen. Discussion of issues that impinged on traditionalist values was avoided and, when such issues were brought up, this was seen as an apocalyptic "opening of the floodgates" to the "permissive society" in which the unborn would be "murdered."

Thus the referenda, according to O'Carroll, had certain implications for Ireland, the first being the importance of Irish identity in defending cultural myths. Abortion, which was already illegal, was not going to be changed, but a particular version of Irish identity was going to be asserted and defended. In addition the absolutist posture, construing debate as a means to condemn the moral order of one's opponents, was hardly conducive to the development of democracy. The manner in which the traditionalists approached the abortion controversy— defining the issue as morally absolute, framing the debate in apocalyptic terms, and seeing victory as delegitimizing the point of view of opponents—undermined the possibility of development and change in social values and the possibility of negotiating acceptable norms.[46] But changing social values were not undermined as much as traditionalists might have liked. From the mid-1980s up to the late 1990s the amount and type of change with respect to women accelerated. We return to the divorce issue and then consider changes in other realms of policy with respect to women.

Taking nearly a decade to return to the national agenda in the form of a referendum, divorce was again put before the public in 1995. The Fianna Fail had moved away from opposition to divorce by the early 1990s and the government had commissioned a report, titled *Marital Breakdown: A Review and Proposed*

Changes, in 1992.[47] The report reviewed the difficulties created by the lack of a divorce law and the measures in place to deal with the circumstances of separation and divorce, such as the 1989 Judicial Separation and Family Law Reform Act. Promising legislation that would deal with maintenance, ownership of property, and recognition of foreign divorces, the coalition government that came to power in 1992 proceeded with a plan to hold a referendum in 1995.

The proposed amendment stated that a court could dissolve a marriage when the couple had lived apart for four of the last five years and there was no reasonable prospect of reconciliation. The court would deal with the problem of spousal support and provisions for the children. Conflict on the issue broke out immediately when the government proposed to spend $60,000 on promoting the pro-divorce amendment to the public. Opposition members of the Dail challenged that expenditure, saying that it should be spent to put forward both sides of the question.[48] The real campaign, as in 1986, was a contest between the Church and those in favor of a traditional Ireland and the liberals. Liberals saw the change as needed to allow minorities to avail themselves of divorce or as a way to eliminate the punitive legal limbo resulting from the absence of a law addressing the reality of broken marriages, separation, new relationships, and children of second unions. Women's groups, liberals such as the Irish Council for Civil Liberties, and others saw these claims as legitimate rights that the Church and state had denied the individual in the name of Church doctrine.

The Church Hierarchy took an aggressive position on the referendum. The Archbishop of Cashel asserted that divorced people had more automobile accidents and a greater incidence of physical and mental health problems. The Bishop of Ferns claimed that the all party consensus on the bill rendered the people "voiceless" and angry, while the Archbishop of Dublin said that the issue was not just about Catholic teaching but about the nature of the social order: Divorce was part of the swelling secularization of Ireland, a "new individualism" that would undermine the Irish family. This sentiment was echoed by Cardinal Cahal Daly, who argued that divorce would damage society, and by the Bishop of Cork and Ross, who stated that "the good of society must be put before the welfare of the individual."[49] The Church stumbled a bit, however, when Bishop Thomas Flynn, the spokesperson for the Hierarchy, warned that Catholics would be denied the sacraments if they divorced and remarried. This warning ignored the fact that Catholics were forbidden to divorce and remarry whether the state allowed them to or not. Thus the heavy-handed threat of removal of the sacraments from Catholics in Ireland could only be interpreted as an indirect means to coerce them into a "no" vote on the referendum. The public, however, was unmoved by the warning; over 80 percent of those surveyed thought people in such circumstances should be able to receive the sacraments.[50] A month before the vote the Catholic Hierarchy issued a million copies of a statement in which they reaffirmed that marriage was an unconditional vow and that changing the law would threaten first marriages. The Hierarchy felt the additional reasons offered by the pro-divorce groups and the government, such as the rights of minorities and the Northern Ireland question, were insufficient to justify the removal of the prohibition against divorce.

The Church was joined by the Anti-Divorce Campaign and the more militant No-Divorce Campaign, which were supported by the Public Policy Institute of Ireland and Opus Dei. The leading figures of each campaign were William Binchey and Ger Casey, respectively. Mark Hamilton provided intellectual support in *The Case Against Divorce*. This book described the pro-divorce argument as being an autonomous claim of the freedom of individuals to manage their own relationships, a claim that Hamilton saw as selfish and attempting to place the individual above the general welfare of the society.[51] Pragmatic arguments against the amendment were that one partner might want a divorce but not the other, the taxpayer would be supporting second families, desertion would be rewarded, the stability of society would be threatened, succession rights would be damaged, and, echoing similar battles in the United States, family values would be threatened.[52]

The government publication for the referendum, *The Right to Remarry,* while carefully declaring the government's adherence to the value of the stability of the family, reiterated the problem of marriage breakdown and the need to address the problems it created. Advocates of the amendment pointed out that divorce laws existed in other countries where there were Catholics and marriages there were as good (or as bad) as in Ireland. The amendment would actually add stability to society because it would eliminate the number of difficult situations in second relationships. Some argued for the rights of minorities, for whom their was no religious doctrinal issue about divorce, others for the protection of women, who ended up in the position of being poor and legally less protected than men after separation, a point recognized by the public and supported by the evidence.[53]

As the date of the referendum approached support for the amendment began to erode. Fianna Fail was supporting the government at the official level, but at the grassroots opposition to the amendment was growing among its members. The anti-divorce campaign and the Church began to have an impact on the voters, who were now exposed to pastoral letters and other materials critical of the amendment. Some of the same fears that had been raised in 1986 were raised again, on questions of children and property. Public opinion polls prior to November showed 69 percent of respondents supporting divorce; in early November this dropped to 61 percent, then to 52 percent, and only two weeks later to 45 percent. In the last week before the vote John Hume, leader of the Social Democratic and Labour Party of Northern Ireland, urged a "yes" vote on the basis of tolerance and relations with the north; he was up against no less a figure than Mother Theresa, who urged a "no" vote.[54]

The vote resulted in a paper-thin margin of victory of 50.3 percent for the amendment to 49.7 percent against. The upward shift in the yes vote from 1986 was slightly over 15 percent and was a reflection of the better legislative preparation of the government; the increasing influence of the women's movement; and, the very thing that traditionalists feared, an increasing sense on the part of the Irish people that there was less need for the Church or the state to decide how they should behave. Divorce would now be available in Ireland. The wrath of the traditionalists was no better expressed than by activist Una Bean nic Mhathuna, who, on the day of the vote, denounced the supporters of the amendment with her admonition; "Go away, ye wife-swapping sodomites." The response of a pro-divorce campaigner was: "If only we had that much fun during the campaign."[55]

Women's Status in the 1990s

By the 1990s formal legal discrimination against women had been minimized through court decisions, legislation, and regulations. Sexism, however, remained widespread in Ireland's paternalistic society and this brought about a shift in the agenda of the women's movement from equality issues to equity issues. That sexism was, and is, widespread in Ireland in the home, the workplace, education, the professions, and the political sphere is well documented.[56] Style, language, agendas, practices, and, above all, values in the society are male dominated. Women are devalued by sexual innuendo, patronized, and subjected to violence in the home. The exclusion of women from juries, for example, was not only a manifestation of the idea that women should be in the home but also left a male imprint on the rendering of justice. Exclusion from business was reinforced by the marriage bar but also reinforced the notion that women could not make the tough decisions necessary in the combative world of commerce.

In 1985 the Working Party on Women's Affairs and Family Law Reform published *Irish Women: Agenda for Practical Action*, which reviewed the existing situation and identified areas still requiring action. The report recognized that progress had been made in removing discrimination but that it was possible to adopt measures "to promote actively and to facilitate greater participation by women in economic and social life."[57] In the realm of employment the report focused on the barriers to advancement in the trade unions, in entrepreneurial initiatives, and in apprenticeship and training for different occupations than those traditionally associated with women. In the realm of education the emphasis was on the removal of gender stereotyping, opening opportunities, improving access to traditionally male subjects such as physics, increasing the number of mixed-gender schools, and increased funding for young women. An area of concern was the absence of adequate child care facilities. The absence of all types of opportunity for rural women, support for single parents, and (as noted above under the divorce issue) family law reform on matters of children and property remained in need of attention. Progress on these issues was obvious, although that progress could be seen as a glass half empty or half full depending on one's perspective.

The report's evaluation of women in the workplace showed marginal to significant improvement. In 1993, 33.5 percent of the workforce was women; in 1960, only 29.7 percent was women. Thirty-three years had passed with an increase of only 3.8 percent. On the other hand, were those jobs better than those of thirty years ago? The answer is yes; for example, women significantly increased their participation in higher civil service positions. Has women's pay improved also? With higher differentials than the rest of the European Union, women in Ireland in both 1982 and in 1992 earned about 68 percent of men's hourly wage and about 60 percent of men's weekly wage. In 1990 the rate was 59 percent of men's earnings, approximately the same as the United States in 1955, altogether not a dazzling performance.[58]

Legislation Affecting Women's Rights and Status

The 1991 Social Welfare Act improved social welfare rights for part-time employees, and the 1991 Worker Protection (Regular Part-Time Employees) Act extended the scope of legislation regarding notice, maternity leaves, unfair dismissal, worker participation, and holiday entitlement to regular part-time employees, most of whom are women. In 1990, the Pensions Act provided for the equal treatment of men and women in occupational pension schemes. The Child Care Act of 1991 provided for reform of child care and protection, especially for youngsters at risk, charging health boards with promoting the welfare of children and providing more support services, supporting intervention when children are at risk, providing for the removal of children from parents when they are in danger, and providing for the provision and support of day care services, all to be phased in by 1996.

In 1994 a National Code of Practise on Sexual Harrassment was promulgated, to be monitored by the Employment Equality Agency and given statutory recognition under the Employment Equality Act.[59] Harsher than the penalty for sexual harassment was that for rape, which was defined under the 1981 Criminal Law (Rape) Act as unlawful sexual intercourse without a woman's consent. This restrictive definition was tied to the potential of pregnancy and thus involved seeing women as a man's property rather than being based on the inviolability of a woman's body. The Law Reform Commission's *Consultation Paper on Rape* and the *Report on Rape* recommended in 1988 that the definition of rape be changed to treat it as an act of violence even if there was no other assault involved. The 1990 Criminal Law (Rape) (Amendment) Act abolished the rule that a husband cannot be found guilty of raping his wife and introduced gradations into the act of rape, including aggravated sexual assault (penetration and violence), sexual assault, sexual assault against both sexes, and the penetration of other orifices. The public, but not the media, was excluded from attending rape trials.

Other notable legislation in this period included the Status of Children Act of 1987, which eliminated discrimination against children born outside of marriage, and the 1989 Judicial Separation and Family Law Reform Act, which extended the grounds for granting a decree of judicial separation and allowed the courts in separation agreements to order maintenance, lump sum payments, and property disposition. The 1995 Family Law Act dealt with the issues of maintenance and other issues concerned with separation and dissolution of marriage. Regional Health Boards set up day care centers. The Advertising Standards Authority for Ireland code was used to cleanse advertising of the sexist and demeaning way in which women were depicted to sell products; the media in general were called upon to eliminate sexism in language and portrayals of women that treated them as sex objects or appendages of men.[60]

In 1988 The Joint Oireachthas Committee on Women's Rights issued three reports that limned a picture of changing views: *Attitudes Toward the Role and Status of Women 1975–86, Issues Related to Employment Opportunities,* and *Attitudes Toward Moral Issues in Relation to Voting Behavior in Recent Referenda.* The reports indicated that there had definitely been a positive shift in the attitudes of men and women toward opportunity for women in matters of work, pay, education, child rearing, and the home. Employment opportunities and mobility were increasing, but women perceived discrimination in the workplace at the same or higher levels in 1986 as they had in 1975 and indicated that there was a long way to go to achieve equal pay and careers. In addition, while the Irish people would accept grounds for divorce, they remained opposed to abortion under all but very limited circumstances.

Changes in Education

Education was the key, as it so often is, to further possibilities for women and is illustrative of changes for women. Education issues covered in the reports included access to education, gender discrimination in subject areas, sexism in textbooks, and practices and behavior in the schools. The *First Report of the Joint Committee on Women's Rights, Education* (1984) and *Irish Women: Agenda for Practical Action* (1985) echoed the 1983 Economic and Social Research Institute report, which noted: "Sex differentiation in our education system is very deeply institutionalized: in the ideological and cultural presumptions underlying the provision of subjects and the design of curricula by the different school owning authorities, in the expectations of parents and teachers, and in the self definitions and educational attitudes and expectations of the students themselves."[61]

Pressure from the European Union was represented by the 1987 *Action Handbook: How to Implement Gender Equality,* which called for the elimination of gender stereotyping in the schools of the European Union. The first Irish government policy statement on this issue was the 1990 document *Department of Education —Gender Equality,* calling for gender equity in administration, curriculum, teaching materials, management, and in-service training. Starting in 1990 the Department of Education pursued the policy goal of creating co-educational schools because they were shown to help eliminate the stereotypes and behaviors that exacerbated sexism. The elimination of sexist statements and images in

186	The Role of Irish Women

textbooks and teaching materials was also addressed. Studies of primary school readings showed that, "Males outnumbered females, boys created things, showed initiative, were brave and strong. Girls were dependent, small and fearful."[62] The department also created incentives for girls to take up studies in areas of the curriculum that were traditionally seen as masculine, such as physics, science, and math. Teachers were to be trained in gender-free language and teaching. Grants were to be provided for older women to continue their education, especially in non-traditional areas such as computers and technology. Policy was adopted with respect to eliminating sexism in that most sensitive area of the curriculum, sex education. The Department of Education stated explicitly in the 1987 *Guidelines on the Development of Sex/Relationships Education*: "The primary responsibility for sex/relationships education must rest with the parents." It was also true that the number of teenage pregnancies from 1980 to 1987 was about one-third of all births outside of marriage, and the department felt some obligation to address the issue. The rationale for some form of sex education was based on earlier maturation of children; earlier sexual activity; the informal acquisition of sexual information; and health issues connected to sexual practice, such as sexually transmitted diseases and AIDS.[63] A goal of the curriculum was to help eliminate gender stereotypes and the highly immature attitudes toward relationships among Irish youth.[64]

The area of education was notable for the increase in women going on to higher education after 1970, almost the same number as men overall and more specifically in the universities. Women were enrolled disproportionately in the field of education and men in the field of engineering. A large discrepancy existed in the number of women on the faculty at the university level, with only 10.5 percent in 1970 and 15.5 percent in 1984. While some improvement has been made, that gap remains wide.

Official Organizations for Women's Issues

The efforts of the Council for the Status of Women have been important as a catalyst for organizing women, for research, and for collecting information but not as important in terms of political pressure. The Council had itself evolved out of the association of women's groups that had come together to respond to the 1967 United Nations call for councils of women to be established in the member states. The initial group of twenty women's organizations created a board to do research on women's issues, the results of which were then presented to the Taoiseach Jack Lynch with the request that a Commission be formed to report on women's issues. The Council disbanded when the first Commission was created in 1970 and then was reborn when the 1972 report called for an organization to represent women's interests.

From 1973 to 1979 the organization was voluntary and self-funded, and its main work was developing policy input to the Women's Representative Committee, a governmental body set up to monitor the 1972 report. That Committee was transformed in 1979 into the Employment Equality Agency, created to monitor the provisions of the Employment Equality Act of 1977. Publicly funded after 1979, the Council for the Status of Women was given the tasks of representing women's interests and continuing to oversee the implementation of the 1972 report. Political scientist Yvonne Fitzsimmons noted two difficulties the organization faced in its first two decades. First was the detachment of the Executive Board from the larger body, producing conflict over activities and strategies, and charges of unresponsiveness on the part of the Executive. A second difficulty was the expansion of the organization by radical feminists of the second wave, which brought greater ideological diversity and thus greater difficulty in achieving agreement over policy and strategy. This led to the adoption of minimalist positions on women's demands and nonconfrontational strategy on some of the most contentious issues concerning a woman's control of her fertility, economic activities, and autonomy.[65] After 1985 the organization became more professional in its priorities and advocacy of positions. The perception of the Council and women's groups was that hostility toward women's issues increased in the late 1970s and early 1980s. Budget cuts in social programs and the emergence of the conservative pressure groups discussed above pushed the women's agenda to the margins of Irish politics. Even the appointment of a minister of state for Women's Affairs by Garret FitzGerald in the 1982–1987 government did not accomplish as much as expected. Nuala Fennell was a visible feminist in the Dail but ran into the territorial obsessions of various departments on policy issues and also into the inflated expectations of the Council's leadership. The result was a lack of equal status legislation during the period. The Women's Affairs ministry was eliminated by the Fianna Fail government in 1987, both a symbolic and a real diminution of women's influence in terms of access to ministers. Fitzsimmons concludes that the political influence of the Council on government policy in the 1980s had "been minimal"; nor had the Council had much influence "on the policies of the political parties over this period."[66]

One area of success in the political arena was in the promotion and creation of the Second Commission on the Status of Women, called for by Council in 1989 and appointed in 1990. The Commission issued a final report in 1993. The report includes over 200 recommendations; the most crucial, however, were the request for an Equal Rights Amendment, a Cabinet Minister for Women's Affairs, a referendum on divorce (carried out in 1995), remediation of the gender balance in political organizations to increase the number of women in the Dail and in government, penalties for organizations that discriminate against women, and revising the tax system to remove the disadvantages for women. Unlike the first report, which was backed by European directives, Yvonne Galligan's question about the implementation of the 1993 report was: "How long can the collective goodwill of the cabinet toward gender equality be sustained?" In January 1993 a minister for Equality and Law Reform was appointed for the first time. The Council for the Status of Women, now called the National Women's Council, has played an important and difficult role as the intermediary between a diverse and sometimes irreconcilable collection of women's groups and a male-dominated government slow to respond to the women's agenda.

A Woman President

The most visible symbol of the new role of women in Ireland, Mary Robinson, was elected president in 1990. Her election, the public reaction to it, and the political consequences, were genuine surprises and had a significant effect on Ireland.

A daughter of a well-off family, Mary Bourke (later Robinson) studied law at Trinity College and then spent a year at Harvard in 1967 earning an LL.M. and absorbing the swirling political currents of the anti-war and civil rights protests. She ran for the Seanad and won in 1969, using her seat as a forum to address issues such as birth control, divorce, family law, and Northern Ireland, in each instance driving the national agenda . . . but very slowly. She was elected the first president of the Woman's Progressive Association (later Woman's Political Association), founded in 1970 to encourage women to enter political life. Her pressure to change the law to remove the stigma from "illegitimate" children helped to create Cherish, the organization devoted to advocacy for single parents. Robinson remained president of Cherish from 1973 until her election as president of the Republic in 1990. The Dail passed the Status of Children Act in 1987 after Robinson won a case in 1986 in the European Court of Human Rights, in which she argued that an "illegitimate" child under Irish law was deprived of rights under the European Convention on Human Rights and Fundamental Freedoms of 1950.

Among the notable cases upon which Mary Robinson served as counsel were the *McGee v. Attorney General* case on contraception in 1973 and the *Mairin de Burca v. Attorney General* case brought against the 1927 Juries Act. This act limited juries to taxpayers and compelled men to serve, while women had to volunteer should they wish to serve. In her brief Mary Robinson pointed out that in the period 1963 to 1973 only three women had served on juries in the Republic. De Burca lost the case on the first round, but while the case was on appeal to the Supreme Court the Dail passed legislation in 1977 that democratized participation on juries.[67] Mary Robinson was also involved in the *Airey* case in 1977, in which the European Court of Human Rights ordered Ireland to provide legal aid in civil cases and ruled in favor of Ms. Airey being granted a full judicial separation from her husband. Robinson represented the claims made by married women against the government for not giving them their payments due under the terms of the European Economic Community's 1978 Social Welfare Equality Directive. The government delayed implementation because of the cost and fought each case until it lost. Eventually the High Court in 1995 ordered the state to pay the amount in arrears to 70,000 women.[68]

Homosexuality was illegal in Ireland. In 1977 David Norris, a professor at Trinity and a professed homosexual, with Robinson as counsel, challenged the 1861 Offences Against the Person Act, which outlawed homosexual practices. Lesbian relationships, as it happens, were not illegal because the law did not specify them as such, due as much to the fact that men wrote the law as to the social invisibility of such relationships in the 1860s. The High Court rejected the Norris claim in 1980. In the appeal to the Supreme Court of Ireland in 1982, Robinson argued that in a similar case in Northern Ireland the European Court of Human Rights had rejected that part of the 1861 Act concerning homosexual practices. The Supreme Court, however, voted three to two to uphold the High Court. Robinson and Norris then took the case first to the European Commission of Human Rights and then to the Court of Human Rights, where they won in 1988. The provisions of the 1861 law were judged to be in violation of the European Convention; the Dail passed the Criminal Law (Sexual Offenses) Act in 1993, which decriminalized homosexual behavior between adults.

In 1976 Robinson formally joined the Labour Party because she felt its progressive agenda coincided with her own. In 1977 she stood as a Labour candidate for a Dail seat in Dublin but was defeated in a Fianna Fail sweep and returned to the Seanad. In the 1981 election for a Dail seat she ran poorly and again returned to the Seanad. In 1982 she did not run in the Dail election and resigned from the seat on the Dublin Corporation (City Council) that she had won in 1979. Her political career was at a low ebb due to her conflicts with the Labour Party leadership and her loss in the Dail elections.

In 1983 Robinson served as a delegate to the Forum for a New Ireland and, as one might expect, pressed for inclusion of statements on the equality of women. At this time the position of attorney general came within her grasp when Peter Sutherland became Ireland's delegate to the European Economic Community Commission. The Labour Party leader, Dick Spring, had the opportunity to select Robinson for the position but he chose to nominate an old friend and advisor, John Rogers. Robinson was clearly disappointed but also recognized that she was not deeply connected to the inner circle of the Labour Party. She completely disconnected herself from the Party in 1985 when the Anglo-Irish Agreement was signed between Dublin and London. In her view the Agreement had been negotiated without any consultation with the Protestant unionist majority community, while the Catholic Nationalist Social Democratic and Labour Party had input through discussion with political leaders in Dublin. Robinson felt that she, and others, had been excluded from contributing to the process but were assumed to be in support of the result. The resulting Agreement, she judged, would exclude the unionists and be counterproductive to the achievement of peace. An election was called for 1989; Robinson announced she would not run again for the Seanad and would devote her attention to the new Centre for European Law at Trinity College. Her resignation from the party was a surprise to many.

In 1990 Patrick Hillary's term as president of Ireland was ending. The usual pattern was that Fianna Fail would name a candidate and that person would win the election; the position had gone uncontested since 1973. Dick Spring, however, decided that it was time to contest the presidential election and use the campaign as a locus to present different positions on Ireland's future. After some persuasion he chose Mary Robinson as the Party's candidate, much to her pleasure and surprise. Negotiations over whether she would rejoin the Labour Party or just run as the Party's choice were resolved in Robinson's favor. Given her highly visible resignation, she thought formally rejoining the Party would be a signal that she would choose ambition over principles. Robinson was not considered to have much of a chance to win the presidency because Brian Lenihan of Fianna Fail was by far the favorite. The probable winner, had he entered the race, would have been former prime minister Garret FitzGerald of Fine Gael, but he chose not to be a candidate. Fine Gael considered nominating a woman candidate or backing Mary Robinson, but instead turned to a former Northern Ireland civil rights activist, Austin Currie, who accepted reluctantly and left Fine Gael in a relatively weak position. The lineup appeared to clinch the win for Fianna Fail senior party stalwart Lenihan, who was Tanaiste and minister of Defense (and, for good measure, former minister for Justice, Education, Foreign Affairs, Fisheries, and Agriculture). Lenihan was recovering from a liver transplant and while under medication earlier in the campaign had given an interview to a graduate student indicating that he had tried to persuade the president of Ireland back in 1982 to not dissolve the Dail and to invite Charles Haughey, the leader of Fianna Fail, to form a new government after a Fianna Fail election loss. When this news was revealed Lenihan denied it, and Haughey was put under pressure from his coalition partners in government, the Progressive Democrats, to ask Lenihan to resign. Lenihan refused and Haughey fired him as the presidential election approached. Public support for Lenihan dropped.

Mary Robinson benefited not only from Lenihan's problems but also from a skillfully organized campaign. Although in the past she had been confrontational and her positions left of center and feminist, she re-created herself as a centrist symbol of moderation and modernity. Changing her appearance and style and running a grassroots campaign, Robinson connected to the electorate, especially rural and urban women. Robinson's Leftist past appeared to be a fixation with Fianna Fail; party members attacked her during the election. Padriag Flynn impugned her commitment to her husband and children and John Browne's speculation as to whether she was going to have an abortion referral clinic in the President's House generated what observers felt was a backlash of support for her.[69]

Despite Lenihan's problems he did receive the most votes, 44.1 percent to Robinson's 38.9 percent and Currie's 17 percent. The Irish electoral system, however, requires that a candidate receive 50 percent of the vote to win. Currie's votes were eliminated and the candidate whom voters had designated as their second choice on Currie's ballots was allocated those votes. Seventy-seven percent of

Currie's second preference votes went to Robinson, bringing her total to 52.8 percent. Lenihan had only 47.2 percent; thus Robinson was the winner.

While Robinson's victory as the first woman president and the first non-Fianna Fail winner was surprising, the reaction of the public was more so. Despite the fact that Brian Lenihan would clearly have won had not the scandal occurred, and despite the fact that he almost did win, scandal and all, the Irish people decided that they had deliberately chosen Mary Robinson as a symbol of the new Ireland, and her popularity escalated accordingly. She became the spokesperson for the emigrant Irish abroad, for women, and for a resurgent Ireland undergoing an economic regeneration. She connected the Irish Famine and the diaspora with the plight of the starving, and malnourished, and the refugees of the developing world. She enhanced the reputation of the Irish as international humanitarians. The Irish people loved having a highly accomplished and highly charismatic president, and her travel and visibility were even more popular because her term coincided with the second Irish cultural renaissance. Her major legacies were, first, to embody the new-found self-confidence and pride of the Irish people and, second, from the point of view of the women's movement she was a highly visible symbol; she had been part of virtually every important women's case or issue in the prior twenty years. When she ended her term and took a position with the United Nations the third, and perhaps most surprising, legacy of Mary Robinson appeared.

The major candidates to replace her as president were all women. Fine Gael chose Mary Banotti, an accomplished politician and member of the European Parliament; Fianna Fail chose Mary MacAleese, a law professor from Queen's University in Belfast; and the Labour Party chose Adi Roche, a committed and highly visible environmentalist. In addition, a conservative Catholic vocalist from Northern Ireland living in Alabama, Rosemary Brown Scanlon, known as Dana, ran to restore a traditional Catholic Ireland. This completed, as journalist Fintan O'Toole noted, the panoply of images of what Ireland should become: McAleese's borderless Ireland, Banotti's European Ireland, Roche's global Ireland, and Dana's Christian Ireland. Mary McAleese, representing Ireland's largest party, won easily in November 1997. On the first round she garnered 45.2 percent of the vote and Banotti had 29 percent. Surprisingly, Dana Scanlon received 13.8 percent, virtually double that of Roche, an established party candidate. On the second round McAleese received 58.7 percent to Banotti's 41.3 percent. McAleese's election can be said to reveal the many threads woven together in the mind of modern Irish voters. The election of a second woman as president of Ireland indicates the degree to which Irish women are now both venerated and, at least symbolically, included in the highest levels of the state. As a law professor she represents the capabilities and professional accomplishments of women. As a devout Catholic and as a member of Fianna Fail, McAleese embodies the deep religious and nationalist dimensions of Ireland. As a northerner elected president of the Republic, she represents the aspiration for a borderless Ireland. Robinson and McAleese are not Queen Maeve, nor Cathleen ni Houlihan; they are the archetypes for a new concept of the Irish woman and her place in Ireland.

How the Women's Agenda Changed

The changes in the women's agenda are aptly summed up by Yvonne Fitzsimmons: "The organizational perspective on equality shifted from a pursuit of measures to implement formal equality in the mid-1970s to an understanding of equality based on justice in the late 1970s and in the mid-1980s to an equality that recognized and valued gender difference."[70] We can conclude with three observations about public policy agenda for women in Ireland in the decades to come. The first is that there is still much to be done: A glance at the research on women in disadvantaged situations reveals still-unachieved goals in the areas of marriage breakdown; support for homemakers; sexual harassment in the workplace; funding child care; elderly, disabled, and imprisoned women; farm families and rural women; increased participation in government, educational opportunities; job training; maternity, family planning, and mental health; equality in the arts and sports; and the representation of women in the media.[71] Second, the agendas of women will be as different as the various ways in which they define themselves in relation to men, the society, the economy, and the state. The term *feminism* holds a multiplicity of meanings. Rebecca West may have been too modest when she offered her acid definition: "I have never been able to find out precisely what feminism is: I only know that people call me a feminist whenever I express sentiments that differentiate me from a doormat or a prostitute."[72] The term can cover the spectrum from a claim to equality of opportunity to emancipation from oppression from the values, laws, and mores of society to an assault on the deep and pervasive sexism of a patriarchal language, social organization, and culture. Moreover, the meaning can be shaped by different contexts for women of different color, different religions, different classes, and different cultural values. The aggregation of different perspectives into a common political agenda is difficult, as the work of the Council for the Status of Women has shown. Conflict will continue within the women's movement and the reconciliation of groups with differing regards for established social values and institutions will prove to be a daunting task. Third, opposition to the agenda of the women's movement has been mobilized and articulated by the organizations that supported the pro-life and the anti-divorce campaigns. The reaction of these groups has been to defend traditional religious and conservative values and in doing so, almost inevitably, to define themselves as increasingly anti-feminist. Anti-feminist values are delineated in *Woman Scorned*, the conservative Public Policy Institute of Ireland's response to the 1993 *Report of the Commission on the Status of Women*: "Many political feminists have unfortunately allowed themselves to be too influenced by individualism and its associated economic thinking allowing personal gain to become the motor which drives everything."[73] Carol Coulter quotes a report included in the conservative Responsible Society newsletter, *Response*, revealing somewhat more homophobic attitudes in describing women at a CSW meeting:

Mary Robinson, in 1996 when president of Ireland, with Sister Lena Deevy, LSA, executive director of the Irish Immigration Center in Boston. Making the continuing connection with the Irish communities abroad was a theme of Robinson's presidency, which she symbolized by keeping a lit candle in the window of the president's residence in Dublin's Phoenix Park.
Photo by Harry Brett, Image Photo

"It had a definite 'women's group look.' . . . The core of the CSW seems to be aging feminists and lesbians."[74] However unrepresentative of average conservative views this may be, the quote indicates the type of opposition that will confront the women's movement in the decades to come. A complex agenda, highly differentiated positions, and a formidable opposition indicate that the achievement of the full rights of women in Ireland still requires traversing difficult waters.

Notes

1. Founded by the Quakers Anna Haslam and Thomas Haslam, the IWSLGA was considered a pioneer organization in Irish feminism although it never had very many members and operated mostly as a letter-writing organization. Anna Haslam was one of the first women to exercise the right to vote (at age eighty-nine) after the passage of the 1918 Act. This organization, as well as many other small suffrage groups, was absorbed into the Irish Women's Suffrage Federation in 1911.

2. Margaret Ward, " 'Suffrage First—Above All Else': An Account of The Irish Suffrage Movement," in *The Irish Women's Studies Reader,* ed. Ailbhe Smyth (Dublin: Attic Press, 1993), p. 25. This section draws heavily on this excellent account. Margaret Ward also published a biography, *Hannah Sheehy-Skeffington: A Life* (Dublin: Attic Press, 1997), in which she chronicles the critical role of this most important feminist and nationalist. The founder of the Irish Women's Franchise League, Sheehy-Skeffington was a graduate of the Royal University. She was married to Francis Sheehey-Skeffington, a noted feminist and pacifist. Both were secular progressives. She was arrested for militant activity in 1912, for protesting against the fact that the third Home Rule bill did not include the women's vote. She supported the Rising of 1916, in which her husband was murdered in the form of an execution by a kangaroo court martial held by a British officer later judged to be insane. From 1916 to 1918 she was in the United States to gain support for Sinn Fein. She met with President Wilson to lobby for Irish independence (with no more success than others had had in trying to persuade this anglophile president to actually implement the doctrine of self-determination in Ireland). Arrested by the British in Ireland, she was released only after a hunger strike. She served on the Executive Committee of Sinn Fein and chose the anti-Treaty side in the Civil War, but also tried to prevent the Civil War. She opposed the 1937 Constitution as anti-feminist. She died in 1946.

3. Louie Bennett, the founder of the Irishwomen's Sufferage Federation, came from a well-off Protestant family in Dublin and aspired to be a writer. She was not sympathetic to the nationalist cause and was a pacifist. The number of feminist activist groups and their political interactions is too extensive to depict in this account, but Inhghinidhe na hEireann, The Irish Women's Suffrage and Local Government Association, The Woman's International League for Peace and Freedom, The Women's Social and Political Union, and the Ladies School Dinners Association represent a complex web of friendship and political connections that was part of the feminist tapestry in Ireland in the period after the turn of the century. See Ward, *Hannah Sheehy-Skeffington,* for a discussion of these groups.

4. The question of the value of militant tactics divided the women's movement. The (tactically) moderate ILGWSA criticized the IWFL, and especially the WSPU, for turning Irish public opinion against the women's movement. Militant tactics cost support among the political parties that would cast the votes necessary for women to win the vote. Hannah Sheehy-Skeffington argued that ladylike behavior had accomplished nothing for fifty years and that the vote for women was a matter of right, not a matter of seducing some advantages for women by behaving properly. This argument came to a head in 1912–1913 when the press chose to decrease coverage of the suffrage movement and militants saw confrontational acts as necessary to get the public's attention.

5. Success in mobilizing women through many organizations and activities rather than just the most militant is discussed in Louise Ryan, "Women Without Votes: The Political Strategies of the Irish Suffrage Movement," *Irish Political Studies* 9 (1994), pp. 119–139.

6. Countess Constance Markievicz is one of the most singular women of the period. Born in 1868, she married a Polish count and then separated from him. Her only daughter was reared by her grandmother. The Countess was a supporter of Sinn Fein but did not support the pacifism of Arthur Griffith. She founded a youth organization, Fianna Eireann, in 1909; wrote a pamphlet, *A Call to the Women of Ireland,* the same year; and was a supporter of women's suffrage. In the 1916 Rising she was second in command at Saint Stephen's Green and was sentenced to death for her actions. Her sentence was commuted, however, allowing her to remain active in the republican movement. She was elected to the British Parliament from Ireland in the 1918 election but would not take her seat and instead went into the revolutionary Dail Eireann with Sinn Fein, holding the position of minister for Labor. An opponent of the Anglo-Irish Treaty, she sided with Sinn Fein and was an implacable opponent of the Free State. She died in 1927.

7. Ward, "Irish Sufferage," p. 43. However, Louise Ryan's "Women Without Votes," pp. 119–139, argues that the actions of the Irish suffrage movement were consequential in penetrating the male-defined space of civil society and that to focus exclusively on the militant movement and the failure to get the vote for women is to miss the constitutional efforts and the broader women's agenda raised by the suffrage movement. Moreover, to stress the degree to which Ireland sought to place women in the home as a function of the confessional aspects of the Irish state ignores the fact that in other countries, in other cultures, and among women themselves, many saw the place of women as in the home. Mary Daly, "Oh Cathleen ni Houlihan Your Way Is a Thorny Way: The Condition of Women in Twentieth Century Ireland," in *Gender and Sexuality in Modern Ireland,* ed. A. Bradley and M. G. Valiulus (Amherst: University of Massachusetts Press, 1998), pp. 106–107.

8. Carol Coulter, *The Hidden Tradition: Feminism, Women and Nationalism in Ireland* (Cork: Cork University Press, 1993), p. 22.

9. David Barry, "Female Suffrage from a Catholic Standpoint," excerpted in *Women in Ireland: 1800–1918,* ed. M. Luddy (Cork: Cork University Press, 1995), pp. 280–281.

10. Quoted in Ronan Fanning, *Independent Ireland* (Dublin: Helicon Press, 1983), p. 56. Liam Cosgrave, the prime minister, was so disposed to concede authority to the Church on matters of health education and sexual morality that he obtained a dispensation to have a private altar in his house and suggested a "Theological Senate" for the Free State that would examine legislation for doctrinal orthodoxy. Mercifully for Irish democracy, the idea went nowhere. On the divorce issue, Cosgrave rejected any grounds for allowing divorce through private bills after Dr. Byrne, the Archbishop of Dublin, indicated that it would amount to acceptance of the principle of divorce. It was pointed out to the Archbishop by Edmund Duggan that this policy would force those who wanted a divorce to move out of the Free State of Ireland. The Archbishop's response was that Ireland would not lose anything by their departure, illuminating the Church's commitment to the prevalence of doctrine over individual rights and the concession of Free State politicians to that position. Objections from no less a figure than W. B. Yeats, who fulminated that this was a policy "which a minority of this nation consider to be grossly oppressive" made little difference. Fanning, pp. 55–56.

11. P. C. Jackson, "Managing the Mothers: The Case of Ireland," in *Women and Social Policies in Europe,* ed. J. Lewis (Brookfield, Vt.: Edward Elgar, 1993), pp. 72–91.

12. Frances Gardiner, "Political Interest and Participation of Irish Women 1922–1922: The Unfinished Revolution," in *Irish Women's Studies Reader,* ed. Smyth, p. 48.

13. Catherine Shannon, "The Changing Face of Cathleen ni Houlihan: Women and Politics in Ireland 1960–1996," in *Gender and Sexuality in Modern Ireland*, p. 263.

14. First Report of the Second Joint Committee on Women's Rights, *Changing Attitudes to the Role of Women in Ireland* (Dublin: Stationery Office, 1988), p. 13.

15. Commission on the Status of Women, *Report to the Minister of Finance* (Dublin: Stationery Office, 1972), pp. 87, 97.

16. Ibid., pp. 38–39.

17. Shannon, "Changing Face of Cathleen ni Houlihan," pp. 263–266; A. Smyth, "The Women's Movement in the Republic of Ireland; 1960–1990," in *Irish Women's Studies Reader*, ed. Smyth, pp. 251–266.

18. Yvonne Fitzsimmons, "Women's Interest Representation in the Republic of Ireland: The Council for the Status of Women," *Irish Political Studies* 6 (1991), pp. 37–51.

19. A. Smyth, "Women's Movement," in *Irish Women's Studies Reader*, ed. Smyth, p. 252.

20. Ibid., pp. 257–262; and Linda Connolly, "From Revolution to Devolution: Mapping the Contemporary Women's Movement in Ireland," in *Women in Irish Society: A Sociological Reader*, ed. A. Byrne and M. Leonard (Belfast: Beyond the Pale Publications, 1997), pp. 557–558.

21. Women's Representative Committee, *Progress Report on the Implementation of the Recommendations in the Report of the Commission on the Status of Women* (Dublin: Stationery Office, December 1976), pp. 3–10.

22. In the 1981 *Bradley v. Power Supermarkets t/a Quinnsworth* case, the court held that overtly discriminatory language, such as "lady required for cleaning work," in advertising for a job was illegal In the same year the equality officer found a job interview in which the interviewer focused on the woman's marital status and duties at home and not on her qualifications for the job to be in breach of Section 3 of the Employment Equality Act. In 1990, in a case involving employment at RyanAir, an interviewer focused on the difficulties of carrying out the job while being married and questioned the candidate on her commitment to her marriage. Ultimately he did not hire her and his actions were found to be discriminatory.

23. The leave is paid at 80 percent and must include four weeks before and four weeks after the birth; if there are complications, an additional four weeks is granted.

24. Additionally, the Pro Life Action Campaign (PLAC) recognized that the Offenses Against the Persons Act of 1861, which forbade abortion, could be changed relatively easily by an act of the Dail, which in turn could be swayed by pro-abortion pressure, as had happened with legislatures in the United States and Britain. Another fear of the anti-abortion forces was that the judicial activism of the U.S. courts would be emulated by the Irish Supreme Court, which might find a personal right to abortion in Article 40.3.2, just as they had found a right to marital privacy to support their decision in the *McGee* case.

25. C. O'Leary and T. Hesketh, "The Irish Abortion and Divorce Referendum Campaigns," *Irish Political Studies* 3 (1988), pp. 46–47.

26. B. Girvin, "Social Change and Moral Politics: The Irish Constitutional Referendum of 1983," *Irish Political Studies* 34 (1986), p. 68.

27. O'Leary and Hesketh, "Referendum Campaigns," pp. 50–51.

28. T. Hesketh, *The Second Partitioning of Ireland: The Abortion Referendum of 1983* (Dublin: Brandsma Books, 1990).

29. The lack of clarity of information on pregnancy and attitudes of shame led to painful events for young women such as Ann Lovett, who in 1986 gave birth to a stillborn child and died of the consequences alone, in front of a statue of the Virgin Mary, without anyone in the town acknowledging that she was pregnant . . . although they all knew it.

30. B. Girvin, "The Referendums on Abortion, 1992," *Irish Political Studies* 8 (1993), p. 118.

31. Alpha Connelly, "The Constitution," in *Gender and the Law in Ireland*, ed. A. Connelly (Dublin: Oak Tree Press, 1993), p. 11.

32. Garret FitzGerald had sought to clarify with the hierarchy of the Catholic Church why he wanted to have the wording of the amendment changed after Peter Sutherland's report and found that he was to deal only with an intermediary. The Church endorsed the original wording without adequately dealing with its consequences because, as FitzGerald saw it, the Hierarchy was under pressure from pro-life Catholic conservative organizations not to be swayed by the government. G. FitzGerald, *All in A Life: Garret FitzGerald, an Autobiography* (Dublin: Gill & Macmillan, 1991), pp. 440–444.

33. M. Holmes, "The Maastricht Treaty Referendum of June 1992," *Irish Political Studies* 8 (1993), pp. 105–110.

34. Carol Coulter, "'Hello Divorce, Goodbye Daddy': Women, Gender and the Divorce Debate," in *Gender and Sexuality in Modern Ireland*, ed. Bradley and Valiulis, pp. 277–278.

35. Minister of Justice, *Marital Breakdown: A Review and Proposed Changes* (Dublin: Stationery Office, 1992), p. 29.

36. M. Leane and E. Keily, "Single Lone Motherhood-Reality Versus Rhetoric," in *Women and Irish Society*, ed. Byrne and Leonard, pp. 296–297.

37. In 1967 a Committee on the Constitution found that the universal prohibition was unfair to those for whom the tenets of their religion did not prohibit divorce and also pointed out that the provision was unfair to Catholics whose marriages had been annulled. The Commission recommended changes to rectify these injustices. Other groups pointed out that divorce did not allow any recognition of new relationships and left people in tax and social welfare difficulties, nor was there legislation to protect the children of the new relationship, who were considered illegitimate. See *Report of the Joint Committee on Marriage Breakdown* (Dublin: Stationery Office, 1985), pp. 72–85.

38. O'Leary and Hesketh, "Referendum Campaigns," p. 56.

39. Coulter, "'Hello Divorce, Goodbye Daddy'," pp. 280–281.

40. O'Leary and Hesketh, "Referendum Campaigns," pp. 56–57.

41. B. Girvin, "The Divorce Referendum in the Republic; June 1986," *Irish Political Studies* 2 (1987), p. 98.

42. With respect to women in this perspective, see C. Coulter's observations about some feminists in *The Hidden Tradition, Women Feminism and Ireland* (Cork: Cork University Press, 1993), pp. 40–41; see also John Waters, *Living at the Crossroads* (Belfast: Blackstaff Press, 1991) for a view from the west of Ireland on the Dublin elite's opinions about the west of Ireland; see also John Ardagh, *Ireland and the Irish: Portrait of a Changing Society* (London: Hamish Hamilton, 1996) for a foreigner's somewhat patronizing ("gosh, the Irish are doing *so* well!") view of change in Ireland. Journalist Desmond Fennell sees Dublin's circles of university, media, arts, and political figures as interlocking; their image of Ireland, in his opinion, is myopic.

43. Richard B. Finnegan, "The Irish Vote Was Against Divorce, Not Against Union," *The Patriot Ledger* 20 August 1986, p. 33.

44. Tom Garvin, "The Politics of Denial and of Cultural Defense," *The Irish Review* 3 (1988), pp. 1–7; and J. P. O'Carroll, "Bishops Knights and Pawn? Traditional Thought and the Irish Abortion Referendum Debate of 1983," *Irish Political Studies* 6 (1991), pp. 53–72.

45. Garvin "Politics of Denial," p. 6.

46. O'Carroll, "Bishops Knights and Pawn?," pp. 58–68.

47. Department of Justice, *Marital Breakdown: A Review and Proposed Changes* (Dublin: Stationery Office, 1992).

48. The government went ahead only to have the Supreme Court rule in the last week of the campaign that the spending was improper. The validity of the amendment was challenged after the referendum, again on the grounds that the government had spent public money to promote one side. In 1998 the Supreme Court rejected the argument and ruled that the amendment was valid.

49. Brian Girvin, "The Irish Divorce Referendum, 1995," *Irish Political Studies* 2 (1996), pp. 176, 178–179. In this section I draw heavily from Girvin's excellent report on the referendum.

50. M. Marsh, et al., "Irish Political Data,1995," *Irish Political Studies* 11 (1996), p. 248.

51. Mark Hamilton, *The Case Against Divorce* (Dublin: Lir Press, 1995).

52. Coulter, "'Hello Divorce, Goodbye Daddy'," pp. 283, 287; Girvin, "Divorce Referendum, 1995," p. 177.

53. Marsh et al., "Irish Political Data, 1995," p. 248; and A. Byrne, "Revealing Figures: Official Statistics and Rural Irish Women," in *Irish Women's Studies Reader*, ed. Smyth, pp. 156–158.

54. Despite Christopher Hitchens's attacks on Mother Theresa for consorting with right-wing moneymen, she still carried weight in Ireland . . . and most everywhere else. The Pope also weighed in with a reiteration of the Church's doctrine on the indissolubility of marriage.

55. Quoted in Coulter, "'Hello Divorce, Goodbye Daddy'," p. 275.

56. See, among many other works, Jenny Beale, *Women in Ireland, Voices of Change* (Dublin: Gill & Macmillan, 1986).

57. *Irish Women: Agenda for Practical Action* (Dublin: Stationery Office, 1985), p. 29.

58. United Nations Fourth Conference on Women, *National Report of Ireland* (Dublin: Stationery Office, 1994), p. 20; and Second Commission on the Status of Women, *Report to Government* (Dublin: Stationery Office, 1992), pp. 100, 102.

59. The courts earlier were contributing to the shift in equal treatment; for example, in 1988 the Labor Court found that a case of sexual harassment (company's senior executives broke into a female employee's hotel room and arranged room items into a phallic symbol) violated Section 2 (a) of the Employment Equality Act, "less favorable treatment on the grounds of sex," and held the company responsible. The senior executives also spread her used underclothing on her bed, spotlighting the adolescent mentality of some Irish men, however "senior" their company position.

60. Third Report of the Joint Committee on Women's Rights, *Portrayal of Women in the Media* (Dublin: Stationery Office, 1986); and *The Development of Equal Opportunities March 1987–September 1988, Coordinated Report* (Dublin: Stationery Office, 1988), p. 26.

61. Economic and Social Research Institute, quoted in *Irish Women: Agenda for Practical Action*, p. 95.

62. Quoted in the Second Report of the Third Joint Committee on Women's Rights, *Gender Equality in Education in the Republic of Ireland (1984–1991)* (Dublin: Stationery Office, 1992), p. 43; and the 1984 and 1991 Department of Education reports with the same name: *Guidelines for Publishers on Sexism and Sex Stereotyping in Primary School Textbooks*.

63. *Report of the Expert Advisory Group on Relationships and Sexuality Education* (Dublin: Stationery Office, 1995), p. 7.

64. A. B. Ryan, "Gender Discourses in School Social Relations," in *Women and Irish Society*, ed. Byrne and Leonard, pp. 26–39.

65. Y. Fitzsimmons, "Women's Interest Representation in the Republic of Ireland," *Irish Political Studies* 6 (1991), pp. 41–42.

66. Ibid., p. 46.

67. John Horgan, *Mary Robinson: An Independent Voice* (Dublin: O'Brien Press, 1997), p. 55.

68. Ibid., p. 119.

69. Keogh, *Twentieth Century Ireland*, p. 378.

70. Y. Fitzsimmons, "Women's Interest Representation," p. 41.

71. This list is drawn from the Women's Rights Committee Work Programme for 1996 in the *1995 Annual Report of the Fourth Joint Committee on Women's Rights* (Dublin: Stationery Office, 1995), p. 24; see also the various articles on women and education, work, welfare, mental health, reproduction, violence, rural life, and alcohol in *Women and Irish Society*, ed. Byrne and Leonard.

72. Quoted in Brid Connolly, "Women in Community Education and Development: Education or Domestication?" in *Women in Irish Society*, ed. Byrne and Leonard, p. 45.

73. Quoted in Coulter, " 'Hello Divorce, Goodbye Daddy'," p. 282.

74. Quoted in ibid., p. 280.

7

CATHOLIC STATE OR CATHOLIC NATION: POLITICAL CULTURE, CONSTITUTION, AND POLITICAL STRUCTURE

The government of Ireland is a republic, parliamentary in form, a structure not unlike that of Great Britain and other parliamentary democracies of Europe but with elements and flavors that are, of course, distinctively Irish. The blend of parliamentary institutions and Irish political values and processes produces a governmental system reflecting the historical and cultural dynamics that have shaped modern Ireland.

Political Culture

Irish political culture is the unique outgrowth of three significant and mutually reinforcing forces of the twentieth century: nationalism, Irish Catholicism, and the influence of Great Britain.[1] Ireland's political culture, moreover, illustrates the ongoing impact of the process of economic and social modernization.

Nationalism

The cumulative growth of nationalism in Ireland culminated in the war for independence from 1919 to 1921 under the aegis of Sinn Fein. Catholicism, Gaelic identity, and political independence from Britain occupied the Irish mind. The Gaelic and Catholic form of nationalism widened and exacerbated the split between the Catholic community and the Protestant community on the island. The Sinn Fein commitment to an independent republic of Ireland was contrary to the Protestant community's commitment to union with Great Britain. Thus the version of Sinn Fein nationalism intensified the differences between Irish Catholic nationalists and Anglo-Protestant unionists. Clearly Gaelic nationalism is not only responsible for widening the chasm between the two communities, it is also a product of that chasm. Irish nationalism was a reaction to the historical dominance, land confiscation, and religious oppression that had stimulated the polarization of the communities. The inclusive vision of Wolfe Tone's Irish nationalism shifted, however, to the more Celtic and Catholic exclusive version at the end of the nineteenth century. Virtues and values were ascribed to the Irish in inverse ratio to their presence in the English. The English were material, the Irish spiritual; the English were urban, the Irish rural; the English were industrial, the Irish agricultural; the English were Protestant, the Irish Catholic; the English were warlike, the Irish peaceful (well, . . . sometimes); the English spoke English, the Irish spoke Irish; the English "nation" oppressed the Irish for 700 years, the Irish "nation" resisted for 700 years . . . and so on right down to the choice of colors, Green for the Celtic Irish and Orange for the Ulster Protestants.[2]

The nationalism that had exacerbated the split between the Anglo and Irish communities itself split in 1921 over the question of the Anglo-Irish Treaty and polarized Sinn Fein into pro-Treaty and anti-Treaty wings. These factions ultimately took the form of opposing political parties. Thus the partisan dimension of Irish electoral competition is rooted in the nationalist movement's debate over the strategy of obtaining the objective of an independent Ireland and the acceptable degree of separation from Britain. When de Valera agreed to enter the Free State Dail in 1927, he pragmatically accepted an opposition role in the Free State. The remaining members of Sinn Fein, who felt that de Valera had "sold out" to the Free State, split from Fianna Fail and held to their position of "pure" nationalism. The three nationalisms (pro-Treaty Cumann na nGaedhal, anti-Treaty Fianna Fail, and republican Sinn Fein) were shaped by the partition of Northern Ireland. Thus the republican nationalism of Sinn Fein and the IRA remained in the Irish political culture, resonating to the issue of Northern Ireland.

The ultimate promise of Irish nationalism was never fulfilled, and it was often advantageous for Free State and Republic of Ireland politicians to fuel the flames of nationalism by reminding the people of Ireland of the problem of Northern Ireland. Irish condemnation of historical British oppression, however rhetorical, was valuable politically only as long as Ireland remained partitioned, and Irish memories retained their enormous capacity for citing a cascade of British excesses in Ireland. There was hardly any advantage for politicians in stressing the virtue of close ties with Britain, however pragmatic or necessary they might be given the substantial intercourse between the two countries. The effect of dwelling on past grievances was to perpetuate among the Irish an already existing attitude of mistrust and hostility toward Britain. The real strength of Anglophobia in the Republic of Ireland is diminishing, but it remains a subdued element in the political culture of Ireland. Nationalist sentiment thus contributed to ambivalent governmental relationships with Great Britain.

Finally, the nationalist component of Irish political culture politicized the issue of the Irish language. It is certainly not surprising that Sinn Fein nationalism should elevate the Irish language to an apogee in the affirmation of Celtic culture. When Sinn Fein was in power the expression of Irish nationalism produced a narrow, exclusive cultural and legal environment within which intolerance flourished.

Irish nationalism has contributed to polarization among the broad communities on the island; the foundations of electoral partisanship within the Sinn Fein movement; the centrality of the language question; the constricted provincial political environment; the Catholic nature of the state; and, among a small segment of the population, the persistence of the view that the governments of Ireland, both north and south, were illegitimate.

Catholicism

Catholicism, the second important element of the Irish political culture, was and is a powerful presence in the Republic of Ireland. Historically, the faith became associated with the nationalist movement and with the Irish-Ireland cultural revival. Religion and the Church became a focal point in the political development of Ireland as well as an important part of the private sphere of personal convictions. The political influence of Catholic values in the past and present has been substantial. The Irish version of Catholicism was cultivated in relative isolation from the ebb and flow of theological currents in Europe and North America. Thus the Irish Church remained relatively free of secular intellectual influences and the radicalism manifest in some versions of liberation theology. The conservatism of Irish Catholicism has had the historical impact of diminishing attempts to generate social reform (until the 1960s), let alone radical or socialist doctrines, in the labor movement or elsewhere. The Leftist movements that did spring up were battered by the conservatism of Irish society and condemnation by the Catholic Hierarchy.

The agenda of political and social issues in Irish politics has been shaped by the Catholicism of the people and the influence of the Hierarchy. As noted in Chapters 4 and 5, the constitutional ban on divorce, laws pertaining to abortion and contraception, support for censorship, and control of education were particularly notable manifestations of Catholic influence. The power of the Church in the political culture was clear in the formative years of the state, and although Church power over specific legislation has diminished, the political culture still is not highly secular. On the contrary, the issues, the way they are framed, their place on the Irish agenda, and the very language used to discuss elements of public policy reflect the degree of religious conviction among the Irish people and the pervasiveness of Catholicism in shaping the Republic.

British Influence

The influence of Britain on Ireland is so extensive as to defy brief description. The impact on the political culture has been to infuse Irish political attitudes with British ideas, institutions, and processes while the Irish either deny that influence or explicitly reject it. Four manifestations of this influence are especially notable. The first is the English language, which is the language of Ireland and has been dominant since the latter part of the nineteenth century even though Irish is revered as a manifestation of the distinctly Gaelic heritage of Ireland. The widespread use of English and geographical propinquity to the United Kingdom contribute to the emphasis on language as a mark of identity for the Irish. The second manifestation of British influence is the extensive interaction between the two countries. British television is watched in Ireland; books, newspapers, and magazines from Great Britain abound in Ireland. The massive emigration to Britain of Irish workers creates a constant flow of people between the two countries for personal reasons, family visits, holidays, and marriages. The extensive commerce creates another conduit of influence, to say nothing of the professional interactions in medicine, education, and the sciences. The foundation of the law in Ireland, the way organizations are structured, the patterns of management, the features of property ownership, the foundations of labor unions, the rivalries in sport, all display a similarity to the British that is as unseen to the Irish as it is obvious to the outsider.

The third impact of British influence is the structure and style of government. The inherent legitimacy of such institutions in Irish political culture is indicated by the forms of government adopted. The revolutionary Dail Eireann in 1919, the Treaty-based Irish Free State in 1922, and the Irish 1937 Constitution were democratic in form and shared a structure of parliamentary government resembling the "Mother of Parliaments" in London. The British civil service model was absorbed.

The fourth factor, the economic relationship of Great Britain and Ireland, has always been extensive and interdependent. Political, cultural, and economic domination of Ireland by Great Britain isolated Ireland from extensive contact with the Continent. Even after entrance into the European Economic Community in 1973 and the development of an export-oriented economy, Great Britain remains Ireland's largest trading partner. Moreover, British law does not recognize Ireland as a foreign state; the Irish were classified as citizens of the Commonwealth in the

1948 British Nationality Act. Thus the Irish are exempt from restrictions put on immigration to Britain from the former Commonwealth colonies.

Constitutional Foundations

Parliamentary government has taken three forms in modern Irish history: the revolutionary Dail Eireann, the Irish Free State Constitution, and the 1937 Constitution.

The Dail Eireann

The Dail Eireann, set up in 1919, was the embodiment of the Republic declared by the rebels of 1916. The most notable feature of this government was its parliamentary structure, modeled on that of Great Britain. The idea that sovereignty flowed from the people, not from the Crown, was significantly different, of course. The Irish had internalized the idea of popular sovereignty after the rebellions of 1798 and 1803. The Constitution itself was brief and created a unicameral Dail, a cabinet called the Ministry, a president, and four executive officers (later expanded to ten, then reduced to six), with the Ministry responsible to the Dail. The structure was the initiation of the nationalist constitutional tradition for independent Ireland and lasted until April 1922.

The first Dail met in January 1919 and had only twenty-seven representatives. They had been elected in the 1918 Sinn Fein landslide but would not take their seats in the British Parliament. Most of those who were elected could not attend because they were in jail or running from the British in the Anglo-Irish War. The British saw the first meeting in the Mansion House as a charade but later banned Dail Eireann, in September 1919. The Dail adopted a Declaration of Independence, elected Cathal Brugha president of the Ministry, and set out to create a parallel government to that of the British in Ireland.[3] The government paid the members of the Dail and full-time officials with the money raised by Michael Collins. After the Dail was banned the ministers were harassed by the British and had a difficult time operating as a formal government. Land courts, which were able to operate to some degree, were established in the west of Ireland, and most of the local governments shifted their allegiance to the Dail.

The Ministry was not effective in asserting control over the whole revolutionary movement because of the ambiguity of relationships between the key organizations. The Ministry and the Dail government sought to control the IRA, which operated pretty much independently. The Irish Republican Brotherhood saw itself as the "real" government of Ireland. The IRA saw civilian Sinn Fein as using the Dail to assert control over them and responded with disdain.[4] All of these organizations were older than the new revolutionary Dail and saw it as in service of their ends rather than vice versa. The IRA was much more successful in hampering the British government than in making the writ of the Dail extend over

Ireland. Yet the success of Dail Eireann is still remarkable: While fighting a war with Britain under martial law and operating underground it laid a foundation for constitutional authority based on popular sovereignty.

The Free State Constitution

The second manifestation of parliamentary government was the Free State Constitution, crafted in accord with the Anglo-Irish Treaty in 1922 and lasting until 1937. The Treaty negotiations did not produce a constitution for Ireland but did set down the parameters for the form of government that would exist in the south of Ireland. The Treaty called for a provisional government to make the transition.

For one day, January 14, 1922, three different governments governed southern Ireland.[5] The British government would not recognize Dail Eireann, which required the elaborate fiction that the Anglo-Irish Treaty was actually approved by the Southern Parliament created by the British 1920 Government of Ireland Act. Griffith, as leader of the Irish delegation that was party to the Anglo-Irish Treaty, had to convene some of those elected in 1921 (sixty pro-Treaty members of Sinn Fein, three from Dublin University) under that Act as a sort of kangaroo Parliament and submit the Anglo-Irish Treaty to them. (As a matter of fact, the rump legislative body was not itself legally constituted because it was not convened by the lord lieutenant of Ireland.) They approved the Treaty and chose the provisional government, and for that one day had the formal power to constitute the Irish government, after which they adjourned and never met again. The authority of that body, derived from the Government of Ireland Act of 1920, was based on English parliamentary legislation but was never accepted by Irish nationalists. Sinn Fein, representing the Irish, saw Dail Eireann, declared in 1919, as having the authority to govern Ireland. Dail Eireann was never accepted as legitimate by the British. Michael Collins was elected chairman of the provisional government chosen on January 14. Constituted by the Anglo-Irish Treaty, this government was viewed as legitimate by the British and by the pro-Treaty wing of Sinn Fein but not by the anti-Treaty wing of Sinn Fein. The British formally turned over power to the provisional government in January 1922.[6] Dail Eireann and the provisional government coexisted for four months, from January to April, when the Dail Ministry was essentially absorbed by the provisional government.

The structure of the Free State was delineated in the Constitution written by the provisional government and approved by the Dail and the British Parliament. It went into effect December 6, 1922. The provisional government's members were trying to square the circle by constructing a constitution that could put their ideas of republican government in place, potentially allow the moderates of de Valera's anti-Treaty section of Sinn Fein to accept participation in the new government, and also satisfy London that the government and its officials were consistent with the Anglo-Irish Treaty.[7] Collins was trying to avoid civil war and the British were trying to prevent the Irish squirming out of the Treaty obligations through the much-debated "election pact" between Collins and de Valera. A draft constitution submitted in May allowed for "External Ministers" in the Free State government as a means to bring anti-Treaty Sinn Fein members into the government. London rejected this and Winston Churchill, the colonial secretary, indicated that any members of the new government had to declare their adherence to the Anglo-Irish Treaty in writing. Ireland meanwhile slipped into civil war in June 1922. The provisional government then restructured the Constitution with no incentives to draw in their former comrades. A draft based on a constitutional monarchy, including a Senate and the Anglo-Irish Treaty provisions, was ultimately approved. The result was a hybrid of the Irish attempt to put a republican government under the Crown and the British attempt to create a colonial government beholden to the Crown.

In the end the Irish Free State was considerably more autonomous than London would have preferred and considerably closer to the Crown than Irish republicans would have preferred. The very symbol of the Crown's presence in Ireland, the governor general, reflects the ambiguous balance. The first governor general was Timothy Healy and the second was James MacNeill. Both accepted the diminished role of the position, legislatively and ceremonially, from 1922 to 1932. When de Valera took power he predictably clashed with MacNeill even over the limited role of governor general and had him dismissed. De Valera appointed a member of Fianna Fail, a grocer, Donal Buckley, to sign the necessary papers. Buckley was hardly a typical regal symbol.[8]

Another example of ambiguity in the Constitution was in the doctrine of sovereignty, which in British constitutional theory flows from the Crown. The Free State Constitution mentioned the sovereignty of the Crown in several articles including Article 17, the oath requiring members of the Free State government to be "faithful to H.M. King George V., his heirs and successors." At the same time, Article 3 of the Constitution indicated that sovereignty actually resided in the people of Ireland: "All powers of government and all authority, legislative, executive and judicial in Ireland, are derived from the people of Ireland." The very same oath that required fidelity to the Crown also demanded "true faith and allegiance to the Constitution of the Irish Free State," which recognized both regal and popular sovereignty.[9]

In the 1920 Government of Ireland Act, the Senate was a non-elected body representing a variety of societal interests, designed to protect the interests of southern unionists. In the new Free State Constitution southern unionists wanted half of a forty-seat body nominated from the professions and the other half elected by property owners. What they got, however, was considerably different. A sixty-seat body with very limited powers, one-third nominated by the Senate and two-thirds by the Dail, was to be elected by the public. Nominations were to take into account "the representation of important institutions and interests in the country." Southern Protestants were disproportionately represented in that body, as Griffith had promised, but it was not the Senate of 1920.

The presence of the Anglo-Irish Treaty provisions in the Constitution was clearly in the colonial mode. They included dominion status, the partition provision, British military bases in Ireland, acceptance of payment of the land annuities, and limitations on the size of the military. Yet at the same time the Constitution guaranteed the rights of citizens to liberty, privacy, freedom of opinion, assembly, association, religious freedom, no established church (Articles 6, 7, and 9), and judicial review (Article 65). These provisions reflected the influence of U.S. law and were unprecedented in British law. The Constitution thus was not the "sellout" to British colonial rule that Sinn Fein claimed but rather much closer to the "freedom to achieve freedom" that Collins argued the Anglo-Irish Treaty would provide.[10]

When de Valera came to power he began the process of removing the symbols of imperialism, as he said, "one by one so that the state that we control may be a Republic in fact."[11] Legislation introduced in 1933 removed the oath of allegiance to the Crown, cropped the powers of the governor general, and ended the right of appeal from Irish courts to the Privy Council in London. In 1936 de Valera abolished the Senate and legislated the elimination of all references to the king and governor general in the Free State Constitution. By 1936 the Free State Constitution was tattered; the constitutional foundation of Ireland was already shifting to the ideas embodied in Catholic nationalism. De Valera planned to introduce a new constitution and was working on the ideas as early as 1935.

The 1937 Constitution

The development of the new Constitution was placed in the hands of John Herne, the legal officer of the Department of External Affairs, who produced a draft that was later reworked by a committee in close coordination with de Valera. The request was introduced into the Dail in March 1937 and a final version of the new Constitution, called Bunracht na hEireann (Constitution of Ireland) was approved by the Dail in June, approved in a referendum in July, and made operative in December. This Constitution not only defined the formal relationships of the components of government, but also reflected the political culture of Ireland and de Valera's personal vision of a united Ireland. The result was a tenuous blend of Irish Catholicism, Fianna Fail nationalism, and Western liberal democracy.

The Constitution identified Ireland as Eire, a "sovereign, independent, democratic state" (Article 5) whose sovereignty was rooted in the people of Ireland. In all essential forms this was a republic, but de Valera refrained from that explicit designation so as to not exclude the possibility that Northern Ireland could again become part of Ireland. A complete break with the Commonwealth of Nations, de Valera believed, would diminish the possibility of eliminating partition.[12] In a piece of tortured rhetoric concerning external relations, the Constitution specified that the state could use "any organ, instrument, or method of procedure" used by "any group" with which the "State is or becomes associated with for the purpose of international cooperation" (Article 51). This was de Valera-speak for the 1936 External Relations Act, which identified the "group" as the Commonwealth and the "instrument" as the king. All of this was an attempt to provide a bridge to the uniting of Ireland. Yet de Valera produced a constitutional formula that reduced the Crown, that very Crown to which the unionists were so loyal, to obscure bureaucratic language. De Valera sought, as he said, to have a Constitution that would require no fundamental change "when the unity of Ireland was accomplished."[13] Not likely. The Constitution contained this and numerous other articles that contributed to the alienation of unionists from Eire.

The careful abstention from the use of the word "republic" did not preclude a constitutional claim to sovereignty over all of Ireland in Articles 2 and 3 of the Constitution. Article 2 claims jurisdiction over "the whole island of Ireland, its islands and territorial seas." This bold claim is circumscribed by declaring that the state's laws will not have force in Northern Ireland, "pending the re-integration of the national territory" (Article 3). This claim had self-evident validity to Irish nationalists from a moral and historical point of view, but it was infuriating to unionists from a political point of view and was less than persuasive from a constitutional law point of view.[14] These articles were changed under the Good Friday Agreement of April 1998 to define the Irish nation in terms of the people who are part of it, and choose to be so, rather than the territory it covers. The articles remain significant, however, as a manifestation of state irredentism for sixty years.[15]

Elements of Catholic thought pervade the Constitution as well. The preamble reads: "In the name of the Most Holy Trinity from Whom is all authority and to Whom, as our final end, all actions of both men and States must be referred, we, the people of Eire, Humbly acknowledging all our obligations to our Divine Lord, Jesus Christ, Who sustained our fathers through centuries of trial, Gratefully remembering their heroic and unremitting struggle to regain the rightful independence of our Nation."[16] Political scientist John Whyte has asked, appropriately, "Whose fathers?" because it appears from that history of Ireland that Protestants are not included among those who are to be remembered. Historian Joe Lee adds that this conjunction of "Irish", "Catholic", and "Nation" implied that Protestants "must jettison their heritage" to become truly Irish under a Constitution that claims to rule them.[17] The Constitutional Review Group appointed in 1995 suggested that the language of the preamble "reflecting the ethos of the 1930s, is overly Roman Catholic and nationalist in tone, is gender biased, and would be objectionable to many in Ireland today."[18]

Notable also for Catholic thought are Articles 41, 42, and 43. In Article 41 the family is defined as the natural, primary, and fundamental unit of society. Antecedent to positive law the family has inalienable rights rooted in Catholic doctrine and in the natural law. The state guarantees to protect the family and thus the institution of marriage is protected to the degree that no law could be passed that allows for divorce. (In 1995 the Divorce Referendum eliminated this provision.)

Article 42 defines the family as the natural educator of the child. Under this provision the state both takes on the obligation to provide "a certain minimum education" and at the same time exempts the parents from being obliged to send their children to schools established by the state. Choosing Catholic schools was a family right, while the obligation of the state was to provide a minimum education. The state resolved this contradiction by funding Catholic schools run by religious orders and parishes as the national school system.

Article 43 grants the right to property as a "natural right" and forbids any law to abolish private property but qualifies this right with the right of the state to limit property rights in accord with the common good. The underlying philosophical perspective is that the laws of the state are just only insofar as they are in accord with natural law. That natural law is a manifestation of the mind of God. Thus Church thought and philosophy is present in these articles, but the only explicit Church doctrine present was the prohibition against divorce.

Article 44 patently recognized the state's Catholic nature and itself was a compromise between the liberal and the Catholic dimensions of the Constitution. The original draft of March 1937 contained far stronger language on the relationship of Church and state than eventually emerged. That draft acknowledged that the "true religion" is the Catholic Church and that it is the interpreter of "true morality." The Church is recognized as a "perfect society" and the "civil and political order is rightly subject to the supreme authority of the perfect society." The state's function is to "procure the temporal well being of society"; thus the state was to be subordinate to the Church. In any Church–state conflict, the state could come to a special agreement with the Church on matters "civil, political and religious."[19] Such a hierarchical formulation, God–Church–state–law–people, was satisfactory to the Catholic Church and to the Vatican but would not have been very satisfactory to the minority Protestant community in Ireland, to adherents of liberalism, or for that matter to Britain, which held that Ireland was still bound by the Anglo-Irish Treaty provision of 1922.[20]

A visit to Rome was necessary to get assurance that the Vatican would not interfere in the constitutional formulation because it appeared that the Vatican would not approve a new Constitution unless the Church was formally recognized. The Bishop of Armagh, Cardinal MacRory did not think the text went far enough in separating what was in his mind the true Catholic Church from other erroneous denominations. The final version of Article 44 was a mixture of primacy and toleration that stated: "The State recognizes the special position of the Holy Catholic Apostolic and Roman Catholic Church as guardian of the faith professed by the great majority of the citizens. The State also recognizes the Church of Ireland, the Presbyterian Church in Ireland, the Methodist Church in Ireland, the Religious Society of Friends in Ireland, as well as the Jewish Congregations and the other religious denominations existing in Ireland at the date of the coming into operation of this constitution."[21] In addition, the Constitution protects freedom of conscience and practice, no religion is to be endowed by the state, and the state cannot discriminate on the basis of religion. De Valera attempted to avoid discriminating against other religions to ensure that in a united Ireland all religious beliefs would be respected. The actual text is far less apodictical than the draft, shifting from "true religion" to "special position," yet de Valera was more solicitous of the concerns of Rome and the bishops than he was of southern Protestants and Ulster unionists. The promise, for example, in Article 44, Section 2:3, that "The State shall not impose any disabilities or make any discrimination on the grounds of religious profession" seemed to be violated right from the start with the ban on divorce.

Article 44 remained controversial until its elimination in 1972, prompted in part by the troubles in Northern Ireland. Critics argued that it only exacerbated the Protestant view that Ireland was a "Catholic" state that had little toleration for other beliefs and constitutionally enshrined the Catholic Church in a special position. *The Report of the Committee on the Constitution* in 1967 called for the elimination of Article 44, in part based on the Northern issue, in part based on liberal principles. In 1969 the Primate of Ireland, Cardinal Conway, said he personally "would not shed a tear if the relevant sections of Article Forty Four were to disappear" and was supported by the Hierarchy.[22] A referendum removed the "special position" sections in 1972. Article 44 did not in fact have much practical effect because the real manifestation of the Catholic state was in the legislation that enshrined the Catholic moral code into public policy.

The "Directive Principles of Social Policy" included in Article 45 of the Constitution reflect the social values that were to undergird the state and are based on Catholic social thought. De Valera read widely on Catholic doctrine and consulted Father John Charles McQuaid, who provided him with then current documents such as the "Rerum Novarum" of Leo XIII and "Quadragesimo Anno" of Pius XI. Included in Article 45 are mandates to the state to provide a livelihood; have a just and charitable social order; prevent the abuse of men, women, and children in employment; have concern for the economically disadvantaged; and establish families on the land. The explicit market directives called on the state to see that the distribution, ownership, and control of the material resources of society served the common good. These were guidelines for the Dail not "cognizable by any Court," but the High Court did suggest they could be taken into consideration "when deciding whether a claimed constitutional right exists."[23] Given the slow expansion of implicit rights found in the Constitution by the courts since the 1970s, this is not an unimportant point.

The composition of the Senate in the new Constitution was also a reflection of the corporatist emphasis in Catholic thought during the 1930s.[24] De Valera appointed a commission to examine the idea of a vocationally organized upper body, which agreed on the idea but disagreed on the size and manner in which it should be elected. If the Dail was the electoral body for the Senate it would be a repository of patronage for party faithful; if it was to be chosen by vocational bodies it could be insufficiently obedient to the Dail's (or Fianna Fail's) wishes.

The result was a compromise in which eleven of the sixty members were selected by the Taoiseach, six were elected from the universities, and forty-three were nominated from the following sectors—"National Language and Culture, Literature, Art, Education. . . .; Agriculture and allied interest and Fisheries; Labour, whether organized or unorganized; Industry and Commerce . . . ; Public Administration and social services"—with no less than five coming from each sector (Article 18).[25] The election of the candidates was not put in the hands of the vocational panels, however; that task fell to the Dail, the Senate, and the members of every council of a county or county borough (that is, about 1,100 people). The election procedure ensured that the apolitical innovation of vocational voices would quickly be supplanted by the Fianna Fail partisan dimension; as historian Joe Lee puts it: "Genuine vocational representatives were swamped beneath the avalanche of party loyalists."[26] Historian Dermot Keogh describes the resulting Senate as "Mr. de Valera's poodle," but the presence of vocationalism was at the least a nod to the Catholic social thought of the time.[27]

The Constitution was hailed by Cardinal MacRory as a "great Christian document" in 1937.[28] The provisions, from the preamble to the "Principles of Social Policy," indicate that Cardinal MacRory should have used the term "Roman Catholic" document. The Constitution of 1937, of course, did not make the Irish people Catholic, but it came as far as liberalism would stretch to making the Irish state Catholic.

Article 8 provided that Irish "as the national language" would be the first official language of the state, with English as the second official language. The ideological goal of Gaelic Ireland clashed with two facts: Irish was not in fact the national language because most people in the Free State spoke English and the ultimate unification of Ireland would include nearly 1 million English-speaking Protestants of the north. The contradictory aspirations of a Gaelic-speaking Ireland and a united Ireland were reconciled by a rhetorical nod to "the national language" of Irish combined with the rapid assurance that the people of Ireland, however great their reverence for Irish, could go on speaking English. The Constitutional Review Group, noting that "English is the language currently spoken as their vernacular by 98% of the population of the State," in 1996 urged that both languages be designated official and that special care be taken to nurture Irish.[29]

The broad structure of government created by the Constitution was liberal, being, of course, a democracy with regular, free, secret elections and majority rule. The civil rights of citizens are guaranteed in Article 40, which states: "All citizens shall, as human persons, be held equal before the law." The rights elaborated by this article include protection by the state of the "life, person, good name, and property rights of every person" and due process of law. The rights of habeas corpus, inviolability of one's dwelling, free speech, assembly, and association are guaranteed.[30] Article 40 has been the vehicle through which Irish judges have elaborated additional implied rights of the citizen, including "bodily integrity, the right to work, the right to belong to a trade union, the right of a union member to take part in the decision-making process of his union, the right to a career, the right to free movement, the right to marry, and a general right to privacy."[31] The Constitutional Review Group, noting the advantages of letting rights be discovered and interpreted and the disadvantages of allowing a wide latitude to judicial interpretation, concluded that the rights that have been articulated by the judges through decisions should be defined; it recommended an amendment that would "provide a comprehensive list of fundamental rights which could specifically encompass the personal rights which have been identified by the high courts to date."[32]

The Constitution has been changed since 1937 not only by the process of judicial interpretation but also by amendment through referenda. Twenty times the voters have gone to the polls; fifteen times they have voted for an amendment. The changes include the adoption of the Constitution itself (1937), discussed below, and matters pertaining to the structural features of government. These include lowering the voting age to eighteen (1972), altering the representation of universities in the Senate (1979), and extending voting rights to non-citizens (1984). Changes involving relations with Europe include entering the European Economic Community (1972), ratifying the Single European Act (1987), ratifying the Maastricht Treaty (1992), and ratifying the Amsterdam Treaty (1998). A third group of changes involves issues of Church and state, including eliminating the special position of the Church (1972), changing rules on adoption (1979), the prohibition of abortion (1983), the right to travel freely (1992), access to information on services in another state (1992), and eliminating the ban on divorce (1995). A last change was to the restrictions on the right to bail (1996).

The referendum in 1937 was accompanied by a call for a general election so that the voters would decide on both a new government and a new Constitution. De Valera expected that the Constitution vote would spill over onto his party vote, and he campaigned with great vigor. The turnout was high. Even though de Valera's opponents ran a tepid campaign, the votes for Fianna Fail dropped that year by 90,000 votes and 4.4 percent. More surprisingly, the Constitution was approved by only 56.5 percent of the electorate. The margin is seen to be even smaller when spoiled ballots (9.9 percent) are taken into account. Political scientist Richard Sinnott points out that the effective turnout was 68.3 percent; thus "the 'yes' vote amounted to only 38.6 percent of the registered electorate—hardly an overwhelming endorsement."[33]

The Structure of Government

The hallmark of Irish government is its unadulterated concentration of power, making it, as political scientist Alan Ward notes, "one of the most highly centralized in the democratic world."[34] The general relationship of the components of the Irish government is one of subordination. The Cabinet is subordinate to the prime minister, the Dail is subordinate to the Cabinet. The Seanad is secondary to the Dail. The civil service departments are closely controlled by the Cabinet. Local government is controlled by the minister and Dail members. The components of the political system can be illustrated in light of this power concentration, starting with the center.

The Cabinet

The center of power is in the Cabinet, the policymaking body. The center of the Cabinet is the Taoiseach. The prime minister in the 1937 Constitution was created on the model of the British prime minister, but de Valera seemed to have something more powerful in mind, as his choice of the title Taoiseach indicates. The word means "chieftain" in Irish, as opposed to Priomh-Aire, which means "prime minister."[35] The Taoiseach appoints the members of the Cabinet and can dismiss them as well. The prime minister sets the policy agenda for the government, controls the budget process, and oversees the implementation of policy. The concentration of constitutional power and the increasing centralization of policymaking power through the impact of personality, party leadership, and media attention have made the Taoiseach the center of the Irish government in both formal and informal respects.

Changes in election techniques in the late 1970s, which placed a great emphasis on presenting the party leader as a national figure in the media, strengthened the position of prime minister. Not all of those who held the office had de Valera's charismatic power of personality and place in the Sinn Fein–Fianna Fail history. His personality shaped the perception of the position apart from its constitutional powers. The role of other prime ministers, as political scientist Brian Farrell has pointed out, is often more that of chairman than of chief.[36] Farrell judges leaders such as de Valera (1933, 1951, 1957) and Lemass (1959) as chiefs. Jack Lynch (1966, 1977) and Costello (1954), on the other hand, were chairman. Since 1971 the names of Ahern (1997), Bruton (1994), Reynolds (1993), and Cosgrave (1973) would not stand out as towering chieftains. Haughey (1979, 1982, 1987) and FitzGerald (1981, 1982), who dominated Irish politics from the late 1970s to the early 1990s, stand above the rest, though for completely different reasons.

Haughey's talent as a politician and a leader was unquestionable. He used those skills on the margins of dubious moral and legal behavior and old boy cronyism and presided over the demise of his party's dominant position. FitzGerald, with his superior intellect and quality of character, led Fine Gael to a position near that of Fianna Fail in 1982 only to have his own administration be seen as inconsistent and uninspired.

Coalition government has increased. Six of the eight governments after 1981 were coalitions, which tends to limit the dominant role of the Taoiseach because Cabinet positions must be shared and policy based on compromise. In this light the most effective chieftain recently may not have been the Taoiseach at all but the Labour Party leader, Dick Spring, who led his party in 1992 to the highest number of seats in the Dail, thirty-three, a third higher than its previous highest total (twenty-two in 1927 and 1965) and put his party into several coalition governments.

The Cabinet consists of the prime minister (Taoiseach), deputy prime minister (Tanaiste), and between seven and fifteen party leaders who are appointed to various ministries by the prime minister. The majority party in the Dail, of course, has the claim on the right to rule, and the president "invites" the leader of the majority party to form a government. If no party has a clear majority, attempts are made to form a coalition of parties, which then takes on the responsibility for forming a government. Of the twenty-seven governments after 1922, ten have been coalition governments (and twelve have in fact been minority governments). The Cabinet then is divided among the party leaders of the coalition. The cabinet members are at once party leaders and ministers for various governmental departments: External Affairs; Health; Agriculture, Food, and Forestry; Arts, Culture, and the Gaeltacht; Social Welfare, Defense, and the Marine; Finance; Transport, Energy, and Communication; Enterprise and Employment; Environment; Justice, Equality, and Law Reform; Tourism and Trade; and Education. An additional seventeen ministers of state are assigned to the Cabinet departments or to other executive departments by the majority party or coalition, but they are not members of the Cabinet.

The Cabinet operates on the basis of collective responsibility. Whatever differences exist in the Cabinet before a decision, all ministers will support the decision after it is made. The minister who opposes a policy has two choices after a decision has been made: resign over the issue or support it. The effect is to create a great deal of secrecy around Cabinet decisions, thus "erecting a formidable barrier between the legislature and the government."[37] The Supreme Court in 1993 upheld this secrecy in *Attorney General v. Hamilton* (no.1) when it ruled there was an obligation by a former minister not to reveal Cabinet discussions in response to a demand by a Judicial Tribunal that he do so.[38] The information in a department is held closely by the minister and the senior civil servants. They are bound by the Official Secrets Act of 1963, which prohibits their revealing official information. The Taoiseach, as party leader and head of the government, generates the policy agenda; legislation is drafted in the department of government. The Dail legislative agenda is set by the Cabinet. The effect of this structure is to centralize the power of government in the Cabinet in a way that is more akin to Gaullist France than the United States.

The Oireachtas

The power to make the laws for the state is in the Oireachtas, made up of the Dail (Assembly) and Seanad (Senate). Government policy may be considered and discussed in both houses but the government of Ireland is responsible to the Dail alone. Composed of 166 members, the Dail is drawn from forty-one multi-member constituencies. Members of the Dail each represent no more than 30,000 and no fewer than 20,000 people, and an attempt is made to balance out the numbers so that the number is roughly the same for each constituency. The Dail and Seanad must revise the constituencies at least every twelve years to take into account population growth and shifts. The maximum time between elections for a member of the Dail is five years, but there is no minimum and the prime minister can call an election any time before the five-year limit is up. A series of committees carry out the legislative tasks.

Among the more important committees are the Dail committees, set up in 1983. They are Social Affairs, Finance and General Affairs, Enterprises and Economic Strategy, and Legislation and Security. The joint committees are Foreign Affairs, Women's Rights, European Affairs, Irish Language, and Sustainable Development and Family. No more than two senators can sit in the Cabinet, and the Constitution specifies that the Taioseach, Tanaiste, and minister for Finance must be members of the Dail. In practice only two members of the Cabinet have been members of the Senate since the adoption of the Constitution.

Dail debate is usually a forum to gain local publicity; strong party discipline ensures that the Cabinet will have its way when the vote comes on legislation. Checks on the government ministers, such as "question time," in which members are free to challenge the ministers on the conduct of government, all too often become a capricious exercise in nit-picking on local matters such as why mail delivery was delayed in Mayo. The members of the Seanad and Dail are not equipped with the staff (each member of the Dail has one secretary), the expertise, or the time to be able to independently challenge the government in any effective way. The salary is not very large, and a member of the Irish Parliament would envy the resources of a state legislator in the United States, to say nothing of a member of the U.S. House or Senate.

The introduction of private bills by the members is usually only a tactic to gain publicity because they have no impact in the Dail. No committee chairman has the kind of legislative power exerted in the U.S. Congress by committee chairs. To speak of the Dail as if it existed outside of the political parties is to miss the point that the operation of the Dail is marked by party discipline. Every member is expected to be loyal to the party. Not only does his or her nomination come from local party conventions, but it must be approved by the national executive of the party, and the candidate is compelled to sign an oath of loyalty and obedience to the party. The members of the Dail have very little autonomy and thus the dance of legislation is marked more by the stability of party discipline than by the judgment of the member (Teachta Dala, or TD) or the structural features of the Dail.

The Dail member is far more concerned with the provision of services or favors to his or her constituents than with developing independent legislative expertise. This clientelist system or "brokerage" politics comes from a traditional environment in which the constituents do not have resources, capabilities, organization, or access to the government and need an intermediary to speak for them. People with low levels of trust in distant and unfamiliar institutions seek a patron or broker to extract what is due them, seek a favor, or right a wrong. The emergence of this system in a country with a relatively authoritarian culture, a dominant political party, and the relatively backward west of Ireland is no surprise. The maintenance of this system today in face of near universal literacy, higher education levels, and mobilization through intermediary pressure groups is more surprising.[39] The persistence of the brokerage system is testimony to the relative powerlessness of the Dail and the discipline of party government. In the perception of voters the task of serving as an intermediary between the citizen and the bureaucracy is more important than the role of policy maker and legislator.

The duty of the TD to the constituents includes everything from attending wakes, weddings, and retirement parties to solving problems for supporters on matters concerning pensions, land, licenses, and jobs. The attitude of the Irish voter toward those in the Dail is aptly summed up by Brian Farrell: "Continuous demands for grants, services and special treatment for local needs . . . a steady stream of supplicants seeking assistance."[40] The requests can run to 110 per week and the public assumes that they are getting the services because they are asking their TD. Dispensing these favors is a form of "massive deceit," according to TD Michael Keating, because it conveys the idea that they would not obtain the benefits anyway.[41] The administrative departments of government are caught up in the process; they devote time, paperwork, and money to the endless stream of idiosyncratic requests to meet the TDs' needs.

The voters in Ireland have powerful parochial loyalties. The successful candidates cultivate that loyalty and reinforce it with constituent service. Ireland is a small country, and the TD returns to his or her constituency regularly to perform the rituals that ensure electoral success. Historically the quality of legislators appeared to be commensurate with the challenge of the tasks. Many talented people sought business, academic, or professional careers instead. Politics then tended to become a family business, with sons, wives, and grandchildren following fathers into local and national government.[42] In 1973, 30 percent of the members of the Dail had a family relationship with a former member; in 1992 the figure was 25 percent. Those who have performed the various services well over time gain the electoral loyalty of the voters and are more likely to be re-elected. Thus the pattern of clientelist politics is reinforced by the electoral victories of the member and the perceived service for the citizen.

In the latter years of the twentieth century the level of education in the Dail climbed significantly. In 1922, 40 percent of the Dail had only a first-level education and only 26 percent a third level. In 1992 a scant 2 percent had only a first level and 72 percent had a third-level education or beyond.[43]

Because of the vocational organization and the lack of power, the Seanad is part of the legislative process only in a very limited way. The body can make amendments to bills but must do so within ninety days; these can be overridden by the Dail. On money bills the Seanad can only make recommendations and then only during a period of three weeks. The power that the Senate has to amend bills is used infrequently, perhaps on no more than 10 percent of the bills passed. Recommendations on money bills are used even less frequently. The Senate meets less often than the Dail, sitting only three-fifths to three-quarters of the days that the Dail sits in a year. The Seanad serves as a place to put prominent people through the prime minister's nominations, to make a name for rising stars, and to put up one's feet for defeated or declining political figures.

The role of the Senate, going back to the Free State, has always been problematical. In the Free State one-half of the Senate was nominated by the head of the government and one-half was elected by the Dail. When de Valera took power the Free State Senate was in opposition to the Dail. He sought to create a Senate in 1937 that would be useful but not oppositional. The resulting entity has been unsatisfactory as a vocational body and superfluous as a legislative body. The Commission on Vocational Organization in 1943 sought to strengthen the vocational basis of the Seanad through election by vocational councils rather than local politicians. In 1958 de Valera appointed a Seanad Electoral Law Commission, which recommended in 1961 that twenty-three seats of forty-three be elected directly by vocational constituencies. The 1967 Committee on the Constitution considered a number of recommendations to reform the Senate elections, composition, and nominations, but rejected changes in each of these areas as creating more problems. Suggestions in the 1990s from the Fine Gael party emphasize strengthening the Seanad, while the Progressive Democrats want it abolished. The 1996 Constitutional Review Group, under the chairmanship of T. K. Whitaker, reviewed the issues of the existence of the Senate, its composition, and the electoral system and recommended that a separate, independent, comprehensive examination of all issues relating to the Seanad be made. The tradition of dissatisfaction with the Senate is accompanied by the tradition of setting up commissions to study it.

Local Government

Contributing to the centralization of Irish government is the structure of local government. Local government is prevented from the exercise of real power over local affairs. Local governments in Ireland control only 10 percent of public spending, compared to an average of 30 percent in the countries of the European Union (EU). Elected local councils represent a relatively large number of people compared to other countries. In 1977 the source of revenue for local councils was removed when taxes on land and houses were eliminated. The councils are filled with members of the Dail, who see them as part of the apparatus for providing service to constituents in return for electoral support. The local governments are actually run by managers not elected locally at all but rather appointed by Dublin through the Local Appointments Commission. The most important tasks of local government are housing and building, roads, water and sewage, development, environmental protection, recreation, and agriculture, which fall under the responsibility of the minister for the Environment.

Health services, physical planning, and regional development bodies have been established in eight regional boards. In practice these bodies are closely controlled by federal government departments. More and more administrative power is in the hands of the manager, collaborating with national agencies and relatively un-fettered by the local councils or regional boards. Efforts to reform local govern-ment have been inversely related to the exhortatory rhetoric to do so. Thomas Barrington, a retired civil servant, is the most vociferous critic of local govern-ment in Ireland, suggesting that it will be ineffectual unless decentralized. He chaired an advisory committee which, in the 1991 *Report of the Advisory Expert Committee on Local Government Reorganization and Reform*, called for fairly sub-stantial decentralization of power and financing. Political scientist Basil Chubb, however, offers no solace to reformers: "The truth is that the system as it is still both suits the central administration, which has it in its thrall, and answers the needs of most politicians, who are able to manipulate it to the extent necessary to supply a satisfactory service to their constituents and who therefore block any proposal for reform that does emerge."[44]

The President

Turning to the more symbolic level of Irish government, the president (Uachtaran) is the head of state. Elected by popular vote for a seven-year term, the president may be re-elected only once. The president does have certain powers. The president appoints the Taoiseach (prime minister) on the Dail's recommen-dation. On the prime minister's recommendation and with the Dail's approval, the president appoints the ministers of the government. On the recommendation of the Taoiseach the president convenes and dissolves the Oireachtas. All legisla-tion must be signed by the president. He or she is the Supreme Commander of the Armed Forces. The president may exercise several important powers in con-junction with the Council of State,[45] including submitting legislation to the Supreme Court if he or she deems that it raises a constitutional question. The president may refer legislation to the people for a referendum or wait until a new government is in power to sign that legislation. In response to a request from a majority of the Seanad and more than one-third of the Dail, the president may re-frain from signing a bill until the will of the people has been ascertained. The president may call the Dail and Senate into session (actually done only once, on the occasion of the fiftieth anniversary of Dail Eireann in 1969). The president may, without the Council of State, choose not to dissolve a Dail in which the Taoiseach has lost a vote of confidence, calling upon the members to try to nego-tiate a new government.

Two of the president's powers have led to political crises. The first is the referral of legislation to the Supreme Court. From 1940 to 1992 eight bills had been sent to the Court and three of those had been deemed unconstitutional. In 1976 this process led to the resignation of President Cearbhall O'Dalaigh. The president

Mary MacAleese was elected president of Ireland in 1997, following Mary Robinson's term, and represents the growing power and visibility of women on the political stage of Ireland.
Photo by Harry Brett, Image Photo

was an experienced lawyer, a former attorney general, a member of the European Court of Justice, and Chief Justice of the Irish Supreme Court. He had reservations about an Emergency Powers Bill, which had been passed in the face of a series of IRA attacks. The Fine Gael–Labour coalition government of the time had a conservative minister for Justice, Mr. Patrick Cooney, who sought a rather extensive expansion of police powers under the bill. Minister for Defense Patrick Donegan called the president "a thundering disgrace" for his quite appropriate and legal constitutional action. O'Dalaigh expected Donegan's resignation and in fact Donegan offered to resign. Prime Minister Liam Cosgrave instead urged Donegan to apologize to the president, which he did, but O'Dalaigh found this insufficient. The Fianna Fail party, in opposition, called for Donegan's resignation and lost the vote in the Dail. O'Dalaigh then resigned the presidency because he found he could not get any satisfaction from the government for such an insult.

Eventually Donegan did resign and the Supreme Court found the bill constitutional. The episode is a catalog of folly; it could have been avoided by prompt action by Cosgrave in accepting Donegan's resignation and preventing a Dail vote on partisan lines that was bound to embarrass the president. The event strengthened the presidency in that it discouraged criticism of the president for exercising constitutional powers.[46]

The second power that has generated controversy is the power to not grant a dissolution of the Dail after the government has "ceased to retain the support of the majority" (Article 13). The lack of clarity in the phrase can lead to ambiguity because it does not specify the loss of a majority to be in a vote of confidence. In 1982 Garret FitzGerald, after a loss on a budget vote, went to the president and asked for a dissolution of the Dail. Charles Haughey, the opposition leader, thought it possible to form a new government without an intervening election and made this known to President Patrick Hillary. Fianna Fail leaders made telephone calls to the president trying to persuade him to allow a new government to be negotiated without dissolution of the Dail. The pressure backfired and made President Hillary so angry that he dissolved the Dail.

Later Fianna Fail and the Tanaiste Brian Lenihan were accused by members of the Dail of improperly trying to intimidate and influence the president. Lenihan explicitly denied that the calls took place and was then embarrassed by the publicizing of a tape recording of him admitting he had spoken to the president whom, he noted, "was clearly annoyed at the whole bloody lot of us."[47] Lenihan continued his denial and said the interview occurred when he was under the influence of medication. His denial led to a crisis over his resignation from the Haughey government, forced by his coalition partners, in 1990 while he was a candidate for president. Arguably the crisis cost him that election. While some ambiguity exists over the definition of retention of the support of a majority, it is clear that the president has the power to refuse a request for dissolution and let the parties in the Dail attempt to form a government, especially if there has been a recent election and all the possible coalitions have not yet been negotiated.

The role of the president may be changing. Mary Robinson promised to restore an active presidency, although actually there never had been any such thing. She strove to emphasize the symbolic nature of the office as spokesperson for the nation and promised to make the Council of State more representative (which she did, appointing more women, a farmer, and the iconic T. K. Whitaker). She chose to speak to larger issues of charity, development, and the Irish abroad as well. As expansive as her view of the presidency was, Robinson assured the voters that at no time was she suggesting anything outside of the constitutional limitations of the office. The Irish may come to expect this increase in the visibility and presence of the president, but an attempt to formalize an expanded presidency in 1990, pushed by Alan Dukes, the head of Fine Gael, went down to defeat in the midst of criticism that such a change would tamper with the Constitution.

State Sponsored Bodies; the Electoral System

The Irish political system is marked by two anomalies that contribute to less centralization: the governmental grant of authority to autonomous functional organizations called State Sponsored Bodies and the adoption of an electoral system that potentially limits single-party control of the Dail.

The State Sponsored Bodies, as attachments to the various civil service departments, emerged from no plan, design, or ideology. Beginning in 1927 with the Electricity Supply Board and the Agricultural Credit Corporation, these entities were created to address the problems that came up on the national agenda in the process of state building. The state in the 1920s and 1930s was not endowed with a wealth of resources to allocate to the development of business, and the private sector was capital starved as well. Sean Lemass noted in 1961: "Even the most conservative among us understands why we cannot rely on private enterprise alone, and state enterprise in fields of activity where private enterprise has failed or has shown itself to be disinterested, has not only been accepted but expected."[48]

Thus the State Sponsored Bodies began to emerge to fulfill three different functions. First is the production of needed goods and services (for example, Aer Lingus and Radio Telfis Erieann), second is the development and/or promotion of industry and commerce (for example, the Industrial Development Authority and the Irish Tourist Board), and third is the provision of social services or administration and regulation of social and economic activity (for example, the Higher Education Authority and the Employment Equality Agency). Socialism as a doctrine of state ownership and control of productive resources had little or nothing to do with the evolution of these semi-state organizations. Hardly anything was nationalized, and there was in fact in Ireland a firm belief in the marketplace (albeit somewhat circumscribed by anti-material attitudes). The belief that the government departments were not the appropriate structures to take on these functions, recruit the necessary personnel, or develop the necessary strategies led to the pragmatic creation of these highly different and idiosyncratic bodies. The ministers of government departments produced them as they were seen to be needed and the boards of directors, structure, regulation, financing, and staffing differed for each depending on the circumstances.

The number of State Sponsored Bodies is not clear. Alan Ward cites a 1980 Fine Gael report that identifies 87, a text on Irish government identifies 133, and Basil Chubb identifies 96.[49] Whatever the precise number, it is clear that these bodies employ over 70,000 people, about 30 percent of public sector employment, and are responsible for as much as 10 percent of Ireland's Gross Domestic Product.

The number of these bodies exploded after World War II. Their impact on the public finally raised the issue of their accountability to the ministers, the government, and the Dail. State Sponsored Bodies needed autonomy to fulfill their functions, especially the state enterprises, which operated in a competitive arena; thus they were relatively free of close control. On the other hand, the governments of the day raised concerns about financing of these bodies and the political ramifications of their policies.

The Public Services Organizational Review Group, known as the Devlin Group after its chair Liam St. John Devlin, was appointed in the late 1960s to examine public services. Increasing demands were being put on existing government departments and State Sponsored Bodies after the adoption of *Economic Development*. The conclusions of the Devlin Group directed at the civil service departments were implemented in the 1970s but with the same lack of quality and comprehensiveness and the same protection of bureaucratic turf, that had engendered the Devlin Group in the first place. Addressing State Sponsored Bodies, the Devlin group saw that ministerial control had eroded as the bodies grew in number, size, and functions.[50] The Devlin group saw the state enterprise bodies and the development/regulatory bodies as different. They concluded that the non-commercial bodies were carrying out activities that could be done by the government departments but that commercial bodies should also be more answerable to the minister in terms of goals and results. Little came of these recommendations and a steady stream of reports and calls for accountability have not had much effect. With their own structures, their linkage to the departments, and their lack of accountability, State Sponsored Bodies remain one of the more incoherent features of Irish government.

The electoral system of Ireland, proportional representation with a single transferable vote, is an anomaly that is mystifying to the world beyond Eire. While rarely used elsewhere, it has been very satisfactory to the Irish voter. The choice to incorporate this system into the 1937 Constitution comes from its adoption in the 1922 Constitution. At that time proportional representation (PR) was widely discussed in Europe as being more democratic in representing the spectrum of parties in the electorate. Arthur Griffith was a member of the Proportional Representation Society of Ireland and Sinn Fein favored the adoption of the PR system. Griffith promised London that it would be used in elections in Ireland during the negotiations on the Anglo-Irish Treaty. The British favored the adoption of PR in Ireland, although Britain itself did not use that system, because it ensured representation for the southern Protestants and the unionists in any future assemblies. Incorporated into the Free State Constitution, one of the first effects of PR was to prevent a defeat for de Valera's anti-Treaty wing of Sinn Fein. Under a single-member district plurality system, such as Great Britain and the United States have, Sinn Fein might have been eliminated in the 1920s. If the voters had had only one vote to cast in those early elections, they might have been less and less ready to cast it symbolically for a party unwilling to take their seats.

Under PR the constituencies are multi-member: twelve districts return three members, fifteen return four members, and fourteen return five members each. No constituency can return fewer than three. The parties put forth more candidates than there are seats, and the members of a particular party are running against each other as well as against the opposition parties. The number that are to run in a given constituency is determined by the national party leadership. Not all seats are contested by the Labour Party and the minor parties, but Fine Gael and Fianna Fail usually contest all the seats. The party does not attempt to guide the voters regarding which of its own members to vote for. Election material urges the electorate to vote for the candidate of their choice within the party.

The actual voting system is more complicated to explain than to operate. The central feature is the ability of the voter to rank order his or her preference for the candidates. The voter puts the number "1" beside the candidate he or she prefers first, the number "2" beside the second preference, the number "3" beside the third, and so on. The voter is getting a chance to express a choice of candidate, that is number "1," but also to express with a greater degree of subtlety how he or she views all the candidates. Voters are able, by using a lower preference, to vote should they choose for a candidate from a party other than their own. All the valid votes for a district are counted by putting them on a table and lining them up by first preferences. The "quota" for election is then determined. The quota is the total of all valid votes cast divided by the number of seats in the constituency plus one, and then one is added to the product. If there were 40,000 votes cast in a four-seat district, the quota would be 40,000 divided by 5 (the number of seats plus one). The result is 8,000 plus one for a quota of 8,001. The candidates who achieve the quota are declared elected. If no candidate achieves the quota on the first count, the candidate with lowest number of votes is eliminated and those ballots are redistributed based upon the second preference listed. To run a candidate must put up a deposit of £100 ($150), which is forfeited if the candidate does not get votes equal to one-third of the quota. When a candidate is elected by achieving the quota, the "surplus," second preference votes are transferred to the other candidates and added to their totals. This continues until the seats are filled by candidates getting the quota. If a seat is left and no one reached the quota, the person with the highest total would be elected.

The PR system has been praised by some as being capable of registering voters' preferences with greater sensitivity than other electoral systems. Critics have suggested that PR creates splinter parties, coalitions, and unstable government.[51] Every ideological sector on the political spectrum can organize as a party and hope to win a proportion of seats, however small, rather than integrate into a larger party. The Irish experience has tended to affirm the view of proponents of the system and confute the critics. The record shows that Irish government has been stable. Fianna Fail dominated the government of Ireland from 1932, ruling for forty-six of seventy-six years. In two periods, 1932 to 1948 and 1957 to 1973, Fianna Fail enjoyed sixteen years of unbroken rule. As political scientist Basil Chubb noted in 1978, "Clearly Ireland has not had unstable government. 'Stagnant' might sometimes have been a more appropriate term."[52] The Irish system has not had the effect of multiplying parties because the rise and fall of minor parties had been generated by periodic discontent with the major parties and subsequently most minor parties disappeared within a decade. The same three parties have dominated Irish politics since the 1930s.[53]

The distribution of votes among parties has of course varied, and it is this variation that has made the parties reconsider PR. The most notable, some would say egregious, efforts were made by Fianna Fail in 1959 and 1968. Fianna Fail had a claim on four to five out of every ten voters in Ireland after 1932, achieving a high of 52 percent in 1938. The PR system has been favorable to Fianna Fail, providing a slightly greater percentage of seats in the Dail than their popular vote. The temptation for Fianna Fail to change to the U.S. and U.K. system was irresistible, however, because their percentage of votes would produce staggering majorities in the Dail. The single-member district plurality system, or "first past the post," has the effect of multiplying the percentage of seats of the winning party considerably beyond the popular vote and thus is favored by those seeking consistent governing majorities.

In 1959 Fianna Fail put forward an amendment to abolish PR. The referendum was held the same day as the de Valera presidential election. In a close vote the voters chose to reject a change to the PR system by a margin of 33,667 votes while at the same time electing de Valera president by a majority of over 120,000. Clearly the Irish voters preferred both their PR system and de Valera. In 1968 Fianna Fail tried again. Nine years is a short time and Irish memories are long. The press coverage of the Fianna Fail ploy was embarrassing, pointing out that under a first-past-the-post system Fianna Fail would command over 90 seats of a chamber of 144 (63 percent). The referendum was defeated by a three to two margin. Recognizing that this effort was patently self-aggrandizing, nevertheless Fianna Fail was still prescient in trying to ensure the party's dominant majorities and pluralities in the Dail, because they have become a thing of the past. In the 1992 election Fianna Fail received 39 percent of the vote, 68 seats out of 166 in the Dail (41 percent). Five of the governments after 1981 were coalitions, and the last two Fianna Fail governments after 1981 have been minority governments. The age of coalition government has arrived, and the PR electoral system will reinforce that pattern.

Neo-Corporatist Policymaking

The impact of corporatist doctrines in the Church's social thought on Ireland is usually discussed in terms of the composition of the Senate. Lee and others quickly point out that de Valera and others were not interested in any structures that would diminish the power of Fianna Fail and thus vitiated the embryonic corporatism of the Senate through the election process.[54] Corporatism, however, manifested itself in Ireland in other forms, such as the flirtation with corporatism by Fine Gael in the early 1930s and the *Commission on Vocational Organization Report* of 1943. The Church in its social thought had sought to find an alternative ideology to capitalism and communism, articulating the idea of the vertical organization of society into vocational sectors. The sectors would govern themselves and bring people together to develop national policy based upon their shared concerns rather than on class or partisan foundation.

To the degree that corporatism would appeal to any party in Ireland, Fianna Fail, with its Catholic, Gaelic, and mystical nationalism and mixed record on democracy, would have been the obvious choice. However, when Fianna Fail came to power in 1932 it triggered the merger of the Blueshirts, the National Centre Party, and Cumann na nGaedheal into Fine Gael. Intellectuals such as John Horgan, professor of history at University College Cork, and Michel Tierney, later president of University College Dublin, tried to push Fine Gael toward the corporatist model. According to their view individualism and collectivism represented distortions of human nature, the former mired in self-interest and alienation and the latter in class conflict and the obliteration of individual differences. The answer was corporatism as put forth in the papal encyclical *Quadragesimo Anno* in 1931. The development of corporatist councils would generate self-governing social sectors and would diminish the power of the state bureaucracy. Corporatism would rectify the weaknesses of democracy: a lack of authenticity and the inability to respond to crisis. The government so constructed would be "a practical alternative which is based upon the principles of Christianity."[55] The intellectual underpinnings of Catholic corporatism were dressed up with something a little more sinister, however, in the rhetoric of Eoin O'Duffy, leader of the Blueshirts and of Fine Gael: "We shall be masters of Ireland in three years. . . . [W]e do not want politics and politicians: we want a disciplined well governed country."[56] Eventually the segment of Fine Gael based upon the old Cumann na nGaedheal emerged under William Cosgrave to take over the party. Fine Gael returned to being a conservative commonwealth party and the corporatist doctrines faded. O'Duffy resigned and later led a brigade to the Spanish Civil War to fight for Franco.

However, Michael Tierney suggested to de Valera in 1938 that a commission of inquiry be set up to look into vocational (corporatist) organization. De Valera agreed, but with reservations, because his ardor for vocationalism was dimmed by his adherence to the "right," so to speak, of Fianna Fail to govern Ireland. The report of the twenty-five-person Commission in 1943 offered both a comprehensive critique of the existing policymaking and bureaucratic system and an alternative based on elected vocational councils ascending in layers to a national council, which would recommend national policy to the Parliament. The structure envisioned substantial intervention in the society to carry out the corporatist ends of the report. De Valera essentially ignored the report; he clearly was not going to tamper with a Constitution that he had written and a government that was dominated by his party. The bureaucracy was held in contempt by the report, which would hardly make them an ally of substantial change in the state structures. Because the Commission reported during the war, and despite the Commission's asseverations that their report owed absolutely nothing to fascism, Joe Lee points out that "opportunist critics could impute guilt by semantic association."[57]

Corporatism returned to the language of political analysis after World War II when governments in Europe began to bring together the key sectors of society—government, labor, industry, and agriculture—to agree on the direction of national policy. The governments, attempting to rebuild, sought economic stability, taxes, and freedom from the labor unrest that produced social tensions. The industrial sector sought a stable and predictable economic environment in which they could grow and profit. Labour sought a living wage, job security, and social benefits such as health care and pensions, which would allow a decent life. The process and the "bargain" was identified by different names such as co-determination, social partnership, and neo-corporatism. The aggregate organizations, such as the Irish Farmers Association and the Irish Congress of Trade Unions (ICTU), not only represent their members as advocates to the government but bargain for them in a policymaking process. The resulting agreements are considered binding and are policed by the organizations. In Ireland the policy process, historically authoritarian and relatively closed, was centered in the Cabinet and the top level of the civil service, a pool consisting of no more than perhaps 600 people. This process was not wholly insensitive to organized interests, especially those of the Church, but could hardly be described as porous.

The goals of national development and the adoption of economic and social incentive planning meant bringing in the relevant interests to make them stakeholders in the outcomes and to draw upon their information and policy advice. Boards were set up (for example, the National Industrial Economic Council in 1963). The first, second, and third economic programs and their successors increasingly depended upon the cooperation of aggregate groups from education, agriculture, industry and labor, and the professional bodies. Ad hoc boards and commissions of these groups were created. *A National Partnership* in 1974 and *National Development 1977–1980* explicitly called for the agreements necessary to execute national goals from 1976 to the early 1980s. The Employer Labour Conference, consisting of employers, labor, and government representatives, negotiated wage agreements in the 1970s that were binding upon the companies, the workers, and the state.

Aggregate groups have been institutionally woven into the fabric of government. For example, ICTU representatives are on at least twenty-four bodies involved in public policy and representatives of the Federation of Irish Employers on forty-one. The National Economic and Social Council has almost taken on the role of a quasi-government. Political scientist Alan Ward notes that the Council in 1991 "not only agreed to a three year plan of pay increases and tax cuts, but to a comprehensive strategic program for the 1990s. The Program . . . dealt with . . . tax policies, social reform and welfare, health, education, housing, transport, construction, commercial state bodies, the environment, arts and culture, agriculture, forestry and other matters."[58]

Such extensive policy development and neo-corporatist policymaking outside of the Dail raises the question of the democratic deficit in Irish government. The transfer of policy responsibility out of the hands of parties and parliaments can lead to rule by technocrats not accountable to the public through an explicit democratic connection. A criticism often directed at Brussels bureaucrats of the European Union, the democratic deficit could apply to Ireland as well. Neo-corporatism coupled with a relatively authoritarian policy process, a small policy elite, a weak parliament, and sophisticated policy technocrats could produce a pallid form of democracy in Ireland. The voters are connected to government through parties sitting in a parliament. The policy process comes from a Cabinet, which sends ministers to bargain as equals with monopolistic aggregate groups to form binding agreements on a vast array of public matters. The public is "represented" in this arrangement, to be sure, but their linkage to public policy and the policy maker's accountability to the public could be increasingly evanescent.[59]

The Impact of Europe

Centralization and neo-corporatism are not the only features contributing to the democratic deficit in Irish government. Participation in the European Union, as political scientist Brigid Laffan points out, has created "a 'Europeanization' of government in the Republic."[60] Entry into the EU required a constitutional amendment in 1972, which accepted that EU law was part of the law of the Republic without the specific approval of the Dail. A further amendment was necessary in 1985. The Single European Act strengthened European Economic Community institutions and introduced qualified majorities in the Council of Ministers, thus eliminating the veto power of individual states. In 1992 the Maastricht Treaty, which brought security and foreign policy into the European Union treaties, also required a constitutional amendment.

The laws of the Community flow into the laws of the Republic through the instrumentality of the Irish bureaucracy. The EU has a great impact on the work of the ministers and the senior civil servants, especially in departments that have a close European interface, such as Agriculture, Foreign Affairs, Finance, and Industry and Commerce. These government figures are regularly in Brussels at meetings of the Commission of the European Union and the Council of Ministers. The Commission has twenty-three directorates, functionally divided and staffed by over 13,000 people. The laws that enter Irish law, so to speak, are passed by the European Commission in a process of consultation with the Council of Ministers and the European Parliament. The actual process in fact much more closely resembles the neo-corporatist policy process because the collection of large aggregated interest groups, the ministers of the member governments, and the bureaucrats of the EU interact in a series of policy circles. The process involves developing positions, bargaining, reshaping, and bargaining in an extended negotiation until the point of approval.

The directors of the European departments are at once policymakers, legislative negotiators, and policy implementers. Aggregations of interest organizations at the European level include the Committee of Professional Agricultural Organizations, the Union of Industries of the EC, the European Trade Union Confederation, and a host of sectoral organizations (banking, chemicals, textiles, etc.). Moving easily through the European bureaucracy, these groups work closely on policy with an eye to both their interests and the impact on the home country. The expansion of the EU from six states to twelve and then to fifteen has diluted the commonality of these interest groups, however, because they reflect the differences in levels of development of the new member states. The regulations then go out to the member states and are integrated into law and practice by the bureaucracy and courts of the member states. Presiding over the process is the European Council of the prime ministers of the member states, which meets three times a year and provides broad policy direction and approval. In addition, each member state must chair the EU for a period of six months. During that period each state wants the European agenda to be positive and to show accomplishments of worth, thus creating a constant diplomatic pressure to move on the European matters and generating obligations of reciprocity among the states.

Policies made in Brussels can have a far greater impact on areas such as agriculture than the policies made in Dublin, as is illustrated by pressure group activity. In the Irish case, as a small country the number of people who represent aggregated interests in Dublin and Brussels is small, as is the number of ministers and civil servants. Their connection with a small group of Brussels technocratic specialists in policy means that the state level neo-corporatist model is replicated in two ways in the European policy process. Overall EU policymaking is neo-corporatist; for the microcosm of Ireland-in-Europe the Irish circle of policymakers and shapers is small and close knit and need refer policy positions back no farther than their respective clienteles.

Members of the Dail are not focused on the European Union; despite their rhetorical nods, their view is distinctively constituency bound. The Dail does not deal with European matters. The rare exception, such as the debate on the place of Irish neutrality in a European security policy, proves the rule. The Irish focus on the economic dimensions of the EU, and Ireland's relative weakness made it possible for Ireland to be reasonably effective at getting the benefits of the Common Agricultural Policy and the Structural Funds (allocations for development in regions, training, and agriculture) in the early years of its membership. Since then Ireland has had to compete with poorer new members, such as Greece and Portugal (and later Poland and Hungary), for these funds and has been less effective in mobilizing to get them.[61]

The line between domestic law and European law is not clear, and the European law expands into domestic law to a greater and greater degree. The European Court is to resolve conflicts between domestic law and EU law; domestic courts can, and at the highest level must, refer cases to it. The effect is to have the European court deciding on breaches in domestic observance of EU regulations. Domestic law is declared void if it conflicts with EU obligations such as access to services in another member state, a situation that arose in relation to the abortion issue. The EU is restricted to those matters covered by its treaties, but that is a very wide area indeed. Agriculture, fishing, industry, trade, working conditions, monetary and tax policy, training, and environment are all covered, and the policy impact is significant. The powers of the state and the EU are not clearly defined because it is not a federal system in which the definition of the powers of each layer would be specified. The EU, especially since 1985, has been expanding horizontally with new members and vertically through the elimination of trade barriers, the adoption of common standards, and the move toward a single currency. Vertical integration involves a greater degree of policy direction from Brussels, with European law augmenting and supplanting Irish law. A British judge, not surprisingly lamenting this development, said it is "like an incoming tide. It flows into the estuaries and rivers. It cannot be held back."[62]

Irish Democracy

Questions about the foundation, character, and stability of Irish democracy are intriguing to scholars because Ireland at the time of the Anglo-Irish War was a relatively backward society and was essentially in a colonial situation (although formally integrated into the United Kingdom, and the Irish nationalist movement was badly split over the question of the degree of autonomy from their colonial master. A number of theories address the question of why democracy emerged and stabilized in Ireland while the cultural features of the Irish society at the time appeared to be similar to those of less-developed nations and presented a most inhospitable environment for democracy to flourish.

Political scientist David Schmitt and sociologist Jeffrey Prager point out that while Ireland did possess a modern urban elite, the society as a whole was marked by values antithetical to democracy. For these scholars a connection is required to resolve the incongruity between the traditional culture of Ireland and modern democracy. Schmitt sees Ireland at the time as a developing nation with a peasant culture, deference toward authority, and a strong religious presence that rejected the legal or rational basis for the authority of the state. For Schmitt the transition occurs with a fusion of the traditional and modern sources of authority in Cumann na nGaedheal in 1922–1923. By accepting the Anglo-Irish Treaty, writing a democratic constitution, and fighting a civil war against Sinn Fein, Cumann na nGaedheal became the bridge between traditional culture and modern democratic structures.[63] Prager depicts the Irish culture as divided deeply by two traditions: the Anglo-Irish-rationalist-individualist-Enlightenment tradition and the Gaelic-Catholic-organic-communal-Romantic tradition. Prager's view is that the tension between the Enlightenment and the Romantic traditions prevented the legitimization of the state that was formed in 1922 because the Gaelic Romantic dimension was not validated.[64] The bridge for Prager is the five-year period when Fianna Fail entered the Dail in 1927 and took power in 1932.

Cumann na nGaedheal built democratic structures and Fianna Fail reconciled those modern structures with the traditional cultural values.[65] In this view, the resulting democracy displays the traditional culture in, for example, the clientelist brokerage role of the TD, the inclusion of censorship and Church doctrine in the state's laws, and the authoritarian style of governing. The modern Enlightenment dimensions are exemplified in the constitutional tradition, the guarantees of civil rights and liberties, and the professional bureaucracy.

Political scientist Tom Garvin also identifies the division in the nationalist tradition, focusing on the anti-Treaty moralistic and elitist dimension of the republican movement, which he sees as contemptuous of democracy and possessing a certitude of a right to rule. The pragmatic tradition of the pro-Treaty nationalists was committed to building a civic culture and a democratic order. For Garvin the political culture was still essentially traditional; the triumph of democratic government in Ireland was a function of the virtually heroic actions of the Cumann na nGaedheal leadership after 1922.[66]

Political scientist Bill Kissane takes issue with Schmitt and Prager (and by implication Garvin) and argues that they make several questionable assumptions. The first is that Irish society was substantially pre-modern, the second is that the pre-modern society does not support modern democracy, and the third is that Irish democracy succeeded because it adapted itself to the pre-modern society, so that to some extent Irish democracy is an anomaly. Kissane overstates his position when he summarizes the other authors' arguments thus: "The Irish state remained democratic, not because it imposed its rules on Irish society but because it compromised them. So rather than saying the outcome was undemocratic, they say it was amazing."[67] Kissane argues that Irish democracy is not so amazing when a series of changes that occurred in the nineteenth century is taken into account. The rise of democracy is associated with the rise in the pluralization of power in Ireland, although it would not appear so at first glance.

The Crown had implemented certain policies in Ireland that were creating autonomous centers of power, which facilitated democracy. The power of the landed aristocracy in Ireland, so dominant in the eighteenth century, was diminished in the nineteenth after the Act of Union through the dissolution of the gentry's militias, the tax policies adopted during the Famine, the extension of Catholic rights, the extension of the franchise and secret ballot, and the dis-establishment of the Anglican Church. At the same time the peasant and tenant farmer class was being transformed into small property owners through the 1885 Purchase of Land Act and the 1903 Land Act. A radical peasantry angry over rents in 1870 had turned into a class of conservative family farmers by 1890. Three percent of the farms were owner occupied in 1870, 64 percent in 1916, and 97 percent in 1929.

Adding to the argument that Ireland was not so backward are scholars such as Basil Chubb and Brian Farrell, who point out that Irish democracy advanced by the absorption of the ideas of British democracy. Ireland had been a part of the United Kingdom since 1800 and had developed mass parties and a stable bureaucracy.[68]

The rise of the mass movement under O'Connell became a foundation for the parties that emerged at the end of the century. The Irish Parliamentary Party was operating in a democratic environment, mobilizing, recruiting, campaigning, and participating in Parliament in London. Despite repression from London, splits over Parnell, and competition from undemocratic secret organizations, the Irish Parliamentary Party was a significant mobilizer of the Catholic middle class and an instrument of the democratic process. The bureaucracy had been developed by the British, was autonomous from the nationalist movement, and, while not understating the chaotic situation in 1922, was a stabilizing element in that it was meritocratic and "neutral."

The Catholic Church was increasingly autonomous, creating its own education system and shaping public opinion, and although it accepted union with Britain at the institutional level it was associated with Irish nationalism at the functional level. The press was free and there was a free market economy. The conditions that foster democracy and stabilize it thus were present in Ireland. Ireland had developed institutions without a backward peasantry or a dominant landlord class, as well as family farms and autonomous institutions of church, press, and political parties.[69] The institutions of society were in effect modern and even somewhat pluralistic even though the values were traditional and organic. Kissane argues that Prager and Schmitt overstate the traditional values while not recognizing the level of development of a civil society that supported democracy. Kissane is applying the ideas developed by Robert Putnam et al. in *Making Democracy Work: Civic Traditions in Modern Italy.*[70] Putnam argues that the emergence of stable democracy is based on the presence of what he calls the civic community, or civil society, and not just the character of the government and its relationship to the market. The horizontal organizations in society that bind people together and provide a sphere of un-coerced public discussion and debate, such as those enumerated by Kissane above, shape a political culture. A political culture that has traditions of "social capital" or strong bonds between people concerning trust, cooperation, equality, and community is often more important for the foundation and development of democracy than the vertical links between citizen and government. Thus the long-term social capital or civil society built in Ireland since O'Connell contributed to the establishment and stability of democracy even in the face of the split in Sinn Fein over the Anglo-Irish Treaty.

Irish democracy is not an anomaly but rather is congruent with the mass and elite culture and society of Ireland. The Treaty and the Civil War contributed to the initial instability of Irish democracy, but as Kissane argues: "The significance of the Civil War may well have been to provide a salutary warning to both sides, that the unity and legitimacy of the new state was more important than anything else."[71] The two sides in the Civil War shared common values about the establishment of democracy and the political agenda of the state, which of course were masked by the bitterness of that conflict.[72] The division threatened democracy to the extent that Sinn Fein rejected the will of the party and the public and Cumann na nGaedheal adopted draconian security measures, but the convergence on the legitimacy of the state came with the 1937 Constitution, which for Kissane "signifies the end of civil war politics."

The Irish form of democracy blended together Catholicism, constitutionalism, authoritarianism, neo-corporatism, and Europeanization in the environment of a traditional culture with a developed civil society undergoing a process of transformation. The parties and pressure groups that emerged in the Free State and Republic were the vehicles of political competition over public policy in the new state.

Notes

1. Chubb, *Government and Politics of Ireland*, pp. 1–23.
2. Richard B. Finnegan, "The Blueshirts of Ireland in the 1930s: Fascism Inverted," *Eire-Ireland* 24, no. 2 (Summer 1989), p. 80.
3. Brugha lasted until de Valera escaped from prison and was elected president in April 1919. The split over the Anglo-Irish Treaty caused de Valera to resign and Arthur Griffith was elected president in January 1922.
4. Tom Garvin, *The Evolution of Irish Nationalist Politics* (New York: Holmes & Meier, 1981), pp. 127–129.
5. Because the 1920 Act was still the governing law in Northern Ireland, the separate Northern Parliament had authority over the six counties of Ulster; the British Crown also ruled over the north because it was part of the United Kingdom. Thus Ireland as a whole on January 14, 1922, had five governments.
6. Collins was late for the transfer of power at Dublin Castle; purportedly this led to the following exchange between him and Lord FitzAlan. FitzAlan said to Collins, "You are seven minutes late," and Collins replied, "We have been waiting 700 years . . . you can have the seven minutes." Coogan, *The Man Who Made Ireland*, p. 310. Even if Collins did not say it, the story is too good not to repeat.
7. De Valera was always more moderate than his own rhetoric, as shown in the election pact of 1922, which called for the pro- and anti-Treaty Sinn Fein members to be on the ballot together. His ideas about "external association" and his willingness to take an oath to an Irish constitution that included a place for the Crown in Dominion matters is also evidence of his willingness to compromise. In fact, historian Roy Foster argues that Collins and de Valera would have been more appropriate in each other's role. Collins was the uncompromising hardline soldier and de Valera the politician and diplomat. Events thrust Collins into the roles of diplomat on the Anglo-Irish Treaty, political leader of the provisional government, and soldier supporting the IRA; then he was thrust into civil war with his compatriots. De Valera ended up being elected president and chief executive of the "Irish Republic" by a rump Dail convened by the IRA in October 1922 and then leading them, sort of, into civil war. Personalities and personal loyalties played as much a part in people's stands on the Anglo-Irish Treaty as political positions, to the detriment of Irish interests overall. R. F. Foster, *Modern Ireland, 1600–1972* (Hammondsworth: Penguin, 1988), p. 509.
8. In 1936 the Dail passed the Constitution (Amendment Number 27) Act, which abolished all reference to the king and governor general from the 1922 Constitution, effectively abolishing the office of governor general.

9. Alan Ward, *The Irish Constitutional Tradition* (Washington, D.C.: Catholic University Press, 1994), p. 181. This section of this chapter owes a great deal to Ward's excellent analysis of responsible government in modern Ireland.

10. Ibid., pp. 187–188.

11. Ibid., p. 225.

12. He stated in the Dail that, "If the Northern problem were not there . . . in all probability there would be a flat downright declaration of a republic in this Constitution." Quoted in Chubb, *Government and Politics of Ireland*, p. 43.

13. Lee, *Ireland 1912–1985*, p. 203.

14. Roger Hull, *The Irish Triangle* (Princeton: Princeton University Press, 1975), pp. 91–121, provides a close examination of legal evolution of the law determining sovereignty over Ulster.

15. J. J. McElliot, secretary of the Department of Finance, objected to these provisions when the Constitution was being drafted in 1936. Keogh, *Twentieth Century Ireland*, p. 98. A Commission on the Constitution reporting in 1967 called for elimination of these articles. Liberals have been claiming for years that any similar claim by another country would be seen as provocative and illegitimate (for example, a constitutional claim by the United States on sections of Canada on the basis that their territories were joined in the eighteenth century).

16. Basil Chubb, ed., *A Source Book of Irish Government* (Dublin: Institute of Public Administration, 1964), p. 20.

17. Whyte, *Church and State*, p. 48; and Lee, *Ireland 1912–1985*, p. 205.

18. Government of Ireland, *Report of the Constitutional Review Group* (Dublin: Stationery Office, 1996), p. 4.

19. Adapted from the complete provision quoted in Keogh, *Twentieth Century Ireland*, pp. 98–99.

20. The Anglo-Irish Treaty states that the Irish government shall "make no law so as to either directly or indirectly endow any religion." Endow may not have been the formal status, but it came as close to endow as it could get.

21. Chubb, *Source Book of Irish Government*, p. 58.

22. Chubb, *Government and Politics of Ireland*, p. 47.

23. Ibid., p. 48.

24. Reacting to the vigorous spread of liberalism in the nineteenth century and the spread of socialist ideas in the twentieth, the Church was drawn to the ideology of corporatism, which seemed to be a way to avoid what was perceived as the excessive individualism of liberalism and markets driven by the unrestrained greed of capitalism and also the idea of class conflict, revolution, and collectivization advanced by socialism. Corporatism was based on the idea of vertical sectors of society, or vocational groups, representing people; corporatist boards would decide common goals and the social good would ameliorate the excesses of liberalism and socialism. Versions of these ideas were discussed in the 1920s and 1930s and were connected to the rising fascist movements in Europe. However, the association of corporatism with fascism, fascism with Germany, and Germany with aggression, war crimes, and genocide took the luster off this political doctrine.

25. Chubb, *Source Book of Irish Government*, pp. 199–200.

26. Lee, *Ireland 1912–1985*, p. 272.

27. Keogh, *Twentieth Century Ireland*, p. 103.

28. The Earl of Longford, Thomas P. O'Neill, *Eamonn de Valera* (London: Arrow Books, 1974), p. 296.

29. *Report of the Constitutional Review Group*, p. 15.

30. Chubb, *Source Book of Irish Government*, pp. 55–56.

31. Chubb, *Government and Politics of Ireland*, p. 49.

32. *Report of the Constitutional Review Group*, p. 259.

33. Richard Sinnott, *Irish Voters Decide* (Manchester: University of Manchester Press, 1995), p. 220.

34. Ward, *Irish Constitutional Tradition*, p. 320.

35. Taoiseach literally means "chieftain or captain"; Priomh Aire literally means "high nobleman," but denotes prime minister.

36. Brian Farrell, *Chairman or Chief: The Role of the Taoiseach in Irish Government* (Dublin: Gill & Macmillan, 1971).

37. Ward, *Irish Constitutional Tradition*, p. 275. Ward also points out that the ministerial responsibility for the departments of government, responsibility to the Dail, and the legal status of the minister as an entity, "corporation sole," which embodies the legal existence of the department in the minister, contribute to the separation.

38. This judgment involved the Beef Tribunal, set up to investigate alleged abuses by a large beef exporting concern (discussed in Chapter 8). Ministers were alleged to have known about the abuses and campaign contributions were alleged to be involved. See below.

39. Chubb identified the centrality of this task for the TD in 1963 and he does not see it as any different in the 1990s. B. Chubb, "Going About Persecuting Civil Servants: The Role of the Irish Parliamentary Representative," *Political Studies* 11, no. 3 (1963), pp. 272–286; and Chubb, *Government and Politics of Ireland*, pp. 292–293.

40. Farrell, *Chairman or Chief*, p. 85.

41. Chubb, *Government and Politics of Ireland*, p. 292; and Keating, quoted in Ward, *Irish Constitutional Tradition*, p. 280.

42. If the TD is the son or nephew of a man who served in the rebellion in the years 1916 to 1921, this would increase his chances of being elected or re-elected. A final patina adding luster to the candidate would be to have achieved some reputation in sport. A few prime ministers serve as instructive examples of these attributes: Garret FitzGerald, prime minister in 1981, is the son of Desmond FitzGerald, minister for Foreign Affairs under the 1922 to 1932 Cosgrave government; Charles Haughey is the son of a prominent IRA man and son-in-law of Sean Lemass, prime minister from 1959 to 1965. Haughey's predecessor, Jack Lynch, was an All-Ireland hurling star from Cork, and Lynch's predecessor, Liam Cosgrave, is the son of William Cosgrave, who headed the Free State government from 1922 to 1932. This pattern repeats itself, although direct connection to 1916 obviously will diminish over time.

43. Chubb, *Government and Politics of Ireland*, p. 208.

44. Ibid., p. 284.

45. The Council of State consists of the Taoiseach, the Tainaiste, the chief justice, the president of the High Court, the chairs of the Dail and the Seanad, any past prime ministers and chief justices, and seven members appointed by the president. The Council was created to "aid and counsel" the president and is thus convened by the president when needed.

46. Liam Cosgrave brought a bill on contraception to the floor of the Dail while he was prime minister and then voted against it. While it was considered a free vote, Cosgrave did not let his party know he was going to oppose it. Such mismanagement of the legislative process may reflect why Cosgrave mishandled the O'Dalaigh situation so thoroughly. Ward, *Irish Constitutional Tradition*, pp. 289–290.

47. Quoted in ibid., p. 292.

48. Quoted in Chubb, *Government and Politics of Ireland*, p. 249.

49. Ward, *Irish Constitutional Tradition*, p. 300; Chubb, *Government and Politics of Ireland*, pp. 324–325.

50. Ministers can appoint the boards, approve capital expenditure in line with government policy, intervene in the activities of the body, and request information and reports as needed.

51. For an overheated exposition of this thesis, see F. Hermens, "The Dynamics of Proportional Representation," in *Comparative Politics: A Reader*, ed. H. Eckstein and D. Apter (New York: Free Press, 1963), pp. 254–280.

52. B. Chubb, "The Electoral System," in *Ireland at the Polls: 1977*, ed. H. Penniman (Washington, D.C.: American Enterprise Institute, 1978), p. 27.

53. G. Satori, in "European Political Parties: The Case of Polarized Pluralism," in *Political Parties and Political Development*, ed. J. LaPalombara and M. Weiner (Princeton: Princeton University Press, 1966), argues that PR does not fragment an already institutionalized party system. However, the Irish party system was in formation from 1918 to 1932 and it has a PR system.

54. Lee, *Ireland 1912–1985*, p. 271.

55. Manning, *Blueshirts*, p. 227.

56. *Irish Times*, 8 August 1933, p. 10.

57. Lee, *Ireland 1912–1985*, p. 275.

58. Ward, *Irish Constitutional Tradition*, p. 302.

59. Dermot McCann, in "Business Power and Collective Action: The State and the Confederation of Irish Industry 1970–1990," *Irish Political Studies* 8 (1993), pp. 37–53, argues that state intervention in the economy prompted the creation of business trade associations that acted in close concert with government but not following a neo-corporatist model. Stressing the divisions between business sectors as weakening their common voice, McCann nevertheless notes that the enhancement of structural power (that is, market presence, growth, profits) may be best achieved by "collective, organized power," that is, aggregate pressure group associations. This may still be pressure group activity and not policy participation, but it is a pretty fine distinction.

60. Brigid Laffan, "Managing Europe," in *Political Issue in Ireland Today*, ed. Neil Collins (Manchester: Manchester University Press, 1994), p. 53.

61. Brigid Laffan, "'While You Are Over There in Brussels, Get Us a Grant': The Management of the Structural Funds in Ireland," *Irish Political Studies* 4 (1989), pp. 43–57.

62. Lord Justice Denning, quoted in Chubb, *Government and Politics of Ireland*, p. 51.

63. David Schmitt, *The Irony of Irish Democracy* (London: Lexington Books, 1973).

64. Jeffrey Prager, *Building Democracy in Ireland* (Cambridge: Cambridge University Press, 1986). This summary, of course, does not do justice to Prager's and Schmitt's complete argument; Prager makes a distinction, for example, within each tradition between

values and norms, identifying four distinct positions on the structure of the state and the nature of the community (pp. 38–52).

65. Ibid., pp. 185–214.

66. Tom Garvin, *1922: The Birth of Irish Democracy* (Dublin: Gill & Macmillan, 1996).

67. B. Kissane, "The Not So Amazing Case of Irish Democracy," *Irish Political Studies* 10 (1995), p. 52.

68. Ibid., pp. 44–48. This section draws from Kissane's analysis.

69. Ibid., pp. 61–64.

70. Robert Putnam, Robert Leonardi, and R. Y. Nanetti, *Making Democracy Work: Civic Traditions in Modern Italy* (Princeton: Princeton University Press, 1993).

71. Kissane, "Irish Democracy," p. 65.

72. With respect to rejecting the illegitimate activity of both the Blueshirts and the IRA in the 1930s and the agenda of Church-state relations, among other things, the common elements between Fianna Fail and Fine Gael are clear.

8

THE CHOSEN FEW: PARTIES, PRESSURE GROUPS, AND POLICY

The Irish Voter

The typical voter in Ireland in 1922 was an older, rural male engaged in agriculture, with a first-level education, who was concerned with the national question. By the 1980s the picture could not have been more different. The demographic revolution that took place in Ireland caused a shift from old to young and rural to urban, increased education levels, and shifted occupations from the farm to industry and services. Emigration had a great impact on the rural west of Ireland and also prompted an inner migration from the countryside to the cities. In 1922 two-thirds of the Irish lived in rural areas (and the definition of living in a town or city was very generous); by 1990 that number had dropped to 44 percent. The most dramatic example of this change was Dublin, which contained 17 percent of the population in 1926 but over 30 percent in 1990. The decline in the agricultural population was of course accompanied by a decline in agricultural employment. Fifty-two percent of the working population were employed in agriculture in 1926; by 1995 only 11 percent were. The move to cities meant employment shifts to industry—which increased from 13 percent in 1926 to 28 percent in 1995—and services, which went from 35 percent in 1926 to 61 percent in 1995.

The class structure of Ireland changed in the period from 1961 to 1981; an upper middle professional class, a lower middle class, and a skilled working class emerged at the expense of the agricultural sector.[1] As the upper and middle classes grew they pushed urban growth into a new phenomenon, the suburb. The demographic shift resulted in a drop in the average age of the population of the Republic: in 1981, 48 percent were under age twenty-five and in 1991, 44 percent still were. Not only was Ireland younger, but after the 1972 referendum the voting age was reduced to eighteen. The revolution in education prompted by the 1965 *Investment in Education* began to show its effects: more young people in school longer, more leaving certificates, more young people in third-level education acquiring the skills to work in the new economy Ireland was creating. The typical voter in 1998 was young; well educated; urban or suburban; female as likely as male; in a service occupation, and concerned about employment, emigration, and home ownership.

All Irish voters have been influenced by the society's economic and social transformation. The economic changes, urbanization, and a young electorate brought a different agenda of issues into the political mix. The younger voters are not particularly radical—they have supported the major parties since the 1960s—but they have sought a different legislative response in the realm of social and economic issues. From 1969 to 1992, when voters were asked to rank the most important issues in those nine elections, unemployment ranked first five times and second twice. Inflation ranked first three times and second twice. Other high-ranking concerns were education and welfare (1969), health (1989), and taxes (1987, 1989, 1992). Northern Ireland as an issue ranked less than "other" and "don't know" in all the years but 1973.[2] In 1981, when the hunger strikes carried out by IRA prisoners in the "H" block of the Maze prison had supercharged political attitudes about Northern Ireland, surveys indicated that the electorate in the Republic was still primarily concerned with economic issues.

Despite the persistence of partition and the constant violence and agitation in Northern Ireland, the Irish voters have consistently judged their governments by their economic promise and their economic performance. The referendum on the Good Friday Peace Agreement for Northern Ireland in 1998 drew a turnout of only 57 percent in the Republic, even though it involved changing the Constitution and approving a landmark step for peace in Ireland. The changes in Ireland, government expansion into development, welfare, environment, economic growth and retrenchment, emigration, and engagement with Europe produced a new agenda of issues for the new electorate. How did the parties change in light of the changes in the voters and their agenda?

Political Parties

The two major political parties in Ireland have their roots in the nationalist movement Sinn Fein; the third, Labour, arose independently of the nationalist movement. The critical factor for the formation of a party system is the mass mobilization of the electorate and the cleavages that separate them at the time. For Ireland that event was the 1918 election, when the electorate expanded by two-thirds. Intense political conflict prior to the election and during the following fifteen years defined the agenda and concentrated the political loyalties of the Irish public.

Sinn Fein

Holding the Labour Party aside for the moment, Sinn Fein is the mother of all major parties. Founded in 1905, Sinn Fein was at that time another of the many nationalist organizations in Ireland and did not have any special place on the political landscape. The 1916 Rising, carried out by the Irish Republican Brotherhood and Connolly's Citizen Army, was attributed to Sinn Fein, and the nationalist leaders were quick to re-create the organization as a nationalist umbrella under which they could consolidate the movement. Three events determined both support for Sinn Fein and its strategy. The execution of the leaders of the 1916 Rising triggered a backlash of public opinion in support of the rebels, which crystallized around Sinn Fein. The by-election of Count Plunkett on an explicit Sinn Fein platform and his refusal to take his seat provided Sinn Fein with a strategy. The imposition of conscription on Ireland (although never implemented) in World War I also added to the anti-British and pro-Sinn Fein sentiment. In the election of December 1918 Sinn Fein swept away the Irish Parliamentary Party, winning 73 out of 105 seats in Ireland and 70 of the 75 seats in the twenty-six county territory that would ultimately become the Free State.[3]

The consequences were momentous. First was the removal of a class-based labor/capital split in Irish party loyalties. The Labour Party was persuaded to not contest the 1918 election to ensure a uniform vote on the national question. Further, the Irish were mobilized around a single national movement on the issue of independence. Sinn Fein had not masked its militant positions and intentions in the election, and the Irish people had chosen to oppose Britain. Their rejection of a more conciliatory position could not be more clear. The success of the Anglo-Irish War was overshadowed by the debate over the Anglo-Irish Treaty, which split the nationalist movement although not yet into distinct parties. The 1922 electoral pact of Collins and de Valera was an attempt to keep Sinn Fein together until a solution to the impasse could be reached, but it failed. The 1922 election is difficult to interpret, but it was both a test of public support for the Anglo-Irish Treaty and the event that created the opposing party organizations. De Valera's Sinn Fein received 21.3 percent of the vote, while Collins's Sinn Fein received 38.5 percent. An additional 39.7 percent of the votes were cast for other pro-Treaty parties; the total in favor of the Anglo-Irish Treaty was 78.2 percent. The conflict then shifted from ballots to bombs as the Civil War began.

Sinn Fein was essentially in abeyance while the anti-Treaty IRA fought the provisional and then the Free State government. After losing the Civil War, de Valera's strategy was to contest the 1923 election, abstaining from recognizing the legitimacy of the Free State and offering to set up an alternative government that would draw the support of the Irish people. The result was both a victory and a defeat. The victory was that a party that had just lost a civil war against a government that had popular support managed to gain 27 percent of the vote for an abstentionist position. The defeat was that it was well short of the support needed to overthrow the Anglo-Irish Treaty. The vote given to the pro-Treaty Sinn Fein party, now called Cumann na nGaedheal, and to the other parties elected to the Dail came in at 73 percent. The fortunes of Sinn Fein did not improve: It lost seven of nine seats in the 1925 by-elections and de Valera began to see the political wilderness he inhabited. Remaining in the shadows of government prevented Sinn Fein from exercising any power other than condemnation. The party's efforts to set up parallel governmental institutions failed. As the funds and organization of Sinn Fein began to deteriorate, de Valera attempted to get Sinn Fein to accept seats in the Free State Dail, based on the condition that the oath of allegiance to the Crown would be abolished. The party split on this issue and rejected de Valera's idea. In May 1926 he founded Fianna Fail and took most of Sinn Fein with him to the new party.

Sinn Fein was now a wisp of the former nationalist movement. In the 1927 election Sinn Fein received 3.6 percent of the vote and five seats. Thereafter Sinn Fein drifted into the political margins of Irish politics, along with the anti-Treaty IRA, until the 1960s.[4] Sinn Fein was re-energized by the rebuilt Provisional IRA in the new troubles of Ulster. Sinn Fein served as the political front for the provisional IRA after 1970 but did not contest elections in Northern Ireland or the Republic. When an election strategy was implemented in 1981 Sinn Fein managed to get less than 2 percent of the votes in the Republic. However, the Party has had an important impact in the 1980s and 1990s in the north.

Fianna Fail

Abstention turned out to be a trap for Fianna Fail because to abandon this principal would be transparently hypocritical, while to adhere to it was to be excluded from the exercise of power. While de Valera danced around this question, the solution was provided by the Cumann na nGaedheal government of William T. Cosgrave. After the assassination of Minister of Justice Kevin O'Higgins, the government passed a law requiring a promise at the time of nomination that a candidate would take his or her seat and thus also take the oath to the Crown. In the election of 1927 Fianna Fail won forty-four seats and, more important, took them. Cumann na nGaedheal dropped from sixty-three seats to forty-seven, prompting Cosgrave to call another election in 1927, which Cumann Na nGaedheal won with sixty-two seats; but Fianna Fail also consolidated its position, gaining fifty-seven seats. Fianna Fail founded a newspaper, *The Irish Press*, in 1931 and consistently developed its organization at the grassroots level.

The combination of Fianna Fail's growing strength and the conservative, almost inert, policies of the Cosgrave government brought Fianna Fail into power in the election of 1932. The election was significant for a number of events, not the least of which was the transfer of power by Cumann na nGaedheal to a party with which they had fought a bitter civil war only nine years earlier. That transfer was not without tension; Sean Lemass of Fianna Fail referred to his party as "slightly constitutional," while Cosgrave's government was focused on law and order. The electorate was also choosing a particular vision of Catholic Gaelic nationalism as embodied in de Valera's Fianna Fail. In addition, the legitimization of Fianna Fail's rule validated the mobilization of the public around the partisan polarities of Cumann na nGaedheal and Fianna Fail and thus set the foundation for the party system. De Valera called a snap election in 1933 that pushed his total seats to seventy-seven. The Fianna Fail party was to rule without interruption from 1932 to 1948. During this period the policies of de Valera about the old and new constitutions, protectionism, the economic war, and neutrality fixed Fianna Fail as the dominant party in Irish politics (although the ineptness of its opponents was no small factor in the party's success).

After World War II Fianna Fail began to exhibit signs of old age and an absence of initiative on the problems facing Ireland. Even though challenged by a weak opposition, Fianna Fail was still excluded from power by a five-party coalition from 1948 to 1951, from which it learned little, doing nothing more than waiting for a return to power, which the party saw as its birthright. Defeated again in 1954 to 1957, the party appeared to be insensitive to economic inertia and hints of corruption. The policies of both the coalitions and Fianna Fail appeared either unwilling or unable to address the economic decay of Ireland. In 1957 de Valera formed his last government, the eighth in twenty-five years, only to resign two years later to become president and turn over leadership to Sean Lemass.

Lemass is among the most important of Ireland's leaders after 1922. Four changes occurred under Lemass that determined the direction of modern Ireland. First was the acceptance and management of the role of the state in generating economic growth, thereby jettisoning the protectionist, pastoral paradise of Fianna Fail ideology and recognizing that the survival of Ireland depended on economic growth. Second was the emphasis on entry into Europe as essential to the future of Ireland. Third was Lemass's meeting with Terence O'Neill, the prime minister of Northern Ireland, and his acceptance of a new approach to the north. The fourth change was Lemass's receptivity to the younger members of Fianna Fail who had emerged after the war.[5]

The party in fact experienced a form of intergenerational conflict in the 1950s as de Valera held leadership in the hands of the aging chieftains of the revolution. Lemass had reorganized the party from 1954 to 1957 and opened positions for such men as Charles Haughey and Dr. Patrick J. Hillary. When Lemass resigned from leadership in 1966, he provoked a battle within Fianna Fail among those leaders who had emerged in the prior decade. Charles Haughey, a representative of the "new" entrepreneurial leaders; George Colley, a traditionalist; Neil Blaney, a republican; and Jack Lynch all sought the leadership. Each candidate, except

Lynch, was unacceptable to some segment of the Fianna Fail TDs, and Lynch emerged as the new leader of Fianna Fail, defeating Colley after the withdrawal of Blaney and Haughey. Lynch led the party in a low-key manner but nevertheless was caught up in the impact of the violence in Northern Ireland.

Lynch responded to the crisis with a powerful declaration on August 13, 1969, and appointed Minister of Finance Charles Haughey to head a committee designed to revamp the Irish Army, administer relief funds, and monitor events in Ulster. This committee set up accounts to disburse money, the manner and amount to be determined by the minister of Finance, to provide aid for the victims of the violence. The leadership of Fianna Fail was later shattered when Cabinet members were arrested and tried on charges of arms smuggling to the north. Fianna Fail at this point went through a crisis that would have caused most governments to fall.

Prime Minister Lynch maintained that he was unaware that members of his Cabinet were engaged in the illegal importation of arms (although he supposedly had been informed in 1969). Called upon to respond to allegations of such misdeeds by the opposition leader, Liam Cosgrave, Lynch responded forcefully, requesting the resignation of his minister of Justice for not informing him of the events. Charles Haughey and Neil Blaney, minister of Agriculture, were suddenly dismissed from the Cabinet in April 1970 and Kevin Boland, minister of Local Government, resigned in sympathy. Blaney and Haughey were arrested and tried for conspiracy in August 1970. The case against Blaney was dismissed. In a sensational trial in which Cabinet members told completely contradictory stories and witnesses implicated Haughey, he was found not guilty.

The episode is a morass of conflicting testimony and evidence. A clear portrait of the events is still hard to compose, but evidence supports the fact that he knew what was going on and was involved.[6] Boland resigned not only as a minister of the government but also from the Fianna Fail party in 1970. Blaney was expelled from Fianna Fail in 1971. The crisis highlighted two concurrent developments in Fianna Fail: the question of the commitment to the republican nationalist ideology upon which the party was built and the factionalism within the party among different groups with different leaders. Before the arms crisis Blaney and Boland had been most vociferous in their criticism of the leadership of Lynch on the Northern question. Blaney issued calls that the use of force against the north not be ruled out and hinted that he would accept the leadership of the party. Lynch represented the pragmatic Fianna Fail. He acknowledged the heritage of the party but also recognized the limitations on his choices: "The plain truth—the naked reality—is that we do not possess the capacity to impose a solution by force." He also knew the consequences of simplistic republicanism: "Do we want to adopt the role of an occupying conqueror over the one million or so Six-County citizens?"[7] Lynch's policy, although distasteful to hardline republicans, won the day and Fianna Fail thereafter dealt with the north within the framework of peaceful negotiation even when Haughey changed the party's position upon his accession to power.

After his trial Haughey, also seeking to lead Fianna Fail, called for Lynch to step down and be replaced by, of course, him. Lynch, however, pressed the party with a demand for a vote of confidence, which he won by seventy to three, and also a vote of confidence in the Dail in November, which his government won by seventy-four to sixty-seven. Voting with Lynch, Haughey was, as historian Joe Lee put it, "swallowing short term defeat to secure the basis for long term victory, convinced that outside the party there was no redemption."[8] Haughey returned to the back benches to begin the slow climb back to leadership.

In the election of 1973 Fianna Fail went into opposition. The results of the election revealed not a loss of electoral support—the election was quite close—but rather the threat of a well-organized opposition, something Fianna Fail had rarely faced. Lynch set out to revitalize the party, adopting a professional approach to organization, recruiting young people, and improving relationships with the press.[9] The first major effort at public relations professionalization occurred in preparation for the 1977 election. Lynch appointed a full-time press and information officer to achieve a more sophisticated use of the media. Other methods were drawn from U.S. election techniques. Fianna Fail had commissioned polls of the electorate prior to the election to assess the support for the national coalition and the issues most salient to the voters. Following the direction of the polls and subsequent market research, the campaign identified those issues and areas of support that could be turned to the party's favor.

Notable was the effort not only to create a comprehensive program different from that of the coalition government but also to target certain programs to segments of the electorate. The party offered a forty-seven page manifesto to the voters that had been crafted to appeal to every sector.[10] Fianna Fail used three different advertising agencies. The principal firm promoted the general program while the other two directed specific appeals at women and young people. As the campaign proceeded Fianna Fail's campaign committee adjusted its advertising to include segments of the electorate not included at the outset. Adding to this strategy were slick jingles, buttons, hats, Lynch's face on T-shirts, and a presidential-style election tour by Lynch. Although polling had shown a diminution of support for the coalition government since 1976, Fine Gael leaders had dismissed the evidence, while Fianna Fail capitalized on it. Organizationally Fianna Fail had geared up as early as a year and a half before the election. Senior party members had formed a campaign committee and the party had chosen a new general secretary. Program development drew upon the younger members of the party. By the time the election was called Fianna Fail had selected its candidates, identified critical constituencies, and unleashed a slick advertising campaign

The sweeping victory of Fianna Fail in 1977 brought about another change in leadership because Lynch, who had been on top since 1966, began to be seen as unable to handle the intractable problems of Northern Ireland and economic growth. In 1979 he stepped down under the pressure of a "backbench" revolt within the party, and Charles Haughey was chosen to head Fianna Fail. Haughey had patiently bided his time after the arms trial until he was brought back to the Fianna Fail inner circle in 1975 as minister for Health. He then won the party's leadership position after a bitter intraparty fight that left his opponents less than completely loyal to him. Haughey's position on the north, his wealth, and his baronial style were divisive factors.

In a period of governmental instability from 1979 to 1982 there were three elections. Haughey was Taoiseach from 1979 to 1981 and then again in 1982 for only seven months. The government's instability was mirrored by instability within Fianna Fail: Three challenges to Haughey's leadership occurred during 1982 and 1983. In February 1982 Desmond O'Malley challenged Haughey, but the party leaders rallied to his support and O'Malley withdrew. In March of that year Haughey put together a minority government by purchasing the vote of Tony Gregory, an inner-city independent TD, in the form of largesse to his district, only to have the government founder on a poor budget and embarrassing actions by members of Haughey's Cabinet. A murderer was arrested in the home of the attorney general, the Taoiseach's ability to listen in on phone calls in Leinster House was revealed, and the minister for Justice was found to have authorized phone taps on prominent journalists (resulting in a High Court judgment in 1987 against the government for illegal actions and compensation for the journalists). In October 1982 another challenge to Haughey occurred; he beat that back, but he lost the general election in December 1982.[11] Corruption charges based on Haughey's knowledge of the phone taps and ineffective leadership brought the party to challenge Haughey's leadership a third time in February 1983, but he again survived on a vote of forty to thirty-three.

Haughey took power once again in 1987 with a solid majority and undertook the decreases in government spending and borrowing that no government since the 1970s had had the stomach to confront. To his credit Haughey was willing to face the inevitable public dissatisfaction. In the next election in 1989 Fianna Fail had no clear majority. Haughey chose to break a Fianna Fail tradition by forming a coalition government, a most unpopular move. The party regulars saw the ruling tradition of Fianna Fail being threatened. They believed that if they adhered to a policy of no coalition the opposition either had to form a government or submit to a Fianna Fail minority government because Fianna Fail had more seats than any other party. On the other hand, the two-and-one-half-party system was changing to a multiparty system, and gaining power increasingly meant accepting coalition government. The bone that stuck in the party's throat was that the 1989 coalition partner was the Progressive Democrats. Founded by Desmond O'Malley in 1985, this group was a breakaway from Fianna Fail, and Fianna Fail leaders were not ready to govern in partnership with them. Added to this was the personal animosity between Haughey and O'Malley. Mutual loathing is an understatement of their relationship.

The creation of the coalition allowed the survival of the Haughey government, but by negotiating the agreement alone and then announcing it to his leadership

team Haughey created the very angry opposition within his party that would ultimately oust him. His government lasted until 1992 when, in February, under further clouds of scandal, Haughey was replaced by Albert Reynolds as Taoiseach.
Journalist Bruce Arnold (whose phone was tapped) noted of Haughey's extended
departure: "He had overstayed and worn out all welcome and support."[12]

The coalition with O'Malley of the Progressive Democrats, the departure of
Haughey, and the rise of Reynolds are not the only ways in which these names
were intertwined. When the coalition government of 1989 was formed
O'Malley became minister for Industry and Commerce; he immediately canceled export credit insurance for the Goodman Beef company, a very aggressive
and successful marketer of Irish beef abroad. O'Malley also ordered Goodman
to dispose of his interests in another meat company on the basis that it was monopolistic. Rumors and allegations of special favors to Goodman had been cir-
culating since 1987, when Haughey had put together a large development
scheme for Irish beef that involved direct state investment. A bid to purchase
the Irish Sugar Company by a Goodman subsidiary revealed conflicts of interests for a Fianna Fail minister who had a financial interest in the Goodman
company. This prompted questions by members of the Dail about the actions of
the Goodman companies, which in turn revealed that Goodman had been fined
by the European Union for misusing funds, a transgression known by the
Haughey government. Despite Goodman's abuses Fianna Fail had, in fact, extended a large export credit insurance scheme that gave special preference to the
company, arranged by none other than Albert Reynolds. The increasing
scrutiny revealed not only a pattern of collusion and corruption but also that
the Goodman company was deeply in debt due, in part, to its dealings with
Iraq, which owed Goodman $270 million.

In May 1991 the television show "World in Action" broadcast an investigation
of the Goodman Group that confirmed what all had suspected. Haughey was
clearly associated with the scandal, both through his defense of Goodman and because of his failure to stop preferential treatment and confront illegal activity.
O'Malley would not support an attempt by Haughey to evade the issue and forced
the creation of a judicial tribunal to investigate the whole affair. The tribunal, itself a first in Irish politics, held hearings in Dublin Castle under Judge Liam
Hamilton. In his testimony Haughey attacked Reynolds for having made the export credit decisions without his knowledge, thus foisting the responsibility onto
his successor as prime minister. O'Malley's earlier testimony had done the same,
asserting that Reynolds had recklessly risked the state's money in a special deal for
Goodman. Reynolds used his testimony before the tribunal to attack O'Malley in
very contentious language, accusing him of dishonesty while dancing around or
denying the evidence against him. The tribunal's report in 1994, although exonerating Reynolds, revealed a pattern of party donations and corruption in the beef
industry and in the industry government-connection that only confirmed the parade of abuses adorning the Haughey government from 1987 to 1992.[13]

The coalition government broke down, of course, in bitter accusations of dishonesty. What Reynolds wanted was an election to bring about his principal campaign promise, which was to make Fianna Fail the majority party free of the need for minority or coalition government. What Reynolds got in 1992 was the lowest level of support for Fianna Fail in sixty years. This set off a round of negotiations in which the Labour Party, with thirty-three seats, was kingmaker. Reynolds and Dick Spring struck an agreement that gave Labour a prominent role in the government. The coalition lasted until 1994 when Reynolds appointed Attorney General Harry Whehelan to be president of the High Court without consulting Labour. In addition, the attorney general's office delayed the extradition of a pedophile priest to Northern Ireland, withholding information on that issue from the Dail. Reynolds was forced to resign as Taoiseach and then as leader of Fianna Fail. He was replaced by Bertie Ahern. No election was held and a new government was formed with Labour in coalition with Fine Gael under the leadership of John Bruton. In June 1997 an election was held in which Fianna Fail bounced back with seventy-seven seats, seven short of a majority but enough to form a coalition government with the Progressive Democrats under their new leader, Mary Harney.

As the dominant government party of Ireland for so many years, Fianna Fail saw itself as a movement more than a party and as the embodiment of a special vision of Ireland that warranted a right to rule. The ability of Fianna Fail to accumulate support through the distribution of patronage and favors for so many years was a distinct advantage over the opposition parties. Moreover, those who sought a future in politics found the potential for reaching positions of power much greater in a party where ruling was the tradition, while the opposition had only an intermittent opportunity to rule. It has been left to Bertie Ahern at the end of the 1990s to repair the damage done to Fianna Fail by Haughey and Reynolds in the form of corruption, bad decisions, poor policy, and electoral decline.

Fine Gael

The role of almost permanent opposition in Ireland fell to the party that ruled for a decade at the creation of the Irish Free State, Cumann na nGaedheal. When the split occurred in Sinn Fein, the leadership of the pro-Treaty side was in the hands of Arthur Griffith and Michael Collins. However, both died in 1922, and leadership passed to William T. Cosgrave, a far less towering figure. At that point the pro-Treaty group was not a political party, but by April 1923 the formal trappings of party structure were adopted and the group took the name Cumann na nGaedheal. Cosgrave set out to restore civil order after the Civil War, disband the army, inspire confidence in the Free State government, and manage the economy. Given the difficulties faced by the new state, Cosgrave's success was not inconsiderable: He managed to create the Shannon hydroelectric plan and the Electricity Supply Board. Other issues, such as the severe penalties imposed on their opponents in the Civil War, the outcome of the Boundary Commission, and budgetary restraints, were politically damaging. Cosgrave was cautious and conservative, Catholic and conformist. Support for Cumann na nGaedheal among voters began to leak away in the late 1920s.

In the first 1927 election Cumann na nGaedheal dropped from sixty-three to forty-seven seats while the minor parties and independents won sixty-two seats. The absence of Fianna Fail had allowed Cosgrave to continue to rule, but legislation that forced Fianna Fail to take their seats legitimized them even against their will. Unable to govern with the Dail so fragmented, Cosgrave called another election in 1927 in which the voters could express their clear preference for Cumann na nGaedheal or Fianna Fail; the two parties won sixty-two and fifty-seven seats, respectively. The greatest loss was suffered by the minor parties, which found the expense of contesting another election too great and their appeal as an alternative to Cumann na nGaedheal stolen by Fianna Fail.

While capable of ruling until 1932, Cosgrave was incapable of doing any more than continuing the same policies which, by 1932, appeared inert and lifeless to the electorate. Cumann na nGaedheal's election strategy then was to paint Fianna Fail as the embodiment not of the national vision but of all that was anathema to Ireland.[14] Political scientist Richard Sinnott quotes a Cumann na nGaedheal campaign advertisement warning that Fianna Fail rule would bring "sporadic Revolution, Irreligion, Poverty and Chaos." Ireland would be susceptible to "those doctrines of Materialism and Communism which can so effectively poison the wells of Religion and Natural Traditions."[15] The zealous use of capital letters in their campaign notwithstanding, Cumann na nGaedheal lost the 1932 election.

The party was becoming more conservative, which drew conservative elements in society to its banner and prevented a sharp drop in 1932. However, in the intensely fought 1933 election Cumann na nGaedheal won only forty-eight seats, prompting the merger of the National Centre Party, the National Guard, or Blueshirts, and Cumann na nGaedheal into Fine Gael ("Irish Race"). The leader of the party, General Eoin O'Duffy, was from the Blueshirts, and the party did not thrive in the turmoil of its association with ersatz fascism. William T. Cosgrave took over the party in 1935 and restored it as the successor to Cumann na nGaedheal in ideology and support. The party was hollow in the 1930s, weak in organization, leadership, and ideas. In the 1937 election the party achieved the same number of seats as in 1932 but the percentage of its vote was less than that of its three predecessors combined. In the 1943 election the seats fell to thirty-two. Cosgrave resigned but the new leadership of Richard Mulcahey did little to strengthen the party. Mulcahy was seen as part of the crackdown on republicans during the Free State era, a divisive factor within his own party let alone among the electorate. In the 1944 election Fine Gael did not even contest all the constituencies and won only thirty seats, the lowest in the party's history.

The 1948 election produced a government of all parties that were in opposition to Fianna Fail. Although the stimulus for this coalition had come from the new

Clann na Publachta Party, Fine Gael, at thirty-one seats, was still the largest opposition party and provided the new prime minister, John A. Costello. The bizarre
anomaly was that Costello was not the leader of the party, Mulcahy was. Clann na
Publachta had forced a choice of Taoiseach other than the leader of the largest
party in the coalition, an embarrassment to say the least. The hallmark of the government was the formal declaration of Ireland as a republic by Costello and the
conflict over the Mother and Child Health Plan, both divisive issues. Although
Fianna Fail was back in power from 1951 to 1954, Fine Gael won forty seats in
1951 and fifty seats in 1954. In combination with the Labour and the Farmers
parties Fine Gael was able to rule again from 1954 to 1957 as the dominant party
in the coalition. Thus a party that was clearly slipping away in 1944 was charged
with ruling responsibility for six years out of twelve after the end of World War II
and no doubt was saved from political oblivion.

The 1957 election brought a drop in Fine Gael's seats to forty, partly due to the
deflationary economic policy of the government, burgeoning emigration, and a
growing sense of malaise in the 1950s. James Dillon, the son of the last leader of
the Irish Parliamentary Party and a founder of the National Centre Party, became
party leader in 1959. Fine Gael held forty-seven seats in the two Dillon elections
in 1961 and 1965, fully a third fewer than Fianna Fail each time. Liam T. Cosgrave,
the son of William T. Cosgrave, became the leader of the party in 1965. The only
viable partner in a coalition against Fianna Fail, the Labour Party, decided to opt
for an independent strategy in the 1960s and would not run in tandem with Fine
Gael. Shut out from the possibility of governing, Fine Gael appeared to be destined to spend its new strength in the frustration of opposition. Even though Fine
Gael gained ten seats in the elections from 1952 to 1969 (from forty to fifty) the
growth did not diminish the strength of Fianna Fail but came from the minor
parties and independents.

Some Fine Gael members saw the image of the party as rather negative and
conservative. In response to the economic growth generated by Fianna Fail in
the 1960s, Fine Gael responded with a program titled "The Just Society."
Accepted in 1965, the program represented an attempt to present alternative
policies of economic and social change to the voters. The program also precipitated a split between the more conservative leadership, attuned to the party's
traditional middle class and agricultural support, and the younger, more liberal
members, who wished the party to present a positive social democratic alternative to Fianna Fail.

In 1973 Fine Gael and Labour defeated Fianna Fail and took power. The crucial
element in the victory of the coalition was the agreement on a common policy,
"The Fourteen Point Program," and the discipline of the voters in giving their second preference vote to the partner party in the coalition. The number of Fine
Gael voters giving second preference votes to Labour, and vice versa, was substantial and had the effect of increasing the seats of both parties, despite the fact that
Fianna Fail actually increased its percentage of the total vote.[16]

Fine Gael held power from 1973 until 1977 as the senior partner of a coalition government. The party had available to it the political initiative and the power of the ministries. But true to its history of ramshackle organization and conservative policies, the party did not take the opportunity to reorganize internally and retained the paternalistic autonomy of the TDs, a tendency toward authoritarianism, and cautious policies. Liam Cosgrave was not a dynamic leader and embodied an older, conservative attitude toward party and policy. While the coalition was governing Fianna Fail was girding for the next election with substantial changes in organization and style. While in power Fine Gael let the opportunity to do the same slip away. When Cosgrave called elections in 1977, his own party was less prepared to campaign than the opposition.

The coalition had placed an inordinate degree of faith in the redistricting of electoral constituencies implemented by the minister for Local Government from the Labour Party, James Tully. The prior districting had been done by Kevin Boland with the same attention to Fianna Fail's advantage as Tully was now lavishing on their disadvantage. Nicknamed the "Tullymander," the plan substituted the number of TDs from larger to smaller districts and from urban to rural with an eye to preventing a small Fianna Fail gain in votes from pushing the coalition out. What he did not account for was a Fianna Fail landslide, which had the effect, under his plan, of sweeping out the government. Fine Gael again returned to opposition; Fianna Fail obtained eighty-four seats while Fine Gael dropped to forty-three and Labour lost two, leaving them seventeen. Fianna Fail had garnered over 50 percent of the total vote, and the damage to Fine Gael was considerable. Three ministers in the government lost their seats and eighteen Fine Gael TDs were defeated.

The effect of the election on Fine Gael was dramatic. Liam Cosgrave resigned as leader and, after a brief flurry of candidates, the party settled on Garret FitzGerald, who had served as foreign minister in the 1973–1977 coalition government. FitzGerald wasted no time in undertaking the changes he wanted. A new party secretary was appointed as well as new officers for press relations, youth, and European affairs. FitzGerald commissioned a survey from Market Research Bureau of Ireland to assess the crucial issues in the electorate and the reasons for the Fine Gael loss of 1977. This process was continued up through the election of 1981. This polling led FitzGerald to seek out, as Fianna Fail had done, the votes of youth, women, and the suburbanites.

FitzGerald personally set out to revitalize the constituency organizations with a direct appeal to young people to join Fine Gael. A Young Fine Gael organization was created that was relatively autonomous from the senior party organization. FitzGerald himself often proved to be the most important element in attracting new adherents. FitzGerald's intellectual qualities, character, and leadership not only helped to prevent Fine Gael from sinking into a demoralized apathy but in fact molded the party into a more competitive, aggressive, and professional political opponent to Fianna Fail. As one young woman at the time put it, Fianna Fail was seen as "an unshakable monolith of gombeenism (jobs-for-the-boys), provincialism, insular thinking, and mediocrity. It embodied the mentality that prevented Ireland from becoming a modern pluralist state."[17] FitzGerald was identified with the liberal wing of the party and had taken relatively bold positions in the past on Northern Ireland and social issues such as divorce and contraception. FitzGerald not only attracted a new youth movement but also brought visible progressive figures such as Nualla Fennell and Maurice Manning into the party. In a symbolic gesture, FitzGerald even moved the Fine Gael headquarters in Dublin. The party, much to the dismay of the conservative wing, shifted leadership and momentum to the liberals and replaced a loose and paternal organization with a modernized and integrated structure buttressed with young, enthusiastic campaign workers.

As Fianna Fail had done in 1977, Fine Gael mounted campaigns in 1981 and 1982 characterized by public relations techniques, a focus on FitzGerald as national leader, and a program geared to the various sectors of the electorate the party needed to reach. This approach was not totally without cost, however, because Fine Gael's base of support had always been socially and economically conservative and the changes alienated some of the old guard who preferred tradition to victory.

The election of 1981 revealed the degree to which FitzGerald had succeeded. The weakness of Fianna Fail and the strength of the reborn Fine Gael produced the largest victory for Fine Gael up to that point in its history. Fine Gael took support away from Fianna Fail and also Labour, going from forty-three to sixty-five seats. Labour slipped to fifteen and Fianna Fail dropped to seventy-eight. FitzGerald formed a coalition government with the support of Labour and some independents. However, in 1982 as a result of an austerity budget proposal that included a tax on children's shoes, the FitzGerald government lost to Fianna Fail. This setback was quickly overshadowed by the eight-month Haughey "GUBU government"; in the second election of 1982 Fine Gael reached the high-water mark of seats in the Dail, seventy, and went into coalition government with Labour from 1982 to 1987.

The largest victory ever for the party was a vindication for the leadership of FitzGerald and the professionalization of the party. FitzGerald, the son of the foreign minister in the Cumann na nGaedheal government and himself foreign minister in the Liam Cosgrave government, had done what no other Fine Gael leader could: achieve virtual parity with Fianna Fail in seats. FitzGerald acted on the Northern question through the Anglo-Irish Agreement of 1985 and on liberalization of divorce in 1986. The coalition foundered in 1987, again on the issue of budget austerity.

In the 1987 election Fine Gael's seats dropped to fifty-one; Labour lost four seats as well. FitzGerald resigned and Alan Dukes took over as leader. Dukes was from the liberal wing of the party and was opposed by traditionalists in Fine Gael who saw the party as better positioned in its older conservative mode. Dukes chose to support the austerity budgets introduced by Fianna Fail at the time. His reasoning was that the country would be better off and that austerity was what Fine Gael would have chosen anyway were they in power. This so called "Tallaght Strategy" increased Dukes's unpopularity with the traditional wing of Fine Gael. The gain of four seats by Fine Gael in the 1989 election did not strengthen Dukes's hold on the scepter, nor did Mary Robinson's victory in the presidential race, in which the Fine Gael candidate, Austin Currie, was obliterated. Dukes had ignored advice from his senior party members to support Robinson and thereby strengthen her chances and associate Fine Gael with the victory of a very popular candidate. Dukes was voted out and replaced by John Bruton, a technocrat with a long record of service to the party but certainly deficient in charisma.

To Bruton's surprise, the collapse of the Reynolds coalition with Labour left him Taoiseach in 1994 as head of a rainbow coalition of Fine Gael, Labour, and the Democratic Left. Acquitting himself well on the Northern Ireland issue, Bruton was riding a surge of popularity that evaporated when the election was held in June 1997. Fine Gael won fifty-four seats to Fianna Fail's seventy-seven. Labour also lost seats and Fine Gael was unable to form a coalition government.

Labour Party

The Labour Party, the third of the major Irish parties, is unique in that it did not originate in the Sinn Fein movement, a mixed blessing indeed. Founded in 1912 by the Irish Trades Union Congress, the party was a political arm of that organization, which in 1914 changed its name to include Labour Party. The party had been founded by the eminent labor figures James Larkin, who led the party from 1912 to 1914, and James Connolly, who led from 1914 to 1916. No real party organization structure existed until the party prepared to enter the 1918 election. The trade unions had to confront what then was the crucial political question, Home Rule. Recognizing that worker solidarity was supposed to transcend local loyalties, the party leaders also knew that Belfast industrial workers were bitterly opposed to Home Rule and intensely loyal to the Orange Order. The Labour Party took no stand on Home Rule in an effort to preserve the illusion of worker unity, north and south. Despite James Connolly's participation in the 1916 Rising, the Labour Party was outside the enormous wave of support that was building behind Sinn Fein.

Preservation of unity with the workers of Ulster was to be costly for the Labour Party because social and economic issues were not a sufficient bridge to hold the two groups together in the face of the independence movement. The 1918 election, which Sinn Fein won with widespread support, proved to be damaging to the Labour Party. Labour decided not to contest the 1918 election despite growth in numbers and popular support. Sinn Fein exerted pressure to keep the national question front and center. The Labour Party strategy was designed to allow the nation to vote on its political future and to preserve labor solidarity in the face of Sinn Fein and unionist combat. In fact, the workers in the two regions were polarized on the question of independence, and Labour did not gain or hold the allegiance of Ulster workers. The party excluded itself from the election that was to set the pattern for Ireland in years to come. The effect was to accomplish the worst of both worlds: a split among the workers and abdication of any Labour voice in Sinn Fein.

When the Free State was established, Labour chose to accept its legitimacy and participate in the Dail. In the first election in which Labour participated in 1922 its candidates received one out of every five votes and seventeen seats. Labour became the official opposition to Cumann na nGaedheal and took on the role of advocating more generous social policies. Thomas Johnson took over leadership during the critical years after 1916 until he lost his seat in 1927. In 1927, when Fianna Fail entered the Dail, Labour gained twenty-two seats. In the second election of 1927, however, Labour's seats dropped to thirteen. Fianna Fail pre-empted the role of the Labour Party and became the opposition party committed to social and economic reforms. Johnson was then replaced as leader by Thomas O'Connell, who led the party until his own defeat in 1932, whereupon William Norton took over and led the party until 1960.

In 1936 the Labour Party called for the creation of a "Workers Republic" and for a nationalization of industry. This bold move caused the Catholic Hierarchy to let it be known that such notions were at odds with the Church's position; in response Labour diluted its commitment to socialism in 1939. Labour's thirteen seats in the 1937 election meant that Fianna Fail needed the party to form a government, but the 1938 election found Labour with only nine seats and in a state of decay as profound as that of Fine Gael. The difficulty in the early years was that if Labour moved closer to Fianna Fail and took a more nationalist tone workers would have no reason to vote Labour and could vote for Fianna Fail. If the party moved to a more militant socialist tone it ran into opposition from the Church. If the party sought to be a broader-based Leftist social movement it encountered the social conservatism of an agricultural economy of small farmers. If it stayed close to industrial workers and trade unions in agricultural Ireland its base would always be small and the party would become, as it did, embroiled in the conflicts of the trade union movement. The success of the party in the 1943 election during the Emergency, which nearly doubled the party's seats, was vitiated in the 1944 election by a split in the labor movement that led to the creation of the National Labour Party. The labor vote was divided: Labour got eight seats while National Labour received four seats; in 1948 National Labour got five seats.

In 1948 Labour's fourteen seats brought it into the Inter-Party Government; in 1954 Labour was in coalition with Fine Gael. In both terms Labour was junior partner and under Fine Gael leadership could hardly press for extensive social and economic reform. The deflationary economic policies of the 1950s, which Labour endorsed, did little to endear the party to its supporters. Participation in government, however, had the effect of reviving Labour electorally and it actively sought coalition government in the 1954 election. Labour paid a high price for this coalition, as did Fine Gael. In the 1957 election Labour dropped from nineteen to twelve seats. Labour had chafed under Fine Gael in the coalitions and after the defeat of 1957 opted to forego electoral coalitions in the future. The defect in this strategy, of course, was that electoral alignments were not quite that supple, and rejecting coalition meant potentially permanent rule by Fianna Fail.

Brendan Corish became head of the party in 1961. The party modernized, seeking new members, professionalizing its staff and activities, drawing intellectuals to its banner, and moving toward the status of a majority party. Labour believed that the electoral trend of the future would be toward socialism and that Labour would then be prepared to become a majority party. Labour's support grew from twelve seats in 1957 to sixteen in 1961 and to twenty-two in 1965. Corish's strategy appeared to be working; the party was experiencing growing confidence and optimism when, in the election of 1969, it lost four seats. Labour did not seem to be as much a wave of the future as the Party had anticipated. In fact, Fianna Fail had achieved another extended period of unbroken rule, from 1957 to 1973.

The weakness of Fianna Fail in the early 1970s, coupled with the disappointing results of 1969, prompted the Labour Party to reconsider coalition. Although this was not a popular option with the left wing of the party, the pragmatists won the day. Talks were begun with Fine Gael in 1972 culminating in a common program and electoral cooperation in the 1973 election. Labour increased by one seat and entered the coalition, which ruled from 1973 to 1977. (Labour was also part of the FitzGerald coalition government in 1981, the FitzGerald government of 1982 to 1987, and the Reynolds and Bruton governments from 1993 to 1997.)

When the coalition ended in a defeat for Labour in 1977 a new leader, Frank Cluskey, was chosen. Labour adopted the strategy of running in elections independently and then negotiating a coalition if it seemed appropriate. The 1981 election was a test of that commitment, but embarrassingly Frank Cluskey lost his own seat. The new Labour leader, Michael O'Leary, had to negotiate the coalition, which lasted only until 1982, whereupon O'Leary joined Fine Gael, another embarrassment. Dick Spring, the next Labour leader, then faced the 1982 election and formed a coalition with FitzGerald that lasted until 1987. This coalition foundered on the question of an austerity budget to deal with the public debt. Labour was not doing particularly well. Its twelve seats were more reminiscent of 1927, 1937, and 1957 than a harbinger that "the seventies will be socialist."

The "Tallaght Strategy" of Alan Dukes helped Labour to the extent that Fine Gael was voting with Fianna Fail, leaving Labour in the role of critic and opponent of the government's policies. Spring's adroit leadership brought the party fifteen seats in the 1989 election and his idea of supporting Mary Robinson for president in 1990 brought Labour to its greatest victory in its history. In 1992 Labour received 19.3 percent of the vote, the highest percentage since 1922, winning thirty-three seats. Labour then went into coalition governments, with Fianna Fail until 1994 and then with Fine Gael until 1997. Spring, as foreign minister in these governments, was in the center of the events in Northern

Ireland and his leadership was critically instrumental in achieving the 1998 Good Friday Agreement. In the 1997 election, however, Labour seats fell to earlier levels of support, with only 10.4 percent of the first preference votes producing seventeen seats. Spring had vowed not to go into coalition government with either Fianna Fail or the Progressive Democrats and thus Labour returned to opposition in 1997. Spring, the most successful leader of the Labour Party, stepped down and Ruairi Quinn, former minister for Labour in the FitzGerald government and minister for Finance in the Bruton government, took over the leadership of the party.

Progressive Democrats

A recent addition to the Irish political spectrum, the Progressive Democrats had the capacity to make or break governments in the late 1980s and 1990s because of the fragmentation of votes that led to coalition government. The Progressive Democrats were formed by Des O'Malley. O'Malley, from a distinguished political family, had a reputation in Fianna Fail as a thinker, which was not always a good thing in that patronage- and power-based party. He served in the Cabinet in Lynch and Haughey governments as minister for Justice and minister for Industry and Commerce. He chafed under Haughey's baronial style and was repelled by the repetitive charges of corruption, real or alleged, that clung to the Haughey governments. He was opposed to Haughey as party leader and led a challenge against him in 1982. It was, however, the issue of the New Ireland Forum that eventually separated O'Malley from his party and its leader.

The New Ireland Forum was an attempt by John Hume of the Social Democratic and Labour Party of Northern Ireland to inject some life into the constitutional approach to the Ulster question. Sinn Fein had scored an election victory in Northern Ireland in 1981. Garret FitzGerald, with his liberal views on social and constitutional questions, was open to new approaches to the north and called for a forum of all parties on the island to meet to discuss the relationship of the north and the south and the creation of a "new Ireland." The Forum began in 1983 and took on a life of its own, catching the attention of the press and public and producing research and position papers, extended discussion and reports, and a final report in 1984. The Forum challenged Fianna Fail's exclusionary nationalism and outdated rhetoric. Its final report grappled with the reality of the beliefs of the people who actually lived on the island, not the illusionary inhabitants who resided in Fianna Fail's republican ideology. The report recommended various forms of government for Ireland, including joint authority over Northern Ireland, a federal system, or a united Ireland.

Haughey repudiated the report immediately in spirit and content and claimed that it had actually only called for a united Ireland because that was the only position his party could accept ideologically. O'Malley could not support this position, seeing it as a regressive approach to the north that involved forcing a united

Ireland onto those who did not want it in the name of a religion, language, and identity they did not share. When the Family Planning Bill of 1984 was debated O'Malley gave a notable speech in the Dail. In it he rejected the position of his party and tied the contraception issue to the Northern question. O'Malley accepted a pluralism of values and opposed the legislating of morality. When the vote on the bill was taken O'Malley abstained and he was expelled from the Fianna Fail party in February 1985.

Haughey's opposition to the Anglo-Irish Agreement signed by FitzGerald and Thatcher in 1985 was based on the idea that it contradicted the Irish Constitution and acknowledged that Ulster was part of Britain. O'Malley voted for the Anglo-Irish Treaty, as did Mary Harney, another disillusioned Fianna Fail TD. She also was forced to resign from the party in 1985. In December O'Malley announced the formation of the Progressive Democrats with Mary Harney, two other Fianna Fail TDs, and Michael Keating from Fine Gael. The party's position was conservative and market oriented on the economy, liberal on social issues such as Church-state relations, and open to alternative policies on the north.

The party could be seen either as a necessary antidote to the Fianna Fail of Charles Haughey or another quixotic effort to found a party that would disappear when the political wind changed. In 1987 the party got about 12 percent of the vote and fourteen seats, quite impressive for a new party. Haughey's weak government of 1987 to 1989 led to another general election that resulted in a loss of eight seats by the Progressive Democrats, who went into a not altogether successful coalition government with, of all parties, Fianna Fail. In the 1992 election the Progressive Democrats rebounded to ten seats and were in opposition. In 1993 Des O'Malley stepped down from leadership of the party and Mary Harney took over. Her performance during the 1994 Reynolds crisis displayed her talent and her capacity to hold the minor party together. In 1997, despite a drop to only four seats in the Dail, the Progressive Democrats went into coalition government with Fianna Fail and Mary Harney became Tanaiste.

The party that broke away from Fianna Fail has been in coalition government with Fianna Fail twice. The creator of the party has stepped down and the party holds only 30 percent of the seats that it did after its creation. The future of the Progressive Democrats clearly rests with Mary Harney and her ability, in government and out, to distinguish the party from Fianna Fail to justify its separate existence while at the same time going into power with Fianna Fail to try to effect policy as a minute percentage (four of eighty-one) of the government's plurality of seats.

Democratic Left

An exemplar of the jagged heritage of the original Sinn Fein party of 1916 –1922, the Democratic Left traces its roots to the original wisp of Sinn Fein remaining after the creation of Fianna Fail. In 1969 and 1970 that Sinn Fein split into Provisional and Official wings over the questions of electoral participation in a

British-run government and the use of physical force. The Provisional arm evolved into the Sinn Fein party of Gerry Adams and came to play a major role in both the terrorism and the peace process in Ulster. Official Sinn Fein eschewed violence after an internecine war with the Provisional IRA and chose a constitutional path based on its radical socialist ideology. The party changed its name to Sinn Fein The Worker's Party in 1977 and then in 1982 dropped the Sinn Fein from the title. After the fall of communism in the Soviet Union and eastern Europe the radical socialist element clashed with the parliamentary representatives who sought to be a democratic socialist party. The new name, the Democratic Left, was adopted when the parliamentary representatives split from The Worker's Party. Proinsias De Rossa had been the leader of The Worker's Party and now leads the new party.

The electoral strength of the Sinn Fein/Sinn Fein The Worker's Party/The Worker's Party/Democratic Left has never been significant. In 1981 they got one seat in the Dail, reaching a high of seven seats in 1989 with 5 percent of the vote. After the split the Democratic Left earned four seats and 2.8 percent of the vote. The politics of the crisis in Fianna Fail in 1994 put the Democratic Left in government from 1994 to 1997 with Fine Gael and Labour and perhaps helped to give it some measure of mainstream electoral acceptance that its earlier Marxist Leninist ideology had denied it.

Minor Parties

Minor parties can be identified by the number of seats they have held as a percentage of the Dail. Using 5 percent of the Dail as a cutoff to be considered a minor party, only the Farmers Party, with fifteen seats in 1923 and eleven in 1927, and the National Centre Party, with eleven in 1933, qualified. From 1937 to 1944 only Clann na Talmhan, with eleven seats in 1943 and nine in 1944, made the cut. From 1948 to 1957 the only party over 5 percent was Clann na Publachta, with ten seats in 1948 helping to trigger the creation of the all-party coalition that ended one of Fianna Fail's epochs. From 1961 to 1977 no minor party reached 5 percent. Since 1981, 5 percent of the Dail has been 8.3 seats, and the Progressive Democrats in 1987 and 1992 achieved that number.

Smaller parties and independent candidates have had an impact on the pattern of Irish electoral support only marginally. Only in the 1920s, when Sinn Fein was not taking its seats; in the 1940s, when Clann na Publachta appeared to be on the rise as a real alternative to the major parties; and in the late 1980s and 1990s did third parties make a difference. At no time did the first preference votes for the three major parties fall below 70 percent (in 1948), and in the last five elections minor parties and independents have garnered only between 3 and 17 percent of the first preference votes. The Irish party system is a stable multiparty pattern with a dominant party that has ruled alone or in coalition for most of the years since 1932 but that has an increasing need to seek coalition partners.

This situation elevates the importance of smaller parties that would otherwise be marginal, such as the Progressive Democrats and Democratic Left, and makes the job of Fine Gael even harder.

Bases of the Irish Party System

In a well-known article on Irish political parties, John Whyte pointed out that unlike other party systems, the parties in Ireland were based upon the Civil War split in 1922 and are not differentiated on the basis of distinctive social class foundations.[18] The evidence suggests that this is true. Fianna Fail drew voters and support from across all social classes and, while more middle class, Fine Gael was also not fixed in class-based support. Nor for that matter was Labour, which drew some working class support, but more people from the working class voted for Fianna Fail.

Political scientist Richard Sinnott assesses this explanation and suggests that, while it is undoubtedly valuable in historical terms, three other explanations can be offered that reframe the foundation of the Irish party system. Sinnot calls a second explanation "covert class conflict." The party split apparently was based on the Anglo-Irish Treaty, but the split was really based on the quest for stability, order, and the protection of economic interests on the part of Cumann na nGaedheal/Fine Gael on the one hand and a nationalism that had become intertwined with a "radical" quest for equality and economic advancement on the part of Sinn Fein/Fianna Fail on the other.[19] The evidence, however, does not support this interpretation because the best explanation for support of Fianna Fail is that it is rural, Irish speaking, and Catholic. Fine Gael appears to be a residual party that drew non-Fianna Fail votes from all sectors of the society, although at different rates.[20] A third possible explanation that Sinnott notes is a conflict between rural and urban, tradition versus modernization, and periphery versus center, with Fianna Fail representing the former in all categories and Fine Gael the latter. The difficulty with this view, argues Sinnott, is that the categories fit both parties: They shared cultural nationalism and Catholicism almost completely; they were parties of both the rural areas and the cities, although at different levels; and they both favored agriculture and then became economic modernizers.

Sinnot suggests a fourth explanation that places the Irish party system into the framework of cleavages devised by political scientists S. M. Lipset and S. Rokkan to explain the foundations of party systems. When the masses of people are politically mobilized in a country, the divisions around which they polarize provide the foundation for their partisan allegiance and the alignment of the parties. These cleavages are the center versus the periphery; Church versus state; land versus industry; and owners versus workers.[21] The mobilizing election for Ireland was definitely 1918, with the expanded electorate, the mobilizing party/movement Sinn Fein, and the defining issue of independence from Great Britain. The center/periphery conflict took the form of a struggle between Ireland and England. The majority of voters were mobilized by Sinn Fein in the periphery, Ireland.[22] The center, London, uniformly opposed the periphery on the question of independence and was willing to use force and then diplomacy to retain Ireland. The issue of center periphery was incomplete because full independence was not achieved (and the unionists stayed connected to the center through partition). Sinn Fein split over the degree of Ireland's independence, which led to the Civil War. Sinnot notes: "Voters underwent a further process of nationalist mobilization, this time into strongly peripheralist and moderately peripheralist or strongly nationalist or moderately nationalist camps."[23] Thus the party system is rooted, not only in the sharp differences that resulted in Civil War, but also in similarities between Fianna Fail and Fine Gael. The shared values about the stability of the Irish State and the major cleavages were often masked by Civil War bitterness.[24]

The other cleavages are illuminating when Ireland is placed in this framework. Church–state relations put the Catholic Church of Ireland in conflict with Britain on a host of issues in the nineteenth and early twentieth centuries. The uniformity in Church–state relations under the two political parties after the founding of the Free State indicates that they shared values on this issue, however sharp their differences on other matters. The agricultural versus industrial cleavage is also congruent with the Irish case; Ireland represented the rural sector and England the industrial. Within Ireland both parties drew votes and support from the agricultural sector and both saw it as central to Irish life, but both parties shifted to support of industry when conditions demanded. The final cleavage, workers versus owners, was not that dramatic in Ireland because it was a less-industrialized country. The absence of the Labour Party in the 1918 election pushed class issues to the margin and kept center-periphery questions at the heart of the development of the Irish party system in the critical years from 1918 to 1932.

The absence of a Left–Right spectrum in the Irish parties as well as a flexibility on the cleavage issues was possible because of the absence of ties to a particular class base in the parties.[25] The parties had the capacity to become "new wine in old bottles" and to shift their base of support depending on specific issues and specific leaders and form alliances across the political spectrum. The Fianna Fail election program of 1977, the appeal of Garret FitzGerald in 1982 and Dick Spring in 1992, and the coalition government that included both Fine Gael and the Democratic Left in 1994 are notable examples. The major parties could appropriate parts of the socialist agenda when it suited them, act statist (creating semi-state bodies) or laissez faire (privatizing semi-state bodies), be conservative on social issues (both parties initially favored the abortion amendment), or be liberal (both parties chose to quietly watch censorship fade) as they preferred. The exception to this flexibility is the one issue that refers back to the true fissure in the formation of the Irish system: the national question. Fianna Fail will always be more nationalist as long as the north is partitioned. The differences in the degree of nationalism, especially as conditions change, may be subtle but they will persist.

The shared perspective on the major cleavages meant that both major parties were relatively "traditional" on secular versus confessional issues, agricultural versus industrial issues, and class issues. Thus the political conflicts that emerged after the 1960s are based on different response rates to the pressures of modernization in the economy, society, and electorate. Retaining or jettisoning protectionism, expanding or constricting contraception, modifying the divorce law, providing down payments on houses, taxing farmers, expanding the opportunities of women, joining the European Community, and similar agenda items reveal that the parties have different positions unconnected to past positions or to a core constituency. The different rates of response to the modernizing agenda could perhaps stabilize the parties around particular class bases in the future. But oscillation is evident in the influence of particular leaders, and public concern tends to spike around specific issues and then move on to others. The parties may be lucky enough to find a FitzGerald or a Spring or may find they have caught the wave of change as Fianna Fail did in its about-face on the economy after 1960, but these are not long-term moorings. The fluid character of the parties will probably continue as they construct policy priorities that they hope will bring victory as the agenda of post-industrialism unfolds.

Pressure Groups

The major parties have learned that their appeal has to be targeted at the segments of the differentiated electorate that modernization has produced. The explicit organized voices of those segments are the array of Irish interest groups.

Numbering in the thousands, large and small, those considered here represent important social sectors and carry particular weight. The functions of these groups, as of pressure groups anywhere, are to recruit and organize members; proselytize their interests; and, most important, persuade the government to listen to their advice in implementing policy that will bring the group advantages. All groups tend to rationalize their specific interests in terms of benefits to the common good. In most cases this is at best a partial truth that in fact represents an attempt on the part of one segment of society to enlarge its slice of the pie. Crucial to the success of interest groups are public legitimacy, size, resources, and organization.

The Catholic Church

Of the major pressure groups, the Church is the most visible and considered by some to be the most powerful. Identifying the "power" of the Church per se, however, is difficult in a country that is 94 percent Catholic and devout at that. To determine whether the "Church" or the people have promoted or prevented a policy is sometimes difficult. Examples abound of political figures simply ignoring the official pronouncements of the Church, especially on the national question, up to the point of excommunication, including, for example, as devout a Catholic as de Valera. On the other hand, Brendan Corish, former leader of the Labour Party, stated in the Dail: "I am an Irishman second; I am a Catholic first. . . . If the Hierarchy gives me any direction with regard to Catholic social teaching or Catholic moral teaching, I accept without qualification in all respects the teaching of the Hierarchy and the Church to which I belong."[26]

Virtually all leaders in the major parties, civil service, and pressure groups are Catholic; thus ascertaining the difference between the personal convictions of those leaders and "pressure" from the Church in supporting a particular policy is not at all easy. Moreover, the position of a single cleric, bishop, or cardinal is not always the position of the Church. Single voices, such as that of Cornelius Lucey, the former Bishop of Cork, who badgered the government constantly, may not represent the collective thinking of the Irish Catholic Church. Clearly in the past the conservative voice of the Hierarchy did not always parallel the political convictions of the local clergy, committed as they were to the Irish nationalist movement. In the contemporary setting the younger clergy are not always of the same mind as the Hierarchy of a Church very responsive to papal authority under John Paul II. Finally, the Church's opposition or support for a policy may find expression not from the Hierarchy but from the Catholic lay associations such as the conservative Knights of Columbus, Catholic Action, or the Pro Life Action Committee. Often the community pressure brought about by such groups is extremely effective and precludes the need for direct intervention by the Church.

Commenting on the influence of the Church in 1970, Morely Ayearst wrote: "It is obvious that no Irish political party can afford to advocate policies that are contrary to the Church's view concerning education, the family or moral questions generally. Nor can a politician who hopes for a successful political career, especially within one of the two main parties, afford to flout Catholic opinion in such matters."[27] That which Ayearst apodictically declared so unlikely has in fact transpired, beginning just about the year he wrote. The first changes were in the adoption in the 1970s and 1980s of public policies that the Church opposed. The second stage has been the decline in the legitimacy of the Church in the 1990s, eroding its credibility on public matters. Clearly political parties today advocate policies contrary to Church doctrine, and public opinion no longer can be simply equated with unquestioning adherence to Church doctrine.

Political scientist John Whyte has examined two ways in which we might view the Church as a pressure group. The first is that the Church is like any other organization in Irish society such as industry and trade unions and can express its opinion on public matters and press its views on decision makers. The second view is that the Church is the ultimate authority in the state and that what it wishes will occur and what it forbids will not happen, especially in the realms of moral behavior and Church doctrines. The role of the Church as a pressure group also varies over time. The "just another group" construction does not bear too much scrutiny because the Church at the outset does not see itself as being like any other institution in society, a position articulated with clarity by Bishop Lucey in 1955 when he said: "The Church is the divinely appointed guardian of the moral law . . . in a word their [the Irish Bishops] position was that they were the final arbiters of right and wrong even in political matters."[28] The ministers of government were not willing to treat the Church as just another claimant among the welter of political supplicants. As Whyte notes of de Valera when he got a letter from the bishops protesting a Health Bill: "The effect on Mr. de Valera was electric. He dropped all his engagements and drove off to see the Primate."[29] Hardly the response he would have given to a letter from the Irish Housewives Association. The repeated declaration of politicians during the Mother and Child Health Plan controversy that they would not put the state in conflict with Church moral teachings indicates a power that transcended conventional status. In the early years of the state the Church was particularly powerful: Public and governmental deference was intact, the Church tended to speak with one voice, and the creation of the state as Catholic was an affirmation of Irishness as well as religious conviction.

The Church has been successful in the past in directly and indirectly shaping public policy in Ireland because the Irish people and the Church were symbiotically united and the authoritarian sway of the Church was matched by a complementary deference among the people. The fact that over 90 percent of the schools in the Republic were run by the Church built a faith and loyalty among the people to the Church. The Church took an integralist approach to the society, seeking to permeate and control institutions with the values of the Church. The boundaries between the Church and the state, as political scientist Basil Chubb notes, were to be set by the Church, and other institutions and the government were to defer to its moral authority.[30] John Whyte has pointed out that the Church has exercised that sort of direct intervention on issues only "three or four dozen" times since 1923.[31] Whyte's assessment is of course based on specific policy issues raised between the government and the Church and not on the atmosphere in which it was unthinkable to bring an entire array of policy choices about women, education, censorship, gay rights, and the like to the political arena. Anyone who contemplated such an action would quickly realize that the price was too high socially as well as politically. Thus what is notable is not the issues included on Whyte's short list but the extensive agenda that was excluded.

To jump to the opposite conclusion that the state was a theocracy and that the Church held ultimate authority is also erroneous because Irish governments have advocated policies that the Church opposes and put them into law. Although the first generation of leaders has passed from the scene, in the first years of the state they had differences with the Church on the national question, on the use of force, and on resistance to authority. Many were excommunicated for their beliefs and activities. Their deference to the Church stopped where their nationalism began.

In the 1980s and 1990s some of the more notable instances of this independence were the change in the laws on the availability of contraception and divorce, the diminishing of censorship, the shifting control of the schools, and laws on abortion information and travel, all of which have been very significant to the Church. In the Forum for a New Ireland, the Church was asked if Catholics in Northern Ireland were devout without Church doctrine imbedded in their laws, why it was needed in the laws of the Republic? In the face of the welter of issues that arose after the 1970s and Vatican II the Church stopped arguing that the state was obliged to do what it said and began to argue that what the Church advocated would help prevent the deterioration of the society into secular materialism. Party leaders, however, were evaluating policy in terms of the new pressures from the electorate. The Hierarchy was one voice, an important one to be sure, but not the only or ultimate or determinative voice. Gemma Hussey, member of the Cabinet, noted in her diary when the 1985 contraception bill passed: "Today we defeated the Bishops and Fianna Fail," a comment far from the politics of Corish's Ireland.[32]

The power of the Church as a pressure group was affected by which party was in power (Fianna Fail was somewhat more accommodating), whether the Hierarchy was itself split on the issue, and whether it was before 1970 or after. The slow erosion of deference after 1970, then its sudden collapse in the 1990s, has placed some of the people in the Republic outside of, and in some cases in heated opposition to, the writ of the Church. Education, urbanization, relative affluence, and increasing sophistication, flowing from the modernization process, have eroded deference among people and politicians. Revelations of corruption, illegal, and immoral behavior among priests diminished the Church's moral authority as a pressure group in the 1990s.

Farmers

Farmers in a rural country with agriculture as an important industry would be expected to speak with a strong voice. In fact, the farmers in Ireland never developed the kind of pressure group, or groups, seen in Europe in the last century. This is not to suggest that the farmers are without influence—on the contrary. It is to suggest, however, that the acquisition of property in the late nineteenth and early twentieth centuries produced a country of small proprietors who were socially and economically conservative and provincially oriented. The farmers are fragmented as well, broken down into over 200 specialized organizations concerned with, for example, sugar beets, beef exports, cattle breeding, and milk production.

The single largest agricultural organization is the Irish Farmers Association (IFA) created in 1970 from a collection of other farming organizations. It represents about 80,000 farmers and publishes the *Farmers Journal*. The national executive of this group has a staff of fifty-five and a budget of over £4.5 million and is charged with the responsibility of monitoring agricultural developments at home and abroad to enhance the future of Irish agriculture and livestock. The organization has a committee that reviews proposed bills before the Dail. In close contact with the minister for Agriculture, the IFA presents its point of view on agricultural policy. The Irish Creamery Milk Suppliers Association is smaller, with 53,000 members, but it is an active lobby as well.

The principal interest of farmers in the latter years has been the effort to protect their incomes when the market declines. For the most part they have been successful in controlling taxes, although less so in recent years because the government imposed income and wealth taxes. The farmers' resistance to such taxes and discussion of additional levies took the form of protest marches, road blocking, and demonstrations in the late 1960s.

The greatest impact on the farmers was Ireland's entry into the European Economic Community. The effect on the Irish farmers was not only a sharp increase in their incomes but also the development of organizational skills needed to operate in Dublin and in Brussels. The complexities of the Common Agricultural Policy meant that farmers had to exert pressure on the formation of policy directly in Brussels. Journalist Tim Pat Coogan notes the sophistication that has been developed: "The Irish Farm Association, with a high powered office in Brussels, a top class secretariat of young economics graduates, and a range of business activities related to farming would make an old-time, fork-in-hand, muck-spreading farmer blink in amazement."[33] The farmers have shifted their interests to protecting their incomes, which rose in the wake of subsidies after entry into the EEC and then in the mid-1970s and the 1980s took severe drops as Brussels FEOGA grants were adjusted. The difficulty of Irish farmers remains the structural problem of farms that are too small and insufficiently mechanized and a labor force that is aging. While immense improvements have been made in technology and in agricultural education, the smaller farmers of the west are still not competitive with the larger farm cooperatives of the east of Ireland, to say nothing of their European Union competitors. The farmers have been pressuring the government for the transfers that they have traditionally enjoyed from other sectors of the economy, but they are in fact being subjected to increasing taxes and increasing competitive pressure. Farmers in late 1998 again demonstrated in Dublin because their incomes have been decreasing for years, but their clout does not resonate as it did in years past. The romance associated with rural Ireland always glorified a rather bleak economic existence, however rich the village life. Now the romance has shifted to the dynamic, urban, youthful Ireland and farmers have lost influence and their ideological claim on the public weal.

Labour

Labour shares with farmers the propensity to proliferate; there are about fifty small unions. Half of the Irish trade unions have 2,500 or fewer members and only seven have memberships over 15,000. Among the larger unions is the Irish Transport and General Workers Union. The largest is the Services, Industrial, Professional and Technical Union, with 205,000 members. About fifty-one of the unions are members of the Irish Congress of Trade Unions (ICTU), which speaks for over 95 percent of all union members. Total union membership in the Republic of Ireland is approximately 0.5 million. The ICTU speaks for unions in the various state councils and bodies in the same manner that the IFA speaks for the farmers. The ICTU has become the voice of the working class in a way that the Labour Party is not. The Labour Party is seen as a group of politicians espousing an egalitarian point of view but not very connected to the bread and butter issues of the shop floor. In practice the ICTU is not the clarion voice of a united labor movement but rather a loose harness of autonomous unions. Union membership has been growing since 1961 both in absolute terms and as a proportion of all employed workers and is fourth highest in the European Union.

The policy process of corporatism, which involved a partnership of industry, government, and labor on national economic goals, had brought labor into national wage agreements in the early 1970s and especially in three agreements since 1987. Labour has benefited from the agreements and also from breaking them. Beginning with Sean Lemass in 1963, after much bargaining a national agreement on a wage increase of 12 percent for two years was struck. While the rate was high, industry conceded on the basis that the two-year agreement gave them stability in projecting their costs. Unfortunately the building trades struck in 1964 and were in effect in breach of the deal made by the ICTU. The minister of Industry and Commerce set up a Labour Court and the strike was settled. The employers were disenchanted with both the ICTU and the government. They had thought that the high rate of wage increases pressed by the government would preclude strikes; instead they got both high wages and a strike. The Federated Union of Employers also had to capitulate to the maintenance workers in a bitter strike in 1969. An agreement of 1966 was being re-negotiated and the workers were asking for an increase in wages of 35 percent. The Employers wanted to grant 12 percent. The unions violated an agreement to go to a Labour Court and struck. A settlement was reached but then breached by the unions, putting 30,000 people out of work. The Employers were outraged. The end of the strike was a loss for the Employers but was also a disgrace for the unions and a display of the powerlessness of the ICTU over its own members and of the government over the ICTU.

In the early 1970s successful National Wage Agreements were negotiated to curb the rampant inflation and keep wages in line with productivity increases. In abeyance for the mid-1980s, Haughey after 1987 sought to curtail the national debt and sought similar comprehensive agreements. These agreements have now become institutionalized. Rampant inflation in the 1970s and 1980s put pressure on the unions, which felt that the workers were bearing the high cost of living while at the same time being asked to cure it with low increases in wages. In the early 1990s the decrease in the rate of inflation produced conflict with the government over the demand of unions for pay increases greater than the rate of inflation to recover their purchasing power. The government resisted to prevent wage push inflation.

The array of concerns for labor is wide: rates of employment, employee disputes, insurance benefits, unemployment compensation, industrial relations, holidays, and safety. The representation of workers on management boards has been
a growing trend, with Telecom Eireann and Aer Lingus, for example, drawing
one-third of their boards from the unions. Following the German model of integrating labor into the management structure, the Irish are slowly entering this
form of relationship.

Industry

In addition to the Church, agriculture, and labor, a host of groups with varying degrees of power speak for established sectors of Irish politics. Industrial and commercial interests are represented by over 200 associations, most of which traditionally were relatively weak and lacking in resources. The two largest organizations are
the Confederation of Irish Industry, which has over 2,500 associated firms, and the
Federation of Irish Employers, which deals with labor matters and has 3,200 members. The period of economic growth after 1960 pushed trade and industry associations to organize to a much greater degree. Industry leaders sit on the government boards and monitor legislation that affects their interests. The leaders of the
industrial and commercial organizations have a close working relationship with
the government, in part because Ireland is a small world, in part because of the
neo-corporatist policy process, and in part because individuals have given large
campaign contributions, legally and illegally (Ben Dunne and Larry Goodman for
example) to party leaders. Consumers are not very well organized in Ireland and
there is only one large organization devoted to issues of consumer protection, the
Consumer's Association of Ireland. It is supported by the government to a small
degree, by the European Union, and by its membership. Political scientist Basil
Chubb points out that the improvement in consumer protection legislation has
come from pressure from the European Union far more than from pressure within
Ireland.[34] Professional associations for doctors, teachers, architects and engineers,
among others, also vie for a say in the policies that affect their livelihood.

Single-Issue Groups

Groups that have long been advocates of a particular interest include the promotion of Irish by the Gaelic League, Gael Linn, and Nasiunta na Gaeilge (the
National Convention of the Irish Language). The Pioneer Total Abstinence
Association, which swims upstream against the apparently ineradicable stereotype
of the Irish as drunks, persuades its members never to drink and lobbies the government to stop encouraging drinking. The Gaelic Athletic Association promotes
specifically Irish games. Newer on the scene are groups advocating women's rights;
rights for gays and lesbians; protection of the environment; and help for the traveling people, deprived children, single parents, battered women, and the homeless.

Groups come into existence to address a specific policy issue, such as those that mobilized around the abortion and divorce referenda in the 1980s, and then disappear while others continue to exist and pick up new agenda items.

Groups have emerged in response to a particular government policy and have had important effects on that policy. The Irish Anti-Nuclear Movement is an example. In response to the increasing energy demands in the 1960s and 1970s, the Fianna Fail government initiated in the early 1970s, and approved in 1978, a nuclear power plant at Carnsore Point. The Fine Gael/Labour coalition government of the mid-1970s also approved the plan until the development of an Anti-Nuclear Movement challenged the policy on the grounds of the danger to the surrounding population, the danger of mining uranium, and the disposal of nuclear waste. The increasing pressure of these groups, national and local, brought public attention to the issue. They held an anti-nuclear "festival" at Carnsore Point and a national meeting at the Mansion House and provoked discussion of the issue on "The Late Late Show" in 1978. The parties began to react to public pressure, with Labour calling for a national referendum and a public inquiry. Fine Gael and Fianna Fail, in power at the time, also agreed to a public inquiry with the goal of defusing the public opposition to nuclear power. Political scientist Susan Baker notes that the idea backfired: "Opposition to nuclear power widened and deepened and the concession of the inquiry only served to make the Government's energy policy all the more subject to public scrutiny."[35] An inquiry begun by an Interdepartmental Committee in 1979 was never published. Fine Gael backed away from its support of nuclear power in its 1980 document *Aspects of Energy Policy*. In 1980 the minister of Energy announced the postponement of the Carnsore plant; as Baker points out: "There is little doubt that the emergence and subsequent development of the Irish Anti-Nuclear Movement was a major contributing factor in the Government's decision to abandon its nuclear energy policy."[36] No nuclear power plants have been built in the Republic.

Interest group activity has increased significantly in the Republic of Ireland for two reasons: increased acceptance of the social partners in a previously highly centralized policy process and the increase in more and different organized interests as the society became more pluralist after 1960. Citizens began to feel that their actions would have some political effect but, of course, not at the same rate and intensity. Gay and lesbian advocates, for example, do not lunch with the minister and senior civil servants as often as, say, the head of the ICTU or the IFA do; they are less likely to belong to the same club, golf at the same links, attend the same parties, or drink at the Shelbourne Hotel after work. There is an access to decision making that is as much a part of the social structure of Ireland as it is of the policy process. Because the members of the Dail are not critical in the policy formation process, interest groups do not seek them out as they do members of Congress in the United States. The key figures are in the party leadership who are setting policy goals; the Cabinet, which develops legislation; and the senior civil service, which develops and implements policy. The key policy makers, both in the creation and implementation stages, meet with figures from interest groups on a daily basis.

Interest group activity can have three effects on legislation: first, that the group advocates for its interests and gets what it wants; second, that legislation is shaped in ways large and small by multiple groups in regular consultation with the policy makers; and third, that the group has a veto over changes in the current status of policy and can delay, deflect, or stop a particular policy option. While of course examples abound of groups getting what they want, in fact most pressure group activity consists of shaping policy and sometimes vetoing it. The constellation of countervailing groups means that few interest groups get an unchallenged say in the design of policy and few get to completely reject policy, but most get some say in the process.

Policy Issues: The Environment

Mr. John Hanrahan's cattle began to die mysteriously and rust began appearing on metal faster than normal in Ballycurkeen in Tipperary in the early 1980s. The Hanrahans and their four children were considered model farmers on their 265-acre holding and had run the farm as a family since 1942. Then 114 cattle died in thirty months. The Hanrahans were not the only family having problems with their animals. Bertie Kennedy found his cattle behaving in unexpected ways, such as all gathering in one end of the shed on top of each other or running around the fields in an erratic manner. Both Kennedy and Hanrahan believed these problems were the result of chemicals emitted from the nearby plant of Merck, Sharp and Dohme in Ballymeeny, which was built in 1976. In 1981 one farmer, Paddy O'Meara, found himself and his cattle engulfed in a kind of fog in the fields that made him and his cattle quite sick. The local doctor told him his body was full of poison; it took months for him to recover. His cattle never did; they wasted away until he had to sell them for half their value. Other farmers supported the Hanrahan claims about the particular chemical releases in 1981; one neighbor said he would never leave a window open in his house. Others complained of heart trouble, bleeding, running eyes, and sick sheep. Veterinarian Tom De Lacy became convinced that the erratic behavior of the Hanrahan cattle, their labored breathing, and their deaths were caused by chemical emissions from Merck, Sharp and Dohme. Local doctors chimed in on both sides of the issue, some saying there was little or no pollution in Ballycurkeen while one said he had never seen so many skin disorders. Some farmers nearby had no trouble with their cattle.

Hanrahan's complaints to the county engineer, begun in 1978, were dismissed on the basis of the information given to the engineer by Merck, Sharp and Dohme. Calls for examination of the air were made based on the presence of sickening smells, but the county council argued that there was no emission greater than what was allowed by the European Union. A series of meetings were called by the local residents in 1978 to protest, but a report at the time by the county council said that there was nothing wrong with the air. The company embarked on a public relations campaign, inviting people to the plant and issuing statements about the plant's safety.

A study done by the botany department of Trinity College found that the area was subject to high pollution levels, including the grass and soil on Hanrahan's farm, which "indicated a higher level of bromine and chlorine than would have been expected and that . . . higher levels of bromine had been present during the Summer of 1981."[37] The report indicated that the pollution came from the emissions of Merck, triggering a spate of other reports designed to contradict or minimize the Trinity Report. The Hanrahans then sued the company for damages. In 1985 the High Court found against the Hanrahans and the family began to have financial difficulties. The farm was put up for sale and all the equipment sold off. No one bought the farm itself, so Mary Hanrahan lived on the deserted farm with her sister while the rest of the family moved away for health reasons. Appealed to the Supreme Court, the case went on for another three years, during which environmentalists, scientists, and solicitors supported the Hanrahans. In 1988 the Supreme Court ruled against Merck, Sharp and Dohme and found them liable for the illness of Mr. Hanrahan and the death of his cattle.[38]

Because Merck employed 250 people, attacks on the company were not welcomed by all. In 1976 the people in the same region had raised objections to another chemical company, Schering Plough, which eventually chose to build its plant in Puerto Rico. The concern in Carrick on Suir and by the Industrial Development Authority was that job creation would be halted and the jobs already in place would be threatened by a diminishing return on investment for companies in Ireland. Journalist Colm Toibin points out that, "The objectors were called 'cranks and publicity seekers' in the Senate by James Tully, the Minister for Local Government."[39] The tension between development and employment and the preservation of the environment is no better exemplified than in this case. The Industrial Development Authority (IDA)would like to have dozens of Mercks and is willing to accept the company's word that it is adhering to environmental regulations as long as the jobs are forthcoming. Environmentalists argue that the IDA is willing to take "dirty" industries such as micro-electronics, pharmaceutical, and chemical companies, which use large quantities of water and discharge air and fluid effluent. While discharge of such effluent is forbidden by the Local Government Water Pollution Act of 1977, it was not all that clear that local government had the clout to stop such activities. The 1990 Water Pollution Amendment Act strengthened the powers of local government to impose penalties.

Production of industrial waste since the process of industrialization began in the late 1960s has increased sharply. Over 52,000 tons of toxic waste and one and one-half times as much "problematic waste" are produced in the Republic each year.[40] The problem of what to do with this waste triggered the Irish version of "Not in My Back Yard," and plans for a toxic waste incinerator have been stymied by the opposition of local environmental groups. Less poisonous waste has increased as well. Solid waste is being dumped into landfills that can create other environmental problems such as the creation of methane gas and the problem of biodegradability. Efforts to recycle ordinary waste have been increased in accord with environmental regulations of the European Union.

Agriculture, the preservation of peat bogs, and air pollution have been addressed in the government's 1990 Environmental Action Programme, the first of its kind in Ireland. Excessive peat extraction has caused concern that there will be no peat bogs left in Ireland after 2000. The government has set aside certain types of bogs for preservation. Agriculture has modernized in Ireland and that has brought about the intensive production of animals, such as chickens who are held in cages and force fed, then given antibiotics because such conditions generate disease. The chemicals are then put back into the food chain, to the dismay of environmentalists and natural food advocates. The pens build up the effluent from the animals, which is then run off into the local water. The poisons pollute the water and kill the fish. The government has adopted policies to curtail this activity and has supported with £450,000 ($675,000) the Irish Organic Food Growers Association, which advocates alternate food production processes less reliant on pesticides and chemicals.

As the development of Dublin mushroomed, the amount of air pollution did as well. The use of soft coal and diesel fuel turned the buildings in the city black with soot. Visitors who were in Ireland in the 1970s easily notice the difference in the odor of the air and the cleanliness of the buildings today. Because two thirds of the houses in Dublin burned coal, the prevention of the use of soft coal produced an enormous change in air quality. The expansion in the number of cars in Dublin also contributes to the air pollution (and major traffic jams in Dublin) and the country is shifting to use of unleaded gas to cut down on emissions. The Air Pollution Act of 1987 empowers the minister of the Environment to control the sources of air pollution.

The pressure groups for the environment in Ireland include transnational groups such as Earthwatch and Irish groups such as An Taisce, which has a very powerful environmental voice because planning bodies have to send their plans to it, giving it a semi-official role as a watchdog of the environment. The government has two bodies to monitor the environment: the Environmental Research Unit, which provides a wide variety of information on infrastructure, and Eolas, which "provides services to industry in such areas as information technology, construction, energy and the environment."[41]

Social Problems and Issues

Some clichés about Irish social behavior have undergone remarkable modifications (although they are perpetuated in songs and jokes). Irish marriage in the past was between two older people steeped in sexual puritanism, which, ironically, produced large families. The structure of these marriages was driven by post-Famine property considerations, leading to a high percentage of unmarried older men and women, women married to much older men, and unmarried sons and daughters languishing on the farm. The character of those marriages as depicted in stories and novels was often one of emotional distance, male dominance, and separate lives: the pub and sport for the man, and children and home for the mother. The traditional pressures that bedeviled Irish marriages included sex, drink, and deterioration. While it is not true, an old joke says there were no orgasms west of the Shannon. It is true that there were reports of a less than robust interest in sex among Irish men. Among the reasons were the doctrines of the Church holding that intercourse was for the purposes of procreation and that sin was personal and sexual. The prevalence of drink contributed as well. Social life oriented around male groups, which led to an immature attitude toward women reinforced by male dominance in the home, which made men less accountable for their behavior. Domestic violence was and is not uncommon and reflected the incapacity of the men to deal with the pressures of marriage and family with any other response but force fueled with alcohol. Until the recent change in the divorce law through the referendum of 1995 and a dismissal of a challenge to the results by the Supreme Court in 1996, the lack of divorce law made it hard to estimate the real extent of problems in Irish marriage. Alcohol abuse, sexual immaturity, male chauvinism, large numbers of children, economic hardship, and the lack of divorce did make marriage stressful.

The Family

After 1960 a demographic change abruptly reversed the prevalent pattern. The Irish, at the same time that they were gaining increased access to education, were marrying younger, at the same average age as other European states. In addition, the average number of children within marriage dropped off to the same rate as western Europe. The quality of the relationships in marriage reflect the changes as well. The novelist John McGahern describes the changes: "Marriages have become more equal, couples are closer to each other and they have less ignorance of each other's sexuality."[42] Viewing sex as a bond between couples and not as tied to procreation; increased awareness of sexuality; and increased exposure in uncensored media, cinema, and books led to changes in attitudes toward sexual behavior. Increasingly people believe sexual relations before marriage are morally acceptable and are more tolerant of gays.

Homosexuality

The place of gays in Ireland has been at once a mixture of invisibility, exclusion, and condemnation. This treatment was produced by the intersection of the Church's view of homosexuality as sinful with a conservative society marked by a rigid adherence to an external moral code. Homosexual practices were outlawed under an 1861 British law carried over to Ireland under the Act of Union. Prosecutions under the Act, however, were relatively rare. The lives of gay people remained in the closet because the social disapproval and family embarrassment were as much deterrents to coming out as was the law. At the same time it should be said that the genial side of the Irish personality was aware of and tolerated the behavior of certain men as long as it did not threaten to crack the facade. Transformations in the rest of Irish society after the 1960s inevitably opened this door and by the 1980s there were gay and lesbian organizations on the university campuses, AIDS action groups, and highly visible gays who had come out.

The most prominent of these individuals is David Norris, a professor at Trinity College, a member of the Labour Party, and a member of the Senate. Norris challenged the 1861 law, arguing that it was an infringement of his civil rights under Article 40 of the Constitution. The High Court ruled against Norris in 1983 and the Judge, C. J. O'Higgins, made clear that his decision was based on the Preamble to the Constitution, which identifies Ireland as a Christian state. The court, he said, could not nullify laws "prohibiting unnatural sexual conduct which Christian teaching held to be gravely sinful."[43] Norris took his case to the European Court of Human Rights, arguing that the 1861 law was in violation of the European Convention on Human Rights. In 1988 the European Court found in his favor and mandated that Irish government change the law. Alacrity is not the first word that comes to mind in describing the government's response. Five years later, in 1993, the law decriminalizing homosexual behavior between consenting persons over the age of seventeen was passed. The Irish people, John Ardagh notes with a patronizing, weary shrug, "want to have their moral cake and eat it, i.e. to keep their old ideals yet accept social change."[44] What the Irish people want is tolerance for individual homosexuals while still disapproving of homosexual behavior and the glorification of the homosexual lifestyle, an attitude that prevails in the United States and other countries as well. What Ardagh dismisses as Irish hypocrisy is actually widespread tension that people worldwide feel about the line between discrimination, tolerance, and approval in the gray terrain between civil rights and the moral code of the community. Proposals that the Constitution be amended to prohibit discrimination were supported by the 1996 Constitutional Review Group, which urged the adoption of an addition to Article 40: "No person shall be unfairly discriminated against, directly or indirectly, on any ground such as sex, race, age, disability, sexual orientation, color, language, culture, religion, political or other opinion, national, social or ethnic origin, membership of the traveling community, property, birth or other status."[45]

Alcoholism

Among the most sturdy of clichés about the Irish is their love of drinking. Comedy routines, songs, and jokes are stuffed with references to drunkenness, outrageous behavior, pubs, and pints. The cliché is not in and of itself supported by the evidence; it is perhaps attributable to the excessive celebration of drinking rather than the drinking itself. Drinking in Ireland does not take place in the home but in the pub and thus is highly visible, associated with good times, conversation, and perhaps music, which accentuates the exuberance associated with drink. The habit of buying rounds means that one will drink as many drinks as there are people at the table. The Irish spend a large proportion of their disposable income on drinking and have a high rate of admission to hospitals for alcohol-related problems. An effect of the surge of prosperity and independence among young women is that they drink more than they used to when the pub was more of a male enclave.

Sorting out the statistics on drinking can be daunting because they support contrary conclusions. The consumption of alcohol per capita in Ireland in 1994 was 11.2 litres. Compared to the other European Union countries that amount is low: the British consume 20 percent more, the Italians 30 percent, the French 50 percent, and the Germans 60 percent. However, because about 25 percent of the Irish do not drink, the average overall may be low but the average for specific groups such as younger people and males may be quite high. Until recently the tolerance for the consequences of drinking was quite high. Hangovers, being late for work, automobile accidents, the problem drinker in the family, and public drunkenness were often more the source for a story than a social or political issue. The government's policy on alcohol in the past was ambivalent. The members of the Dail, themselves reared in the drinking ethos, saw the pattern of drinking as normal. The taxes from the drink industry were high and they were large employers.

In the late 1970s policy began to change when clerics and doctors began to point out the damage done and the costs borne by society in work lost, hospitalization, and family problems. *The National Youth Policy Committee Final Report* in 1984 recognized the problem of youth drinking and recommended, among other things, that no one under eighteen be admitted to a pub and that it be an offense to sell to the underaged. With the adoption of strict penalties for drunk driving the government attitude changed from seeing drinking as something taken for granted to regarding it as a behavior that, in excess, is damaging to society. The Road Traffic Act of 1933 defined drunkenness, but it was seen "not as the normal outcome of drinking too much, but of the failure to behave appropriately."[46] The government's reservations about testing for blood alcohol in the 1933 and 1961 Acts was overcome in the 1968 Road Traffic Act, which set a relatively generous blood alcohol level as being too drunk to drive. The 1978 amended Act lowered the acceptable level, allowed roadside testing for blood alcohol, and increased the enforcement, doubling the number of proceedings against drunk drivers. In 1993 the government introduced the "just two will do" campaign and additional efforts at persuading the public not to drink and drive. In 1994 the government lowered the blood alcohol level for the second time, setting a demanding standard. Regulations on the advertising of alcohol in the media were adopted. A national alcohol policy was adopted in 1995 that defined alcohol as a public health problem. The government has taxed alcohol at a high rate, which discourages drinking. The shift is more than merely tightening standards; it is a change in attitudes that defines drunkenness as having too much to drink and not as a personal flaw of an individual or an acceptable cultural norm.

Drinking has declined, especially among the more well educated and well off. Drinking habits have changed to some degree, with wine being chosen more often than ever before but still confined to a small percentage of the total consumption of alcohol, which still consists primarily of beer. As in the United States, there is a clear connection between the amount and type of drinking and smoking and class position in society. Smoking still is widespread in Ireland but to the extent that it has diminished in the professional classes. But alcohol and nicotine are not the only drugs of choice.

Drugs and Crime

Ireland, like other nations, is not free of the problem of illicit drug use. The use of marijuana, cocaine, and heroin has become so widespread as to be seen as a national crisis. The National Co-ordinating Committee on Drug Abuse, the first to address this problem, was appointed in 1985 and reported in 1986. The increase in admissions to drug rehabilitation units escalated exponentially in the 1990s. The availability of the drugs seems to be unimpaired: "ecstasy" is available to the twenty-somethings in the clubs and heroin is easily found on the worn-out streets of the poor neighborhoods. The profit from drug sales is so high that new gangs and criminals come into a market as soon as the Garda arrest someone. Local studies show not only increased use but shifts from softer to harder drugs. The bleak tenements of Ballymun are rife with dealers and the environment of unemployment, dysfunctional families, and low education does not help. Unmarried mothers bear 25 percent of the children born in the Republic, and most of them are poor, subjecting the children to the same degraded and dangerous environment.

The connection between drugs and crime produced one of the more shocking events of 1996. A prominent journalist, Veronica Geurin, was murdered, purportedly by members of major Dublin criminal gangs involved in the drug trade. Geurin was widely known and liked in political circles and was considered a fearless reporter for *The Sunday Independent*. She had broken big stories on politics and crime in Dublin and had interviewed Bishop Eamonn Casey in Ecuador in 1993. She had in fact been shot in the leg in 1995, indicating that she was treading dangerous waters. According to the Garda, her murder was planned by John Gilligan, a well-known Dublin gangster with twelve convictions whose drug gangs earned an estimated £16.8 million ($25.2 million) from 1994 to 1996. Gilligan was arrested at Heathrow Airport in 1996 with £330,000 ($495,000) in his briefcase on his way to Amsterdam.[47] Clearly the level of drug sales and the level of usage to support it point to a serious drug problem in Ireland. The attendant problems orbit around drug use: the destruction of families, the abuse of children, and crime to support the habits of users. The rise in the rate of crime connected to drugs, or otherwise, has become a great concern to the public, which expressed a willingness to accept draconian reforms in the 1997 anti-crime package. Sections of some cities are seen as being as dangerous as any big city in the world; Limerick, with its high violent crime rate, has earned the dark sobriquet "Stab City."

AIDS

Also connected to drug use is the rise in the incidence of AIDS. In 1986 there were nine cases and all had been contracted outside of Ireland. The response of the public, to the degree that there was one at all, was that it had to do with other places like the United States or London and was associated with homosexuality. By 1989 there were 81 cases in Ireland, 36 people had died, and there were over 800 carrying the virus. By 1994 the number of identified HIV positive people was 1,450, but there are undoubtedly many more unidentified cases, with some estimates that in Dublin alone there are 3,000.[48] Almost half the cases come from intravenous drug use and almost half from homosexual contact; the remaining cases are from heterosexual contact, hemophiliacs, and babies born to drug users. The increase in the cases of AIDS led to increasing the availability of condoms, although the general attitude of the government is still conservative. The attitude of the Church is that homosexuality is morally reprehensible, they cannot approve of condoms for such acts, and in fact condoms don't help anyway.

Poverty

AIDS, crime, drink, and drugs always thrive in an environment of poverty. Poverty has been in the past, and continues to be at present, a serious problem in the Republic. The agrarian poverty of the nineteenth century was appalling and the pestilential slums of Dublin at the turn of the last century were among the worst in Europe. The current manifestations of misery include the denizens of public housing, the unemployed, the rural poor, single parent women, elderly women, the homeless, and abused wives and children.

As a relatively poor agricultural country well into this century, Ireland's indigence relative to other European countries was not surprising. Poverty was coupled with conservative social doctrines, which prevailed for a half century after independence, and the anti-statist ideology of the Church. Not only were there few resources to distribute to the disadvantaged, there were few who were willing to undertake the task. The old system of workhouses, dispensaries, county homes, and general hospitals was less than adequate to serve the needy, who had to pass a means test to qualify for their services. Essentially unchanged from the nineteenth century, this system lasted until 1945. After World War II expenditures for health care substantially increased. Services were made available to those who could pass a rather stringent means test, which in 1958 was 28 percent of the population.

In 1952 Fianna Fail unified the patchwork of different welfare programs into the Social Welfare Act, which provided national health insurance, unemployment insurance, and benefits for widows and orphans. The state contributed 40 percent of the costs and the participating entities provided the remainder. The level of payments was low and not all workers were covered although the elderly, widows, and orphans were cared for by the state. The health care system today is a combination of state-run hospitals, Church-run hospitals with state funding, and private hospitals with no state funding. The combination makes it difficult for the minister of Health to adopt consistent management of health policies and also brings the Church and its institutional perspective heavily into health care.

The eight regional health boards do more than run hospitals. The community care component of their responsibility includes child care services, community nursing, and welfare services such as home help and income maintenance schemes for the indigent. These programs account for one-fourth of the budget.[49] Not everyone is eligible, and under the Health Care Act of 1991 standards are set that make all medical care and welfare service open to one-third of the entire population and two-thirds of the elderly population. Everyone is eligible for certain limited services for a limited charge but not for the full range of services. People may purchase the voluntary health insurance, which pays for a wider range of services and certain preferential treatment and is tax deductible. Purchasing private insurance has been increasing since it was introduced in 1957, especially when cutbacks in public health spending resulted in fewer available services. The rise in the cost of health care in Ireland, as elsewhere, has caused scrutiny of the health services and various plans for reorganization. The critical problem for the Republic is that the system is a mixture of funding sources, going to a mixture of management bodies, with a major non-government institution, the Church, running a large number of the services while delivering welfare services as well as health services.

Poverty can be measured in various ways, but in the Republic the conditions of old age, unemployment, and single parenthood always mean poverty, especially for women. The cutbacks in the late 1980s to bring government spending into balance also meant a slowdown in spending on the services, housing, and health for the disadvantaged. The emergence of Ireland as the "Celtic Tiger" should not blind us to the fact that wealth is unevenly distributed geographically and in class terms and that as many as 20 percent of the people in Ireland remain locked in urban squalor or rural indigence.

Conclusion

In 1965 only two people in the Republic were charged with drug offenses; in the early 1980s there were no known cases of AIDS; in 1961 there were eight murders in Ireland; in 1997 there were fifty murders. The changes in Ireland that have produced greater prosperity and cosmopolitanism have also produced behavior problems, crime, disease, and drugs, which are shocking to the Irish people. The key to understanding their shock and disillusionment is the rapidity with which they have had to change their expectations. The crime rate is relatively low (The city of Boston, with 3 million people, has 100 murders a year, which is low relative to New York or Dallas.), the incidence of AIDS is less than other European states, and the quest for gay rights in Ireland is minuscule compared to the gay pride parades and pressure group activity in the United States. But such developments have occurred within forty years in Ireland among a people who were inculcated with the perspective that de Valera's simple, rural, spiritual world was the ideal society. Adjusting to these changes has been and will continue to be hard. The deterioration of the moral aura of the Catholic Church leaves some less moored than they would like to be in the face of this gritty darker world within the new Ireland.

Notes

1. R. Breen, et al., *Understanding Contemporary Ireland: State, Class and Development in the Republic of Ireland* (Dublin: Gill & Macmillan, 1990), pp. 58–60.

2. Richard Sinnott, *Irish Voters Decide* (Manchester: Manchester University Press, 1995), p. 178.

3. Ibid., p. 25.

4. Still maintaining the fiction that the true government of Ireland was the second Dail Eireann, that government, members of Sinn Fein, turned the power of the Republic over to the Army Council of the IRA in 1938. Sinn Fein separated from, and then reconnected with, the IRA in 1949. Sinn Fein even scored a minor electoral victory in 1957, winning four seats in the Dail during the period of the IRA's Border Campaign of 1956–1962. The differences between their ideas on strategy in the 1950s and the 1956–1962 campaign caused the IRA Army Council to take direct control of Sinn Fein in 1962. In the 1960s Sinn Fein became a Marxist organization in the north. When the troubles broke out in 1968 the IRA and Sinn Fein were rejected by the Provisional IRA Army Council and its provisional political wing, Sinn Fein, which separated formally in 1970, with the Provisionals claiming the true line of succession from 1916.

5. Lemass rises steadily in the estimation of analysts as time goes by. Arriving too late and leaving too early, he did not accomplish Ireland's entry into Europe, nor did he see his economic reforms or his administrative reforms go through, but in retrospect he was the hinge between the old Fianna Fail and the new and thus between the old Ireland and the new. It is not a coincidence that he was Taoiseach during the early 1960s, the time to which we now ascribe the genesis of the vibrant Ireland we see today. See Paul Bew and Henry Patterson, *Sean Lemass and the Making of Modern Ireland* (Dublin: Gill & Macmillan, 1982); and John Horgan, *Sean Lemass: The Enigmatic Patriot* (Dublin: Gill & Macmillan, 1997).

6. D. Keogh, *Twentieth Century Ireland*, pp. 307–313; Bruce Arnold, *Haughey: His Life and Unlucky Deeds* (London: HarperCollins, 1993), pp. 80–109; and Dick Walsh, *The Party: Inside Fianna Fail* (Dublin: Gill & Macmillan, 1983), pp. 100–120.

7. Quoted in Keogh, *Twentieth Century Ireland*, p. 306.

8. Lee, *Ireland 1912–1985*, p. 460.

9. R. Sinnott, "The Electorate," in *Ireland at the Polls*, ed. H. Penniman, pp. 60–61.

10. Their manifesto included the abolition of domestic rates (local property taxes) and cutting taxes by £160 million ($240 million). Policies aimed specifically at younger voters included the abolition of taxes on small cars and motorcycles and a grant of £1,000 ($1,500) to people purchasing their first house. Appealing to the unemployed as well as to those young people entering the job market, Fianna Fail promised creation of 20,000 new jobs in one year and more jobs thereafter. How all of this was to be paid for indicates the degree to which Ireland is a country of great faith.

11. In describing the events of the arrest, Haughey used the terms "grotesque, unbelievable, bizarre, and unprecedented" and Conor Cruise O'Brien dubbed the 1982 Haughey period the "GUBU government."

12. Arnold, *Haughey*, p. 282.

13. These include Greencore, the Irish Sugar Company; Micheal Smurfit; Dermot Desmond; the Carysfort Training College land; and the government building an electrical generator on Haughey's private island. See ibid., pp. 261–267. Additional revelations about a contribution to Haughey of $2 million from Ben Dunne of Dunne's Stores, which Haughey denied and then admitted in 1997, add to the tale. In 1997 Ray Burke, the minister for Foreign Affairs, resigned from the Cabinet and Dail after admitting taking $45,000 in 1989 while he was in the Haughey cabinet.

14. A radical socialist wing of the republican movement, called Saor Eire, did emerge at this time outside of Fianna Fail under Peadar O'Donnell. It provided the justification for the heated campaign rhetoric.

15. Sinnott, *Irish Voters Decide*, p. 44.

16. Maurice Manning, "The Political Parties" in *Ireland at the Polls*, ed. H. Penniman, pp. 80–81.

17. Pat Brennan, "The New Face of Fine Gael," *McGill* (July 1981), p. 18.

18. J. Whyte, "Ireland: Politics Without Social Bases," in *Electoral Behavior*, ed. R. Rose (New York: Free Press, 1974), pp. 619–651.

19. Sean O'Faolain quotes Liam Mellows, a leader of the republican anti-Treaty forces, emphasizing the class differences: "The commercial interests and the merchants were on the side of the Anglo-Irish Treaty. We are back to Wolfe Tone . . . relying on the men of no property." Sean O'Faolain, *The Irish* (Hammondsworth: Penguin, 1980), p. 152.

20. Sinnott, *Irish Voters Decide*, pp. 280–281.

21. S. M. Lipset and S. Rokkan, "Cleavage Structures, Party Systems and Voter Alignment: An Introduction," in *Party Systems and Voter Alignments*, ed. S. M. Lipset and S. Rokkan (New York: Free Press, 1967), pp. 1–64.

22. Not all of the people of Ireland, however; the Unionist Party vote shows there was a group loyal to the center but living on the periphery.

23. Sinnott, *Irish Voters Decide*, pp. 282–283.

24. Finnegan, "Blueshirts of Ireland," p. 84.

25. This entire conception is drawn from Sinnott, *Irish Voters Decide*, pp. 284–286.

26. Quoted in Chubb, *Government and Politics of Ireland*, p. 103.

27. M. Ayearst, *The Republic of Ireland* (New York: New York University Press, 1970), pp. 222–223.

28. Whyte, *Church and State*, p. 367.

29. Ibid., p. 368.

30. Chubb, *Government and Politics of Ireland,* p. 118.

31. Whyte, *Church and State,* p. 365.

32. Quoted in Arnold, *Haughey,* p. 224.

33. Tim Pat Coogan, *The Irish, A Personal View* (London: Phaidon Press, 1975), p. 160.

34. Chubb, *Government and Politics of Ireland,* p. 114. This section on interest groups draws heavily on Chubb.

35. Susan Baker, "The Nuclear Power Issue in Ireland: The Role of the Irish Anti-Nuclear Movement," *Irish Political Studies* 3 (1988), p. 12.

36. Ibid., p. 13.

37. Colm Toibin, *The Trials of the Generals* (Dublin: Raven Arts Press, 1990), p. 126.

38. Keogh, *Twentieth Century Ireland,* p. 386.

39. Toibin, *The Trials of the Generals,* p. 131.

40. Susan Baker, "Environment," in *Political Issues in Ireland Today,* ed. Collins, p. 189.

41. Ibid., p. 207.

42. Quoted in J. Ardagh, *Ireland and the Irish* (London: Hamish Hamilton, 1994), p. 205.

43. Quoted in T. Brown, *Ireland,* p. 350.

44. Ardagh, *Ireland and the Irish,* p. 187.

45. *Report of the Constitutional Review Group,* p. 230.

46. T. Cassady, "Just Two Will Do," in *Encounters with Modern Ireland,* ed. M. Peillon and E. Slater (Dublin: Institute of Public Administration, 1998), p. 166.

47. U. Halligan and L. Walsh, "The Real Veronica," *Magill* (May 1998), p. 30.

48. O. MacBride, "When Death Comes Calling," *Irish America* (July/August 1993), p. 45.

49. L. Carswell, "Health Policy," in *Political Issues in Ireland Today,* ed. Collins, p. 154.

9

NORTHERN IRELAND: THE GORDIAN KNOT TIED

Introduction

In Belfast on Good Friday, April 10, 1998, a group of nationalist and unionist political leaders from Ulster signed a groundbreaking agreement that had eluded the best efforts of diplomats, officials, politicians, and the Church for the past three decades, and for that matter for the past 300 years. That agreement established a structure for the sharing of power and rule in Ulster between the divided communities and the creation of cross-border councils to deal with issues common to Ireland as a whole and between Dublin and London. How did such an agreement come to be reached in light of the history of diplomatic failure and the depth of hostility between the communities in Northern Ireland? How did these people manage to escape the snares of history? Have they, like Alexander the Great, cut the Gordian knot that no one could unravel?

Arnold Toynbee said that history is something unpleasant that happens to other people. The unpleasantness provides justification for much that happens in the world. Northern Ireland exemplifies this more than most places. Irish nationalists in the late nineteenth century sought to claim Irish history in support of their ideology of republican nationalism. They constructed in retrospect a seamless history of the Irish people from the invasion of Ireland by Strongbow in 1170 in which all events were coherently placed in the framework of an Irish nation valiantly fighting the monomaniacal oppression of the English. That history often had little or nothing to do with what happened in Ireland but it certainly did demonize the British. (Of course, given the record of the British in Ireland, this was not all that difficult a task.) One of the foremost historians of Ireland asked the question: "Have we in our entanglement with history locked ourselves into a hall of mirrors so grotesque that we can no longer distinguish the realities of what has happened in this island from the myths we chose to weave about certain events?"[1] Maybe, but we must examine that elusive past nonetheless so that we can, at the very least, recognize the hall of mirrors and, at best, empathize with different constructions of the past.

The Creation of Northern Ireland

The conditions that were institutionalized politically in Ulster in 1920 and 1922 had a long history. There had perhaps been an even greater sense of antagonism in Ulster between Protestants and Catholics in the seventeenth and eighteenth centuries due to the particularly comprehensive nature of the plantations after 1607 and the fact that the planters were alien in culture and religion. A common bond emerged between Presbyterians and Catholics in the late 1700s because both suffered under the Penal Laws, the former to a lesser and the latter to a greater degree. Although not negligible, that bond was certainly only one part of the Protestant–Catholic relationship. The symbolic union of the two faiths in the Society of United Irishmen and the 1798 Rebellion occurred at the same time, however, as the emergence of the Orange Order and persistent violent clashes between Catholic and Protestant secret societies. The nineteenth century saw an increasing separation of Ulster from the rest of Ireland. The Industrial Revolution occurred only in that province, and added to religious and ethnic differences were those of prosperity and an urban, industrial way of life.

Presbyterian liberalism at the end of the century declined and was attacked by the Ian Paisley of the nineteenth century, Henry Cooke. Cooke associated his conservative brand of religious evangelism with the political and ethnic views of the Orange Order. Throughout the century antagonism between Catholics and Protestants boiled over into rioting between the two communities. On occasion this resulted in numerous deaths (for example, in 1834, 1864, 1886, and 1893). Thus, at the same time that Ulster was drawing away from the rest of Ireland, antagonism between the two communities within Ulster was increasing as well.

Home Rule was the forge on which Protestant Ulster was formed. The alliance of Ulster Protestants with British Conservatives emerged from this dispute, as did the increased reputation and power of the Orange Order and the Ulster Unionist Council (later to become the Unionist Party). Prime Minister Asquith put a Home Rule bill through the British Parliament in 1912. In the period 1912–1914 Ulster Protestant intransigence rose to a crescendo and ignited the formation of the Ulster Volunteers, the near mutiny of British Army officers, near treasonous statements by Conservative politicians, and the threat of civil war.

Several reasons lay behind the negative posture of the unionists. The Conservative politicians in London exploited and inflamed their traditional antipathy to

Catholics so as to buttress their position against any risk of dissolution of the Empire. That the traditional antipathy existed, there is no doubt. The hostility built up between Protestants and Catholics had grown since the Reformation, and the unionists coupled this hostility with anti-Catholic cultural superiority. Because they would be a minority in a Home Rule assembly, the Protestants could not accept being governed by people they considered their cultural, religious, and ethnic inferiors. Finally, economic interests were at issue: Industrial Ulster had a huge stake in not threatening its advantageous position within the British free trade area.

In an attempt to seek a way out of the impasse of Ulster's ardor for union and Sinn Fein's warfare for independence, Lloyd George sponsored the 1920 Government of Ireland Act, which called for separate parliaments for the six counties of Ulster and the other twenty-six counties of Ireland. The Ulster unionists accepted their separate Parliament only reluctantly. They did not ask for devolution, let alone demand it, because they preferred that all of Ireland remain united with Britain. The remaining provisions of the 1920 bill were aborted as Sinn Fein transformed the southern Parliament into the second Dail Eireann. The Council of Ireland, which was supposed to have representatives from both parts of Ireland, never met. The 1921 Treaty contained a provision that Ulster could merge with the Free State or, if it chose, opt out. Ulster opted out immediately.

In the 1914 Home Rule crisis the spokesman for Ulster unionism, Sir Edward Carson, had demanded that all of Ulster be retained in the Union and that home rule apply only to the other twenty-three countries of Ireland. At that time the population of the province of Ulster consisted of only slightly more Protestants than Catholics, and five of the nine counties had Catholic majorities. When the boundary was determined for Ulster in 1920, the province was collapsed to only six counties—Down, Armagh, Derry, Tyrone, Antrim, and Fermanagh—in which there were 820,000 Protestants and 430,000 Catholics. Clearly the design was to maintain a Protestant majority.[2]

That the Catholic nationalists would immediately dispense with their feelings of religious and cultural identity, eliminate their political opposition, and embrace with open arms a state designed to preserve a form of rule they had died trying to destroy was most improbable. The 1920 Act provoked brutal sectarian rioting in Belfast, and over 500 people had been killed by 1922. The Catholic nationalists, still strongly identified with Sinn Fein, saw the government of Ulster as not yet permanent while the guerrilla war with the British continued. When the Treaty of 1921 was signed and partition accepted by Sinn Fein, the nationalists in Ulster were left only with the promises of Michael Collins that the Treaty would be a stepping stone to an all-Ireland republic and a never fully implemented agreement with James Craig that would provide some legal protection for the Catholic minority. The anti-Treaty forces promised only more fighting and were not supported by the Irish people in the other twenty-six counties. Without even the balm of living in a free state, the Catholic nationalists in Northern Ireland were left bearing the consequences of the split in Irish nationalism and, what was worse, were ruled by an Ulster government controlled by their local Protestant opponents.

The Stormont government (named after the Stormont Castle, located outside of Belfast) consisted of a House of Commons with fifty-two members and a weak Senate elected by the House. It was cabinet government, like that of Britain with executive power in the hands of the prime minister, the leader of the majority party. The monarch was represented by a lord lieutenant. Although the British government circumscribed the powers of the Stormont government—retaining control over foreign affairs, the post office, taxation, customs, and foreign trade—it gave substantial local authority to the Ulster Parliament, which tended to absorb the functions of local government as well. Stormont had responsibility for local law and order and the court system; its ministries were Finance, Home Affairs, Health and Social Service, Education, Agriculture, Commerce, and Development—all a bit elaborate for a province of 1,250,000 people. James Callahan, a former British prime minister, commented: "Here they are with all the panoply of government—even a Prime Minister—and a population no bigger than a few London boroughs."[3] The Stormont government was forbidden to pass laws aimed at religious discrimination or laws contrary to those of Westminster. The effective power of the Northern Ireland government, however, was increased by the reluctance of the British government to involve itself in the affairs of Ulster for the next fifty years.

The nationalists, in the tradition of Sinn Fein, ran for seats in the Stormont Parliament and then refused to take them when elected. Thus, over the next half century, a social structure emerged that was based on the Catholics being members of an underclass and Protestants being a dominant class. Each segment of the society had its institutions to support its traditions and prejudices—for the Protestants: their churches, the Unionist Party, and the Orange Order; for the Catholics: the Church and the Nationalist Party. Each community developed separate institutions to preserve its beliefs, which had the result of reinforcing the negative stereotype of each. Not every Catholic nor every Protestant fit into the established pattern, but the vast bulk of each of the ethnic communities did.

The founding of the Ulster government was bathed in blood, and the ritual response of the Protestant Unionist Party was to view all the Catholics as Sinn Fein nationalist supporters of the Free State of Ireland, a judgment that was substantially correct. Thus the initial governing premise of the unionists was that the Catholics were not only papists and thus inferior, but also traitors to the Stormont regime. As the years went by tensions cooled, and some Catholics came to an accommodation with the fact that Ulster was self-governing. By that time, however, the Catholics found that they were excluded from positions of power. The unionists, for psychological as well as for political reasons, continued to consider all Catholics traitors. Sir Basil Brooke, the minister of Agriculture in Ulster in 1934, commented: "The fact must be faced, however, that ninety-seven, if not one hundred percent of the Roman Catholics of Northern Ireland were disloyal and disruptive."[4] By the 1930s, the certitude (to say nothing of the statistics) of this comment reflects prejudice rather than common sense. For fifty years such attitudes created a pattern of discrimination and separation. The two groups perpetuated and reinforced the disparaging portraits that they had of each other.

Character of the Conflict

One's hopes for the solution offered in the 1998 Agreement, amelioration of the conflict, and potential cordiality between the Ulster unionists and Irish nationalists depend on the explanation one favors as to the fundamental cause of the conflict in Ulster. John Whyte discusses three Marxist and six non-Marxist interpretations of Northern Ireland, and Arendt Lipjhart offers ten different portraits of Northern Ireland, each emphasizing a facet of the crisis such as religion, colonialism, and pseudo-democracy.[5] The principal explanations rest on political, economic, psychological, geographic, sociological, and theological foundations and combinations thereof. Northern Ireland is certainly a multi-dimensional conflict, but it still collapses into political terms. Layers of antagonism between the communities, and the countries, produced intractable political consequences.

Religion

Religion plays a powerful role in the Northern Ireland conflict. The very labels used, Protestant and Catholic, ascribe an overtly religious antagonism and submerge the religious differences within each community. Religion, however, plays the role of an integrating value system at the center of a broader network of community features that provide for each group a distinct ethnic character. Cynthia Enloe, offering one among a plethora of definitions, sees an ethnic group as a group of people who are culturally distinct and view themselves as being so. The group shares common beliefs and values that to some degree set them apart.[6] The common bonds in such groups include such characteristics as religion, race, language, social mores, and national identity. In the province of Ulster the two communities are ethnically distinct; the central, but not sole, difference is religion. Religion, however, is accompanied by subtle, but real, differences in ethnic heritage, speech, and interpersonal relationships. More overt differences include those of sport, social life, music, dance, and education. Education provides distinctive differences in the community's view of history, tradition, and national identity.

In the historical development of the identities of the two ethnic communities, religion defined the distinction between them and consequently the political center of power around which they would revolve (and the symbolic color they would choose). In the case of the Catholics, it was Sinn Fein, Catholicism, Dublin, Ireland, and green; in the case of the Protestants, it was unionism, Protestantism,

London, Britain (or its regional center Belfast/Ulster), and orange. The lack of in-termarriage to any great degree also preserved a racial stock in each case, Anglo-Saxon and Scottish on the one hand, Celtic (or a Celtic blend) on the other. None of the identified differences in the two ethnic communities need necessarily lead to the incandescent hostility between them. On the contrary, the communities ex-hibited extensive similarities: They were all white European people who were deeply Christian and lived similar lives. Clearly the key ingredient was that which turned ethnic difference into ethnic hatred.

From the outset the interests that divided the Ulster planters and the indige-nous Catholics—land, religion, and power—were almost mutually exclusive. The conflict hinged on the expropriation of land owned by Catholics and transferred to Scots, Anglicans, and Presbyterians. History is replete with examples in which such actions engendered severe conflict between the groups involved, even if they shared the same ethnic identity and faith. The religious conflict was not exclu-sively a doctrinal debate as much as it was the use of political (i.e., legal) power to eradicate the Catholic faith through the Penal Laws.

Power

The clash of political interests was over the fundamental question of who would have the authority to rule. Picking a specific issue to represent the opposition of political interests must be symbolic only because such opposition has deep roots. Home Rule, however, represented for the Ulster Protestants the blunt threat of rule by the Catholic ethnic community. However constructed, Home Rule, explic-itly or by implication, meant that the Catholic majority would wield power over the Protestant minority in an Ireland including Ulster. The Catholic Church had become identified not only with the religious issue but also with the land issue and with the political thrust for Home Rule. To the Protestants this reinforced the ethnic divide, in which religion was central. (The irony in this is that the Hierarchy of the Catholic Church in Ireland had almost invariably supported British authority.)

The Irish-Ireland movement at the end of the nineteenth century had the effect of evoking in the Catholics of Ulster a powerful cultural identity that helped to define their national identity. This cultural nationalism was obviously not shared by the Protestants, who in turn reinforced their British national identity. Ethnic distinctiveness was strengthened by political conflict, which ran along the fault line of the ethnic divide, mapping the cultural differences onto the differences of national identity.

There are political contests in which power is diffused among multiple groups with cross-cutting interests of moderate intensity. These take place in arenas in which political institutions have multiple access points and are considered plural-ist. Favorable or unfavorable outcomes are shared among the contestants. Such contests will occasionally but not exclusively reinforce ethnic and cultural identity as opposed to political identity. However, when the political contest is between two groups and the favorable outcomes always favor one group, then the two groups not only will reinforce their ethnic identity but will do so in the context of superiority and inferiority, or oppressor and oppressed.

In Northern Ireland the movement from union with the United Kingdom to Home Rule to Partition created the political reality of dual minorities and the consequent impact on ethnicity. The Catholics are a minority in Northern Ireland and have been discriminated against politically and economically; thus they have reinforced their already strong ethnic identity, especially the religious and nationalist components. The Protestants are a minority in the whole of Ireland and consequently fear integration into a Catholic-dominated state in which their privilege would be eradicated; this coalesced their identity. Each group points to the practice of the other. The Catholics point to fifty years of unionist/Protestant/Orange rule in Ulster, the Protestants point to seventy-five years of nationalist/Catholic/Green rule in the Republic of Ireland. It is not difficult then to translate political differences into religious difference as a marker of different interests.

Under pressure ethnic groups in conflict tend to reinforce their own communal values and to stereotype their vision of the "out group." The other group is seen not only as different but as inferior. In the case of the Protestants this took the form of seeing the Catholics as garrulous, lazy, dirty, and superstitious. The Catholics, on the other hand, viewed the Protestants as cold-blooded, ruthless, inhumane, and oppressive. In Northern Ireland the "out group" or underclass was the Catholics. Political and economic advantage blended into and reinforced the Protestant stereotype of superiority. In Ireland as a whole, the Protestants were not an underclass, being traditionally ascendant, but they feared that they would become so in an Irish Catholic state. The antagonism between the two communities is rooted in political conflict that is split along ethnic lines. It is reinforced in emotional intensity by the perceptions of minority status by both communities and is expressed in the language of the central ethnic values, religion, and nationality.

Nationality

For the Ulster Protestant, however, the question of nationality is more difficult. The conflict in national terms is between Irish Catholics and Ulster Protestants. The Ulster Protestants, being Irish, that is residents of Ireland for nearly 400 years, do not have quite the same attitude about asserting their Britishness as do the Catholics their Irishness. The Ulster Protestant identifies with Britain in symbolic and political loyalty. This is the alternative to the identification the Irish Catholic asserts. Their British nationality remains qualified, however, by the fact that the claim is really Ulster-in-Britain nationality. A powerful pull on the Protestants in Northern Ireland is their identification with Ulster. The Ulster Protestant may not really have a nationality at all, that is, an Ulster nationality, but adopts the British nationality for essentially negative reasons, to not be part of Irish-Ireland.

The result for the Ulster Protestant is an absolutely frantic claim to Britishness, adopted about a century ago to preserve a dominant economic and political position. Interestingly enough, this has been expressed in a language of religious bigotry that repels a great number of British. The British in fact did not see the Ulster Protestants as British. Rather, they were seen as Irish, and though attached to the United Kingdom, they had been left alone and regarded as quite distinct. Many British had little or no identification with the Protestants of Ulster, and that number has increased to a large degree. This leaves the Ulster Protestants feeling extremely vulnerable and ultimately mistrustful of the British.

Historically the Irish nationalist position has been that the partition of Ireland was London's imperial theft of an Irish province thwarting the natural outcome of the Irish independence movement. So repugnant to the unionists was this position that their clasp on British identity exceeded their common bond with the mainland British. The claim by unionists to British identity also masked the differences within the Protestant unionist community as they were driven together to form a common front in the face of the constitutional question of Ulster. In fact, the unionist community was polarized by different views of what it meant to be Protestant and to be British. The Democratic Unionist Party of Ian Paisley represents a view of Ulster that makes fundamentalist Presbyterianism and the preservation of that religion by remaining in the United Kingdom the dominant agenda item. Union is a necessity to preserve faith and insofar as London does not advance or protect that interest then the "contract" with Britain is invalidated.[7] The conditional nature of their support for the Crown, coupled with their tradition of seeing themselves as people of the book, as having a covenant with God, and as a people under siege, magnifies the Democratic Unionists' mistrust of everyone and leads to a paranoid style of politics. Thus the virulent rejection of the Agreement of April 1998 by some Ulster unionists.

For the Church of Ireland/England confessants the prime issue is being British and the Union with Britain and a justification for that goal is the question of freedom of religious practice. The Official Unionist Party held this point of view with somewhat more self-confidence and less of a trapped-in-a-corner approach to politics. Class differences are clear: The Democratic Unionist Party drew from the petite bourgeoisie and the working class while the Official Unionist Party drew from the business community and landed gentry.

Discrimination and Separation

Discrimination

Governmental discrimination in Northern Ireland fell into several categories: voting, employment, housing, regional development, and law enforcement. In the realm of voting (after 1920) Ulster retained property qualifications for local government voting and provided additional votes for businessmen. The effect, of course, was to discriminate against the poor or non-property owner. Because historically the Catholics were poorer, the exclusion fell most heavily on them. When property qualifications were coupled with the pattern of gerrymandering districts to the advantage of the unionists, the effect was to dilute the vote of the Catholics. The most oft-cited example is the city of Derry, in which a majority of the population, 60 percent, was Catholic. Property qualifications allowed only 40 percent of the Catholics to vote but 50 percent of the Protestants. The three districts were aligned to allow slender Protestant majorities in two districts to elect twelve members to the city council, while a massive Catholic majority in the third elected only eight. The net effect was that 60 percent of the voters elected 40 percent of the members. Catholic nationalists were not prevalent in government on the local or Stormont levels.

Not surprisingly, a great number of Catholics rejected the idea of serving the Stormont regime, but even given that reticence, Catholics held a disproportionately low number of government positions in those years: in the Royal Ulster Constabulary, 10 to 12 percent; in the judicial system, 8 percent; in the higher-level civil service, 5 percent; and in local government, Derry 15 percent and Belfast 5 percent.[8] In the allocation of public housing the local governments used the location and the tenants as a way to reinforce control of an area. The practice varied from place to place, but the cumulative effect was both a form of political manipulation and a denial of housing to Catholics.

The Catholic and Protestant populations in Ulster were mixed together in a patchwork quilt fashion. Within the cities the sections were also mixed, but in the province as a whole more Catholics lived in the western section, separated from the eastern part by the Bann River. The Stormont government did little to prevent the decay of that region or to rebuild it when the population began to decline. Industrial development, new towns, and transportation were all focused in the east. In 1965, for example, a new university was located in Coleraine, in the northeast. This rejection of Derry's claim from the west occurred despite the fact that Derry was four times the size of Coleraine.

Perhaps the most frustrating form of discrimination for the Catholics was in the area of law enforcement. In 1922, under conditions of intense sectarian conflict, the Stormont government passed the Special Powers Act. Renewed regularly, it was made permanent in 1933. The Act empowered the home secretary to put forth a wide array of regulations, including curfews, searches without warrant, the banning of organizations as illegal, legal forcible entry, and arrest and detention of individuals on mere suspicion. In 1951 the Act was augmented to include the prohibition of offensive flags and emblems and public meetings. The effect of the Act was to create somewhat elastic powers to curtail threats to civil disorder. Catholics were opposed to the Act, not only because it was legally questionable in its extraordinary grant of authority but also because it was used almost invariably only against the Catholics. The Catholic political associations were banned but not the Protestant. The IRA was, of course, banned, but Protestant paramilitary organizations weren't forbidden until the 1960s. The internment provisions were used exclusively against Catholics.

Adding fuel to the fire was the Royal Ulster Constabulary (RUC). Almost completely Protestant in composition, this police force persistently directed its threats and coercive acts at the Catholic community. The RUC was rarely used against Protestant mobs or during Protestant demonstrations, but the Catholics felt the brunt of it for fifty years. The B Specials, a third component of law enforcement, was an auxiliary force. The B Specials were completely Protestant, poorly trained, heavily armed, overtly anti-Catholic, and responsible for a number of deaths in clashes with Catholics. For Catholics the law in Northern Ireland was an instrument of harassment, not a guarantee of equal treatment.

Nongovernmental discrimination occurred in the economic sphere. The Ulster Unionist Party was anti-labor, devoid of a social or economic policy worthy of the name, and committed only to the preservation of the Union with Britain. When established, the government of Northern Ireland was to turn its revenues over to London, but by 1938 London was the financial guarantor of a debt-ridden Northern Ireland. Unemployment in the 1920s began to rise as the linen and shipbuilding markets diminished. By the late 1920s the unemployment rate had reached approximately 20 percent, and the Depression drove the rate to over 25 percent for a decade. No ships were built in Belfast in 1933 for the first time in a century, and 90 percent of the workers in that industry were unemployed. The steady downward spiral in the economy meant that the competition for jobs was fierce, and the resulting animosities augmented both discrimination and separation. Catholics blamed the government for both their unemployment and their exclusion from the work that did exist. Protestant employers hired Protestants under the impetus of their traditional enmity against Catholics and the prodding of organizations such as the Ulster Protestant League. In 1935 violent clashes left 12 dead and 600 wounded as economic deprivation and sectarian hatred combined.

World War II brought prosperity to Northern Ireland, but although economic growth was sustained to some degree, the pattern of discrimination in employment continued. Unemployment was higher in the area west of the Bann and in Catholic areas of all cities in Ulster. Extreme cases are necessarily only illustrative of the problem, but they are revealing. The Harland and Wolf Shipyard in 1971 employed 9,000 manual workers, of whom 500 were Catholic; Mackies Engineering employed 8,500 workers and of them 120 were Catholic. From 1929 until 1972, when it was suspended by London, the Stormont government either overtly discriminated against Catholics or encouraged such oppression.

Separation

Coupled with, and encouraged by, discrimination was the separation of the two ethnic communities. Separation, however, was voluntary because each group sought to preserve its heritage and identity. The principal conservators of the separate traditions were the schools and the churches, which socialized the children into separate value systems.

In a rare display of unanimity, all the churches in Ulster opposed a bill put forth in 1923 that called for mixing the children in the public schools and hiring teachers without regard to religion. The Catholic Church had fought this battle before, from 1831 to 1883, when the Church had slowly transformed the British system of education in Ireland into a denominational one. Clearly, in Protestant-dominated Ulster, the Catholics resisted non-denominational schools, even at the cost of losing state support, and the Protestant churches and the Orange Order also challenged the "godless" schools. By 1925 the law had been undermined, and by 1930 education was again denominational. The state supported Protestant education financially but did not provide any money for Catholic education until 1930. After 1939 the government subsidized Catholic education at 50 percent of cost; that figure was raised to 65 percent in 1947 and later to 80 percent. This differential could be seen as discrimination toward the Catholics rather than separation, but in fact financial independence preserved Church control over the schools.

The resulting differences are obvious, not only in the realm of religious education but also in the children's views of their culture and identity. Catholics learn Irish history and absorb a view of the world of religion, politics, and social life that is rooted in nationalist images. Protestants learn British history and a unionist view of the world.[9] Clearly the education system was designed to reinforce identity with each community, not to transcend it. In an utterly divided sectarian atmosphere such thinking was no surprise, but it contributed little to empathy between the communities then, nor does it today.

Church affiliation in Northern Ireland is extremely tenacious. Over 40 percent of the people are Catholics and one-third Presbyterians—the rest are Anglicans and Methodists—and these religions make strong claims on the life of a person. In the period from 1920 to 1972 the Catholic Church in the Free State/Republic gave no indication to Protestants in the north that the Church's influence was diminishing in the south. The Catholic aspects of the 1937 Constitution hardened the Presbyterians' exaggerated claim that Eire was a theocratic state. Those preachers who had a vested interest in the sectarian division in Ulster could use the Catholicity of the Republic to pull their flocks politically ever closer to Protestant fundamentalism and separation from the Catholics in their own province. Catholic doctrines—such as those on divorce, interfaith marriage, abortion, birth control, and the Papacy—were seen by the Protestants as proof that Catholics submissively conformed to the dictates of an authoritarian church.

Church and school reinforced a pattern of separate social life and values. Church-related social organizations drew the people of each ethnic community together for song, dance, and companionship—Orange halls for Protestants and parish halls for Catholics. Sports were another cause of division, especially after the creation of the Gaelic Athletic Association. For Catholics the principal sports were hurling and Gaelic football; for Protestants, rugby and cricket. The professional associations, or special-interest organizations devoted to art or film, were non-sectarian in a gingerly way, especially in the later years. The closer such groups got to the working class, however, the more they were divided into Catholic or Protestant organizations.

Symbols reinforced the division. The Orange parades on July 12 of each year to celebrate the victory of King "Billy" at the Battle of the Boyne in 1690 were an extraordinary display of Protestant triumphalism that alienated the Catholics. Conversely, playing the Republic's anthem "The Soldiers Song" (or "A Nation Once Again"), flying the tricolor, and celebrating the Easter Rising all grated on the Protestant community. More than once such observances led to severe sectarian violence in Belfast and Derry.

Less formal differences have become magnified over the years into sectarian separation. The Ulster Protestants are laconic in speech, the Catholics are more effusive; Catholics use Sunday for recreation, most Protestants do not. Catholics have higher rates of unemployment, which is transmuted by the Protestants into a stereotype of lazy irresponsibility. Catholics react to Protestant taciturnity and reserve with a stereotype of cruelty and coldness. Perpetuation of both discrimination and separation was ensured as children absorbed their community's values and hatreds. Violence was regular enough in each generation so that the sectarian hatreds were annealed by looting, bloodshed, burning houses, and police searches, which ensured that there would be little or no diminution of the rift.

For the entire fifty-year span of the Stormont regime Northern Ireland was governed by one party, the Unionist Party. Leadership was stable; James Craig, the first prime minister, ruled for twenty years. The Unionist political program was simple, to maintain the Union with Britain. Unionist organization was powerful, interlocked as it was with the Orange Order, which in turn interlocked with the Ulster Protestant churches of all social levels. The political opposition ran the gamut from minuscule to nonexistent. Labour could not transcend the sectarian split in the working class in Ulster and so could never mobilize non-sectarian voting on economic issues. Thus voters remained in the Unionist or Nationalist parties. Sinn Fein sporadically contested elections, but elected candidates would not take their seats. The Nationalist Party, representing the Catholic community, could never hold enough seats to make any political difference and was relegated to the work of ameliorating problems for the Catholic community.

The British government after World War II forced a reluctant Unionist Party to accept the program of social welfare that was being enacted in London. Payments for unemployment, illness, orphanhood, retirement, health care, housing, and a host of other programs flowed into Ulster from London. One effect was an improvement in the standard of living of Catholics. Another effect was a reinforcement of the difference between the two regions of Ireland. Political differences were now multiplied by significant differences in state-supported welfare programs. By 1955 a backward Ulster had gone through a social transformation. The change in Northern Ireland had some effect on the Unionist Party; it developed a liberal wing—liberal, that is, in Unionist terms. The possibility of a Catholic being a Unionist candidate was even raised; the Orange Order, however, quickly put a stop to that notion.

Educational opportunity increased when Catholics took advantage of 1945 and 1947 British acts that provided for free secondary schooling and then went on to gain a university education. Catholics moved into the middle class in growing numbers as the professions of teaching, medicine, and law were opened to them. Many of these Catholics were less interested in the older nationalist dream of Irish unification than in obtaining first-class citizenship in Northern Ireland.

The IRA

A diminishing impact, splits in the ranks, imprisonment, and a political position now well out of the mainstream of public support left the Irish Republican Army a powerless, pallid shell of its earlier incarnation in the fight for Irish independence. A last gasp in the 1950s seemed to signal the end of the IRA. Between 1956 and 1962 the IRA, now long disconnected from its heroic past but very much a prisoner of it, attempted to bomb away the border of Northern Ireland. Clearly devoid of a Clausevitz in their ranks, this effort was a dismal failure and provoked security crackdowns on both sides of the border. The IRA lamented the lack of public support and said that Irish "minds had been deliberately distracted from the supreme issue facing the Irish people—the unity and freedom of Ireland."[10]

The IRA was rebuilt, however, in the 1960s upon decidedly Leftist lines under the influence of Ray Johnston, and it engaged in sporadic violence and political propaganda.[11] The Marxist influence, however, disconcerted old-line republicans who were uncomfortable with socialist ideology but who supported the militant stance.

In the Republic the rise of Sean Lemass represented a new stage in Fianna Fail's traditional leadership and policies. In Ulster the choice of Terence O'Neill as prime minister in 1963 represented the victory of the liberal wing of the Unionist Party. To the ultraloyalists O'Neill's actions were shocking, to liberals they were ground-breaking, to people used to politics outside of Northern Ireland they were quite ordinary and would scarcely warrant such a fuss. O'Neill, for example, visited a Catholic school in 1965 and exchanged visits with Sean Lemass in the same year, thus initiating official contacts between the two regions of Ireland.

Tensions in Northern Ireland had cooled, the IRA campaign had been a failure, and talks between the two governments were proceeding tentatively on economic matters. To all appearances every indication was that Ireland was entering a new stage in intergovernmental and intercommunal relationships, but less attention was directed at the more negative developments that were occurring during the same period. It was true that Ireland was entering a new stage, but that stage was to be one of the most bitter and bloody in the long history of antagonism between Catholics and Protestants.

Ian Paisley

The Reverend Ian Paisley, a Presbyterian fundamentalist minister and a dema-
gogue, was attacking the Unionist Party from the right and denouncing the drift
toward liberalism by the O'Neill wing. In the mid-1960s Paisley broke away from
the Unionists to form the Protestant Unionist Party (later to become the
Democratic Unionist Party) to organize the more militant loyalists. Paisley directed his attacks not only at the unionists but also at all attempts to establish a
dialogue with Catholics. Paisley's demagogic appeal to working-class Protestants
and his militant tactics earned his party seats both in the Stormont Assembly and
in Parliament. In 1966 a Protestant paramilitary force was created and took the
name of the old Ulster Volunteer Force of 1913. This group announced that it
would execute IRA members; it did, killing two Catholic men. That same year the
organization was outlawed by the Special Powers Act, but it did not disappear.
The year 1968 was marked by the political activity of the Northern Ireland Civil
Rights Association and what Conor Cruise O'Brien had called "the frozen violence" in Ulster promptly melted.

British Policy in Ulster, 1922–1968

It is a commonplace to ascribe to the British a bumbling passivity in the realm of
political initiatives on Northern Ireland on the one hand and an unsheathed ruth-
lessness in the realm of security on the other. Both pictures may be overdrawn to
the extent that it is easy to pillory London for its more than obvious deficiencies,
vacillations, and duplicity. On the other hand, the actions of a relentless group of
IRA paramilitaries who murdered families and then later "apologized" while at
the same time demanding the highest standards of civil rights and judicial procedures to protect them from an "unfair" judicial system must lead to a modicum of
caution in making glib judgments about either side of the political divide. Was
British policy so ineffectual, or to put it another way, what have been the British
initiatives on the north and what have been their effects? To better understand the
conflict-regulation processes in Ulster we can examine the structures of the political institutions and the model of conflict regulation underpinning them, the degree to which the structures of government in Ulster aligned with the landscape
of conflict, the degree of political will in London to put political reforms in place,
and the consistency of the goals of British policy.

The Stormont government, created in 1920 by a legislative act, was designed to
remedy the failure of the Home Rule Act of 1912 by creating two Parliaments for
the island of Ireland. The unwillingness of the Ulster unionists to be part of a
state governed by Catholic nationalists was accommodated by the separate assembly. When the Anglo-Irish Treaty went into effect in 1922 that structure was in
place. London's goal in dealing with the Irish question was to find a means to keep
Ireland in the Commonwealth, accommodate Irish demands for autonomy (in

the south), and deal with unionist intransigence (in the north). Having set up the Stormont government, London essentially ignored Ulster for fifty years. The structure was federalist with respect to the United Kingdom and democratic majoritarian with respect to internal rule. In reality it was a form of political isolation and majority oppression. The Unionists used this form of government to preserve their dominant position unfettered by London and the price was paid by the Catholic minority. That the minority community in a situation of ethnic conflict may be deprived of basic rights or access to the goods of society is not a surprise. Successful or effective forms of managing conflict in divided societies often involve deviations from the majoritarian democratic model.[12] The question is, were there ways to manage conflict better than abdicating central authority to a federal unit governed by a permanent ethnic majority that was bitterly antagonistic to another permanent ethnic minority? The answer to that question is certainly yes, as is shown by the record of discrimination and abuses in the realm of police and judicial functions provoking regular and severe outbursts of violence in the fifty years of the Stormont government.[13]

The form of ethnic conflict management that the British used in the Stormont government of Northern Ireland ensured that the minority was "unlikely to accept highly unpalatable governmental decisions or procedural rules which invest the majority with the authority to impose its will on the minority."[14] Thus the initial form of government in Ulster was marked by structures likely to polarize the communities, oppress the minority community, and exclude the metropolitan capital, London, from responsibility. Education policy passed by the Parliament in London, for example, was rejected in Ulster, and police powers were draconian.

The United States and Northern Ireland, 1922–1968

Irish immigration to the United States after the Great Hunger was extensive. Assimilation and success followed for these emigrants in later generations. The election of John F. Kennedy to the presidency symbolically sealed the Irish Americans' place in the U.S. social fabric. The role of the United States in the Irish question has been significant from the nineteenth century up to 1998. The Good Friday Agreement was brokered by a former U.S. senator in negotiations undertaken in no small part because of the efforts of U.S. President Bill Clinton. The role of the United States in Northern Ireland is considered here in parallel to the unfolding of events in Ireland.

Many observers have noted the "arcadian," romantic vision of Irish nationalism held by Irish Americans from the Famine to the Free State. The post-Famine migration from Ireland brought to the United States not those who felt they were making a free choice to seek a new life in the New World but rather those who felt they were in exile from their homeland as a result of British policy.[15] American Irish bore a deep and enduring hatred for the British that was in no way ameliorated by the events of the early part of the twentieth century, when

Britain reneged on the Home Rule Bill of 1912, crushed the Rising of 1916, and attempted to defeat Sinn Fein in the Anglo-Irish War from 1918 to 1921. Irish Americans played a not unimportant role in that period, using their wallets as a means to express their rancor by supporting Sinn Fein.

After the formation of the Free State in 1922, which the Irish Americans by and large favored, their interest in Ireland dropped off sharply.[16] Irish American nationalists' view of Ireland and Northern Ireland remained unchanged to the point of sometimes making the Irish American a figure of derision to American nativists as a stereotyped "professional" Irishman: fighting, drinking, and hating the British.[17] After the creation of the Free State prosperity did not come to the Irish, but it did come to the Irish Americans. As Andrew Greeley has shown, the Irish Catholics in the United States became the most successful gentile group in the country.[18] The Irish Americans were assimilating so successfully that the situation in Ireland slipped down their political agenda to the point of invisibility. Intense, specifically Irish ethnic identity came to reside in older urban neighborhoods, in Irish social clubs, in civil service unions, and in the Ancient Order of Hibernians. Irish American nationalism was nurtured for more than a half century, at a low temperature to be sure, but always sustained by the long memory of British excesses in Ireland. All nationalisms are, of course, a bouillabaisse of myths, historical facts and historical fiction, posited values, and ascribed national characteristics, and in this respect Irish nationalism did not differ from any other version. In the United States, however, it was not subject to slow evolution engendered by the inexorable passage of time and events. Irish Americans held their myths antiseptically intact.

Years of Violence, 1968–1972

The Northern Ireland Civil Rights Association (NICRA), formed in 1967, did not set out to destroy the Stormont government, drive the British from Northern Ireland, or unite with the Republic. The group was composed of both Catholics and Protestants, and their objective was to reform the political system by ending discrimination in hiring and housing, eliminating the B Specials, ending the Special Powers Act, redistributing electoral boundaries, and expunging electoral restrictions. The methods they adopted were those of the U.S. Civil Rights Movement: nonviolent demonstrations and marches. The Unionist Party became completely disoriented by a change in Catholic political demands and methods. The spark that lit the tinder was a demonstration in Derry in October 1968. The demonstration had been banned by government officials because they feared violent confrontation with Protestants. Violence did occur, but it was between the RUC and the demonstrators; the police attacked the crowd, and eighty-eight police and demonstrators were injured. Feelings were aroused among the civil rights people, especially the more radical student movement (called People's Democracy) at Queen's University. Of lasting importance was the television exposure to the wider world of the Republic of Ireland and Britain of the "normal" procedures of the Ulster government and police. The glare of the camera brought international pressure on London to institute reforms, which then brought pressure on Belfast.

Unionist politicians could never quite comprehend why the world viewed the Stormont government as a backward group of oppressive bigots. Conservative Unionists were incapable of differentiating between the middle class civil rights activities and the Catholic nationalist irredentist politics of fifty years earlier. Terence O'Neill knew the difference, but he was caught in a trap between the loyalist Unionists and the British government, which was urging reforms along the lines demanded by the civil rights movement. In a 1968 speech O'Neill said Ulster stood at the crossroads between perpetual violence and an attempt to provide justice. O'Neill's personal commitment to reform was sincere, but he pressed the reforms on an increasingly recalcitrant Unionist Party. The reforms included replacing the local government in Derry with a Development Commission, appointing commissioners to investigate governmental discrimination, and rearranging housing allocation procedures into a more equitable system. Promised, but not implemented, were changes in the election laws and limitations on the Special Powers Act. O'Neill also dismissed William Craig, the conservative Unionist minister for Home Affairs, whose response to the civil rights agitation was simply to yell, "No surrender," and crush it.

The reforms had several effects, the first of which was to harden the position of the conservative Unionists against both O'Neill, who they believed was selling out, and the Catholics, who needed to be controlled (the civil rights movement, from their perspective, was simply Catholics up to their old tricks). The reforms also split the civil rights movement. The moderates, responding to O'Neill's plea, wished to wait and see if the government would undertake additional reforms. On the other hand, the People's Democracy, the radical student movement at Queen's University Belfast, wished to continue pressure on the government until complete reform was forthcoming. The next march from Belfast to Derry was organized by the People's Democracy because Protestants and moderates were slipping away from the NICRA. At Burntollet Bridge in January 1969 the marchers were viciously attacked by both Protestant mobs and the police. The antiwar demonstrators in the United States used to chant, "The whole world is watching," when police would break up demonstrations. Burntollet was watched with revulsion by British, U.S., and European television viewers as marchers were beaten with clubs and pipes. The Catholic community in Derry was attacked by the police as well. Tension was high in the following months, and there were additional clashes in Newry, Strabane, Derry, and Belfast.

In February 1969 an election was held for the Stormont Parliament, and the results revealed the polarity of Ulster politics. O'Neill was embarrassed by the strength of the hardline Unionists, who were mobilized by Craig and Paisley. The Nationalist Party virtually disappeared and was replaced by the Catholic civil rights activists led by John Hume and Austin Currie. The Unionists were frag-mented, and the liberal Unionists certainly gained no mandate from the people. Under pressure from London and his Unionist colleagues and beset by the violent demonstrations and marches, O'Neill stepped down in April. Major James D. Chichester-Clark became prime minister. In April an election was held in mid-Ulster for a parliamentary seat and Bernadette Devlin, a young leader of the People's Democracy, won. The result made Catholic sentiment clear: In July Devlin, a member of Parliament, was hurling paving stones at the police during riots provoked by the Orange Parade.

The Apprentice Boys' March in Derry is held each August 12 by Protestants to celebrate the siege of Londonderry in spring 1689, when the city held out against the forces of James II. Two hundred and eighty years later the city was to be the site of another form of siege. The parade in 1969 sparked a confrontation that es-calated into a virtual civil insurrection. The RUC tried to enter the Catholic dis-trict, the Bogside, and was driven out. The district was sealed off by the residents, who denied entry to the police resulting in the forming of "no go" areas. The B Specials were called in and restraint disappeared on all sides. In Belfast rioting and confrontation between Protestant and Catholic mobs broke out on August 14 as the violence continued in Derry. Over 100 homes were burned out as Protestant mobs attacked Catholic areas. In August 1969, mob violence, sniping, and police charges were completely without restraint in Derry and Belfast. The Catholic districts had been sealed off; the Royal Ulster Constabulary—never a wholly non-sectarian body—was under pressure and exhausted. The B Specials, clearly a sectarian organization, had been called in. The result: Police fire killed a nine year old and five men were killed.

The Stormont government could not keep order; British troops entered Derry on August 14 and Belfast one day later. The violence continued, but it subsided substantially. On August 13 the prime minister of the Republic, Jack Lynch, stated on television, "The Irish Government can no longer stand idly by and see innocent people injured and perhaps worse," and raised the specter that haunted the Protestant community: "Reunification of the national territory can provide the only permanent solution of the problem."[19] The Protestants became con-vinced that a united Ireland, not civil rights, was the fundamental objective of the Catholics.

The Chichester-Clark government was no more effective than O'Neill's had been at containing extreme unionist sentiment or the violence. A number of sig-nificant reforms were enacted at this time under British pressure, such as elimina-tion of the B Specials, disarming the RUC, reforming local election laws, passing an Incitement to Hatred Bill, and creating a Central Housing Authority. By now, however, reform was seen by the Unionists as a concession to the "rebels" and by Catholics as mere window dressing in the face of RUC and B Special violence.

In the Catholic neighborhoods of Derry and Belfast in 1969 the statement, "IRA-I Ran Away," was written on the walls. Such comments were an embarrassment to that organization, which until the mid-1960s had seen its role as protector of the Catholic community. The initial response of the IRA to the introduction of British troops into Ireland in August 1969 was essentially throwing stones and occasionally a petrol bomb. The IRA is said to have had available at that time only ten guns.[20] In early 1970, under the pressure of events, the IRA split in two. The Northern Ireland IRA developed its own command, and at the same time the new Provisional IRA broke away from the old Official IRA.[21] The Provisionals (Provos) sought to provide protection to the Catholic community by using guns and working toward the restoration of a united Ireland. The Provos drew support from traditional Irish nationalists, especially in the United States, and after the split sometimes only an uneasy truce existed between the two IRA organizations.

In June 1970 the Conservatives came to power in London, and a combination of circumstances caused the situation in Northern Ireland to deteriorate rapidly. Although the Unionists were more politically in tune with the Conservative Party in London, the Conservatives knew little or nothing about Ulster. Ted Heath, the British prime minister, appointed Reginald Maudling home secretary, with responsibility for Ulster. Maudling's efforts were decidedly less than spectacular. The tail of Stormont wagged the dog of London during this period, and the use of the Army and of repressive measures was approved by Maudling because he was relying on the perceptions and inclinations of the Unionists. The army began using CS gas, which, though not lethal, is debilitating and indiscriminate. The British Army entered Ulster to keep the peace. Initially the Catholics were buoyed by the arrival of troops who represented security from both Protestant mobs and the RUC. At this point, however, several inexorable pressures began to converge. First, the direction of the security policy was in the hands of the Unionist leaders in the Stormont government; second, the British Army is an army and given time will act like an army, not, for example, like social workers, policemen, or officers of the judiciary; third, the IRA made an effort to drive a wedge between the Catholics and the Army, identifying the Army's measures as those of the traditional enemy, Britain.

Neither the Heath government in London nor the British Army knew anything about Ulster. They relied on the Ulster Unionists for policy guidance and the Unionist vision of Catholic agitation could not differentiate between the current civil rights activities and the nationalist politics of 1918–1923. In fact, the Unionists treated the former as if it were the latter, thus ensuring in due course that the former would become the latter for some nationalists. In June 1970 Catholics were not defended by the Army even when attacked by Protestant mobs.

Also in June the Army imposed a thirty-six-hour curfew and began searching for weapons. Armies are good at searching for weapons, but their approach is characterized by a certain insensitivity. At the end of the curfew, five civilians were dead and sixty injured. As Tim Pat Coogan notes: "The result was a morass of brutality, and propaganda fodder—kicked down doors, ripped up floorboards, beaten up young men and, worse, occasional bursts of ill directed rifle fire that claimed civilian life."[22] In 1972 alone there were more than 36,000 house searches conducted mostly by the Army and directed overwhelmingly at Catholic homes. From 1969 to 1972, 129 civilians were killed by the Army or security forces. The use of rubber bullets, a purportedly minimum-force weapon, by the Army and police led to three reported deaths and numerous injuries.

This fertile ground was exploited by the IRA during these years to build support and to redefine the enemy. In 1971 the IRA began killing British soldiers which, of course, caused the Army to react. They turned on the Catholic community from whence the threat emerged; they increased security measures; and they were instruments and/or were portrayed by the IRA to be instruments of the Unionists. The circle was complete: Army activity alienated Catholics, Catholics supported and joined the IRA, the IRA attacked the Army, the Army cracked down on Catholics. The original bond between the Catholics and the British Army was broken and the Army was now seen as another arm of the Stormont government, imposing its will by force on the Catholics. The RUC, the Ulster Defense Regiment (a part-time security force), and the Army were all at the service of Chichester-Clark, who was on a complete law-and-order path.

The "marching season" of July and August 1970 brought bloody clashes in Belfast and Derry. The anti-Unionist groups welded together in August to form the Social Democratic and Labour Party (SDLP). The title reflects the variety of political forces brought to the new party. The first leader, Gerry Fitt, hewed to a republican-labor standard, and John Hume, presently the head of the SDLP, came from the civil rights movement; other members were from the Nationalist Party and the Northern Ireland Labour Party. The SDLP's program was socialist and non-sectarian and advocated the reunification of Ireland through peaceful, democratic processes. However, the reunification position offset the non-sectarian posture, so the bulk of the party's supporters were Catholic.

Early 1971 brought fresh rounds of violence, and the first British soldier was killed by the IRA in February. Chichester-Clark's response was to demand more troops. In March Chichester-Clark was replaced by Brian Faulkner as prime minister, and the right wing of the Unionists agitated for an increasing crackdown on the violence. Faulkner took a two-pronged approach: He continued to implement reforms but also pressed for an increase in law and order. The situation was no better throughout summer 1971, however, and the shooting of two men in Derry by the British Army prompted the SDLP to withdraw from Stormont. This action was ineffectual, but it did indicate, along with the persistent violence, that the Stormont regime could do nothing more than satisfy an increasingly truculent Unionist right wing.

The Provisional IRA had undertaken a bombing campaign throughout the summer, which added to Unionist fury. The response was internment, which was introduced on August 9, 1971. Approximately 350 people were arrested at the outset and put in detention centers. The Catholic community was quickly radicalized because the policy of internment was directed solely at the IRA. The manner in which internment was carried out did not help either: people were beaten, homes were searched, and innocent people arrested. Those interned were often older men or had been inactive IRA members for many years. Internees were overwhelmingly Catholic; moreover, they were treated harshly, virtually up to the point of torture. The current leaders of the IRA were not interned, and the movement surged with the addition of new members who were totally alienated from the London and Belfast governments. The effect of internment was antipodal to its intent. The Catholic community was galvanized into unity, support for the IRA soared, violence escalated rapidly, and the number of deaths in the next four months was almost six times as high as in the previous seven months. The Catholic community withheld rents, and Catholics withdrew from public office and local government. In October the SDLP set up an alternative assembly, indicating the degree to which the two communities were distant and hostile.

The Catholics, in effect, had been driven into the hands of the IRA. The government lost all ability to govern in the Catholic ghettos. Normal patterns of living disappeared and were replaced by a form of anarchy, with troops in the streets, fires at night, homes burned out by the hundreds, bombs exploding in businesses, and snipers shooting at soldiers. Presiding over this chaos were Brian Faulkner and the Unionists. Ian Paisley formed the Democratic Unionist Party because Faulkner was not being harsh enough for his taste. Faulkner was caught between the Unionists and the Catholics. Unionists saw reform as the destruction of their statelet and were willing to shoot Catholics to preserve the Stormont rule. Catholics had abandoned civil rights and were now fighting for survival under British troops.

In January 1972 paratroopers shot thirteen men dead and wounded more when they encountered an unauthorized civil rights march in Derry. It would be hard to conceive of a way to drive the Catholics to further fury and alienation, but Bloody Sunday, as the event was called, accomplished that end. In the Republic of Ireland the British Embassy was burned to the ground by a mob a few days later. The specifics concerning the provocation of the paratroopers were submerged in the bloody encounters that followed. William Craig drew the conservative, or traditional, Unionists together in a new organization entitled the Vanguard Movement, which included a young Unionist named David Trimble. Craig drew strong working-class support for an extremely militant line on the preservation of Stormont. Protestant paramilitary organizations such as the Ulster Defense Association were linked to the Vanguard Movement. Protestants, in fact, feared a united Ireland more than they loved the Stormont government. The society they had preserved for fifty years was shattered, but they could still preserve the raison d'être of Ulster, political separation from the Republic. Thus the Protestants directed violence against the Catholic community because it was with the Catholics that the ultimate threat to Ulster resided.

In March 1972 the Heath government finally prorogued the Northern Ireland Parliament "temporarily," and the Unionist Party no longer had a political structure through which to maintain its domination. William Whitelaw, the new secretary of state for Northern Ireland, was charged with finding a new foundation for governing because the Stormont regime demonstrably could not do so. The collapse of the Stormont government was not the destruction of a stable civic order based on popular support. On the contrary, the regime was capable of little more than perpetuating itself. Economic growth and employment came as a result of World War II, and as soon as the war ended the economic situation began to decay to levels only slightly above the prewar years. Social welfare and social services were pressed on Stormont by London, paid for by London (because the tax base of the province could not support such programs), and monitored by London.

In matters of local authority and law enforcement the record was one of anti-Catholic discrimination and heavy-handed brutality. The regime did only one thing well: It preserved the colonial relic of the nineteenth-century Protestant ascendancy through the instruments of the Unionist Party and the Orange Order, which were based on opposition to a united Ireland. The regime had little will or incentive to transform or create. Unionist politics was a politics of preserving the abusive use of power under the guise of majority rule in a provincial backwater supported by British taxpayers. Few tears were shed by Ulster Catholics, citizens of the Republic, citizens of Britain, or even some Ulster Protestants when Stormont collapsed after half a century of being "a Protestant Parliament and a Protestant State."[23]

British Policy in Ulster, 1968–1972

After the explosion of violence in 1969 the British government found itself in the position of attempting to protect the Catholic community while the law enforcement powers were in the hands of the local Unionist government. The Unionist government responded to the emerging civil rights movement, the student radicals at Queen's University, and the protests of the local citizens at police abuses as they always had, with the truncheon, arrest without warrant, internment, and repression. When the British entered this environment in 1969 they had no grasp of the political and security dynamics of Ulster or the changes in the Catholic community and the absence of change in the Unionist community, and they found themselves willingly or unwittingly partners or instruments of the Unionist law enforcement policies. Within months the Catholics were at odds with the British troops, and it finally became clear to London that the Stormont government could not maintain order but in fact was, proverbially, part of the problem not part of the solution. The British answer was direct rule, and they suspended the Stormont government.

The United States and Northern Ireland, 1968–1972

In 1969, in the immediate aftermath of the violence in Northern Ireland, Irish Americans were galvanized into action to help the Catholic nationalists of the north. The only ideological garb available to put the Northern conflict into a political context was the well-worn cloak of Irish American nationalism. The most militant of the IRA factions reinforced this perspective to gain political and, more important, financial support. Thus grassroots Irish Americans were reviving and/or adopting a conception of the Ulster crisis that was relatively clear, simple and . . . well out of date. The irony was that the particular blend of U.S. working class conservative attitudes and traditionally militant Irish nationalism produced a group of people who did not share an agenda about Ulster with any group in Ireland, north or south.

Irish American nationalism was initially amorphous. Apart from the Ancient Order of Hibernians, which was founded in the nineteenth century, the first militant organization was the Northern Aid Committee, formed in 1970 and known as NORAID. Support for Sinn Fein and the IRA by NORAID was explicit despite the fact that the Irish Americans shared little of the left-wing, socialist, revolutionary ideology of the Official IRA and later the Provisional IRA. The Irish National Caucus followed in 1974, with the goal of lobbying Congress and mobilizing public opinion on the Ulster question. Many smaller groups followed.

What of Irish American elites? In the early 1970s their response was not unlike that of the grassroots, condemning British policy and calling for a united Ireland. Senator Edward M. "Ted" Kennedy, for example, made frequent statements that compared the British in Ulster to the United States in Vietnam, and in a 1971 Senate resolution he called for a withdrawal of all British forces from Ulster and for a united Ireland. He repeated that call when he held hearings on Northern Ireland in the Senate in 1972. In 1973 he published an article in *Foreign Policy* in which he argued that Ulster was an international issue and warranted intervention by the international community (although by this time Kennedy's views were beginning to move beyond his 1969–1971 positions).[24] Kennedy was not alone in this response; Congressman Thomas P. "Tip" O'Neill had collected the signatures of 100 members of Congress on a letter to President Nixon calling upon him to protest the discrimination against Catholics in Northern Ireland. O'Neill indicated to John Hume that he had been a contributor to NORAID during this period.[25] Then Congressman, and later Governor, Hugh Carey of New York introduced a resolution into the House similar to Kennedy's in the Senate and called the British Army "thugs" in 1971.[26] Sharing similar views at the time, Congressman Mario Biaggi, a former police officer whose political reputation had been made on the strength of his hardline law-and-order attitudes, was later to become the somewhat improbable herald of Sinn Fein ideology.

Few have been as influential on American relations as Senator Edward M. "Ted" Kennedy. Pictured on a 1994 visit to Boston with the then Prime Minister of Ireland Albert Reynolds and his sister Jean Kennedy Smith, the United States Ambassador to Ireland. *Photo by Harry Brett, Image Photo*

Irish American elites had however accumulated a new set of values as a result of their successful ascent up the socio-economic ladder. Calls for violence did not immediately trip to the tongues of politicians, business leaders, journalists, academics, doctors, and lawyers. Nor were they in great sympathy with Official Sinn Fein and its Third World revolutionary ideology, insofar as they were aware of the situation in Northern Ireland at all. The events of the early and mid-1970s brought about the slow mobilization of this sector of the Irish American community. Initially less vocal than the more militant grassroots ethnic Irish Americans, by the end of the 1970s they had joined forces with highly visible political leaders to shoulder aside the grassroots neighborhood and labor union interests.

Northern Ireland, 1972–1981

Security Measures

What security measures were adopted during 1972 to 1977? The Special Powers Act of 1922 had remained in effect in Ulster until 1973. A particular target of the civil rights movement, the Act was the legal tool for police harassment of Catholic nationalists for fifty years. This Act was replaced by the Northern Ireland Emergency Provisions Act of 1973, the most notable provisions of which were that the Army could detain someone without a warrant for four hours and the police could do the same for three days. An alleged terrorist could be tried before a single judge (Diplock Court) and convicted on the testimony of a member of the security forces. The 1973 Act incorporated many of the powers from the earlier Special Powers Act. These legal practices were justified by London as a necessary response to terrorist violence and intimidation.

Internment without warrant, with no time limit, was also empowered by the Emergency Provisions Act. In fact, however, internment was phased out in 1975 after approximately 1,800 people had been detained for various periods of time. Of that number 200 were Protestant militants. A companion law, the Prevention of Terrorism Act, was passed by Parliament in 1974 for the United Kingdom after bombs went off in Birmingham. This Act allows the holding of a suspected terrorist for two and then five days, allows for "deportation" of suspects to Ulster, forbids travel by suspects into Britain, and forbids political activity in support of terrorist organizations. The use of these Acts by the security forces in Northern Ireland led to the practice of constantly picking up members of the Catholic community, interrogating them, and then releasing them, and in doing so increasing the information available in security dossiers. The normal policing procedures gave way to harassment, intelligence gathering, and abusive and rough interrogations. Convictions were based on "confessions" based on the interrogations.

After 1970 the B Specials were abolished and the RUC disarmed. The B Specials were replaced by the Ulster Defense Regiment, a mainly part-time auxiliary to the Army. In fact, police procedures improved substantially after 1970. But the perception on the part of the Catholic community was somewhat different. Under the Emergency Provisions Act, for example, 60,000 people were arrested and interrogated (an equivalent proportion in the United States would be 10 million people). Only 12 percent, mostly young people and virtually all Catholic, were charged with crimes.

From 1969 to 1978 the prison population in Northern Ireland went from about 700 to 3,000. Clearly the number was a direct result of the violence, the rise in paramilitary organizations, and the rise in conventional crimes that were related to paramilitary fundraising. The increase in prisoners fostered what Padraig O'Malley calls the "prison culture."[27] While in prison the IRA members created a new sense of community among themselves and with those on the outside. O'Malley describes this world: "Thus the prison culture: solidarity and camaraderie, adding to the myth of continuity, isolation, deprivation and breeding a separate community more committed, more tested, more cohesive and more removed from the reality of Northern Ireland itself. And for every prisoner there are mothers, fathers, brothers, sisters, wives, children, networks of friends who feed off the prison culture, adopting its values, sharing its ethics and cultivating its resentments, their perception of reality mirroring and often magnifying the perceptions of the prisoners themselves."[28] O'Malley notes the paradox in the efforts of the security forces: the more effective they were at prosecuting the IRA, the more prisoners there were. The more prisoners, the more dominant the ethos of the prison culture and "the more viselike the grip of the IRA."

Under direct rule from 1972 to 1977, the practices of the Army did not essentially change from the period after 1969. The number of house searches remained high until 1978, with 72,000 in 1973; 72,000 in 1974; 30,000 in 1975; 34,000 in 1976; 20,000 in 1977; and 15,000 in 1978. Although not all house searches were carried out by the Army, the majority were. The police and Army shifted from rubber bullets to plastic bullets in 1973. In the ensuing years the bullets were responsible for an estimated twelve deaths and over sixty injuries. Among the dead were two girls, one fourteen, one twelve. The security forces fired over 45,000 such bullets.

The monitoring and surveillance of the population of Ulster became an extraordinarily sophisticated enterprise. The data held by the security forces on the people of Ulster, the Republic of Ireland, and Britain ran to approximately 500,000 files and included names, employment, registration, crime records, and political activity. These data were linked to that of Northern Ireland Social Services and were augmented by phone tapping and bugging. Journalist Roger Faligot quotes Gerry Fitt, MP and head of the SDLP at the time, on these procedures: "It's like something you would find in the Soviet Union or South Africa. . . . Big Brother is watching you."[29]

In sum, then, under the aegis of direct rule from London, the Army and security forces had extensive emergency powers and used them. The net effect of these uses and abuses of interrogation, the courts, imprisonment, surveillance, and plastic bullets was to create an atmosphere in the Catholic community that nourished the IRA and which the IRA nourished through their propaganda.

After 1977 the British government adopted the policy of "Ulsterization," to turn the principal direction and responsibility for security in Ulster over to the RUC and the UDR. The Army was to take a low profile. In fact, from a high of 24,000 in 1974, the British Army had only 10,000 soldiers in Ulster in 1983. The RUC had 7,800 members in 1983 and a 4,800-member reserve. The UDR had 7,200, about a third of whom were full time. After 1977 it is more correct to talk about the acts of the Ulster security forces than just the British Army.

From the point of view of the Catholic community not a great deal of change occurred. The nature of the violence changed, but the basic pattern of security measures remained the same. In 1977–1978 more than 2,800 people were arrested and interrogated under the three-day power. Of these only 35 percent were charged with a crime. The use of plastic bullets escalated dramatically in the rioting and confrontations of 1981 in the wake of the hunger strikes, with 29,665 fired that year. In late 1984 a plastic bullet killed a demonstrator at the Martin Galvin speech in Belfast, the speech which led to the RTE protest of Section 31.

The IRA

The Provisional IRA was structured along the lines of a traditional army, with officers, brigades, and battalions. Its activity from 1969 to 1972 was enhanced by recruitment of young people and by increasing the supply of guns, but it remained essentially the same: throwing stones or petrol bombs, sniping, mob violence, and, until July 1971, manning the barricades around the Catholic "no-go" areas. Internment, introduced in 1971, produced an outpouring of recruits for the IRA, widespread mob violence, and shootouts with the Army. By 1972 the IRA "were part guerrilla army, part local defense force, part neighborhood police force."[30] IRA guns accounted for the deaths of over 200 members of the security forces by 1972, including over 100 soldiers in 1972 alone, with over 1,300 bomb explosions. The IRA was becoming increasingly skilled at bombing during this period, although the inexperience of the new recruits was costly: Twenty-five IRA members killed themselves with their own bombs.

The strength of the IRA was such that six leaders were flown to a meeting with Northern Ireland Secretary William Whitelaw in June 1972. They made demands and agreed to a cease fire, which soon crumbled. The IRA flourished with popular support and fresh recruits. The demand on the part of the IRA that Stormont be abolished, a goal shared with other groups, also sustained their public support. IRA propaganda at this time focused on British Army abuses, Protestant Unionist domination, and British rule. The growth of IRA violence was linked to Army security activities. In 1971 twenty-seven bombs were exploded in Belfast, earning the name "Bloody Friday." Bloody enough to the 7 killed and the 150 injured, it also signaled the beginning of two trends: an upsurge in bombing as a tool and the loss of support from some in the Catholic community who were outraged at the Belfast bombing.

With the abolition of Stormont and the inception of direct rule, British security policy changed and rioting and mob violence slowly diminished. IRA activity over the next few years included changes in leadership, bombing, developing international linkages for supply of arms, the adoption of sectarian murder, and attacks on Great Britain. The organization passed into the hands of younger guerrillas whose politics were more Left wing.

The security measures taken by the British Army began to take their toll after 1972. The IRA shifted its tactics in response to Army infiltration and the arrest of some members. The IRA adopted the booby trap bomb, car bomb, and remote controlled bomb. Gun battles were out, sniping was in. The targets for bombing included RUC stations and Army trucks but also shops and pubs. The destruction of property was immense, to say nothing of the loss of life.[31] These tactics, however, had the effect of hurting or killing civilians and threatened to erode IRA support among the Catholic community. The peak years of the bombing campaign were 1971 to 1976. In 1970 the number of bombing incidents was 170; in 1972 it was 1,853. The number remained above 1,000 until 1974, then dropped to 635 in 1975.

Associated with the bombing campaign was the forging of international links for training and arms supply. One arm of this linkage was to overseas revolutionary and terrorist groups and arms suppliers. The IRA purchased Czechoslovakian and Bulgarian arms in the Middle East. In 1977, Palestinian-provided arms were intercepted in Amsterdam. Libya apparently provided support to the IRA in the form of a substantial arms shipment on a ship, *The Claudia*, intercepted in 1973. Political links existed between the Palestine Liberation Organization and the IRA and INLA and also the Basque separatists. The PLO is said to have trained IRA members in the Middle East.

These linkages, however, were dwarfed by the supply of guns and money that flowed from the United States. The principal source of funds to purchase weapons was NORAID. The money was supposedly intended for the Green Cross to feed the hungry and provide for the homeless victims of violence. In fact the money went for guns for the IRA. NORAID leaders have been connected with gun running, including, in 1982, an effort to purchase five SAM missiles. A finely tuned propaganda effort accompanied the NORAID efforts. The IRA wore "green" when reaching Irish Americans.[32]

The response in the Protestant community to the increase in IRA bombing and shooting was to generate organizations that in many ways mirrored the IRA. The Ulster Defense Association (UDA), founded in 1971, was the largest and most well known. The Ulster Volunteer Force, the Ulster Freedom Fighters, and the Red Hand Commandos were also active. From 1971 to 1976 especially, but not ending at that point, the UDA began to murder Catholics, intimidate them out of their homes, and respond to the IRA with countervailing violence. The IRA acted in kind, and a spiral of murder began in which the victims were randomly chosen and often had no political affiliations. Twenty-five Catholics were murdered in a period of ten months in 1976 by a UDA gang. The IRA engaged in retaliation and, in a particularly gruesome episode in 1976, took ten Protestant workmen out of a van and murdered them in cold blood. From 1972 to 1976, 909 civilians died in Ulster by explicit sectarian assassination. The IRA and the UDA and related paramilitaries were responsible for approximately two-thirds of those deaths. Although this deadly exchange diminished after 1976, sectarian murder continued.

The IRA also responded to the increase in British security measures with attacks on Great Britain. In 1972 bombs were exploded at the Old Bailey and Whitehall. The bombing escalated to a savage level in 1972, then dropped off during a 1975 cease fire, but the fire never really ceased. In February 1972 a bomb went off at the Officer's Mess in Aldershot, killing seven people. In March 1973 a car bomb in London killed 1 and injured 200 others. In July 1974 a bomb in the Tower of London killed one and injured forty-one children. In February, October, and November, three more bombings took twenty lives. In Birmingham in November 1974 two bombs in pubs killed 19 and injured 182.

Public support for the IRA's "heroic" struggle was badly tarnished by the bombing and by an ugly internecine battle with the Official IRA in 1975, in which eleven people were murdered in as many weeks. Provisionals shot a seven-year-old girl, and the Officials shot Owen McViegh, a man who had nothing to do with the Provisionals. Finally, the IRA took control of businesses, pubs, taxis, and housing allocation in West Belfast. Threats, pressure, and extortion in the Catholic districts led to an image in the press and in the public that the IRA were no more than local gun-toting criminals. Jack Holland notes: "This kind of behavior was hardly a good advertisement for the new Ireland and the IRA. There were other rumors of growing corruption and gangsterism through 1975, until it seemed that the guerrillas were turning into a local mafia."[33]

By the end of 1975 the IRA had reached a low point. Sporadic negotiations with the British in 1972 and 1975 had neither legitimized the IRA nor brought it success. The British had consistently increased security measures. The pattern of indiscriminate bombings in Ulster and in Britain had tarnished their image with innocent blood. Murder—sectarian, internecine, capricious, and vicious—drained public support. Finally, criminal corruption compromised the political integrity of the IRA. The British claimed that the IRA was no longer a politically motivated insurrection but sheer gangsterism.[34] The policies of Ulsterization and criminalization were making a difference. Between 1976 and 1977 the RUC managed to get over 2,500 murder, attempted murder, arms, and explosives convictions. "We were almost defeated," admitted a Provo leader at the time.[35]

In 1977 the IRA reorganized in a rather dramatic fashion. Sean Mac Stiofain, Joe Cahill, and David O'Connell had led the IRA up until 1975. O'Connell had presided over splits in the IRA between those opting for more violence. He was arrested in 1975; this marked both the degeneration of the IRA and the advent of younger, more Left-wing leaders to rescue it. Gerry Adams emerged as vice president of Provisional Sinn Fein and a leader of the IRA.[36] The IRA disbanded its military structure of brigades, battalions, and companies based upon specific geographical areas. A cell system was put in place with "active service units" of four to six people. The cells are autonomous, and the members know only each other. The leader knows only his or her immediate superior. This reorganization was coupled with a purge of the gangster elements in the IRA. Restructuring to active service units contracted the IRA from perhaps 2,000 members in 1972 to perhaps 300 by the 1980s. Inversely related to the number, however, was the degree of professionalism. The British General John Glover stated in 1978: "The provisionals cannot attract the large members of active terrorists they had in 1972/73. But they no longer need them. PIRA's organization is such that a small number of activists can maintain a disproportionate level of violence."[37] The new units possessed sophisticated weapons and material and were capable of such acts as the Brighton bombing of 1984, in which massive damage was done to a hotel housing the Conservative Party convention, nearly killing members of the British Cabinet and Prime Minister Thatcher.

After 1977 the IRA changed tactics, focusing its attacks on prison officials, bureaucrats, businessmen, judges, and RUC and UDR members, who were seen as servants of Britain, the "imperial" power in Ulster. Major political figures in Britain and the British Army became targets. On August 27, 1979, Lord Mountbatten was murdered on his boat with three others in Donegal Bay, and eighteen British soldiers died in an ambush at Warrenpoint. The IRA's continuing penchant for the murder of innocent civilians, however, was displayed in the 1983 Christmas-time bombing at Harrod's department store in London, in which six people died.

The IRA now has chosen to fight a war of attrition, in part because of a decline in public support for widespread IRA activities, in part to maintain security, and in part because they had no choice. They risked losing hardcore support from the Catholic community because the active service units and professional terrorists were not as broadly based in the neighborhoods as the old military structure had been. In the face of such a risk and the surges of popular revulsion at particular assassinations, the IRA needed a tool to pump up popular emotions and support. The hunger strikes of 1981 were just such a tool. The demands were "reasonable"; the IRA prisoners and their demands were legitimized by the government, religious, and popular outcry; the British were made to appear intractable and brutal; and the streets were again filled with rioters.

The Political Situation in Ulster

The events that had occurred since 1969 had split Unionists into several shards, the first being an extreme dissident wing, Paisley's Democratic Unionist Party. Craig now transformed his Vanguard Movement of militants into the Vanguard Unionist Progressive Party, with the Ulster Defense Association and Loyalist Association of Workers as its paramilitary wing and working class base, respectively. The remaining Unionists followed Brian Faulkner and represented a moderate view, moderate that is in relation to the Paisleyites.

The Catholic Nationalists, contrary to the Unionist pattern, had politically coalesced into the Social Democratic and Labour Party, thus eliminating the variety of representation that had existed in the Catholic community since 1920. The SDLP took the position that Ulster could find a way to be governed without violence. Sinn Fein was lurking behind the Provisional IRA, but the party entered into community organizing with a will and later, in 1982, began contesting elections.[38]

The only other party of any weight was the Alliance Party, which had grown out of the New Ulster Movement founded in 1969 as a liberal-centrist pressure group. In 1971 it became a political party. The supporters of Alliance could accept neither the extremists of the Unionist Party nor the radicals of the nationalist movement and stood for non-sectarianism, a constitutional settlement of Ulster's problems, and a concern for justice for all citizens. The sectarian gorge was so wide, however, that Alliance could garner only a small number of seats for its centrist position.

In March 1973 the British government put out a white paper titled *Northern Ireland: Constitutional Proposals*. The central feature was power sharing and the whole arrangement was an earlier model of the 1998 Good Friday Agreement. Ulster was to have a new Assembly of eighty representatives elected by a system of proportional representation. Firm guarantees of Catholic civil rights were to be accompanied by guaranteed seats on an executive committee in proportion to the party representation in the Assembly. The powers of the Assembly were to be more circumscribed than those of the Stormont government. Elections were held in June 1973. The results indicated that the "moderate" Faulkner Unionists still had somewhat of a grip on the party; they won twenty-three seats. SDLP won nineteen, Alliance had nine, and the loyalist Unionists together had twenty-seven votes, spread among the Democratic Unionist Party (DUP), Vanguard, and other hardline Unionists. The majority of those elected (about fifty-one) were committed to making the new government work. In the following months a power-sharing Executive Committee was formed, composed of one Alliance member, four SDLP members, and six Faulkner Unionists. In December 1973 a meeting was held in Sunningdale, England, to discuss a Council of Ireland, which had been proposed in the white paper. The power-sharing Executive of Northern Ireland and cabinet members from Dublin and London hammered out a plan for an elected all-Ireland Assembly and a ministry of fourteen members, half from Belfast, half from Dublin, which would have consultative power only.

As so often happens in Ulster, the extremists acted because their objectives were not served by moderation. Sinn Fein and the IRA denounced the whole idea of power sharing as the continuation of British rule. To the IRA elimination of British rule was the real solution, not "puppet" assemblies. The Craig and Paisley forces denounced the plan as a step toward a united Ireland (because of the Council of Ireland proposal) and as a sellout of majority (i.e., Protestant) rule. The final blow to the power-sharing Executive Committee came from the extreme Unionists in the following year.

In many ways what was important about the Sunningdale meeting was not only the new Council of Ireland proposal but the policy changes, assumptions, and directions of the governments involved. For London the very proposal of a Council of Ireland in the 1973 white paper was a major departure from the traditional posture that Ulster was exclusively British. It was no less than a formal recognition of what the SDLP called "the Irish dimension," the long-term connection between north and south historically and politically. In the Ireland Act of 1949 the British had committed themselves to no change in the status of Northern Ireland without the consent of a majority of the people. London's attitude had changed as British public opinion shifted against the unionists and London recognized that Northern Ireland was never going to have peace unless it took account of its geographical, historical, and cultural ties to the Republic.

The Dublin Officials went to Sunningdale optimistic that with a policy of power sharing their co-religionists in the north could experience some peace and stability in the province. In time, then, the two governments could move slowly to expand the all-Ireland aspects of Sunningdale, which would perhaps ultimately lead to a united Ireland. Liam Cosgrave, the prime minister of the Republic, promised to recognize Northern Ireland as a British territory as long as the citizens of Ulster chose to remain so. For the Republic this concession was a repudiation of the constitutional claim, a step away from rhetorical claims on the north, and a step toward dealing with the reality of 1 million Protestants who did not want to be unloaded onto the Republic by London and refused to be bombed into it by the IRA.

The Republic of Ireland's response to the Northern problem displayed a lot of ambivalence. The traditions of Fianna Fail and the deep-seated feelings of the people pushed the Republic toward powerful condemnations of the Stormont regime and sympathy and support for the Catholics in Ulster. The Arms Trial and the fact that southern Ireland was a refuge for IRA men influenced this attitude. On the other hand, when bombs went off in Dublin in 1972, 1974, and 1975 and the British ambassador was assassinated in 1976, Dublin responded with an Emergency Powers Bill and a declaration of a state of national emergency. IRA men were interned and tried without juries and civil liberties took a back seat to preventing the violence of Ulster from sweeping into the Republic. The early 1970s saw a debate in Ireland on the nature of the Constitution and the Catholic nature of the state. In response to liberal pressure, the special position of the Catholic Church was deleted from the Republic's constitution in 1972. Overall, however, the impact of the Northern Ireland crisis on the Republic had been less than one might have expected. Businessmen worried about investments, the Tourist Board worried about declining rates of tourism, and large numbers of ordinary people talked of Ulster as an alien place from which they feared violence but toward which they felt no sense of passionate nationalism. Only one person in seven in the Republic had ever visited Northern Ireland. While unification was part of the aspiration of Irish nationalism, as noted above, polls showed that it fell far down the agenda of voter concerns in the Republic.

In an atmosphere charged with hope, the power-sharing Executive assumed its duties in early 1974. The Assembly contained a group of more extreme Unionists who saw the Assembly as illegitimate; they withdrew in January. The Executive struggled along despite the handicap of the extreme wings of sectarian community engaging in persistent violence. Power sharing, the Council of Ireland, and the issue of police power in Northern Ireland being questioned, changed, or controlled by Catholics were too much for some members of Faulkner's Unionist party to bear. They abandoned Faulkner to join with other extreme Unionists in the United Ulster Unionist Council (UUUC). The Executive now contained only a sliver of the original Unionist Party members, and what fragile consensus it ever had was gone.

The end of the Executive came in May 1974 when the Ulster Workers Council (UWC) called a general strike in Belfast to demand that the Council of Ireland be eliminated. The UWC received support from the extreme Unionists and paramilitaries. The strike put the Faulkner Unionists in the Executive under a great deal of pressure. In a conciliatory gesture the SDLP agreed to the postponement of the Council of Ireland for four years. The extremists then demanded the resignation of the Executive members and called for new elections. Polls at the time in Ulster indicated that while only 40 percent of the people supported the Council of Ireland, 70 percent supported power sharing. The pressure proved too great, and Faulkner resigned. In two weeks the strike had destroyed the power-sharing Executive. Once again the extremists, in this case the Protestants, had caused the center to crumble.

Harold Wilson, the British prime minister at the time, bore a great deal of the responsibility for the failure. Although the Executive was too slender a reed to support the hopes that were built upon it or to surmount the opposition against it, Wilson made the struggle impossible. Bringing too few troops far too late to be effective in the strike, Wilson belied his assurances that he would preserve the government and the Executive. The new government in Northern Ireland was suspended after five months. Brian Faulkner, a traditional Unionist, was far ahead of his time in accepting the new structures, but the threat of change to the Unionist world created an untraversable chasm.

The efforts to create a new government had done little to diminish the violence, which poured forth in a steady stream. The extreme ends of the two communities had hardened their respective and irreconcilable positions and proceeded to shoot, burn, and bomb to achieve them. The Provisional IRA on the one hand and the UDA on the other engaged in a minuet of sectarian assassinations followed by reprisals, followed by revenge, followed by funerals, followed by lives ravaged by tragedy. By the autumn of 1974 over 1,000 people had died in the violence and 2,400 had been injured. Nearly 20,000 British troops were stationed in the province, and the bombings spread to Dublin where, in May 1974, twenty-three people died and hundreds were wounded.

Once again London attempted to create a government in Ulster. In 1974 another British white paper called for elections to a Constituent Assembly, which would then form a government. The government, however, had to include power sharing and an "Irish dimension" and guarantees of civil rights and had to be acceptable to the British Parliament. The election to the Constituent Assembly displayed the support for loyalist Unionists, who took forty seats, whereas Faulkner Unionists won only twelve seats, Alliance took only eight seats, and the SDLP won seventeen seats.

In summer and fall 1975 the Assembly met in an atmosphere of tension that was not conducive to compromise. The hardline UUUC splintered because Craig was willing to come closer to power sharing than Paisley, but in the end the loyalists pulled together and proposed to London a government that rejected power sharing and the Irish dimension. Based as it was on majority rule, the scheme was designed to restore the domination of the Protestant Unionists.

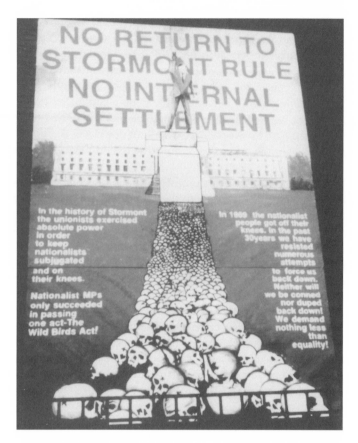

The murals on the ends of housing blocks in Northern Ireland have become something of
a political art form. This nationalist mural rejects any of the proposed British settlements,
which recreated a form of Stormont rule that the nationlist community believed was a
restoration of unionist majority oppression.
Photo by David Margarita

London rejected the plan, and the Assembly ended with Paisley spewing sul-
furous invective at his opponents.

The Women's Peace Movement

In 1976 the stage shifted from the corridors of Whitehall and Stormont to the
streets of Belfast. Mauread Corrigan and Betty Williams, residents of Belfast,
were repulsed by the continuing violence, especially when three youths were
killed by a runaway vehicle driven by an IRA man. The women contacted other

women who lived in fear and began a series of small silent marches and vigils to protest the violence around them. To the shock of the militant groups, who assumed they had the complete support of their respective communities, the movement mushroomed rapidly into a series of marches every weekend. The numbers were extraordinary, running from 5,000 to 20,000. What was more surprising is that the participation was non-sectarian and tapped a wellspring of feeling against the mayhem in both communities. Clergy of different faiths marched together, thousands of people signed petitions, and activists flocked to the movement. The media in Ireland and Britain, and later in Europe and the United States, focused on the marches. Money poured in from around the world. A massive march in London in November 1976 riveted attention on the peace movement, putting the militant groups on the defensive. In fall 1976 the two women won the Norwegian People's Peace Prize and then the Nobel Peace Prize in February 1977.

Known as the Women's Peace Movement, this group also had behind the scenes a former journalist, Ciaran McKeown, who developed the movement's program while the two women drew public attention to the frustration in Ulster. McKeown wrote a manifesto for the movement that stressed its pacifist and grassroots orientation. He called for a movement that would be community based and oriented toward solving problems, such as needed playgrounds and health clinics, in an approach that would be relatively free of traditional doctrinal positions. The nonsectarian aspect was emphasized in the focus on common problems across the two ethnic communities at the local level instead of the constitutional status of Northern Ireland. At its peak of success through 1977 and 1978 the movement did more to bridge the sectarian divide than had been done for a long time. Small groups of women from both communities would meet for tea and discuss common fears and suffering. Organizations sprang up in the towns, newsletters were printed, and local activities were initiated. These accomplishments were limited but not negligible. Williams and Corrigan kept the Ulster problem highly visible as they traveled extensively to raise funds.

In the period from 1978 to 1980 the movement began to decay. The leading figures began to have differences of opinion, and the two women were sharply criticized for keeping the Nobel Prize money and not donating it to the movement. Betty Williams quit in 1980, and the movement finally ended up as a modest community-action group still operating in Belfast. The Women's Peace Movement confronted some deeply held bitterness and some hard men. The Protestant and Catholic communities' collective memories could not be swept away in the burst of emotional frustration, nor were the men of the UVF and the IRA simply going to drop their guns and join a peace march. The movement's attempt to be nonpolitical was a difficult if not impossible task. Initiated by emotional energy, the movement mobilized that emotion into a visible and constructive force. Such an effort requires money, time, and expertise and thus organization becomes necessary. The group then was confronted with choices that in the highly charged atmosphere of Ulster became divisive. John Hume noted in 1977 that after the emotions of the peace movement wore away, the political divisions of Northern Ireland would remain.[39] At best the Women's Peace Movement could only foster the climate for a settlement of the issues; it could not provide a settlement.

Trying to Take Back Self-Government

In 1977 another failure of a more sectarian nature occurred. Ian Paisley, who had emerged as a powerful spokesman for the loyalists, decided to return to an earlier strategy to force the British to restore self-government to Ulster. He called a general strike in May similar to the one of 1974 that had brought down the power-sharing government. Paisley had the support of the extreme loyalists and the Protestant paramilitaries, but the strike was a failure. Far fewer men stayed out of work than Paisley had expected, despite the efforts of the paramilitaries to force workers to stay home. Paisley's lack of success in this effort indicated that the Protestant workers had been powerful enough in 1974 to bring down a government that included the Council of Ireland but that they were not powerful enough in 1977 to force London to restore a government to the province. They had a veto power over British initiatives, but as strong as this power was it could not be translated into power to compel London to restore a government to their liking.

Exposing the Security Forces' Excesses

Violence continued throughout the years. A wave of fire bombings occurred, and two soldiers were killed when the Queen visited Belfast in August 1977. When the initial confrontations had ignited across Ulster, the British government had pressured Stormont to appoint commissions to investigate them. In 1969 two of these, the Cameron Commission on the August riots and the Hunt Commission on the police in Northern Ireland, reported. The reports were damaging to the Stormont regime and embarrassing to London, because the Commissions called for the elimination of the B Specials and made forty-seven recommendations for changes in the RUC. The Cameron commission reported that members of the B Specials had been part of the mob that had attacked the People's Democracy demonstrators at Burntollet Bridge in 1969. The RUC was described as anti-Catholic and, in the case of the Burntollet riot, charged with brutality in Derry. The reports were sensitive to the difficulties the RUC faced, such as manpower shortages and widespread violence since 1968, but the weight of the reports was clearly against the police. In 1972 the Hunt Commission reached similar conclusions concerning the RUC and its abuses of Catholics. To Catholic nationalists this was hardly breaking news, to the British it was embarrassing, and to the

Unionists it was cause for befuddlement because what the police did was perfectly "normal" and appropriate in their view.

After internment was introduced in 1971 reports of physical and psychological abuse of the internees increased; leaving prisoners naked, hooding (i.e., putting hoods over prisoners' heads), white noise, and beatings were alleged to be common practices at Long Kesh Prison. In 1971 the Compton Report investigated the interrogation of internees and found evidence of ill treatment. In 1972 Amnesty International reported on the abuse of internees and concluded that the ill-treatment amounted to brutality. Although internment ceased in 1975, the Republic of Ireland brought the accumulated evidence before the European Human Rights Commission because both the Republic and the United Kingdom were by then members of the European Community. In 1976 London was embarrassed by the report of the European Commission that, in fact, the interned prisoners were subjected to cruelty and to brutal treatment. Prime Minister James Callahan then asked the Republic of Ireland not to take the Commission's evidence to the European Court of Human Rights. Callahan argued that such an act would only exacerbate tensions because internment had been terminated and Dublin and London were cooperating on the control of cross-border terrorism. Prime Minister Lynch decided to go ahead and submit the evidence. In 1978 the European Court ruled that the techniques used to interrogate were "inhumane and degrading treatment" and violated the European Convention on Human Rights, the first such judgment since the founding of the European Economic Community.[40] In May of the same year Amnesty International reported again, indicating that the treatment of prisoners was abusive and that the legal rights of suspects were regularly violated. Stung, Roy Mason, the secretary of state for Northern Ireland, denied the allegations but appointed the Bennett Committee to investigate. That committee concluded that, in fact, prisoners were beaten, and it suggested reforms. The position of London on the whole question of the treatment of prisoners essentially was that they were not abused, but if they were, such treatment was necessary and not excessive.

More Violence

The year 1979 brought a series of brutal assassinations. Killed were Richard Sykes, the British ambassador to the Netherlands; Aery Neave, a member of the British Parliament and a close associate of Margaret Thatcher; as well as Earl Mountbatten and his grandson. At the time of Mountbatten's death an IRA ambush also killed eighteen soldiers in Northern Ireland. This trail of blood did little to further the IRA cause; public revulsion was matched by Margaret Thatcher's determination not to be bombed out of Ulster. Thatcher, who took power in 1979, had a series of meetings with Jack Lynch that led to an increased emphasis on cross-border security.

British Policy in Ulster, 1972–1981

In March 1972, after the explosion of communal violence beginning in 1969, London prorogued the Stormont government and thus became directly responsible for government on the ground in Ulster. A period of poorly thought out direct rule followed, which might be classified as "metropolitan coercion" because the grounds for rule were not based on any local consensus from either community. Moreover, the administration of the province was in the hands of the Northern Ireland Civil Service, a Unionist bureaucracy whose very raison d'être was to be responsive to their Protestant Unionist clienteles. London sought only orderly rule at this point and used the provisions of martial law to keep order in the cities. Although British politicians and bureaucrats were getting a better grasp on what was going on in Ulster, by now the IRA was revivified, in no small part due to the security policies of the British Army.

Anxious to turn the governing authority in Ulster back to the province but unwilling to simply recreate the Stormont government, London called upon the political parties to elect an Assembly on the basis of proportional representation. The British white paper of March 1973 calling for these arrangements sought to reassure the Unionists of the guarantee of British rule in the north, while inclusion of the Council of Ireland would reassure the nationalists that the British were serious about recognizing their position. The effort was destroyed by the Ulster Workers Council. Why did this occur?

Power sharing had effected some truly significant differences in the traditional perspectives on Ulster. The participation of the Irish government at Sunningdale indicated, for the first time since partition, that Dublin recognized the validity of British rule over Northern Ireland. The British government's acceptance of the role of the Irish government indicated that they recognized the Irish dimension to the problem. The participation of the Official Unionist Party (although not all Unionists) indicated the acceptance of the principle that the Nationalists had a right to share power. The participation of the Social Democratic and Labour Party indicated the acceptance on the part of the Catholic nationalists (though not all Republican nationalists) that they were willing to be part of a British government of Northern Ireland that recognized them.

Power sharing is seen as an effective means to manage conflict in a divided society. Political scientist Eric Nordlinger notes that governmental power and scarce resources "are proportionately reserved for particular segments rather than being entirely up for grabs by anyone who can grab them."[41] The basic cause of failure of this model, one of the most promising in the history of Northern Ireland, was that the majority of the unionist parties were not motivated to become stakeholders in a system which for them entailed a loss of power, positions, control, and guarantees. As one prominent Unionist politician remarked, "I was elected to exercise power not to share it." Unionists were not going to rush to support a system that guaranteed positions and power for those they saw as irredentists willing to use violence to destroy "their" state. The power-sharing system was not a product of negotiation and compromise among all the political groups in Northern Ireland; in fact militant Unionists rejected it and the IRA hoped it would fail. It was in part imposed by London, which then had an obligation to make it work. When a general strike occurred among unionists, Prime Minister Wilson acted pusillanimously and his actions signaled to unionists that they could undermine any political initiative on Northern Ireland. Thus London's policy was rejected by the Ulster Unionists, who claimed the highest degree of loyalty to London . . . but only on their terms.

The British government sought to hurdle the impasse of Unionist objection to the power-sharing executive through the device of the constitutional convention, which would allow all the parties of Ulster to meet and develop a set of institutions upon which all could agree. The polarization produced by the violence prevalent in Ulster during this period hardened the positions of the communities and their political parties. The 1973 election for the House of Commons in Northern Ireland, for example, produced greater support for the hardline Unionists. In the white paper of 1974 London called for the inclusion of power sharing and an Irish dimension and arrangements that would command "widespread acceptance" in the province. The eighty-member convention elected was dominated by hardline Unionist parties in intense opposition even to the moderate Unionists who had participated in the power-sharing Executive. The Unionist hard liners took the narrow position that the law creating the convention called for institutions that would command widespread acceptance in the community, which to them meant a return to the majoritarianism of the Stormont regime. The Catholic Nationalists took the mandate of the white paper as requiring power sharing and an Irish dimension seriously and found the Unionists to be evading the responsibility that the British Parliament had laid upon them. The convention, having voted through on a majority basis a majoritarian government unacceptable to the British government, ended in complete deadlock and was dissolved by an Order in Council in March 1976.

In this instance the British government sought to ground the new form of government in Ulster on compromise between the parties representing the two communities. The ability to exercise power over the province, a goal of the Unionists; to share that power, a goal of the nationalists; and to unload power onto the local level, a goal of London, were supposed to converge in a compromise that would produce a deal which, while not pleasing anyone, would purchase their participation in government. Why did it fail? One procedural deficiency was giving the Convention a parliamentary format, which created the atmosphere in which debate took the form of adherence to party pronunciamentos and left little room for political movement, let alone constitutional development.

But far deeper than that were the pressures on the Unionist parties that shattered their singular but brittle unity on governing the province. Each party was more politically intransigent in dealing with the fact that the British government was actually governing or demanding that the Unionists do so under new conditions. Parties leapfrogged over each other in degrees of intransigence, which made their positions more and more uncompromising. The Protestant community stood for zero compromise with the nationalist community and a militant crackdown on the IRA. Their parties were competing to articulate that position. There was no political payoff for Unionists to support a consensus, let alone one so fragile, that would mean giving up political power on the one hand and electoral support on the other. Thus the political arrangements did not have any congruence with the political techtonics of Ulster and the British government did not have the will to impose them on the Unionists.

Power sharing was dead. No British politician or secretary of state for Northern Ireland was going to attempt once again to get the parties to bridge that gap. Merlyn Rees, the secretary of state for Northern Ireland, began the next phase of British policy, "Ulsterization." Ulsterization involved a number of initiatives that fell under the general umbrella of direct rule. From 1971 to 1973 London had used direct rule only as a damage limitation measure while seeking to re-institutionalize a slimmed-down, effective, devolved government in Ulster. London now was determined to accept for the near term the lack of consensus in the province and take a more active role in governing.[42]

The most notable change was the process of "criminalization" of charges made against those engaged in political opposition to the regime. Up to this point prisoners arrested due to the conflict had been given "special category" status and had been free from the usual prison regimen. Now all prisoners were to be treated as criminals based upon the acts they committed. Journalist Tim Pat Coogan notes: "The policy was legally dubious as most IRA men are convicted under the Emergency Provisions Act, which justifies extraordinary measures in order to deal with terrorists and then defines terrorism as using violence for political ends. There is little doubt that the actions of IRA men were politically motivated and that they could be subjected to arrest for questioning, detained for three to seven days, tried without a jury and subjected to pressure to give confessions. Although these factors seem to make involving the policy of criminalization a contradiction, they still do not necessarily justify special treatment in prison."[43]

The laws of the province were brought into line with British legislation and Britain extended the reforms initiated in 1969–1970, eliminating the most blatantly discriminatory statutes (a barn door closed). In addition, the presence of the Army was reduced from 21,000 to 12,000 by 1980. The security forces were increased through the creation of the Ulster Defense Regiment, a part-time reserve force of the British Army that was located only in Ulster and used as a backup to the Royal Ulster Constabulary. The men came from the Protestant unionist community, leading historian J. J. Lee to call Ulsterization "Protestant-ization."[44] This period of "normalization" in the life of Ulster and depoliticization of security issues actually led to some of the most egregious abuses of the law enforcement and judicial process. The Royal Ulster Constabulary were accused of brutality and torture in extracting confessions from nationalists suspected of violence. The police were accused of adopting a "shoot to kill" policy with respect to suspected IRA activities. The Diplock, or juryless, courts gave wide-ranging power to Protestant Unionist judges. Prisoners were given extraordinary rewards to squeal on their political associates, rewards so great as to encourage naming those who were innocent as well. Attempts to investigate the RUC were thwarted, most notably in the case of John Stalker, appointed to examine the RUC but given little support. When he came close to uncovering the abuses and reporting them he was removed and discredited with flimsy charges of misconduct in Manchester.[45]

What was the outcome of a more substantial exercise of direct rule and the changing of security measures to "criminalize" violent political opposition to British rule? Essentially the policy foundered on the basic contradictions in British policy, which saw the direct rule and reforms as necessary, forced on London because of the deficiencies of Unionist politicians (oblivious as they were to their own ineptitude). Thus London denigrated the Unionist politicians and parties and shouldered them aside while at the same time stating that the ultimate goal of direct rule was to turn the province over to them. On the one hand, the British government did not attack substantively the fundamental problems of Ulster because it wanted to limit its commitment to direct rule. On the other hand, it did not want to endure the necessary political heat to put in place in Ulster a devolved government that actually gave one-third of the citizens a say in the governing of their lives, guarantees of fair police procedures, equal justice under the law, and access to opportunity in social and economic life.

The nationalist constitutional party, the Social Democratic and Labour Party, was marginalized to an even greater extent than the Unionists. With no political outlet in Ulster the party was a powerless fragment within the context of British politics as a whole. This produced from the SDLP, at one and the same time, a demand that London produce a power-sharing devolved government and a demand that the British withdraw from Northern Ireland. It also produced at one and the same time from the Unionist demands that Ulster be integrated wholly into the United Kingdom and a demand that there be a restoration of a Stormont-type government in Ulster. The apparent contradictions are explained by the lack of consistency in British policy.[46]

The United States and Northern Ireland, 1972–1981

In the first violent years of the conflict the voice of Irish Americans was essentially unified, but by the late 1970s it was divided. What had brought about the transformation in the attitudes of the Irish American elites in the early 1970s? The answer was a combination of John Hume, Sean Donlon, and Michael Lillis. Each had concluded that the NORAID/Caucus perspective among Irish Americans was entirely too pervasive and encouraged the contribution of money that ended up in the hands of the IRA. Biaggi, for example, came to sail under the banner of the Caucus and the statements and viewpoints of other leading politicians were at odds with those of the SDLP and the Irish government, especially after Sunningdale in 1973. John Hume had been contacted by Ted Kennedy in 1972 and began a relationship, both political and personal, which was to play an important part in the marginalization of the NORAID/Caucus version of Irish American nationalism. Hume's regular visits to the United States and his stay at the Harvard Center for International Affairs in 1976 extended his influence with Kennedy and other U.S. politicians and Irish American leaders.

Hume was friendly with Sean Donlon, who was appointed ambassador to the United States in 1978 by Dublin. He joined Michael Lillis, who had been appointed to the Irish Embassy in the United States in 1976 as second counsellor. Lillis struck up friendships with people in Washington and shaped their views to such an extent that the influence of the Irish government was out of proportion to the place of Ireland and Irish interests on the U.S. foreign policy agenda. Lillis began a friendship with Tip O'Neill, who became Speaker of the House in 1976. At the same time Hume was also entering the speaker's circle, spending Thanksgiving in 1976 at O'Neill's house on Cape Cod. Barry White, in his biography of Hume, postulated "almost a father and son relationship developing" between them. Garret FitzGerald, however, noted that "Kennedy was more responsive to Hume, the Irish government had a better connection with O'Neill."[47]

The central thrust of the message of these three figures was that traditional Irish American nationalism was out of date in terms of the situation in Ulster. In fact, while not minimizing their differences on security matters, the British and Irish governments had in common their opposition to the IRA, the quest for a devolved government in Ulster, and a peaceful solution to the violence based upon negotiation. While Irish Americans might share the ultimate goal of a united Ireland with the Irish government and the nationalists of the north, supporting Sinn Fein and the IRA meant that they were extending and legitimizing the violence.

Traditional Irish nationalism had never addressed the existence of 1 million Ulster unionists, placing the onus for the political divisions of Ulster at the feet of London. Irish American nationalism was equally obtuse. As Garret FitzGerald observed, "I was too impatient with Irish American groups and too willing to tell them to stop supporting violence in our country." On the other hand, FitzGerald noted, "British efforts to condemn the violence in the North were counterproductive in the United States for it involved their justifying their presence."[48] The importance of Hume, Donlon, and Lillis was to articulate these issues, with an Irish accent and condemn U.S. support of the violence. The ironic twist of this policy was not lost on Congressman Brian Donnelly, who observed that "the role of the Irish diplomats was to make the American Irish less green."[49]

Events of the mid-1970s illuminate the diverging approaches of Irish American groups to the Ulster crisis. Congressman Mario Biaggi, under the auspices of the Caucus, visited Ireland to meet with leaders of Sinn Fein and the IRA, as well as representatives of other political groups. The IRA, Biaggi asserted, focused attention on the problem of the north. But to the Irish government, as Jack Holland put it, "the IRA did not focus attention on the problem—the IRA *was* the problem."[50] In November 1976 presidential candidate Carter issued a statement after meeting with Father Sean McManus of the Caucus to the effect that the United States should play a more active role in the Ulster issue, that the Democratic Party favored a united Ireland, and that human rights abuses in Ulster should be investigated. This was not all that far away from the positions that Senator Kennedy had advocated four years earlier, but it was now seen as a sign of the growing influence of the Caucus in defining the problem of Northern Ireland and framing the policies the U.S. government should adopt.

A statement by Speaker O'Neill, Senators Kennedy and Moynihan, and Governor Carey issued on Saint Patrick's Day in 1977 condemned Irish American support for the violence in Northern Ireland and by implication the groups, such as the Caucus, that supported it. The statement did not neglect to chide the British for their less than scintillating political initiatives in the north and the excesses of their security policy.

With the election of a Democratic president in 1976, Tip O'Neill emerged as the key figure on Irish issues for the next decade. His influence was felt on numerous developments: President Carter's statement on Ulster; preventing hearings on the north; the State Department ban on gun sales to the Royal Ulster Constabulary; the Sean Donlon affair; changing Thatcher's position on Ulster; and U.S. aid to the International Fund for Ireland. The first mark of his influence was the Carter statement on Northern Ireland in August 1977. Carter and his staff were not very familiar with the Ulster issue and there had been a long tradition of the United States having no foreign policy position on Northern Ireland because it was seen as part of the United Kingdom, one of the major U.S. allies, no less. O'Neill convinced Carter in the face of these difficulties to make a statement on Northern Ireland. The statement, drafted by Michael Lillis, had to meet the approval of so many constituencies that it was the quiddity of tepidity. It was far more interesting for having been made than for what it said. The United States pledged to prosecute those who transferred money or guns illegally to groups in Ulster (an obligation it had anyway), called for a form of government acceptable to both communities (not very far out on a limb there), and promised job-creating investment to benefit all the people of Northern Ireland (implying that it was lack of jobs that led to ethnic conflict).

The speaker had blocked any effort to convene hearings on Northern Ireland after those of 1972. Mario Biaggi had formed the Ad Hoc Congressional Committee for Irish Affairs in 1977, consisting of approximately 100 members of the House, and had pressed for hearings that would include representatives from Sinn Fein. The speaker was unwilling to grant a forum to this group after having deplored Sinn Fein's support of bullets and bombs and condemned their politics as undemocratic. O'Neill indicated to the chair of the Foreign Relations

Committee that hearings would provide an opportunity for Sinn Fein and the IRA to gain credibility. Biaggi revealed both his frustration and the speaker's power when he said: "There is no question that the Irish government's representatives in Washington have been very close to Speaker O'Neill and as a result we have not been able to have hearings."[51]

Although thwarting Biaggi on the hearings the speaker supported his position on the approval of licenses for the sale of guns to the Royal Ulster Constabulary in 1979. Biaggi's Ad Hoc Committee had been informed that the Royal Ulster Constabulary had ordered 3,000 handguns and 500 automatic rifles from Sturm, Ruger and Company in Connecticut. Biaggi sought to have the transaction halted on the basis that the State Department considered itself impartial in the Northern conflict and thus the sale of the guns was incompatible with that impartiality. Moreover, the Foreign Assistance Act forbade the sale of weapons to groups that had violated human rights. As human rights were a centerpiece of the Carter administration's foreign policy, this charge had a particularly strong bite. Carter had, in fact, embarrassed the British government by including the United Kingdom on the annual list of states that had violated human rights, based on their treatment of prisoners in Northern Ireland. Biaggi proposed an amendment to the State Department's Appropriations Bill that forbade the granting of the export license from the Munitions Control Division. O'Neill's power over Irish issues was never more strongly demonstrated than in this case, when he let the amendment go forward. Biaggi later agreed to withdraw the amendment in exchange for hearings, which would further embarrass the British government because they would bring out the reports by Amnesty International and the decision of the European Court of Human Rights on the treatment of prisoners in the Maze, the prisoners "on the blanket," and the like.

Tip O'Neill and the other leading spokesmen strengthened the Saint Patrick's Day statement of March 1979 because they felt that there were no British initiatives on Northern Ireland while there were significant abuses of Catholic nationalists by the security forces and the judicial system. In April of that year O'Neill had visited Ireland and Northern Ireland and had made the statement: "There is no more serious problem on the agenda of British politics than a crisis which has claimed 2,000 lives and caused almost 20,000 serious injuries. The problem had been treated as a political football in London, or has otherwise been given a low priority."[52] The reaction to O'Neill's statement was explosive; there was an election going on in Britain. Along with the calls in the British press to stay out of the domestic affairs of the United Kingdom was a comment by Stanley Orme, a former minister of state in the Northern Ireland Office, who said, "The Irish-American community has very little idea of the truth of the situation in Northern Ireland." It could also be said of Mr. Orme that he had very little idea of the truth of the situation among Irish Americans, for he had confused the NORAID/Caucus viewpoint with that of the speaker and other political leaders whose knowledge of the situation in Northern Ireland had increased immensely in sophistication since 1971. (Mr.

Orme also seemed to think that a knowledge of the situation in Northern Ireland would lead to no other conclusion than to agree with British policy, a position that, at the very least, invited debate.)

By July 1979 the Speaker was in no mood to be accommodating to the British. To calm his ire and avoid high profile hearings on security policy and human rights abuses in Northern Ireland, the State Department suspended the sale of weapons to the Royal Ulster Constabulary. Adrian Guelke, assessing the results, saw a "tremendous boost for the Ad Hoc Committee and its associate, the Irish National Caucus."[53] This assumes that Mario Biaggi and Speaker O'Neill had equivalent influence over the events that took place within the House of Representatives, the Congress as a whole, or the executive branch. While it is true that at this time Carter was moving away from Kennedy because Kennedy was going to challenge him for the 1980 Democratic nomination, he still had need for a cooperative relationship with the speaker. The record was clear. In Congress Biaggi's group could not move without the speaker's nod and the very "boost" that the Biaggi/Caucus received was only because of the willingness of the speaker to cooperate.

The dominance of Tip O'Neill and the "four horsemen" over Irish matters was illuminated by the Sean Donlon affair. Donlon's importance in shaping the approach of Irish American leaders cannot be overestimated. Garret FitzGerald, prime minister of Ireland at the time, has stated: "Sean Donlon was the most important connection to the Irish American Congressmen."[54] Appointed ambassador to the United States at the age of thirty-eight, Donlon was unquestionably on a fast track. He arrived the same year that Michael Lillis went back to Dublin but there was no diminution in Lillis's two-pronged approach: Lobby the O'Neill group to pressure the British government to adopt policies in the north that would involve support of power sharing and justice for the nationalist community, and at the same time mount attacks on the NORAID/Caucus groups of Irish Americans for supporting the IRA. Donlon had alienated a variety of Irish American groups who felt that their legitimate viewpoints about Sinn Fein and the British record in Ulster were being dismissed. Dealing with the perspective of some of these groups and their monocausal view of Ireland could be less than delightful.[55] In Ireland there were those on the republican edge of constitutional politics who listened with greater favor to the Biaggi/NORAID/Caucus viewpoint than to that of the four horsemen. Not surprisingly such republicans were in Fianna Fail, and when Charles Haughey took power in 1980 the Caucus and others saw it as an opportunity to amplify the voice of the more republican-oriented groups in the United States.

The efforts by Irish American republican groups to delegitimize the British presence in Ulster consisted of a constant stream of information about the British abuses in the prisons, the legal system, and police procedures. The British activities in realm of security produced such a cascade of abuses of individual rights and threats of violence that the message was not all that difficult to convey. The police in Ulster searched homes with brutality and violence; used plastic bullets for the control of demonstrations; shot unarmed demonstrators; used juryless trials; convicted on the uncorroborated word of a single police officer; used physical abuse to obtain confessions; fabricated or suppressed evidence as suited their case; closed off investigations of their own police abuses; and, apparently, adopted a police policy of "shoot to kill" when encountering suspected IRA types.[56]

Kevin Boland had visited the United States and heard the Irish American group's criticism of Donlon and the fact that their perspective had been frozen out of the top circles of power. The Caucus had been unable to gain access to the White House since early 1977. Garret FitzGerald's closeness to Lillis and Donlon exacerbated matters; FitzGerald and Haughey rarely bothered to disguise their contempt for each other. At the end of June Haughey called Donlon back to Dublin and told him he was moving to a post at the United Nations. Donlon returned to the United States, reportedly stopping at Cape Cod for a visit with Tip O'Neill. Within the week the press was reporting the anger and dismay of the three horsemen (Carey was out of the country at the time) at the decision.

Their efforts to get a plank in the Democratic Party platform calling for a united Ireland apparently were not appreciated by Haughey, to say nothing of their persistent activities on behalf of Ireland. The four indicated that there would be no new initiatives on Ireland from the United States and that cooperation with the Haughey government would not be forthcoming. The heart of the matter, however, was which Irish American groups were to have the ear of the Irish ambassador, which perspective was to prevail? Haughey bowed to the pressure and announced that Donlon was not being moved. Haughey, however, was unwilling to dissociate himself completely from the republican wing of Irish American opinion. John Hume and FitzGerald called for Haughey to repudiate Biaggi, NORAID, and the Caucus. The Taoiseach in July 1980 condemned NORAID, waffled on the Caucus, and did not mention Biaggi. The whole affair was an embarrassment to Haughey and illustrated the power of O'Neill and Kennedy to dictate the choice of the Irish ambassador to the United States and delegitimize the perspective of certain Irish American groups in the corridors of power in Dublin.

Notes

1. F. S. L. Lyons, "The Burden of History" (Rankin Lecture, Queen's University, Belfast, 1978), p. 8.

2. The collapsed boundary is a reflection of the problem with the consistency of the British Parliament. In 1914 the Parliament concluded that it would be unjust and unfair to place a 25-percent Protestant minority in a state controlled by a 75-percent Catholic majority. But in 1920 Parliament placed a 33-percent Catholic minority under the domination of a 66-percent Protestant majority. L. McCaffrey, *Ireland from Colony to Nation State* (Englewood Cliffs, N.J.: Prentice-Hall, 1979), p. 174.

3. Quoted in O'Hanlon, *The Irish,* p. 244. Callahan found the problems of Ulster a tad more difficult than those of a few London boroughs when he was prime minister of Britain.

4. Basil Brooke, speech in Newtownbutler, 12 July 1933, quoted in *Great Irish Speeches of the Twentieth Century,* ed. M. McLoughlin (Dublin: Poolbeg, 1996), p. 155.

5. J. H. Whyte, "Interpretations of the Northern Ireland Problem: An Appraisal," *Economic and Social Review* 9, no. 4 (1978), pp. 257–282; and A. Lijphart, "Review Article, The Northern Ireland Problem: Causes, Theories, Solutions," *The British Journal of Political Science* 5, no. 1 (1975), pp. 83–106.

6. Cynthia Enloe, *Ethnic Conflict and Political Development* (Boston: Little Brown, 1973), p. 15.

7. See David Miller, *Queens Rebels* (Dublin: Gill & Macmillan, 1980).

8. John Darby, *Conflict in Northern Ireland* (Dublin: Gill & Macmillan, 1976), pp. 48–49.

9. Darby cites a study that asked children in Northern Ireland to name the capital of the country in which they lived. One-half of the Catholics answered Dublin and two-thirds of the Protestants answered Belfast. Such was sectarian education in Ulster that more than half the children were wrong.

10. "IRA Statement," quoted in Coogan, *The IRA,* p. 418.

11. Ibid., p. 419.

12. Eric Nordlinger, *Conflict Regulation in Divided Societies* (Cambridge: Center for International Affairs, 1972), pp. 34, 35.

13. J. H. Whyte, "How Much Discrimination Was There under the Unionist Regime, 1921–1968," in *Contemporary Irish Studies,* ed. T. Gallagher and J. O'Connell (Manchester: Manchester University Press, 1983).

14. Nordlinger, *Conflict Regulation,* pp. 34–35.

15. See Kerby Miller, *Emigrants and Exiles* (Oxford: Oxford University Press, 1985).

16. John P. McCarthy, "Northern Ireland: Irish American Responses," *The Recorder* (Winter 1986), pp. 43–52.

17. Thomas Brown, *Irish American Nationalism* (New York: Lippincott, 1966).

18. Andrew M. Greeley, *The Irish Americans* (New York: Warner Books, 1981), pp. 3–4.

19. Quoted in Conor Cruise O'Brien, *States of Ireland* (New York: Vintage Books, 1973), p. 179.

20. Jack Holland, *Too Long a Sacrifice* (Hammondsworth: Penguin, 1982), p. 123.

21. Both segments used the name Sinn Fein for the public political wings of their organizations. This situation led to some confusion, and for some time the streets on which their headquarters were located in Dublin became the means of differentiating them: the Officials were Gardiner Place Sinn Fein and the Provisionals were Kevin Street Sinn Fein.

22. Coogan, *The IRA,* p. 437

23. James Craig, the first prime minister of Ulster, said this about the Stormont government in 1934, quoted in Darby, *Conflict in Northern Ireland,* p. 84.

24. Edward M. Kennedy, "Ulster Is an International Issue," *Foreign Policy* 57 (Summer 1973), pp. 57–71.

25. Barry White, *John Hume: Statesman of the Troubles* (Belfast: Blackstaff Press, 1984), p. 188.

26. Jack Holland, *The American Connection: U.S. Guns, Money, and Influence in Northern Ireland* (New York: Viking Press, 1987), p. 116.

27. Padraig O'Malley, *The Uncivil Wars: Ireland Today* (Boston: Houghton Mifflin, 1983), p. 272.

28. Ibid.

29. Roger Faligot, *Britain's Military Strategy in Ireland* (Kerry: Brandon Books, 1983), pp. 124–125.

30. Maurice Tugwell, "Politics and Propaganda of the Provisional IRA," in *Terrorism: Theory and Practise*, ed. Y. Alexander, D. Carleton, and P. Wilkinson (Boulder, Colo.: Westview Press, 1979), pp. 13–40.

31. Anthony McIntyre is quoted by journalist Jonathan Stevenson on the period—"We went to jail, our people hunger striked, we suffered in protest, we died, we killed an awful, awful lot of people in the process . . . we lost a lot of our own lives, we blew up London, we blew up Belfast, we wrecked the place"—giving Stevenson the title of his book, *We Wrecked the Place* (New York: Free Press, 1996), p. 1.

32. Tugwell, "Politics and Propaganda," p. 22. Tugwell quotes from Maria McGuire's book *To Take Arms* on the briefing of speakers visiting the United States: "There should be copious references to the martyrs of 1916. . . . By no means should anything be said against the Catholic Church and all references to socialism should be strictly avoided."

33. Holland, *American Connection*, p. 138.

34. Scott Anderson, "Making a Killing: The High Cost of Peace in Northern Ireland," *Harpers* (February 1994), pp. 45–54. Anderson argues that the gangster organizations from both communities with ties to the paramilitaries were deeply imbedded in Northern Ireland. Their influence was based on the influx of money into the north from the British government.

35. Ed Maloney, "The IRA," *Magill*, 1 September 1980, p. 14.

36. Edgar O'Ballance asserted that Adams was Chief of Staff of the IRA in 1978 in "IRA Leadership Problems," in *Terrorism: Theory and Practise*, ed. Alexander, Carleton, and Wilkinson, p. 79.

37. James Glover, "Northern Ireland: Future Terrorist Trends" (November 1978), a secret report made public by the IRA and included in Faligot, *Britain's Military Strategy*, pp. 221–242.

38. There is not a little irony in this; the Provisional IRA was created in 1970 because it rejected a strategy of elections and Left-wing ideology.

39. John Hume, Interview by R. Finnegan, Boston, April 1977.

40. See text of decision in B. H. Weston, R. A. Falk, and A. A. D'Amato, eds., *International Law and World Order* (St. Paul, Minn.: West Publishing, 1980), p. 523.

41. Nordlinger, *Conflict Regulation*, p. 23.

42. Paul Bew and Henry Patterson, *The British State and the Ulster Crisis* (London: Verso, 1985), p. 95.

43. Coogan, *The IRA*, p. 464.

44. Lee, *Ireland 1912–1985*, p. 685.

45. John Stalker, *Stalker* (London: Harrap, 1988).

46. Bew and Patterson, *British State and the Ulster Crisis*, p. 95.

47. B. White, *John Hume: Statesman of the Troubles* (Belfast: Blackstaff Press, 1984), p. 188; and Garret FitzGerald, Interview with R. Finnegan, Dublin, 18 June 1991.

48. FitzGerald, Interview.

49. Brian Donnelly, Interview with R. Finnegan, Quincy, MA, 12 July 1991.

50. Holland, *American Connection*, p. 120.

51. *New York Times*, 21 April 1979, p. 4.

52. Holland, *American Connection*, p. 131.

53. Adrian Guelke, *Northern Ireland: The International Perspective* (Dublin: Gill & Macmillan, 1988), p. 141.

54. FitzGerald, Interview.

55. An example would be John J. Finucane, editor of the *American Irish Political Education Newsletter*, who wrote in December 1990: "Britain's record, often condemned by the Soviet Union, would have shamed the likes of Hitler and Stalin. She has resorted to mass murder, torture, censorship, shoot to kill, juryless courts, politics of exclusion, discrimination of every sort. Britain has even attempted genocide. Worst of all she has done this in the name of democracy." To parse this statement so as to bring it in any way in line with the events that actually happened in Northern Ireland would require so many pages as to run the risk of deforesting Canada. It exemplifies the particular, and peculiar, world view of some militant Irish Americans. This view is so locked into its own construction of reality that it cites the testimony of the former Soviet Union (with its renowned commitment to historical fidelity) as evidence in a statement that compares Britain's behavior with that of Stalin. It is a world view that bludgeons the capacity of words to provide distinctions in meaning, however fragile those meanings may be in this post-modernist age.

56. See O'Malley, *Uncivil Wars*; Bell, *The Irish Troubles*; and Stalker, *Stalker*.

10

▄▄▄▄▄▄▄▄▄▄

NORTHERN IRELAND: THE GORDIAN KNOT UNTIED?

Developments in Northern Ireland, 1981–1992

In 1981 Bobby Sands, a member of the Irish Republican Army, died of a hunger strike in the Maze Prison near Belfast, and the streets exploded in violence. Sands's hunger strike and death wove together a number of the most heroic and tragic strands of Irish history and contemporary Northern Ireland. The tactic of the hunger strike evoked memories of the death of Terence MacSwiney in 1920 from a hunger strike in a British prison. Shortly before his death Sands had been elected to the British Parliament, whose rule over Northern Ireland he rejected; Sinn Fein had used the same tactics in 1918 to create the first Dail Eireann. Sands was jailed for possession of firearms and involvement in the blowing up of a warehouse; the IRA had taken the path of the gun against British rule from 1918 to 1921. During Sands's hunger strike violent confrontations had occurred in the streets of Belfast, and on Easter Sunday in 1981 they resulted in the death of two youths who were crushed by a British Army truck. Their funerals were two more in a long string of funerals in Belfast and Derry, not only from the violence since 1968 but from trouble in the 1920s and 1930s. The British were adamant in refusing to make concessions to Sands's demands for better treatment in prison, reflecting the "not-an-inch" position that the Ulster unionists had adopted toward Catholic demands for half a century. International opinion favored a concession,

331

but the British prime minister felt that such a move would cause a backlash from the Protestant community, a pressure not unfamiliar to Lloyd George in 1921.

Sands's death was the culmination of a series of British policy decisions. In 1972 William Whitelaw, secretary of state for Northern Ireland, responded to a hunger strike by IRA and loyalist prisoners by granting them a form of prisoner-of-war status that included wearing their own clothes, being able to mix freely, and doing no prison work. In 1975, however, the government rejected the prisoner-of-war status and adopted the policy of "criminalization." Acts committed by IRA and loyalist paramilitaries were to be considered ordinary crimes and the perpetrators ordinary criminals.

In 1976 the government began to phase out the special status of those IRA men who were in the H Block section (so called because of its shape) of the Maze Prison outside Belfast. This section contained over 900 prisoners, 600 of whom were IRA members. This change resulted in protest from 417 of the prisoners, who refused to wear prison clothes, covering themselves with blankets; refused privileges; and smeared their cells with excrement. The British government's response was to label their demands as a maneuver to achieve political status and thus open the possibility of amnesty later. At the end of 1980 some of the prisoners went on a hunger strike to achieve five demands: (1) freedom to not wear prison clothes; (2) ability to freely associate or mix; (3) no compulsion to do prison work; (4) one letter, one parcel, or one visit a week; and (5) full remission on sentences (remission is one day off a sentence for each day of good behavior). After fifty-three days the strike was settled, or at least it appeared to be so. After the turn of the year, however, the prisoners felt that the government had reneged on the agreement, and Bobby Sands, a spokesman during the earlier hunger strike, began his own fast in January 1981. Sands was followed by others; eventually Sands and nine other men died. The hunger strike put the British government in an embarrassing position because the prisoner's demands appeared to be reasonable.

Public opinion turned against Prime Minister Thatcher's policy. Thatcher's uncompromising stand turned the complaints of the prisoners into the broader question of the whole situation in Northern Ireland. The IRA increased violence in the streets, and the situation reverted back to that of the early 1970s. The hunger strike ended when the families of some of the strikers ordered that they be tube fed after they were comatose. The IRA did not want this to be done but the families were convinced, correctly as it turned out, that the death of more hunger strikers was not going to change the status of prisoners. The IRA wanted to take advantage of the negative response of the public to British policy, not only with respect to prisons but with respect to Northern Ireland as a whole.

Another attempt at a devolved government for Northern Ireland was generated in 1982 by the secretary for Northern Ireland, James Prior, who saw that direct rule would lead not to conflict regulation in Ulster but only to continued uncertainty and violence. He thought that any movement to completely integrate

Northern Ireland into the United Kingdom would alienate the Catholic community, encourage the violence of the IRA, and terminate the steady cooperation with Dublin on Northern matters. In a 1982 white paper Prior proposed returning to the idea of an assembly. The major innovation in his proposal was the idea of "rolling devolution." Under this arrangement a Northern Assembly would begin with an oversight function but no power. Should legislators achieve a 70 percent consensus on policy in six areas of administration, the Assembly would "earn" the right to control that legislation. Parliament would then approve the grant of devolution. If the rolling devolution did not happen after four years the secretary could prorogue the Assembly, call new elections, or revert to direct rule.

The Assembly elections were held in October 1982 and the results reflected the changes in the politics of Ulster since 1973. The Unionists divided into the devolutionist camp (the Democratic Unionist Party) and the integrationist camp (the Official Unionists). The SDLP ran on an abstentionist position. The SDLP argued that in 1974 they had been part of a power-sharing Executive, in 1975–1976 London had assured them that there would be a power-sharing government, and now in 1982 London wanted them to participate in a powerless Assembly without even a nod to the Irish dimension. The SDLP's commitment to nonviolent constitutionalism was rewarded by London with less and less power and responsibility, and as a consequence they would not participate. Sinn Fein, running as the party in support of the IRA, vowed they would not take their seats. Sinn Fein held that the British had no right to create assemblies for Ireland. The SDLP never took their seats, nor did Sinn Fein. In 1983–1984 the Official Unionists withdrew for six months. The Assembly was never able to approach even remotely the possibility that it would "roll" the power from Parliament over to the Province.

The first, and most well-known hunger striker, Bobby Sands, had been elected to the British Parliament at Westminster while in prison in 1981. This prompted Sinn Fein to contest the 1982 Northern Ireland Assembly elections in Ulster, something they had refused to do up to this point. Benefiting no doubt from the wellspring of support for Sinn Fein that resulted from the hunger strike of 1980–1981, Sinn Fein received 64,191 votes and five seats. The results of the election identified Sinn Fein as a political force. The party garnered 10 percent of the vote in the election and one-third of the vote of the Catholic nationalist community. When debating whether to enter electoral politics, Danny Morrison said: "Will anyone here object if, with a ballot paper in this hand and an Armalite in this hand, we take power in Ireland?"[1]

Events, however, were overtaking the Assembly even as the truncated membership took their seats. The SDLP, stung by the Sinn Fein vote, went to Dublin and sought to generate a fresh initiative on the Northern issue. The government of Garret FitzGerald agreed and convened a Forum for a New Ireland from May 1983 to May 1984. While initially seen as a public relations effort by the SDLP, the Forum began to take on a life of its own. The major parties in the Republic and a wide variety of groups participated, studies were done, interviews conducted, and

hearings held. The result was an examination of the shibboleths of Irish nationalism that had rarely taken place in the Republic in the prior sixty years. The resulting report was seen by its creators as something of a breakthrough on the Irish
question. The policy proposals on the north to create a "new Ireland" included a
united Ireland under a single government, joint authority under Dublin and
London, and a confederation of the two states. Each alternative, however, was unacceptable respectively to the unionists, the British, and the IRA.

Haughey and Fianna Fail rejected the second and third alternatives as soon as
the ink was dry, interpreting the Forum only as a call for a united Ireland so as to
bring it in line with the nationalist tradition of that party. Despite this hypocrisy,
the Forum did contribute to the dialogue on Northern Ireland in the same way
that the Sunningdale agreement did, helping Irish nationalists to recognize that a
"solution" to the problem would have to take into account the validity of the
unionist tradition on the island. After the Forum for a New Ireland issued its report in 1984 there was a feeling of optimism among some Irish that the Forum
had opened the possibility for change in the north. Prime Minister Thatcher
quickly disabused everyone of that notion when she rejected the Forum's three
proposed alternatives for the future of Northern Ireland in a press conference,
curtly dismissing the three alternatives with the words "out . . . out . . . out."

A concatenation of pressures led the British government to change the grounds
upon which it dealt with Northern Ireland. These included increased pressure
from the United States and President Reagan to adopt a more flexible position on
the north. In addition, a series of meetings among high-level civil servants from
London and Dublin had begun on a regular basis in the early 1980s. Also, the
wide international attention given to *Report of the Forum for a New Ireland* contrasted with the obvious ineffectiveness of the Northern Ireland Assembly. The
Assembly was to be supplanted by the shift in conflict regulation on the part of
the British government in 1985 when it signed an agreement with Dublin.

The IRA killed six people in a bombing of a hotel in Brighton in 1984 where
the Conservative Party of the United Kingdom was having its annual conference.
That Margaret Thatcher came close to being assassinated by the IRA was a reminder of the power of that organization and its political and military impact.
Thatcher's policy of criminalization and her rejection of the Forum's recommendations suggested that she would not be likely to take a bold step on the Ulster
problem, but she did. Negotiated in secret, the treaty the government put forward
was an attempt to move the peace process in Ulster forward in effect "over the
heads" of the communities on the ground. The inclusion of the SDLP in consulta-
tions on the Dublin side, however, was not matched by the inclusion of the
unionists on the London side, so the treaty was not only politically unpalatable to
the unionists but was a surprise as well.

The governments of Ireland and Britain signed the Anglo-Irish Agreement in
November 1985. Lodged with the United Nations, the Agreement was negotiated
at the level of sovereign governments. The principal thrust of the document was

to create a British-Irish Intergovernmental Conference composed of ministers from each of the governments. They were to consult on matters of mutual concern on Northern issues, recognizing the rights and identities of the two traditions and seeking to promote human rights, economic development, and reconciliation. The substantive areas of concern were politics, security, justice, and cross-border cooperation. The Agreement called for the creation of a devolved government in Northern Ireland that would "secure widespread acceptance." The Irish government supported that goal.

The significance of the treaty, like Sunningdale, was not only its provisions but its very existence. The treaty elevated the Irish dimension to the center of the British approach to the problem of Ulster. Because the Irish government's role was consultative there was no derogation of British sovereignty, yet for London to accept that the Irish nationalist community in the north would have no confidence in political or security arrangements without the participation of Dublin is a considerable distance from Margaret Thatcher's assertion years earlier that "Ulster was as British as Finchley."

The unionists were furious and felt that they had been betrayed; their loyalty to the United Kingdom had been repaid with the treachery they had always feared. The unionist penchant for reading the most expansive, and ultimate, consequences into every political situation ensured that they would view the treaty as the first step in a chain of events that would inevitably lead to a united Ireland under Dublin. Interestingly enough, in a mirror image, critics on the nationalist side saw the treaty as mere window dressing to fob off the nationalists with meaningless "consultation" while Britain, as usual, retained control of the north.

The actual governance of the province had not changed. Political scientist Paul Bew described it as "direct rule with a coat of green paint."[2] In fact the treaty had a paradoxical quality. By generating such explosive anger in the unionist community, London demonstrated that it would (finally) take steps that would run contrary to the unionist position and take the political consequences. Yet in doing so Britain also drove the unionists, paranoid as they are, into a frenzy of political intransigence that undermined London's ability to create the devolved institutions called for by the treaty. The Unionists withdrew from Parliament at Westminister, would not participate in government, and stopped paying their taxes to back their demand that the treaty be rescinded. The SDLP were in no better shape because, since they were in on the negotiations and the Unionists had been excluded, the Unionists did not now trust them (as if they ever did). Yet the treaty was of no particular advantage to the SDLP because they had no role in the governance of Ulster.

Clearly the British had demonstrated that they now had the resolution to undertake new arrangements, if they could just find them. In the period after the signing of the Anglo-Irish Agreement discussion was frozen by the militance of the unionists. By 1990 it appeared that progress could be made, and that period was marked by "talks about talks." In 1991 it was agreed that the talks would have three strands: unionist and nationalist in the north; Dublin and Belfast in Ireland; and Dublin and London at the international level. In fact, the talks proceeded in fits and starts as conditions were advanced that were unacceptable to one side or the other. The grounds of conflict were again negotiations on devolved government, with the Unionists vetoing any power-sharing structure and the inability/unwillingness of the British to do anything about it.

British Policy, 1981–1992

Responses by the British to the hunger strikes of 1980–1981 can be framed in two ways. The first view is that Thatcher held to a tough line and would not be intimidated by the creation of martyrs or by pressure from the global community, the Church, the media, and the Irish government. The hunger strike petered out after ten men died and the families of strikers who were comatose ordered that they be fed. The British government did not give in to criminals and terrorists and indicated that such strategies would not work in the future. A second view is that Thatcher was a cruel autocrat so blinded by her own sense of righteousness that she could not see, or did not care to see, that the hunger strikes symbolized the complete failure of British policy in Northern Ireland since the end of the nineteenth century. After the hunger strikes the crystalization of opinion on the illegitimacy of British rule in Ulster was palpable and the long-term effect was to corrode the credibility of the British government's claim on Northern Ireland under the existing political arrangements.

The Forum for a New Ireland was not a British policy initiative on Northern Ireland, but it fits into the same category as the response to the hunger strikes. In this instance a Report on a New Ireland generated by the Forum set up by the Irish government had a much greater degree of political legitimacy than the coercive pressure from the hunger strike. Thatcher's response, however, was essentially the same. When presented with the three alternative institutional arrangements that the Forum advanced, Thatcher rejected them all out of hand. Since the Forum had presented the arrangements as places to begin the process of overall discussion and diplomacy on the north (as opposed to increased coercion in prison policy), Thatcher's dismissal was both an insult to Irish Prime Minister Garret FitzGerald and a cold display of Thatcherite arrogance that only alienated the Irish and Irish American political figures. Clearly external initiatives, whether reasoned or coercive, were not going to move Ms. Thatcher.

The rolling devolution Assembly was a good idea in the abstract because it focused on the need to build cross-community consent through political institutions. The Assembly, however, was out of synch with the political landscape of Ulster at the time. The contradictory pressures of direct rule had driven the parties in Ulster to more polarized positions. Sinn Fein, representing the IRA, won five seats, and at the other end of the spectrum Paisley's DUP won twenty-one. Thus 32 percent of the vote went to the extremes. If we add the percentage given to the Official Unionists (the party that emerged out of the ruins of the old Unionist Party), 64 percent of the electorate would have to be characterized as extremely rigid. There was little common ground on the questions of local rule and the relationship with the Republic among the voters in Ulster.

Prior's conceptualization of the Ulster problem as one of building consent between the two political positions implies an equality of position that was incomprehensible to the SDLP. Moreover, London was devoid of the political will, except in the security realm, to make the playing field level by confronting the intransigence of the unionists with the same energy that the unionists put into the denial of participation by the nationalists.

The Anglo-Irish Agreement reflected London's shift to dealing directly with Dublin in a formal treaty and indicated major change in the level at which London would deal with the Ulster problem. It was in fact an important step for both governments in the long term. Dublin took the risk of buying into British political and especially security policy in Ulster while not having authority over that policy. London took the risk of signaling to the unionists that Dublin had a "say" in the politics of Northern Ireland and that to pretend otherwise was to maintain the unionist mythology that there once was a happy, well-governed little province full of hard-working, God-fearing people whose political autonomy was threatened by some Dublin-sponsored intransigent terrorists. The process of dealing with the politics of Ulster required that both governments, and both communities, go through a learning process that involved shedding cherished assumptions about the past and the present. The Forum for a New Ireland and the Agreement were points on a learning curve, the trajectory of which can be said to have led to the Good Friday Agreement of 1998.

The United States and Northern Ireland, 1981–1992

In 1981 a loose network of representatives and senators who shared the O'Neill-Kennedy approach to Northern Ireland and Irish matters in general became the Friends of Ireland, with O'Neill as leader. A number of instances illustrate their pressure on London. During the hunger strikes Speaker O'Neill, Senator Kennedy, and others sent a telegram to Margaret Thatcher urging her to change British policy. The Friends, and especially O'Neill, played a significant role in what was seen as the most important change on the Ulster issue in sixty-three years. After the Forum for a New Ireland had issued its report and Thatcher had quickly rejected it, Sean Donlon contacted the speaker and asked that he ask President Reagan to intervene with the prime minister on the Irish question. In the meantime the prime minister had been sharply criticized by the Friends of Ireland, who had written to the president that: "The destructive alienation and violence that plague the people of that land are also unfortunately becoming an increasing source of contention between the United States and Great Britain."[3] Thatcher was also criticized for her intransigence by the *New York Times* and the *Washington Post*.

The connection with Speaker O'Neill was not, of course, the only effort of the Irish government to enlist the aid of the United States. Donlon also asked William Clark to ask President Reagan to urge Ms. Thatcher to be somewhat less inflexible. President Reagan did bring up the matter in December 1984, prompting a bevy of denials from the prime minister that there was any breakdown between the Irish government and London on Ulster.

In February 1985, when Thatcher was in Washington to address Congress, Speaker O'Neill asked the president to raise the question again; requested the British Ambassador, Oliver Wright, to ask Ms. Thatcher to include a reference to Northern Ireland in her speech; and, finally, met with her personally to express his concerns and to pledge his support for reconstruction efforts should there be a breakthrough on the Northern question.[4] It would be presumptuous to think that the U.S. interventions in these negotiations made all the difference, but it also would be unrealistic to think that they made no difference at all. The Anglo-Irish Agreement was signed in November 1985, on a day that found Speaker O'Neill in the Oval Office with President Reagan, who promised to implement the pledge of aid to Northern Ireland made by Reagan's predecessor Jimmy Carter. This represented, no doubt, the only time Reagan praised Carter.

Garret FitzGerald had sent Donlon to confer with O'Neill about getting the president's support. O'Neill agreed to talk to the president about it and did so at one of their breakfast meetings in October. The result was an announcement that displayed the triumph of Irishness over partisanship and the influence of the speaker on the president when it came to Irish matters. Fulfilling the promise that O'Neill had given to Garret FitzGerald in May 1985, a bill went through the House by Saint Patrick's Day of 1986. This was the last term of the speaker, so it represented something of a going away present to him from the members of the House. When the Senate approved the bill it was for one year for $50 million, the same amount as the House bill. This aid was subsequently extended for two more years at $35 million a year. Congressman Brian Donnelly of Massachusetts became the head of the Friends of Ireland group in the Congress at the request of O'Neill on his retirement.

Tip O'Neill balanced dissatisfaction with British policy and pressure to change it without endorsing the violence of the IRA and their bloodshed. Militant republican nationalists in the United States, and their counterparts in Ireland and Ulster, were excluded from framing the Ulster issue in exclusively republican nationalist terms as a British "occupation" of the north.

External Influences on Northern Ireland

Northern Ireland is among the more illustrative cases of the jagged intersection of the forces working in world politics today. Converging on this polarized province were the ethnic transnational pressures from the United States and increased pressures from the supranational level, the European Union, and international non-governmental human rights organizations challenging the legitimacy of British security policy.

It is commonplace to note the increasing porosity of international borders. The extension of complex interdependence, increased density of economic interaction, and increased flow of communication shape the entire grid of global politics.[5] Particular to the conflict in Northern Ireland is the ethnic transnational interaction through which external groups in other nations, Irish emigrants who live in Britain and the United States, support the Catholic nationalists. The Protestant unionists also draw support from their co-religionists in Australia, Canada, and elsewhere, although to a considerably smaller degree. The Irish American groups illustrate the enduring influence of the transnational linkage between people with a primordial bond of ethnicity.[6]

Human Rights

The erosion of sovereignty within political systems has been accompanied by the bounding of sovereignty through the growth of increasingly independent international organizations acting on global issues. Britain's membership in the European Union, despite London's reservations about the expansion of the power of Brussels, does not exempt the United Kingdom from the human rights pressures that emerge from Europe. International non-governmental organizations such as Amnesty International and other ad hoc human rights organizations, while devoid of the power to compel, are not devoid of the power to mobilize pressure and thus, at the very least, to embarrass.

With respect to the United Nations, the Irish government requested that the Security Council send peacekeeping forces to Northern Ireland in August 1969, arguing (correctly, as it turned out) that British troops would exacerbate the problem. The Security Council met and the British representative spoke against the proposal, arguing that Ulster was a local problem. The initiative was shelved when the Security Council adjourned without dealing with the issue.

At the regional level, however, the European Union is a different matter. Both Britain and Ireland entered the EU in 1973. Northern Ireland did not come onto the European agenda until 1980. Transnational pressure during this period accelerated when the hunger strikes of 1980–1981 brought about widespread criticism of the British government. British policy was seen in the United States and Europe as inflexible and callous, and the Thatcher government was subjected to a media blitz generally sympathetic to Irish nationalism. Northern Ireland was seen by Europeans, and in fact by the larger world, as an illegitimate and anachronistic remnant of colonialism. The peculiar status of Ulster as part of the United Kingdom, but capable of succession if it so chose, ascribes to it a status of something more than a colony but something less than an integrated part of the United Kingdom.[7]

In 1980 an Irish MEP sought to have the Legal Affairs Committee of the European Parliament investigate human rights violations in Ulster but the Committee would not do so. After the hunger strikes of 1981, however, a resolution was passed by the Parliament expressing concern about the hunger strikes and the violence. That year the European Parliament also established a working group to examine the conditions in Northern Ireland and in 1982 passed a resolution banning the use of plastic bullets in Northern Ireland. Much to the dismay of the British government, the European Parliament in 1983 mandated that its Political Affairs Committee conduct an inquiry into the crisis. The Committee produced a balanced report, endorsed by the European Parliament in 1984, urging British-Irish joint cooperation on the Province, thus indicating a rejection of the British position that Ulster was purely a local or internal matter. Adrian Guelke notes: "It put added pressure on the British government to reach agreement with the Republic of Ireland through the Anglo-Irish Process."[8] Not content with its earlier resolution, the Parliament condemned the use of plastic bullets again in 1984 and called for an inquiry into the British Prevention of Terrorism Act in 1985. In 1986 the European Parliament passed three resolutions questioning the convictions of the Birmingham Six, the Guilford Four, and the Maguire Seven, all cases in which evidence was either suppressed or manufactured by the British police. The Parliament also endorsed the Anglo-Irish Agreement of 1985 which, in this instance, had the effect of taking some of the European pressure off the United Kingdom.

Human rights have been, and remain, the area of greatest vulnerability for the United Kingdom. Police and prison practices and judicial procedures in Ulster have been scrutinized by numerous organizations. The Women's Peace Movement mentioned above was awarded the Norwegian People's Peace Prize in 1976 and the Nobel Peace Prize in 1977. This attention was an embarrassment to the purveyors of violence in Ireland and it put them on the defensive, at least briefly. London, attempting to appear as an anti-terrorist peacemaker, was no less embarrassed because its political policies since 1968 seemed pallid and ineffectual while its security policy appeared to perpetuate the problem.[9] A report by Amnesty International in 1978 also created pressure on London. It documented strong evidence of physical abuse of seventy-eight prisoners during interrogations by the Royal Ulster Constabulary at Castlereagh Prison. Especially damaging was the determination of the European Court in 1978 that the treatment of prisoners in the Maze Prison was cruel and abusive.

Amnesty International again issued a number of reports in 1988, 1989, and 1990, which brought international visibility to the issues of killings by the security forces, the use of defendants who indict other offenders for a reduction in their sentence, the mistreatment of prisoners, and the question of fair trials in the Guilford and Birmingham bombings. The International Helsinki Federation for Human Rights issued a report in 1990, titled *Irish Terrorism or British Colonialism: The Violation of Human Rights in Northern Ireland.* Amnesty issued another report in 1991, titled *United Kingdom: Human Rights Concerns,* which encompassed earlier concerns and included references to the killing on Gibraltar, both calling attention to the United Kingdom's protestations about the violence of IRA terrorists and charging the SAS with shooting down unarmed suspects. The stream of reports and studies continues unabated up to the present, following a regular pattern of British denunciation, press and pressure group condemnation, and a further erosion in the legitimacy of British police and judicial procedures in Ulster.[10]

Sovereignty

The degree to which the international community in various forms plays a part in softening the concept of sovereignty in the definition of policies as domestic or international is mirrored in the elastic concept of sovereignty utilized by various groups in Northern Ireland. Unionists and nationalists prefer a rather classical notion of sovereignty as absolute coercive power located in London when they want the British government to take action against their opponent. Nationalists, for example, call for London to "crack down" on the unionists to force them to accede to equal political participation in government and to curb the abuses of police and judicial power in Ulster used to oppress the nationalist community. When it comes to the application of British sovereignty to the nationalist community, however, they claim a degree of autonomy from London in being Irish not British, deny the legitimacy of London's rule over them, and deny the political authenticity of the province of Ulster. Yet they want that same London to send imperial thunderbolts of coercion onto the heads of the unionists. The unionists are no different. In matters of controlling terrorism and use of police powers, unionists demand that London "crack down" on nationalists and give them back their B Specials. On the other hand, when it comes to the application of London's sovereignty over the unionist community they resist, based on a conditional loyalty that did not accept any actions from London that threatened the preservation of the Protestant community or that tampered with the institutions of "their" state. Outside groups bought into these definitions. For example, Irish Americans demanded that the British do things to the unionists that if done to the nationalist community would have been seen as heavy-handed oppression. In fact, in spite of the historical record, the degree of political autonomy of both unionists and nationalists in the latter years of the twentieth century limited British options.

The Peace Process, the Good Friday Agreement of April 1998, and the Prizes of Peace

The path to the Good Friday Agreement was a process of weaving together the numerous threads of Ulster politics into a fabric of potential peace. The role of the United States moved from the transnational grassroots ethnic linkages and pressure from Irish American political elites to the diplomatic channel of presidential intervention. British policy in Ulster was transformed initially by the policies of Conservative Party Prime Minister John Major and more directly by the election of Labour Party Prime Minister Tony Blair in 1997. The positions of the political parties in Northern Ireland were changing, at a glacial pace to be sure, and included the receptivity of Sinn Fein and the Official Unionist Party to negotiations. Finally, the posture of the loyalists, and especially the IRA paramilitaries, shifted to acceptance of negotiations. The peace process of 1993 to 1998 can be said to be a culmination of political activities, secret negotiations, open negotiations, international treaties, elections, cease fires, and violence, marked by successes, failures, false starts, posturing, pontificating, compromises, and promises made and broken, all culminating in a moment when former U.S. Senator John Mitchell found a threshold of consensus among these groups and gave it structure in the form of the April 10, 1998, Good Friday Agreement.

Negotiations and Setbacks

The fact that the Northern question was being dealt with on a government to government level was accentuated by the declarations that emerged in 1993 and 1995 from the British and Irish governments. Critical steps, however, were being taken outside the conference room that would lead to a breakthrough in 1994. Talks were going on between the British government and Sinn Fein/IRA from 1991 to 1994. This was revealed in 1994 and caused a certain degree of distress to those, such as Prime Minister Thatcher and President Reagan, who had constantly reiterated the principle of not negotiating with terrorists. It put Sinn Fein on a different footing with London. Sinn Fein's electoral strength had ebbed from a high point in 1983 of 13.4 percent to less than 9 percent and in 1992 Gerry Adams, the head of Sinn Fein, had lost his district's Northern Ireland seat in Parliament. In the European elections of 1989, John Hume, the head of the SDLP, had received 25 percent of the vote and his Sinn Fein rival Danny Morrison 9 percent. In the elections in the Republic in 1987 Sinn Fein received 1.7 percent of the vote, dropping to an even more insignificant 1.2 percent in 1989.

In addition, John Hume had initiated an effort to talk with Gerry Adams in 1985, which was aborted by the militancy of the IRA. In 1988, however, they finally met, Hume stressing that it appeared that the IRA strategy was more sacred than their goals and that identifying the British in Ireland as the sole cause of the problem was simplistic to say the least. Members of Sinn Fein were willing to admit privately that the "long war" strategy could not guarantee victory and would probably alienate the public and that the bombing at Enniskillen in 1987, in which eleven innocent civilians were killed, was a particularly gruesome illustration. Those talks ended inconclusively but did set the stage for the IRA and Sinn Fein leadership to question the certitude of their approach, as well as contributing to the creation of the Sinn Fein report, *Toward a Lasting Peace in Ireland.* The report recognized, at long last, that the unionist community and its fears in

Northern Ireland would have to be acknowledged and that British withdrawal would take place over a long period of time. The report also discussed the role of the European Union, acknowledged the existence of the two traditions in Ireland, and recognized that self-determination for Ireland as a whole must include the rights of the minority in the north.

The back channels had been widely used by the Irish and British governments, both of which had continuing communication with Sinn Fein in the early 1990s. In 1993 the talks between Hume and Adams resumed, leading to a declaration of principles that included the acceptance of the two traditions on the island, self-determination for the north, and national reconciliation. The Irish government's Prime Minister Reynolds and Foreign Minister Spring in the middle of 1993 were also attempting to find common ground with the British government.

At the time, the revelation of the length and depth of the talks between Hume and Adams generated a huge amount of criticism of John Hume. More than most Hume was seen as a pillar of integrity and as committed to peace through negotiation without the degree of egocentrism found in most political figures. After the Shankill bombing by the IRA (see below) Hume was blistered with condemnation. The unionists gloated, claiming that the bombing only proved what they had been asserting for years—that nationalists really were all alike—and that Hume was consorting with terrorists. Conor Cruise O'Brien saw Hume "dancing to Gerry Adams's tune." Hume was frozen out of the negotiations and fell ill from the pressure. In the long term, however, Hume had helped convince Gerry Adams of two things: that the unity of Ireland was not going to come through IRA violence and that the idea of self-determination for the whole island could be conceived as having two parts, the south and the north, and the process should be directed at trying to achieve an expression of that public will. Hume's efforts with Adams not only advanced the peace process but, after Shankill, eventually drew substantial public support. Hume's risk helped to legitimize Adams's actions in 1994 and 1995.

Talks had been going on in 1991 and 1992 between the constitutional parties of Northern Ireland about the basis on the three strands: the relationships between the two communities in the north, between the north and the south, and between Dublin and London. The talks started and stopped amid killings and bombings and a lack of political consensus. The election of Albert Reynolds, former show band and pet food magnate, as prime minister of the Republic, who took office in 1993, would not have immediately led to the conclusion that an important initiative on the north would come on his watch. Reynolds, however, not carrying any particular ideological baggage about the north and being a pragmatic problem solver, shared the goal of addressing the violence in Ulster with his coalition partner Dick Spring, the head of the Labour Party. Reynolds sought out John Major and indicated that it was time to break the logjam. Secretly both the Irish and the British governments had been maintaining contacts with Sinn Fein and Gerry Adams, looking for a formula that could be used to start a dialogue while at the same time allowing the British government to assure the unionists that nothing would change in the north without a majority vote and that unionist interests would be protected.

The efforts of Hume and Adams and the British and Irish governments were nearly derailed in October 1993 by a horrifying bombing in a fish shop on the Shankill Road, in which the IRA was attempting to kill the leaders of the Ulster Defense Association, the Unionist paramilitary group. Thomas Begley, an IRA man, killed himself and nine other people in the shop and near it when the bomb went off prematurely. Fifty-six people were severely injured; among the dead were four women and two girls, ages seven and thirteen. Gerry Adams took part in the funeral of Thomas Begley and carried the casket in the procession. This picture was flashed across the television screens of Britain and Ireland and undercut Adams's credibility as a person seeking peace. Adams was compelled to participate in the funeral despite his own reservations about the bombing, to retain credibility with Sinn Fein and the IRA, but Reynolds, Spring, and John Major were appalled and their efforts were frozen for a period of time.[11] Not to be outdone in their ruthless minuet of death, the UDA a week after the Shankill bombing sent two young men into a pub in a Catholic neighborhood in Graysteel in Derry on Halloween night. They shouted "trick or treat" then opened fire with AK 47s, wounding nineteen people, of whom eight died. The climate for compromise was hardly auspicious.

In December 1993 some rather intense and confrontational diplomacy took place in which Prime Ministers John Major and Albert Reynolds tried to find common ground on a declaration in light of the Hume-Adams initiative. London wanted no association with Adams because the violence in October hardly promoted a generosity of spirit toward the republicans and the loyalists. Despite the violence, or perhaps because of it, the two prime ministers issued the Downing Street Declaration. It was a delicate compendium of position papers that had been part of the sub-rosa dialogue for years. This included the IRA's paper on peace, which had been passed to the Irish government in 1992 and which moved beyond the simplistic "Brits Out" position of years past. The Declaration called for a new approach to the north, recognizing the two traditions, with no preconditions, and open to all parties. The prime ministers asked that the paramilitaries lay down their arms and enter into negotiations to create new governing arrangements for Ulster. The nationalists were assured that Britain had "no selfish strategic or economic interests" in Northern Ireland. London indicated that it supported the democratic will of the people of the north whether they preferred a united Ireland or maintenance of the Union with Britain.

The unionists were assured that the British guaranteed that there would be no change in the status of Ulster until a majority of the people in the province democratically expressed their choice for another option. The government of Ireland assured the unionists that "it would be wrong to attempt to impose a united Ireland in the absence of the freely given consent of a majority of the people of

Northern Ireland." The rights of the people of Northern Ireland to freedom of thought and of religion, democratic participation, and equal opportunity would be part of any arrangements. The document indicated that there was no need for the continuation of violence because the future of Ulster was to be determined democratically with respect for all views. The British government stated in the Declaration: "It is for the people of Ireland alone, by agreement between the two parts respectively, to exercise their right of self determination on the basis of consent, freely and concurrently given, North and South, to bring about a united Ireland if that is their wish." The two governments recognized the absence of trust but asserted that they could break the cycle of violence: "Democratically mandated parties which establish a commitment to exclusively peaceful methods and which have shown that they abide by the democratic process, are free to participate fully in democratic politics and to join the dialogue in due course between the Governments and the political parties on the way ahead."[12]

Responses to the Declaration were both predictable and yet at the same time hopeful. The Unionists, ever vigilant in searching for a sellout by London, condemned the Declaration because it did not affirm the position of pre-1972 unionism and thus could only be to their detriment. The Protestant community as a whole, however, was less intense in its opposition than in the case of the 1985 Anglo-Irish Agreement. What was the reaction of the republicans? The response of Sinn Fein was that the Declaration had to be examined closely. That measured response was in fact disappointing to John Hume, who felt that the Declaration was very close to the position taken by the as-yet unseen Hume-Adams statement and the Sinn Fein proposal of 1992. The Declaration could not satisfy Sinn Fein *in toto* of course, because it would have been impossible for the British government to endorse any such document, but the Declaration did send out a signal about the nature of long-term British interests in Ulster and that Irish self-determination was open to negotiation.

In retrospect no more could have been expected from the various parties. The Unionists had to process the idea that there actually could be a change in Northern Ireland and that the possibility of real peace could be as frightening to their perspectives and assumptions as the institutionalized violence. Nor could the IRA, on the basis of the Declaration alone, instantaneously unload all their assumptions and entrenched values and behaviors. The period after the release of the Declaration was marked by fifteen shootings, four hijackings, and twenty bombings carried out by the IRA. Nor was there good reason for either community to put a lot of trust in the word of the British. However destructive the paranoid siege mentality of the Unionists and the long memories of Irish nationalists were to the politics of Ulster, they had in common their deep mistrust of London.

The onus had shifted to Sinn Fein, putting them on the defensive about why they should not declare a cease fire and join the talks. The fact of the matter was that Sinn Fein/IRA violence since at least the mid-1980s, however destructive, was ineffectual politically. No shifts in the fundamental political alignments did occur, or would occur, as a result of the next IRA bomb or bullet. The violence could be efficient, deadly, and repetitive but could produce no political repercussions of any importance, let alone a united Ireland. Thus it became sterile and cruel; more than one incident caused more revulsion than applause among supporters of the IRA.[13] The Unionist paramilitaries would retaliate and the cycle of death would continue. Gerry Adams, the head of Sinn Fein, recognized that the overall strategy of Sinn Fein had to change. The slow shift in Sinn Fein attitudes toward the peace process took place from 1990 to 1994. The Downing Street Declaration offered by the prime ministers of Ireland and the United Kingdom in December 1993 was an opportunity, albeit a dangerous one, for Adams.

When Adams persuaded the IRA to undertake the cessation of hostilities in August 1994, he was choosing compromise to avoid the IRA becoming a marginal purveyor of unpopular, pointless violence that would sink Sinn Fein politically. The public relief in Ulster at the 1994 IRA cease fire was palpable and it became clear that the IRA "long war" strategy in the long term was not an asset to Adams, as had been commonly thought, but a liability. The IRA was not going to bomb its way into a united Ireland because then, as now, 1 million unionists would not give in, and nor would Dublin or London. The intermediate position for Adams was to bargain for guaranteed rights of nationalists in the north, their political partic- ipation in a new government for Ulster, respect for their tradition, fair and just treatment by the police and judiciary, and an Ireland-wide demonstration of self- determination. A united Ireland would have to remain an aspiration only until a majority of those in the north chose it. It was the most Adams could get and he wisely took it.

Throughout the first half of 1994 the various sides were operating from differ- ent perspectives. The IRA continued bombing to show London its determination, launching mortars at Heathrow Airport in March 1994. This prompted President Clinton to call for an IRA cease fire and made Albert Reynolds impatient. The public in Ireland was also becoming impatient with the Sinn Fein/IRA position. A poll taken in February 1994 on an all-Ireland basis found overwhelming support for the principle that the future of Ulster and a united Ireland should be deter- mined by the principle of consent. Only one group did not agree: Sinn Fein sup- porters. Supporters of all parties thought that the Downing Street Declaration should lead to a cessation of violence; again, Sinn Fein did not agree.[14] Reynolds called the Heathrow attack "politically naive" and viewed an IRA Easter cease fire of three days with disdain, reflecting what he saw as the flouting of his and others' genuine efforts to address the republicans' concerns.

Within Sinn Fein some were ready to talk to the British and the other parties about the future of Ulster, but others were reluctant to give up the long war. Eventually the view of Gerry Adams and Martin McGuiness prevailed and the IRA Army Council and Sinn Fein approved the cessation of violence in July. In August 1994 the IRA declared a "cessation of military operations." Although Protestant paramilitaries also had escalated the violence in 1994 and in April,

May, and June had killed sixteen Catholics, six weeks later they also declared a cease fire. True to his promise made earlier in the year, Albert Reynolds invited Gerry Adams and John Hume on to Dublin for a highly visible symbolic handshake on September 6. From that point on media focus was on Gerry Adams and the legitimization of Sinn Fein (much to the elation of Irish Americans and the disgust of the British). A Forum for Peace and Reconciliation was convened in Dublin in October 1994 under Judge Catherine McGuiness and included Sinn Fein in the deliberations. The 1996 Report of this Forum addressed the definition of nationality, the question of consent, and the assurance of parity of esteem for the two traditions and religions, the issues that were to be later dealt with in the Good Friday Agreement.[15]

Although not easy in coming, the declaration ending violence was a watershed event in the modern troubles of Ireland. Some nationalists saw the future of Ireland as bright and unification as imminent. Unionists were far more skeptical but recognized that this was seemingly more than another IRA cease fire for public relations purposes or tactical advantage. Although later broken and altogether more fragile than some adherents would believe, the 1994 end of the violence remains a crossroads in the history of Ulster. It was both the culmination of such events as the Anglo-Irish Agreement and the Downing Street Declaration and the turning point toward such important events as the Mitchell Report and the Good Friday Peace Agreement. The cessation of violence was the most significant adjustment in the values and behavior of the Sinn Fein/IRA to the political reality surrounding them since they ended the spasmodic IRA campaign of violence in 1956–1962 or since ending the Civil War in 1923.

The question of the IRA arms being laid down before they could engage in negotiation with the other parties to the conflict now moved to the top of the peace agenda. The British government was reluctant to embrace the idea that the IRA had actually ended the violence and was slow to respond to the circumstances. The discussion shifted from the cessation of violence to the issue of arms, and there were no formal meetings between the British and Sinn Fein until December 1994 and spring 1995. This delay was accompanied by the demand that the IRA decommission its arms before negotiations took place. Nationalist leaders, Hume, Adams, and Reynolds asserted that the declaration was permanent and urged that the talks should proceed more quickly. Garret FitzGerald commented that if you ask people to cease violence on the promise to talk to them if they do, you cannot then change your mind because they have done unacceptable things in the past.[16] Prime Minister John Major's delay, because he doubted that the cessation was permanent, created a situation in which it probably would not be permanent because he was freezing Sinn Fein out of negotiations. Ironically he shared this position with the hardliners of the IRA, who felt that the cessation was conditional upon the British facing up to their responsibility to engage in open negotiations on an open agenda.

The Framework for Agreement

The British and Irish governments produced "A Framework for Agreement" in February 1995, which was not to be considered "a rigid blueprint" but rather a starting point for negotiation. What is remarkable about the document is that the key agreements of the past are all incorporated into one long "framework." The fundamental shift in the two governments' positions with respect to each other and Northern Ireland recognized at Sunningdale (and many statements thereafter) was present (Articles 10, 11, 12); the British guarantee to the Unionists was present (Article 17); power sharing was present; and the three strands of the relationships over Ulster and institutions designed to express them were suggested or already present, such as the Intergovernmental Conference, set up by the Anglo-Irish Agreement, which was also in the Framework. Guarantees of protection of human rights through legislation were suggested, which reflects the changes in the laws to eliminate discrimination that took place under direct rule. The Framework was actually a coherent summary of the changes in thinking about the north in London and Dublin over two decades and the revivification of institutional structures already attempted or accepted. Were it implemented, it would provide something closer to joint sovereignty than British rule or a united Ireland.

There was a highly negative Unionist reaction to the Framework document. David Trimble called it a "foolish document" and said, "We don't see any point in discussing what we would regard as a purely nationalist agenda."[17] Unionist intransigence on the question of the IRA decommissioning their arms pushed the Major government into a harder position. Sir Patrick Mayhew, secretary of state for Northern Ireland, declared in May 1995 that Sinn Fein would have to accept the principle of disarming, establish a process, and actually decommission arms as a sign of good faith before negotiations could take place. London and the Unionists took the position that evidence of decommissioning was a precondition for talks. The polarity of positions on this issue could not be clearer: Sinn Fein also called for disarmament, but it was a reduction in the British Army, the police, and the loyalist paramilitaries that they sought, not just the IRA. The IRA position was that decommissioning before negotiations was a form of surrender and that a laying down of arms would be "the price for getting *up* from the negotiating table rather than for sitting *down* at it."[18]

The positions of all parties hardened in summer 1995, with the Unionists intransigent on the disarming issue and Sinn Fein withdrawing from talks in June. It was difficult to find a formula that would bring the Unionists and Sinn Fein to the same table. In June 1995 the Orange Order prepared to march their July Orange parade down the Garvaghy Road in Drumcree near Portadown, the traditional path of the parade. In doing so the Order revealed the depths of the loyalist commitment, the fissures ever-present in the province, and the balancing act required of the police. The nationalist community in Drumcree resisted, demanding a change in the route of this triumphalist Orange exercise. The Orange Order refused and the police were put in the middle of a confrontation when the parade did go down its traditional route. (Drumcree in 1995, as intense as it was, would pale beside the 1996 and the 1998 confrontations at the same place and over the same issue.) The situation was deteriorating and the peace process was under threat as the positions of the parties hardened.

U.S. Involvement

The visit to Northern Ireland by President Clinton in November 1995, the first by a U.S. president, drew great attention to the peace process and brought pressure on London to move on the talks. Clinton's visit was an enormous success: crowds gathered everywhere and speeches proclaimed the advent of a new day of peace. In fact the visit came at a low ebb in the process. The IRA had already secretly decided to break the cease fire, the British and Irish governments were incapable of moving the process forward, and the Unionists were intransigent. The main barrier to progress was that the parties would not talk while the IRA still had weapons. The problem was solved in that most enduring bureaucratic fashion, by appointing a commission. The International Commission was chaired by former Senator George Mitchell of Maine. Mitchell was joined by former Finnish Prime Minister Harri Holkeri and retired Canadian General John de Chastelain.

Mitchell was already involved in Northern Ireland because he had helped President Clinton set up investment conferences in the United States in 1995 to show the players in the Northern drama that there could be an economic reward for peace in the province. The three-member group was endorsed by President Clinton. In its final report the Commission called for the initiation of talks before decommissioning arms if all parties agreed to six principles, which in effect committed them to ultimately decommissioning their arms, to verification of the process, to peaceful negotiation, and to acceptance of the outcome without resorting to violence. The talks would proceed on two tracks: the issue of arms and the issues related to the three strands.

The president's visit to Northern Ireland and the recommendations of the International Commission were not enough to pressure London to begin the twin-track, all-party talks. The Commission had in effect rejected Prime Minister Major's position. Major countered with a call for elections in May 1996 to a Forum in Northern Ireland as a "confidence building measure" before negotiations could begin. The new Forum, Major promised, would not be a return to earlier Ulster assemblies. It would be part of the negotiating process, it would not preempt the outcome of the talks, and it would give all parties a fresh mandate reflecting the new realities in Ulster. Opposition to this idea was uniform: The Irish government wanted proximity talks and saw the elections as a useless delay; Sinn Fein wanted all-party talks, saw the election as a delay, and announced that it would boycott the assembly because it would not participate in any body to which it had not consented in negotiations; the SDLP took the position that if the

George Mitchell, former senator from Maine, served as the chairman of the talks which produced the Good Friday Agreement. Representatives from every political position offered praise of Mitchell's patience and skill in bringing the negotiations between the historically intractable parties to a successful conclusion.
Photo by Harry Brett, Image Photo

Forum was powerless (as it turned out to be) then it was unnecessary and a massive amount of overkill to produce three-member negotiating teams. Conversely, if the Forum were genuinely part of the process it would be used by the Unionists to frustrate the real negotiations. Elections were by definition divisive as parties tried to differentiate themselves from each other and thus hardly a productive prelude to negotiations that required compromise.

The only ones to approve of the proposal, the Unionists and their leaders, Paisley and Trimble, were pleased because it gave them the assembly they wanted to ensure that the strand one talks between the communities of Ulster were insulated from what they saw as the meddling of Dublin. Without an Assembly the Unionists were subject to political pressure and proposals that threatened to put them too far out in front of their electorate. They had dismissed the Mitchell Report as the finding of an international body which not only compromised British sovereignty but was an abandonment of the British position that some decommissioning should take place before negotiation. In effect, in allowing policy to be dictated by the Unionists, Major's Forum was a return to some of the traditional characteristics of British policy: misunderstanding the problem and trying to "manage" the conflict to a politically tolerable level rather than trying to solve it. Major was adopting a policy that was riddled with the potential for replicating past mistakes.

President Clinton's decision to involve himself to the degree that he did in Northern Ireland is itself puzzling given the history of the issue and the panoply of problems that confront any president. It has been seen as part of his overall strategy of "democratic enlargement" in world politics, designed to expand the areas of democratic capitalism to allow for the expansion of U.S. investment. President Clinton had spent time in Britain as a Rhodes scholar after he graduated from college, and all those who discussed Ulster with him indicated that he had an in-depth knowledge of the problem and a personal interest in Northern Ireland. Despite Joseph O'Grady's assertions that the president was responding to the Irish American constituency in the politically critical states as a ploy to get Irish American votes, it appears that only his initial response in the New York State primary was designed to get votes.[19] After that it appears that his increasing commitment emerged from a constellation of pressures, including his close connection to Senator Kennedy of Massachusetts; the pressure brought by a group of prominent Irish Americans, Americans for a New Irish Agenda (ANIA); the serendipitous timing of events in Northern Ireland; and, finally, his willingness to pay the price of British ire for not following the State Department's preordained policy path, which treated the north as a domestic matter in British politics. To promote the issue of Ulster to his foreign policy agenda, from its place on the transnational and congressional agenda, required that the president take the risk that his actions would not produce any results while at the same time alienating London.

Senator Kennedy's sister, the U.S. ambassador to Ireland, had aligned herself in Ireland with those who thought there was a possibility of traversing the Northern impasse.[20] She persuaded her brother, now the most influential congressional figure on Irish matters and a close friend of John Hume, to support the president's decision to issue a visa to Gerry Adams in January 1994. Hume had also been trying to convince the Irish government at that time to give Adams more room for maneuvering and told Senator Kennedy the same.[21] The ANIA was composed of figures such as former Congressman Bruce Morrison; Niall O'Dowd, the editor of the *Irish Voice*; Joe Jamison, a trade union executive, and Charles Feeney and William Flynn, both prosperous businessmen. This group convinced both Sinn Fein and the White House that they had credibility with the other. Sinn Fein was convinced of the importance of U.S. support in gaining a political settlement and getting concrete benefits for the north, and the White House was convinced that the word of Sinn Fein was good on promises to take actions toward a peaceful settlement.

Clinton had taken office in January 1993; serendipitously, 1993 saw the culmination of the Hume-Adams talks, the arrival of Albert Reynolds as prime minister of Ireland with Dick Spring as his Tanaiste, and the agreement of John Major to the Downing Street Declaration. That Declaration appeared to be the needed trigger to move the peace process to a breakthrough and convinced the president that á risk was worth taking on the issue. In 1993, following traditional policy, Clinton had twice turned down requests for visas from Gerry Adams to visit the United States. In January 1994 the President considered allowing Gerry Adams to visit the United States on a visa to attend a conference in New York City. Nancy Soderberg said of the president's decision: "He weighed the pros and cons of taking a risk for peace or missing what might have been a historic opportunity. He decided it was worth the risk of reaching out to Adams a little bit in the hopes he would then help deliver on the cease fire."[22] President Clinton's willingness to break the pattern of decision making on Ulster was opposed by his own key advisors, Attorney General Janet Reno, Secretary of State Warren Christopher, the FBI, the CIA, and the U.S. ambassador to Britain, all of whom thought issuing the visa to Adams would appear to be an endorsement of international terrorism.

The British government was angered by the president's action and subsequent acts such as Adams meeting Anthony Lake at the White House in October 1994. Yet the president was willing to challenge the accepted path of conceding to the British on this issue, at the risk of cooperation on others, because he believed that the fundamentals of the situation in Ulster had been realigned and he wanted the United States to be on the positive side of the movement for peace.[23] As it turns out, the president's judgment was correct, although casting the weight of the United States into the equation in fact changed the equation itself and facilitated the peace process. By issuing a visa in 1994, visiting Ireland in 1995, appointing Mitchell as the chair of the talks, and making phone calls at critical moments during the April 1998 negotiations, the president, and through him the United States, became key players in the outcome of the peace process.

The Peace Process Derailed

Despite the Mitchell Report of January 1996 the year was to be one of violence and political upheaval. On February 9, 1996, the IRA set off a bomb at Canary Wharf in London that killed two people and injured thirty-six. The cease fire was over and the peace process was derailed. The IRA's position was that after almost sixteen months the British were still dithering on the question of setting a date for negotiations that included all parties and by calling for an election were clearly in the thrall of the Unionists. The Major government had been too confident that the cease fire had boxed in the IRA politically and that they would not return to violence, displaying once again the British inability to understand the IRA's position. The IRA, on the other hand, showed that their word was less than trustworthy and thus fueled the Unionist conviction that negotiation was impossible because if the IRA did not get what they want they would bomb you. The Bruton government in Dublin was also seen by the IRA as too accommodating to the British position. The decision to renew the violence had, in fact, been under consideration since the prior November. It had been taken by a majority of the IRA Army Council but with not all members present and was not universally supported within the republican community.

The effect on a variety of players was shocking. Gerry Adams was put in the embarrassing position of appearing to be unable to deliver on the promises he had made and unaware of such an important decision. If he were not able to speak for the IRA, should not the governments of Ireland and Britain be talking to someone who could? What use was the promise of the IRA cease fire being permanent when it clearly was not? The governments of Britain, Ireland, and the United States were alienated immediately and key figures, whatever their position on decommissioning and elections, felt betrayed. The Irish government had believed the cease fire to be permanent and found its relationship with London cooling. The Irish people blamed Britain's dilatory tactics regarding the negotiations as the cause of the renewal of violence and complained that the British were unresponsive to attempts to find conditions that would effect a new cease fire. Later in the year the Irish government broke off relations with Sinn Fein because Dublin was extremely pessimistic about producing long-term results. Differences appeared within the Irish government in April: The leader of Fianna Fail, Bertie Ahern, criticized John Bruton, the prime minister, for being too accommodating to the Unionists; Bruton, in turn, accused Ahern of "a disturbing lack of political judgment." The Irish and British governments announced on February 28 a date to begin the talks—June 10, 1996—in conjunction with the Forum election.

The Forum Election

The election to the Forum took place on May 30, 1996. The hallmark of the election was the bitter reaction to the proposal that there be an election at all and that it be carried out by the proportional representation electoral system proposed by Major. The election of a powerless assembly was something that had no attraction for the SDLP, which had not taken its seats in the ineffectual 1982 Northern Ireland Assembly. The delay of negotiations was seen as a dilatory tactic to appease the Unionists. The electoral system was unique in the election history of the United Kingdom. Not used in Ulster, it required choosing from a party list without designating a candidate. Ninety seats were allocated by electing five members from each of the eighteen constituencies. The effect was to force the voter to one party choice, with the likely effect of weakening the support for small parties. An additional twenty seats were to be allocated on the basis of the total percentage of the vote in the province, with the top ten parties getting two seats from another list of candidates submitted by the parties. The smaller parties were potentially able to gain representation in this manner. To get enough votes to reach the top, ten parties had to run candidates in all the constituencies. In all, 926 candidates were on the constituency lists and 181 on the regional party lists.[24]

The Unionist parties clawed at each other for the Protestant unionist community votes. Their positions were not surprising, with Paisley's Democratic Unionist Party promising to preserve the union and accusing David Trimble of the Ulster Unionist Party of treachery and a sell-out to the "pan-nationalist front" of Sinn Fein and the SDLP. Trimble's party indicated that the electoral system was designed by an "unholy alliance between Dr. Paisley and John Hume" to split Unionists and that it had to be met with a united front of votes for the UUP. Trimble had to assure Unionists that he was going to be as vigilant in protecting the Union as the DUP and yet be open to negotiation. That position was somewhat disingenuous electorally although oddly necessary in the long term, because only when unionism could address the changes that had occurred in Northern Ireland was there a chance for a settlement.

The results of the vote were somewhat skewed by the electoral system.[25] The UUP received 24 percent of the vote and 28 seats, and an additional 2 seats, for a total of 30 seats of the 110 in the Forum. The DUP under Paisley received 18.8 percent and 22 seats plus the additional 2 from the list. The SDLP received 21.4 percent of the vote and 19 seats plus 2, for 21 seats. Sinn Fein received 15.5 percent of the vote and 15 plus 2 seats, for a total of 17 seats. The remaining seats went to the Alliance Party (7); the Unionist Party of the United Kingdom (3); The People's Unionist Party, a small party associated with the paramilitary Ulster Volunteer Force (2); the Ulster Democratic Party, associated with the paramilitary Ulster Defense Association (2); the Labour Party, a party not associated with the Labour Party of Britain (2); and the Northern Ireland Women's Coalition (2).

The votes received by the parties associated with the loyalist paramilitaries were an interesting reflection of the fact that in many respects the loyalists were out in front of the mainstream Unionist parties on the peace process. They had a virtual truce with the IRA for the period from the cease fire to the IRA renewal of violence in 1996. They initially chose not to reciprocate, although they later engaged in sporadic violent acts. The paramilitary parties gained political support for their position, garnering altogether 5.7 percent of the vote, a figure less than 1 percentage point from that of the Alliance Party.

The Northern Ireland Women's Coalition was a rather interesting development in the male chauvinist world of Ulster politics. The NIWC was a non-sectarian, cross-party group of women founded in 1966. They ran seventy candidates in the Forum election and came in in the top ten finishers with 1 percent of the vote and thus elected Monica McWilliam and Pearl Seger to the Forum. The group sought a multicultural, multi-ethnic, multi-religious society that would include women on an equal footing with men. That women would seek representation separate from the established parties was a reflection of their attitudes. In a 1996 poll asking women which party in Northern Ireland represented the interests of women, 26 percent said their own party, 18 percent identified another party, but 57 percent said no party did.[26]

The rise in the Sinn Fein vote raised eyebrows because it appeared to be a repudiation of Major's position. In fact the increase was significant because the highest vote total of Sinn Fein had been achieved in 1983, and in 1996 they gained more than 2 percentage points over that figure. That did not gain them entry into the peace talks because there had been no cease fire since February and thus no adherence to Mitchell's six principles. The Forum itself turned out to be much ado about nothing; the SDLP withdrew in protest at Unionist support of Orange violence that summer.

The eighteen delegates to the talks were chosen from the Forum members, with three from each of the larger parties and two from the smaller. Not surprisingly, David Trimble led the UUP; Ian Paisley, the DUP; John Hume, the SDLP; John Alderdice, the Alliance; and Robert McCartney, the United Kingdom Unionist Party (UKUP). The talks opened on June 10 with Gerry Adams, the uninvited guest, making the most of the media attention, blaming the British government for causing the IRA violence and illegitimately excluding Sinn Fein from the talks. George Mitchell chaired the plenary session and a subcommittee on decommissioning. The Unionists objected to his place in the chair because they saw him as a Catholic representing the pro-nationalist U.S. point of view. The Unionist perception of Americans was usually staggeringly wide of the mark, and it certainly was not accurate with respect to Mitchell, who proved himself to be scrupulously fair in the negotiations in the ensuing twenty months.[27] John de Chastelain presided over the north-south strand portion of the talks.

The issue of decommissioning arms had hovered over the negotiations up to that point and did not depart with the advent of the Forum. With the DUP and the UUP both at the talks the competition over commitment to the Union was only overshadowed by the demand that the IRA put down their arms and give them up. Adams responded repeatedly that such an arrangement must be reciprocal; the IRA was not the only armed body in the north; and the police, army, and paramilitaries must also be accountable for their violence and their weapons.

The talks dragged on in 1996 and 1997. They were not very productive because they were focused on the decommissioning issue. In May 1997 a breakthrough occurred in the form of the election of Tony Blair of the Labour Party as the prime minister of Britain. Blair had a very substantial majority in Parliament and thus was free of the need the Conservatives had for the votes of Ulster Unionists. Blair was also personally disposed to initiate change because he did not want to be seen as wedded to the rigid positions of the past. His party had always taken a responsible, but more flexible, position on the Northern problem than the Conservative Party with its traditional affinity for the Ulster Unionists and their tradition of empire. In May Blair visited Northern Ireland and approved of opening up talks with Sinn Fein, reversing the policy of the Major government. Blair appointed Majorie "Mo" Mowlam secretary of state for Northern Ireland. A blunt, vigorous, and talented figure, Mowlam quickly established a working relationship with all the parties to the conflict. She almost immediately faced a crisis, the brutal murder of two RUC police in June 1997 by the IRA. This act prompted the British government to break off talks with Sinn Fein and the Irish government followed suit. Blair was not deterred, however; he had said in May: "My message to Sinn Fein is clear. The settlement train is leaving. I want you on that train. But it is leaving anyway and I will not allow it to wait for you. You cannot hold the process to ransom any longer. So end the violence. Now."[28]

The change in government in London was accompanied by a change of government in Dublin. Dick Spring took his party out of coalition with Fine Gael and a new government under Bertie Ahern of Fianna Fail came to power in June 1997. The convergence of the Ahern government, the Blair government, the Forum, the multi-party talks, external pressure, and internal pressure finally brought the IRA to declare another cease fire in July 1997. Reactions were as predictable as the behavior of characters in Kabuki theater. The Unionists saw this as another manifestation of the duplicity of the IRA, the nationalists saw it as a sign that the IRA had accepted the Mitchell principles and was committing itself to a peaceful path of negotiation (although that was not at all clear), and the Blair government saw it as an opportunity to move the Ulster crisis toward a solution. After a suitable interlude negotiations began in September with Sinn Fein at the table. The DUP under Paisley and the UKUP under Robert McCartney then withdrew from the talks, which put great pressure on David Trimble and the UUP. They were now subject to the traditional unionist charge of selling out to the terrorists. Trimble received assurances from Ahern, Blair, and President Clinton that the IRA would not break the cease fire again and he remained in the talks.

The hard bargaining began over such contentious issues as police powers, the release of prisoners, the protection of civil rights and liberties, the governing arrangements in the north, and the linkages of north and south. Each side was committed to the process in the context of its own political positions; that is, Sinn Fein was still operating under the assumption that the long-range goal was to be a united Ireland, while the Unionists insisted that the new arrangements were to exist in the context of the Union with Britain. Both were also operating out of an unspoken subtext, which for the Unionists was a recognition that London was no longer going to serve as the guarantor of Unionist ascendancy; that the number of Catholics in the north was growing faster than the number of Protestants and the balance of power was going to shift at some point; and that the unionist business and religious leaders, the middle class, and, surprisingly, the loyalist hardliners were reaching a point where they thought that ending the conflict was more productive than perpetual conflict. The subtext for Sinn Fein was that the violence had reached a politically counterproductive point; that the public in the Republic did not support their position, nor did a substantial number of the nationalists in Ulster; and that support from the outside world depended heavily on the promise of ending the violence. Adams and McGuinness could not but take notice of the ebullience that exploded in the nationalist community when the first IRA cease fire was declared. The negotiations operated at these two levels throughout.

Strong positions and rhetoric produced obstinacy fueled by intransigence and a sense of grievance, yet those positions perched paradoxically on the surface of a sense of impending weakness and uncertainty at the core of both the militant unionist and nationalist positions.

The Good Friday Agreement

The discussions lasted from September through April, at which point Mitchell felt that they had reached a point where a resolution was possible. He noted in May that, "It had become obvious to me that the longer these negotiations dragged on the better the chance those outside the process had to ruin them."[29] Mitchell set a deadline of April 9 and got the promise of Ahern and Blair that they would stay with the negotiations until the process was over whether an agreement was reached or not. In the last few days the delegates got hardly any sleep, crafting agreements on the powers of the cross-border authorities; the release of prisoners that each side viewed as heroes or murderers, respectively; participation in the Assembly; and assurances that weapons would be turned in by paramilitaries. President Clinton called Blair, Adams, Hume, Ahern, and Trimble in the final hours. On Good Friday, April 10, at five o'clock Prime Ministers Ahern and Blair announced that a comprehensive agreement had been reached. Journalist Kevin Cullen noted later that the Agreement had put aside "the baggage of history" and that "in Ireland where the dead have always wielded a disproportionate influence, a decision had been made for the living."[30]

The Agreement reached in the multi-party negotiations was summarized sardonically by Seamus Mallon, the deputy leader of the SDLP, as "Sunningdale for slow learners" and his observation was not far off the mark. The parallels were there—the non-support of the DUP, power sharing, and cross-border institutions—but the times had certainly changed since 1974.[31] What had been agreed to in 1998?

The Agreement begins with a Declaration of Support calling for "reconciliation, tolerance, and mutual trust" as well as "partnership, equality and mutual respect as the basis of relationships," and while recognizing the differences in political aspirations the parties offer a "commitment to exclusively democratic and peaceful means of resolving differences." The section on constitutional issues recognizes that the future of Northern Ireland can only be determined by the consent of a majority of the people, whether remaining in the Union or a united Ireland, and the respective governments will amend their laws and constitutions to reflect that decision.

Strand 1 concerned the democratic institutions in the north and sets up an Assembly of 108 members with devolved legislative powers over the province. It also sets up a qualified voting arrangement in the Assembly to ensure parallel consent or weighted majorities to reflect the will of both communities. The executive will have a first minister and deputy first minister from the different communities and ten members who will serve as departmental ministers. Appointments will be made according to party strength and there are extensive guarantees to protect the rights of both communities. Strand 2 creates a north/south Ministerial Council, which is purely consultative and is designed to develop cooperation on matters of mutual interest. The Council is to meet regularly and include members of the Republic's Cabinet and Northern Ireland's executive to consult on a number of issues, such as agriculture, education, transport, and environment. The two legislatures should "consider" a joint parliamentary forum to foster cooperation between them. Strand 3 creates a new British-Irish Council, which has representatives of the two governments and of the devolved governments of Northern Ireland, Scotland, and Wales. The goal is the mutually beneficial development of the totality of relationships among the peoples of what used to be called the "British Isles," although that is now a politically incorrect term. In addition, a British-Irish Intergovernmental Conference is created to deal with matters of common concern, especially security matters in the north.

The Rights, Safeguards, and Equality of Opportunity section identifies a list of human rights to be protected and respected, including "freedom from sectarian harassment" and the right of women to "full and equal political participation." Human rights commissions are to be created in the north and in the Republic and are to meet as a joint committee periodically. Economic opportunity and development are pledged, with special attention to "seek to remove, where possible, restrictions which would discourage or work against the maintenance and development of the (Irish) language" in the north. The issue of decommissioning arms is addressed by setting a limit of two years for the elimination of all paramilitary arms, to be monitored by the Independent International Commission on Decommissioning. The British government pledges in the realm of security to reduce the armed forces deployed in Northern Ireland to "levels compatible with normal peaceful society." The most contentious issues of policing and justice are dealt with by creating an independent Commission on Policing for Northern Ireland to ensure that "policing arrangements including composition, recruitment, training, culture, ethos and symbols, are such that in a new approach Northern Ireland has a police service that can enjoy widespread support from, and is seen as an integral part of, the community as a whole." Prisoners who are part of organizations that are parties to the Agreement will have their situations reviewed and be released, with all prisoners to be let out by the end of two years after the commencement of the Agreement. Finally, the Agreement calls for a referendum in both Northern Ireland and the Republic on May 22. If the two referenda are passed by majorities the two governments are to introduce the legislation necessary to put the Agreement into effect.

The referenda campaigns in the Republic and the north produced two sets of statistics on voter turnout that were clearly opposite to those from the vote approving the Good Friday Agreement. In the Republic the turnout was 56.3 percent, which was rather small given the position that partition and the north played in modern Irish history. Yet the evidence that the north did not have primacy of place on the agenda of politics in the Republic had long been clear. The issues of economic development, jobs, wages, and the social changes in the years since 1960 in education, media, and Church–state relations had topped the list of concerns in the Republic. The goal of a united Ireland was undoubtedly an aspiration for a vast majority but had less traction as a salient bread-and-butter issue. The issue of whether the questions on the Agreement and the changes in the Constitution should be separated was about as much controversy as could be found on the referendum. The outcome was overwhelmingly positive, with 94.4 percent of the voters approving the Agreement and the constitutional changes necessary to implement it.

The north was another story altogether. Conflict over the Agreement raged right up to the afternoon of April 10, and the tense divisions among the delegates spilled out into the larger electorate in the referendum. The opposition to the Agreement in the north formed around Ian Paisley and the DUP, the UKUP, and the dissident members of the UUP (six of ten of that party's members of Parliament). Called the United Unionists, this group campaigned on the well-worn ground that the Agreement was a slippery slope to a united Ireland that would not respect the Protestant culture of Ulster. Choosing to emphasize the change in the 1920 Government of Ireland Act, they ignored the corresponding elimination of the Irish Constitution's claim to the whole island. The unionist population's concerns, however, were closer to the ground and focused on prisoner release, reform of "their" police, and the decommissioning of weapons.[32] The critical moment for the UUP occurred when David Trimble was supported by fifty-five to twenty-three in the UUP Executive and later by a 72 percent majority in the party's Council.

The republican movement also had criticisms of the Agreement. The changes in the Republic's Constitution recognized the legitimacy of Ulster, the Assembly was de facto partitionist, and the Unionists had vetoes on various bodies all of which were closer to reformist than republican. The debate took place on grounds that had an eerie similarity to the treaty debates in 1921. Militant republicans asked, Is this what we have sacrificed and died for? Sinn Fein had an Ard Feis (party convention) in Dublin at which the delegates voted overwhelmingly to accept the Agreement, which lined up republican support both north and south.

The voter turnout in Northern Ireland was 81.1 percent, reflecting the importance of the Agreement as a turning point for Ulster. The votes came in at 71.1 percent for and 28.9 percent opposed. Assuming a large positive vote in the nationalist community, the key question is the degree to which the unionists had opposed the Agreement. Surveys and polls taken later indicate that it was supported by a very slender majority of the unionist voters. In seventeen of the eighteen constituencies the Agreement was passed. The one exception was Ian Paisley's North Antrim district. On the island as a whole the majority was 85 percent. In numerical terms support was clear, but numerical majorities did not reflect the intensity of those opposed to the Agreement that would be later displayed at Drumcree and Omagh.

The elections to the new Assembly followed in due course on June 25, 1998. The splits within unionism continued with the problem of candidate selection. The rules of the UUP require that there be special permission for a sitting member of Parliament to run for another office. The Party gave the dispensation to Trimble, of course, and to his deputy, John Taylor, but refused it to Jeffrey Donaldson, the only UUP MP who sought a nomination. Jeffrey Donaldson had walked out of the negotiations on the final day in opposition to prisoner releases. He then opposed the Agreement in the referendum. The Party felt no obligation to support his candidacy or allow him to undermine the Assembly they supported. The decision, however, split the party again and a member of the UUP executive even ran against David Trimble, while UUP members opposed to the Agreement cooperated with the DUP and UKUP candidates based on a promise to attempt to frustrate the work of the Assembly. The DUP opposed the Agreement, and thus the Assembly, and sought votes to ensure that there would be enough seats (thirty) in the Assembly to constantly require all legislation to be declared "key decisions." This would require the cross-community voting procedures and allow them to stall the work of the Assembly. With only a few more seats (six) the work of the Assembly could be brought to a standstill.

The nationalists also were not free of division. Sinn Fein's Gerry Adams suggested an electoral pact with SDLP in the Assembly elections after the referendum. John Hume refused this offer, however, recognizing that the nationalist community could too easily transfer the hard-earned legitimacy of the SDLP onto Sinn Fein, which had nothing to lose and much to gain, while SDLP had much to lose and little to gain.

The Prizes of Peace

The results of the election were encouraging for the SDLP and Sinn Fein and discouraging for Trimble and the UUP. The vote for the SDLP was the highest in the election, 22 percent. This was the first time a nationalist party had received the highest number of first-preference votes in an election in Northern Ireland. The votes translated into 24 of the 108 seats. Sinn Fein received 17.6 percent, up 2 percent from the 1996 Forum election, and won 18 seats. The UUP lost almost 3 percentage points compared to their total vote in the Forum election, but due to the electoral system and districts they gained 28 seats. The DUP percentage dropped just 0.7 percent and earned 20 seats. The remaining seats went to the Alliance Party (6), the UKUP (5), the PUP (2), the NIWC (2), and independent Unionists (3). The electorate was not quite as mobilized for this election as for the referendum; the turnout was only 77 percent.

One in every four voters voted for anti-Agreement parties, giving them twenty-eight seats, while pro-Agreement seats numbered eighty. Exit polls revealed that those middle class voters in the unionist community who thought that the peace process would succeed voted for UUP; the same group in the nationalist community voted for SDLP. Sinn Fein gained a significantly larger share of the votes of young people in the nationalist community. Political scientist Richard Sinnott points out that a positive dimension of the Assembly election was the shift in attitudes of those who voted "no" to the Agreement. Fifty-eight percent of those voters in May believed that IRA paramilitary violence would resume. By June a 34 percent drop in that belief indicated that many had changed their minds. In fact, two of every five of the "no" voters wanted the Assembly to succeed, while only 14 percent wanted their representatives to work to bring the Assembly to an end.[33]

The Assembly met on July 1, 1998, electing David Trimble first minister and Seamus Mallon deputy first minister. The debate in that session turned on the question of the Parade Commission's decision to prevent the Orange Order from marching down the Garvaghy Road in Drumcree. The route of the parade came to be the least of the problems at Drumcree.

The Orange Order had been marching at Drumcree in Portadown for 200 years. The parade commemorates the loss of the Ulstermen in the Battle of the Somme in World War I as well as other historical events in the unionist vision of Irish history. The Orange Order remained one of the few organizations that cut across class and party lines in the unionist community. The symbolic militance; the songs such as the "The Sash My Father Wore," celebrating the Battle of the Boyne in 1690; the generally triumphant manner of the parades; and the attitude that the Orangemen have the right to "walk the Queen's highway" anywhere in Northern Ireland have been particularly offensive to the nationalist community, which had been banned from walking those same "highways" many times. The nationalist community had been protesting this behavior for years to no avail, and from time to time the marches led to dueling symbols, flags, and songs, and violent confrontations. The nationalists, including Sinn Fein, had organized the nationalist community in a housing project in Drumcree, which was on the route of the march. Confrontations in 1995, 1996, and 1997 had provoked bitter political tensions and violence but the police had let the marches go down their traditional route.

In 1998 a newly appointed Parade Commission was created to address just such issues. The Commission ordered the Orange Lodges to reroute the parade. The decision, coming as it did at the time of the Agreement referendum and the Assembly vote, appeared to unionists, even some not enamored of the Orange Order, to be evidence of a further decline in their position in Northern Ireland. The traditional paranoia of the unionist was fueled in this instance by the belief among some Unionist leaders that the police were acting "under Dublin orders."[34] The Orange Order saw this as the kind of apocalyptic conflict that fit their slogan from a hundred years before: "no surrender." Each night more Orange supporters arrived in Drumcree, camping on the hillsides and becoming increasingly more confrontational. The police put up barbed wire in front of a trench and at night some of the more alcohol-fueled minions would try to storm the police lines. As the days went by the numbers increased, raising the potential of the police being overrun. David Trimble and Seamus Mallon tried to defuse the confrontation, but Mallon encountered resistance in the housing project. (Although this was nothing compared to the problems Trimble had had when he marched down the Garvaghy Road in 1995 in support of the Orange demonstrators.) Trying to balance his role as head of the new Assembly produced by the peace process and his long connection to the militant Orange and Unionist community, Trimble would not flatly state that the Orangemen should call off their protest. Nothing good could come of the situation for the protesters, the police, or the fragile peace process.

In the early hours of July 12, 1998, a bomb was thrown into an apartment in a housing project in Ballymoney. The family was mixed, the mother a Catholic, the father a Protestant, and the four children attended a Protestant school. The fire killed three of the Quinn children, ages eleven, ten, and eight (the fourth was away), and generated a wave of revulsion against the brutality of the act, the innocence of the victims, and the motivation of the perpetrator. Because the housing project was militantly unionist, it was assumed that a loyalist extremist had thrown the bomb because the woman was a Catholic. Leaders of the Protestant churches, the police, and David Trimble denounced the act and associated it with the confrontation at Drumcree. The Reverend William Bingham, a chaplain to the Orange Order, called for the protest to end. He was roughed up for his comments, although ultimately most people in the unionist community came to share his views. The Orange Order militants tried to dissociate themselves from the bombing but the spine went out of the protest, the Orangemen went home, and in a few days the police sent the remainder away. Journalist John Lloyd commented: "This horror was Irish Luck," in a most infelicitous juxtaposition of terms. (The death of three children hardly constitutes "Irish Luck" under any circumstances unless one defines "luck" as, for example, being ruled by the British during the Famine.) Ultimately the Orange protests led to four deaths, with RUC officer Frank O'Reilly dying from shrapnel in October. The spokesperson for the Orange Lodge, David Jones, said the officer's death was the responsibility of the Parade Commission. The president of the Lodge, Harold Gracey, was re-elected and Drumcree flared again in July 1999. Attention was deflected from the issue in 1998 by the murder and the question that nationalists would ask of the management of Orange parades was left unanswered: How is the idea of "parity of esteem" to be achieved in the face of these triumphalist exercises?

But profoundly heartless acts are not confined to one side or another in Northern Ireland. There have always been in the republican community those who oppose the Sinn Fein/IRA, which sees the IRA as not militant enough. Only a few days after the Drumcree confrontation, on July 15, a car bomb was set off in the city of Omagh. Twenty-nine people died and 220 were injured in the worst single bombing since the troubles began in their modern form in 1968. Misleading phone calls indicating different times and places prompted the police to move the crowds in the city center toward the bomb rather than away from it. The carnage was appalling and indiscriminate: Young and old, pregnant women, Protestant and Catholic, foreign tourists from Spain, visiting youths from the Republic, and children were all murdered by the car bomb. The city was a peaceful community with a mixed population, a large number of whom were out shopping that day for school uniforms and supplies. Condemnation of the murderers flowed from every point on the political spectrum and in the community. John Hume called them "fascists" and Tony Blair labeled it "an evil act of savagery." Bertie Ahern and Blair introduced more stringent anti-terrorist legislation in Ireland and Britain aimed at the "Real IRA," the group that set off the bomb.

A former IRA supporter who broke with the organization over the Peace Agreement, Mickey McKevitt, who is married to the sister of hunger striker Bobby Sands, is seen by police as one of the leading figures in the "Thirty Two County Sovereignty Association," which was associated with the Real IRA. People in the Republic shunned and harassed McKevitt's family after the bombings. His wife said that she and her children did not feel safe . . . although they were apparently a lot safer than the shoppers in Omagh. A month later eighteen members of the Real IRA admitted responsibility for the Omagh bombing, accompanying the admission with a pompous declaration of a cease fire. The statement said that warnings had been issued, the target was commercial, and they had not intended to kill civilians. Few would disagree with Mo Mowlam's comment that the statement was a "pathetic attempt to apologize for and excuse mass murder."

By far the most telling effect of the bombing in Omagh was the universal condemnation of the act by every leader and the utter revulsion displayed by the public. The Omagh bomb represented the logical extreme of action of the utterly undemocratic terrorist nationalist. Regardless of every manifestation of public will, the terrorists take unto themselves the right to determine what is politically acceptable rather than what the people want. Gerry Adams had the insight in the late 1980s to recognize that the logic of the strategy of the Provisional IRA was ultimately destined to be as politically arrogant and quintessentially cruel as the Real IRA. He adroitly avoided that cul de sac while keeping his vision of Irish republicanism intact and leading his party into both the peace process and the political process.

The Assembly reconvened in fall 1998 and was immediately frozen on the issue of decommissioning arms. Adams and Sinn Fein felt they had a right to a place on the executive in proportion to their percentage of seats in the Assembly and wanted their place on the All-Ireland Council. They were pushing for the structures of the Agreement to be put in place and for ten departments in the executive to be set up. Trimble and the UUP held that there would be no movement on those issues until the arms issue was addressed. The other provisions of the Agreement were slowly being implemented. The last British Army street foot patrol was in September 1998. Prisoners were released, the British were closing army bases, and life was approaching normality . . . almost. The beating of

Gerry Adams, leader of the Sinn Fein Party, on a 1994 visit to Boston. Adams's political astuteness was on display in the peace process as he had to balance the demands of the nationalist community, the IRA's strategy of violence, the opposition to new governmental institutions by the Unionists, and the diplomatic pressures from Washington, Dublin, and London.
Photo by Harry Brett, Image Photo

Catholics and Protestants by the paramilitary organizations for sectarian offenses continues at a problematic level and those organizations are willing to kill informers past or present.

In October 1998 the Nobel Committee announced that the Peace Prize would go to John Hume and David Trimble. The Belfast Agreement was a clear and direct step toward peace in a historically intractable problem. John Hume had been nominated before and his visibility and commitment to peace in Ulster were beyond doubt. The selection of Hume only underlined the towering place he holds in the modern history of Ireland. From the initial outbreak of the new troubles in 1968 Hume has been at the center of every significant stage in the conflict. Important developments—the civil rights movement, the founding of the SDLP, the involvement of Irish American politicians, the Forum for a New Ireland, and the breakthrough Hume-Adams talks, to mention only a few—were all shaped by the leadership of John Hume. His fidelity to a peaceful democratic process marked by compromise and negotiation never let him lose sight of his ultimate

John Hume, leader of the Social Democratic and Labour Party, on a visit to Boston in 1996. Hume emerged in the early days of the conflict in the late 1960s and has played a leading role ever since. He has been at the crossroads of every major positive development in the "Troubles" and won the Nobel Peace Prize for his three decades of effort to achieve peace. *Photo by Harry Brett, Image Photo*

goals. His connection to the United States and his membership in the European Parliament eventually extended the esteem in which he was held far beyond Ireland. There is virtually no figure in Northern Ireland, friend or foe, who did not think that John Hume deserved the Nobel Peace Prize.[35] When he was notified Hume characteristically said he did not see it as a personal award but as "more a powerful statement of international support and goodwill for the peace process and an endorsement of all those who played a role in the process." Both before and after winning the Nobel Prize Hume has been showered with accolades.

David Trimble is another matter. The choice of Trimble represents a balance in the selection; it takes more than one side to make peace. Trimble is a relative latecomer to the politics of peace although not to the politics of Ulster unionism. A member of the quasi-paramilitary Vanguard Party in the 1970s and part of the armed and militant Ulster Clubs in the 1980s, Trimble was also a leader in the Orange Order. Elected to Parliament in 1990, Trimble made his reputation in the unionist community and the UUP party by his militant stand at Drumcree in 1995. A law professor at Queen's

David Trimble, leader of the Ulster Unionist Party, on a visit to Boston in 1998. Trimble, a hard-line Unionist leader, had earned his reputation in the party through his uncompromising fidelity to Unionism. His leadership in taking his party into the Good Friday Agreement was rewarded with the 1998 Nobel Peace Prize.
Photo by Harry Brett, Image Photo

University, Trimble was an unreconstructed unionist with a keen intelligence but also with an irascible and explosive temper. When the former leader of the UUP, James Molyneaux, resigned Trimble entered the leadership fight although it seemed that the position would go to Ken Maginness. The conservative UUP Council then chose Trimble over Maginness and another popular UUP leader, John Taylor. Trimble was viewed by the Irish and British governments as unlikely to be in the least supportive of the peace process because he had made numerous legal and constitutional arguments about why the position of unionists in Northern Ireland was non-negotiable.

When Trimble was awarded the Peace Prize with Hume the reaction of the DUP was to denounce the award and Trimble with it because to them it was a symbol of a sell-out of the unionist community. His own supporters were muted in their praise. Trimble seemed stunned and said he hoped the award was not premature. Brid Rogers of the SDLP, however, identified the critical element in

Trimble's leadership. He was the first Unionist leader "prepared to take risks and acknowledge the need for equal recognition of unionism and nationalism." But then if the Peace Prize goes to Trimble, why not Gerry Adams? Many leaders acknowledged the key role of Adams in the process, including Mitchell, Hume, and President Clinton. On the other hand, given Adams's history with the IRA, awarding him the Nobel Peace Prize may have been a little too much like giving the "Firefighter of the Year" award to a repentant arsonist. Yet if the Nobel Committee was going to go beyond Hume to Trimble but not Adams, then George Mitchell is perhaps as deserving as anyone. During the negotiations his brother died while he was in Ireland, he rarely saw his newborn son, and his patience with the imperious positions and vehement arguments of the nationalists and unionists was infinite. He spent a total of three-and-one-half years in ascending roles of responsibility on the Ulster crisis and at the end was admired by all the parties to the negotiations (except, of course, Ian Paisley, who referred to him as "the pope").[36] There were many important people in the unfolding peace process. Tony Blair put the process back on track after his election. Bertie Ahern made a significant contribution. Important figures in the peace process were out of office by April 1998, including Albert Reynolds, Dick Spring, and John Major. Still and all, to use an oft-spoken phrase in Northern Ireland, at the end of the day the Peace Prize should have gone to John Hume alone.

Explaining the Conflict; Explaining the Peace

If the participants in the conflict had all read the mountains written about Northern Ireland peace would have broken out long before 1998. Not because of the solutions contained therein, but because they would have had no time to do anything else.[37] That voluminous literature is replete with theories about the conflict organized along virtually any axis that can be identified in Ulster, including class, religion, national identity, imperialism, irredentism, the British government, the Irish government, the Catholic Church, fundamentalist Presbyterianism, political parties, government institutions, education, songs, flags, and sports. We examine those theories that seem to connect to the events that have produced some of the most incandescent confrontations, heart-breaking violence, and giant steps toward peace.

John MacGarry and Brendan O'Leary have organized with clarity the basic framework of explanations for the conflict in Northern Ireland.[38] They cluster external explanations and internal explanations, focusing on the degree to which the primary reason for the conflict lies outside of Northern Ireland or inside that troubled province. The external explanations undergird the classical models of Irish nationalism and Ulster unionism, while the internal explanations focus on religion, culture, and economic conditions. The explanations evoke political solutions for the north that flow from the different perspectives.[39]

Integration

Integration into a united Ireland or into the United Kingdom was, of course, the preferred option of classical nationalism and classical unionism. Recognizing the differences in Irish nationalism, the claim to a united Ireland was still central to all of them. The "naturalness" of this ultimate political arrangement was fed by the creation of the nineteenth-century Irish identity marked by Celtic heritage, Gaelic language, and Catholic faith, which justified self-determination for the people on the island. The British partition of the island was illegitimate, nationalists hold, because the Irish people as a whole have a right to self-determination and the "unionists have no justification for opting out of their birthright."[40] Unionists in this view have been sold a bill of goods by London, which told them they are British and rewarded them with a dominant status over Catholics, to get unionists to do the job of preserving British interests. Once Britain withdrew, or was forced to withdraw, from Ulster the unionists would face reality, reconcile themselves to their Irish identity, and become a national minority with their minority rights protected. Unionists' material interests would, in fact, be served better in a united Ireland. This classical nationalist view, of course, ignored some facts and made colossal assumptions about others to preserve intact the nationalist ideology. In this view unionists have rights only as future Irish citizens; unionists will be moved to enter a united Ireland on the basis of material gain; and unionist commitment to their values and ideals, and their willingness to fight for them, will simply dissipate in the absence of British rule. The view is not only deluded, it is patronizing. Are we to believe that, faced with minority status in a united Ireland, the unionists will dispense with their ethnic and national identity, dispense with their beliefs that the Republic is a Gaelic Catholic state, dispense with their militance, and go along merely for the punts and pence? Were the situation to be reversed, do nationalists believe this is what they would do, is this what nationalists have done since 1922?

The unionist perceptions of the nationalist community, with respect to integration into the United Kingdom, were in fact a mirror image of those of the nationalists. The unionists held that theirs was a peaceful, hard-working, loyal province of the United Kingdom, which always was in a state of uncertainty because of the presence of Irish nationalists being encouraged by Dublin to engage in violence and terror. These acts of violence both exacerbated unionist anxiety and inflamed nationalist aspirations. London, by fully integrating Ulster administratively within the United Kingdom, would reassure the unionists of their Britishness, convince the nationalists in Dublin to stop their irredentism, and convince Irish nationalists within Ulster to forsake their Irish identity so that they could fully enjoy the rights and economic benefits of being British. This unionist view of nationalists was as deluded as the Irish nationalists' view of unionists. Both selectively read history so as to affirm their perspective. Both ideologies eschewed responsibility for their own discriminatory and violent behavior and placed the villain outside of Ulster, in London and Dublin, respectively. Both found that their patron state let them down, the nationalists when Dublin rejected the violence of Sinn Fein/IRA and the unionists when London made it clear that the status of Ulster was negotiable. Both groups ignored the contradictions in their own ideology with respect to the situation of dual minorities in Ireland. Self-determination is the most obvious but not the only example. Nationalists demanded self-determination for Ireland as a whole relative to Britain but rejected the unionist claim for self-determination relative to Ireland. The unionists claimed self-determination as a majority in Ulster relative to Ireland but rejected it when the majority in the United Kingdom threatened to change the status of Ulster. Both visions underestimated the beliefs and will of their opponents and both ideologies were willing to grant the other community full rights and opportunities only if they were to become what they were not. It is not surprising that these solutions canceled each other out. Political scientist Paul Mitchell notes that "they are an assault on their rival's national identity, they are exclusionary, unbalanced and unfair." [41]

The Locus of Sovereignty

What of the other explanations of the conflict in Ulster? Religion and culture are distinctively different in the two communities of Northern Ireland. They remain, however, markers of the difference between unionists and nationalists. As discussed in Chapter 9, the cause of the conflict in Northern Ireland is the presence of two competing ethno-national groups. The unionists were in a superior position in terms of land, power, and wealth and when the Irish nationalist movement crested at the turn of the nineteenth century. Unionists believed that British identity and British authority would best preserve their privileged position and resisted the creation of an independent Ireland. Nationalists believed they would never control their own destiny and create their own identity in a British state. The partition of Ireland created a contested political region that could not resolve the question of political authority. Co-existing in the same state, nationalists seek to have their state ruled by their nation and unionists seek to have their nation protected by their state.

Britain was a mature nation-state when Ireland was partitioned but never promoted sufficient reform in Ulster, nor would Ulster unionists, to incorporate Catholic nationalists into the British state. The new Free State/Republic of Ireland went through a process of state building, which incorporated the Gaelic Catholic dimension to a degree that was not welcome to Ulster Protestants. Eventually the Republic evolved into an economically advanced, mature democracy with a vibrant culture. In 1922 in Northern Ireland, however, a residue of Irish nationalists remained as well as an enclave of Ulster unionists incapable of building a state (or province) at all. Democracy in Northern Ireland was stunted, citizenship was stratified, opportunity was absent for some, violence was a constant threat, and bigotry pockmarked the culture.

Thus at the end of the day, although the conflict expresses itself in many different ways, it is at root a question of ethno-national identities competing over the
issue of who is to rule—that is, the locus of sovereignty—in Ulster. The quest for
other explanations in the polarity of the communities, the disparities in power
and money, educational practices, or the exclusive character of Catholicism and
Presbyterianism, may uncover facets that exacerbate the conflict and sustain it but
they do not explain the conflict.[42] Paul Mitchell states succinctly: "Thus the conflict is not primarily religious, cultural, or class based; it is not imperial, colonial
or even settler-native—although elements of all of these have been contributory
in the past or the present."[43] The path toward a settlement then had to be based
on the issue of rule: rule in Northern Ireland, rule in Ireland, and rule in the
British isles. Claims that Ulster be exclusively British or be exclusively Irish left
the conflict in all or nothing terms.

Two steps had to to be taken to move toward a settlement on these lines. The
first required alterations in the two most self-encapsulated versions of nationalism and unionism, the two ideologies most impervious to change. These groups
had to shift out of the absolutes of unification and union into the blurred realm
of shared sovereignty. The neo-nationalist view of Hume and the SDLP came to
slowly adjust the Sinn Fein nationalist viewpoint and thus allow for a discussion
of the future of Ireland that allowed for a settlement not created by violence, recognized unionism, and shifted to the long term the goal of a united Ireland.[44] The
unionists had to shift from the cultural unionism of the DUP and the liberal
unionism of the UUP to a form of what Norman Porter calls "civic unionism."
They had to adjust to the reality that Irish nationalists had legitimate rights in
Ulster, British rule was conditional, and the Union was guaranteed now but negotiable over the long term.[45] How did this happen? In the nationalist community
the catalyst was the decreasing effectiveness of violence coupled with the efforts of
John Hume and Gerry Adams to find a formula through which the absolutist version of Irish nationalism's doctrines of self-determination and unification could
be framed as negotiable. In the unionist community it was the 1985 Anglo-Irish
Agreement, which signaled to the unionists that London would deal directly with
Dublin on Ulster and that the unionist veto on British policy had ended.
Eventually Unionists in the UUP under David Trimble modified their absolutist
position in a slow recognition that change was going to come and that they
should negotiate matters that were previously off the unionist agenda.

The second step required that the negotiations produce a settlement that addressed the change in the two community's positions in the form of institutional
arrangements that would (1) assure the rights of the communities in Ulster with
guarantees of their most cherished political values; (2) commit the Irish and
British governments to institutions that blurred the sovereignty issue and placed
both governments into the structures of rule, and (3) exclude the Irish and British
governments from the inclusive claims of citizenship on one community or the
other. As noted above, the Good Friday Agreement is structured in this manner

and appears to have a better chance than any other effort to contain the hereto-fore irreconcilable, engage the uncompromising, and spin into a web of peaceful political relationships those for whom the gun and the bomb were all too often their way of life . . . and their way of death.

Notes

1. British Information Services, "Provisional Republican Movement: Sinn Fein" (New York: British Information Services, February 1984).

2. Paul Bew, conversation with R. Finnegan, 7 September 1986.

3. Sean Cronin, *Washington's Irish Policy: 1916–1986, Independence, Partition and Neutrality* (Dublin: Anvil Books, 1987), p. 322

4. Holland, *American Connection*, p. 146; and Garret FitzGerald, *All in a Life* (Dublin: Gill & Macmillan, 1991), p. 535.

5. James N. Rosenau, *Turbulence* (New York: Free Press, 1990); R. O. Keohane and J. S. Nye, *Power and Interdependence: World Politics in Transition*, 2nd ed. (Boston: Little Brown, 1989).

6. J. F. Stack Jr., "Ethnic Groups as Emerging Transnational Actors," in *Ethnic Identities in a Transnational World*, ed. J. F. Stack (Westport, Conn.: Greenwood Press, 1981).

7. Guelke, *Northern Ireland: International Perspective*, p. 4.

8. Ibid., p. 160.

9. Richard B. Finnegan, "Human Rights in Northern Ireland: The Peace People, The Emergency Provisions Act of 1972, and the 1978 European Court Decision on the Treatment of Prisoners," in *Great Events in Human Rights*, ed. F. N. Magill (Salem, Oreg.: Salem Press, 1992).

10. Richard B. Finnegan, "Transnational Pressures and Institutional Responses in Northern Ireland: The Softening of Sovereignty," in *The Ethnic Entanglement*, ed. J. F. Stack Jr. and L. Hebron (New York: Praeger, 1999).

11. Eamon Mallie and David McKittick, in *The Fight for Peace* (London: Heinemann, 1996), quote a security officer to the effect that Gerry Adams had no alternative: "Anyone who would castigate Adams for carrying that coffin could have no concept of republican-ism. If he were involved in a process to turn the republicans away from violence for him to have credibility there wasn't any way he could shun being closely identified with the funeral" (p. 203).

12. Included in John McGarry and Brendan O'Leary, *Explaining Northern Ireland* (Oxford: Blackwell, 1995), pp. 408–413.

13. Some of the more gruesome acts of violence include the killing of a Sinn Fein Councilor by the UFF and three UDR soldiers in a bomb attack in 1991, eight Protestant workmen killed by an IRA bomb, three Sinn Fein men shot dead by an RUC officer, five Catholics shot by loyalists in 1992, a bomb at Warrington killing two children, ten people killed by an IRA bomb at a fish shop, and eight people gunned down in a pub attack in Graysteel in 1993. The list goes on . . . and on . . . , reaching a particularly heart-rending peak in July 1998, when three children were burned to death because the mother, a Catholic, was living with a Protestant man and feelings were running high because of the confrontation at Drumcree between the Orange Order and the police. The worst carnage of the entire troubles was exacted by the dissident "Real IRA" in August 1998, when a bomb

went off in the shopping district of Omagh, killing twenty-nine, including two pregnant women, mothers, and children and injuring 200 doing their school shopping in the center of the city.

14. Brian Girvin, "Northern Ireland and the Republic," in *Politics in Northern Ireland*, ed. Paul Mitchell and Rick Wilford (Boulder, Colo.: Westview Press, 1999), p. 235.

15. See *Building Trust* (Dublin: Stationery Office, 1996).

16. Garret FitzGerald, conversation with R. Finnegan, March 1996.

17. Quoted by James McCauley, "Flying the One Winged Bird: Ulster Unionism and the Peace Process," in *Who Are "The People": Unionism, Protestantism, and Loyalism in Northern Ireland*, ed. Peter Shirlow and Mark McGovern (London: Pluto Press, 1997), p. 161.

18. Brendan O'Brien, *A Pocket History of the IRA* (Dublin: O'Brien Press, 1997), p. 145.

19. Joseph O'Grady, "An Irish Policy Born in the U.S.A.," *Foreign Policy* 75, no. 3 (May–June 1996), pp. 2–7; and Andrew J. Wilson, "From the Beltway to Belfast: The Clinton Administration, Sinn Fein and the Northern Ireland Peace Process," *New Hibernian Review* 1, no. 3 (Autumn 1997), pp. 23–39.

20. Her appointment, in fact, had been made by President Clinton as a favor to Senator Kennedy; there were many people well-qualified by experience and connections for the position.

21. As events developed, Kennedy's foreign policy advisor, Trina Vargo, could communicate with Sinn Fein through U.S. contacts for a New Irish Agenda and in turn communicate with Nancy Soderberg of the National Security Council and in turn with Anthony Lake, the president's National Security advisor in the White House. Wilson, "Clinton Administration," p. 30.

22. Quoted in ibid., p. 31.

23. The facts that the British Conservative Party had sent representatives to help the George Bush campaign in the waning days of the 1992 election and that the British government had searched its intelligence files for information deleterious to Clinton to aid the Bush effort no doubt dulled Clinton's sensitivities to the concerns of John Major and the Conservative Party.

24. Sydney Elliot, "The Northern Ireland Forum/Entry into Negotiations Election 1996," *Irish Political Studies* 12 (1997), p. 118.

25. Geoffry Evans and Brendan O'Leary, "Frameworked Futures: Intransigence and Flexibility in the Northern Ireland Election of May 30, 1996," *Irish Political Studies* 12 (1997), pp. 23–47.

26. Rick Wilford, "Women and Politics," in *Politics in Northern Ireland*, ed. Mitchell and Wilford, p. 215.

27. The Unionists' perceptions of U.S. citizens have been monolithic and almost impervious to correction. In 1993 and 1995 Unionists were surprised to discover that there were Irish Americans who did not support the IRA. Joe English, a paramilitary leader, commented in an interview with Kevin Cullen of the *Boston Globe*, "I thought all Irish Americans were Provos," when he visited Boston College and was disabused of that notion. *Boston Globe*, 19 April 1998, p. 361. The Unionists' views were so congealed that any effort to communicate them to the outside world was clumsy and confrontational, and they often provoked the hostility that they assumed to be directed at them or assumed their position to be so self-evidently correct that they were astounded when people differed with them.

28. Quoted in Paul Arther, "Anglo-Irish Relations and Constitutional Policy," in *Politics in Northern Ireland*, ed. Mitchell and Wilford, p. 243.

29. Quoted by Kevin Cullen in the *Boston Globe*, 19 April 1998, p. A37.

30. Ibid.

31. In 1974, 1,150 had died and the communities were as polarized as much as they had ever been; by 1998, 3,250 had died and large segments of the communities in the north were sick of the violence.

32. Rick Wilford, "Epilogue," in *Politics of Northern Ireland*, ed. Mitchell and Wilford, p. 299.

33. Richard Sinnott, "Vote Shows Peace Optimists on the Increase," *The Irish Times*, 27 June 1998, p. 8.

34. McCauley, "One Winged Bird," p. 159.

35. However, Gregory Cambell of the DUP felt that Mr. Hume did not deserve the prize and in fact accused him of instigating the entire thirty years of strife.

36. In an essay in the *Economist*, R. Bagehot, "The Disturbing Niceness of George Mitchell," 11 April 1998, the author was dismayed that Mitchell was *not* as disliked as Dennis Ross in the Middle East and Richard Holbrooke in the Balkans at the end of the negotiations in Northern Ireland. You have to love the *Economist*, often smarmy and often wrong, but with style.

37. One of the better efforts to make sense of that literature was John H. Whyte's *Interpreting Northern Ireland* (Oxford: Clarendon Press, 1990).

38. McGarry and O'Leary, *Explaining Northern Ireland*. At this point there is no better analysis than this book of the different explanations for events in Northern Ireland and the consistency and inconsistency of the evidence and arguments within each explanation. In this chapter I touch only briefly on those discussions and the reader who seeks a first-rate elaboration of the theories of conflict in Ulster should read the entire book. Another analysis that stresses the dynamics of power, dominance, and equality is Joseph Ruane and Jennifer Todd, *The Dynamics of Conflict in Northern Ireland* (Cambridge: Cambridge University Press, 1995).

39. Two perspectives can be ruled out immediately, not only because of their lack of feasibility and their unlikelihood but also because they lack substantive support in either Ulster community or either state. The first is repartition to create an Ireland that has the Catholic Nationalists in the north as part of the Republic and a smaller enclave of Unionists in Ulster remaining in Britain. This simply would not do what it was intended to do because significant segments of each community would remain in the other political area. Another option to be ruled out is independence. The proposal hinges on the idea that if the Irish and British governments are out of the conflict the communities can resolve their difficulties. This does not appear likely in a political entity that would potentially be riddled with violence and, moreover, economically not viable.

40. Paul Mitchell, "Futures," in *Politics in Northern Ireland*, ed. Mitchell and Wilford, p. 269.

41. Ibid., p. 270.

42. This is again not to suggest that examination of this issue does not reveal something of the dynamics of Ulster and the potential amelioration of community relations. See, for example, Martin Dillon, *God and the Gun: The Church and Irish Terrorism* (New York:

Routledge, 1998); and B. K. Lambkin, *Opposite Religions Still: Interpreting Northern Ireland After the Conflict* (Belfast: Avebury Press, 1996).

43. Mitchell, "Futures," p. 266.

44. Sterile stereotypes are not helpful and the polarities I am describing represent political paradigms more than social. The Catholics in Northern Ireland are no more like those in the 1920s or 1950s than are the unionists. See Fionnuala O'Connor, *In Search of a State: Catholics in Northern Ireland* (Blackstaff: Belfast, 1993); and Shirlow and McGovern, *Who Are "The People."*

45. Norman Porter, *Rethinking Unionism, An Alternative Vision for Northern Ireland* (Belfast: Blackstaff Press, 1996). Porter argues that cultural unionism is defined by a rather exclusive definition of the Protestant way of life and requires union with Great Britain for its preservation and that liberal unionism has as its center British citizenship. Both are exclusive, the former in terms of rejecting parity of esteem with the Catholic ethos of the nationalists and the latter because it undermines the integrity of British sovereignty. Both contribute to unionism's "paltry forms of political conduct." Civic unionism, in Porter's view, focuses on Northern Ireland's civil society, that band of public space that is apart from the state and not in the private domain that would allow for a wider participation, openness to difference, and tolerance of Catholic nationalists. Arthur Aughey, a unionist intellectual, suggests in a review of Porter's book that Porter is advocating a form of politics in which "unionists are no longer unionists and nationalists are no longer nationalists." *Irish Political Studies* 12 (1997), p. 129.

11

IRELAND IN THE WORLD: POLICY, PEOPLE, AND THE ARTS

Irish Foreign Policy

To state that the impact of Ireland on world politics is modest is not to engage in irresponsible understatement. The geographical position of Ireland, its size, and the absence of critical resources place it among nations that are destined for lesser roles on the world stage. Ireland's physical insularity was matched by its insular foreign policy from 1922 until the 1960s. In 1996, however, the government of Ireland published a white paper on Irish foreign policy titled *Challenges and Opportunities Abroad*, the first comprehensive white paper on foreign policy since the founding of the state in 1922. That no such paper was considered necessary until seventy-four years after the founding of the state is a reflection of the increasing globalization of Irish economics and politics. Heretofore Irish foreign policy has been dominated by relations with London over the question of independence and Northern Ireland. Those central questions shaped Ireland's position in the Commonwealth in the 1920s and 1930s, Ireland's position at the League of Nations in the 1930s, Ireland's constitutional and economic actions in the 1930s, and Ireland's neutrality in the 1940s. Northern Ireland and Anglo-Irish relations, surprisingly, were not included in the white paper, not a reflection of their lack of importance but rather manifesting the degree to which the European Union has moved to the center of Irish foreign policy. Yet Irish foreign policy today in many ways reflects the initial efforts of the Free State in the 1920s and 1930s to escape the dominance of London. Now Ireland is escaping British dominance through the European Union and resolving the question of Northern Ireland through the peace process.

The Irish Free State

After 1922 the fledgling Irish state slowly began to expand its representation abroad, beginning with its delegation to the League of Nations in Geneva and a High Commissioner to London in 1923. Berlin and Paris and the Vatican received permanent representatives in 1929. Dublin sent a representative to Washington in 1924 as the volume of emigration to the United States brought the relationship with Washington to the forefront. Irish American immigrants adhered to a particularly incandescent version of Irish nationalism and sought to advance Irish independence from Britain through political pressure on U.S. politicians and the U.S. government.[1]

The Anglo-Irish Treaty establishing the Free State was registered with the League of Nations. The Free State signed the Kellogg Briand Agreement in 1929 and also signed on to the optional clause of the Permanent Court of International Justice at the Hague, which obliged states to submit disputes to international adjudication. Most important to Ireland was the Statute of Westminister passed by the British Parliament, which exempted Commonwealth states from laws passed by the British Parliament unless they consented. Noting the development of increasing autonomy for Ireland in the 1920s and 1930s historian Desmond Keogh states: "The Treatyites had been proven correct"; the Anglo-Irish Treaty was a means of becoming independent of Britain.[2]

The failure of the League of Nations as an instrument of peace in the 1930s was clear when Italy invaded Ethiopia and the League attempted to impose economic sanctions. De Valera supported those sanctions, arguing before the League that if the sovereignty of small states was taken away then the League was meaningless. When those sanctions failed de Valera pressed for the use of troops, an idea with little likelihood of realization. De Valera argued that the sovereignty of all small states was subject to the whims of great power politics unless sanctions against Italy were upheld and she was forced to rescind the invasion of Ethiopia. While de Valera's was a principled position consistent with Ireland's history and size, the League's consensus on security matters was too slender to support this sort of collective security action.

In the same period de Valera pushed the British on the 1922 Treaty provisions, provoking the Anglo-Irish "Economic War." Relations with London deteriorated until 1938, when an Anglo-Irish Agreement was signed. Yet as the storm clouds of World War II approached, de Valera recognized that he could not support the United Kingdom in the war because he had portrayed London as the violator of Ireland's unity and independence; nor, for patently obvious pragmatic reasons, could he support the Germans. Ireland's military weakness and geographical position meant that the only course open to de Valera was neutrality.

The legal position of Ireland during the war was absolute neutrality. The actual policies of Ireland were favorable to the United Kingdom but apparently not to a degree sufficient to satisfy U.S. Ambassador to Ireland David Gray. Gray made every effort to induce de Valera to give up neutrality and put the resources and ports of Ireland in the service of the war effort. When Winston Churchill offered to eliminate the partition of Ireland after the war in exchange for the end of Irish neutrality, Gray pressed de Valera to agree. De Valera would not do so and Gray then set out to discredit him among Irish Americans and more broadly in U.S. public opinion. He arranged for a diplomatic note to be sent to Ireland in March 1944 calling for the expulsion of the Japanese and German missions from Dublin on the basis that they were potential centers of espionage. De Valera refused to expel the two missions and Gray had the note released to the press, provoking a negative reaction toward Ireland and Irish neutrality in the United States.

After the war relations with the United States were cold because neutrality had not endeared Ireland to the nations that had fought in what all now agreed was an absolutely necessary war against a profoundly evil regime. Ireland did receive Marshall Plan aid of $36 million in the form of loans, but it was considerably less than Ireland had hoped to get. Discussion about Ireland joining the North Atlantic Treaty Organization did not reach the state of a formal invitation. Dublin would not consider entry other than as a united Ireland, thus setting the ending of partition as a precondition of entering the European alliance. Washington, and not surprisingly London, took this as a lack of serious interest in NATO. In the early 1950s Ireland did seek to get military aid from the United States and forged links with the Central Intelligence Agency. Despite Ireland's absence from NATO, formal declarations on the part of Irish prime ministers left no doubt where they stood on the Cold War. John A. Costello, for example, asserted that Ireland's influence "would always be directed against the threat of communism" and Sean Lemass stated that Ireland was "clearly on the democratic side and that is where we belong."[3]

The United Nations

Ireland's entry into the United Nations was delayed by the impasse between the United States and the Soviet Union over the admission of new states and did not occur until 1955. The Soviet Union formally opposed Irish entry on the basis of Ireland's policy of neutrality, although in fact Moscow was merely attempting to exclude another state in what they perceived as the Western bloc. In the United Nations the Irish delegation adopted a position, under Frank Aiken, the minister for External Affairs, of non-alignment with any particular bloc and asserted that Irish votes on resolutions would be based on the merits of the issue. On the issues of decolonization, disarmament, apartheid, and especially the People's Republic of China, Ireland took independent positions from the western European states and the United States. Conor Cruise O'Brien was an influential member of the Irish delegation and sought to have Ireland diplomatically placed more in the role of Sweden. When Ireland voted to allow for discussion of the issue of Chinese representation, that is replacing Taiwan with Beijing, a furor of diplomatic pressure and criticism emerged from the United States. When in 1957 Aiken suggested that both the United States and the Soviet Union should withdraw troops from Europe, the diplomatic pressure on Ireland became intense and Ireland backed away from that position. While no lap dog of London and Washington, it should also be noted that Ireland's positions, for the most part, were not all that far from the positions of the other European neutrals and still supported Ireland's goal of "preserving the Christian civilization of which Ireland was a part."[4] The blend of a western European orientation with an independent stance produced Ireland's criticism of Britain in the Falklands-Malvinas War and of the United States in Central America, especially during the Reagan administration.

The Irish have contributed to the United Nations most notably in the area of peacekeeping. Irish soldiers were used in the Congo crisis of 1960–1964 and ten lost their lives there. The commander in chief of the United Nations forces in that operation was Sean MacEoin, and Conor Cruise O'Brien served as the United Nations representative in Katanga. Subsequently more than 16,000 Irish soldiers have participated in Lebanon, Cyprus, and numerous other UN peacekeeping operations.

The policy of neutrality, which had emerged as a pragmatic response to the conditions in the 1930s, was after the war somewhere between a practically grounded policy choice and an enduring principle of Irish foreign policy. The question of whether this sacralization of neutrality represented a form of self-delusional moral superiority is raised by historian J. J. Lee, who argues that the Irish chose the policy for pragmatic reasons but could not resist transforming that choice into moral posturing against Great Britain while relying on the Royal Navy and Air Force to protect Ireland's interests.[5] Having enshrined the policy, the Irish now had to live with it. Anti-British in origin, the policy acquired additional resonance in later years through opposition to nuclear deterrence, Cold War confrontation, and colonialism. Joining the European Union, or European Economic Community as it was then known, raised the question of neutrality insofar as the long-term objective of the European Union was political and thus eventually would involve security policy.

The European Economic Community

When Ireland's entry into the EEC was to be put before the people in a referendum, the economic pragmatists argued that there was no threat to Irish neutrality in joining the Community and further demoted neutrality to a policy that was temporal and conditional. Their position was that political integration would come at the end of a long process of economic integration and that in the mean-time Irish neutrality would be maintained. The opponents of membership, on the other hand, elevated neutrality to an eternal principle guiding the Irish state. Neutrality was at least problematic because Article 224 of the Treaty of Rome specifies that the European Economic Community could take common action during war, which would clearly imply actions that could ultimately be inconsistent with Irish neutrality. The Irish public, to the degree that neutrality entered their consideration at all, overwhelmingly opted for economic pragmatism and Ireland entered the EEC in 1973.

In practice since 1970, European Political Cooperation (EPC) had evolved pragmatically into common declarations and support for members' actions. Based on a process of consultation, consensus between foreign ministers was to be sought on matters of general interest to the member states, but the result was hardly a common EU foreign policy. In 1986 the European Economic Community adopted the Single European Act, which gave treaty status to the for-mulation of a European Union foreign policy. The Maastricht Treaty of 1992 es-tablished the Common Foreign and Security Policy (CFSP) formally as part of the new EU structure, set broad EU foreign policy objectives, and required member states to pursue these goals.

In 1982 the European Economic Community imposed economic sanctions on Argentina in support of Great Britain after Argentina invaded the Falkland Islands (if you support London) or recovered the Malvinas Islands (if you sup-port Argentina). The Irish went along with the sanctions until the British were prepared to invade the island. The Irish opted out, saying that continuation of Irish sanctions was inconsistent with neutrality in the context of an armed con-flict. Although creating much friction with London, the Irish action was not chal-lenged by other European Economic Community members.

In 1986, however, when the Irish government adopted the Single European Act (SEA) through legislative rather than constitutional means, the process was chal-lenged by William Crotty, a private citizen who argued that the Irish government could not legislatively approve an Act that itself contained provisions that were potentially unconstitutional and required approval in a referendum. The High Court did issue an injunction to prevent the ratification but ultimately rejected the legal argument. In *Crotty v. An Taoiseach* in 1987 the Supreme Court, on ap-peal, held that the section of SEA codifying EPC did require an amendment to the Constitution for ratification. Three of the five judges thought that the SEA was fundamentally changing the nature of the European Union from an economic union to a political one. Two, however, saw the EPC process as essentially consul-tative, not a concession of sovereignty, and thus not an eschewing of Irish neutral-ity. When Ireland approved the SEA through a constitutional amendment in 1987, it lodged a statement of neutrality declaring that the Act "does not affect Ireland's right to act or refrain from acting in any way which might affect Ireland's international status of military neutrality."[6] Eventually the issue would come to a head in the 1992 referendum in Ireland on the Maastricht Treaty, which called for the further development of a common foreign and security policy for the European Union by taking the western European Union and making it the defense arm of the European Union.

The 1996 white paper on foreign policy noted that neutrality "has taken on a significance for Irish people over and above the essentially practical considerations on which it was originally based. Many have come to regard neutrality as a touchstone for our entire approach to international relations, even though, in reality, much of our policy is not dependent on our non-membership of a military alliance." Having said that, the white paper also noted that since 1973, "successive governments have indicated that Ireland would be prepared to enter into discussion with other member states on the development of common arrangements in relation to security and defense matters." Finally, the white paper indicates that the ratification of the Maastricht Treaty bound Ireland to a "Common Foreign and Security Policy."[7] Although at no point does the document say so, the juxtaposition of the statements makes clear that the Irish policy of neutrality clearly does not prevail over participation in the European Union, up to and including security issues.

The European Union

Challenges and Opportunities Abroad "illustrate(s) the extent to which Ireland, . . . has come to express its foreign policy through the medium of the European Union," and we can clearly see that impact.[8] Membership in the EU has definitely enhanced the diplomatic status of Ireland. A small state on the perimeter of Europe, Ireland now has direct and regular access to the policy elites of all the major countries of Europe. The presidency of the EU Council rotates every six months and Ireland gains high-profile visibility for the issues that it has selected to emphasize during its term. Participation in the EU brings Ireland into development and trade policy issues in the global arena that would be beyond the country's scope as an individual state.[9] The permanent delegation to the EU in Brussels is the largest of all Irish diplomatic missions.[10] In addition, Ireland's membership in the Council of Europe, established in 1949 to promote European integration, has involved the country in human rights issues. The Council runs the European Court of Human Rights and has done much to promote democracy and human rights in Europe.

Participation in the European Union has been very popular with the Irish public, and issues that have become confounded with being part of Europe, such as neutrality and abortion, have not dimmed their enthusiasm. Membership in the European Economic Community was endorsed by 83 percent of those who voted for accession in 1972. The SEA referendum in 1987 drew the support of 70 percent, although with a low turnout, and the Maastricht Treaty in 1992 was supported by over 69 percent of the electorate.

The most significant impact of the EU on Ireland has been in the economic realm (see Chapter 4). Ireland underwent a transition from having a relatively closed and backward economy to internationalization in three stages. The first was the adoption of planning after 1959 that rejected protectionism and began shifting the basis of the economy from agriculture to industry and from being hampered by the paucity of domestic capital to attracting foreign capital. The second stage was entry into the European Economic Community in 1973 and the effects of the Common Agricultural Policy (CAP) on the farmers of Ireland, the European Monetary System, and the effects of the structural funds. The rapidity of these shifts and the global oil crises, however, resulted in inflationary spirals, costly job creation, balance of payments difficulties, government deficits, continued emigration, and the failure of non-competitive Irish companies from the late 1970s to the late 1980s. The third stage began around 1987 and involved the development of indigenous industry, the control of inflation, increased productivity, decreased emigration, and spectacular growth rates exceeding those of all other European states.

Political scientist Brigid Laffan sees the development as "a process of learning how to manage internationalization and the emergence of international governance."[11] Laffan argues that the Irish managed internationalization of the economy through the use of the social partnership. The Irish created a continuing series of national planning documents in which the major sectors of society—employers, labor, agriculture, and government—agreed to constraints on wage increases, agreed on tax policy, and agreed on social services. All the social partners approved Ireland's participation in the international economy and all recognized that a small economy must maximize domestic policy consensus to be internationally competitive.[12]

Negotiating the social partnership reveals the degree to which being in the EU creates a new kind of politics for Ireland. The intersection of Irish and European public policy represents an intermediate step between domestic and foreign policy. The regulatory areas of the EU are extensive, covering infrastructure, fisheries, farm incomes, research and development, conservation programs, social policies, education, and other areas of domestic policy. The areas of policy falling under the EU have expanded with the SEA and the Maastricht and Amsterdam Treaties of 1992 and 1997. Irish public agencies in Dublin are looking simultaneously toward both Brussels and Cork and Galway. An extensive body of EU law applies in Ireland and the citizens of Ireland can make claims in the European Court.

Government departments such as Foreign Affairs, with overall authority for European matters; Agriculture, with respect to the CAP; and Finance, with respect to EU funding are continuously and deeply involved in negotiations with their counterparts from other EU countries, the representatives of interested pressure groups, and party leaders in Ireland. The prime minister's department is central to setting the overall direction of Irish policy and assessing the policy consequences of EU initiatives, especially during Ireland's Council presidencies.[13]

The growth in European integration and the expansion of the EU since 1973 have allowed Ireland to expand its bureaucratic and institutional capacity as the EU extended its institutionalization and regulation.[14] Nevertheless, the Irish policymaking process was relatively unprepared for entry into Europe and the pragmatic approach to policy-making that prevailed in Ireland has led to three deficiencies in the Irish/EU interface. The departmental autonomy of the Irish civil service caused poor management of issues that cut across departments, which needed to be addressed by interdepartmental committees. The Irish government can respond to issues in the short term, but no planning structures examine problems emerging from the EU for the medium and long terms. In addition, the Irish government pays little attention to the institutional development of the European Union itself and tends to react to institutional reforms proposed by the other states instead of proposing reforms itself.[15] The SEA, Maastricht, and Amsterdam have streamlined decision making and introduced qualified majorities for EU decisions, speeding up the EU policy-making process and thus accentuating the Irish deficiencies.

European Union policies have had a significant impact on the institutional development of the Irish government in three areas. The EU directives on equality of pay and opportunity have influenced Irish law (see Chapter 6). These directives led to the creation of the Employment Equality Agency. That agency is deeply imbedded in the European policy process. Another example is the Health and Safety Authority, which handles issues that traditionally were under the Department of Labor. The increasing amount of EU legislation directed at this area to ensure common safety guarantees that this agency and its directives are woven into that intermediate zone between Brussels and Dublin. An additional example of the impact on local government is the EU policy of distributing local development funds in accordance with plans drawn up in partnership by the EU Commission, the national government, and regional and local government. For Ireland the plans were formulated by Dublin with its tradition of strong central government. The necessity to respond to the EU requests for plans emerging from the grassroots level prompted the inclusion of local government and community groups in the Irish planning process. The revitalized institutions and groups were a direct result of EU policy processes.[16]

The Irish parties and the Parliament have had relatively little influence on Ireland EU matters. The absence of a committee system in the Parliament, the orientation of the TDs to their constituencies, and the centralization of policy-making in the Cabinet have made the Dail traditionally weak. The absence of a committee system eliminated a continual accounting on the part of the executive on European matters. The governments were left alone and had secure majorities on European matters. The Joint Committee on Secondary Legislation, appointed in 1974 to monitor the implementation of the European directives, did not engage in a critical oversight role. The appointment of a Joint Committee on Foreign Affairs in 1993 appeared to be a step in the right direction, but the committee had inadequate time and resources to consider the plethora of European matters affecting Ireland, so another Joint Committee on European Affairs was established in 1995. As Brigid Laffan notes, the record of both committees is mixed. Lacking resources and attendance, the committees are dependent on the Department of Foreign Affairs for information and policy analysis; the lack of independent sources of information prevents genuine oversight.[17] Political Scientist Neill Nugent bluntly states, "The fact is that in Ireland EU policy tends to be in the hands of a small, government dominated, network of politicians and officials who listen to Parliament only as they see fit . . . ."[18]

The Irish parties align themselves with their ideological confreres in the European Parliament. This was easy for the Labour Party, which had connections to the international socialist organizations and joined the Socialist Group in the Parliament while opposing Irish entry into the EU. The choices for Fine Gael and Fianna Fail were somewhat different. Both were essentially conservative parties and for reasons of domestic competition could not join the same group. The Fine Gael party joined the International Union of Christian Democrats. This group is the most vigorous in asserting the need for a common European Economic Community defense policy, putting Fine Gael in an awkward position when asserting Irish neutrality. Fianna Fail, traditionally the most isolationist Irish party, was left looking for a home and eventually formed a pragmatic alliance with the French Gaullists in a group consisting essentially of those two parties. They share little other than a lack of connection with the other parliamentary groups and a pro-CAP stand to protect small farmers. As the power of the European Parliament grows within the EU the voice of Fianna Fail is weaker than that of Fine Gael. The members of the Dail who are elected to seats in the European Parliament hold both positions until the next election and then have to decide if they are going to hold their Dail seats and make their political careers in national politics or keep the MEP position and spend their careers consuming Belgian waffles.

Despite the distance between the Irish Parliament and the European Parliament, the decision makers in the Irish government have moved smoothly into the EU policymaking style and skillfully negotiate their way through committees, advancing the interests of Ireland. As noted in Chapter 8, interest groups have also thrived in the Brussels environment: "Groups in Ireland can play nested games at the national level and connected games in the Brussels arena."[19]

Attempting to create a balance sheet to measure the benefits of Irish membership in the European Union involves the difficulty of counterfactually speculating on what would have happened had Ireland not become a member.[20] The weight of the evidence, however, indicates that membership has benefited Ireland in numerous tangible and intangible ways. In support of the goal of Irish industrialization, foreign investment funds have been brought to Ireland by companies seeking access to the EU market while expanding the market for Irish goods beyond Britain. Although Ireland has received more of the EU structural funds per capita than other states and the funds have been and are helpful for Ireland to achieve infrastructure development. The CAP increased Irish agricultural productivity and opened new markets. CAP funds from Brussels were considerably greater than the structural funds and significantly influenced Irish agricultural policy.[21]

In the realm of foreign policy the ambiguity about the commitment to neutrality has been more than offset by the access the Irish government has to a sophisticated diplomatic network and participation in a larger framework of global trade and development policy. Membership has diminished the country's dependence on the United Kingdom.[22] As a small country with few resources, suffering from bureaucratic overload in European matters, one benefit is often an intangible sense of being "European."

Evaluating the EU's impact on the Irish government and the social agenda depends on one's point of view. Plunging into the European policy process has increased the sophistication of Irish policymakers and bureaucrats. The policies that the EU has pushed onto the Irish agenda include women's rights, consumer law, and health and safety. The education system has been influenced by the extensive student exchange programs, the pressure to eliminate sexist stereotypes in texts, and the encouragement of the study of continental foreign languages (although without much success). The overall effect has been to diminish the provincial procedures and policies of traditional Ireland, although for many Irish, as we have seen in earlier chapters, that is a detriment. All of these changes are not without critics from both the Left and the Right. Anthony Coughlan, among others, argues that in every domain discussed above, Ireland has abdicated power over its own sovereignty to the disadvantage of Ireland, turning economic policy, foreign policy, and control of the fate of the Irish worker over to multinational corporations and to Brussels— in effect, to the larger European states, which can manipulate the European community to their advantage.[23]

People

The New Irish Emigrants

From the mid-nineteenth century through much of the twentieth century, Irish immigration has represented one of the largest and most culturally influential movements in the history of the Atlantic world. Each successive generation of Irish has left a lasting image: the famine migrants of the 1840s and 1850s, the female domestic servants of the turn of the century, the sons and daughters of rural Connemara during the 1950s, and the "undocumented" Irish of the 1980s. Today the "New Irish" of the 1990s are forging a vastly different persona in the United States. Riding the back of the "Celtic Tiger" they are seen as ambitious, highly educated, talented, and successful. Indeed, their impact and presence in the United States has been one aspect of a remarkable renaissance of Irish culture that has been felt around the globe.

During the second half of the twentieth century there was a pronounced ebb and flow in Irish immigration to the United States. In the years following World War II the pace of Irish immigration quickened, becoming a stream that soon turned into a flood by the 1950s. Nearly 50,000 Irish arrived in the United States during that decade, a movement prompted by narrowing opportunities at home and the promise of jobs in the post-war United States. Many of these voyagers traveled from the west of Ireland, bound for the "next parish" of Boston or New York. This exodus, however, was not to continue indefinitely.

In 1965 a new immigration act passed by the U.S. Congress extended the same quota—20,000 immigrants—to every country. The criteria for entry also changed. Henceforth those immigrants who had close family connections in the United States or had specific job skills would be given first preference. This piece of legislation would haunt the Irish twenty years down the road.

More immediately, Irish immigration was slowed by events at home. During the 1970s a temporary boom in the Irish economy was brought about by Ireland's entry into the EU. Many young men and women found gainful employment at home and the need to emigrate diminished. However, by the mid-1980s Irish unemployment figures had risen significantly and as job prospects dwindled young Irish set their sights on "the farther shore" yet again and crossed the Atlantic by the thousands. Unable to fulfill the requirements of the 1965 Immigration Act, they entered as tourists, quickly found jobs (albeit "under the table"), and overstayed their visas. While the precise number of these "undocumented" Irish is unknown, perhaps as many as 100,000 were working and living illegally in America by 1987.[24]

Those Irish immigrants who made landfall during the 1980s were generally young, single, and urban. Most tended to settle in established Irish American neighborhoods such as Dorchester, Massachusetts, or Woodside Queens, New York, where they traveled almost exclusively among Hibernian networks. Many of the Irish men worked in construction jobs (often at a lower wage scale than their legal counterparts) and women found employment as waitresses or in child care. For many it was a precarious existence. They often lived in crowded apartments, worked at low-paying jobs, and were cut off from security and medical benefits because of their undocumented status. They were constantly looking over their shoulders and could not visit Ireland for fear of losing their jobs or not clearing customs upon their return.[25]

The plight of these illegal immigrants came to the attention of the Irish American community. Newspapers such as the *Irish Voice* published exposés of their experience and a grassroots organization, the Irish Immigration Reform Movement, lobbied Congress for reform. Several Irish American politicians stepped forward to assist the new Irish, most prominently Senator Edward (Ted) Kennedy and U.S. Representative Brian Donnelly, whose Dorchester congressional district in Boston contained a plethora of undocumented Irish. Over the period 1987–1990 Donnelly secured more than 18,000 visas for Irish immigrants (visas that did not require applicants to have family networks or special skills). This boon was followed in the early 1990s by 48,000 Morrison visas—named after congressional sponsor Bruce Morrison of Connecticut—that were earmarked for Ireland. Although many of these lottery visas were secured by Irish at home, they also offered amnesty to many of the undocumented already in the United States.[26]

During the 1990s the image of the Irish immigrant experience changed dramatically. Gone are the days of the Irish "exile" from Erin squeezed out by lack of jobs and opportunity. Today the "Celtic Tiger" has spawned a new breed of Irish immigrant, represented in the media as "adventure seeking, talented, ambitious, and successful."[27] Indeed, the New Irish—free from the restraints of undocumented life in the shadows—have done well for themselves. Their ranks include actors, writers, international bankers, lawyers, engineers, and musicians. As one writer remarks, they "arrived in droves, university degrees at the ready, complementing immigrants with more traditional professions—carpenter, accountant, barman."[28]

For many of these new arrivals, Ireland is just a short plane ride away, a fact that has muted somewhat the emotional baggage of separation and displacement that accompanies every immigrant. Indeed, the "American Wake," which celebrated the leave-taking of Irish immigrants, is something from the distant past. Today the New Irish are characterized by a self-confidence that is bolstered by prosperity and vitality at home. Writer Helena Mulkerns describes this metamorphosis, a sea change that has particular power for the growing Irish artistic community in the United States:

> It simply is not possible for Ireland to fade into sentimental memory these days, because its culture has become a vibrant, respected international force. . . . Ireland has finally established a post-colonial identity, which has inspired the New Irish community with the confidence to create their own output in America, in almost every art form there is.[29]

The new Irish are also part of a larger "virtual community" of Irish worldwide. Today Ireland is only a heartbeat away thanks to new technology and communications. One can phone or e-mail the family at a moment's notice, read the *Irish Times* on the Internet, and keep up with the global doings of Irish immigrants via the World Wide Web. As Ray O'Hanlon asserts: "The Irish have long spoken of the next parish. The world is finally catching up."[30]

Despite this ever-shrinking distance across the Atlantic and a commuter lifestyle that allows the new immigrant to work in the United States and vacation in Ireland, one still detects a restlessness among the New Irish. This is expressed perhaps most dramatically in return migration to Ireland. For the first time in living memory Irish immigrants are confronted with a novel decision: stay in the United States, the "land of opportunity," or go home to an increasingly vital and booming Ireland. Previously in U.S. history, trans-Atlantic movement was a one-way ticket. As historian Kerby Miller notes: "Irish immigrants longed to return, at least sentimentally, but they realized it was impractical or impossible."[31] Today, however, new jobs at home and the promise of peace in Northern Ireland exert a strong pull on Irish immigrants from both sides of the border. Moreover, Irish families are coming back to Ireland to raise their children in a more tranquil pace of life. As one immigrant put it, "New York is a wonderful city to come and work in and earn money. But New York is not the place to raise a family and grow old in. There is no place like home after all."[32] Irish government figures confirm this growing pattern. In 1997 and 1998, 13,000 more Irish returned to Ireland than emigrated out of it.[33] This trend has even prompted Ireland's Department of Social Welfare to issue a pamphlet titled "Thinking of Returning to Ireland?" It provides the potential returnee (some who have been away for a decade or more) with practical information on housing, taxes, health care, and pensions.

The revolving door migration of the 1990s has prompted glowing descriptions of immigrant success in the media. The New Irish are educated, talented, and successful—so much so that several writers have identified a new breed of "Mid-Atlantic dual citizen" who "fly over and back from Ireland setting up their deals, putting on their productions . . . [and] keeping in touch by fax-modem and e-mail."[34] While this image has some truth to it, it neglects those Irish who still live on the fringe in the United States. We seldom hear of the illegal immigrant who is trapped by increasingly stringent anti-immigration laws or the university graduate from Claremorris who is waitressing in the Boston suburbs until "something better comes up." True, Irish immigration in the 1990s represents exciting opportunities and experiences for many. Yet, as Mary Corcoran warns, by only framing the story in those terms we lose track of "the collective necessity of emigration for those who still see no place for themselves in Irish society."[35]

Immigration into Ireland

While return migrants are going home in the thousands, Ireland is also experiencing an unprecedented movement of a different kind: immigration from Europe and the Third World. Between April 1996 and April 1997 over 44,000 immigrants settled in Ireland, many of them drawn by a thriving economy and the creation of new jobs. While more than one-half came from the United Kingdom and EU countries (some of these return migrants), over 9,000, or approximately 20 percent, journeyed from former Eastern Bloc countries such as Romania and developing nations such as Bangladesh, the Congo, and Algeria.[36] Many have come to Ireland seeking asylum, while others have entered illegally, attracted by one of the most liberal social welfare systems in Europe. This new influx, while holding the promise of a new diversity, has also stirred the ugly pot of racism in Ireland.

In 1997 and 1998, Dublin witnessed an increase in racial tension along with several unprovoked attacks on black asylum seekers. Part of the problem has been a less-than-enlightened migration policy. In an effort to clamp down on illegal immigration via Britain and Northern Ireland, Garda and immigration officers have selectively targeted people of color or those travelers who do not meet "the normal criteria."[37] Moreover, bona fide refugees and asylum seekers are regularly housed in working class and deprived inner city neighborhoods in Dublin. In these environments home-grown unemployment and poverty breed a heightened suspicion of newcomers on state relief. Indeed, immigrants say they live in constant fear and have been attacked on several occasions in Dublin. As one refugee laments: "We lost our freedom in our own countries and now we are going to lose it here in Ireland."[38]

It is difficult to project how immigration policy or public awareness will evolve in Ireland.[39] There are some promising signs, however. The government has lately established a national agency for refugees and has set up training courses in the inner cities to increase public awareness and foster understanding between both immigrant and native communities.[40] It is hoped that in the future Ireland will extend "Cead Mile Failte" (one hundred thousand welcomes) to all its people, not just its native born or U.S. cousins "returning home" across the Atlantic.

Irish America

In her first Christmas message in 1990, the new Irish president, Mary Robinson, sent out greetings of peace and reconciliation to "all Irish people at home and abroad . . . to our emigrants everywhere." She addressed a great diaspora of Irish and their descendants, a commonwealth of talent, energy, and kinship that numbered 70 million worldwide.[41] In this message Robinson presented a new vision for the 1990s, one that embraced a more open and inclusive Ireland. Indeed, she projected an Irish community, a sense of belonging if you will, that was no longer predetermined by geography, birthright, or political identity. Hers was a new outlook in which, according to Ray O'Hanlon, "the idea of Ireland as a small inward-looking island on the edge of Europe was out the window and the notion of "Irishness" was suddenly a globally marketed concept."[42]

During the 1990s the image and impact of Irish culture skyrocketed worldwide. Blockbuster films, Pulitzer and Nobel Prize winners, and dance productions that conquered London, New York, and Sydney all heralded the arrival of the Irish. The cultural effects of this "second Irish renaissance" were nowhere more keenly felt than in the United States, where both countries had long drawn on each other's talents. In fact, as several writers suggest, the coming of age of Ireland in the 1990s is often inseparable from that of Irish America, both of them "inventing fresh ideas of Irishness, cross-pollinating across the ocean, eliciting critical interest and, in the process, enjoying commercial success."[43]

This renaissance is a phenomenon that few would have expected thirty years ago in the heartland of Irish America. During the 1950s and 1960s the Irish urban enclaves of Boston, New York, and Chicago were rapidly changing. Post-war affluence and social mobility prompted a move to the suburbs, away from the old Irish neighborhood, the parish, and the precinct. Along with this move came the rapid assimilation of Irish American identity. Indeed, the new Irish middle class never looked back. Many became homeowners, moved up the corporate ladder, sent their children to public rather than parochial schools, and watched as this new generation went off to college—now perhaps "at Harvard rather than Holy Cross."[44]

This post-urban assimilation of Irish America, however, was gradually reversed between the 1970s and the 1990s. Many of the young who grew up in suburbia, starting with the baby-boom generation, have rediscovered their Irish roots—and in a dramatic fashion quite unlike that of their parents. Gone are the Kelly green sweaters, the Clancy brothers, and the porcelain leprechauns. Now there is a more sophisticated appreciation of Irish American identity and an explosion of interest in things Irish ranging from traditional music to Irish history to Celtic Christianity.[45] This transformation is exemplified in the experience of Chris Byrne, the uillean pipes player with the rock band Black 47. In an article appearing in *The Washington Post*, Byrne remembers growing up in Brooklyn during the 1970s and hiding his interest in Irish music from his friends. Not any more. "Now it's cool," declares Byrne. "All these kids in my neighborhood come up to me and they want to learn the tin whistle. It's like a watershed moment."[46]

The momentum that led to this "Irish moment" had been building for several years. The Irish arts, once shunned in the United States by the doyens of culture, have enjoyed a broad wave of support well beyond an Irish-interest audience. Irish theater, literature, and music have taken the United States by storm. There have been Tony awards for Martin McDonagh's "The Beauty Queen of Leenane"; a national infatuation with the Celtic dance spectacular "Riverdance"; and the success of Frank McCourt's *Angela's Ashes*, which has sold 4 million copies worldwide and won the Pulitzer prize for literature. Indeed, critics speak of an "Irish Chic" that has taken over the arts scene. In New York City people line up for tickets to literary readings by novelist Roddy Doyle or poet Nuala Ni Dhomhnaill, and Altan, Ireland's premier traditional music ensemble, recently signed a major recording contract with Virgin Records.

Young people in particular have caught the Irish wave in the United States. This is nowhere better illustrated than in the prolific growth of academic programs in Irish studies. Schools ranging from the University of California–Los Angeles and Notre Dame to New York University offer an Irish studies curriculum and sponsor study-abroad programs in Ireland. In part, these programs reflect the growing interest in ethnic studies in the United States. Many students today are attracted to rediscovering their Irish "roots" but also to connecting these with the larger context of multiculturalism. Irish history, with its legacy of colonialism, emigration, and ethnic conflict, allows students to make this connection as well as to make parallels with peoples of other cultures.[47] On a different level, Irish studies have also benefited by the coming of age of an Irish American elite who have an avid interest in the Irish experience. Indeed, several programs have been made possible, in part, through the financial support of wealthy benefactors, including Donald Keough, former CEO of Coca-Cola, who funds the Irish studies program at Notre Dame, and Brian Burns, who sponsors a similar program at Boston College and who recently put his world-class collection of Irish art on tour.[48]

Why is there an overwhelming popularity for things Irish, and why are U.S. youth increasingly drawn to Irish studies, Guinness stout, or The Cranberries? Journalist Peter Finn suggests that today's Irish-interest boom is "driven by changes in the Irish-American psyche as much as by the creativity of a modern Ireland."[49] While an earlier generation of Irish were preoccupied with moving up and out into the mainstream of the United States, a younger generation of Irish Americans are reexamining who they are. Many of these youth have grown up in a multicultural society and have been taught to "embrace what makes them different."[50] And what they are learning is that being Irish is "different"; Celtic Christianity, U2, Oscar Wilde, and Roddy Doyle's *The Commitments* have an offbeat edge to them, an irreverence for conformity. Novelist Peter Quinn concurs; they are "discovering there is an interesting marginality to Irish culture. It is a culture that is on the periphery and is now coming into the center and bringing with it a lot of energy."[51]

The U.S. embrace of Irish culture has produced a number of commercially successful ventures in recent years. The Irish pub and cafe, while long a fixture in Irish America, has found a lucrative home outside the ethnic enclaves and has expanded its repertoire beyond that of a simple taproom. In New York City, for example, drinking establishments such as the Sin E Cafe in the East Village have hosted literary readings by the likes of Roddy Doyle and uptown pubs such as Rocky Sullivan's feature traditional Irish bands as well as more eclectic crossovers such as Paddy A Go-Go, an Irish American rap/rock ensemble. While Irish neighborhood bars still exist throughout the city, there is an increasing emphasis on what can only be described as "Celtic trendy." As Mick Maloney maintains: "All over America Irish pubs thrive, with live Irish music providing a backdrop to the animated gossip of the crowds who flock to them in record numbers."[52] The Irish theme pub, in particular, is gaining popularity in the United States. (One Atlanta-based company has built "Irish Country Cottage" and "Victorian Dublin" pubs around the world.) One of the more "authentic" reconstructions has been Thady Con's, on Second Avenue in Manhattan. Entering its warm interior, one is temporarily transported by its hearth fire, Irish country furniture, and old black bicycle leaning against the wall. It has the taste of nostalgia to it, especially for those patrons who have never been to Ireland.[53]

The Irish theme pub or concept shop is a highly marketable item in the United States. Bewley's, the Dublin Coffeehouse, has recently acquired a major cafe chain in Boston, where they plan to purvey their fine Irish blend. More self-consciously Irish is "Morrissey's," a specialty shop designed to look like an Irish corner grocery (but built within a supermarket setting). Morrissey's is a cooperative venture between the Irish Food Board, Bord Bia, and Star Markets, a U.S. chain. The first Morrissey's was opened in Dorchester, Massachusetts, in early 1998. Here both New Irish immigrants and their U.S. cousins can choose from a line of Irish rashers and sausage and anything from tin whistles to Tayto Crisps. It's the next best thing to being home.[54]

For those who can't get to Ireland there are huge Irish festivals that fill the horizons in Boston, New York, Chicago, and San Francisco. Typical is the Stonehill College Irish Festival, sponsored by the Irish Cultural Centre in Canton, Massachusetts. Each June the festival welcomes over 40,000 visitors, who can listen to top-flight Irish bands; take in show jumping, cultural exhibits, or lectures on 1798; or see a reconstruction of the Ballinasloe Agricultural Fair. In New York City, likewise, one can attend the Guinness Fleadh, a huge outdoor extravaganza billed as "the ultimate Irish music and culture festival." Here one is attracted to a diverse melange of performers ranging from Irish groups such as the Chieftains and Sinead O'Connor to U.S. bands such as Los Lobos. This lineup reflects the impressive versatility of Irish music today and its ability to draw fellow travelers from jazz, folk, and the blend of African, Asian, and Latin music that is emerging as "world music." Indeed, Irish music has been one of the great ambassadors for Ireland, acting as a gateway to exploring other avenues of Irish culture.

The Arts

Music

Perhaps more than any other medium, music has been a major exponent of Irish culture to the world. During the 1980s and 1990s Irish music and performers achieved international stature and had an impact on popular music well beyond their small island. Sinead O'Connor, Van Morrison, U2, The Cranberries, The Cars, and Enya, among others, are recognizable anywhere from Tipperary to Tokyo. U2, arguably the most important rock band of the 1980s, has sold millions of records worldwide and continues to have an avid following on both sides of the Atlantic. One of the most original products of the Emerald Isle is Van Morrison, from Belfast. Over the years his recordings have forged a unique blend of jazz, blues, and gospel to produce such recognizable anthems as "Brown Eyed Girl" and "Moondance."

Ireland's music scene today is as diverse as its landscape. Balladeers in Dublin, country music in the midlands, traditional sessions in Galway, and samba bands in Drogheda are all part of the musical pastiche in the Emerald Isle. Traditional music, however, takes pride of place in Ireland, and one of the finest exponents of this genre is Altan. Largely comprising musicians from Donegal, Altan sets off traditional reels and jigs with vigor and mixes its repertoire with Gaelic songs sung with verve and beauty by Mairead Ni Mhaonaigh. Her voice can turn heads in music stores and attracts many followers outside the Irish-interest market. This universal appeal was not lost on Virgin Records, which signed Altan to a major recording contract and is promoting Altan in mainstream music circles. The band is already making progress on the pop charts in Europe. The United States no doubt will be next.

As Ireland and the "Celtic Tiger" are making strides on the world stage, so has traditional Irish music. During the past few decades Irish traditional music has increasingly opened its arms to a wide range of musical idioms: folk, jazz, eastern European, and African rhythms. The pioneers are the Chieftains, who over the years have infused their traditional playing with influences and guest artists as diverse as country singer Emmy Lou Harris and Carlos Nunez, who plays the Galician pipes. This world-music baton has been taken up by other Irish ensembles, notably Clannad, Davey Spillane, Afro-Celt, and Donal Lunny, who is collaborating with Kodo, a twenty-piece percussion troupe from Sado Island in Japan.

Fiddle player Eileen Ivers, born of Irish parents in New York City, is another performer who has blended Irish traditional music with other idioms. Steeped in traditional Irish music forms, her scintillating style has also been influenced by jazz, blues, and "old timey" music. She has appeared as a featured musician with "Riverdance" and also fronts a dynamic band that mixes Irish fiddle, blues organ, and African percussion. Over the years there have been critics of this pattern of Celtic fusion, purists who would have the music remain within established conventions. Ivers, however, suggests that old and new are not mutually exclusive. Certainly in a traditional Irish session there is no place for flashy innovation, but "you do have to take on your own character within the music." For her this works best by playing within a number of musical settings and finding a creative spark that links the traditional with the new.[55]

Ivers underlines that one has to be rooted first in Irish traditional music. Indeed, the wellspring of energy that characterizes Irish music today is (and has been) found at the grassroots level. Much of traditional music is organic, nurtured locally and supported in the community. Its seedbed in Ireland can be found at the Fleadh Cheoil, music workshops, and competitions, as well as at Ceilis (local dances), house parties, family get-togethers, and pub sessions.[56] In such settings the music is personal and immediate; a symbiotic energy develops between musician and audience that keeps the music fresh and alive. Irish traditional music, according to Micheal O'Suilleabhain, is by definition "music which is passed down by ear, passed on, interestingly, by human contact."[57] The value of this tradition was recognized in 1980 when the music department at University College Cork voted to admit students who could not read music.[58]

Traditional music is thriving in modern Ireland and gaining new popularity. One of the catalysts behind this resurgence is Iarla Leonard, Ireland's most prominent exponent of Sean Nos singing, an ethereal, unaccompanied style that is passed down orally and difficult to master. He played to a packed house at the Town Hall Theatre, Galway, a show that, while traditional in style, was accompanied by multi-media programming and innovative use of lighting and mood. Here Leonard has taken the traditional—the pure drop—and made it popular to a wider audience without diluting its origins. Yet what is also striking to the observer is Leonard's evolving musical identity. A product of the Irish-speaking uplands of west Cork, he nonetheless is always seeking out new musical land-scapes.[59] In addition to Sean Nos singing, he is a vocalist with the band Afro-Celt, a heady blend that mixes Irish melody with the rhythms of East Africa. It embod-ies what musician and folklorist Mick Maloney calls a "healthy tension" between old and new. "Doing things in a traditional way involves taking responsibility for the future and also being respectful of the past. It is a truly humble act but also a supremely assertive one."[60]

In keeping with the theme of cross-pollination, Irish American performers are slowly moving into the forefront of Irish music. Virtuoso musicians such as Eileen Ivers and Seamus Egan (a multi-instrumentalist from Philadelphia), as well as bands such as Solas and Cherish the Ladies, have brought new ideas and energy to music and have achieved success on the popular music charts. In addition, a vari-ety of Irish-born musicians now ply their craft in the United States, working out of a variety of locations ranging from New York City to Portland, Oregon.

This should not come as a surprise. First, the Irish music scene in New York City has long been of high caliber and one that has shaped Irish music. Early in the twentieth century emigrant musicians such as uillean pipes player Patsy Tuohey and Sligo fiddler Michael Coleman recorded with U.S. record compa-nies. As Mick Maloney reminds us, these early recordings found their way back to Ireland, "where they had a profound effect on the evolution of the tradition in the home country."[61] This same pattern—albeit with a new generation of Irish Americans and new musical grooves informed by jazz, blues, and country—was replayed in the 1990s. A second factor that underscores the importance of Celtic music in the United States is that there are simply more venues where tra-ditional music and dance are performed. During one week in June, for example, Boston and environs hosted Sinead O'Connor and the Chieftains at Harborlights pavilion, Donal Lunny's new band at McGann's, De Dannan and Black 47 at the Stonehill College Irish Festival, and the Scottish band Capercaillie (which features Donegal fiddler Manus Lunny) at the Somerville theater.[62] The great market for Celtic music, in other words, is not in Ireland—it is in the United States.

Yet it is not only in the great concert halls and clubs that Irish music finds its mark in the New World. In the 1990s Celtic music and step-dancing could be heard in a variety of locations, enjoying a revival in parish halls, bars, and local festivals. And it is not only Hibernian-American bands pursuing the Irish muse. Bar bands regularly cover songs by Van Morrison and The Cranberries; even big bands have taken up the Irish beat. Over the 4th of July, 1998, for example, the U.S. Navy Band—the Commodores—played in St. Stephen's Green in Dublin. After playing jazz standards, "Cherokee," and "Caravan," the multi-racial band finished with "A Tribute to Ireland": a syncopated, electrifying version of "Riverdance." They received a standing ovation from the lunchtime audience—nothing like bringing it all back home.

Dance

Irish dance, like music, has taken the world by storm and produced its share of headline performers, many of them from the United States. The flagship of this revival has been "Riverdance," an extravaganza that has captured a generation of admirers worldwide and made Irish dance fashionable. Originally designed and presented in the 1994 Eurovision Song Contest television broadcast, "Riverdance" only lasted seven minutes. American Michael Flatley was asked to choreograph the dance, which was based on music by Bill Whelan. Choosing another American, Jean Butler, as his partner, Flatley combined the elements of traditional Irish dancing with a freedom of movement, black costumes, and pounding rhythms. The response was extraordinary; after the performance calls poured in from all over Europe for the video. A CD was recorded; it sold out and the show was transformed into a full-length evening of dance and music, which swept London, New York City, and the world. Today in towns and cities around U.S. boys and girls are taking up step-dancing in record numbers. This is a far cry from years past. As Peter Quinn remembers from his childhood growing up in the Bronx: "The joke was the kids who took Irish dancing lessons were the ones who couldn't run faster than their parents."[63] Not any more.

"Riverdance" not only prompted a revival of Irish dance, it succeeded in transforming the style and cultural meaning of the genre. Previously Irish step dancing was stiff, unemotional, and straight laced, with the dancers keeping their arms at their sides and a stoic, almost distant visage. In "Riverdance," however, featured dancers Michael Flatley and Jean Butler used expressive movement, a touch to the hair, high leaps, and even a flamenco flourish to convey a new style. There is a pounding sexuality to the dance that was unheard of in the Catholic Ireland of old. Indeed, several observers of "Riverdance" and the boom of Irish culture worldwide have explained this emergence, in part, to the decline of the Catholic Church in Ireland. Many of the old pieties are gone, and what has emerged are new ideas, experimentation, and boundless creativity that are unfettered by conformity, censorship, and inhibition. In short, "Riverdance" is emblematic of the new self-confidence and spirit that Ireland has enjoyed in the age of the "Celtic Tiger." It also reflects the cross-pollination of Irish culture: a mix of Irish creativity, Irish American dancers, Atlantic marketing, and a world beat.[64]

Theater

The most notable figure in Irish theater has undoubtedly been Brian Friel, whose "Dancing at Lughnasa" won Tony awards for the best play on Broadway, best actress (Brid Brennan), and best director (Patrick Mason) in 1992. The play opened at the Abbey Theatre in Dublin in 1990 to critical praise. The drama captured the absence of potential and possibility for women in the Irish rural social structure of the 1930s and the indomitable spirit with which the five sisters of the Mundy family, individually and collectively, cope with their fate. The play was later made into a movie, discussed below, starring Meryl Streep and directed by Pat O'Connor, which was released in 1998. Friel's earlier well-known plays include "Philadelphia Here I Come" in 1965. Another of his plays is "Translations," originally produced by the Field Day Theatre Group in 1981 and brought to Broadway in the late 1990s with Brian Denehy in the lead role. "Translations" creates a nineteenth-century mythical past in which the juxtaposition of the language of the British conqueror and the Irish conquered is explored through names and language. The importance of translation, of language, the death of the Irish language, and the failure of language to convey common meaning are woven throughout the play.

Friel was born in 1929, was raised in Derry, and chose the priesthood. He attended Maynooth but withdrew, finding the experience rather distasteful. He turned to writing, and although he is quiet and introspective in demeanor, his characters crackle with sharp words and wit.

In 1980 Friel was a co-founder, with the actor Stephen Rea, of the nationalist Field Day Theatre Company in Derry. The theater provided an outlet for promising young playwrights and produced Friel's "Translations," Thomas Kilroy's searing "Double Cross," and Seamus Heaney's "The Cure at Troy." After a decade the Field Day Theatre was in difficulty financially and also in terms of the quality of productions. When Friel choose to have his new play, "Dancing at Lughnasa," open at the Abbey instead of at Field Day it caused a rift with Stephen Rea, who by then had himself become widely known for his role in *The Crying Game.*

Two other writers of Friel's generation—Hugh Leonard, born in 1926, and Tom Murphy, born in 1935—dominated Irish theater through the late 1980s. Leonard's 1973 "Da" was also made into a movie starring Martin Sheen, while Murphy's "Famine" and his 1984 "The Gigli Concert" have brought him belated critical and popular recognition.[65] Younger than both is northern Catholic Frank McGuinness, whose play "Behold the Sons of Ulster Marching to the Somme" is a powerful representation of the mind and soul of Ulster loyalists and their both sturdy and fragile sense of identity. His "Carthaginians" is a bitter exploration of Derry residents coping with the impact of Bloody Sunday.

A new generation of young playwrights is emerging, among them Conor McPherson. His play "The Weir" has been received well in Dublin and London and opened on Broadway in 1999. By far the hottest new Irish dramatist is Martin McDonagh. During summer 1997 he had four plays running in the West End of London. Two were taken to Broadway in 1998: "The Cripple of Irishman" and the Druid Theatre production of "Beauty Queen of Leenane." The "Beauty Queen" won four Tonys. McDonagh blends in his characters the idiosyncrasies of the Irish countryside with the patina of the Americanized global culture, and does so with cutting wit. Robert Brustein, director of the American Repertory Theatre, says of McDonagh: "He is the best Irish playwright since Synge; he may be better than Synge. . . . No one writing today can touch him."[66]

Poetry

The premier poet of Ireland is Seamus Heaney. This is not an inconsiderable matter in Ireland, where the people purchase more poetry books per capita than any other English-speaking country. Poets are household names, and lines of poetry are as likely to be quoted at public events as are invocations. Winner of the 1995 Nobel Prize for Literature, Heaney joined the august company of other Nobel Laureates from Ireland: George Bernard Shaw, William Butler Yeats, and Samuel Beckett. Heaney was born in 1929 to a family of eight in Mossbawn County Londonderry. His father was a farmer and the connection to the land is profoundly present in Heaney's work. Nature and images of the earth—land, clay, rooting, fertility, digging, burial, and recovery—fill his poems. His first book, *Death of a Naturalist* (1966), won numerous prizes. The volume included one of his most widely quoted poems, "Digging," in which he notes his ineptitude with a spade but states:

> *Between my fingers and my thumb*
> *The squat pen rests*
> *I'll dig with it.*

Having attended Queen's University in 1961 he returned there in 1966 to lecture in English literature. His second book, *Door into the Dark,* appeared in 1969 and in 1971 he moved to the Republic. In 1972 *Wintering Out* appeared, in which Heaney began to address the issues of violence and sacrifice. Recognition of Heaney increased and he won various prizes for his writing. His next book, *North* (1975), contained poems that were directed at the political violence of Ulster, including "Whatever You Say Say Nothing." His later works include *Field Work* (1979), *Station Island* (1984), and other volumes in 1987, 1991, and 1996. Selected poems from all his works are collected in *Opened Ground,* published in 1998. In 1984 Heaney was asked to be the Boylston Professor of Oratory and Rhetoric at Harvard, and in 1989 he was invited to be visiting professor of Poetry at Oxford. Renowned poet Robert Lowell, himself the Boylston Professor at Harvard, called Heaney "the best Irish poet since Yeats" and his reputation widened, especially in Britain and the United States. Heaney is not without his critics. Some see his poetry as very distant and not very lyrical, more in tune with the forms of minimalist modern poetry rather than emotionally moving or quotable. Heaney himself sees poetry as mediating between the inner mind and the external reality and capable of nurturing the potential of the individual. As Heaney asserted in his Nobel address, poetry has "the power to persuade that vulnerable part of our consciousness of its rightness in spite of the wrongness all around it; the power to remind us that we are the hunters and gatherers of values, that our very solitudes and distresses are creditable."[67]

Composer Michael Holohan and Nobel Prize winning poet Seamus Heaney at Caitlin Ni
Cairbre's Pub Drogheda, County Louth. Taken on the occasion of their poetry reading
and musical performance "No Sanctuary" in February 1997.
Photo by Jimmy Weldon

Heaney was also associated with the Field Day group, as were the poet Tom
Paulin and the musician David Hammond. Field Day, as well as sponsoring the
Theatre, published a group of pamphlets examining the Northern question from
a nationalist, anti-revisionist perspective, generating controversy on all fronts.
Sometimes the Field Day group was seen as an IRA apologist, at others it was condemned for being insufficiently nationalist. Seamus Deane, critic and author,
along with Heaney and others, created the three-volume *Field Day Anthology of
Irish Writing* (1991). Covering 1,500 years and every form of writing, the 4,000-
page opus was quite ambitious. Despite the book's size and coverage, women were
underrepresented and the selection of pieces was seen to be decidedly nationalist
in perspective. Literary and political conflict broke out between Deane, defending
the volumes, and literary critic Edna Longley, who attacked them. A fourth volume was promised that would be devoted to women's writing, and eventually the
literary slash-and-burn between Deane and his critics subsided.

In Heaney's generation the most well-known and talented poets were Michael
Longley, Derek Mahon, Richard Murphy, and Eavan Boland. The next generation
of poets, born after World War II, feel less obligation to write about Ireland only

in terms of her history . . . her rural landscape. . . . her oppression . . . her Catholicism . . . her nationhood. The younger highly regarded poets include Paul Muldoon, Tom Paulin, Paul Durcan, Medbh McGuckian, Paula Meehan, Mary O'Malley, and Greg Delanty. Peter Fallon, who founded Gallery Press, Ireland's foremost publisher of poetry, is also a noted poet. Known as a "Belfast poet," Ciaran Carson has published relatively few works, but his prize-winning *The Irish for No* (1987), *Belfast Confetti* (1989), and *First Language* combine accessibility of the poems with subtle, sophisticated wordplay. Critics see Carson as a truly gifted poet destined to rise in stature. Nuala Ni Dhomhnaill is considered the premier poet in the Irish language. In 1993 Wake Forest University Press published two of her books, with translations by outstanding poets.

Literature

As highly regarded as Irish poets are, novelists and short story writers are not far behind. The present generation of writers has been notable for its freedom from the traditional image of Ireland and also from the spell that Yeats and Joyce had cast over the writers of the previous generation. Dublin writer Ferdia Mac Anna says of the new generation of writers: "They saw Ireland not as some ancient colonial backwater full of larger than life 'characters' boozing their heads off in stage Irish pubs but as a troubled modern entity, plagued by drugs, unemployment, high taxes and emigration. . . . Anyone expecting a Dublin of garrulous chancers and Joycean characters will be either disappointed or shocked . . . or both."[68]

Some writers born after World War II who have made a particular mark on modern Irish writing are Roddy Doyle, Dermot Bolger, and John Banville.[69] Banville, born in 1945, is the literary editor of the *Irish Times*. He writes in high intellectual style, with dense and symbolic explorations of the interiors of a disturbing world. Banville feels no obligation to speak to Irish themes or to have his writing be a commentary on Ireland. Books such as *The Newton Letter* and *The Book of Evidence* are set in Ireland. His other novels, intellectual explorations of the intersection of personality and truth—*Doctor Copernicus* (1976) and *Keppler* (1981)—are far outside the Irish context. His prize-winning *Book of Evidence* (1989) is a profound and chilling exploration of a morally inert, self-delusional central character, a murderer named Freddie Montgomery. The Irish context is relatively incidental and the setting could as easily be Russian as Irish. Critics found the book dazzling, labeling it a masterpiece. Banville is considered the best novelist in Ireland today.

If Banville is considered to be in the company of Vladimir Nabokov, then Roddy Doyle is in the company of Sean O'Casey. Doyle, born in 1958, is a graduate of University College Dublin and was a teacher for fourteen years until he took up the pen full time. The most widely known of any contemporary Irish writer, his Barrytown Trilogy—*The Commitments, The Snapper,* and *The Van*—has made him internationally recognized. The gritty portraits of working class life in the north side of Dublin would not have been so widely acclaimed had not Alan Parker made the first novel, *The Commitments,* into an outstanding film in 1991. The novels are based almost entirely on dialogue and the writing snaps with the banter and wordplay of the characters. Doyle says of his writing: "Don't expect any message about the world, politics or the dole, as far as I am concerned, the message is the characters."[70] The themes of the three novels are bleak: The Commitments, the soul music band, is not very good and doomed to failure at the talent, as well as at the personality, level; the snapper is a child born of a pregnancy that is the result of a drunken assault by an older man on Sharon Rabbitte; and the van is a successful hamburger business enterprise between friends that threatens the friendship. Events unfold through the characters' conversations, which are incredibly funny and display an energy and zest that blends the failures and pain of their circumstances with the triumph of their indomitable resilience.

Although the Barrytown Trilogy is Doyle's most widely known work, *Paddy Clarke Ha Ha Ha* (1993) won the Booker Prize for Doyle's capacity to present the world of a troubled marriage through the eyes of a ten year old. His *The Woman Who Walked into Doors* also was widely praised for his ability to present through the woman's voice the disintegration of her marriage and herself. Doyle has subsequently worked on a television series, "The Family," which is somewhat less warm and funny than his Barrytown novels. Critics, in fact, sometimes find the novels sentimental and disingenuous in the face of the unrelenting dark side of urban life.

Another chronicler of the seamy side of urban life is Dermot Bolger. Born in 1959, the son of a seaman, Bolger is a denizen of the cold housing estates of north Dublin. His first novel, *Night Shift,* and his second, *The Women's Daughter,* portrayed the loneliness of urban and suburban life in Dublin. In 1990 he published *The Journey Home,* a slashing portrait of a journey through political corruption, the Church, drugs, unemployment, rural city dwellers, and the emptiness of urban life. The evil family of corrupt tycoons, named Plunkett, engages in all forms of bribery, sexual escapades, and cruelty. In the end the main character, Hano, finds refuge in the countryside and in the wisdom of a wise old woman who lives in a caravan. Bolger explicitly rejects the canonical templates of the earlier generation: "Nationalism and 'Irishness' do not interest me—even if my books *are* very much about Ireland. And what is Irishness anyway? A novel set on the Finglas motorway is every bit as Irish as one set in Connemara featuring some half mad priest. Or as *Dancing at Lughnasa.*"[71] The literary scholar Declan Kiberd, however, argues that Bolger, in his depiction of the city as virtually uninhabitable and the escape to rural wisdom, was closer to validating the Ireland of de Valera than he would perhaps admit.[72]

Bolger and Doyle are part of a group of writers who convey a freshness of perspective; a sometimes grim vision of modern Ireland; and a feel for the peculiarities, contradictions, ironies, and hypocrisies of the politics of Ireland's rapid development and the violence in Northern Ireland. Patrick McCabe's *The Butcher Boy* (1992) drew wide praise. His *The Dead School* (1995) and the *Breakfast on*

Pluto (1998) complete the trilogy begun with *The Butcher Boy*. Other writers gaining recognition for quality work include Colin Bateman, Colum McCann, John MacKenna, Diedre Madden, Joe O'Connor, Emer Martin, Niall Williams, and Robert McLiam Wilson. The journalist Colm Toibin, in addition to his newspaper and travel writing, has penned two prize-winning novels, *The South* and *Heather Blazing*.

Film

Ireland had long supplied settings and actors, from *Ryan's Daughter* to *Barry Fitzgerald*, for Hollywood movies. However, it could be said that Irish film came of age in 1990, when *My Left Foot*, directed by Jim Sheridan, was nominated for five Academy awards. The film, made with a modest $2 million, premiered at the Dublin Film Festival in 1989. The U.S. distributor Miramax managed to draw the attention of the U.S. public and critics to a film devoted to the story of writer Christy Brown, who was crippled so badly by cerebral palsy that he could only write with his left foot. The film won Oscars for best actor, best supporting actress, and best adapted screenplay in the face of formidable competition, including Tom Cruise in *Born on the Fourth of July* and Robin Williams in *Dead Poet's Society*. The film featured a compelling performance by Daniel Day Lewis and the rest of the cast; superb writing by Shane Connaughton, who adapted the screenplay; and fine directing. The film won six other international awards for, variously, directing, acting, and writing. The film's high-profile Hollywood visibility prompted recognition of Sheridan and other Irish directors and actors, to say nothing of providing access to the funding needed to produce major films.

Prior to *My Left Foot* Irish directors had made a number of high-quality films with Irish settings, actors, and themes. Pat O'Connor did a first-rate job in bringing Bernard McClaverty's novel *Cal* to film in 1984. Helen Mirren starred as the wife of a murdered RUC officer who has an affair with Cal, a young man who had participated in her husband's death. He is seeking escape from the IRA and the convolutions of their relationship are a reflection of the pain and personal barriers produced by the politics of the north. Neil Jordan wrote and directed *Angel* in 1982 (released as *Danny Boy* in the United States), which starred Stephen Rea as a musician who sees his manager and a mute girl killed in the north. Clumsily he attempts to solve the murders. The story takes Rea into an increasingly surrealistic world of humorous encounters and casual violence. Jordan also wrote and directed, to critical acclaim, a small gem of a film, *Mona Lisa*, in 1986. It starred Bob Hoskins as the driver of a prostitute with whom he is in love.

The 1990s brought forth a group of films that not only drew attention to Ireland but also added to the development of the genre. Three Irish directors stand out in particular: Pat O'Connor, Jim Sheridan, and Neil Jordan. All of these directors have done non-Irish theme films as well, but their expressive gifts have illuminated facets of life in Ireland and Northern Ireland particularly well.

Pat O'Connor took a Maeve Binchy novel of young love in Dublin in the 1950s and made *Circle of Friends* in 1995. The film presents the simple tale of attraction between two young people with an ease and sensitivity that is neither saccharine nor overdrawn. Chris O'Donnell gives a fine performance as a young student in Dublin, but Minnie Driver commands the film as Benny, a young woman of great size and spirit. O'Connor avoids falling into a simplistic ugly duckling template by focusing on the power of the character. In creating a film symmetrically matched to the story, O'Connor produced a richly etched portrait both of young Benny and of 1950s Ireland. In 1998 O'Connor turned his hand to Brian Friel's "Dancing at Lughnasa." Meryl Streep brought the star power to a cast of first-rate actors. The arrival of their brother, a missionary priest from Africa, upsets the delicate balance among five sisters that has been achieved in the house through the fierce discipline of Kate (Streep). As the place of each sister is revealed the audience can see beneath the surface of the family. Critics preferred the stage version. Although few thought it was a poor film, few thought it was as great as its source.

In the 1990s Jim Sheridan produced some the best of Irish films. *The Field*, although based on a play by John B. Keane, was a somewhat less than successful effort. The story reflects the deep connection of the Irish to the land in terms of sense of place, making a living in the hard life of rural agriculture, and the connection of property to village life. Richard Harris in the lead role plays a man who has worked to make a rented field productive; the widow who owns it wants to sell it at auction to an American, no less. This action leads to a crisis, a murder, and lots of people in the village saying things about the connection of people to the land. While Harris gives a thundering performance, earning an Oscar nomination for best actor, the rest of the story lacks verisimilitude and the overall quality of the film is not compelling. Sheridan then collaborated with Gabriel Byrne on the film *Into the West*, with Sheridan writing the screenplay. The story is highly symbolic. Two boys ride a mystical white horse from their miserable circumstances in Dublin into the west of Ireland with help from the traveling people. The film evokes the classic theme of the west as the redemption of Ireland but also treats the life of the traveling people with texture and depth rather than clichés.

In 1993 Sheridan directed *In the Name of the Father*. The film starred Daniel Day Lewis and Emma Thompson and was nominated for seven Oscars, including best picture, best actor, best director, best film editing, best supporting actor and actress, and best writing. The nomination for best picture gave *In the Name of the Father* the visibility and acclaim of *My Left Foot*. The movie is a fictionalized account of Gerry Conlon and the Guilford Four. Conlon, a reckless Belfast youth, was convicted of a bombing on trumped-up evidence, with exculpatory evidence suppressed. He was later released after spending years in prison. The story of the abuse of the law by the British police is tied to the emotional story of the bond between father and son and the concurrent maturation of Conlon. The viewer is connected to the characters and thus feels the injustice done them. Emma Thompson stars as the attorney who discovers the illegal use of evidence, and Peter

Postlewaithe is mesmerizing as Conlon's father. A big film in terms of stars, cost, and promotion *In the Name of the Father* remains one of the most popular films about Ireland among viewers, a first-rate film in cinematic terms as well as a telling representation of the power of the police and the British authorities in Ulster.

Sheridan used Northern Ireland as the locale for his next two films as well. In 1996 he produced and wrote *Some Mother's Son* and in 1997 he wrote and directed *The Boxer*. *Some Mother's Son* stars Helen Mirren as Kathleen Quigley, the mother of a middle class family whose son is a Republican activist. He goes on a hunger strike and Mirren connects with the mother of another hunger striker from working class Republican origins. After the sons go into a coma the mothers must decide whether they are to be fed intravenously or allowed to die. The dilemma is torturous for Mirren, a pacifist and schoolteacher, who did not even know her son was involved with the IRA. Annie Higgins, the other mother, is convinced that her son should die and that it is the British who are killing him. The transformation in Mirren's character's inner emotional structure and her connection to the Republican political landscape bring her to a new awareness of the personal moral dilemmas in the Green and Orange world of Ulster. Mirren's capacity as an actress to convey those changes keeps the film at a complex level of questions about sacrifice, willing sacrifice, the love of a son, and the understanding of his beliefs.

In *The Boxer* the director of photography, Chris Menges, creates a powerful and dark panorama of Belfast (using Dublin) that matches the delicate balances holding the relationships within the film together. The local IRA chieftain supports the peace process, but his nemesis in the IRA wants to undermine it. Entering this balance is Daniel Day Lewis as a promising boxer, Danny Flynn, who was arrested at age eighteen and spent fourteen years in prison because he would not name his IRA companions. After his release he wants only to build his life around teaching kids to box. Emily Watson plays Maggie, his girlfriend of many years ago and still the love of his life. She has married another IRA man who is in prison. Their relationship is finely balanced within the film; they must choose not to act on their mutual attraction because it could be personally and politically dangerous. The drama is played out in such a way that the politics are not reduced to leaden slogans. The complication of the relationships in a small community, with serious consequences for one's beliefs and actions, is felt in every scene, whether it is Danny receiving a gift of boxing gloves from the RUC or Danny and Maggie walking on the other side of the city. A stark ending sums up the possibility of change in Ulster only through the means of violence, which is the very problem of Ulster.

While critics see Sheridan as producing some of the very best Irish films, Neil Jordan would have an equal claim to that praise. Four of his films in the 1990s displayed different facets of Irish life, some with stunning success. In 1991 Jordan wrote and directed *The Miracle*. The construction of the location and the story were free of Irish clichés yet rooted in deeper Celtic images. Two youngsters go around a seaside town making up stories about the people they see, using wildly imaginative scenarios to keep themselves amused. A sophisticated and mysterious woman appears in town (Beverly D'Angelo as Renee Baker), and the two children make up a story to fit her arrival that involves murder and more. The imaginary worlds they create through their stories reflect the Celtic notion of the power of words to cross the evanescent barrier between this world and the world of dreams and fantasy. One of the young men begins to fall for Ms. Baker, and the movie then looses its charm and whimsy, slipping into a somewhat forced ending that is not really as much a surprise as was intended. Critics appreciated the images and dialogue in *The Miracle* but thought the ending weakened the film.

Not content with the "surprise" ending in *The Miracle*, Jordan really decided to surprise his viewers in his *The Crying Game*. Fergus, an IRA killer played by Stephen Rea, decides to opt out of the killing game after forming a relationship with a British soldier that the IRA plans to (and does) execute. Moving to London, Fergus tracks down the girlfriend of the dead soldier, Dil, played by Jaye Davidson, and finds himself falling in love with her. Miranda Richardson, from the IRA, tracks him down to get him to participate in another bombing. This description of the film, however, is much like describing the Grand Canyon as an old riverbed. The keys to the film are the characters, who are real and engage the viewer in their emotional changes; the dialogue, which is clever and both conceals and reveals at the same time; and the very character of the relationships, which create and break conventional expectations. Richardson is a tough, violent woman who toys with Fergus sexually, while Dil is a gentle male transvestite who cares deeply for him. Fergus is completely confused by the lure and the repulsion he feels for both, first toward the IRA and the killing and the second toward the "woman" he loves—who is a man. The writing and acting behind the play of identities and the switching of gender role expectations earned the film six Oscar nominations: best writing for the screen, best actor, best director, best film editing, best picture, and best supporting actor. The film won the Oscar for best writing for the screen as well as eight other film awards. *The Crying Game* explicitly shifts away from the politics of the Northern conflict in the middle of the film, but in Jordan's next feature the political content is the centerpiece.

Michael Collins appeared in 1996 after Jordan had worked on the screenplay for years. The possibility of Kevin Costner making a film about Collins had delayed Jordan's effort. In the screenplay Jordan sought to counterbalance the traditional view that Griffith and Collins had been hoodwinked at the Anglo-Irish Treaty negotiations and that the republican movement, the IRA and Sinn Fein, should never have accepted partition. Collins was, of course, as critical to the success of the IRA and Sinn Fein as anybody, including de Valera. Jordan wanted to add some complexity to the history of the period and move beyond the simple adulatory historical mythology that had grown up around the events of the Anglo-Irish War and the Anglo-Irish Treaty. The visual representation of Ireland in the 1920s is superb, earning Chris Menges an Oscar nomination. The story hinges on the role Collins (Liam Neeson) played in the war with his adoption of guerrilla tactics, his command of intelligence, and his willingness to use violence. Collins is contrasted with de Valera, played by Alan Rickman, and de Valera comes out as selfish, priggish, authoritarian, and inflexible. When the split occurs in Sinn Fein and Civil War in Ireland breaks out, in the film the responsibility is put at the feet of de Valera. When Collins dies in County Cork in 1922, the film suggests that de Valera is aware of, and perhaps actually complicit in, the ambush. This is revisionist history at its most explicit. The film introduces a love interest with Kitty Kiernan, played by Julia Roberts, but rather than adding dramatic personal counterpoint to the plot it seems to get in the way. Among the more memorable aspects of the film is the portrayal of de Valera by Rickman. His demeanor, accent, posture, and dramatic intensity are truly remarkable.

As good as Rickman was, Eamonn Owens as Francie Brady in *The Butcher Boy* was even more compelling. Jordan released this film in 1998. It was drawn from Patrick McCabe's novel of the same name. The twelve-year-old boy Francie lives in a small Irish town in the early 1960s. His mind is a collection of cartoon or comic book figures. He holds his disintegrating life—his mother is suicidal and his father a drunk—at bay by creating an imaginary world with his closest friend, played by Alan Boyle. His mortal enemy is Mrs. Nugent, played by Fionna Shaw, who says he and his family are pigs. The narration is from the point of view of Francie and his description of his life, real and imagined, is presented as childhood hijinks even though his actions and thoughts become more extreme, grotesque, and surreal as the film progresses. After the death of Francie's mother and father, hospitalization, abuse, and betrayal, the black comedy ends in a murder done by the boy. Jordan's balancing of the jaunty narrative, the life of the town, the desperate events circumscribing Francie, and the comic images is truly masterful. With *The Butcher Boy* Jordan reached a new level of integration of loopy fantasy and surrealism with the realism of savage mental illness and death. Jordan was described in *Film Comment* magazine as "possessed of that rare Irish gift for dark wicked poetry."

While O'Connor, Sheridan, and Jordan toiled on these films other filmmakers were at work as well. Of the wave of films in the 1990s Alan Parker's *The Commitments* must head the list. Parker captured the bleak housing estates that are Doyle's landscape in the novel but also the spirited engagement with life of the inhabitants and the central characters, the Rabbitte family. Parker changes the band to be better than it was in the novel so that the viewer cares what happens to them as a group as well as what happens to them as individuals. Robert Arkin as Jimmy Rabbitte, the band's manager, and Johnny Murphy as Jimmy "The Lips" Fagen put in particularly strong performances, and Andrew Strong as Deco is as good a singer as many of the vocalists in the bands whose songs they used. The images of working class Dublin are unvarnished and not drenched in ersatz anguish. The pushing, vibrant, abrasive, and endearing people spilling out of this film are a proof of Yeats's dictum: "romantic Ireland's dead and gone, it's with O'Leary in the grave." And all to the good as far as Doyle's novels and Parker's film are concerned. Stephen Frears made *The Snapper* and *The Van* into good films as well, although they lack the polish of Parker's effort. Colm Meaney plays the father in all three movies, giving a particularly good performance in *The Snapper* as a father at the center of a nexus of contradictory pressures and values.

Michael Lindsay-Hogg made a fine film of Chet Raymo's novel *The Dork of Cork*, naming the film *Frankie Starlythe*. The story is about a dwarf born of a French woman in Ireland and befriended and cared for by Jack Kelly, played by Gabriel Byrne. The dwarf, played by Corbin Walker, moves through the strange chapters of his life using his love of the stars to find his way to fulfillment as a writer. *Waking Ned Devine*, directed by Kirk Jones III, has an engaging charm in the manner of the films of Bill Forsythe. The winning lottery ticket in a small Irish village is held by a dead man, and two friends decide one should impersonate the winner so they can collect the funds. Nothing can be that simple, and the obstacles become more complicated, eventually involving the entire village. The performances by Ian Bannen and especially David Kelly as the masterminds of the scheme are outstanding. The intimacy and quirkiness of Irish village life give the film its appeal. We are presented with what appears to be an uncontrived community that sustains both closeness and individuality. John Boorman's 1998 *The General* garnered numerous awards for Boorman's directing. Brendan Gleeson plays Martin Cahill, a crime lord of Dublin with something of a Robin Hood reputation. His unique personality and tough demeanor are offset by the capacity of the film to make us like him. Although the film skirts the issue of politics, it is Cahill's dealings with the Ulster Loyalists which bring about his downfall at the hands of the IRA. This well-crafted film displays Ireland not as a rural heaven but as possessing modern urban problems such as charming crime bosses and questionable police practices, things not unknown to New York City. These films, and others too numerous to mention, indicate the degree to which the Irish have adapted this twentieth-century medium to their creative ends.

Conclusion

Ireland's enthusiastic embrace of membership in the European Union is seen by many conservative Irish as only the final step in the homogenization of Irish culture and the dissolution of the Irish identity into the larger global, U.S., and European cultures. From whatever source the danger springs, the permeability and vulnerability of Irish culture are taken as a given by those fearful of the disappearance of what is uniquely Irish. As noted previously, a rather powerful uniform and stable conception of Irish identity prevailed in the Free State/Republic from 1922 until the 1960s. Celtic, Catholic, closed, and conservative, that identity was formed in opposition to the British identity of their colonial master. After Irish society opened up in the 1960s and the Northern conflict raised the question of what it meant to be Irish, Irish identity became much more fluid in conception as did the conception of fixed Irish culture. That fluidity is seen by some as a

vacuum into which has gushed U.S. popular culture—an MTV-ized lifestyle coupled with shallow consumerism, and European modernity, marginalizing what is
truly Irish.

Despite the lamentations of those who see the changes in Ireland as the erosion
of a strong identity and vibrant culture, they could not be more wrong. In the first
instance, the Irish identity being "lost" was synthetic. Supported by the institutions of government and Church with censorship and shame, Irish identity and
culture were a post-colonial product within the Republic. The cramped result was
far from defining the totality of Irishness and Irish culture. Such a concept of
Irishness excluded the Irishness of 1 million Protestants of Ulster and the millions
who had emigrated and displayed their Irish identity in the world and repressed
any other concept of identity within Ireland, such as that of women. Moreover,
the attempt to preserve Irish culture in Ireland resulted in an ossified caricature of
both Celtic romanticism and the Catholic Church. The supposed deterioration of
Irish identity and culture in the 1980s and 1990s is, as we have seen, actually a creative explosion in Irish culture and a bold, unprecedented assertion of Irishness in
the global environment. While the first Irish renaissance at the turn of the nineteenth century produced the masterpieces of Yeats, Joyce, and O'Casey, the second
Irish renaissance at the turn of the twentieth is global in scope; expressed in all
manner of cultural media including music, theater, literature, poetry, dance, and
film; and more self-confidently Irish because it is less self-consciously Irish. The
global culture has entered and enriched the Irish culture, but the flow is not one
way, and the Irish creative spirit is enriching the global culture in a manner not
seen since the Middle Ages.

NOTES

1. Ireland's place in the world has actually been marked more by transnational relations
in the realms of emigration, religious missionaries, and educational missionaries. The diaspora has had great influence in the countries to which the Irish have gone and in the continuous connection that they have had with Ireland. The Irish have placed priests, brothers,
and nuns all over the world in the work of development, health care education, and prosely-
tization. For a brief consideration of the place of Ireland in U.S. foreign policy, see Richard
B. Finnegan, "Ireland" and "Northern Ireland" in *The Encyclopedia of U.S. Foreign Relations*,
ed. B. W. Jentleson and Thomas G. Paterson (New York: Oxford University Press, 1997).

2. Keogh, *Twentieth Century Ireland*, p. 51.

3. Patrick Keatinge, *A Singular Stance: Irish Neutrality in the Eighties* (Dublin: Institute
of Public Administration, 1984), p. 22.

4. Keogh, *Twentieth Century Ireland*, p. 234.

5. Lee, *Ireland 1912–1985*, pp. 262–270.

6. Patrick Keatinge, "Security Policy," in *Ireland and EC Membership Evaluated*, ed.
Patrick Keatinge (New York: St. Martin's Press, 1991), p. 161.

7. Department of Foreign Affairs, *Challenges and Opportunities Abroad* (Dublin:
Stationery Office, 1996), pp. 51–52.

8. Ibid., p. 52.

9. Keatinge, "Foreign Policy," in *Ireland and EC Membership*, ed. Keatinge, pp. 150–151.

10. Ireland is underrepresented abroad. All the smaller states of Europe maintain twice the number of overseas missions and have twice the number of diplomats that Ireland has. Brigid Laffan and Rory O'Donnell, "Ireland and the Growth of International Governance," in *Ireland and the Politics of Change*, ed. Crotty and Schmitt, p. 172. I draw heavily on the work of Brigid Laffan in this entire section because she has done extensive and excellent work on Ireland in the EU.

11. Ibid., pp. 157–158.

12. Ibid., p. 165.

13. Brigid Laffan, "Ireland," in *The European Union and the Member States: Towards Institutional Fusion?*, ed. D. Rometsch and W. Wessels (Manchester: Manchester University Press, 1996), pp. 294–295.

14. Laffan and O'Donnell, "International Governance," in *Ireland and the Politics of Change*, ed. Crotty and Schmitt, p. 166. This is an advantage that Ireland had over the new members who are both adapting to membership policies in the EU and trying to build the institutions necessary to adapt.

15. Brigid Laffan, "Government and Administration," in *Ireland and EC Membership*, ed. Keatinge, pp. 193–194; and Brigid Laffan, "Ireland," in *Parliaments and Parties: The European Parliament in the Political Life of Europe*, ed. R. Morgan and C. Tame (New York: St. Martin's Press, 1997), pp. 262–263.

16. Laffan and O'Donnell, "International Governance," in *Ireland and the Politics of Change*, ed. Crotty and Schmitt, p. 170.

17. Ibid., p. 168.

18. Neill Nugent, *The Government and Politics of the European Union*, 3rd ed. (Durham: Duke University Press, 1994), p. 418.

19. Laffan and O'Donnell, "International Governance," in *Ireland and the Politics of Change*, ed. Crotty and Schmitt, p. 169.

20. Patrich Keatinge, Brigid Laffan, and Rory O'Donnell, "Weighing Up Gains and Losses," in *Ireland and EC Membership*, ed. Keatinge, pp. 279–291.

21. Rory O'Donnell, "Regional Policy," in *Ireland and EC Membership*, ed. Keatinge, pp. 72–73. O'Donnell points out that some EU policies, such as the structural funds, are designed to create convergence among poorer regions, while others, such as the CAP, have the consequence of creating greater differences.

22. Being out of the orbit of the United Kingdom does not necessarily mean opposition to the United Kingdom. Dublin and London have shared interests in European matters such as opposition to a strong European Parliament, Ireland because its representation is so small and Britain because it seeks to guard its sovereignty; both opposed majority rule for foreign and security policy, Ireland because of neutrality and Britain because of sovereignty; both governments opposed extensive extensions of European social policy, Ireland because of the financial burden and Britain because of sovereignty.

23. Anthony Coughlan, *The EEC: Ireland and the Making of a Superpower* (Dublin: Irish Sovereignty Movement, 1979).

24. Ray O'Hanlon, *The New Irish Americans* (Niwot, Colo.: Roberts Rinehart, 1998), p. 45.

25. Mary P. Corcoran, "Emigrants, Eirepreneurs, and Opportunists: A Social Profile of Recent Irish Immigration in New York City," in *The New York Irish*, ed. Ronald H. Bayor

and Timothy J. Meagher (Baltimore: The Johns Hopkins University Press, 1996), pp. 461–480.

26. For a full picture of the efforts to secure Irish immigration reform, see O'Hanlon, *The New Irish Americans*, especially chapters 3–6.

27. Mary Corcoran, "Heroes of the Diaspora?" in *Encounters with Modern Ireland*, ed. Michel Peillon and Eamonn Slater (Dublin: Institute of Public Administration, 1998), p. 135.

28. Helena Mulkerns, "The New Irish Chic: The Irish Arts Scene," in *The Irish in America*, ed. Michael Coffey, with text by Terry Golway (New York: Hyperion, 1997), p. 231.

29. Ibid.

30. O'Hanlon, *The New Irish Americans*, p. 16.

31. Quoted in Mike Allen, "Ireland, New Promised Land," *New York Times*, 31 May 1998, sec. 4, p. 4.

32. Linda Dowling Almeida, " 'And They Still Haven't Found What They're Looking for': A Survey of the New Irish in New York City," in *Patterns of Migration*, ed. Patrick O'Sullivan (New York: Leicester University Press, 1992), p. 206.

33. Mike Allen, "Ireland, New Promised Land," *The New York Times*, 31 May 1998, sec. 4, p. 1.

34. Joe Carroll, "Letter from America," *The Irish Times*, 2 May 1998; and O'Hanlon, *The New Irish Americans*, p. 219.

35. Corcoran, "Heroes of the Diaspora?" in *Encounters with Modern Ireland*, ed. Peillon and Slater, p. 139. See also Dick Hogan, "Fighting the Glossy Spin on Emigration," *The Irish Times*, 17 June 1997.

36. Paul Cullen, "Immigration to Ireland Reaches Record Levels," *The Irish Times*, 30 October 1997.

37. Kevin Myers, "An Irishman's Diary," *The Irish Times*, 22 April 1998.

38. Paul Cullen, "Asylum-seekers Advised Not to Go Out at Night," *The Irish Times*, 28 April 1998.

39. Maol Muire Tynan, "Policy on Immigrants Draws Sharp Criticism," *The Irish Times*, 20 May 1998.

40. Paul Cullen, "Black Immigrants Living in Constant Fear of Attack," *The Irish Times*, 7 July 1998.

41. O'Hanlon, *The New Irish Americans*, pp. 132–133.

42. Ibid., p. 131. Also see Richard Kearney, "The Fifth Province: Between the Global and the Local," in *Migrations: The Irish at Home and Abroad*, ed. Richard Kearney (Dublin: Wolfhound Press, 1990), p. 109.

43. Peter Finn, " 'Riverdance' and the Eire Sensation: How America Got Its Irish Up," *The Washington Post*, 29 July 1997, sec. G, p. 1.

44. This quote, as well as a good overview of the process of Irish American assimilation, can be found in *The Irish in America*, ed. Coffey, pp. 221, 228.

45. Andrew Greeley, *The Irish Americans* (Warner, 1981).

46. Peter Finn, " 'Riverdance' and the Eire Sensation: How America got its Irish up," *The Washington Post*, 29 July 1997, sec. G, p. 7.

47. Carol Coulter, "The Tiger and the Leprechaun," *The Irish Times*, 10 June 1998.

48. On the growth of Irish Studies programs in America, see ibid.

49. Peter Finn, "'Riverdance' and the Eire Sensation . . . ," *The Washington Post*, 29 July 1997.

50. Coffey, *The Irish in America*, p. 247.

51. Finn, "Riverdance," p. G7.

52. Mick Maloney, "Old Airs and New: From Reels to Riverdance," in *The Irish in America*, ed. Coffey, p. 188.

53. On Thady Con's, see Dan Barry, "A Thousand Welcomes for the Culture of the Celts," *The New York Times*, 17 March 1997, p. 1.

54. Sean McConnell, "Bord Bia to Promote Irish Shop Idea in the U.S.," *The Irish Times*, 7 June 1997; and Anna Mundow, "On the Pig's Back in Boston," *The Irish Times*, 29 July 1997. While Morrisey's strives to capture an Irish "flavor" in Boston, there are more authentic bakeries and shops that carry the same types of products in Dorchester or Brighton.

55. Eileen Ivers's insights come from an interview with Ms. Aine Ni Cairbre, 14 April 1996, on the latter's world music and arts program, Smidirini, on LMFM in Drogheda, County Louth. Ms. Ni Cairbre has kindly allowed me to use a portion of this interview.

56. A good description of the local, intimate foundations of traditional Irish music can be found in Henry Glassie, *Passing the Time in Ballymenone: Culture and History of an Ulster Community* (Philadelphia: University of Pennsylvania Press, 1982), especially pp. 95–105.

57. The quote is taken from the video production "Bringing It All Back Home" (BBC Enterprises Ltd., 1992). On the character of traditional music, see also Brendan Breathnach, *Folk Music and Dances of Ireland* (Dublin: Mercier Press, 1971); and Ciaran Carson, *Irish Traditional Music* (Belfast: Appletree Press, 1986); and Fintan Vallely, ed., *The Companion to Irish Traditional Music* (Cork: Cork University Press, 1999).

58. Nuala O'Connor, *Bringing It All Back Home: The Influence of Irish Music* (London: BBC Books, 1991), p. 174.

59. Dave Caren, "Old Style for a New Age," *Irish Music* III, no. 3 (October 1997), p. 7.

60. Mick Moloney, "Old Airs and New: From Reels to Riverdance," in *The Irish in America*, ed. Coffey, p. 188.

61. Ibid., p. 188.

62. See the *Boston Irish Reporter* 9, no. 6 (June 1998).

63. Finn, "Riverdance," p. 1.

64. For a discussion of the cultural dimensions of Riverdance, see Fintan O'Toole, "Unsuitables from a Distance: The Politics of Riverdance," in *Ex-Isle of Erin: Images of a Global Ireland* (Dublin: New Island Books, 1997). For a different slant, see Barbara O'Connor, "Riverdance," in *Encounters with Modern Ireland*, ed. Peillon and Slater, pp. 51–60.

65. Other playwrights who also should be noted from just prior to the Friel generation include Brendan Behan, who wrote "The Quare Fellow" in 1954 and "The Hostage" in 1958, and, of course, the Nobel Prize-winning Samuel Beckett, whose "Waiting for Godot" of 1953 is more widely known than perhaps any of the other plays. Beckett is seen as less of an Irish author and more of an existential continental author seeking to use words to find the silence of meaning in the universe.

66. Maureen Dezell, "Playwright McDonagh Crosses Borders," *Boston Sunday Globe*, 1 November 1998, p. M6.

67. Seamus Heaney, *Crediting Poetry: The Nobel Lecture* (Old Castle, Meath: Gallery Press, 1995), p. 29.

68. Quoted in Ardagh, *Ireland and the Irish*, p. 245.

69. Many Irish authors of the post-Yeats and Joyce generation achieved recognition between about 1940 and 1970, and some after: Brendan Behan, John B. Keane, Sean O'Faolain, Mary Lavin, Brian Moore, Jennifer Johnston, Benedict Keily, John McGahern, William Trevor, Edna O'Brien, and the extraordinary Brian O'Nolan (Flann O'Brien, Myles Nn nCopaleen); there are also writers bridging the two periods, such as Bernard MacLaverty.

70. Quoted in Ciaran Carty, *Confessions of a Sewer Rat: A Personal History of Censorship and the Irish Cinema* (Dublin: New Island Books, 1995), p. 159.

71. Quoted in Ardagh, *Ireland and the Irish*, p. 249.

72. Declan Kiberd, *Inventing Ireland: The Literature of the Modern Nation* (London: Vintage, 1996), p. 609.

Select Bibliography

Aalen, F. H. A., Kevin Whelan, and Matthew Stout, eds. *Atlas of the Irish Rural Landscape.* Toronto: University of Toronto Press, 1997.

Anderson, Scott. "Making a Killing: The High Cost of Peace in Northern Ireland." *Harpers* (February 1994), pp. 45–54.

Ardagh, John. *Ireland and the Irish: Portrait of a Changing Society.* London: Hamish Hamilton, 1994.

Arnold, Bruce. *Haughey: His Life and Unlucky Deeds.* London: HarperCollins, 1993.

Ayearst, M. *The Republic of Ireland.* New York: New York University Press, 1970.

Baker, Susan. "The Nuclear Power Issue in Ireland: The Role of the Irish Anti-Nuclear Movement," *Irish Political Studies* 3 (1988), pp. 12–13.

Bardon, Jonathan. *A History of Ulster.* Belfast: Queen's University Press, 1992.

Bartlett, Thomas. *The Fall and Rise of the Irish Nation: The Catholic Question, 1690–1830.* Dublin: Gill & Macmillan, 1992.

Bartlett, Thomas, Kevin Dawson, and Daire Keogh. *The 1798 Rebellion.* Niwot, Colo.: Roberts Rinehart, 1998.

Bartlett, Thomas, and Keith Jeffrey, eds. *A Military History of Ireland.* New York: Cambridge University Press, 1996.

Barton, Brian. *Northern Ireland in the Second World War.* Belfast: Ulster Historical Foundation, 1995.

Beale, Jenny. *Women in Ireland, Voices of Change.* Dublin: Gill & Macmillan, 1986.

Bell, James Bowyer. *The Irish Troubles: A Generation of Violence 1967–1992.* New York: St. Martin's Press, 1993.

Bell, James Bowyer. *The Secret Army: History of the Irish Republican Army 1916–79.* Dublin: Academy Press, 1979.

Bew, Paul, and Henry Patterson. *The British State and the Ulster Crisis.* London: Verso, 1985.

Binder, L., et al. *Crises and Sequence in Political Development.* Boston: Little, Brown, 1971.

Bowman, John. *De Valera and the Ulster Question: 1917–73.* Oxford: Clarendon Press, 1982.

Boyce, D. George, and Alan O'Day, eds. *The Making of Modern Irish History: Revisionism and the Revisionist Controversy.* London: Routledge, 1996.

Bradley, A., and M. G. Valiulus. *Gender and Sexuality in Modern Ireland.* Amherst: University of Massachusetts Press, 1997.

Brady, Ciaran, ed. *Interpreting Irish History: The Debate on Historical Revisionism.* Dublin: Irish Academic Press, 1994.

Breen, R., et al. *Understanding Contemporary Ireland: State, Class and Development in the Republic of Ireland,* Dublin: Gill & Macmillan, 1990.

Brown, Noel. *Against the Tide.* Dublin: Gill & Macmillan, 1986.

Brown, Terence. *Ireland: A Social and Cultural History, 1922–1985.* Rev. ed. Dublin: Fontana, 1985.

Byrne, Anne, and Madeleine Leonard, eds. *Women and Irish Society.* Belfast: Beyond the Pale Publications, 1997.

Carney, James. *Medieval Irish Lyrics.* Dublin: Dolmen Press, 1985.

Chubb, Basil, ed. *The Government and Politics of Ireland.* London: Oxford University Press, 1974.

_____. *The Government and Politics of Ireland.* 3rd ed. London: Longman, 1992.

_____. *A Source Book of Irish Government.* Dublin: Institute of Public Administration, 1964.

Coffey, Michael, ed., with text by Terry Golway. *The Irish in America.* New York: Hyperion, 1997.

Collins, Neil, ed. *Political Issues in Ireland Today.* Manchester: Manchester University Press, 1994.

Connelly, A. "Religion and History." *Irish Economic and Social History* X (1983), pp. 66–80.

_____. ed. *Gender and the Law in Ireland.* Dublin: Oak Tree Press, 1993.

Connolly, S. J. *Religion, Law and Power: The Making of Protestant Ireland, 1660–1760.* Oxford: Clarendon Press, 1992.

Coogan, Tim Pat. *The IRA: A History.* Niwot, Colo.: Roberts Rinehart, 1993.

_____. *The Irish, A Personal View.* London: Phaidon Press, 1975.

_____. *The Man Who Made Ireland: The Life and Death of Michael Collins.* Niwot, Colo.: Roberts Rinehart, 1992.

_____. *The Troubles: Ireland's Ordeal 1966–95 and the Search for Peace.* London: Hutchinson, 1995.

Cooney, John. *The Crozier and the Dail: Church and State 1922–1986.* Cork: Mercier Press, 1986.

Corkery, Daniel. *The Hidden Ireland: A Study of Gaelic Munster in the Eighteenth Century.* Dublin: Gill & Macmillan, 1967.

Coulter, Carol. *The Hidden Tradition: Feminism, Women and Nationalism in Ireland.* Cork: Cork University Press, 1993.

Crotty, William, and David E. Schmitt, eds. *Ireland and the Politics of Change.* New York: Longman, 1998.

Cullen, L. M. *The Emergence of Modern Ireland 1600–1900.* Dublin: Gill & Macmillan, 1983.

_____. "The Irish Diaspora of the Seventeenth and Eighteenth Centuries." In *Europeans on the Move: Studies on European Migration, 1500–1800,* edited by Nicholas Canny. New York: Oxford University Press, 1994.

Cullen, Louis. "The Hidden Ireland: Reassessment of a Concept." *Studia Hibernica* 9 (1969), pp. 7–47.

_____. *Life in Ireland.* London: B. T. Batsford, 1979.

Curtin, Nancy. *The United Irishmen: Popular Politics in Ulster and Dublin, 1791–1798.* New York: Oxford University Press, 1994.

Darby, John. *Conflict in Northern Ireland.* Dublin: Gill & Macmillan, 1976.

Dickson, David, and Hugh Gough, eds. *Ireland and the French Revolution.* Dublin: Irish Academic Press, 1990.

Dickson, David, Daire Keogh, and Kevin Whelan, eds. *The United Irishmen: Republicanism, Radicalism, and Rebellion.* Dublin: Lilliput Press, 1993.

Dowling, Michele. " 'The Ireland That I Would Have': De Valera and the Creation of an Irish National Image." *History Ireland* 5, no. 2 (Summer 1997), p. 40.

Doyle, David Noel. *Ireland, Irishmen and Revolutionary America, 1760–1820.* Dublin: Mercier Press, 1981.

Duffy, Sean, ed. *The Macmillan Atlas of Irish History.* New York: Simon & Schuster/Macmillan, 1997.

Eliot, Marianne. *Wolfe Tone: Prophet of Irish Independence.* New Haven, Conn.: Yale University Press, 1989.

Elliot, Sydney. "The Northern Ireland Forum/Entry into Negotiations Election 1996." *Irish Political Studies* 12 (1997), p. 118.

Evans, Geoffry, and Brendan O'Leary. "Frameworked Futures: Intransigence and Flexibility in the Northern Ireland Election of May 30, 1996." *Irish Political Studies* 12 (1997), pp. 23–47.

Faligot, Roger. *Britain's Military Strategy in Ireland.* Kerry: Brandon Books, 1983.

Fanning, Ronan. *Independent Ireland.* Dublin: Helicon Press, 1983.

Farrell, Brian. *Chairman or Chief: The Role of the Taoiseach in Irish Government.* Dublin: Gill & Macmillan, 1971.

Finnegan, Richard B. "The Blueshirts of Ireland During the 1930s: Fascism Inverted." *Eire-Ireland* 24, no. 2 (Summer 1989), pp. 79–99.

_____. *Ireland: The Challenge of Conflict and Change.* Boulder, Colo.: Westview Press, 1983.

_____. "The United Kingdom's Security Policy and IRA Terrorism in Ulster." *Eire-Ireland* 23, no. 1 (Spring 1988), pp. 87–110.

Finnegan, Richard B., and James L. Wiles. "The Invisible Hand or Hands Across the Water?: American Consultants and Irish Economic Policy." *Eire-Ireland* 30, no. 2 (Summer 1995), pp. 42–55.

Finnegan, Richard B., and James L. Wiles. *Irish Official Publications: 1972–1992.* Dublin: Irish Academic Press, 1995.

Finnegan, Richard B., and James L. Wiles. *Women in Ireland Public Policy Since 1922: A Documentary History.* Dublin: Irish Academic Press, forthcoming.

Fitzpatrick, David. *Politics and Irish Life, 1913–1921: Provincial Experience of War and Revolution.* Dublin: Gill & Macmillan, 1977.

Fitzsimmons, Yvonne. "Women's Interest Representation in the Republic of Ireland: The Council for the Status of Women." *Irish Political Studies* 6 (1991), pp. 37–51.

Foster, R. F. *Modern Ireland 1600–1972.* London: Allan Lane, 1988.

Foster, R. F., ed. *The Oxford Illustrated History of Ireland.* New York: Oxford University Press, 1989.

Gahan, Daniel. *The People's Rising: Wexford 1798.* Dublin: Gill & Macmillan, 1995.

Gallagher, T., and J. O'Connell. *Contemporary Irish Studies.* Manchester: Manchester University Press, 1983.

Galligan, Yvonne, Eilis Ward, and Rick Wilford, eds. *Contesting Politics: Women in Ireland, North and South.* Boulder, Colo.: Westview Press, 1999.

Garvin, Tom. *The Evolution of Irish Nationalist Politics.* New York: Holmes & Meier, 1981.

_____. *1922: The Birth of Irish Democracy.* Dublin: Gill & Macmillan, 1996.

_____. "The Politics of Denial and of Cultural Defense." *The Irish Review* 3 (1988), pp. 1–7

Gerald of Wales. *The History and Topography of Ireland.* New York: Penguin Books, 1982.

Gibbons, Luke. *Transformations in Irish Culture.* Cork: Cork University Press, 1996.

Girvin, B. "The Divorce Referendum in the Republic; June 1986." *Irish Political Studies* 2 (1987), p. 98.

_____. "The Irish Divorce Referendum, 1995." *Irish Political Studies* 2 (1996), pp. 176–179.

_____. "The Referendums on Abortion, 1992." *Irish Political Studies* 8 (1993), p. 118.

_____. "Social Change and Moral Politics: The Irish Constitutional Referendum of 1983." *Irish Political Studies* 34 (1986), p. 68.

Goldthorpe, J., and C. T. Whelan, eds. *The Development of Industrial Society in Ireland.* Oxford: Oxford University Press, 1992.

Gray, Peter. *The Irish Famine.* New York: Harry N. Abrams, 1995.

Gray, Tony. *The Irish Answer.* London: Heinemann, 1966.

Guelke, Adrian. *Northern Ireland: The International Perspective.* Dublin: Gill & Macmillan, 1988.

Guinnane, Timothy W. "The Vanishing Irish: Ireland's Population from the Great Famine to the Great War." *History Ireland* (Summer 1997), pp. 34–35.

Hachey, Thomas E., Joseph M. Hernon Jr., and Lawrence J. McCaffrey. *The Irish Experience: A Concise History.* Rev. ed. Armonk, N.Y.: M.E. Sharpe, 1996.

Hepburn, A. C., ed. *The Conflict of Nationality in Ireland.* New York: St. Martin's Press, 1980.

Hesketh, T. *The Second Partitioning of Ireland: The Abortion Referendum of 1983.* Dublin: Brandsma Books, 1990.

Holland, Jack. *The American Connection: U.S. Guns, Money, and Influence in Northern Ireland.* New York: Viking Press, 1987.

_____. *The American Connection: U.S. Guns, Money, and Influence in Northern Ireland.* Rev. ed. Niwot, Colo.: Roberts Rinehart, 1999.

_____. *Too Long a Sacrifice.* Hammondsworth: Penguin, 1982.

Holmes, M. "The Maastricht Treaty Referendum of June 1992." *Irish Political Studies* 8 (1993), pp. 105–110.

Holohan, Francis T. "History Teaching in the Irish Free State, 1922–35." *History Ireland* 2, no. 1 (Winter 1994), pp. 53–55.

Hug, Chrystel. *The Politics of Sexual Morality in Ireland.* New York: St. Martin's Press, 1999.

Hull, Roger. *The Irish Triangle.* Princeton: Princeton University Press, 1975.

Inglis, Tom. *Moral Monopoly: The Rise and Fall of the Catholic Church in Modern Ireland.* Rev. ed. Dublin: University College Dublin Press, 1998.

Jones, W. R. "England against the Celtic Fringe: A Study of Cultural Stereotypes." *Journal of World History* XIII, no. 1 (1971), pp. 155–171.

_____. "Giraldus Redivus: English Historians, Irish Apologists, and the Work of Gerald of Wales." *Eire-Ireland* IX (1974), pp. 3–20.

Keatinge, Patrick. *A Place Among the Nations: Issues of Irish Foreign Policy.* Dublin: Institute of Public Administration, 1978.

Keatinge, Patrick, ed. *Ireland and EC Membership Evaluated.* New York: St. Martin's Press, 1991.

Kennedy, Edward M. "Ulster Is an International Issue." *Foreign Policy* 57 (Summer 1973), pp. 57–71.

Kennedy, Kieran A., Thomas Giblin, and Diedre McHugh. *The Economic Development of Ireland in the Twentieth Century.* London: Routledge, 1988.

Kennedy, Michael J. *Ireland and the League of Nations.* Dublin: Irish Academic Press, 1997.

Keogh, Daire, and Nicholas Furlong, eds. *The Mighty Wave: The 1798 Rebellion in Wexford.* Dublin: Four Courts Press, 1996.

Keogh, Dermot. *Twentieth Century Ireland: Nation and State.* Dublin: Gill & Macmillan, 1994.

Kiberd, Declan. *Inventing Ireland: The Literature of the Modern Nation.* London: Vintage, 1996.

Kissane, B. "The Not So Amazing Case of Irish Democracy." *Irish Political Studies* 10 (1995), pp. 44–64.

Laffan, Brigid. "'While You Are Over There in Brussels, Get Us a Grant': The Management of the Structural Funds in Ireland." *Irish Political Studies* 4 (1989), pp. 43–57.

Lee, J. J. *Ireland 1912–1985: Politics and Society.* Cambridge: Cambridge University Press, 1989.

———. *The Modernization of Irish Society 1848–1918.* Dublin: Gill & Macmillan, 1973.

Lijphart, A. "Review Article, The Northern Ireland Problem: Causes, Theories, Solutions." *The British Journal of Political Science* 5, no. 3 (1975), pp. 83–106.

Loughery, Patrick, ed. *The People of Ireland.* Belfast: Appletree Press, 1988.

Luddy, Maria, ed. *Women in Ireland, 1800–1918: A Documentary History.* Cork: Cork University Press, 1995.

Luddy, Maria, and Cliona Murphy, eds. *Women Surviving: Studies in Irish Women's History in the Nineteenth and Twentieth Centuries.* Dublin: Poolbeg, 1990.

Lyons, F. S. L. *Culture and Anarchy in Ireland: 1890–1939.* Oxford: Oxford University Press, 1979.

———. *Ireland Since the Famine.* London: Fontana, 1973.

MacDonagh, Oliver. *The Emancipist: Daniel O'Connell, 1830–1847.* London: Weidenfeld & Nicolson, 1989.

Mallie, Eamon, and David McKittick. *The Fight for Peace.* London: Heinemann, 1996.

Maloney, Ed. "The IRA." *Magill*, 1 September 1980, p. 14.

Manning, Maurice. *The Blueshirts.* Dublin: Gill & Macmillan, 1970.

McCaffrey, L. *Ireland from Colony to Nation State.* Englewood Cliffs, N.J.: Prentice-Hall, 1979.

McCann, Dermot. "Business Power and Collective Action: The State and the Confederation of Irish Industry 1970–1990." *Irish Political Studies* 8 (1993), pp. 37–53.

McCarron, Edward T. "A Brave New World: The Irish Agrarian Colony of Benedicta Maine." *Records of the American Catholic Historical Society* 105, no. 2 (Spring 1994), pp. 1–15.

———. "Altered States: Tyrone Migration to Providence, Rhode Island in the Nineteenth Century." *Clogher Record* 16, no. 1 (1997), pp. 145–161.

———. "In Pursuit of the 'Maine' Chance: The North Family of Offaly and New England, 1700–1776." In *Offaly History and Society: Interdisciplinary Essays on the History of an Irish County,* edited by William Nolan and Timothy O'Neill. Dublin: Geography Publications, 1998.

McCarthy, John F., ed. *Planning Ireland's Future*. Dublin: Glendale Press, 1990.

McCarthy, John P. "Northern Ireland: Irish American Responses." *The Recorder* (Winter 1986), pp. 43–52.

McGarry, John, and Brendan O'Leary. *Explaining Northern Ireland*. Oxford: Blackwell, 1995.

McDowell, R. B. *Ireland in the Age of Imperialism and Revolution, 1760–1801*. Oxford: Oxford University Press, 1979.

Miller, Kerby. *Emigrants and Exiles: Ireland and the Irish Exodus to the United States*. New York: Oxford University Press, 1985.

Mitchell, Frank, and Michael Ryan. *Reading the Irish Landscape*. Dublin: Townehouse Publications, 1997.

Mitchell, George J. *Making Peace*. New York: Knopf, 1999.

Mitchell, Paul, and Rick Wilford, eds. *Politics in Northern Ireland*. Boulder, Colo.: Westview Press, 1999.

Munck, Ronnie. *The Irish Economy: Results and Prospects*. London: Pluto Press, 1993.

Ni Dhonnchadha, Mairin, and Theo Dorgan, eds. *Revising the Rising*. Derry: Field Day Press, 1991.

Nolan, Janet. *Ourselves Alone: Women's Emigration from Ireland, 1885–1920*. Lexington: University of Kentucky Press, 1989.

Nordlinger, Eric. *Conflict Regulation in Divided Societies*. Cambridge: Center for International Affairs, 1972.

Nowland, Kevin B., and Maurice O'Connell, eds. *Daniel O'Connell: Portrait of a Radical*. Belfast: Appletree Press, 1984.

O'Brien, Brendan. *A Pocket History of the IRA*. Dublin: O'Brien Press, 1997.

O'Brien, Conor Cruise. *States of Ireland*. New York: Vintage Books, 1973.

O'Buachalla, Seamus. *Educational Policy in Twentieth Century Ireland*. Dublin: Wolfhound Press, 1988.

O'Carroll, J. P. "Bishops Knights and Pawn? Traditional Thought and the Irish Abortion Referendum Debate of 1983." *Irish Political Studies* 6 (1991), pp. 53–72.

O'Clery, Conor. *The Greening of the White House*. Dublin: Gill & Macmillan, 1996.

O'Connor, Fionnuala. *In Search of a State: Catholics in Northern Ireland*. Belfast: Blackstaff Press, 1993.

O'Donahue, Tom A. *The Catholic Church and the Secondary School Curriculum in Ireland: 1922–1962*. New York: Peter Lang, 1999.

O'Faolain, Sean. *The Irish*. Hammondsworth: Penguin, 1980.

O'Ferrall, Fergus. *Catholic Emancipation: Daniel O'Connell and the Birth of Irish Democracy, 1820–1830*. Dublin: Gill & Macmillan, 1985.

O'Grada, Cormac. *Ireland: A New Economic History 1780–1939*. Oxford: Clarendon Press, 1994.

_____. *A Rocky Road: The Irish Economy Since the 1920s*. Manchester: Manchester University Press, 1997.

O'Hanlon, Ray. *The New Irish Americans*. Niwot, Colo.: Roberts Rinehart, 1998.

O'Hanlon, Thomas J. *The Irish: Portrait of a People*. London: Andre Deutsch, 1976.

O'Hearn, D. "The Irish Case of Dependency: An Exception to the Exceptions." *American Sociological Review* 54 (1989), pp. 578–596.

O hEithir, Breandan. *The Begrudger's Guide to Irish Politics*. Dublin: Poolbeg, 1986.

O'Leary, C., and T. Hesketh. "The Irish Abortion and Divorce Referendum Campaigns." *Irish Political Studies* 3 (1988), pp. 46–47.

O'Malley, E. *Industry and Economic Development: The Challenge of the Latecomer.* Dublin: Gill & Macmillan, 1989.

O'Malley, Ernie. *On Another Man's Wound.* Dublin: Anvil Books, 1979.

_____. *The Singing Flame.* Dublin: Anvil Books, 1978.

O'Malley, Padraig. *The Uncivil Wars: Ireland Today.* Boston: Houghton Mifflin, 1983.

O'Sullivan, Patrick, ed. *Irish Women and Irish Migration.* London: Leicester University Press, 1995.

O' Toole, Fintan. *Black Hole, Green Card.* Dublin: New Island Books, 1994.

_____. *The Exiles of Erin: Images of Global Ireland.* Dublin: New Island Books, 1996.

O'Tuama, Sean, and Thomas Kinsella, eds. *An Duanaire.* Philadelphia: University of Pennsylvania Press, 1981.

Pakenham, Thomas. *The Year of Liberty: The Great Irish Rebellion of 1798.* Englewood Cliffs, N.J.: Prentice-Hall, 1970.

Peillon, Michel. *Contemporary Irish Society.* Dublin: Gill & Macmillan, 1982.

Peillon, Michel, and Eamonn Slater, eds. *Encounters with Modern Ireland.* Dublin: Institute of Public Administration, 1998.

Penniman, H., ed. *Ireland at the Polls: 1977.* Washington, D.C.: American Enterprise Institute, 1978.

Porteir, Cathal, ed. *The Great Irish Famine.* Cork: Mercier Press, 1995.

Porter, Norman. *Rethinking Unionism: An Alternative Vision for Northern Ireland.* Belfast: Blackstaff Press, 1996.

Power, T. P., and Kevin Whelan, eds. *Endurance and Emergence: Catholics in Ireland in the Eighteenth Century.* Dublin: Irish Academic Press, 1990.

Prager, Jeffrey. *Building Democracy in Ireland.* Cambridge: Cambridge University Press, 1986.

Raftery, Brian. *Pagan Christian Ireland: The Enigma of the Irish Iron Age.* New York: Thames & Hudson, 1994.

Regan, John. "Looking at Mick Again: Demilitarising Michael Collins." *History Ireland* 3, no.2 (Autumn 1995), pp. 17–22.

Rockett, Kevin, Luke Gibbons, and John Hill. *Cinema and Ireland.* Syracuse, N.Y.: Syracuse University Press, 1987.

Rometsch, D., and W. Wessels, eds. *The European Union and the Member States: Towards Institutional Fusion?* Manchester: Manchester University Press, 1996.

Ruane, Joseph, and Jennifer Todd. *The Dynamics of Conflict in Northern Ireland.* Cambridge: Cambridge University Press, 1995.

Ryan, Louise. "Women Without Votes: The Political Strategies of the Irish Suffrage Movement." *Irish Political Studies* 9 (1994), pp. 119–139.

Ryan, Michael, ed. *The Illustrated Archaeology of Ireland.* Dublin: Country House, 1991.

Savage, Robert. *Irish Television: The Political and Social Origins.* Cork: Cork University Press, 1996.

Scally, Robert. *The End of Hidden Ireland: Rebellion, Famine, and Emigration.* New York: Oxford University Press, 1995.

Schmitt, David. *The Irony of Irish Democracy.* London: Lexington Books, 1973.

Shirlow, Peter, and Mark McGovern, eds. *Who Are "The People"? Unionism, Protestantism, and Loyalism in Northern Ireland.* London: Pluto Press, 1997.

Silke, John. "Irish Scholarship and the Renaissance, 1580–1673." *Studies in the Renaissance* XX (1971), pp. 169–206.

Sinnot, Richard. *Irish Voters Decide: Voting Behavior in Elections and Referedums Since 1918.* Manchester: Manchester University Press, 1995.

Smyth, Ailbhe, ed. *The Irish Women's Studies Reader.* Dublin: Attic Press, 1993.

Smyth, Jim. *The Men of No Property: Irish Radicals and Popular Politics in the Late Eighteenth Century.* Dublin: Gill & Macmillan, 1992.

Smyth, William J., and Kevin Whelan, eds. *Common Ground: Essays on the Historical Geography of Ireland.* Cork: Cork University Press, 1988.

Stack, John F., Jr., and Lui Hebron, eds. *The Ethnic Entanglement: Conflict and Intervention in World Politics.* Westport, Conn.: Praeger, 1999.

Stalker, John. *Stalker.* London: Harrap, 1988.

Stevenson, Jonathan. *"We Wrecked the Place": Contemplating an End to the Northern Ireland Troubles.* New York: Free Press, 1996.

Tobin, Fergal. *The Best of Decades: Ireland in the 1960s.* Dublin: Gill & Macmillan, 1984.

Toibin, Colm. *The Trials of the Generals.* Dublin: Raven Arts Press, 1990.

Trench, Charles Chevenix. *The Great Dan: A Biography of Daniel O'Connell.* London: Jonathan Cape, 1984.

Valiulis, Maryann Gialanella. *Almost a Rebellion: The Irish Army Mutiny of 1924.* Cork: Tower Books, 1985.

Valiulis, Maryann Gialanella, and Mary O'Dowd, eds. *Women and Irish History.* Dublin: Wolfehound Press, 1997.

Vaughn, W. E. *A New History of Ireland, Vol. VI: Ireland Under the Union, 1870–1921.* New York: Oxford University Press, 1996.

Walker, Brian. *Dancing to History's Tune.* Belfast: Institute of Irish Studies, 1996.

Wall, Maureen. "The Rise of the Catholic Middle Class in Eighteenth Century Ireland." *Irish Historical Studies* XI, no. 42 (1958), pp. 91–115.

Ward, Alan. *The Irish Constitutional Tradition: Responsible Government and Modern Ireland 1782–1992.* Washington, D.C.: Catholic University Press, 1994.

Whelan, Kevin. *The Tree of Liberty: Radicalism, Catholicism and the Construction of Irish Identity 1760–1830.* Cork: Cork University Press, 1966.

Whyte, J. H. *Church and State in Modern Ireland, 1923–1979.* 2d ed. Dublin: Gill & Macmillan, 1980.

———. "Interpretations of the Northern Ireland Problem: An Appraisal." *Economic and Social Review* 9, no. 4 (1978), pp. 257–282.

Whyte, John H. *Interpreting Northern Ireland.* Oxford: Clarendon Press, 1990.

Wiles, James L., and Richard B. Finnegan. *Aspirations and Realities: A Documentary History of Economic Development Policy in Ireland Since 1922.* Westport, Conn.: Greenwood Press, 1993.

Wilson, Andrew J. *Irish America and the Ulster Conflict: 1968–1995.* Washington, D.C.: Catholic University Press, 1995.

Young, Arthur. *A Tour in Ireland, 1776–1779.* Shannon, Ireland: Irish University Press, 1970.

Index

Note: italic page number indicates picture.

AAC. *See* Anti-Amendment Campaign
Abbey Theatre, xi, 394, 395
Abortion, 170–173, *179*
    interpreting Irish attitude toward, 177–180
Act of Settlement, 10–11
Act of Union, 20, 231
    and Catholic aspirations, 23
    and homosexuality, 273
    O'Connell's attempts to repeal, 23, 24–25
    and socioeconomic conditions of the time, 21–23
Action Handbook: How to Implement Gender Equality, 185
Action Plan for Irish 1983–1986, 118
Active or Passive: Broadcasting in the Future Tense, 150
Ad Hoc Congressional Committee for Irish Affairs, 323, 324, 325
Adams, Gerry, 258, 309, 342, *364*
    and British government, 343–344
    and Canary Wharf bombing, 353
    and cessation of violence, 347, 348, 363
    and Downing Street Declaration, 346
    exclusion from Forum in Northern Ireland, 355
    and Good Friday Peace Agreement, 357
    handshake with Hume, 347
    intermediate position, 346
    role in peace process, 367
    and Shankill bombing, 344
    talks with Hume, 342, 343, 352, 360
    U.S. visit, 351, 352

Adrian IV, Pope, 6
Advertising Standards Authority for Ireland, 185
Aer Lingus, 222, 267
Afro-Celt, 392, 393
Age of Reason, 152
Agricultural Credit Corporation, 222
Agriculture, xi, xvii
    changes induced by Great Famine, 40
    de Valera's vision, 75, 76
    decline in 1950s, 93, 96
    and depression of 1870s, 43
    and environmental issues, 269–271
    farmers as pressure group, 264–265
    and Normans, 6–8
    origins in Ireland, 2
Ahern, Bertie, 214, 248
    coming to power, 356
    and Good Friday Peace Agreement, 357
    and peace process, 367
    response to Omagh bombing, 363
AIDS, 170, 186, 273, 276, 277–278
Aiken, Frank, 153, 377, 378
AIM (Action, Information, Motivation), 166
Airey case, 188
Alcoholism, 273–275. *See also* Drugs
Alderdice, John, 355
Aldershot, 308
Algeria, 54–55, 387
All-Ireland Council, 363
Alliance Party, 310–311, 360
Altan, 389, 391
American Revolution, 17
    and Scots-Irish, 14

Americans for a New Irish Agenda, 351

Amin, Idi, 55

Amnesty International, 317, 324, 339,
    340–341

Amongst Women, 174

Amsterdam Treaty of 1997, 381, 382

An Rinn, 76

An Taisce, 271

Ancient Order of Hibernians, 303

Andrews, Eamonn, 142, 143

Angel, 400

Angela's Ashes, 389

Anglican Church, 291

Anglo-Irish, 14–17

Anglo Irish Agreement, 189, 257, 335, 337,
    338
    and European Parliament, 340

Anglo-Irish Treaty, 68–69, 78, 206, 241, 376

Anglo-Irish War, 66–68

ANIA. *See* Americans for a New Irish Agenda

Anti-Abortion Campaign, 175

Anti-Amendment Campaign, 170, 173

Anti-Discrimination (Pay) Act, 167

Anti-Divorce Campaign, 175, 176, 182

Antrim and Great Famine, 33

Apprentice Boys' March, 298

Aran islands, 48

Archbishop of Dublin, 181

Ard Macha. *See* Armagh

Ardagh, John, 273

Arkin, Robert, 404

Armagh, 5
    Ard Macha, 3–4
    and Great Famine, 33

Arms Trial, 312

Arnold, Bruce, 247

Arts
    dance, 394
    film, 400–405
    literature, 398–400
    music, 391–394
    poetry, 396–398
    theater, 394–395

Asquith, Herbert Henry, 45, 46, 160–161, 282

Assembly (Northern Ireland), 357–358
    and decommissioning of arms, 363–364
    election results, 360–361

Association of Business and Professional
    Women, 165

Association of Secondary Teachers Ireland,
    112

ASTI. *See* Association of Secondary
    Teachers Ireland

*Attitudes Toward Moral Issues in Relation to
    Voting Behavior in Recent
    Referenda*, 185

*Attitudes Toward the Role and Status of
    Women 1975–86*, 185

Attorney General v. Hamilton, 215

*Attorney General v. Open Door Counseling
    et al.*, 171

Ayearst, Morely, 262

B Specials, 290, 296, 298, 305, 316

The Bad Lieutenant, 154

Balbriggan, 67

Balfour, Arthur J., 45

Ballinasloe Agricultural Fair, 391

"The Ballroom of Romance," 174

Ballymoney, 362

Ballymun, 275

Bangladesh, 387

Bank of Ireland, 98

Bannen, Ian, 405

Banotti, Mary, 191

Bantry Bay, 17

Banville, John, 398

Barrington, Thomas, 219

Barry, David, 163

Barry Fitzgerald, 400

Barrytown Trilogy, 398–399

Bartlett, Thomas, 14

Basque separatists, 308

Bateman, Colin, 400

Battle of Clontarf, 5

Battle of Kinsale, 9

Battle of the Boyne, 11, 292

Battle of the Somme, 361

Battle of Vinegar Hill, 17

"Baywatch," 144

BBC. *See* British Broadcasting Corporation

"The Beauty Queen of Leenane," 389, 395

Beauvoir, Simone de, 152

Beckett, Samuel, 108, 396

Beere, Thekla, 166
Begley, Thomas, 344
Behan, Brendan, 152
"Behold the Sons of Ulster Marching to the Somme," 395
Belfast, xii, 297
    Bloody Friday, 307
    industry, xvi
    population, xvi
    violent conflict, 300
Belfast Confetti, 398
The Bell, 152–153
Bennett, Louie, 160
Bennett Committee, 317
Better Government of Ireland Act, 67
"Beverly Hills 90210," 144
Bew, Paul, 335
Bewley's, the Dublin Coffeehouse, 390
Biaggi, Mario, 303, 321–322, 322–323, 323–324, 325, 326
Binchey, William, 182
Bingham, William, 362
Birmingham Six, 340
Birth control. *See* Contraception
Bishop of Clonfert, 126
Bishop of Cork and Ross, 181
Bishop of Dublin, 108
Bishop of Ferns, 181
Bishop of Galway, 108, 145
Bishop of Tuam, 129
Black 47, 389, 393
Black and Tans, 67, 68
    and world opinion, 68
Blair, Tony, 342
    and Good Friday Peace Agreement, 357
    and Northern Ireland peace process, 355–356
    on Omagh bombing, 363
    and peace process, 367
Blake, James, 119–120
Blanchard, Paul, 128
Blaney, Neil, 243–244
Blaskets, 76–77
Bloody Friday, 307
Bloody Sunday, 68, 301, 395
Blueshirts, 79–80, 226, 249
Boland, Eavan, 397

Boland, Kevin, 244, 251, 326
Boland's Mills, 53, 64
Bolger, Dermot, 398, 399
The Book of Evidence, 398
Book of Kells, xi
Boorman, John, 405
Bord Bia, 390
Bord na Gaeilige, 118
Bord na Mona, 82
Born on the Fourth of July, 400
Boru, Brian, 5
Boston, County Clare, 75
Boundary Commission, 72
The Boxer, 402
Boyce, D. George, 53
Boycott, Charles, 43
Boyle, Alan, 404
Breakfast on Pluto, 399–400
Brehon Law, 4, 8
Brennan, Brid, 394
Brighton bombing of 1984, 309
Britain
    arrests of Sinn Fein leaders, 65
    concessions to Catholics, 15
    Cromwellian settlement policy, 10–11
    first incursions into Ireland, 6
    and flight of the earls, 9
    grants vote to women, 161
    Home Rule offers (1916–1917), 63
    and hunger strikes, 336
    imperialism in Ireland, 4
    influence on Ireland, 204–205
    institutes draft in Ireland (1918), 64–65
    Ireland Act of 1949, 83
    Irish condemnation of, 202–203
    and Irish democracy, 231
    and Irish economy, 104–105
    and Irish neutrality in World War II, 82, 377
    and Irish Parliament, 15
    and Northern Ireland peace process, 342, 344
    Penal Laws, 12–14
    plantation of Ulster, 9–10
    policy during Great Famine, 32–33, 35, 36–37

response to Easter Rising of 1916,
    52–53
Statute of Westminster, 376
talks with Sinn Fein, 342
Ulster policy, 294–295, 302, 306,
    311–313, 318–321, 334–337
British Army, 298, 299–300, 306, 307, 363
British Broadcasting Corporation, 142, 143
    and circumvention of film censorship,
    146–147, 154
British-Irish Intergovernmental
    Conference, 334–335
British Parliament
    and Home Rule, 44, 45
    Penal Laws, 12
Broadcasting Act of 1960, 143
Brooke, Basil, 285
"Brown Eyed Girl," 391
Brown, Christy, 400
Browne, Arthur, 14
Browne, John, 190
Browne, Noel, 83–84, 129–130
Brugha, Cathal, 205
Brustein, Robert, 395
Bruton, John, 214, 248, 253
    and Northern Ireland peace process,
    353
Buckley, Donal, 207
Building on Reality 1985–1987, 101
Bulgaria, 308
Bunracht na hEireann. *See* Constitution
"Buntus Cainte," 143
Burke, Edmund, 108
Burns, Brian, 389–390
Burntollet Bridge, 10, 297, 316
The Butcher Boy (film), 404
The Butcher Boy (novel), 399–400
Butler, Jean, 394
Butt, Isaac, 42–43
Byrne, Chris, 389
Byrne, Ernest, 143
Byrne, Gabriel, 401, 405
Byrne, Gay, 144, 146

Cahill, Joe, 309
Cal, 400

Callahan, James, 284, 317
Cameron Commission, 316
Canary Wharf bombing, 352
Cantwell, 7
Capercaillie, 393
Capital Investment Advisory Committee, 96
Capote, Truman, 152
Caravats, 22
Carberry v. The Minister for Social Welfare,
    168
Carey, Hugh, 303, 323, 326
Carlingford peninsula, xi
Carrick on Suir, 270
The Cars, 391
Carson, Ciaran, 398
Carson, Edward, 45, 283
Carter, Jimmy, 323, 324, 325, 338
"Carthaginians," 395
The Case Against Divorce, 182
Casey, Eamonn, 132, 275
    sex scandal, 137–138
Casey, Ger, 182
Castlebar races, 17–18
Castlereagh, Robert Stewart, 20
"Cathleen ni Houlihan," 48. *See also* ni
    Houlihan, Cathleen
Catholic Action, 262
Catholic Association, 23–24
Catholic Church
    and abortion issue, 171, 172
    arrival of, 3–4
    authoritarianism, 124, 128
    ban on attending Trinity College, 108,
        113, 126, 132
    British concessions, 15–17
    and censorship, 151–152, 154–155
    contemporary position, 139–142
    and contraception, 126, 134–135
    corporatist alternative to capitalism
        and communism, 141, 225–226
    and Cosgrave, 124–125, 128
    and dancing, 125, 152
    and de Valera, 125, 128
    decline of monasteries and increasing
        influence of Rome, 5–6
    and development of democracy, 232

diminished numbers and prestige of
   clerics, 140
and divorce, 125–126, 133, 174–175,
   176–177
and education, 41, 44, 107–110, 126
and educational reform, 114
and Free State, 124–130
and Gaelic Athletic Association, 47
on health care, 129
on homosexuality, 136–137, 276
influence on Constitution, 78, 125
internal reconsiderations, 131–132
internal scandals, xii, xiv
and Irish political culture, 203–204
and language of Constitution,
   209–211, 212
and media, 144–146
and modernization in Ireland,
   130–137
moral monopoly, 123
and national identity, 124
and nationalist movement, 41, 42, 44
and Northern Ireland, 135–136
and post-war social doctrine, 83–84
as pressure group, 261–264
and pressures of media, 136
scandals, 137–139
secular challenges, xii, xiv
sexual puritanism, 124, 125, 130, 152
social policy, 126–128
syncretism with Celtic elements, 3–4
and television, 144–145
and Tudors, 9
Catholic Communications Institute of
   Ireland, 145
Catholic Defenders, 18–19
Catholic Hierarchy, 64, 107, 109
   and Censorship Board, 153
   and contraception, 134
   diminished political influence,
      140–141
   and divorce referendum, 181–182
   and education, 126
Catholic Nationalist Social Democratic
   Party, 189
Catholic Truth Society, 151, 154

Catholic University of Ireland, 109
Cavendish, Frederick, 44
Ceann Clogher, 76
Ceannt, Eamonn, 53
Ceilis, 392
"Celtic Tiger" period (1987–1997),
      102–104, 277, 386. *See also* Irish
      renaissance (of 1990s)
Celts and Celtic culture, 3. *See also* Culture
   golden age, 4
   influence on Catholic Church, 3–4
   inversion of vices as virtues, 48–49
   Irish as "barbarous" people, 8
Censorship
   of films, 132, 146–147, 154
   and IRA, 149
   and national development, 154–155
   of television, 148–149
   in World War II, 153
   of written materials, 125, 132,
      151–153
Censorship Board, 92, 108, 152–153,
      154–155
Censorship of Film Act of 1923, 154
Censorship of Publications Act of 1929,
      151–152
Central America, 378
Central Housing Authority, 298
Centre for European Law, 189
CFSP. *See* Common Foreign and Security
      Policy
*Chains or Change? The Civil Wrongs of Irish
      Women*, 166
Challenges and Opportunities Abroad, 375,
      380
Chamberlain, Neville, 78
Chaplin, Charlie, 153
Chastelain, John de, 349
   and Forum in Northern Ireland, 355
Cherish, 166, 188
Cherish the Ladies, 393
Chichester-Clark, James D. (and adminis-
      tration), 298, 300
The Chieftains, 391, 392, 393
Child Care Act of 1991, 184
Childers, Erskine, 70

Christian Brothers, 107, 108, 126, 137
    apology to students, 139
Christianity, arrival of, 3–4
Christopher, Warren, 352
Chubb, Basil, 219, 222, 224, 231–232, 263,
    267
Church of Ireland, 22
    with Catholic graves, *127*
    disestablishment, 41, 45
Churchill, Randolph, 44
Churchill, Winston, 81, 82, 377
Circle of Friends, 401
Cistercian Order, 6
Citizen armies. *See* Irish Citizen Army,
        Irish Volunteers, Ulster Volunteer
        Force
Civil Service (Employment of Married
        Women) Act of 1973, 167
Civil service departments. *See* State
        Sponsored Bodies
Civil War, 69–70, 232–233
Clachans, 40
Clan na Gael, 51
Clann na Publachta, 83, 130, 249–250, 258
Clann na Talmhan, 258
Clannad, 392
Clare, Anthony, 136–137
Clare, Richard de. *See* Strongbow
Clark, Austin, 152
Clark, William, 338
Clarke, Thomas, 49, 52, 53
Class structure, 239–240
Clientelist (brokerage) system, 216–217
Clinton, Bill, 295
    and Adams visit, 352
    on Adams, 367
    and Good Friday Peace Agreement,
        357
    and Northern Ireland, 349, 351, 352,
        356
Clontarf
    Battle of, 5
    monster meeting, 25, 26
Cluskey, Frank, 255
Coleman, Michael, 393
Coleraine, 289
Colleges, 76

of technology, 113
Colley, George, 110, 243–244
Collins, Michael, 63–64, 248, 283
    on Anglo-Irish Treaty, 208
    biographical sketch, 66
    and Bloody Sunday, 68
    chairman of provisional government,
        206–207
    and Civil War, 70
    and Dail, 205
    and de Valera, Eamon, 68, 70–71,
        206–207, 241, 403, 404
    death of, 70
    debate over legacy of, 70–72
    and film *Michael Collins*, 71, 403–404
    and Sinn Fein, 65
    and Treaty of 1921, 68, 69
Comhairle na Gaelige, 117
Commission of the European Union, 228
Commission on Emigration and Other
        Population Problems, 96
Commission on Policing for Northern
        Ireland, 358
Commission on the Status of Women, 164,
        165–166
Commission on Vocational Organization,
        218
    Report, 225
The Commitments (film), 404–405
The Commitments (novel), 390, 398–399
Committee of Professional Agricultural
        Organizations, 228–229
Committee on Irish Language Attitudes, 117
Committee on Women's Rights, 165–166
The Commodores, 393
Common Agricultural Policy, 99, 100, 229,
        265, 381
    benefits to Ireland, 383
    and Fianna Fail, 383
Common Foreign and Security Policy, 379,
        380
Communist Party of Ireland, 166–167
Compton Report, 317
"Condom Train," 166
Confederation of Irish Industry, 267
Confederation of Kilkenny, 10
Congo, 378, 387

Conlon, Gerry, 401
Connally, Peter, 132
Connaught, xvi, 10
    and Great Famine, 33
    and Irish language, 73
    land holdings (early 19th century), 22
Connaughton, Shane, 400
Connemara, 48
Connolly, James, 26, 253
    and Easter Rising of 1916, 52, 53, 54, 57
    and Irish Citizen Army, 50, 51
Connolly, S. J., 13
Conservative Party (Britain), 299, 309
Constituent Assembly, 313–314, 318
Constitution. *See also* Free State
        Constitution
    amendments, 213
    avoidance of "Republic" designation,
        208–209
    and Catholic Church, 125, 133
    and Catholicism, 209–211, 212
    deletion of Catholic Church's special
        position, 312
    "Directive Principles of Social Policy,"
        211
    on divorce, 125–126, 133, 163
    drafting and passage, 78–79, 208
    election approving, 213
    and Irish language, 212
    and John Herne, 208
    1972 amendment giving primacy to
        European law in employment
        and social welfare, 167
    and Northern Ireland, 208–209
    on religion, 210–211
    rights of citizens, 212–213
    on sovereignty, 208
    and women's role, 163–164
    and women's suffrage, 161
Constitutional Review Group, 212, 213,
        218, 273
Consultation Paper on Rape, 184
Consumer's Association of Ireland, 267
Contraception, 126, 134–135, 163, 166, 168
    changes in laws, 169–170
    interpreting Irish attitude toward,
        177–180

Contraception Action Programme,
        134–135, 166–167
Control of Manufactures Act, 96
Conway, Cardinal, 131, 133, 211
Coogan, Tim Pat, 265, 299–300
Cooke, Henry, 282
Cooney, Patrick, 176, 220
Coras Trachtala, 94
Corcoran, Mary, 387
Corish, Brendan, 255, 262
Cork, xvi
    assassination and reprisal, 68
    and Great Famine, 33
    and Irish language, 76
Cork Examiner, 150
Corkery, Daniel, 12–13
Cornwallis, Charles, 20
"Coronation Street," 144
Corporatism, 141, 225–227. *See also*
        Neo-corporatism
    and labor, 266
Corrigan, Mauread, 314–315
Cosgrave, Liam, 84, 135, 220–221, 244, 250,
        251
    promise to recognize Northern
        Ireland as a British territory, 312
Cosgrave, William (and administration),
        72–73, 79–80, 242
    and Catholic Church, 124–125, 128,
        129–130
    as "chairman," 214
    and Cumann na nGaedheal, 248–249
    and Fine Gael, 226, 249
    and Irish language, 116
Costello, John, 83, 129–130, 250, 377
    as "chairman," 214
Costner, Kevin, 403
Cottiers, 21
Coulter, Carol, 178, 192–193
Council for the Status of Women, 166,
        186–188, 192–193. *See also*
        National Women's Council
Council of Education, 107
Council of Ireland, 67, 283, 311–313
Council of Ministers (European Union), 228
County Clare, 66
County Kilkenny, 67

County Louth, 76
County Meath, 76
Cousins, Margaret, 160
Coventry bombing, 80
Craig, James, 45, 283, 292
Craig, William, 297, 301, 310, 313
The Cranberries, 390, 391, 393
Crime, 275–276, 277–278
Criminal Law (Rape) Act of 1981, 184
Criminal Law (Rape) Act of 1990, 184
Criminal Law (Sexual Offenses) Act of
    1993, 189
Criminal Law Amendment Act, 163, 169
"The Cripple of Irishman," 395
Croagh Patrick, 128
Croke, Thomas William, 47
Croke Park, 68
Cromwell, Oliver, 10
Crotty, R., 105, 106–107
Crotty v. An Taoiseach, 379
Crotty, William, 379
Cruise, Tom, 400
The Crying Game, 395, 403
CS gas, 299
Cullen, Kevin, 357
Cullen, Paul, 41, 42, 109
    and creation of modern Irish Church,
        124
Culture. *See also* Arts, Celts and Celtic cul-
        ture, Political culture
    decline after Great Famine, 38–39
    and Gaelic Athletic Association, 47
    and Gaelic League, 47–48
    Irish American cultural baggage, 33
    Irish Americans and 1990s Irish cul-
        tural renaissance, 388–391
    Irish festivals (U.S.), 391
    and modernization, 405–406
    1990s renaissance, 119–120, 388–389,
        406
    two traditions, 230
Cumann na mBan, 161
Cumann na nGaedheal, 70, 79, 151 , 202,
    226, 242–243
    as bridge between traditional culture
        and modern democratic struc-
        tures, 230–231, 232–233

and divorce, 163
and election of 1932, 74
    position in Irish politics, 259
and William Cosgrave, 248–249
Cummins, Nicholas, 33
"The Cure at Troy," 395
Currach Mutiny, 46
Currie, Austin, 190–191, 253, 297–298
Cusak, Michael, 47
Customs House, 14
Czechoslovakia, 308

"Da," 395
Dail Eireann, 65–66, 72, 118. *See also* Irish
        Parliament
    and Cabinet, 216
    clientelist (brokerage) system,
        216–217
    and commercialization of broadcast-
        ing, 150
    committees, 216, 382–383
    constituencies and representation,
        215–216
    coverage by Telefis na Gaelige, 119
    Declaration of Independence, 205
    and election of 1920, 67
    and European Union, 229
    founding, 205
    number of members, 148
    and party discipline, 216
    repudiation of de Valera, 72
    and Treaty of 1921, 68–69
    weakness of, 382–383
    women members, 164, 168–169
Daily Mirror, 150
Dalton, Cardinal, 143
Daly, Cahal, 181
Daly, Gabriel, 139
Daly, Mary, 34
Dance, 394
"Dancing at Lughnasa," 394–395, 399, 401
D'Angelo, Beverly, 403
Danny Boy, 400
The Dark, 108
Daughters of Ireland. *See* Inghinidhe na
        hEireann
Davidson, Jaye, 403

Davis, Thomas Osborne, 18, 27
Davitt, Michael, 34, 43–44
Day Lewis, Daniel, 400, 401, 402
De Dannan, 393
De Lacy, Tom, 269
De Rossa, Proinsias, 258
de Valera, Eamon, 53, 131
    arrested by British, 65
    biographical sketch, 64
    and Blueshirts, 79–80
    and Catholic Church, 125, 128,
        261–262, 263
    and censorship, 153
    as "chief," 214
    and Civil War, 69–70, 241–242
    and Constitution, 78–79, 208–209
    and corporatism, 226
    and Dail, 202
    death of, 84
    economic conflict with Britain, 78
    economic policy, 95, 104
    escape from jail, 66
    and Fianna Fail, 72–73, 242–243
    founding of *Irish Press*, 151
    head of government, 74–77
    and IRA, 72, 79, 80
    and Irish language, 115
    and Irish neutrality in World War II,
        376–377
    leader of Sinn Fein and Irish
        Volunteers, 64
    and Michael Collins, 68, 70–71,
        206–207, 241, 403, 404
    and negotiations with Lloyd George,
        68
    in 1950s, 84
    and partition, 68, 69
    pastoral Gaelic vision, 75–77, 91–92,
        179
    as portrayed in film *Michael Collins*,
        404
    and sanctions against Italian invasion
        of Ethiopia, 376
    summation of career, 84–85
    and symbols of imperialism in Free
        State Constitution, 208
    and television, 143
    and Treaty of 1921, 78
    and women's role, 77–78, 163
    and World War II, 81–82, 376–377
de Valera, Vivion, 151
Dead Poet's Society, 400
The Dead School, 399–400
Deane, Seamus, 397
Deevy, Lena, *193*
Delanty, Greg, 398
Democracy in Ireland, 230–233
Democratic deficit, 227–228
Democratic Left (party), 257–258, 259
Democratic Socialist Party, 170
Democratic Unionist Party, 288, 294, 310,
    311. *See also* Unionists (Northern
    Ireland)
    and Assembly, 360
    and election of 1982, 333, 336
Demographics, 239–240
Denehy, Brian, 395
Department of Customs and Excise, 153
Department of Education, 107, 111, 113
*Department of Education—Gender
    Equality*, 185
Department of Finance, 94, 96
    shortcomings of, 106
Deputy prime minister, 215
    and Dail, 216
Derry. *See* Londonderry
Devlin, Bernadette, 298
Devlin, Liam St. John, 223
Devlin Group, 223
Dickson, David, 13
Dillon, James, 250
Dillon, John Blake, 27
Diplock Court, 304, 321
Divorce, 125–126, 133, 163, 174–177
    interpreting Irish attitude toward,
        177–180
    legislation and referendum,
        180–183
Divorce Action Group, 175
Doctor Copernicus, 398
Doctrine and Life, 131
Doheny, Michael, 41, 42
Dollar Exports, 94
Donaldson, Jeffrey, 360

Donegal
  and Great Famine, 33
  and Irish language, 76
Donegal Bay, 310
Donegan, Patrick, 220–221
Donleavey, J. P., 152
Donlon, Sean, 322, 323, 326
  and Irish Americans, 321, 325, 337,
    338
Donnelly, Brian, 322, 338
  and "undocumented Irish," 385–386
Door into the Dark, 396
The Dork of Cork, 405
Dorrian, Hugh, 39
Dos Passos, John, 152
"Double Cross," 395
Dowling, Brendan, 95
Dowling, Michele, 75–76
Downing Street Declaration, 344–345
Dowth, 2–3
Doyle, Roddy, xi, xiii, 389, 390, 398–399,
    404–405
Dreiser, Theodore, 152
Driver, Minnie, 401
Drogheda, 10
Drugs, 275. *See also* AIDS, Alcoholism,
    Smoking
  and crime, 275–276, 277–278
Druid Theatre, 395
Druidism, 3
Drumcree, xii
  Orange Order parades, 348–349,
    361–362
Drummond, Thomas, 24
Dublin
  AIDS cases, 276
  and air pollution, 271
  Anglo-Irish architecture, 14
  as Anglo-Norman administrative
    center, 8
  and Civil War, 70
  founding by Vikings, 5
  migration to (1950s), 95
  population, xvi
  population as percentage of national
    population, 239

  poverty, 276
  tourism, xi
  Wood Quay, 5
Dublin, University of. *See* Trinity College
Dublin City University, 113
Dublin Corporation, 189
Dublin horse show, xi
Dublin Metropolitan Police, 68
Dublin Primary School, 108
Dublin Well Women's Centre, 170
Duffy, Charles Gavan, 25–26, 27
  formation of Tenants League, 41
Dukes, Alan, 221, 252–253, 255
Dunn, Joseph, 145
Dunne, Ben, 267
Durcan, Paul, 398
Durrell, Laurence, 152

Earthwatch, 271
Easter Rising of 1916, 52–53
  art and imagery of, 54, 56, *56*
  influence on subsequent politics,
    53–54
  memorials, 54
  nationalist interpretation, 53–54
  and Patrick Pearse, 26
  post-revisionist interpretation, 55–57
  public reaction, 53, 63
  revisionist interpretation, 54–55
  seeds of, 51–52
  women's role, 56–57
*Economic and Social Development
    1969–1972*, 99
Economic and Social Research Institute,
    185
Economic Development, 96, 109
Economy, xi–xii
  "Celtic Tiger" period (1987–1997),
    102–104, 277, 386
  consultants' reports (1950s), 94–95
  and foreign investment, 97–98
  and government failings, 106
  interpretations, 104–107
  and Irish character, 106
  and Irish language, 117–118
  1950s, 93–96

1970s and 1980s, 99–102
Second Programme, 98–99
Third Programme, 99
and Whitaker Plan, 96–99
Educational system
Catholic control over, 41
classical curriculum, 107, 113
gaelicization of, 73–74, 76
and Irish language, 116
and nationalist movement, 18
reform, 109–114, 132, 240
teachings on Great Famine in 20th
century, 34
traditional, 107–109
Edward VI, King, 9
Edwards, Ruth Dudley, xv, 34, 55
Egan, Seamus, 393
Electoral system
preferential ranking, 224
proportional representation, 223–225
Electricity Supply Board, 222, 248
Electronics companies, 104
Emergency Powers Bill, 312
Emigration, 384. *See also* Immigration,
Internal migration
and demographic changes, 239
and Great Famine, 33, *39*
and Industrial Revolution, 38
and Irish language, 116
1930s, 77–78
1950s, 92, 95–96, 153
and 1965 U.S. immigration act, 385
1970s, 385
1980s, 385
1990s, 384–387
and population decline, 38, 73
post-war, 385
and return migration, 386–387
"undocumented Irish," 384, 385–386
Wild Geese, 11–12
and World War II, 82
Emmet, Robert, 23
Emmet, Thomas Adis, 19, 23
Employer Labour Conference, 227
Employment Equality Act of 1977, 167,
184, 187

Employment Equality Agency, 167, 184,
187, 222
Encumbered Estates Act of 1849, 40
English Civil War, 10
English language, 204, 212
Enloe, Cynthia, 285
Environmental Action Programme, 271
Environmental issues, 269–271
Environmental Research Unit, 271
Enya, xiii, 391
Eolas, 271
EPC. *See* European Political Cooperation
Equal Rights Amendment, 187
Equality and Law Reform ministry, 187
"ER," 144
European Convention on Human Rights, 172
European Council, 229
European Court, 229–230
European Court of Human Rights, 172,
188, 273, 324, 380
European Court of Justices, 171–172
European Economic Community, 97, 99.
See also European Union
Fourth Equality Directive, 168
Irish participation, 378–380, 381
and Irish women, 167–168
Social Welfare Equality Directive, 188
Third Equality Directive, 168
European Human Rights Commission, 317
European Monetary Fund, 100
European Monetary System, 381
European Parliament, 40, 228
European Political Cooperation, 379
European Trade Union Confederation,
228–229
European Union, 99–102. *See also*
European Economic Community
Common Agricultural Policy, 99, 100,
229, 265
Council, 380
democratic deficit, 228
impact on Ireland, 228–230
Ireland's entry into, 99–100, 107
Irish participation in, 380–384
Regional Fund, 99
Social Fund, 99

Eurovision Song Contest, 144, 394
Evening Herald, 150, 151
Evening Press, 151
Everett, James, 153
External Relations Act of 1936, 209

Failure, romance of, 51–52, 55, 106
"Fair City," 144
Faligot, Roger, 306
Falklands-Malvinas War, 378, 379
Fallon, Peter, 398
"The Family," 399
Family Law Act of 1995, 185
Family Planning Bill of 1984, 257
Famine. *See* Great Famine
"Famine," 395
Farmers
    and European Economic Community,
        265
    as pressure group, 264–265
Farmers Journal, 264
Farmers Party, 84, 250, 258
Farrell, Brian, 214, 217, 231–232
Faulkner, Brian, 300, 310, 311, 312, 313
Federation of Irish Employers, 227, 267
Feeney, Charles, 351
Fenian Brotherhood, 1, 42
    influence on republicans in Northern
        Ireland, 26
    roots in America, 41, 42
    and ruins of Young Ireland, 41
Fennell, Nualla, 169, 187, 252
Fermanagh, 82
Fianna Fail, 70–71, 83, 84, 126
    alignment in European Parliament,
        383
    and Catholic Church, 142
    contesting seats, 224
    and contraception, 135
    and divorce issue, 175, 176, 180–181,
        182
    dominance and reduction, 224–225
    and election of 1932, 74
    and election of 1977, 101, 260
    and election of 1987, 102
    history of, 242–248
    and *Irish Press*, 151

and nationalism, 202
and 1977 election, 245
pastoral Gaelic ideal, 91–92
position in Irish politics, 259, 260
and proportional representation, 225
and RTE, 148
and Social Welfare Act of 1952, 277
woman candidate in 1997, 191
and women, 163, 166, 173
The Field, 401
Field Day Anthology of Irish Writing, 397
Field Day Theatre Group, 395, 397
Field Work, 396
Film, 400–405
Film Appeal Board, 154
Finance Acts, 96
Financial services industry, xvii
Fine Gael, 79–80, 83, 84, 151, 169
    and abortion, 171
    alignment in European Parliament, 383
    coalition with Labour (1980s), 101
    and coalitions, 249–251
    contesting seats, 224
    and contraception, 135
    and divorce issue, 133, 174, 175, 176
    formation and component organiza-
        tions, 226, 249
    and Garret FitzGerald, 251–252
    history, 248–253
    as opposition party, 248
    position in Irish politics, 259, 260
    woman candidate in 1997, 191
Finn, Peter, 390
First Language, 398
*First Report of the Joint Committee on
        Women's Rights, Education*, 185
Fitt, Gerry, 300, 306
Fitzgerald, F. Scott, 152
FitzGerald, Garret, 84, 178, 190, 260
    and abortion issue, 171
    on cessation of violence, 347
    characterization of, 214
    and dissolution of Dail, 221
    and divorce issue, 174, 175, 176
    and Fennell, 169, 187
    and Fine Gael, 251–252
    and Forum for a New Ireland, 333

and Haughey, 177, 326
and Irish Americans, 322, 325, 338
on Irish language, 117
and Northern Ireland, 256
and Thatcher, 336
Fitzgerald, William Vesey, 24
Fitzpatrick, David, 66
Fitzsimmons, Yvonne, 187, 192
Flanagan, Oliver J., 145, 178
Flannery, Austin, 148
Flatley, Michael, 394
Fleadh Cheoil, 392
Flight of the earls, 9
Flynn, Padriag, 190
Flynn, Thomas, 181
Flynn, William, 351
For Whom the Bell Tolls, 152
Ford, Henry, 1
Foreign Assistance Act, 324
Foreign policy, 375–376
    of Irish Free State, 376–377
    membership in European Economic
        Community, 378–380
    membership in European Union,
        380–384
    membership in United Nations,
        377–378
    neutrality, 376–379, 380, 384
Forsythe, Bill, 405
Forum for a New Ireland, 189, 333–334,
    336, 337
Forum for Peace and Reconciliation, 347
Forum in Northern Ireland, 349–350
    delegates, 355
    discussions, 356–357
    election, 353–355
    exclusion of Adams, 355
Foster, Roy, 19, 34–35
Four Courts, 14, 52, 69, 70
Fox Network, 147
"Framework for Agreement," 348–349
Frankie Starlight, 405
Frears, Stephen, 405
Free State Army, 70, 74
Free State Assembly, 69
Free State Constitution, 206–208
    on sovereignty, 207

Freedom movements, 54–55
French Revolution, 15–17
Freud, Sigmund, 152
Friel, Brian, xiii, 394–395, 401
"Friends," 147
Friends of Ireland, 337, 338
Frongoch, 66
"The Fugitive," 144
The Furrow, 131, 132

GAA. *See* Gaelic Athletic Association
Gaeilgeoiri, 115
Gael Linn, 267
Gaelic. *See* Gaeltactht, Irish language
Gaelic Athletic Association, 47, 66, 267, 291
    and Irish Republican Brotherhood, 49
    and television, 143
Gaelic League, 47–48, 64, 66, 267
    and Irish language, 115
    and Irish Republican Brotherhood, 49
Gaelic Revival, 26
Gaeltacht, 73, 76, 116–117, 118, 169. *See
    also* Irish language
Gahan, Daniel, 18
Gallery Press, 398
Galligan, Yvonne, 187
Galvin, Martin, 149, 306
Galway
    and Great Famine, 33
    and Irish language, 76, 119
Galway Cathedral, 145
"The Galway Plains," 49
Garibaldi, Giuseppe, 27
Garvin, Tom, 178–180, 231
Gaullists, 383
The General, 405
General Post Office, 52
Geoghegan-Quinn, Maire, 169
George III, King, 23
George V, King, 45
Gerald of Wales, 6–8
Germany
    and IRA, 81
    and nationalist movement, 51, 52, 65
Geurin, Veronica, 275
Gibbons, Luke, 36, 37–38
Gide, Andre, 152

"The Gigli Concert," 395
Gilligan, John, 275
Girvin, Brian, 178
Gladstone, William, 44, 45
Gleeson, Brendan, 405
"Glenroe," 144
Glover, John, 309
Golden age (7th and 8th centuries), 4
Good Friday Peace Agreement, xii, 240,
        255–256, 281, 311. *See also* Peace
        process (Northern Ireland)
    American participation, 295
    Assembly, 357–358
    British-Irish Council, 358
    conclusion of, 357
    Declaration of Support, 347
    on decommissioning of arms, 358
    Ministerial Council, 358
    points, 357–360
    on policing and justice, 358
    on prisoners, 358
    referenda on, 358–360
    Rights, Safeguards, and Equality of
        Opportunity, 358
Goodman, Larry, 267
Goodman Beef, 247
Gorki, Maxim, 152
Government. *See also* Dail Eireann
    Cabinet, 214–215
    clientelist (brokerage) system,
        216–217
    coalition, 214
    corporatism and neo-corporatism,
        141, 225–228
    democratic deficit, 227–228
    electoral system, 223–225
    impact of European Union, 228–230
    influence of Britain, 204
    local, 218–219
    Oireachtas, 215–218
    policy failures, 106
    popular sovereignty, 205, 207, 208
    President, 219–221
    prime minister, 214, 215
    State Sponsored Bodies, 222–223
    structure, 212, 213–214

Government of Ireland Act of 1920, 206,
        207, 283
Gracey, Harold, 362
Grattan, Henry, 15, 16, 24
    influence on Young Irelanders, 27
    statue, *16*
Gray, David, 377
Gray, Peter, 32, 33, 36, 44
Great Blasket, 76–77
The Great Dictator, 153
Great Famine, 1, 31–32
    British policy during, 32–33, 35,
        36–37
    and contemporary world hunger, 34,
        38
    and decline of Irish language, 38–40
    effect on political activity, 40–41, 44
    and exports of other commodities
        during, 34
    Famine fever, 33
    impact on economy, 40
    legacy of, 38–42
    nationalist interpretation, 34
    and population decline, 38
    post-revisionist interpretation, 35–38
    revisionist interpretation, 34–35
    and soup kitchens, 36–37
    and teachings in school system, 34
Greeley, Andrew, 296
Green Cross, 308
The Green Paper on Education, 112
Gregory, Lady, 48, 56
Gregory, Tony, 246
Griffith, Arthur, 34, 49, 64, 69, 248
    arrested by British, 65
    and Dail, 206, 207
    death of, 70
    and negotiations with Lloyd George,
        68
    and proportional representation, 223
Guelke, Adrian, 325, 340
*Guidelines on the Development of
        Sex/Relationships Education*, 186
Guilford Four, 340, 401
Guinness Fleadh, 391
Guinness stout, 390

Hachey, Thomas, 80
Hamilton, Liam, 247
Hamilton, Mark, 182
Hammond, David, 397
Hanafin, Des, 175
Hanrahan, John, 269–270
Hanrahan, Mary, 270
Harland and Wolf Shipyard, 290
Harney, Mary, 248, 257
    and Progressive Democrats, 257
Harris, Emmy Lou, 392
Harris, Richard, 401
Harvard Center for International Affairs,
    322
Haughey, Charles (and administration),
    84, 135, 148, 171, 190
    characterization of, 214
    and dissolution of Dail, 221
    and Fianna Fail power struggle and
        crisis, 243–245
    and FitzGerald, 177, 326
    and Irish Americans, 325, 326
    and New Ireland Forum, 256–257
    scandals, 246, 247, 248, 256
    on spending, 102
    as Taoiseach and head of Fianna Fail,
        245–247
Health and Family Planning Act of 1979, 169
Health Boards, 184, 185
Health Care Act of 1991, 277
Healy, Timothy, 207
Heaney, Seamus, xiii, 57, 395, 396–397, *397*
Heath, Ted (and administration), 299, 302
Heather Blazing, 400
Heathrow Airport mortar attack, 346
Heinz Corporation, 151
Hemingway, Ernest, 152
Hennessys, 11
Henry II, King, 6
Henry VIII, King, 9
Herne, John, 208
Hesketh, Tom, 171, 178
Higgins, Michael D., 119
Higher Education Authority, 222
Hillary, Patrick, 110, 190, 243
    and dissolution of Dail, 221

History, xiv–xv. *See also* Nationalist histori-
    ans, Post-revisionist historians,
    Revisionist historians
Hobson, Bulmer, 49
Holkeri, Harri, 349
Holland, Jack, 309, 323
Holohan, Michael, 397
Home Government Association, 43
Home Rule, 42
    British offer, 63
    and Parnell, 42, 43–45
    and Redmond, 45–46, 63
Home Rule League, 43
"Home Truths," 148
Homosexuality, 189, 272–273. *See also*
    AIDS
    and Catholic Church, 136–137, 276
    gay and lesbian advocates, 268, 273
Horgan, John, 133–134, 226
Hoskins, Bob, 400
Human rights (Northern Ireland),
    339–341. *See also* Amnesty
    International, European
    Convention on Human Rights,
    European Court of Human
    Rights, European Human Rights
    Commission
"Humanae Vitae," 132
Humbert, Jean-Joseph, 17–18
Hume, John, 297–298, 300, 303, 342, *365*
    on Adams, 367
    on cessation of violence, 347
    on divorce, 182
    and Forum in Northern Ireland, 355
    and Good Friday Peace Agreement, 357
    handshake with Adams, 347
    importance to peace process, 364–365
    and Irish Americans, 321–322, 326
    and New Ireland Forum, 256
    Nobel Peace Prize, 364–365
    talks with Adams, 342, 343, 352, 360
    Trimble on, 354
    and U.S. visa for Adams, 351
    on Women's Peace Movement, 316
Hunger strikes, 310
    Bobby Sands, 331–332

British reaction, 336
  Terence MacSwiney, 68, 331
Hunt Commission, 316
Hunter-gatherers, 2
Hussey, Gemma, 264
Hyde, Douglas, 47
  and Irish language, 115, 118, 120

IBEC Technical Services Corporation, 94
ICTU. *See* Irish Congress of Trade Unions
IDA. *See* Industrial Development Authority
Illegitimate birth, 146
Immigration, xi, 387–388. *See also*
  Emigration, Internal migration
In the Name of the Father, 401–402
Incitement to Hatred Bill, 298
Independent International Commission on
  Decommissioning, 358
Industrial Development Act of 1958, 97
Industrial Development Authority, 93–94,
  98, 102, 222, 270
Industrial Grants Act, 96
*Industrial Potentials of Ireland: An
  Appraisal*, 94
Industry, xvii
  Belfast, xvi
  and foreign investment, 97–98, 102
  post-war, 93–94, 96
  as pressure group, 267
Inghinidhe na hEireann, 56–57
Inglis, Tom, 123, 128
Intergovernmental Conference, 348
Internal migration, 95–96, 239
International Commission, 349, 350–351
International Helsinki Federation for
  Human Rights, 340
International Lesbian Caucus, 166–167
International Union of Christian
  Democrats, 383
INTO. *See* Irish National Teachers
  Organization
Into the West, 401
Investment in Education, 109, 110, 240
The Invincibles, 44
IRA. *See* Irish Republican Army
IRA Army Council, 353
Iran, 54–55

Iraq, 247
IRB. *See* Irish Republican Brotherhood
Ireland
  dependence on Britain, 105
  east-west split, xvi
  economic and social change, xi–xiii
  geography, xv–xvi
  and its history, xiv–xv
  population, xvi, 21
  as post-colonial society, 105
  religious affiliations, xvi
  three Irelands, xi–xv
Ireland Act of 1949, 83, 311
Irish Americans, 295. *See also* Emigration,
    Friends of Ireland, United States
  anti-British sentiment, 295–296
  cultural baggage, 33
  cultural connections to old country, 75
  and current Irish cultural renaissance,
    388–391
  and nationalist movement, 33, 41–42,
    66
  and Northern Ireland, 303–304,
    321–326
  and transnational linkage based on
    ethnicity, 339
  and "undocumented Irish," 385–386
Irish Anti-Nuclear Movement, 268
Irish Association of Civil Liberties, 153
Irish Brigade, 80
Irish character, 106
  forms of religiosity, 128
Irish Citizen Army, 26, 50
  and Easter Rising of 1916, 52, 241
Irish Confederation, 26–27
Irish Congress of Trade Unions, 64, 227,
    253, 266
Irish Council for Civil Liberties, 170, 175
Irish Countrywomen's Association, 164
Irish Creamery Milk Suppliers Association,
    265
Irish Cultural Centre (Canton,
    Massachusetts), 391
Irish Export Board. *See* Coras Trachtala
Irish Family League, 134–135, 176
Irish Farmers Association, 227, 264–265. *See
    also* National Farmer's Association

Irish Food Board, 390
The Irish for No, 398
Irish Free State, 72–75
  and Catholic Church, 124–130
  foreign policy, 376–377
  founding, 68
  and Irish language, 73–74
  neutrality in World War II, 81, 82,
    376–377
  and women's role, 162
Irish Golf, 153
Irish Housewives Association, 164, 165
Irish Immigration Center, 193
Irish Independent, 150, 151
Irish Land Commission, 76
Irish language, xvi, 4. *See also* English lan-
    guage, Gaeltacht
  and all–Irish schools, 119
  and Constitution, 212
  as cultural symbol, 119–120
  de Valera's vision, 75
  decline after Great Famine, 38–40
  decline in number of speakers, 76
  and educational system, 116
  effect of emigration, 96
  and Gaelic League, 47
  groups promoting, 267
  and Irish Free State, 73–74
  and nationalism, 203
  and 1990s cultural renaissance,
    119–120
  reasons for decline in use of, 114–115
  revival efforts, 115–119
  taught on "Buntus Cainte," 143
  and television, 119, 143–144
Irish Medical Association, 84, 130
Irish National Caucus, 321, 322, 324, 325,
    326
Irish National League, 44
Irish National Teachers Organization, 108,
    111–112
Irish National Theatre, 48
Irish Organic Food Growers Association,
    271
Irish Parliament. *See also* Dail Eireann
  dissolution of, 20
  founding, 8

Grattan's Parliament, 16
  and Protestant ascendancy, 15
  and Rebellion of the United Irishmen,
    17
Irish Parliamentary Party, 43, 45, 64, 151,
    232, 250
  and 1918 elections, 65
The Irish People, 42
Irish Press, 150, 151, 242
Irish renaissance
  in literature (c. 1900), 48–49
  of 1990s, xiii, 119–120, 388–389, 406.
    See also "Celtic Tiger" period
    (1987–1997)
Irish Republican Army, xv, 2, 202. *See also*
    IRA Army Council, Official IRA,
    Provisional IRA
  and Anglo-Irish War, 66–68
  and Blueshirts, 80
  and censorship, 149
  and Civil War, 69–70
  and Dail, 205–206
  and de Valera, 72, 79, 80
  and Easter Rising of 1916, 54
  hunger strikes, 240
  Marxist influence, 293
  and Nazi Germany, 81
  in Northern Ireland, 289, 293, 294,
    298–299. *See also* Provisional
    IRA
  opposition to partition, 73
  renaming of Irish Volunteers, 66
  trend of aversion toward, 55
Irish Republican Brotherhood, 42, 66, 241
  and Irish Volunteers, 51
  and Michael Collins, 63–64, 70
  and other nationalist organizations, 49
  regeneration of, 49
Irish Republican Socialist Party, 166–167
Irish rising of 1641, 10
Irish Socialist Republican Party, 50
Irish studies, 389–390
Irish Sugar Company, 247
*Irish Terrorism or British Colonialism: The
    Violation of Human Rights in
    Northern Ireland*, 340–341
Irish theme pubs (U.S.), 390

Irish Times, 150–151, 386, 398
Irish Tourist Board, 222
Irish Transport and General Workers
        Union, 50, 265
Irish Vigilance Association, 151, 154
Irish "virtual" or world community, 386,
        388
Irish Voice, 351, 385
Irish Volunteers, 15, 46, 49
        and Easter Rising of 1916, 52
        and released prisoners, 63
        renamed Irish Republican Army, 66
        and Sinn Fein, 64, 66
        split into two factions, 51
Irish Women: Agenda for Practical Action,
        183, 185
Irish Women's Franchise League, 160–161
Irish Women's Liberation Movement, 166
The Irish Women's Suffrage and Local
        Government Association, 160
Irish Women's Suffrage Federation, 160
Irishwomen United, 166–167, 170
Issues Related to Employment Opportunities,
        185
Ivers, Eileen, 392, 393
IWFL. *See* Irish Women's Franchise League
IWLM. *See* Irish Women's Liberation
        Movement
IWSF. *See* Irish Women's Suffrage
        Federation
IWU. *See* Irishwomen United

James I, King, 9–10
James II, King, 11
Jamison, Joe, 351
John Paul II, Pope, 262
John XXIII, Pope, 131
Johnson, Thomas, 254
Johnston, Ray, 293
Joint Committee on the Irish Language,
        118
Joint Oireachthas Committee on Women's
        Rights, 185
Joint Parliamentary Committee on
        Women's Rights, 169
Jones, David, 362
Jones, Kirk III, 405

Jones, W. R., 8
Jordan Neil, xiii, 71, 400, 402–403
The Journey Home, 399
Joyce, James, 48, 398, 406
Judicial Separation and Family Law
        Reform Act of 1989, 181,
        184–185

Keane, John B., 401
Keating, Geoffrey, 11
Keating, Michael, 217, 257
Kellogg Briand Agreement, 376
Kelly, David, 405
Kelly, John, 131, 132
Kelly, Thomas, 42
Kennedy, Bertie, 269, 353
Kennedy, Edward M. "Ted," 303, *304*, 322,
        323, 325, 337
        and Clinton, 351
        and "undocumented Irish," 386
Kennedy, John F.
        portrayed in cathedral mosaic with
        Christ and Pearse, 54, *56*
        significance of election, 295
Kennedy, Kieran, 95, 105
Kenney, Mary, 166
Keogh, Dermot, 212
Keogh, Desmond, 376
Keough, Donald, 389–390
Keppler, 398
Kerry
        and Great Famine, 33
        and Irish language, 76
Khomeini, 55
Kiberd, Declan, 399
Kickham, Charles, 42
Kilroy, Thomas, 395
Kinealy, Christine, 35
Kissane, Bill, 231, 232–233
Knights of Columbus, 154, 262
Knowth, 2–3
Kodo, 392
Koestler, Arthur, 152

Labor movement
        and nationalist movement, 50
        as pressure group, 265–267

Labour Party, 74, 84, 189, 241, 248, 250, 266
   and abortion issue, 171
   alignment in European Parliament, 383
   and Catholic Church, 128
   coalition with Fine Gael (1980s), 101
   and coalitions, 254–255
   contesting seats, 224
   and contraception, 135
   and divorce issue, 175
   history, 253–256
   vs. ICTU, 266
   and 1918 election, 241
   and Ulster workers, 253–254
   woman candidate in 1997, 191
   and worker solidarity, 253
Laffan, Brigid, 103, 228, 381, 383
Laffan, Michael, 54
Lake, Anthony, 352
Lalor, James Finton, 27, 40
Land Act of 1881, 44
Land Act of 1903, 231
Land Courts, 205
Land League. *See* National Land League
Land reform, 34, 43, 44, 45
   under de Valera, 76
   and nationalist movement, 50
Landlord class
   and Encumbered Estates Act of 1849, 40
   and Great Famine, 32, 35
   and transfer of land ownership to tenants, 45
Larkin, James, 50, 253
"The Late Late Show," 144–145
   and Irish Women's Liberation Movement, 166
"Laudabiliter," 6
Law Reform Commission, 184
League of Nations, 376
Lee, J. J., 115, 320, 378
Lee, Joseph, 35, 53, 55, 57, 178
   on Constitution's Catholic language, 209
   on corporatist report, 226
   on Irish economic development, 105–107

   on Irish Free State, 73–74
   on Michael Collins, 71–72
Leinster, 6, 8
   land colonists from Connaught, 76
Leinster House, 79, 246
Lemass, Sean, 73, 84, 85, 131, 243, 293
   as "chief," 214
   importance to modern Ireland, 243
   and Ireland-in-Europe, 107
   on Ireland's position in Cold War, 377
   on private enterprise, 222
   on RTE, 148
   and Second Programme, 98–99
   and wage agreement, 266
Lenihan, Brian, 132, 190–191, 221
Leonard, Hugh, 395
Leonard, Iarla, 392–393
Lessing, Doris, 152
Libya, 308
Light industry, xvii
Lillis, Michael, 321, 322, 323, 325
Limerick, xvi
   crime rate, 276
   founding by Vikings, 5
Limerick, University of, 113
Lindsay-Hogg, Michael, 405
Lipjhart, Arendt, 285
Lipset, S. M., 259
List, Friedrich, 49
Literature, 398–400
Lloyd George, David, 63, 67, 283, 331–332
   negotiations with Sinn Fein, 68
   and partition, 68
Lloyd, John, 362
Local Appointments Commission, 218
Local Government Water Pollution Act of 1977, 270
Locke, John, 15
Londonderry, xii
   Catholic majority, xvi
   population, xvi, 289
   siege of, 298
   violent conflict, 297, 298, 300
Long Kesh Prison, 317
Longley, Edna, 397
Longley, Michael, 397
Los Lobos, 391

Lovett, Anne, 146
Lowell, Robert, 396
Loyal National Repeal Association, 24–25, 26, 40
Loyalist Association of Workers, 310
Lucey, Cornelius, 132, 262–263
Lunny, Donal, 392, 393
Lunny, Manus, 393
Lynch, Jack (and administration), 84, 134, 149, 169
    as "chairman," 214
    and Fianna Fail power struggle and crisis, 243–245
    and 1977 election, 245
    and Northern Ireland, 298, 317
Lynch, John, 11
Lynch, Liam, 69–70
Lynch, Patrick, 109
Lyons, F. S. L., 96

"M*A*S*H," 144
Maastricht Treaty of 1992, 379, 380, 381, 382
Mac Anna, Ferdia, 398
Mac Stiofain, Sean, 309
MacAleese, Mary, 175, 191, *220*
MacDonough, Thomas, 51, 52, 53
MacEoin, Sean, 378
MacGarry, John, 367
MacKenna, John, 400
Mackies Engineering, 290
MacNamara, Brinsley, 152
MacNeill, Eoin, 47, 49
    and Easter Rising of 1916, 52
    and Irish Free State, 72, 73
MacNeill, James, 207
MacRory, Cardinal, 210, 212
MacStiofain, Sean, 149
MacSwiney, Terence, 68, 331
Madden, Diedre, 400
Madonna, 153
Madonna House, 138
Maeve, Queen, 191
Maginness, Ken, 366
Maguire Seven, 340
Maher, Mary, 166
Mahon, Derek, 397

Mahoney, John, 41, 42
Mairin de Burca v. Attorney General, 188
Major, John, 342, 344
    and cessation of violence, 347, 348
    and Downing Street Declaration, 344–345, 352
    and Forum in Northern Ireland, 349, 353
    and peace process, 367
    and Reynolds, 344
Malachy, 5
Mallon, Seamus, 357
    elected deputy first minister, 361
    and Orange Order parade, 362
Maloney, Mick, 390, 393
Malraux, Andre, 152
Manchester Martyrs, 42
Manning, Maurice, 252
Mansion House, 166, 205
Marital Breakdown: A Review and Proposed Changes, 180–181
Market Research Bureau of Ireland, 251
Markievicz, Constance, 56, 161
Marriage, 174, 176, 271–272
Married Women's Status Act, 163
Marshall Plan, 377
Martin, Emer, 400
Mason, Patrick, 394
Mason, Roy, 317
"Mater and Magistera," 131
Maternity (Protection of Employees) Act of 1981, 167–168
Matthew, Theobald, 31
Maudling, Reginald, 299
Maugham, W. Somerset, 152
Maupassant, Guy de, 152
Maxwell, John, 53
Mayhew, Patrick, 348
Maynooth, 15–17. *See also* Saint Patrick's at Maynooth
Mayo
    and Great Famine, 33
    and Irish language, 76
    and origins of boycott, 43
    and Rebellion of the United Irishmen, 17–18
    and television, 147

Maze Prison, 324, 331, 340
McBride, Sean, 83, 130
McCabe, Patrick, 399, 404
McCann, Colum, 400
McCartney, Donal, 26
McCartney, Robert, 355, 356
McClaverty, Bernard, 400
McCourt, Frank, 389
McCullough, Denis, 49
McDermott, Sean, 49, 53, 57
McDonagh, Martin, 389, 395
McGahern, John, 108, 145, 152, 174
    on marriage, 272
McGann's, 393
McGee v. Attorney General, 169, 188
McGuckian, Medbh, 398
McGuiness, Catherine, 347
McGuiness, Martin, 346
McGuinness, Frank, 395
McKeown, Ciaran, 315
McKevitt, Mickey, 363
McManus, Sean, 323
McMorraugh, Dermot, 6
McPherson, Conor, 395
McQuaid, John Charles, 126, 129, 132, 211
    on contraception, 134
    on divorce, 133
    influence on Irish Church, 130, 131
McViegh, Owen, 309
McWilliam, Monica, 354
Meaney, Colm, 405
Media. *See also* Censorship, Newspapers,
        Radio, Television
    influence, 123–124, 142
    multiplicity of messages, 123–124
Meehan, Paula, xiii, 398
Megalithic architecture, 2–3
Menges, Chris, 402, 403
Merck, Sharp and Dohme, 269–270
Mercy Sisters, 107
Methodist Church, 291
Michael Collins, 71, 403–404
Miller, Kerby, 386–387
The Miracle, 402–403
Miramax, 400
Mirren, Helen, 400, 402
Mitchel, John, 25, 26, 34

Mitchell, George, 349, *350*
    on Adams, 367
    chair of Forum in Northern Ireland,
        355
    and Good Friday Peace Agreement,
        357
    importance to peace process, 367
Mitchell, Thomas, 113
Mitchell Report, 350–351, 352
Modernization, xiii–xiv
    and individual vs. community, 92–93
    intrepreting Irish attitude toward
        birth control, abortion, and
        divorce, 177–180
    Irish view of the downside, 92
Moher, xi
Mokyr, Joel, 37
Molyneaux, James, 366
Mona Lisa, 400
Monasteries, 4
    decline, 5–6
    and Vikings, 4–5
Monster meetings, 25, 26
Moody, F. X., xv
Moody, T. W., 34
Mooncoin, 47
"Moondance," 391
Moravia, Alberto, 152
Morrison, Bruce, 351
    and "undocumented Irish," 386
Morrison, Danny, 333, 342
Morrison, Van, 391, 393
Morrissey's, 390–391
Mother and Child Health Plan, 129–130,
        250, 263
Mother Theresa, 182
Mountbatten, Lord, 310, 317
Movement for a Socialist Republic,
        166–167
Mowlam, Marjorie "Mo," 355–356, 363
Moynihan, Daniel, 323
MTV, 119
Mulcahey, Richard, 70, 249, 250
Muldoon, Paul, 398
Mulgrave, Lord, 24
Mulkerns, Helena, 386
Multiculturalism, 389–390

Munster, 5, 65, 67
    and Civil War, 70
    and Great Famine, 33
    and Irish language, 73
Murders, 277
Murphy, Annie, 137
Murphy, Johnny, 404
Murphy, Richard, 397
Murphy, Tom, 395
Murphy, William Martin, 50
    and *Irish Independent*, 151
Murtaugh Properties Ltd. v. Cleary, 167
Music, 391–394
My Left Foot, 400, 401

Nabokov, Vladimir, 398
Nasiunta na Gaeilge, 267
The Nation, 27
"A Nation Once Again," 292
National Centre Party, 79, 226, 249, 250, 258
National Co-ordinating Committee on
    Drug Abuse, 275
National Code of Practise on Sexual
    Harrassment of 1994, 184
National Convention of the Irish
    Language, 267
National Council for Curriculum and
    Assessment, 111
National Council of Bishops, 126
National Development 1977–1980, 101, 227
National Economic and Social Council,
    102, 227
National Farmer's Association, 148. *See also*
    Irish Farmers Association
National Guard. *See* Blueshirts
National Institutes for Higher Education,
    113
National Labour Party, 254
National Land League, 34, 43
National Museum, xi
National Parents' Council, 111
A National Partnership, 227
National pay agreements, 100–101
National Union of Journalists, 148
National University of Ireland, 47, 109
    branches, 108
    and Irish language, 117

National Wage Agreements of 1972, 167,
    266
National Women's Council, 175, 187–188.
    See also Council for the Status of
    Women
*National Youth Policy Committee Final
    Report*, 274
Nationalism, 202–203. *See also* Nationalist
    movement
Nationalist historians, xiv–xv, 1
    on Daniel O'Connell, 25–26
    and Easter Rising of 1916, 53–54
    and Great Famine, 34
    and Penal Laws, 12–13
    and Rebellion of the United Irishmen,
        18
Nationalist movement. *See also* Easter
    Rising of 1916, Home Rule
    and Catholic Church, 41, 42, 44, 50
    and Catholicism, 26
    and Celtic roots, 4
    and citizen armies, 50
    and educational system, 114
    and Gaelic Athletic Association, 47
    and Gaelic League, 47–48
    and Germany, 51, 52, 65, 81
    ideals, 20–21
    and Irish Americans, 33, 41–42, 66
    and Irish language, 115–116
    and Irish literary renaissance, 48–49
    and labor movement, 50
    and land movement, 50
    and romance of failure, 51–52, 55
    and school system, 18
    and Sinn Fein, 49
Nationalist Party, 284, 292, 297–298, 300,
    319
Neave, Aery, 317
Neeson, Liam, 403
Neo-corporatism, 227–228
New Ireland Forum, 256, 264
New Irish, 386
    and return migration, 386–387
New Ulster Movement, 310
The New York Times, 151
Newgrange, 2–3
Newman, John Henry, 109

Newry, 297
Newspapers, 150–151, 232
    decline of, 147
The Newton Letter, 398
Ni Dhomhnaill, Nuala, 389, 398
ni Houlihan, Cathleen, 191. *See also*
    "Cathleen ni Houlihan"
Ni Mhaonaigh, Mairead, 391
nic Mhathuna, Una Bean, 183
NICRA. *See* Northern Ireland Civil Rights
    Association
Night Shift, 399
Nixon, Richard, 303
Nobel Peace Prize, 315, 340
Nobel Prize for Literature, 396
No-Divorce Campaign, 182
NORAID, 149, 303, 321–322, 325, 326
Nordlinger, Eric, 318
Normans
    and agriculture, 6–8
    first incursions, 5–6
    founding of Irish Parliament, 8
    integration into Irish cultural milieu, 8
    knights (tomb effigy), 7
Norris, David, 189, 273
North Atlantic Treaty Organization, 377
North, 396
Northern Aid Committee. *See* NORAID
Northern Ireland, xii–xiii. *See also* Good
    Friday Peace Agreement, Peace
    process (Northern Ireland)
    agriculture, xvii
    and Better Government of Ireland
        Act, 67
    British policy, 294–295, 302, 306,
        311–313, 318–321
    Britishness of Protestants, 287–288
    Catholic economic advancement, 293
    Catholic underclass, 284–285, 287
    civil rights movement, xiii, 296–298,
        299, 301
    components of conflict, 285–288
    Constituent Assembly, 313–314, 318
    and Constitution, 208–209
    counties, 283
    creation of, 282–285
    discrimination, 288–290

east-west split, xvi
economic discrimination, 288–290
education, 291
and election of 1918, 65
election of 1973, 311
Executive, 312–313, 319
explanations of the conflict, 367–371
expropriation of land, 286
external influences on, 338–341
governmental discrimination,
    288–289
and Great Famine interpretation,
    35–36
and historical interpretation, 2
and Home Rule, 282, 286
and Home Rule issue, 44, 45–46
human rights, 339–341
hunger strikes, 310, 331
industry, xvii
integration into Ireland or United
    Kingdom, 368–369
and IRA, 289, 293, 294, 298–299
and Irish interpretation of history,
    281–282
and Irish language, 73
law enforcement discrimination,
    289–290
nationality and conflict, 287–288
and O'Connell's legacy, 26
political posters, *314*
power and conflict, 286–287
prisoners and prison culture,
    305–306, 317, 321, 324, 332
property qualifications for voting,
    288–289
Protestant dominant class, 284–285,
    287
ranking as an issue, 240
religion and conflict, 285–286
religious affiliations, xvi
security measures, 304–306
separation, 290–293
shipbuilding industry, 290
sovereignty issue, 341, 369–371
sports, 291–292
Stormont government, 284
"Ulsterization" policy, 306, 320

unemployment, 290, 292
and United States, 295–296, 303–304,
    308, 321–326, 337–338
U.S. participation in peace process,
    349–352
Women's Peace Movement, 314–316,
    340
and World War II, 81
Northern Ireland: Constitutional Proposals,
    311
Northern Ireland Aid. *See* NORAID
Northern Ireland Assembly, 333, 336–337
Northern Ireland Civil Rights Association,
    294, 296
Northern Ireland Civil Service, 318
Northern Ireland Emergency Provisions
    Act of 1973, 305
Northern Ireland Labour Party, 300
Northern Ireland Women's Coalition, 354
Norton, William, 254
Norwegian People's Peace Prize, 315, 340
Notre Dame University, 113, 389–390
Nuclear power, 268
Nunez, Carlos, 392
"NYPD Blue," 144

O'Brien, Conor Cruise, 54, 294, 343
    and censorship, 149
    as delegate to UN, 378
O'Brien, Edna, 152
O'Brien, Flann, 92
O'Carroll, J. P., 178–180
O'Casey, Sean, 48, 152, 398, 406
    and Irish Citizen Army, 50
O'Connell, Daniel, xiv, 18, 21, 23, 232
    busts of, 47
    Catholic Association, 23–24
    and Catholic emancipation, 23–24
    on compensation to former slave
        holders in 1840s, 37
    election to parliament, 24
    on English and Irish languages,
        114–115
    nationalist assessment, 25–26
    opposition to Union, 23, 24–25
    post-revisionist assessment, 26–27
    revisionist assessment, 26

O'Connell, David, 309
O'Connell, Desmond, 136–137
O'Connell, Thomas, 254
O'Connor, Frank, 152
O'Connor, Joe, 400
O'Connor, Pat, 395, 400, 401
O'Connor, Rory, 70
O'Connor, Sinead, 391, 393
O'Criomthain, Tomas, 76
O'Dalaigh, Cearbhall, 220–221
O'Donnell, Chris, 401
O'Donnell, Hugh, 9–10
O'Dowd, Naill, 351
O'Duffy, Eoin, 79–80, 226, 249
O'Faolain, Sean, 125, 152
O'Godhra, Nollaig, 118
O'Grada, Cormac, 36, 37
O'Grady, Joseph, 351
O'Hanlon, Ray, 386, 388
O'Hanlon, Thomas J., 153
O'Higgins, C. J., 273
O'Higgins, Kevin, 74, 151, 242
O'Kelly, Kevin, 149
O'Leary, Brendan, 367
O'Leary, John, 42
O'Leary, Michael, 255
O'Malley, Desmond, 246, 247
    and New Ireland Forum, 256–257
    and Progressive Democrats, 256, 257
O'Malley, Donagh, 110–111, 112–113
O'Malley, E., 105, 106–107
O'Malley, Ernie, 69
O'Malley, Mary, 398
O'Malley, Padraig, 305–306
O'Meara, Paddy, 269
O'Morain, Micheal, 148
O'Neill, Hugh, 9–10
O'Neill, Terence, 243, 293, 294, 297
O'Neill, Thomas P. "Tip," 303, 322,
    323–325, 326, 337–338
O'Reilly, Frank, 362
O'Reilly, John, 170
O'Reilly, Tony, 151
O'Shea, Michael, 108
O'suilleabhain, Micheal, 392
O'suilleabhain, Muiris, 76–77
O'Toole, Fintan, 136, 191

Offences Against the Person Act of 1861, 170, 189
Offenses Against the State Act, 80
Official IRA, 309
Official Unionists, 333
    and election of 1982, 336–337
Oil, 100
Oireachtas, 215–218. *See also* Dail Eireann, Seanad
Old IRA, 74
Omagh, xii, xiii
    bombing, 362–363
Open Door Counseling, Well Women Centre et al. v. Ireland, 172
Opened Ground, 396
Opus Dei, 170, 182
Orange halls, 291
Orange Order, 18–19, 22, 284, 292, 302
    Drumcree parades, 348–349, 361–362
    emergence, 282
    and Home Rule, 44
    outlawed in 1837, 24
    and Unionist Party, 293
Orange parades, 292
Organization for European Cooperation and Development, 109
Orme, Stanley, 324–325
Orwell, George, 152
Ostmen. *See* Vikings
Owens, Eamonn, 404

Paddy A Go-Go, 390
Paddy Clarke Ha Ha Ha, 399
Paine, Tom, 17
Paisley, Ian, 288, 294, 310, 313
    call for general strike (1974), 316
    and Forum in Northern Ireland, 350, 355, 356
    on George Mitchell, 367
    and Good Friday Peace Agreement, 359
    and Trimble, 354
Pakenham, Thomas, 18
The Pale, 8
Palestine, 54–55
Palestine Liberation Organization, 308
Pankhursts, 160
Parker, Alan, 398–399, 404–405

Parliament of Northern Ireland, 67, 83, 284
Parliaments. *See* British Parliament, Dail Eireann, European Parliament, Irish Parliament, Northern Ireland Assembly, Oireachtas, Parliament of Northern Ireland, Seanad, Stormont Parliament
Parnell, Charles Stewart, xiv, 18, 21, 41, 232
    founding of *Irish Independent*, 151
    and Home Rule, 42, 43–45
    and Irish National League, 44
    and National Land League, 44
Partition, 68
    and Boundary Commission, 72
Partnership 2000: 1997–2000, 103
Paul VI, Pope, 132
Paulin, Tom, 397, 398
Peace Accord of 1998, 57
Peace process (Northern Ireland), 341–342. *See also* Good Friday Peace Agreement, Women's Peace Movement
    British talks with Sinn Fein, 342
    Downing Street Declaration, 344–345
    Forum for Peace and Reconciliation, 347
    Forum in Northern Ireland, 353–357
    "Framework for Agreement," 348–349
    International Commission, 349, 350–351
    1996 derailment, 352–353
    reassessment of violence and resulting cease fire, 345–347
    three strands of talks, 343, 348
    U.S. participation, 349–352
    willingness of parties to negotiate, 342
Pearse, Patrick, 1, 18
    and Easter Rising of 1916, 51–52, 53–54
    as educator, 51, 57
    on Gaelic nation, 48
    influence on republicans in Northern Ireland, 26
    and Irish language, 115
    on O'Connell, 26
    portrayed in cathedral mosaic with Christ and Kennedy, 54, *56*

post-revisionist view of, 55–57
revisionist view of, 55
romance of failure, 51–52, 55
Peel, Robert, 24, 25, 32, 36
Peillon, Michel, xiii
Penal Laws, 12–14, 15, 109, 282
    and Catholic Church, 124
    nationalist interpretation, 12–13
    post-revisionist interpretation, 14
    revisionist interpretation, 13
Pensions Act of 1990, 184
People's Democracy, 296–297, 298, 316
People's Republic of China, 377–378
Permanent Court of International Justice,
    376
Phytophthora infestans, 31
"Philadelphia Here I Come," 395
Pioneer Total Abstinence Association, 267
Pitt, William, 20, 21, 23
PLAC. *See* Pro Life Amendment Campaign
Plunkett, Count, 64, 241
Plunkett, Joseph Mary
    and Easter Rising of 1916, 51, 52, 53, 57
Poetry, 396–398
Pol Pot, 55
Political culture, 201
    and British influence, 204–205
    and Catholicism, 203–204
    and nationalism, 202–203
Political parties, 240–241. *See also* Alliance
    Party, Clann na Publachta, Clann
    na Talmhan, Conservative Party
    (Britain), Cumann na nGaedheal,
    Democratic Left (party),
    Democratic Socialist Party,
    Farmers Party, Fianna Fail, Fine
    Gael, Irish Parliamentary Party,
    Irish Socialist Republican Party,
    Labour Party, National Centre
    Party, Nationalist Party, Northern
    Ireland Labour Party, Northern
    Ireland Women's Coalition,
    Progressive Democrats,
    Provisional Sinn Fein, Sinn Fein,
    Social Democratic and Labour
    Party, Ulster Unionist Party,

Vanguard Unionist Progressive
    Party, The Worker's Party
    minor, 258–259
    political cleavages in Ireland, 259–261
Poor Law, 24
Population, xvi
    decline between Great Famine and
        1960, 38, 73
    demographic changes, 239–240
    growth in early 1800s, 21
Portadown, 10
Post-revisionist historians, xv, 2
    on Daniel O'Connell, 26–27
    and Easter Rising of 1916, 55–57
    and Great Famine, 35–38
    and Penal Laws, 14
    and Rebellion of the United Irishmen,
        19–20
Post-war era, 83–85
    problems, 92
Postlewaithe, Peter, 402
Potatoes. *See also* Great Famine
    and population growth of early 1800s,
        21
Poverty, 276–277
PR. *See* Proportional representation
Prager, Jeffrey, 230–231, 232
Prendergast, James, 24–25
Prendergast, Maurice, 33
Presbyterianism, 282
    and Democratic Unionist Party, 288
Presentation Sisters, 107
President
    debate over expanded powers, 221
    and power of referral of legislation to
        Supreme Court, 219–221
    and power to dissolve Dail, 210, 221
    powers, 219
Pressure groups
    Catholic Church, 261–264
    farmers, 264–265
    industry, 267
    labor, 265–267
    single-issue groups, 267–269
Prevention of Terrorism Act, 305
Priests' Social Guild, 151

Prime minister, 214, 215, 219
  and Dail, 216
  Farrell's characterization of those who
      have held the office, 214
Prior, James, 332–333, 337
Privatization, 103
Pro Life Action Committee, 262
Pro Life Amendment Campaign, 170
Proclamation of 1916, 161
*Programme for Action in Education
      1984–1987*, 112
*The Programme for Competitiveness and
      Work 1994–1996*, 103
*The Programme for Economic and Social
      Progress 1990–1993*, 103
The Programme for Economic Expansion, 96
*The Programme for National Recovery
      1987–1990*, 103
Progressive Democrats, 247, 248, 256–257,
      259
Proportional representation, 223–225
Proportional Representation Society of
      Ireland, 223
Protestant ascendancy, 14–17
Provisional IRA, 149, 242, 299, 300–301
  attacks in Britain, 308
  bombings and other violence,
      307–310, 313, 317, 345–346
  Canary Wharf bombing, 352
  Heathrow Airport mortar attack, 346
  hunger strikes, 310, 331
  international links, 308
  military structure, 307
  1994 ceasefire, 346–347
  and Official IRA, 309
  prison culture, 305–306
  recruitment, 307
  reorganization of 1977, 309–310
  second cease fire, 356
Provisional Sinn Fein, 309, 310
Provos. *See* Provisional IRA
Public Policy Institute of Ireland, 176, 182,
      192
Public Services Organizational Review
      Group. *See* Devlin Group
Punt, 100

Purchase of Land Act of 1885, 231
Putnam, Robert, 232

Quadragesimo Anno, 226
Queen's University of Ireland, 109
Quinn, Peter, 390, 394
Quinn, Ruairi, 256
Quinn family (bombing incident), 362

Racism, 387–388
"Radharc," 145
Radio, 142
  commercial stations, 149–150
  and government control, 147
Radio and Television Act of 1988, 149–150
Radio Eireann, 117
Radio Telefis Eireann, 222
  American programming, 144
  and Catholic Church, 144–145
  founding, 142–143
  and government control, 147–148
  and Irish language, 143–144
  most-watched shows, 144
  and Northern Ireland issue, 148–149
Rape, 184
Rape Crisis Center, 166, 168
Rath Cairn, 76
Raymo, Chet, 405
Rea, Stephen, 395, 400, 403
Reagan, Ronald (and administration), 132,
      337, 338, 342, 378
Real IRA, 362–363
Rebellion of the United Irishmen (1798),
      17, 282
  consequences, 20–21
  key battles, 17–18
  nationalist interpretation, 18
  post-revisionist interpretation, 19–20
  revisionist interpretation, 18–19
Red Hand Commandos, 308
Redmond, John, 21, 42
  and Home Rule, 45–46, 63
  and *Irish Independent*, 151
  and Irish Volunteers, 51
  opposition to women's suffrage, 160,
      161

Reformation, 9
Relief Act, 24
Religion, 128, 139, 141. *See also* Catholic
    Church, Church of Ireland
Reno, Janet, 352
Repeal Association. *See* Loyal National
    Repeal Association
*Report of a Commission on Higher
    Education*, 112
*Report of the Advisory Expert Committee on
    Local Government Reorganizaton
    and Reform*, 219
*Report of the Commission on the Status of
    Women*, 165–166, 167, 192
Report on Rape, 184
Report to the Minister of Finance, 159,
    164–165
Responsible Society, 170, 176, 192–193
A Review of Industrial Policy, 102
Revisionist historians, xv, 1–2
    on Daniel O'Connell, 26
    and Easter Rising of 1916, 54–55
    and Great Famine, 34–35
    and Penal Laws, 13
    and Rebellion of the United Irishmen,
    18–19
Reynolds, Albert, 173, 214, 247, *304*
    and Adams-Hume handshake, 347
    on cessation of violence, 347
    and coalitions, 247–248
    and Downing Street Declaration,
    344–345
    and Goodman Beef scandal, 247, 248
    and IRA violence, 346
    and Major, 344
    and Northern Ireland peace process,
    343–344, 352
    and peace process, 367
Richardson, Miranda, 403
Rickman, Alan, 404
The Right to Remarry, 182
Right to Remarry Campaign, 175
Ring of Kerry, xi
River Bann, xvi
    and drowning at Burntollet Bridge, 10
River Boyne, 10
River Shannon, 4, 10

"Riverdance," xiii, 389, 392, 393, 394
Road Traffic Act of 1933, 274
Roberts, Julia, 404
Robinson, Mary, 133–134, 164, 170,
    171–172, 175, *193*
    biographical sketch, 188–190
    first woman president, 188, 190–191,
    221, 253, 255
    and Irish world community, 388
    on world hunger, 38
Roche, Adi, 191
Rocky Sullivan's, 390
Rogers, Brid, 366–367
Rogers, John, 189
Rogers, W. A., 39
Rokkan, S., 259
Romania, xi, 387
"Rose of Tralee Contest," 144
Rossa, O'Donovan, 52
Roth, Edward M., 142, 143
Rousseau, Jean Jacques, 17
Royal Irish Constabulary, 22, 42, 66, 67
Royal Ulster Constabulary, 298, 300, 309
    abuse by, 340
    and American gun sales, 323, 324, 325
    anti-Catholic actions, 290, 316,
    320–321
    Catholics in, 289
    disarming of, 305
RTE. *See* Radio Telefis Eireann
RTE Authority, 142, 148, 149
    and IRA ban, 148–149
RUC. *See* Royal Ulster Constabulary
Russell, Lord, 32, 36
Ryan, Thomas, 145
Ryan Commission, 112
Ryan's Daughter, 400

Saint Patrick's at Maynooth, 15–17, 109,
    113, 395
Sands, Bobby, 331–332
Sartre, Jean Paul, 152
"The Sash My Father Wore," 361
Sayers, Peig, 76
Scanlon, Rosemary Brown (Dana), 191
Schering Plough, 270
Schmitt, David, 230, 232

School system. *See* Educational system
Schwarzenegger, Arnold, 147
Scots-Irish
and Penal Laws, 13–14
and Ulster Plantation, 10
SDLP. *See* Social Democratic and Labour
Party
Sean Nos, 392–393
Seanad, 118, 188, 189, 211–212
limited role, 217–218
Second Commission on the Status of
Women, 187
The Second Partitioning of Ireland, 171
Second Programme, 98–99
Second Vatican Council, 131
Seger, Pearl, 354
"Seinfeld," 144
Senate. *See* Seanad
Service industry, xvii
Services, Industrial, Professional and
Technical Union, 265–266
"Seven Days," 148
Sex, 153
Sex education, 186
Sexual harrassment, 184
Sexuality
and Catholic Church, 124, 125, 130,
152, 271–272
Criminal Law (Sexual Offenses) Act of
1993, 189
and marriage, 271–272
Shanavests, 22
Shankill bombing, 343, 344
Shannon, Catherine, 165
Shannon Airport, 98
Shannon Free Airport Development
Company, 98
Shannon hydroelectic plan, 248
Shaw, Fionna, 404
Shaw, Francis, 54
Shaw, George Bernard, 53, 152, 396
Sheehy-Skeffington, Francis, 53
Sheehy-Skeffington, Hannah, 160
Sheen, Martin, 395
Sheridan, Jim, 400, 401–402
Single European Act, 228, 379–380, 381, 382
Single-issue groups, 267–269

Sinn Fein, 241–242
and Assembly, 360–361
and censorship, 149
and Dail, 206
and Downing Street Declaration,
345–346
and election of 1920, 67
and election of 1923, 70
emergence as political arm of republican movement, 63–64
and Forum in Northern Ireland,
356–357
founding, 49
and Free State Constitution, 208
and Great Famine, 34
and Irish Free State, 72
and Irish language, 115
and *Irish Press*, 151
as mother of other political parties,
240, 241
and nationalism, 202–203
and 1916 Rising, 241
and 1918 election, 65
Northern Ireland, 309, 310
and Northern Ireland election of
1982, 333, 336
and O'Connell, 26
outlawed by Britain, 65
position in Irish politics, 259, 260
and proportional representation, 223
repudiation of de Valera, 72
and suffrage movement, 160, 161
Toward a Lasting Peace in Ireland,
342–343
Sinnott, Richard, 213, 249, 259
Sisters of Charity, 138
Sisters of Mercy, 138–139
SKY News, 119
Sky TV, 147
Smith, Jean Kennedy, 304, 351
Smoking, 275
Smyth, Brendan, 138
The Snapper (film), 405
The Snapper (novel), 398–399
Social Democratic and Labour Party, 182,
256, 300, 301, 311, 321
and Assembly, 360–361

and British-Irish Intergovernmental
     Conference, 334–335
and Catholic nationalists, 310, 318
and election of 1982, 333
Social stratification (early 19th century),
     21–22
Social Welfare Act of 1952, 163, 277
Social Welfare Act of 1991, 184
Social Welfare (Amendment) Act of 1981,
     168
Social Welfare (#2) Act of 1985, 168
Socialist Group, 383
Socialists, 26
Society for the Protection of the Unborn
     Child, 170, 173
Society of United Irishmen, 17, 23, 282. *See
     also* Rebellion of the United
     Irishmen (1798)
     O'Connell's membership, 23
     and politicization of popular culture,
          19–20
     Rebellion of 1798, 17–21
Software companies, 104
Solas, 393
"The Soldiers Song," 292
Soloheadbeg, 66
Somalia, xi
Some Mother's Son, 402
The South, 400
Soviet Union, 377
Special Powers Act, 289, 294, 296, 297,
     304–305
Spillane, Davey, 392
Spring, Dick, 171, 189, 190, 248, 255–256, 260
     breaking of coalition with Fine Gael,
          356
     as "chieftain," 214
     and Good Friday Peace Agreement,
          255–256
     and Labour's support for Robinson as
          president, 255
     and Northern Ireland peace process,
          343, 344, 352
     and peace process, 367
SPUC. *See* Society for the Protection of the
     Unborn Child

SPUC v. Grogan et al., 171–172
St. Patrick, 3–4
St. Stephen's Green, 52
Stalker, John, 321
The Star, 150
Star Markets, 390
State Sponsored Bodies, 222–223
Station Island, 396
Status of Children Act of 1987, 184, 188
Statute of Westminster, 376
Statutes of Kilkenny, 8
Steinbeck, John, 152
Stephens, James, 41, 42
Stonehill College Irish Festival, 391, 393
Stormont Castle, 284
Stormont government, 284, 290, 292
     and Britain, 294–295
     collapse, 302, 318
     Special Powers Act, 289
Stormont Parliament, 297
Strabane, 297
*A Strategy for National Development
     1986–1990*, 103
Streep, Meryl, 395, 401
Strike of 1913, 50
Strong, Andrew, 404
Strongbow, 6
Structural Funds, 229
Sturm, Ruger and Company, 324
Suffrage movement
     and Home Rule, 159–161
     opposition to, 160
     in Ulster, 160, 161
The Sun, 150
Sunday Independent, 150, 151, 275
Sunday Press, 151
Sunningdale meeting, 311–312, 318, 348
Supreme Court of Ireland, 134
     on abortion issue, 171, 172
     on contraceptives, 169
     and divorce issue, 174
     and homosexuality, 189
     referrals to, 219–220
     on women's rights, 167, 168
Sutherland, Peter, 171, 189
Swift, Jonathan, 14, 108

Sykes, Richard, 317
Synge, John Millington, 48, 50
Tanaiste. *See* Deputy prime minister
Taoiseach. *See* Prime minister
Tara, 5, 25
Taylor, John, 360, 366
Telecom Eireann, 267
Telefis na Gaelige, 119, 144
Telesis, 102, 105
Television. *See also* Fox Network, Radio
    Telefis Eireann, SKY News, Sky
    TV, Telefis na Gaelige
    arrival in Ireland, 142
    British channels available in east, 142,
      143, 146
    commercial stations, 149–150
    and consumerism, 146
    expansion of, 146
    and government control, 147–148
    as primary news source, 147, 151
    and permissive or liberal society,
      146–147
    and west of Ireland, 147
Temple Bar, xi
Tenant possession of land, 45
Tenants League, 41
Thady Con's, 390
Thatcher, Margaret, 257, 317, 323, 332, 335,
    342
    and Brighton bombing, 309
    and hunger strikes, 336
    and international public opinion,
      339
    and U.S. admonitions, 337, 338
Theater, 394–395
Third Programme, 99
Thirty Two County Sovereignty
    Association, 363
Thompson, Emma, 401–402
Thornley, David, 21, 53–54
Threshers, 22
Tierney, Michael, 226
Tobin, Fergal, 109, 117, 143
Tobin, Liam, 74
Toibin, Colm, 270, 400
Tomb effigies, *7*

Tone, Wolfe, xiv, 1, 18, 19, 20, 23
    busts of, 47
    capture and suicide, 18
    influence on republicans in Northern
      Ireland, 26
    influence on Young Irelanders, 27
    on "men of no property," 24
    nationalism, of, 202
    and Rebellion of the United Irishmen,
      17
    republican ideal, 83
Tourism, xi, xiii, xvii
Toward a Lasting Peace in Ireland, 342–343
Tower of London, 308
Town Hall Theatre, Galway, 392
Toynbee, Arnold, 281
Trade Union Women's Forum, 170
Trainor, Oscar, 153
"Translations," 395
Treason Act, 80
Treaty of Limerick, 11
Treaty of 1921. *See* Anglo-Irish Treaty
Treaty of Rome, 167
Trevaskis, Brian, 145
Trevelyan, Charles, 32, 35, 36
Trevor, William, 174
Trimble, David, 301, 348, *366*
    career summary, 365–367
    elected first minister, 361
    and Forum in Northern Ireland, 350,
      355, 356
    and Good Friday Peace Agreement,
      357, 359, 360
    Nobel Peace Prize, 364, 365, 366
    and Orange Order, 365
    and Orange Order parade, 362
    and Paisley, 354
Trinity College, xi, 14, 108, 113
    Catholic ban on attendance, 108, 113,
      126, 132
    Centre for European Law, 189
    and Merck pollution issue, 270
    statue of Henry Grattan, *16*
"Trom agus Eadrom," 144
Tuatha, 3
Tuberculosis, 92, 129

Tudors, 9
Tully, James, 251, 270
Tuohey, Patsy, 393

Uachtaran. *See* President
UDA. *See* Ulster Defense Association
Ulster. *See* Northern Ireland
Ulster Clubs, 365
Ulster Defense Association, 301, 308, 310
    and Shankill bombing, 344
    violence, 313
Ulster Defense Regiment, 300, 305, 320
Ulster Freedom Fighters, 308
Ulster Plantation, 9–10
Ulster Unionist Council, 282
Ulster Unionist Party, 282, 284, 290, 302,
        318. *See also* Unionists (Northern
        Ireland)
    and Assembly, 360–361
    liberal wing, 292–293, 294
    and Northern Ireland Civil Rights
        Association, 296–297
    and Stormont regime, 292
Ulster Volunteer Force, 46, 49, 294, 308
Ulster Workers Council, 313, 318
Ulsterization policy, 306, 320
Underground gentry, 10, 14
Unemployment Insurance Act of 1920, 163
Unfair Dismissals Act of 1977, 167
Union of Industries of the EC, 228–229
Unionists (Northern Ireland), 45, 318–321,
        333. *See also* Democratic
        Unionist Party, Official
        Unionists, Ulster Unionist Party,
        United Ulster Unionist Council,
        Vanguard Unionist Progressive
        Party
    and British-Irish Intergovernmental
        Conference, 334–335
    and Downing Street Declaration, 345
    and Forum in Northern Ireland,
        349–350, 354, 356–357
    and "Framework for Agreement,"
        348–349
    and integration into United Kingdom,
        368–369
United Irish League, 45

The United Irishman, 49
United Irishmen. *See* Rebellion of the
        United Irishmen (1798), Society
        of United Irishmen
United Kingdom
    integration of Ireland into, 20
    proposed integration of Northern
        Ireland into, 368–369
United Kingdom: Human Rights Concerns,
        340–341
United Nations, 377–378
United Nations National Commissions on
        the Status of Women, 165
United States. *See also* Irish Americans
    Americanized global culture, 144, 147
    and Home Rule issue, 63
    and Irish neutrality in World War II,
        81, 82, 377
    and Northern Ireland, 295–296,
        303–304, 308, 321–326, 337–338
    and Northern Ireland peace process,
        349–352
United Ulster Unionist Council, 312
University College Cork, 392
University College Dublin, 109, 113
U2, xiii, 390
UUP. *See* Ulster Unionist Party
UUUC. *See* United Ulster Unionist Council
UWC. *See* Ulster Workers Council

The Valley of the Squinting Widows, 152
The Van (film), 405
The Van (novel), 398–399
Vanguard Movement, 301, 310
Vanguard Unionist Progressive Party, 310,
        311, 365
Vatican II, 264
Vikings, 4–5
    contributions, 5
    founding of port towns, 5
Voter demographics, 239–240

Waking Ned Devine, 405
Walker, Corbin, 405
Wall, Maureen, 13
Walsh, Edward, 113
Ward, Alan, 213, 222, 227

Ward, Margaret, 161–162
Warrenpoint, 310
Water Pollution Amendment Act of 1990, 270
Waterford
    college, 76
    founding by Vikings, 5
    and Irish language, 76
Watson, Emily, 402
The Way Forward: National Economic Plan 1983–1987, 101
"The Weir," 395
West, Rebecca, 192
West, Trevor, 133–134
Wexford
    founding by Vikings, 5
    and Rebellion of the United Irishmen, 17, 19, 21
Whehelan, Harry, 138, 248
Whelan, Bill, 394
Whelan, Kevin, 14, 19, 20, 37, 48–49
    on land reform, 76
Whitaker, T. K., 96, 221
Whitaker Plan, 85, 96–99
White, Barry, 322
White Paper on Educational Development, 112
Whitelaw, William, 302, 307, 332
Whore, 154
Whyte, John, 209, 259, 285
    on Catholic Church as pressure group, 262–263
Wild Geese, 11–12
Wilde, Oscar, 108, 390
William III, King (William of Orange), 11
Williams, Betty, 314–315
Williams, Niall, 400
Williams, Robin, 400
Wilson, Harold, 313, 319
Wilson, Robert McLiam, 400
Wintering Out, 396
Woman Scorned, 192
The Woman Who Walked into Doors, 399
Woman's Political Association, 188
Woman's Progressive Association, 188
Women. *See also* Suffrage movement
    and abortion, 170–173
    advancements since 1960, 163
    changes in agenda, 192–193
    and changes in contraception law, 169
    and divorce, 133, 174–177
    and drinking, 274
    in Easter Rising of 1916, 56–57
    economic status, 103
    and educational changes, 168, 185–186
    emigration of, 77–78
    and European Economic Community/ European Union, 167, 185
    factors in changed status of, 165
    and Gay Byrne talk show, 146
    and international feminist movement, 165
    and jury duty, 167
    legislation affecting (1980s and 1990s), 184–185
    and modernization, 159
    1980s, 168–169, 183
    1990s, 183
    official organizations, 186–188
    in presidency, 190–191
    radicalized movement, 166
    Report of the Commission on the Status of Women, 159, 164–165, 165–166, 167
    restrictive legislation, 163
    and social welfare, 168
    veneration and deprivation, 162–165
    in the workplace, 164–165, 167–168
Women's Affairs ministry, 169, 187
Women's Aid, 166, 175
Women's Centre, 168
The Women's Daughter, 399
Women's Peace Movement, 314–316, 340
Women's Political Association, 166
Women's Representative Committee, 186–187
Women's Right to Choose (organization), 170
Women's Right to Choose Campaign, 166–167
Women's Social and Political Union (Britain), 160, 161
Woodham-Smith, Cecil, 35

"The Work of Justice," 131
Worker Protection (Regular Part-Time
    Employees) Act of 1991, 184
The Worker's Party, 258
Working Party on Women's Affairs and
    Family Law Reform, 183
"World in Action," 247
World War II, 81–82
    and censorship, 153
World Wide Web, 386
Wright, Oliver, 338
WSPU. *See* Women's Social and Political
    Union (Britain)
Wyndham Act of 1903, 45, 78

X et al. v. Attorney General, 172

Yeats, William Butler, 42, 48, 396, 398, 406
    and Blueshirts, 80
    "The Galway Plains," 49
    opposition to censorship, 125
    on "romantic Ireland," 404
Young, Arthur, 12
Young Ireland, xiv, 25, 26–27, 42
    and aftermath of Great Famine, 40–41
    and Gaelic Athletic Association, 47
    and Irish Americans, 33, 40–41
Young Ireland Association, 79
Young people, xi